MIRROR STUDY BIBLE

VOLUME 2 *of a set of 3*

Paul's Brilliant **Epistles**
&
The Amazing Book of **Hebrews**
also,
James - *The Younger Brother of Jesus*
&
Portions of **Peter**

Behold how beautiful,
valuable,
loved
and innocent
you are!

In the Mirror,
Bible language becomes heart to heart
whispers of grace.

Preparation of HTML Text for App Dawie Blake

Technical assistance with App Laurence Davies

Preparation for Kindle and eBooks: Amol Gavali

Cover Design by: Sean Osmond

Published by Mirror Word Publishing

Should you wish to order printed copies in bulk, [2 or more] pls contact us at info@mirrorword.net

Contact us if you wish to help sponsor Mirror Bibles in Spanish, Shona or Xhosa.

Highly recommended books by the same author: Divine Embrace, God Believes in You, The Logic of His Love.

Children's books: The Eagle Story, by Lydia and Francois du Toit, illustrated by Carla Krige

Stella's Secret by Lydia du Toit and illustrated by Wendy Francisco.

The Little Bear and the Mirror by Lydia du Toit and illustrated by Karlee Lillywhite.

KAA of the Great Kalahari by Lydia du Toit and illustrated by Sanette Strydom.

King Solitaire's Big Banquet by Lydia du Toit and illustrated by @christo_francois_art

The Mirror Bible, Divine Embrace God Believes in You and The Logic of His Love are also available on Kindle. The new updated Mirror Bible App is available on our website

www.mirrorword.net

Subscribe to Francois facebook updates http://www.facebook.com/francois.toit

The Mirror Translation fb group http://www.facebook.com/groups/179109018883718/

ISBN 97817764104910

The Mirror Bible is a work in progress

This is the 11th Edition

Also available on Kindle and other E-Book platforms or as an App in Android as well as in Apple.

www.mirrorword.net

The Mirror Study Bible is a work in progress

Since its 1st Edition print in 2012, the MSB has become a very bulky book.

The single book size of **the 11th Edition** exceeds 1200 pages, so, our Print on Demand Ingram publishers would in future print 3 Separate Volumes of approximately 500 pages each.

This is the Second of our set of 3 Volume Formats.

Volume 1 is dedicated to **Dr Luke**

Luke's brilliant account of the Life of Jesus - The Gospel of Luke

& his account of the Acts of the apostles

Volume 2 features **Paul's** writings as well as **James** and **Peter**.

Paul's Brilliant **Epistles** &

The Amazing Book of **Hebrews**

James - The Younger Brother of Jesus

Priceless **Peter**

Volume 3 - features **John's** writings

John's beautiful **Gospel**
The **Epistle** of John
Revelation - John's Amazing unveiling of the triumph of the Lamb

A 4th Volume will eventually feature **Matthew and Mark.**

At the completion of the New Testament, the MSB will also be printed as a one volume book on thin "Bible-paper"

THE MIRROR STUDY BIBLE

The Mirror Study Bible is a paraphrased translation from the Greek text. While strictly following the literal meaning of the original, sentences have been constructed so that the larger meaning is continually emphasized by means of an expanded text.

Some clarifying notes are included in italics. This is a paraphrased study rather than a literal translation. While the detailed shades of meaning of every Greek word and its components have been closely studied, this is done taking into account the consistent context of the entire chapter within the wider epistle, and bearing in mind that Jesus is what the Scriptures are all about and humankind is what Jesus is all about.

To assist the reader in their study, I have numerically superscripted the Greek word and corresponded it with the closest English word in the italicized commentary that follows. This is to create a direct comparison of words between the two languages.

I translated several Pauline epistles in the eighties, but these were never published.

In 2007 I started with the Mirror Translation. This is an ongoing process and will eventually include the entire New Testament as well as select portions of the Old Testament.

Completed books and chapters as of July 2023 are:

Luke; John; Acts 1-12; Romans; 1 Corinthians; 2 Corinthians;

Galatians; Ephesians; Philippians; Colossians;

1 Thessalonians; 2 Timothy; Titus; Philemon; Hebrews; James; 1 Peter 1,2,3,5; 2 Peter 1

1 John 1-5; Revelation

The 11th Edition Mirror Study Bible is available in 3 Separate Volumes in both Paperback as well as Case Laminate, Hardback formats.
The previous 10th Edition MSB is still available as a single Volume
Because of its sheer size, we recommend the Hardcover version

See website for other languages as well as Children's Books
www.mirrorword.net

I dedicate this book to you, the Reader.
As you ponder these pages,
I pray, that Holy Spirit quicken
your spirit with fresh insight
and resonance as you engage
in the
Romance of the Ages.

Jesus is God's language and message to mankind.

He is the context of Scripture.

To add anything to his completed work in revealing and redeeming the
image of God in human form,

or taking anything away from what God spoke to us in him, is to depart
from the essence of the Gospel.

There is no perfect translation;

there is only a perfect Word: the Logic of God.

The Bible is all about Jesus.

What makes the book irresistibly relevant, is the fact that

Jesus is all about you.

He mirrors the Incarnate word, face to face with the Father

and now unveiled in you! This is the mystery that was hidden for ages
and generations!

It is Christ in you!
God has found a face in you that portrays him

more beautifully than the best theology.

Your features, your touch, the cadence of your voice,

the compassion in your gaze, the lines of your smile,

the warmth of your person and presence unveil him.

INDEX

Soul realm sources its wisdom from information
gathered and interpreted through the senses
and filtered through the familiar avenues of our cultural,
historical, or personal references.
There is another Source though.
Supreme and most significant;
when one's ears begin to hear the whispers
of spirit to spirit resonance -
the Logic of a thought incarnate,
inside of you -
a knowing that you are known,
entirely-
even from before time was-
and that you are loved -
unconditionally and very intentionally.
This understanding cuts like a two edged sword
piercing,
to the division of soul and spirit,
ending the dominance of the sense realm
and its neutralizing effect upon the human spirit.
In this way man's spirit is freed
to become the ruling influence again
in the thoughts and intentions of the heart.
Hebrews 4:12

Reflecting on any translation of Scripture gives one the opportunity to hear our Maker's voice and thoughts, filtered through the interpretation and language of the translator.

In this fresh Paraphrase, Francois du Toit has opened the curtain for readers of any age, culture or language to enjoy amazing insights into the heartbeat of *Agapē* - where everyone feels equally loved, included and valued in the eyes of the Father - and fully redeemed in the union we come from.

Archbishop **Desmond Tutu** - *Legacy Foundation*

In a world where Bible translations and paraphrases are ubiquitous, *The Mirror Study Bible* is uniquely beautiful and helpful. Submitted to the original texts and the abiding guidance of the Holy Spirit, Francois du Toit carefully and meticulously opens and explores the treasures of Scripture. Not only does it satisfy the demands of the intellect, but it overwhelms the heart.

Wm Paul Young - *Author of The Shack*

The Mirror Study Bible is a transforming paraphrased translation that is simplistic, accurate, detailed and comprehensive, captivating and at the same time exuding intriguing spiritual revelation; it is divinely insightful and contemporary.

It's a must read, a befitting guide and manual for all age groups for; Bible study, meditation, devotion, worship, teaching, instruction and scholarship.

Jesus Christ is the epicenter of the entire text.

Believers will not miss the centrality of the translation as there is a finite and delicate thread directing to the revealing and redeeming Christ.

Unbelievers will derive unrivaled comfort from the text as they get captivated by the reality and close proximity of Christ.

This is definitely a life giving and transforming translation. I am humbly convinced that Francois is chosen by God to serve this generation and the next with undiluted truth in the midst of incomprehensible compromises of worldly, heretical and traditional doctrinal interpretations and practices (religion) that have diverted us from the truth.

The Mirror Study Bible is a welcome revelatory and revolutionary development that is divinely sanctioned, inspired and directed. This translation is by no doubt a compelling grounding expository of our century.
To God be the Glory.

Rev. Anouya Andrew Muchechetere - *MBA. MA.*
Former Secretary General of the Evangelical Fellowship of Zimbabwe (EFZ).

The Mirror Study Bible is astonishingly beautiful. The union theme is outstanding.

The gospel is not the news that we can receive Jesus into our lives; it is the news that Jesus has received us into His. Once we discover this reality, beautiful, liberating, and life-giving questions emerge. Who is this Jesus who has received us into his life with his Father and the Holy Spirit?

What is his life all about? How did he receive us? What does this mean for us, and for creation here and now, and hereafter?

The early followers of Jesus knew that he was the center of all creation, the plan from the beginning, the alpha and the omega, the author and finisher of faith. They wrestled deeply with these questions and the staggering implications of Jesus' very identity. They handed down clear and powerful and very relevant insights and answers. Francois has met the Jesus of the Apostles, and through his wrestling with their light, is providing for us all a paraphrase of their work that is as thrilling as it is beautiful and true.

My imagination ignites reading your translation. What a beautiful, breathtaking translation. This is brilliant, and destined to relieve and liberate many. You sing the Father's heart, my brother. May the Holy Spirit continue to use the Mirror to reveal Jesus and his Father and us all around this world! I love it.

This is so beautiful! Poetic and profound.

And, about the book of Revelation: I have plunged myself deep into the Apocalypse, reading articles, books, and commentaries. Francois, your translation rocks. I am so very proud of you and can only imagine what you have had to suffer to give birth to this translation. Union, union, union. Blindness, blindness, blindness. Union wins. Hallelujah. What a beautiful, stunning translation.

John must be in ecstatic joy.

Francois' paraphrase challenges everything you thought you knew about this book.

Astonishingly beautiful, and wonderfully controversial.

Dr. C. Baxter Kruger - *Author of "The Great Dance" and "The Shack Revisited"*

The Bible is God's amazing conversation with us. Here we engage with God's words that crescendo in the revelation of his Son, Jesus Christ. The greatest joy is to realize that you as an individual are included in this conversation.

It was the mission of Jesus to reveal the Father; studying Scripture outside of the context of the finished work of Christ on man's behalf causes one to miss out on understanding and appreciating the Father's loving intention with the human race.

The Mirror Study Bible brings a dimension in which this revelation is facilitated in a way that makes it not only easy to understand, but also life changing in its powerful impact as the revelation dawns in one's heart.

This translation is in all probability one of the greatest contributions in the last few years to the broader church. It is imperative that every Christ follower discovers their true identity mirrored in Jesus. The most liberating revelation is the fact that we have not only died together with Him, but that we were also raised with Him in resurrection life. Then to grasp that we are seated with Him in heavenly places, where we may now live our daily lives from a position of significance and influence within this world. The premise of the Good News of the Gospel is that we are not required to strive to attain something through personal achievement, but rather to discover who we already are and what we already have in Christ, as revealed in the glorious Scriptures.

May *The Mirror* impact your life as much as it has mine, and may it facilitate your spiritual journey to truly relocate your mind, living from the new vantage point of this glorious life in Christ.

Alan Platt - *Visionary leader of* **Doxa Deō** *International*

The mystery concerning God's Own action in Christ, balanced with the nature and necessity of our human response has defined my personal journey for many years.

When I was introduced to Francois du Toit and *The Mirror Study Bible*, much of that mystery were resolved. Often, I found myself 'gasping for breath' as some new aspect of the mystery of Christ and His Kingdom emerged with startling clarity.

Francois' love for the text, his sheer exegetical courage and his astonishing ability to express essential biblical pre-suppositions in the intimate Love language of God, has opened for Judith and me a renewed and transformative biblical understanding.

Bob and **Judith Mumford** - *www.lifechangers.org*

When the 1611 King James team endeavored to compile their English version of the Bible, they quoted Augustine as proof "that variety of translations is profitable for the finding out of the sense of the Scriptures." As an avid collector of translations, I would highly recommend *The Mirror Study Bible* as one of my favorites. Though every scholar attempts to present an objective portrayal of the text, each version is ultimately filtered through the translator's own theological lens. This is not wrong per se—it is impossible to convey the text apart from our own understanding of the work and nature of God. Perhaps this is why Francois du Toit's work brings such a fresh perspective to the table. To rightly divide the Word of God, our interpretative lens must ultimately be the person of Christ Himself and His finished work. Christ is the ultimate Text. Each page of The Mirror drips with grace as we discover our own identity restored in the very Image of the invisible God, the Firstborn of all creation.

John Crowder - Author of "Mystical Union" and "Cosmos Reborn"

I thank God I live today when God is releasing through full hearts like yours the true revelation of His heart and intent in glorious, creative wisdom and words.

In my more than 40 years of believing, I have never had such joy as these last years after becoming involved with your books. I am so grateful, I often cry when reading the Mirror. I have been overwhelmingly transformed by God Believes in You. I am a professional writer myself and ghost write for many Christian leaders.

I have found such treasure in the Mirror Study Bible!

Thank you, Holy Spirit, for singing us this new love song!

Bessie Watson Rhoades

I have been asked at times why God didn't make the Bible easier to understand. If He is able to inspire the writings of Scripture, couldn't He provide a key for unlocking its treasures for us? *The Mirror Translation* you hold in your hand opens the treasure-chest of understanding with that Key. The key to properly understanding the Bible is Jesus Christ. He is the source and subject of its pages. For years I have been asked why there isn't a Bible translation that presents the Scriptures from a pure grace orientation. It is a great encouragement to know that the Mirror Bible is just that. Drawing not only from the literal meaning, but also the historical nuances of the Greek language, Francois Du Toit presents this translation in a way that will enrich your love for our Triune God and ground you in the grace expressed to us all through Jesus Christ. This is a translation you will read again and again. It is one you will share with your friends.

Dr. Steve Mcvey - *Founder of Grace Walk Ministries, Florida*

See your identity clearly portrayed here in The MIRROR! Exhilarating, thrilling, breathtaking beauty overtakes you in this glorious translation. God's empowering, everlasting, all-compassing Gospel of Grace – Christ's Finished Work – is here revealed in depths and dimensions of joy that will rock your world.

You are co-revealed in Christ! Co-crucified, co-included in His death and resurrection, co-buried, co-quickened, co- alive, co-seated with Him in His executive authority in the Throne Room of the heavenly realm (Ephesians. 2:5,6 The Mirror). Herewith, my highest recommendation for this new, powerful, mega-encouraging Bible translation, so rich with fresh, wide vistas of the mystery of our restored innocence in Christ.

May The MIRROR STUDY BIBLE soon be treasured in every home, seminary and School of Ministry in the world!

Rev. **Lani Langlais** - San Francisco, California

We consider it a great honor to be the academic institution that first had the opportunity to recognize your incredible work producing the Mirror Study Bible. The spiritual insight that you reveal along with your thorough exegesis amazes me.

I have had many favorite translations over the years, but none that elevates me to experience such glorious heavenly communion as the Mirror.

The world will be forever indebted to you for such a powerful gift of The Mirror Word, and a true understanding of God's Kingdom and His overwhelming love for His creation and family.

Dr. Douglas J. Wingate - President and Founder

Life Christian University

(On the 11th of June 2022 I was honored with a PhD degree in theology and philosophy, based on the Mirror Study Bible work. FDT)

My philosophy in doing the Mirror Bible is reflected in the following example:

I do not read music, but have often witnessed our son, Stefan, approach a new piece on the piano.

His eyes see so much more than mere marks scribbled on a page;

he hears the music.

His trained mind engages even the subtleties and the nuances of the original composition, and is able to repeat the authentic sound,

knowing that the destiny of the music would never be reduced to the page;

but is always in the next moment,

where the same intended beauty is heard

and repeated again.

The best translation would always be the incarnation.

I so value the enormity of the revelation of the incarnation.

Yet, before flesh, the Word was προς

face to face with God.

And fragile text

scribbled through the ages in memoirs of stone, parchment and papyrus pages -

carrying eternity in thought

and continues to translate faith

to faith.

Now we have the same spirit of faith as he encountered when he wrote...

I believe

and so I speak.

Conversation ignites.

Did not our hearts burn within our being when he spoke familiar text of ancient times, in the voices of Moses and the prophets and David and Abraham,

who saw his day

and announced its dawn in our hearts.

The mystery that was hidden for ages and generations

is now revealed.

In dealing daily with ancient text,

rediscovering thoughts buried in time, I am often overwhelmed and awed at the magnificence of eternity captured in little time capsules,

opening vistas of beauty beyond our imagination- face to face with the same face to faceness of the Logos

and God

and us - conceived in their dream.

And irresistibly intrigued by the invitation to come and drink -

to taste and see -

from the source -

and to hear a saint reminiscing and reminding himself of the utterance of another earth dweller-brother, David, who wrote a song 1000 BC,

Return to your rest, oh my soul.

For the Lord has dealt bountifully with you.

I believe and so I speak.

And with fresh wounds bleeding from the many angry blows he was dealt with, Paul echoes,

We have the same spirit of faith as he had who wrote, 'I believe and so I speak.' We too believe and so we speak.

Let's celebrate the sameness of Jesus

yesterday - yes, as far as history and beyond time can go -

and today. This very finite, fragile moment -

plus, the infinite future.

Inexhaustible, beyond boundaries and the confines of space and time.

The Value of Etymology

Etymology is the study of the origin of words in order to help understand their history and original meaning.

The word etymology is the Greek word, ἐτυμολογία *etumologia.* It too, like most Greek words, have various components, ἔτυμον, *etumon,* true, and λογια *logia,* words. Thus, the study of the true meaning of words.

Obviously, the meaning of many words have evolved over the centuries in their use, and have in time departed from their original meaning. Especially in modern languages we have ample examples where the accepted word today bears no relevance whatsoever to the meaning of their individual components. However, many still do.

My passion therefore, as a treasure hunter, is to uncover and unveil these gems, always bearing in mind the ultimate relevance found in context.

The context of this conversation is beautifully reflected in *John 1:1-3 & 14,* as well as *Hebrews 1:1-3.* And is also powerfully endorsed in Paul's focus in his writings.

The destiny of the word has always been flesh - the Incarnation. *[Latin, en carne]*

John 1:14 Suddenly the invisible, eternal Word takes on visible form - the Incarnation, on display in a flesh and blood Person, as in a mirror. In him, and now confirmed in us. The most accurate tangible exhibit of God's eternal thought finds expression in human life. The Word became a human being; we are his address; he resides in us. He captivates our gaze. The glory we see there is not a religious replica; he is the authentic begotten Son. The glory *(that we lost in Adam)* **returns in fullness. Only grace can communicate truth in such a complete context.**

Colossians 1:19 Jesus is God's happy delight to be human. *Also Colossians 2:9,10. See* **2 Corinthians 3:2,3 The living Epistle speaks a global, mother-tongue language! This conversation is embroidered in your inner consciousness.** *(It is the life of your design that grace echoes within you.)*

In human conscience, we have the invisible written logos fully preserved and recorded to reflect in the Aha! resonance-echo, within us! We are compatible by design to hear with inner-ears.

Romans 1:19 God is not a stranger to anyone; whatever can be known of God is [1]manifest in man. God has [2]revealed it in the very core of our being which bears witness with our conscience. *(The word [1]phaneros Adjective, from phainō, means to shine like light. Then, the same word again, εφανερωσεν [2]ephanerōsen, this time in the Aorist Active Indicative Tense of phainō, God has shone this light into our hearts. The TPT reads, God has embedded this knowledge inside every human heart.)*

> *Note* **Romans 2:14 For even a pagan's natural instinct will confirm the law to be present in their conscience; though they have never even heard about Jewish laws. Thus they prove to be a law unto themselves.**

> **Romans 2:15 The law is so much more than a mere written code; its presence in human [1]conscience even in the absence of the written instruction is obvious.** *(The Latin word [1]conscience means to see together - as in the Greek word συνείδω suneidō.)*

> See also *2 Corinthians 4:4 & 7* and *Colossians 1:27.* Blindfold-mode simply veils, but does not remove the treasure from where it was hidden all along. Every time we love, encounter joy, or experience beauty, a hint of the nature

of our Maker reflects within us; even in the experience of the unbeliever. In the incarnation Jesus unveils God's likeness, not his otherness, in human form as in a mirror.

Paul wrote two thousand years ago…

Ephesians 3:4 In [1]pondering these words you will [2]perceive my [3]insight into the mystery of Christ.

*([1] The word, [1]anaginōskō, suggests an upward [ana] knowledge [ginōskō]; to know again, to recognize, to read with recognition. See my **Notes on An Open Heaven** at the end of Revelation 13.*

*[2] You will comprehend, νοιέω [2]noeō, to perceive; thoughtful understanding. [This is also the word connected with the preposition **meta** [with] in μετανοέω **metanoeō**, to awaken in your understanding. It does NOT mean, to repent! See Luke 5:32].*

*[3] Paul anticipates the impact of his own insight in his audience! The word, insight, [3]sunesis, from συνίημι **suniem**i – **sun** + **eimi**, together with my I am-ness, to resonate; which means a flowing together as of two streams – a seamless merging; a fusion of thought; a joint-seeing; to sync together in order to form a mental picture. It suggests the grasp and comprehension that happens from comparing and combining things. A word only Paul uses; also his colleague, Dr Luke, in Luke 2:47, as well as another disciple of Paul, Mark who uses it in **Mark 12:33**, To love him with all your heart, with all your **understanding**, with all your strength, and to love your neighbor as you love yourself; this is more important than all the burnt offerings and sacrifices.)*

Luke, interviewing the two men who encountered Jesus as a stranger along their journey from Jerusalem to Emmaus, where Jesus endorses the entire context of Scripture

Luke 24:32 They erupted in an avalanche of words, Was our hearts not set ablaze – even while he was speaking along the way and opening the Scriptures to us. (οὐχὶ ἡ καρδία ἡμῶν καιομένη ἦν – ὡς ἐλάλει – διήνοιγεν) *The Authorized Version, as usual, pays no attention to the **graphic Imperfect Tenses** here. They are speaking of something which was in progress: was not our heart burning [finite verb and Participle] while he was speaking, and was opening the Scriptures? [Marvin Vincent.]*

Jesus could easily have just tapped them on the shoulder at the beginning of their journey and immediately told them who he was! But he reveals himself in their familiar language, the Scriptures, knowing that the entire context of the Incarnation is grounded in these profound, prophetic writings. Also, this beats any angelic visitation hands down!

*It pleased the father, Paul later recalls, to unveil his son IN me! The fire now kindled in their hearts, would become a mirror-encounter where the mystery that was hidden for ages and generations would gush out from within them. **Colossians 1:27**.)*

In the study of the ancient languages of Scripture the etymology of very many words in **Koine Greek** as well as the meaning of individual letters of the Ancient as well as *the square letter Aramaic/Hebrew alphabet*, carry significant relevance.

Notes on the Ancient Hebrew Alphabet: With the Babylonian exile, 586 BC, the Jews gradually stopped using the Paleō-Hebrew script, based on *ancient pictographic letters*, [10th century BCE – CE 135] otherwise known as the Phoenician alphabet and instead adopted a *square letter form of the Aramaic alphabet*. See my introduction to Luke chapter 3 in the Mirror Bible…

Notes on Koine Greek LXX Old Testament and the New Testament:

Koine Greek evolved from *the spread of Greek* following the conquests of *Alexander the Great in the fourth century BC* and served as *the lingua franca* of much of the Mediterranean region and the Middle East during the following centuries.

Koine is the language of the Christian New Testament, of the Septuagint LXX *(the 3rd-century BC. Greek translation of the Hebrew Bible),* **and of most early Christian theological writing by the Church Fathers.**

I believe that, just like gold-containing ore, so the Bible contains the Word. Though the ore is a most important pointer to the gold, it cannot be confused with the gold. Jesus is the Word unveiled – He studied scripture with a different intent; he knew that he was reflected there! Familiar with the text, he brought context! Psalm 40:7 and Hebrews 10:7; also, John 5:39.

During my 3-year studies at the University of Pretoria *[1975-1977]*, I was triggered with the intrigue of the richness of the language, and how so much of the nuances and early meanings of words have remained hidden and were ultimately lost in many translations over the years.

I remember one day in an Assembly of God church, which we joined just after we got married *[January 1979]*, we attended a Bible-study meeting. I excitedly shared from John 14:2, The word, *μονή monē*, is only used here and in verse 23. The verb form, *menō* suggests a seamless union. *[John uses menō more than anyone else.]* As in the next chapter, John 15:4. ...the branch *abiding* in the vine.

So, Jesus was not about to become a building contractor in heaven. He is not in the mansion building-business, as some translations will imply! He is standing on the threshold of the cross; in his death and resurrection he would prepare a place for us of restored, intimate *oneness* with himself and the Father in Spirit and in truth. Now we may be where he is, wrapped up in the same, *inseparable union*. See *John 14:20*.

Our pastor immediately stopped me saying, If the King James says it's a mansion then that's what it is!

This early encounter inspired me even more on my journey of regularly referencing the Hebrew and Greek text in studying the Bible. During our Acts Team days *[December '85 – Jan '91]*, I translated several of the Pauline Epistles which were never published; although printed along with other booklets which I wrote and distributed amongst our students.

Oh, how I love the word!

Just look at the first word in the Hebrew Bible, [in the beginning] בראשית *Bereshet, be,* (in) *rosh* (head) We are the idea of Elohim!

As stated earlier, etymology is the study of the history of words, their origins, and how their form and meaning have changed over time. By an extension, the term the etymology of [a word] means the origin of the particular word.

My point is, the words that I pursue in the Greek components are not to contradict the character of God but to rather discover how the context is endorsed in our understanding of the word.

It is my delight, over the years, to seek out these treasures. Some of which you will not find in a lexicon or a dictionary.

Here are a few examples of my use of etymology, with notes following:

1/ χαρακτηρ *charaktēr*;

2/ ἐπιχορηγέω *epichoregō*

3/ ἀγαπάω *agapaō*

4/ ἁμαρτία *hamartia*

5/ ἐξουσία [1]*exousia* & ἔξεστι [2]*exesti* [*exact same components*]

6/ ἐκκλησία *ekklesia*

7/ ᾅδης *Hadēs*

8/ paradise παράδεισος

9/ παρουσία *parousia*

10/ δίκη *dikē*

11/ μετάνοια *metanoia*

12/ διάκονος *diakonos*

1/ The word χαρακτηρ *charaktēr*

From χάραγμα *charagma* – to engrave – translated mark of the beast, in Revelation 13:16,17.

Hebrews 1:3 The Messiah-message is what has been on the tip of the Father's tongue all along. Now he is the crescendo of God's conversation with us and gives context and content to the authentic, prophetic thought. Everything that God has in mind for mankind is voiced in him. Jesus is God's language. He is the [1]radiant and flawless mirror expression of the person of God. He makes the [2]glorious intent of God visible and exhibits the [3]character and every attribute of Elohim in human form. His being announces [4]our redeemed innocence; having accomplished purification for sins, he sat down, enthroned in the boundless measure of his majesty in the right and of God as his executive authority. He is the force of the universe, [5]upholding everything that exists. This conversation is the dynamic that sustains the entire cosmos.

([1] The word απαυγασμα [1]apaugasma, only occurs here, and once only in the Greek Septuagint, LXX, in the book of Wisdom 7:26, For she is the brightness of the everlasting light, the unspotted mirror of the power of God, and the image of his goodness. [The Book of Wisdom 7:26.]

[2] The word, δόξα [2]doxa glory is the expression of the divine attributes collectively. It is the unfolded fullness of the divine perfections. Vincent.

[3] The word χαρακτηρ [3]charaktēr from χάραγμα charagma - to engrave - translated mark of the beast, in Revelation 13:16,17. Either the character of the Father or the character of the fallen mind will influence our actions (hand) because it is what engages our thoughts (forehead).

[4] Having accomplished purification of sins, he sat down ... His throne is the very endorsement of mankind's redeemed innocence. See Ephesians 1:20-23; LXX Psalm 109:1.

[5] The words, φέρων τε τὰ πάντα [5]pherō te ta panta - [5]upholding all things, are not static, they imply sustaining, but also movement. It deals with a burden, not as a dead weight, but as in continual movement; as Weiss puts it, 'with the all in all its changes and transformations throughout the aeons.' Vincent.

More than two thousand years ago the conversation that had begun before time was recorded—sustained in fragments of thought throughout the ages, whispered in prophetic language, chiseled in stone and inscribed in human conscience and memory—became a man. Beyond the tablet of stone, the papyrus scroll or parchment roll, human life has become the articulate voice of God. Jesus is the crescendo of God's conversation with mankind; he gives context and content to the authentic thought. His name declares his mission.

As Savior of the world he truly redeemed the image and likeness of the invisible God and made him apparent again in human form as in a mirror.)

2/ The word, ἐπιχορηγέω *epichoregeō* has 3 components:

This is a keyword in Peter's powerful illustration in 2 Peter 1:1-10, which was traditionally translated, to 'add to', in verse 5.

The etymological values of this word clearly describe a conductor of music. Consider its three components: [1]*epi*, a Preposition of position, over, in charge, indicating continuous influence upon; *[with the idea of a teacher standing in front of a class of students]* + [2]*chorus*, choir, orchestra, or dance + [3]*agō*, meaning to lead as a shepherd leads his sheep.

Sadly, by translating *epichoregeō* as, **add to** your faith virtue, etc..., the Authorized Bibles all repeat the same mistake, which has kept multitudes of sincere believers trapped in the treadmill-mode of striving to become; instead of discovering who you are and what you already have!

This is after Peter clearly states in verse 1 that, to begin with, we already are equal shareholders in a faith of exactly the same, priceless value.

Then, in verse 3 he states that it is by God's divine engineering, that we are gifted with all that it takes to live life to the full.

Gift language puts reward language out of business!

One cannot add to something that is already complete. However, one can engage in the adventure of a limitless discovery.

I often use an 8-piece Babushka doll to illustrate that there is so much more than just the outer image. This is a traditional Babushka Russian doll, beautifully carved out of wood and painted with colorful images.

The outer image is repeated again and again in smaller, identical inner pieces – each one fitting perfectly into the other. Until it almost seems impossible that yet another piece could follow the little figures that emerge. Our 5-year-old granddaughter, Nicola calls this, **the Reflection Doll.**

The outer piece of the Babushka represents **the Faith** which has given everyone an equal standing through God's righteousness and not our efforts.... [verse 1]

This now beautifully unfolds into these amazing attributes which each person is already and equally gifted with. Now, acquaint yourself with these.

1/ Faith; 2/ Elevation; 3/ Spiritual insight; 4/ Inner strength; 5/ Patient perseverance; 6/ Meaningful devotion and worship; 7/ Genuine fondness for others and finally, the heart of faith is 8/ the Agapē of God.

3/ The Greek verb ἀγαπάω *Agapaō* to love, [noun, *Agapē*]

*The word [1]agapaō is a compound word from **agō**, which means to lead as a shepherd leads his sheep, and **paō**, which means rest. His love leads me into his rest; into the full realization of his finished work. Agapē is Psalm 23 in one word. My Shepherd-Lord leads me beside still waters where my soul is restored; [by the waters of reflection my soul remembers who I am]. Now I can face the valley of the shadow of death and fear no evil.*

It does not derive from the Hebrew עגב *Agab* as the dictionaries would imply – Agab is a word that Ezekiel uses 6 times and Jeremiah only once; and every time it is used for lust as in whoredom!

The Hebrew word for love, closest to Agapē is the word, אהב *Ahab* which is used 207 times.

See my use of the word *agapē* here:

John 14:23 Jesus answered him, This is so much more than a mere casual, distant and suspicious, or indifferent observation of me; this is about someone's [1]passionate, loving desire, finding its rest in me; they will treasure my words and encounter my Father's love reflecting in them, and my Father and I will [2]appear [3]face to face to them, and make our [4]abode [5]with each one individually. *To love passionately, [1]agapaō from agō and paō, to lead to rest [Psalm 23] – this word also links to the Hebrew word for love, אהב ahab, to love with passionate desire; like a beating heart or breathing chest. Genesis 22;2 Abraham's love for Isaac. Jeremiah 31:3 I have loved you with an everlasting love: therefore, with lovingkindness have I drawn you.*

4/ Then the word *ἁμαρτία hamartia*

The root of sin is to believe a lie about yourself. To be out of sync with the life of your design.

The word sin, is the word *hamartia*, from *ha*, negative or without and *meros*, portion or form; thus to be without your allotted portion or without form, pointing to a disoriented, distorted, bankrupt identity; the word *meros*, is the stem of *morphē*, as in *2 Corinthians 3:18* - the word *metamorphē*, with form, which is the opposite of *hamartia* – without form. Sin is to live out of context with the blueprint of one's design; to behave out of tune with God's original harmony.

See *Deuteronomy 32:18*, You have forgotten the Rock that begot you and have gotten out of step with the God who danced with you. Hebrew, חול *khul*, also means to dance, as in *Judges 21:21.*

5/ The word *ἐξουσία [1]exousia & ἔξεστι [2]exesti*

Both have the same 2 components:

[1] The 1st one, *exousia*, is often translated as authority. From *ek*, a Preposition pointing to the origin or source, and *eimi*, I am; *thus, out of I am. This gives legitimacy and authority to our sonship.* See *John 1:12*, *... God gives the assurance that they are indeed his offspring, begotten of him; <u>he sanctions the legitimacy of their sonship</u>.*

[2] Then also the word, *ἔξεστι exesti which* is often translated lawful. **See 2 Corinthians 12:4 This person was caught up into paradise. There he heard words that could not be articulated into language; he understood a conversation that did not <u>originate</u> in human thought.** *The word ἔξεστι exesti, <u>again has the same two components</u> as the word, exousia, ek, a Preposition pointing to the origin of something, and eimi, I am, in this case, Paul <u>points to the origin of our beingness</u> in God's authentic thought. See **1 Corinthians 2:7-13**.)*

6/ Here's what Jesus says about the *Ekklesia*:

The 1st time this word is mentioned, is in **Matthew 16:13-19**. Here also, Jesus asks the most important question in the Bible **Who do people say, that I, the son of man, am?**

Luke 9:19 They replied, Some think that you could possibly be John the Baptist reincarnated, or even a re-appearance of Elijah, or another of the ancient prophets resurrected.

Luke 9:20 And you; who am I to you? Jesus asked them; Peter answered, The Messiah of God.

Matthew 16:17 Blessed are you, Simon, <u>son of</u> Jonah. *[<u>Bar Jonah, his surname identity</u>]* **Flesh and blood did not reveal this to you, but my Father.** *(No, I'm not a reincarnate prophet. I am the Incarnate Word in whom all things exist – I gave you birth.)*

Matthew 16:18 Now that you know who I am, allow me to introduce you to you, Mr. Rock! You're a chip [petros] of the old Block [petra]. And upon this revelation, that the son of man is the son of God, I will build my Ekklesia-church, and the gates of Hadēs will not prevail against it.

Matthew 16:19 *[In this revelation, of seeing mankind's authentic identity,]* **I give you to the keys of the dominion of the heavens, and whatever you bind upon the earth shall be, [1]having been bound in the heavens, and whatever you loose upon the earth shall be, [1]having been loosed in the heavens.**

The word, traditionally translated, **church,** ἐκκλησία **ekklesia,** *from* **ek,** *origin and* **kaleō,** *to* **surname;** *[in this context it is clearly reflected in Jesus mentioning Simon's surname, Simon, son of Jonah, flesh and blood did not reveal this to you. Jonah does not define you!] The Perfect Passive tense used in both, having been bound and having been loosed, clearly reveals what Jesus accomplished once and for all in his triumphant mission.*

Thus, the **ekklesia-church** *is the voice of God echoing in man and reveals man's true spiritual origin and identity.*

The keys Jesus refers to here, are the same keys John recorded in **Revelation 1:18.**

Revelation 1:17 Observing all this, I fell at his feet like a dead man. Then, [1]kneeling down, he ordained me with his right hand upon me and said, Do not be afraid. I am the origin and the [2]conclusion of all things. *(See Isaiah 44:6. The word [1]****tithēmi*** *from* **theō,** *to kneel down, lay down, to ordain, purpose, put, set forth. See John 15:16, I have* **ordained** *you - I have strategically positioned you. Also 1 Timothy 2:7 I am an ordained preacher.*

Again the word, **[2]eschatos;** *Jesus, as the Alpha and Omega, defines eschatology.)*

Revelation 1:18 I am also the Living One; I died and now, see, here I am alive unto the ages of the ages and I have the keys wherewith I have disengaged the gates of [1]Hades and death. *(This profound statement of Jesus in verses 17 & 18, is the platform, theme and focus of the entire book. To distract from these words of Jesus is to miss the point of the Revelation. [1]See commentary note in verse 20 and Revelation 2:7 on the gates of Hadēs. Multitudes are in hell on this side of the grave; we have the keys to unlock a door that was already opened when Jesus went there as a man to free the human race from Adam to Noah, to now. Wow, what joy to introduce people to the freedom of sonship. Let's not make the other brother in Luke 15 our reference when we can know the Father's heart.)*

7/ The word ᾅδης *Hadēs*

It has 2 components, *ha*, negative/not, and *eidō*; thus, not to see.

Jesus says in **Matthew 16:18 I say, you are Rock, a chip [petros] of the old Block [petra]. And upon this revelation, that the son of man is the son of God, I will build my ekklesia-church, and the gates of Hadēs will not prevail against it.** *(In a walled city, the gates are the most strategic point - if the gates are disengaged, the city is taken. Thus,* **the blindfold mode of mankind's forgotten identity, will not prevail against your advance.***)*

8/ The word *paradise* παράδεισος

[Which is the opposite of the word **Hadēs***], from* **para,** *closest possible union, and* **eidō,** *to see; thus, to see from a place of our union.*

9/ The word, παρουσία *parousia*

It does not mean 2nd coming!

1 Thessalonians 2:19 We expect nothing less in the context of the gospel than you enjoying a face to face encounter in the [1]immediate presence of our Lord Jesus Christ. This is our delight and wreath of honor. *(The word [1]parousia speaks of the immediate presence of the Lord. From **para**, a Preposition indicating closest possible proximity; intimate connection, and **eimi**, I am.*

*There is not even a hint of judgment or punishment in this word. While there are great and accurate definitions in Strongs, please do not believe everything you read there. G3952 parousia from the Present Participle of G3918 **pareimi**; a being near, that is, advent; often, return; specifically of Christ to punish Jerusalem, or finally the wicked.!?*

The Greek word **parousia**, occurs 24 times in the NT, and 22 times it wrongly implies a 2nd coming or coming judgment.

Only twice it is translated as presence. 2 Corinthians 10:10, Philippians 2:12.

Of all the English translations that I have checked, only the Young's Literal has it correct. What a shame that this word has been so dramatically twisted over the years.

In the Greek Septuagint **Psalm 138:8** *[in the Hebrew it is Psalm 139]* reads, **If I make my bed in Hadēs, your presence already fills it.**

LXX - πάρειμι pareimi your immediate presence - I am.

10/ The word, δίκη *dikē*

This word suggests, to be judged equal; indicating two parties finding likeness in each other - which is also the stem for the word, righteousness, **dikaiosunē** .

Dikē, *[pronounced, Dikay]* reminds of the Greek goddess of Justice by the same name, typically portrayed holding a scale of balances in her hand.

In Ancient Greek δείκνυμι - to bring to light, display, portray, represent; to make known, explain, teach, prove. In Sanskrit it means direction. Sadly this word is translated as vengeance, judgment or punishment in the 4 instances it is used in the NT.

2 Corinthians 6:14 Faith-righteousness has nothing in common with the philosophies of karma and performance-based approval; they could never [1]balance the scales or be evenly yoked together in any context.

> *(1) The word [1]**heterozugeō**, an unequal or different yoke; from the Hebrew word, **zugot**, זוגות indicates pairs of two identical objects; a yoke or a teaching; the yoke of a rabbi or philosopher represented their doctrine; reminds of the Hebrew word for righteousness, **tzedek**, צדק which also includes the idea of the wooden beam in a scale of balances. He that judges his neighbor according to the balance of righteousness, or innocence, they judge him according to righteousness. [T. Bab. Sabbat, fol. 127. 2.] The Greek stem for righteousness is **dikē** - it is interesting to note that the Greek goddess of Justice is Dikē [pronounced, **dikay**] and she is always pictured holding a scale of balances in her hand.*

2 Corinthians 6:15 There is no [1]symphony between the value that Christ reveals in people and the worthlessness that [2]Belial represents. Faith-righteousness and work based-righteousness are two opposites; they are conflicting systems that can never match.

> *(1) Paul uses the word [1]**sumphōnēsis** from **sun**, denoting union and **phōnē**, voice. Faith-righteousness is to know the truth about the redeemed life of your design; whereas a work based-righteousness keeps you trapped in a striving to become something that you already are by design. See 2 Corinthians 11:3 also Genesis 3:22 in notes on Psalm 22:2*

> *(2) The Hebrew word, [2]**beliya'al** בליעל literally means without profit; worthlessness. The etymology of this word has been variously given. The Talmud (Sanh. 111b) regards it as*

21

a compound word, made up of beli and 'ol (without a yoke) which is very interesting in this context. Jesus says, My yoke is easy and my burden is light. Peterson renders it, Walk with me and work with me--watch how I do it. Learn the unforced rhythms of grace. I won't lay anything heavy or ill-fitting on you. Keep company with me and you'll learn to live freely and lightly. Matthew 11:29,30. The Message.

11/ The word μετάνοια metanoia

It does not mean repentance!

It suggests an awakening to the awareness of God's thoughts; from **meta**, together with and **noieō**, to perceive with the mind. It describes the awakening of the mind to that which is true; a re-alignment of one's reasoning; it is a gathering of one's thoughts, a co-knowing. Faith is not a decision; it is a discovery. It has nothing in common with the Latin word **paenitentia** - where the idea of penance and repentance stems from.

Metanoia means to discover God's thoughts about us; literally, to co-know as in Isaiah 55:8-13.

The metanoia moment awakens in us an inevitable returning to our redeemed, authentic Genesis.

See **Psalm 22:27** *-the ends of the earth shall remember, and return to the Lord!* **Jeremiah 1:5;** **1 Corinthians 13:12** *- to know as we have always been known!*

The Shepherd never forsook the sheep, we all like sheep have gone astray!

In the Incarnation Jesus pictures the return of the prodigal son:

In his death he descended with us into the lostness of our hell, and conquered every definition of our darkness; then, in his triumphant resurrection, he co-quickened us and returned us to the bosom of the Father; to awaken from the horror of the nightmare!

See my in depth explanation of this word in **Why The Mirror Translation?**

12/ The word διάκονος diakonos

The word, [1]**diakonos**, deacon or minister from **dia** + **konis** etymologically, **through dust** [*Liddell, Scott & Jones*], which I translated in **2 Corinthians 8:4** as tangible, practical or incarnate.

This word commonly translates as ministry, service, running errands.

I believe that the ultimate service is the expression of the heart of God in tangible human form. In essence, New Testament ministry is a celebration of the incarnation.

I have translated this verse many years ago, and only a few days ago [*October 2023*] discovered the reference in Liddell, Scott & Jones. **Why The Mirror Translation?**

One day I had the pleasure of taking a famous photographer on a scenic boat trip in the bay of our hometown, Hermanus South Africa. I could tell by the size of his camera lenses and equipment that he was not your average tourist.

He explained to me that he needed to sell only two photographs a year to cover his budget. I was impressed to say the least and felt privileged and delighted to watch the artist at work. With fluent skill he would exchange lenses and film and go about his work.

After about two hours with the wonderful Southern Right whales we were on our way back to the harbor when we witnessed a flock of a few hundred Cape Cormorants.

The next moment they all took off in flight; the rhythm and unison of their wings were like a ballet reflecting on the water.

Our photographer friend was happily clicking away when suddenly he shouted, I've got it. I've got it.

It was amazing to witness the joy in the man's face. He knew that he had captured a moment that would be worth more than all the equipment in the boat. He immediately proceeded to pack away his expensive gear and carefully zipped up the waterproof bags. I then watched him relax and sit back, glowing with delight.

I couldn't help but reflect on what must have been the greatest moment when, for the first time in the history of the universe, the invisible Creator witnessed their image and likeness on display in fragile, tangible human form. And God saw everything that he had made and said, Behold, it is very good. And God entered into his rest.

The Sabbath was a celebration of perfection, rather than a break from a busy and exhausting schedule, to observe a religious ritual (Genesis 1:31).

I became absorbed with the thought of photography; magic moments of light, shape, color and movement arrested and stored on film or in memory to be reproduced in a million glossy magazines or framed in art galleries. These exhibitions would be appreciated in any culture or language for countless years to come. I imagined how the artist would document these gems in a way that no virus would flaw the original detail, regardless of what would happen to the prints, whether they be framed, forgotten or destroyed—like words storing images of rare beauty to be repeated at any time in any language or thought.

In one of her classic novels, *Gentian Hill*, Elizabeth Goudge paints the picture of little Stella listening to her stepfather reading from the Bible:

The language would now and then suddenly affect her like an enchantment. The peculiarities of Father Sprigg's delivery worried her not at all. It was as though his gruff voice tossed the words roughly in the air separate particles of no great value, and immediately they fell again transmuted, like the music of a peal of bells or raindrops shot through with sunshine and vista beyond vista of incomparable beauty opened before the mind. It was a mystery to Stella that mere words could make this happen. She supposed the makers of these phrases had fashioned them to hold their visions as one makes a box to hold one's treasure, and Father Sprigg's voice was the key grating in the lock, so that the box could open and set them free. That transmutation in the air still remained as unexplainable as the sudden change in herself, when at the moment of the magical fall her dull mind became suddenly sparkling with wonder and her spirit leaped up inside her like a bird … .

I am fascinated with words; language intrigues me. We are in essence communicators and interpreters of thought and meaning. We live in the amazing age of a global communication explosion. Age-old traditions, interpretations and philosophies are Googled and questioned with deliberate scrutiny.

One wonders why God did not delay the spectacular event of the incarnation of the prophetic word by two thousand years. Imagine our technology recording the Messiah on high definition megapixel cameras, documenting his life, parables, miracles, his love! Then, the dramatic detail of his crucifixion, resurrection and ascension!

No technology, yet to be invented in the far future, could possibly match the enormity of human life. Consider the capacity and wonder of a single DNA strand with its three billion individual characters, mirror repeated seventy five trillion times in the cells in your body. Just to count the individual characters in a single DNA strand, at one character per second, would take 93 years. This dwarfs terabyte technology into insignificance. (1 million seconds equals 12 days, while 1 billion seconds equals 31 years. A trillion seconds is 31,688 years.)

The inaudible voice of trillions of cells in the body, resonates the light of life.

The hearing ear and the seeing eye, the Lord has made them both (Proverbs 20:12). Mankind is the God-kind, designed to live by the complete word that proceeds from the mouth of God.

The heavens are telling the glory of God; and the firmament proclaims his handiwork. Day to day pours forth speech, and night to night declares knowledge. There is no speech, nor are there words; their voice is not heard; yet their sound transmits through all the earth, and their words to the end of the world. In them he has set a tent for the sun, which comes forth like a bridegroom leaving his chamber, and like a strong man runs his course with joy. Its rising is from the end of the heavens, and its circuit to the end of them; and there is nothing hidden from its heat (Psalm 19:1-6 RSV).

All flesh shall see it together. Flesh was designed to recognize and exhibit the glory of God.

A voice cries: In the wilderness prepare the way of the Lord, make straight in the desert a highway for our God (Isaiah 40:3 RSV).

Every valley shall be lifted up, and every mountain and hill be made low; every crooked place shall be made straight, and the rough places smooth. (Isaiah 40:4).

And the glory of the Lord shall be revealed, and the salvation of God shall be globally and fully realized by every individual - all mankind shall see and celebrate their redeemed oneness, for the mouth of the Lord has spoken. *(The word, οψεται from* **horaō,** *to gaze upon; to see for oneself; to discern and perceive within.)* Isaiah 40:5. See Luke 3:4-6; then, 2 Corinthians 3:18.

In the incarnation, God deleted every definition of distance; every possible excuse humanity could have to feel separated or even neglected by God was removed in one day, through one sacrifice, once and for all.

Life documented in the Rock of ages is now inscribed on hearts of flesh. Hear the echo, feel the resonance. Christ is all and in all.

You are a living Epistle, known and read by all. The word incarnate speaks a global, universal, mother-tongue language!

More than two thousand years ago the conversation that had begun before time was recorded—sustained in fragments of thought throughout the ages, whispered in prophetic language, chiseled in stone and inscribed in human conscience and memory—became a man. Beyond the tablet of stone, the papyrus scroll or parchment roll, human life has become the articulate voice of God. Jesus is the crescendo of God's conversation with us; he gives context and content to the authentic thought. Everything that God had in mind for mankind is voiced in him. Jesus is God's language. His name declares his mission. As Savior of the world he truly redeemed the image and likeness of the invisible God and made him apparent again in human form (Hebrews 1:1-3).

The destiny of the *logos* was not the printed page, but you. A mirror can only reflect the object; likewise, the purpose of the page was only to reflect the message which is Christ in you. He completes the deepest longing of every human heart. The incarnation is the ultimate translation.

In the words of the song of Moses, Give ear, Oh heavens, and I will speak; and let the earth hear the words of my mouth. May my teaching drop as the rain, my speech distil as the dew, as the gentle rain upon the tender grass, and as the showers upon the herb. For I will proclaim the name of the Lord, ascribe greatness to our God. The Rock, his work is perfect ... . (Deuteronomy 32:1-4 RSV).

Mankind has forgotten their Maker and in the process, their identity. You were unmindful of the Rock that begot you, and you forgot the God who gave you birth (Deuteronomy 32:18 RSV).

The mission of Jesus was not to begin the Christian religion. His mandate was to reveal and redeem the image and likeness of God in human form.

While none of Jesus' siblings believed in him during the three years of his ministry, his brother, James, discovers his own true identity when Jesus appears to him after the resurrection (John 7:5, 1 Corinthians 15:4-7).

James gives testimony to this life-changing discovery: We did not begin in our mother's womb. It was God's delightful resolve to give birth to us; we were conceived by the word of truth. The incarnation reveals the logic of mankind's origin (James 1:18).

James continues in 1:23-25, By being a mere spectator in the audience you underestimate yourself (you come to an inferior conclusion of who you really are). You are God's poem. The difference between a mere spectator and a participator is that both of them hear the same voice and perceive in its message the face of their own genesis reflected as in a mirror; they realize that they are looking at themselves, but for the one it seems just too good to be true, he departs (back to his old way of seeing himself) never giving another thought to the person he saw there in the mirror.

The other one is mesmerized by what he sees; he is captivated by the effect of a law that frees mankind from the obligation to the old written code that restricted them to their own efforts and willpower. No distraction or contradiction can dim the impact of what he sees in that mirror concerning the law of perfect liberty (the law of faith) that now frees one to get on with the act of living the life (of their original design). This person finds a new spontaneous lifestyle, the poetry of practical living.

The law of perfect liberty is the image and likeness of God revealed in Christ, now redeemed in human life, as in a mirror. Look deep enough into that law of faith that you may see there in its perfection a portrait that so resembles the original that he becomes distinctly visible in the spirit of your mind and in the face of everyone you behold.

Let us briefly consider these two words that James uses here, *parakuptō* and *paramenō*. I translated the word *parakuptō* as mesmerized from *para*, a Preposition which indicates close proximity, a thing proceeding from a sphere of influence, with a suggestion of union of place of residence, to have sprung from its author and giver, originating from, denoting the point from which an action originates, intimate connection; and *kuptō*, to bend, stoop down to view at close scrutiny; *paramenō*, to remain under the influence. The word often translated as freedom, *eleutheria*, means without obligation.

A word in any language can be most fascinating. A seed stores the life energy and the genetic detail of a plant species in much the same way as thoughts and concepts are concealed in words and language. Individual words can greatly influence the meaning and interpretation of any conversation.

For many years deliberate as well as oblivious errors in translations were repeated and have empowered the religious institutions of the day to influence, manipulate and even abuse masses of people.

Consider the Greek word μετάνοια *metanoia*, from *meta*, together with, and, *noieō*, to perceive with the mind; which describes the awakening of the mind to that which is true; a re-alignment of one's reasoning; it is a gathering of one's thoughts, a co-knowing. It has nothing in common with the Latin word *paenitentia*, where the word *penance* stems from;

26

meaning, payback and punishment inflicted on oneself. Then they added the re to get even more mileage out of sin consciousness. Re-penance. This gross deception led to the perverted doctrines of indulgences, where naive, ignorant people were led to believe that they needed to purchase favor from an angry god. Most cathedrals as well as many ministries were funded with this guilt money.

English translations do little to help us understand what repentance truly is. Until Jerome's Latin Vulgate translation, the word *metanoia* was commonly used. For instance, Tertullian wrote in 198 A.D. In Greek, *metanoia* is not a confession of sins but a change of mind. But despite this the Latin fathers begin to translate the word as do penance following the Roman Catholic teaching on doing penance in order to win God's favor.

In 1430, Lorenzo Valla, a Catholic theologian, began a critical study of Jerome's Latin Vulgate and Valla pointed out many mistakes that Jerome had made. Sadly, the Vulgate-Only crowd of Valla's day forced him to renounce many of the changes that he noted needed changing in the Vulgate including the poor translation of *metanoia*.

The business of religion desperately needs paying and returning customers. The entire system that trapped multitudes in their hierarchy of sin-consciousness was challenged and condemned by Jesus. In the genius of God, the Lamb of God took the sin of the world out of the equation.

Isaiah 55:8-11 gives meaning to metanoia: your thoughts were distanced from God's thoughts as the heavens are higher than the earth, but just like the rain and the snow would cancel that distance and saturate the soil to awaken its seed, so shall my word be that proceeds from my mouth.

The Greek Preposition meta, together with, implies another influence. This is where the Good News becomes so relevant since it appeals to our conscience to reason together with the Engineer of our original design where the authentic thought, the mind of God is realized again. The distance caused by Adam's fall, compared to the distance between heaven and earth, is canceled in the incarnation. Metanoia suggests a co-knowing with God. It is an intertwining of thought; it is to agree with God about me.

Adopted meanings to words have over time formed many popular doctrines and have often distracted completely from the original logic of God's prophetic communication culminating in the incarnation. Over the years, the study of the original Greek or Hebrew words have always been a great source of inspiration and enlightenment to me. You do not need to be a Greek scholar to access the root meanings; most Greek words are compound words and with the help of Greek dictionaries like Strongs and Thayers and its numerical system, you can do your own study and highlight the individual components of the word. Do not be distracted though by extended meanings you will find in Dictionaries. See my rendering of the word *parousia* in 1 Thessalonians 2:19, We expect nothing less in the context of the gospel than you enjoying a face to face encounter in the immediate presence of our Lord Jesus Christ.

27

This is our delight and wreath of honor. (Commentary note: Face to face encounter, The word G1715 ἔμπροσθεν, *emprosthen*; from G1722, in and G4314 pros; in front of - in place [literally or figuratively] or time): - face to face, before, (in sight) of. See John 1:1)

The word *parousia* speaks of the immediate presence of the Lord. From *para*, a Preposition indicating close proximity, intimate connection; and *eimi*, I am. There is not even a hint of judgment or punishment in this word. While there are great and accurate definitions in Strongs, please do not believe everything you read there. G3952 parousia from the Present Participle of G3918 *[pareimi]*; a being near, that is, advent; often, return; specifically of Christ to punish Jerusalem, or finally the wicked.!?

Parousia occurs 24 times in the NT, and 22 times it wrongly implies a 2nd coming or coming judgment. Only twice it is translated as presence. 2 Corinthians 10:10, Philippians 2:12. Of all the English translations that I have checked, only the Young's Literal has it correct. What a shame that this word has been so dramatically twisted over the years.

In the Greek Septuagint Psalm 138:8 [in the Hebrew Psalm 139] reads, If I make my bed in Hadēs, your presence already fills it. LXX - πάρειμι *pareimi* your immediate presence - I am.

In Mark 11:22, Jesus says, Have the faith of God. Unfortunately, most translations say, Have faith in God. There is a massive difference between our beliefs and philosophies about God and God's persuasion about us. God's belief in you gives substance to your faith. Jesus is what God believes about you. Your belief in God does not define him; his faith in what he knows to be true about you defines you.

If our point of reference is not God's faith in the finished work of Christ we have no valid gospel to preach. If our faith is not sourced and sustained in him as the mirror image of God revealed and redeemed in us we are deceiving ourselves with yet another religious disguise called Christianity.

There are countless errors bound in expensive leather books, sold over many years under the notion of being the authentic word of God. The book is not the word of God; but the message it contains certainly is. And in spite of the errors in text and translation millions of lives have been ignited, transformed and blessed by the Bible.

I salute the effort and contribution of the multitude of people who have painstakingly preserved, documented, gathered fragments of, scrutinized, compiled, copied and translated texts over the centuries; also those who translated and lost their lives in order to introduce the text in a language that ordinary people could understand.

The Mirror Bible does not replace any translation; it is simply a study tool that will assist both the casual reader as well as the student of Scripture to gain highlighted insight into the promise and the Person documented and revealed in the Bible as the mirror image of the invisible God redeemed in human form.

Jesus blows our definitions and doctrines apart with one statement: No-one knows the Father except the Son. Can you imagine how this shocked the Jews? They thought that they had copyright on God. Then he says, If you have seen me, you have seen the Father. Whatever we thought that we knew about God that is unlike Jesus, is not God. (Matthew 11:27, John 14:9, Luke 15.)

Jesus is the face of the Father. If you have seen me you have seen the Father. This was his purpose, to resonate and redeem the *Abba* echo in every human heart.

You have your heads in your Bibles constantly because you think you'll find eternal life there. But you miss the forest for the trees. These Scriptures are all about me. (John 5:39, *The Message.* See also Luke 24:27, 44, 45.)

Jesus is what the Bible is all about, and you are what Jesus is all about. (John 5:39)

Every invention begins with an original thought. You are God's original thought. You are Their initiative, the fruit of Their creative inspiration, The intimate design and love-dream of Elohim. The first Hebrew word in the Bible, בראשית *bereshet,* from **berosh,** literally means in the head. God had you in mind from the beginning. You are God's work of art; a poem, says Paul in the Greek text of Ephesians 2:10.

Every human life is equally valued and represented in Christ. He gives context and reference to our being as in a mirror; not as an example for us, but of us. The ugly duckling saw reflected in the water the truth that freed the swan.

Psalm 23 says, He leads me beside still waters, and restores my soul or by the waters of reflection my soul remembers who I am. Psalm 22:27 says, The ends of the earth shall remember and return to the Lord.

He has come to introduce us to ourselves again, so that we may know, even as we have always been known. (Jeremiah 1:5, 1 Corinthians 13:12)

Even when illiterate Peter learns to write, he declares, we were born anew by the resurrection of Jesus from the dead. (1 Peter 1:3)

I love his motivation. In 2 Peter 1:13, he says, I make it my business to thoroughly arouse you until these truths become permanently molded in your memory. He continues (verses 16-19): We are not con-artists, fabricating fictions and fables to add weight to our account of his majestic appearance; with our own eyes we witnessed the powerful display of the illuminate presence of Jesus the Master of the Christ-life. (His face shone like the sun, even his raiment was dazzling white. [Matthew 17:2])

He was spectacularly endorsed by God the Father in the highest honor and glory. God's majestic voice announced, 'This is the Son of my delight; he has my total approval.'

For John, James and me the prophetic word is fulfilled beyond doubt; we heard this voice loud and clear from the heavenly realm while we were with Jesus in that sacred moment on the mountain.

For us the appearance of the Messiah is no longer a future promise, but a fulfilled reality. Now it is your turn to have more than a second hand, hearsay testimony; take my word as one would take a lamp at night; the day is about to dawn for you in your own understanding.

When the Morning Star appears, you no longer need the lamp; this will happen shortly on the horizon of your own hearts. (2 Peter 1:16-19).

Now we all with new understanding see ourselves in him as in a mirror; thus, we are changed from an inferior mindset to the revealed opinion of our true Origin. (2 Corinthians 3:18)

By beholding the glory of the Lord as in a mirror you cannot but discover that you are his glory.

May this translation ignite many hearts with the light of life.

The TEXT

New Testament

Westcott and Hort vs.. Textus Receptus

The Codex Sinaiticus [Aleph B 33] and the Codex Vaticanus are considered amongst most current scholars to be the best Greek texts of the New Testament. These were extensively used by Westcott and Hort in their edition of The New Testament in the Original Greek in 1881. Aleph is the famous Sinaiticus, the great discovery of Constantine von Tischendorf, the only surviving complete copy of the New Testament written prior to the ninth century. Also note that The oldest Greek manuscripts were all written in uncials - all upper case letters. See Revelation 22:14 ΠΛΥΝΟΝΤΕΣ ΤΑΣ ΣΤΟΛΑΣ ΑΥΤΩΝ – wash their robes vs. Textus Receptus ποιοῦντες τὰς ἐντολὰς αὐτοῦ - do his commandments.)

Old Testament

LXX [Greek Septuagint] vs. The MASORETIC Text

The LXX was the Jewish Scriptures of the time. The Septuagint, from the Latin, septuāgintā literally seventy; often abbreviated as 70 in Roman numerals, i.e., LXX; sometimes called the Greek Old Testament. It is the earliest extant Koine Greek translation of the Hebrew Scriptures. [It was at the request of Ptolemy II Philadelphus (285–247 BCE) by 70 Jewish scholars or, according to later tradition, 72, with six scholars from each of the Twelve Tribes of Israel.] The discovery of the Qumran scrolls in 1947 reveal that the LXX represents much older manuscripts than our OT, which used the 1000 years later Masoretic text.

For example, one of the main Jewish apologist arguments against the Messianic interpretation of Isaiah 52:13 and 53:11 is that all the references to the suffering 'servant', so they say, are in the plural, making him a symbol of Israel. But in the LXX these are singular; and they refer to ὁ παῖς μου my child; not servant. The word, παῖς *pais*, boy [G3816] - is in the LXX in most places where the Hebrew text prefers עֶבֶד, ebed, slave.

*Also Isaiah 53:4 Surely he has borne our griefs and carried our sorrows; **yet we esteemed him stricken, smitten by God, and afflicted**. Then, Isaiah 53:10 in the Septuagint! **No!** It did not please the Lord to bruise him!! The Lord desires to cleanse his wounds - and in the offering of his life as sacrifice he shall see his seed afar off! See verse 11 - the joy that is set before him! The offspring is the fruit of the travail of his soul! Hebrews 12:2, for the joy that was set before him endured the cross, despising the shame!*

See also my commentary on Hebrews 1:6 and Hebrews 10:5; this reveals an important change in the text!

The most widely accepted view today is that the Septuagint provides a reasonably accurate record of an early Hebrew textual variant that differed from the ancestor of the Masoretic text as well as those of the Latin Vulgate, where both of the latter seem to have a more similar textual heritage. This view is supported by comparisons with Biblical texts found at the Essene settlement at Qumran. The Dead Sea scrolls are multiple copies of the Hebrew Bible along with other literary works of the time untouched from as early as 300 BC.

In Romans 3 there is a large quotation - from Psalm 14:1-7:, where there are six whole verses in Paul's quotation which are not found in the present Hebrew text, but are preserved in the Septuagint!

(See my further notes on The Text in the Introduction to the book of Revelation.)

TEXTUAL CRITICISM

Before mechanical printing, literature was copied by hand, and many variations were introduced by copyists. Reconstruction of the lost original is often aided by a selection of readings taken from many sources. An edited text that draws from multiple sources is said to be eclectic [critical]. In contrast to this approach, some textual critics prefer to identify the single best surviving text, and not to combine readings from multiple sources. The observed differences are called variants. It is not always apparent which single variant represents the author's original work. The process of textual criticism seeks to explain how each variant may have entered the text, either by accident (duplication or omission) or intention (harmonization or censorship), as scribes or supervisors transmitted the original author's text by copying it.

Text appears to have been added first as an explanatory note, and in the process of time crept into the text. Adam Clarke

We have no original manuscript - the thousands of manuscripts we do have are handwritten copies of copies for centuries and what happened was that, from time to time, a scribe's notes became text. The majority of these do not alter the meaning of the text though. But some do, which makes it an important observation.

The first edition of the New Testament with a Greek text was prepared by Erasmus and published in 1516. For Revelation, for instance, he based his Greek text on a single manuscript, minuscule 1r (now numbered 2814 according to the new Gregory-Aland number). This manuscript, however, lacks the final verses of the book of Revelation, and in order to have a complete text, Erasmus re-translated these verses into Greek from Latin. Elements of his translation survive in every edition of the so-called Textus Receptus, which were the standard text of the printed Greek New Testament until the nineteenth century. [See my notes above on the TR.]

There are more than 500,000 variants in the 5300 manuscripts of the New Testament we have access to. These are not necessarily errors but variant readings, the vast majority of which are strictly grammatical; but according to the warning you dare not add or take away any word, in Revelation 22:18 &19.

The question arises, any of which manuscripts are we talking about. See my notes at the end of Revelation 22.

DAVID E. AUNE, writes, In the field of textual criticism, no text poses so great a problem for the critic as does that of the collection of documents making up the New Testament. In contrast to the paucity of extant classical manuscripts, there is a great abundance of manuscripts which witness to the text of the New Testament. There are, indeed, more than 4,000 extant Greek manuscripts of portions of the New Testament, 8,000 of the Latin Vulgate, and more than 1,000 of other versions. Add to this the vast number of biblical quotations found in the Fathers, and we find that the great mass of material, while it gives an unparalleled opportunity for the performance of the critical task, is also the source of enormous difficulties.

*The application of the classical method of textual criticism, **recensio**, [a critical revision of a literary work] **examinado** and **emendado**, is impossible of rigid application to the text of the New Testament. The primary reason for this lies in the extensive process of corruption which has taken place between the various lines of manuscript descent. The presence of contamination makes it difficult, if not impossible, for the critic to decide whether the common errors of manuscripts are due to corruption between various lines of manuscripts or to common descent.*

I believe that, just like gold-containing ore, so the Bible contains the Word. Though the ore is a most important pointer to the gold, it cannot be confused with the gold. Jesus is the Word unveiled - He studied scripture with a different intent; he knew that he was reflected there. Familiar with the text, he brought context. Psalm 40:7 and Hebrews 10:7; also, John 5:39.

Francois du Toit ~ May 2012

[It is a work in progress. The latest 3 Volume-format, 11th Edition, was released in November 2022 and updated in October 2023]

Understanding The Bible - The Incarnation Code

The Bible is a dangerous book. It has confused and divided more people than any other document. Yet its profound and simple message continues to appeal, overwhelm and transform the lives of multitudes of men and women of any age or culture. It is still the best seller on the planet.

Scriptures have been used to justify some of the greatest atrocities in human history. People were tortured, burned at the stake and multitudes murdered based on somebody's understanding of the Scriptures. Jesus, Paul and believers throughout the ages faced their greatest opposition from those who knew the Scriptures.

If it is such a dangerous document, how does one approach the book? What is the key that unlocks its mystery message?

The Romance of the ages is revealed here. The heart of the Lover, our Maker is hidden in Scripture and uncovered in the pages of this book. He says in Isaiah 65:1, I was ready to be found by those who did not seek me. I said, 'Here am I, here am I.' (RSV) This sounds like mirror-language. Here I am echoes within us: Here I am.

What would it be that attracts God to engage with us?

Man began in God. You are the greatest idea that God has ever had.

It is not our brief history on planet Earth that introduces us to God. He has always known us. We are not the invention of our parents. Maybe your arrival was a big surprise to them, but according to Jeremiah 1:5, God knew you before he formed you in your mother's womb.

The Bible records how the invisible Engineer of the universe found image and likeness in visible form in human life.

When God imagined you, they imagined a being whose intimate friendship would intrigue Father, Son and Holy Spirit for eternity. Mankind would partner in God's triune oneness. Their image and likeness would be unmasked in human life.

Jesus says in John 10:30, I and the Father are one. None of the other disciples better captured the conclusion of the mission of Jesus than John in John 14:20, In that day you will know that we are in seamless union with one another. I am in my Father, you are in me and I am in you.

God has found us in Christ before we were lost in Adam. We are associated in Christ from before the foundation of the world (Ephesians 1:4). Elohim knew us, even before we were mystically formed in our mother's womb. Now in Christ, we are invited to know ourselves even as we have always been known (1 Corinthians 13:12).

Jesus Christ is the context and meaning of Scripture; his work of redeeming the image and likeness of God in human form is what the Bible is all about (Colossians 1:13-15).

He reveals that there is no place in the universe where God would rather be; the fullness of Deity physically resides in him. Jesus proves that human life is tailor-made for God. He mirrors our completeness. (While the expanse cannot measure or define God, their exact likeness is displayed in human form. The human body frames the most complete space for Deity to dwell in. See Colossians 1:19 & Colossians 2:9,10)

The entire Bible is about Jesus, and Jesus is all about you. This makes the Bible the most relevant book. Jesus is God's mind made up about you-manity. The meaning of his name declares our salvation. In him, God rescued our authentic identity and innocence.

The prophetic shadow of the Old Testament introduces us to the Promise and the Promise points to the Person. He is the Messiah-Christ, the Incarnate Word. He represents the entire human race. In the economy of God, Jesus mirrors man. The heart dream of God realized in the redemption of humanity; in one man, through one act of righteousness, in a single sacrifice, he rescued the human race.

The conclusion is clear. It took just one offense to condemn mankind; one act of righteousness declares the same mankind innocent. The disobedience of one exhibits mankind as sinners; the obedience of another exhibits mankind as righteous (Romans 5:18, 19 *Mirror Bible*).

We see then, that as one act of sin exposed the whole race of mankind to judgment and condemnation, so one act of perfect righteousness presents all mankind freely acquitted in the sight of God (Romans 5:19 *JB Phillips*). God has shown me that I should not call anyone common or unclean. (Acts 10:28)

When Jesus joins the two confused disciples on their way back from Jerusalem, he introduces himself to them through the eyes of Scripture: And beginning with Moses and all the Prophets, he interpreted to them in all the Scriptures the things concerning himself (Luke 24:27 RSV). Then in Luke 24:44, he does the same when he appears to his disciples: He said to them, 'These are my words which I spoke to you, while I was still with you, that everything written about me in the law of Moses and the Prophets and the Psalms must be fulfilled.' (RSV) Luke 24:45 says, Then he opened their minds to understand the Scriptures. (RSV)

Philip joins the chariot of the chief treasurer and asks him, Sir, do you understand what you are reading? (Philip knew that it is possible to read the right book but get the wrong message.) The passage of the Scripture which he was reading was from Isaiah 53:7, As a sheep led to the slaughter or a lamb before its shearer is dumb, so he opens not his mouth. And beginning with this Scripture Philip told him the Good News of Jesus. (Acts 8:35) Jesus is the context of Scripture. (Isaiah 53:4, 5)

The destiny of the Logos was not to be caged in a book or a doctrine but to be documented and unveiled in human form. Human life is the most articulate voice of Scripture. Jesus is God's language; mankind is his audience (Hebrews 1:1-3).

Diligent research and study is not the key to understanding the Scriptures; Jesus says, You study and search the Scriptures thinking that in them you will find eternal life, but if you miss me, you miss the point.

The Message translation reads, You have your heads in your Bibles constantly because you think you'll find eternal life there. But you miss the forest for the trees. These Scriptures are all about me (John 5:39).

The mission of Jesus was not to begin the Christian religion or to win protest votes against Moses, Mohammed, or Buddha. His mandate was twofold; first to reveal and then to redeem the blueprint image and likeness of the invisible God in human form. Instead of an instruction manual, the Bible is a mirror revealing our redeemed identity.

We are not window-shopping the promises; we gaze into the mirror of our true likeness and discover the integrity of our redeemed innocence.

Any form of striving to become more like Jesus through personal devotion and diligence, no matter how sincere, bears the same fruit of failure and guilt. Jesus did not come to condemn the world but to free the world. Religion has majored on guilt and willpower-driven sentiment, which engaged mankind in futile efforts to save or improve themselves.

The Bible was never meant to be a manual; its message is all about Immanuel. God with us. Every definition of distance is canceled in Christ (Isaiah 40:4, 5). When Scripture is interpreted as a mere instruction manual for moral behavior its message is veiled. 2 Corinthians 3:15 says, Whenever Moses is read the veil remains.

In John 1:17, Moses represents the law; Jesus reveals grace and truth. It is only in the mirror where the miracle transformation takes place and the blueprint image of our Maker is again realized in us (2 Corinthians 3:18).

Jesus did not come as an example for us, but of us. Beholding Jesus in any other way, sentimentally or religiously, will bring no lasting change. Now in Christ we may know ourselves, even as we have always been known (1 Corinthians 13:12).

This is the truth that frees us to live the life of our design (John 8:32).

John writes that this is not a new message; it is the word that was from the beginning. Yet it is new, for that which is true in him, is equally true in you (1 John 2:7, 8).

We know that the Son of God has come, and he has given us understanding to know him who is true; and this is the understanding: we are in him who is true. (1 John 5:20).

Paul brands his gospel with the words grace and peace in order to distinguish the message of the revelation of the finished work of Christ from the law of Moses. It is a matter of grace vs. reward and peace vs. striving, guilt and condemnation. Grace and peace express the sum total of every beneficial purpose of God towards us realized in Christ.

To discover yourself in the mirror is the key that unlocks the door to divine encounter. Tangible beyond touch the genesis of our being is unveiled. Our most intimate and urgent quest is satisfied here.

The days of window-shopping the Bible are over. And we all, with new understanding, see ourselves in him as in a mirror; thus, we are changed from an inferior mindset to the revealed endorsement of our true Origin (2 Corinthians 3:18).

As much as the world of science depends upon the senses to perceive, measure and calculate the facts to then form reliable conclusions, faith perceives the reality of God and extends its awakening to reason. This is the renewing of the mind. Faith is to the spirit what your senses are to your body; while the senses engage the fragile and fading, faith celebrates perfection. Faith is not wishful thinking; Jesus Christ is the substance of faith. He is both the author and conclusion of faith. He is the accurate measure of the blueprint of our design.

The gift of Christ measures the extravagant dimensions of grace; where everyone is equally advantaged. Ephesians 4:7. This is the mystery that was hidden for ages and generations; it is Christ in you (Colossians 1:27). He is not hiding in history or in outer space, or in the future. He is *I am* in you. Anticipate the revelation of Christ within you. There is no greater motivation for studying Scripture.

Jesus did not point to the sky when he gave the address of the kingdom of God; he said, The kingdom of God is within you! (Luke 17:21)

In Matthew 13:44, he says, The kingdom of heaven is like a treasure hidden in an agricultural field, which a man found and covered up. Then in his joy he goes and sells all that he has and buys that field. He saw the joy of his image and likeness redeemed in mankind when he braved the cross and despised the shame of it. (Hebrews 12:2)

There is so much more to the field than what meets the eye. Jesus has come to unveil the real value of the field. Human life can never again be underestimated. The treasure exceeds any agricultural value that any harvest could possibly yield. The treasure defines the authentic value of the field.

Paul says, We have this treasure in earthen vessels. (2 Corinthians 4:7 RSV). Yet our own unbelief veils our minds to keep us from recognizing the image of God, revealed in Christ, as the authentic reflection of our original identity (2 Corinthians 4:4).

We are not designed to live by bread alone. Bread represents the harvest of our own labor. Jesus invites us to look away from our own labor and to lift up our eyes and to see a harvest that is already ripe. A harvest is only ripe when the seed in the fruit matches the seed that was sown.

The single grain of wheat did not abide alone. (John 12: 24, John 4:35, John 2:19-21, Hosea 6:2, Ephesians 2:5).

The destiny of the word was not the book but the living epistle. Human life as revealed and redeemed in Christ is God's voice; mankind is his audience. You yourselves are all the endorsement we need. Your very lives are a letter that anyone can read by just looking at you. Christ himself wrote it—not with ink, but with God's living Spirit; not chiseled in stone, but carved into human lives—and we publish it. 2 Corinthians 3:2-3 —*The Message*

2 Corinthians 3:3 reads, The fact that you are a Christ-Epistle shines as bright as day. This is what our ministry is all about. The Spirit of God is the living ink. Every trace of the Spirit's influence on the heart is what gives permanence to this conversation. We are not talking law-language here; this is more dynamic and permanent than letters chiseled in stone; this conversation is embroidered in your inner consciousness. *(It is the life of your design that grace echoes within you.)*

Any sincere student of classical music would sensitively seek to capture and interpret the piece, so as not to distract from the original sound of the composition. To form an accurate conclusion in the study of our origin would involve a peering over the Creator's shoulder as it were, in order to gaze through his eyes and marvel at his anticipation. His invisible image and likeness is about to be unveiled in human form.

Personal opinion or traditional belief holds no ground against the fountain freshness of his thoughts. The word of truth accurately preserves his original idea in the resonance of our hearts.

Jesus studied scripture with a different intent; he knew that he was reflected there. Familiar with the text, he brought context.

Imagine God finding a word, worthy to hold his ultimate thought; his final, eternal, most intimate message to mankind.

He frames this thought, not in an ancient language of men or celestial messengers, but in an earthen jar, Jesus, the incarnate Word, the one who gives express image to the invisible God in human person.

In his dying humanity's death, he brings closure to every lie that we believed about ourselves, and in God co-quickening us in his resurrection, he powerfully introduces us to the redeemed life of our design.

Now, with every definition of veil removed, we may behold him as in a mirror, and discover and celebrate our own completeness endorsed in him.

ROMANS REVEALED

The Eagle Story

During our honeymoon in January, 1979, in the Blyderiver Canyons in Mpumalanga, South Africa, Lydia and I met a nature conservation officer who told us of a fascinating incident when they released a Black Eagle just the previous week; this bird, with a wingspan of more than two meters, had been in the Pretoria Zoo for ten years. She told us how excited they were when the eagle finally arrived in its wooden crate. This was the day for its release. But their excitement soon turned to frustration when, after opening the cage, the bird refused to fly. Ten years of caged life seemed to have trapped its mind in an invisible enclosure. How could they get the eagle to realize that it was indeed free? No amount of prompting and prodding seemed to help. Then, after some hours the bird suddenly looked up, and in the distance they heard the call of another eagle; immediately the zoo-eagle took off in flight.

This dramatic story left a deep impression on my mind. I knew that in the light of Paul's revelation of the Good News, we are left with one urgent priority, which is to announce to the nations with bold confidence the truth about their original identity and mirror-reflect the integrity of their redeemed innocence. No flying lessons are required when truth is realized.

This gives such clarity and content to the fact that Jesus came to the planet not to upgrade the cage of Judaism or any other religion by starting a new one called Christianity; but to be the incarnate voice of the likeness and image of God in human form. He came to reveal and redeem the image of God in us. His mission was to mirror the blueprint of our design, not as an example for us but of us. (Colossians 1:15, 2:9, 10).

In God's faith mankind is associated in Christ even before the foundation of the world. Jesus died mankind's death and when the stone was rolled away, we were raised together with him. Every human life is fully represented in him (Hosea 6:2).

If the gospel is not the voice of the free eagle, it is not the gospel.

Paul's Gospel

In this pivotal book, Paul immediately introduces himself and his intention: My mandate and message is to announce the goodness of God to mankind. This message is what the Scriptures are all about. It remains the central prophetic theme and content of inspired writing. (Romans 1:1, 2).

Scripture could never again be interpreted in any other way. The good news of the success of the Cross gives content and context to Scripture.

There is nothing to be ashamed of; this message unveils how God got it right to rescue man from the effect of what Adam did wrong. (Romans 1:16, 17)

The dynamic of the gospel is the revelation of God's faith as the only valid basis of our belief (from faith to faith). Paul quotes Habakkuk who prophetically introduced a new era when he realized that righteousness would be founded in what God believes about the redeemed life of our design, and not in our clumsy attempts to be righteous.

From now on righteousness by God's faith defines life. (Habakkuk 2:4, Romans 1:17, 3:27).

Instead of reading the curse when disaster strikes, Habakkuk realizes that the Promise out-dates performance as the basis to mankind's acquittal. Deuteronomy 28 would no longer be the motivation or the measure of right or wrong behavior. Though the fig trees do not blossom, nor fruit be on the vines, the produce of the olive fail and the fields yield no food, the flock be cut off from the fold and there be no herd in the stalls, yet I will rejoice in the Lord, I will joy in the God of my salvation. God, the Lord, is my strength; he makes my feet like hinds' feet, he makes me tread upon my high places. (Habakkuk 3:17-19 RSV).

From Romans chapters 1:18 to 3:20, Paul proceeds to give a graphic display of distorted human behavior as a result of suppressing the truth of their redeemed innocence and likeness.

Romans 1:18 God is not standing neutral to mankind's indifference. This revelation of God's belief in our redeemed righteousness is at the same time an unveiling of God's passionate desire, from a heavenly perspective, towards a humanity who seemed to have lost touch with the romance of their devotion by suppressing the truth about themselves; they have forgotten the delicate art to adore and be adored; while they continue to hold on to an inferior reference of themselves by being out of sync with their true likeness.

Romans 1:19 God is not a stranger to anyone; whatever can be known of God is manifest in man. God has revealed it in the very core of their being which bears witness within their own conscience.

Being a Jew, and therefore to be acquainted with the requirements of the law, offers no real advantage, since it offers no disguise or defense from sin. It bears the same symptoms and consequences. His triumphant statement in verses 16, 17 of chapter 1 and again reinforced in chapter 3:21-24, is set against this backdrop. The good news declares how the same condemned mankind in Adam is now freely acquitted by God's grace through the redemption that is unveiled in Christ Jesus.

He brings the argument of the ineffectiveness of the law to get a person to change their behavior, to a final crescendo in Chapter 7. He states in 7:1 that he is writing to those who know the law. They have first-hand experience therefore of the weakness of willpower to consistently govern a person's conduct.

The best the law could offer was to educate and confirm good intention; but the more powerful law, the law of sin, introduced to mankind through one man's transgression, has to be challenged by a greater force than human willpower.

Because sin robbed mankind of their true identity and awakened in them all kinds of worse-than-animal-like conduct, a set of rules couldn't do it. The revelation of God's righteousness has to be far more effective and powerful than mankind's slavery to sin.

In the typical language of the law, mankind's corrupt behavior deserves nothing less than condemnation. Yet within this context, the grace and mercy of God is revealed; not as mere tolerance from God's side to turn a blind eye and to put up with sin, but as God's triumphant act in Christ to cancel our guilt and to break sin's spell and dominion over us.

For salvation to be relevant it has to offer mankind a basis and reference from which their faith is to be launched. It has to offer a conclusion of greater implication than the stalemate condition they find themselves in under the dispensation of the law.

My inner person agrees that the law is good and desires to obey its requirements yet my best intentions leave me powerless against the demands of sin in my body.

Romans 7:24 It doesn't matter how I [1]weigh myself by my own efforts, I just do not measure up to expectations. The situation is absolutely desperate for mankind; is there anyone who can deliver them from this death trap? *(The word [1]talaipōros occurs only twice in the New Testament - Romans 7:24, Revelation 3:17 - and both times it is translated wretched!? It has two components, **talanton**, which is the word for a scale of balance; that which is weighed, a talent [of gold]; and **poros** from **peira**, to examine closely, to pierce; a test to determine the hidden value of something. You cannot measure temperature with a ruler.*

See 2 Corinthians 3:15 In the meantime nothing seems to have changed; the same veil continues to blindfold the hearts of people whenever Moses is read. (Moses symbolizes the futility of self righteousness as the global blindfold of the religious world. [John 1:17] Against the stark backdrop of the law; with Moses representing the condemned state of mankind, Jesus Christ unveils grace and truth. He is the life of our design redeemed in human form.)

Paul is convinced that whatever happened to the human race because of Adam's fall is far superseded in every possible proportion by the revelation of mankind's inclusion in the life, death and resurrection of Jesus Christ. He places the fall of Adam and every act of unrighteousness that followed, against the one act of righteousness that God performed in Christ as proof of mankind's acquittal.

Romans 4:25 While our sins resulted in his death; our righteousness and redeemed innocence is celebrated in his resurrection!

The revelation of righteousness by God's faith unveils how Jesus Christ represented and redeemed mankind. The etymological essence of the word, righteousness in its stem, dikē, suggesting to be judged equal; it implies the idea of two parties finding likeness in each other; with no interference of any sense of blame, guilt or inferiority. The Hebrew word for righteousness is the word *tzedek,* צדק which also includes the idea of the wooden beam in a scale of balances. When Adam lost the glory of God *(Hebrew,* כבוד *kabod, weight; the consciousness of God's likeness and image)* the law proved that no amount of good works could balance the scale again. Grace reveals how God redeemed his image and likeness again in human form; now the scale is perfectly balanced. No wonder Jesus cried out on the cross, It is finished. *See commentary note on **2 Corinthians 6:14**.*

This is the message that Paul says he owes to the entire world.

I proclaim Jesus Christ according to the revelation of the mystery which was concealed in silence in the sequence of timeless ages, but now is made publicly known, mirrored in prophetic Scripture. *(Surely he was wounded by our transgressions; he was bruised by our iniquities. [Isaiah 53:4, 5] See NB commentary note in 2 Corinthians 5:21)* And now the God of the ages has issued his mandate to make the mystery known in such a way that all the nations of the earth will discover the lifestyle that the hearing of faith ignites. *(Romans 16:25, 26)* Paul gives new definition to obedience when he calls it the obedience of faith. Romans 1:5.

The conclusion is clear: it took just one offense to condemn mankind; one act of righteousness declares the same mankind innocent. The disobedience of one exhibits mankind as sinners, the obedience of another exhibits mankind as righteous. Romans 5:18, 19.

Just as all mankind became exceedingly sinful through one person's disobedience but did not know it until the law revealed it, so all mankind became exceedingly righteous through one act of righteousness but they do not know it until the gospel reveals it. The principle of faith is to see what God sees. God calls things that seem not to be as though they were. Romans 4:17.

While we look not at the things that the senses observe, we look at the revelation of the unseen as it is unveiled in our understanding through the mirror revelation of the Gospel of Christ. See 2 Corinthians 3:18; 2 Corinthians 4:18.

Romans 4:17 finds its context in Romans 1:17 and 10:17, It is clear then, that faith's source is found in the content of the message heard; the message is Christ. (We are God's audience; Jesus is God's language.)

The incarnation is the voice of the free eagle.

(The beautifully illustrated Eagle Story is available on Amazon.)

1:1 Paul, [5]passionately engaged by Jesus Christ, [1]identified in him to [2]represent him. My [3]mandate and [4]message is to announce the goodness of God to mankind. *(Mandate, the scope or horizon of my message, from [3]horitso, meaning marked out. The word, [2]apostelo, means an extension from him, a representative; [5]doulos, means slave from deō, to be bound or knitted together like a husband and wife; [1]kletos comes from kaleō, meaning called, to identify by name, to surname; and [4]eu + angellion, means well done announcement, good news, the official announcement of God's goodness.)*

1:2 This message is what the Scriptures are all about. It remains the central prophetic theme and content of inspired writing.

1:3 The Son of God has his natural lineage from the seed of David; *(In Matthew 22:41-45 Jesus asked the Pharisees, What do you think of the Christ? Whose son is he? They said to him, The son of David. He said to them, How is it then that David, inspired by the Spirit, calls him Lord, saying, 'The Lord said to my Lord, Sit at my right hand, till I put your enemies under your feet'? If David thus calls him Lord, how is he his son? Matthew 22:41-45 You must not call anyone here on earth Father, because you have only the one Father in heaven. [Matthew 23:9]. Yet there is for us only one God, the Father, who is the Creator of all things and for whom we live; and there is only one Lord, Jesus Christ, through whom all things were created and through whom we live. [1 Corinthians 8:6]. For this reason I bow my knees before the Father, from whom every family in heaven and on earth receives its true name. [Ephesians 3:14, 15]. ... there is one God and Father of all people, who is Lord of all, works through all, and is in all. [Ephesians 4:6, 7].)*

1:4 however, his powerful resurrection from the dead by the Holy Spirit, [1]locates and confirms his being and sonship in God. *(The word translated, locates, comes from [1]apo + horizo, meaning to mark out beforehand, to define or locate; literally, horizon. The same word is translated as mandate in verse 1. In Acts 13:32-33, Paul preaches the resurrection and quotes Psalm 2, Today I have begotten you. Jesus locates us and confirms that we have our genesis in God. Peter understands that we were born anew in the resurrection of Christ. The relevance of the resurrection is the revelation of mankind's inclusion in Christ [see 1 Peter 1:3]. Hosea 6:2 is the only Scripture that prophesies the third day resurrection, and here in this single dramatic prophecy, we are co-included in his resurrection. After two days he will revive us, on the third day he will raise us up. [RSV] This is the crux of the mystery of the Gospel. Will the earth be brought forth in one day? Can a nation be born in a moment? [Isaiah 66:8, 9].)*

1:5 The grace and commission we received from him, is to bring about a [1]faith-inspired lifestyle in all the nations. [2]His name is his claim on the human race. *(Paul immediately sets out to give new definition to the term, obedience, no longer by law, but of faith. [1]Obedience, from upo + akoō, means to be under the influence of what is heard, accurate hearing; hearing from above. [2]Every family in heaven and on earth is identified in him. Ephesians 3:15.)*

1:6 In Jesus Christ you individually discover [1]who you are. *(The word, [1]kaleō, means to call by name, to surname.)*

1:7 In addressing you, I address all in Rome. I am convinced of God's love for you; he ²restored you to the harmony of your original design; you were made holy in Christ Jesus; no wonder then that you are ¹surnamed ²saints. His grace gift in Christ secures your total wellbeing. The Father of the Lord Jesus Christ is ours also; he is our God. *(The word, ¹kaleō, means called, identified by name, surname; ²hagios, means saints, restored to the harmony of your original design; He separated me from my mother's womb when he revealed his Son in me, in order that I may declare him in the nations; immediately I did not consult with flesh and blood. [Galatians 1:15, 16]. From now on, therefore, we regard no one from a human point of view; even though we once knew Christ after the flesh, we regard him thus no longer. [2 Corinthians 5:16 RSV].)*

1:8 My greatest joy is to realize that your faith is announced throughout the entire world. The total ¹cosmos is our audience. *(The word, kosmos in the NT refers to the entire human family.)*

1:9 I am completely engaged in my spirit in the gospel of God's Son; constantly including you in my prayers; God is my witness.

1:10 Since I already feel so ¹connected to you I long to also see you face to face. *(¹To beseech, deomai, from deō to tie together, to be knitted together.)*

1:11 I really look forward to finally meet you in person, knowing that my spiritual ¹gift will benefit you greatly; it will cement and establish you in your faith. *(The word, ¹metadidomi, translates as the kind of giving where the giver is not distanced from the gift but wrapped up in it. The Apostles, Prophets, preachers, pastors, and teachers are gifts to the ekklesia to establish them in their faith and to present everyone in the full and mature stature of Christ [Ephesians 4:11-16]. There is such a vast difference between a gift and a reward. We are God's gifts to one another. What God now has in us is gift-wrapped to the world. What we are in our individual expression is a gift and not a reward for personal diligence or achievement. These gifts were never meant to establish one above the other, or to become mere formal titles, but rather to identify specific and dynamic functions with one defined purpose, to bring everyone into the realization of the fullness of the measure of Christ in them.)*

1:12 And so we will be mutually refreshed in the ¹participation and reflection of our common faith. *(The word, ¹sumparakaleō, comes from sum, together; para, is a Preposition indicating close proximity, a thing proceeding from a sphere of influence, with a suggestion of union of place of residence, to have sprung from its author and giver, originating from, denoting the point from which an action originates, intimate connection, and kaleō, meaning to identify by name, to surname.)*

1:13 Until now I have been prevented from coming to you, even though I have frequently desired to reap some harvest in you as much as I anticipate the full fruit of this gospel in all the nations.

1:14 I am so convinced of everyone's inclusion; I am ²indebted both to the Greeks as well as those many ¹foreigners whose languages we do not even understand. I owe this message to everyone, it is not a matter of how literate and educated people are; the illiterate are equally included in the benefit of the Good News. *(The word, [1]barbaros, means one who speaks a strange and foreign language; [2]opheiletes, means to be indebted, obliges one to return something to someone that belongs to him or her in the first place.)*

1:15 Because of this compelling urgency I am so keen to preach to you Romans also.

1:16 I have no shame about sharing the Good News of Christ with anyone; the powerful rescuing act of God persuades both Jew and Gentile alike.

1:17 Herein lies the secret of the power of the Gospel; there is no good news in it until the righteousness of God is revealed. The dynamic of the gospel is the revelation of [1]God's faith as the only valid basis for our belief. The Prophets wrote in advance about the fact that God believes that righteousness reveals the life of our design. Righteousness by his *(God's)* **faith defines life.** *(In David's dramatic, prophetic account of the crucifixion in Psalm 22, he concludes with verse 27, All the ends of the earth shall remember and return to the Lord; and all the families of the nations shall worship before him. And in verse 31, ...they shall declare his righteousness to a people that shall yet be born; that he has done it. The gospel is the revelation of the righteousness of God; it unveils how the Father, Son and Spirit succeeded to put mankind right with themselves. It is about what God did right, not what Adam did wrong. The good news reveals how God's righteousness rescued the life of our design and redeemed our innocence. Mankind's futile efforts to justify themselves, have failed them miserably. [Romans 7] The Good News shifts the emphasis away from our failure and condemnation to highlight what it was that God accomplished in Jesus Christ on humanity's behalf. Look away [from the law of works] unto Jesus; he is the [1]Author and finisher of faith. [Hebrews 12:2]. It is God's faith to begin with; it is [1]from faith to faith, and not our good or bad behavior; we are not defined by our performance or circumstances. The Greek word translated from is the Preposition, [1]ek, which always denotes source or origin. The language of the old written code was, Do in order to become. The language of the new is, Be, because of what was done. Instead of do, do, do, it's done, done, done. Paul refers here to Habakkuk 2:4, The just shall live by his [God's] faith. Habakkuk sees a complete new basis to mankind's standing before God. Instead of reading the curse when disaster strikes, he realizes that the Promise outdates performance as the basis to mankind's acquittal. The curse is taken out of the equation. Galatians 3:13. Deuteronomy 28 would no longer be the motivation or measure of right or wrong behavior. Instead of righteousness as a reward to mankind's efforts to obey the law, Habakkuk celebrates God's righteousness based on God's belief, in the face of apparent disaster, represented in the evidence of all the curses mentioned in Deuteronomy 28. He sings, Though the fig trees do not blossom, nor fruit be on the vines, the produce of the olive fails and the fields yield no food, the flock be cut off from the fold and there be no herd in the stalls, yet I will rejoice in the Lord, I will joy in the God of my salvation. God, the Lord, is my strength; he makes my feet like hinds' feet, he makes me tread upon my high places. [Habakkuk 3:17-19 RSV]. It is interesting to note that Habakkuk -* חבקוק *chăbaqûq, was* *possibly the son of the Shunammite woman and her husband who hosted the Prophet Elisha. They could not have children, until Elisha declared that in a year's time she would embrace - חבק chabaq - a child. When the child grew up to be a young man he died of sunstroke and Elisha stretched himself over the boy and mirror-embraced the dead child, face to face and the boy came back to life. חבקוק Chabaquq is a double embrace - it is the prophetic picture of our mirror-resurrection together with Christ. If anyone knew that righteousness was not by works, but by God's faith, it was Habakkuk.*

The word righteousness comes from the Anglo Saxon word, rightwiseness; wise in that which is right. In Greek the word for righteousness is dikaiosunē, from dikē, that which is right; it is a relationship word and refers to two parties finding likeness in each other. Righteousness points to harmony in a relationship. See 2 Corinthians 6:14. Faith-righteousness has nothing in common with the pagan philosophies of karma and performance-based approval; they could never balance the scales or be evenly yoked together in any context. [The word heterozugeō, an unequal or different yoke; from the Hebrew word, zugot, זוגות indicates pairs of two identical objects; a yoke or a teaching; the yoke of a rabbi or philosopher represented their doctrine; reminds of the Hebrew word for righteousness, tzedek, צדק which also includes the idea of the wooden beam in a scale of balances. He that judges his neighbor according to the balance of righteousness, or innocence, they judge him according to righteousness. [T. Bab. Sabbat, fol. 127. 2.]

It is interesting to note that the Greek goddess of Justice is Dikē, [pronounced, dikay - the stem of the word dikaiosunē, righteousness] and she is always pictured holding a scale of balances in her hand. See also 2 Corinthians 6:15. In Colossians 2:9-10, It is in Christ that God finds an accurate and complete expression of himself, in a human body. He mirrors our completeness and is the ultimate authority of our true identity.)

1:18 God is not standing neutral to mankind's indifference. This revelation of God's belief in our redeemed righteousness is at the same time an unveiling of God's [1]passionate desire, from a heavenly perspective, [2]towards a [3]humanity who seemed to have [5]lost touch with the romance of their devotion, by [4]suppressing the truth about themselves; they have [5]forgotten the delicate art to adore and be adored; while they continue to hold on to an [6]inferior reference of themselves by being out of sync with their true likeness. *(God's belief in mankind's redeemed righteousness is endorsed in the heavens and in sharp contrast to the counterfeit, earthly reference that blindfolds people in their own unrighteousness. The word often translated wrath, [1]orgē, means desire - as a reaching forth or excitement of the mind, passion. The Preposition [2]epi means towards, continuous influence upon; I interpreted it here as contrast. The word for the [3]human species, male or female is anthropos, from ana, upward, and tropos, manner of life; character; in like manner. The word [4]katechō, to echo downwards is the opposite of anochē, to echo upward; see Romans 2:4 and 3:26. In Colossians 3:2 Paul encourages us to engage our thoughts with things above [God's belief], and not below [law of works]. The word, ασεβειαν [5]asebeian, from a, negative and sebomai, to adore, to worship. The word [6]adikia, unrighteousness, is the opposite of dikē, suggesting to be judged equal; it implies the idea of two parties finding likeness in each other; thus, to be out of sync with* *likeness. The law reveals how guilty and sinful mankind is, while the gospel reveals how forgiven and restored to their original blueprint we are. See 2 Corinthians 4:4.)*

1:19 God is not a stranger to anyone; whatever can be known of God is [1]manifest in man. God has revealed it in the very core of our being which bears witness with our conscience. *(Note Romans 2:14 & 15 For even a pagan's natural instinct will confirm the law to be present in their conscience even though they have never heard about Jewish laws. Thus they prove to be a law unto themselves. The law is so much more than a mere written code; its presence in human conscience even in the absence of the written instruction is obvious. See also 2 Corinthians 4:4 & 7 and Colossians 1:27. Blindfold-mode does not remove the treasure from where it was hidden all along. Every time we love, encounter joy, or experience beauty, a hint of the nature of our Maker reflects within us; even in the experience of the unbeliever. In the incarnation Jesus unveils God's likeness, not his otherness, in human form as in a mirror. The word [1]phaneros from phaino, means to shine like light. Colossians 2:9,10 It is in Christ that God finds an accurate and complete expression of himself, in a human body. Jesus mirrors our completeness. While the expanse cannot measure or define God, his exact likeness is displayed in human form. Jesus proves that human life is tailor-made for God. See also Ephesians 4:8 And James 3:9 We can say beautiful things about God the Father but with the same mouth curse a fellow human made in his mirror likeness. The point is not what the person did to deserve the insult. The point is that people are image and likeness bearers of God by design.)*

1:20 God is on display in creation; the very fabric of visible cosmos appeals to reason. It clearly bears witness to the ever present sustaining power and intelligence of the invisible God, leaving mankind without any valid excuse to ignore him. *(Psalm 19:1-4, God's glory is on tour in the skies, God-craft on exhibit across the horizon. Madame Day holds classes every morning, Professor Night lectures each evening. Their words aren't heard, their voices aren't recorded, But their silence fills the earth: unspoken truth is spoken everywhere. — The Message.)*

1:21 Yet mankind only knew him in a philosophical religious way, from a distance, and failed to give him credit as God. Their taking him for granted and lack of gratitude veiled him from them; they became absorbed in useless debates and discussions, which further darkened their understanding about themselves.

1:22 Their wise conclusions only confirmed their folly.

1:23 Their losing sight of God, made them lose sight of who they really were. In their calculation the image and likeness of God became reduced to a corrupted and distorted pattern of themselves. Suddenly a person has more in common with creepy crawlies than with their original blueprint.

1:24 It seemed like God abandoned mankind to be swept along by the lusts of their own hearts to abuse and defile themselves. Their most personal possession, their own bodies, became worthless public property.

1:25 Truth suppressed *(v18)* **became twisted truth. Instead of embracing their Maker as their authentic identity, they preferred the deception of a distorted image of their own making, religiously giving it their affection**

and worship. The true God is the blessed God of the ages, and he is not defined by our devotion or indifference. *(And all this because they traded the true God for a fake god, and worshiped the god they made instead of the God who made them. Message.)*

1:26 By being confused about their Maker they became confused about themselves; which led to all manner of obsessions.

1:27 Men and women alike became inflamed with perverted fantasies. This brought about an intense ¹striving and a ²most exhausting toiling in the pursuit of a ³disillusioned identity - which clearly are the symptoms of an ⁴inferior estimate of oneself. *(The word, ¹orexei describes a reaching out after something. The word ²katergazomai from kata, downward; also to emphasize intensity; and ergatsomai, to toil. Then he uses the word ³aschēmosunē from aschēmōn, deformed, from a, negative or without and schema, form or pattern. The word ⁴antimisthia from anti, against or opposite and misthois, the wage of a hireling; translated here an inferior estimate; or a wage that leaves one disappointed.)*

1:28 Their indifference to their god-identity, veiled God from them.

1:29 Sin snowballs. It spreads like a disease, exhibiting its ugly symptoms in every possible form; this engages one in a ¹wearisome and exhausting lifestyle, occupied with the futile pursuit for counterfeit fulfillment. A life opposed to the righteousness of God *[unveiled in verse 17, but adikia in verse 18]*, remains stuck in the wilderness of a mindset ²filled to the brim with everything that is out of sync with one's design and redemption. The problem with sin is that it ³never satisfies; leaving the victim miserably unfulfilled and constantly craving for more of the same deception: vileness, jealousy, anger and an unnatural obsession with self. Life is cheap, murder doesn't matter; they are steeped in constant quarreling and wickedness; their conversation has become reduced to slanderous ⁴gossip.

(Paul, again and again, emphasises the difference between the two laws governing human life: 1/ The life of our redeemed innocence, [righteousness by God's faith which he also calls, the law of the Spirit of life in Christ Jesus, in Romans 8:2], versus 2/ the life of one's own making. [The one is driven by agapē-love, which is totally value based, or, the counterfeit, which is a fragile, make-belief, performance-based identity, based on self righteousness. In Romans 3:27 Paul calls it the law of faith versus the law of performance. See also John's contribution and my commentary note on the 2 trees - 1 John 3:6-12].

[1] The word, ¹πονηρία - ¹ponēria, from ponēros, full of hardships, annoyances and labor. This concludes in a judgment based on performance; which is the opposite to an opinion of approval, solely based on value. [The word, πορνεια pornea in the Textus Receptus, was a later addition by a copyist. See Bruce Metzger's Textual Commentary of the Greek NT.]

[2] Both these words, πεπληρωμενους which is the Perfect Passive tense of πληρόω plēroō as well as μεστός mestos mean to be filled to the brim.

[3] The word, πλεονεξια ²pleonexia suggests a constant, craving for more.

[4] Gossip, ψιθυριστας ³psithuristēs, a whisperer.)

1:30 No one is safe in their company; they think that by insulting people they can voice their hatred for God; proudly bragging about their latest inventions of filth. They remain [1]indifferent to any definition of [2]parenthood, disregarding the fact that we did not invent ourselves. *(The word [1]apeithēs, where we get the word apathy from, traditionally translated to disobey, in my opinion translates better as being indifferent; from a, negative and peithō, to believe; to make friends, to win one's favor, gain one's good will, or to strive to please one. The word [2]goneus, parent; from ginomai, to be born.)*

1:31 They live [1]dysfunctional, [2]disconnected lives where no [3]sympathy or mercy is shown. *(The words, [1]asynetous, a, negative and sunetos; from suniemi; a joining together like that of two streams; a fusion of thought, a joint-seeing. Thus, with them, there seems to be no compatibility or harmony to connect meaningfully with others. The word [2]asunthetos again, a, negative and suntithemai - to stand in agreement or support with another. They live completely out of sync with others. Then Paul uses the words, [3]astorgos, without natural affection and ανελεημονας aneleēmōnas, no mercy.)*

1:32 It just doesn't make any sense, they started off knowing the [1]righteousness of God, yet by their lifestyle they flirt with death; it is almost as if sin has become a fashionable contest. *([1]dikaioma, righteousness - not judgment, as some translations suggest.)*

Note, from verses 18 to 32 Paul paints the picture of the dilemma and darkness of the fallen mindset - where the distorted picture becomes the norm. This is the language of a law system, which defines people by their behavior rather than their design.

He then concludes in chapter 2:4 with this amazing statement, underlining his conviction as recorded in chapter 1:16,17 about the powerful rescuing act of God announced in the Gospel:

> *Romans 2:4 Do not underestimate God's kindness. The wealth of his benevolence and his resolute refusal to let go of us is because he continues to hear the echo of his likeness in us. Thus his patient passion is to shepherd everyone into a radical mind shift.*

2:1 A presumed knowledge of what is right or wrong does not qualify you to judge anyone; especially if you do exactly the same stuff you notice other people do wrong. You effectively condemn yourself. No one is another person's judge.

2:2 God must judge all transgression, but your judging others does not make them any guiltier.

2:3 God is completely impartial in his judgment; you are not scoring any points or disguising your own sins by telling on others.

2:4 Do not [1]underestimate God's [2]kindness. The wealth of his [2]benevolence and his [3]resolute refusal to let go of us is because he continues to hear the echo of his likeness in us! Thus his [4]patient passion is to [5]shepherd everyone into a [6]radical mind shift. *(The word translated, underestimate is the word,* [1]*kataphroneō, from* **kata***, down, and* **phroneō***, to think, to form an opinion; thus a downcast mind, to despise or take for granted. It is the revelation of the goodness of God that leads us to* [6]*repentance; it is not our repentance that leads God to goodness! The word repentance is a fabricated word from the Latin word,* **paenitentia***, which became penance, and to give religion more mileage the English word became repenance! That is not what the Greek word means at all! The word,* [6]**metanoia***, comes from* **meta***, together with and* **noieō***, to perceive with the mind. It describes the awakening of the mind to that which is true; a re-alignment of one's reasoning; it is a gathering of one's thoughts, a co-knowing. Faith is not a decision; it is a discovery. [See Isaiah 55:8-10] The word,* [2]**chrestos***, kind, benevolent, from* **xeir***, hand which is also connected to the word* **xristos***, to draw the hand over, to anoint, to measure; see also the Hebrew for Messiah,* משיח *to anoint; to measure, from* **mashach***,* משח *to draw the hand over, to measure! [Analytical Hebrew and Chaldee Lexicon, B Davidson.] In Jesus Christ, God has measured mankind innocent, he is the blueprint of our design! The word* [3]**anochēs** *comes from* **ana***, meaning upward;* **ana** *also shows intensity and the word* **echō***, to hold, or embrace, as in echo. He continues to hear the echo of his likeness in us! [See Romans 3:26.] If we are able to invent tracking devices to find stolen property via satellite, God has every person on the planet covered.*

The word, [4]**makrothumias***, means to be patient in bearing the offenses and injuries of others. Literally, passion that goes a long way; fortitude. The word,* [5]**ago***, means to lead as a shepherd leads his sheep.)*

2:5 A calloused heart that resists change accumulates cause to self-destruction, while God's righteous judgment is revealed in broad daylight. *(The gospel openly reveals that God declared mankind innocent.)*

2:6 By resisting him you are on your own; your own deeds will judge you. *(Rejecting his goodness [v 4] keeps you snared in a lifestyle ruled by sin-consciousness and condemnation.)*

2:7 The quest of mankind is to be [1]constant in expressing that which is good and glorious and of imperishable value. We are eager to engage the original blueprint-life of the [2]ages. *(The word,* ὑπομονή [1]*hupomonē - to continue to be present; consciously abiding undisturbed in seamless union with your Source.*

The life of the ages, from [2]aionios, which is the most attractive life we could wish to live; it is the life of our design, yet it remains elusive outside the redemption that Christ achieved on our behalf. Not even the most sincere decision to live a blameless life under the law or any sincere philosophy could satisfy the heart hunger of mankind.)

2:8 Yet there are those who ignore the truth through [2]unbelief. *(The truth about their original identity as sons)* **They continue to exist as mere [1]hirelings, motivated by a monthly wage** *(rather than sonship).* **They believe in their failure and unrighteousness and are consumed by outbursts of anger and displeasure.** *(The word, [1]eithea, comes from erithos, working as a hireling for wages; often translated, self-willed or contentious. The word, [2]apeitheo, means to be not persuaded, without faith, often wrongly translated as disobedient.)*

2:9 Pressures from every side, like an [1]overcrowded room, *(or a cramped foot in an undersized shoe,)* **is the experience of the soul of everyone who does what is worthless. The fact that the Jews are Jewish does not make their experience of evil any different from that of the Greeks.** *(Symptoms of disease are the same in anyone; they are not a respecter of persons. The word, [1]stenochoria, means narrowness of room.)*

2:10 In sharp contrast to this, bliss, self-worth and total tranquillity is witnessed by everyone, both Jew and Greek, who finds expression in that which is good. We are tailor-made for good.

2:11 God does not judge people on face value.

2:12 Ruin and self-destruction are the inevitable results of sin, whether someone knows the law or not.

2:13 Righteousness is not a hearsay-thing, it is faith-inspired practical living, giving new definition to the law.

2:14 For even a pagan's natural instinct will confirm the law to be present in their conscience even though they have never heard about Jewish laws. Thus they prove to be a law unto themselves.

2:15 The law is so much more than a mere written code; its presence in human conscience even in the absence of the written instruction is obvious, condemning or commending personal conduct.

2:16 Every hidden, conflicting thought will be disclosed in the daylight of God's scrutiny, based on the Good News of Jesus Christ that I proclaim. *(The ineffectiveness of good intentions and self discipline to produce lasting change will be exposed as worthless in contrast to the impact of the message of Christ's death and resurrection as representing mankind's death and new birth as our ultimate reference to our redeemed identity and innocence.)*

2:17 Your Jewish identity does not make God your exclusive property,

2:18 even though you boast in the fact that you have the [1]documented desire of God [2]published like an instruction manual in the law. *(The word, [1]dokimatsō, comes from document, decree, approve; [2]diapherō, from to carry through, to publish [Acts 13:49, the word was published throughout].)*

2:19 You promote yourself confidently as a guide for the blind, and a light bearer for those groping about in darkness.

2:20 You feel yourself so superior to the rest of the world that you promote yourself as the kindergarten teacher to the mindless, an instructor of infants, because you believe that in the law you have knowledge and truth all wrapped up in a nutshell.

2:21 However, the real question is not whether you are a good teacher; how good a student are you? What's the good of teaching against stealing when you yourself steal?

2:22 You speak against adultery while you cannot get your own mind off sexual sins. It just doesn't make sense does it? You say idolatry stinks yet you steal stuff from pagan shrines.

2:23 Your proud association with the law is ruined every time you dishonor God by dodging the doing bit.

2:24 This has been going on for hundreds of years; it is all recorded in Scripture. No wonder the Gentiles think that your God is no better than any of their philosophies when it comes to living the life the law promotes.

2:25 The real value of circumcision is tested by your ability to keep the law. If you break the law you might as well not be circumcised.

2:26 The fact that you are circumcised does not distinguish you from the rest of the world; it does not give you super-human power to keep the commandments.

2:27 If it is not about who is circumcised or not, but rather who keeps the law or not, then in that case even uncircumcised people can judge the ones who claim to know it all and have it all. On the one hand you have those who feel naturally inclined to do what is right, yet none of them are circumcised, then you have the circumcised who know the letter of the law but fail to keep it.

2:28 So it is not about who you appear to be on the outside that makes you a real Jew, but who you really are on the inside.

2:29 For you to know who you are in your heart is the secret of your spirit identity; this is your true circumcision, it is not the literal outward appearance that distinguishes you. After all it is God's approval and not another's opinion that matters most. People see skin-deep; God knows the heart.

3:1 Having said all this, you might ask whether there is still any advantage in being Jewish? Is there any significance in circumcision?

3:2 The Jewish nation, entrusted with the Messianic Promise, gives relevance and context to the entire prophetic conversation of God. *(See my notes on The Prophetic Significance of Circumcision at the end of Romans chapter 4. Also my notes on **Politics and Israel** at the end of Acts chapter 1)*

3:3 The question is, how does their failure to believe God affect what God believes? It is impossible for their unbelief to compromise God's faith! *(What we believe about God does not define him; God's faith defines us. See the RSV translation, What if some were unfaithful? Does their faithlessness nullify the faithfulness of God? By no means.)*

3:4 God's word is not under threat. In fact, if all of mankind fails, truth remains intact. Truth is defined in God; it is neither challenged nor vindicated by human experience. Contradiction does not intimidate or diminish God's belief. Scripture records that God stands justified in his own word; it confirms that God's promise and purpose are not compromised through mankind's failure; neither is God's reputation threatened by our behavior. *(Truth does not become true by popular vote. We were convinced for many generations that the earth was flat; yet, our belief does not make something true. It is already as true as it gets because God believes it. There is only one faith and one Source! Romans 4:4 & Hebrews 12:2. It is from faith to faith, says Paul [Romans 1:17]; there is no gospel in it until the righteousness of God is revealed; we can do nothing against the truth. [See 2 Corinthians 13:5 and 8]. David's sin did not cancel God's promise. But my mercy I will not take from him and his house shall be made sure, and his kingdom forever before me, and his throne shall be set up forever. [2 Samuel 7:15-16].)*

3:5 We could argue then that God doesn't have a right to judge us, if our unrighteousness only emphasizes his righteousness.

3:6 This would make God an unfair judge of the world.

3:7 This almost sounds like I am saying that it is not really wrong to sin, if our cheating only serves to further contrast the truth of God.

3:8 Because of my emphasis on God's grace, some people slanderously make the assumption and accuse me that my teaching would give people a license to sin. Let us do evil so that good may come. I strongly condemn such foolish talk. *(But if our wickedness advertises the goodness of God, do we feel that God is being unfair to punish us in return? [I'm using a human tit-for-tat argument.] Not a bit of it. What sort of a person would God be then to judge the world? It is like saying that if my lying throws into sharp relief the truth of God and, so to speak, enhances his reputation, then why should he repay me by judging me a sinner? Similarly, why not do evil that good may be, by contrast all the more conspicuous and valuable? (As a matter of fact, I am reported as urging this very thing, by some slanderously and others quite seriously. But, of course, such an argument is quite properly condemned. — Romans 3:5-8 Phillips Translation.)*

3:9 It is common knowledge that sin holds sway over both Jew and Greek alike. *(Just like disease would show the same symptoms regardless of someone's nationality.)*

3:10 Scripture records that within the context of the law, no-one succeeds to live a blameless life. *(Psalm 14:1-3, To the choirmaster of David. The fool says in his heart, 'There is no God.' They are corrupt and they do abominable deeds, there is none that does good. The Lord looks down from heaven upon the children of men, to see if there are any that act wisely, that seek after God. They have all gone astray, they are all alike corrupt; there is none that does good, no, not one [RSV]. In Genesis 18, Abraham intercedes for Sodom and Gomorrah, If there perhaps are 50 righteous people, will you save the city on their behalf? He continues to negotiate with God, until he's down to, perhaps ten?...there was none righteous, no not one ... This argument is building up to the triumphant conclusion of the fact that there is indeed no distinction; the same people who fell short of the glory of God are now justified through God's work of grace in Christ. If mankind was 100% represented in Adam, then they are equally 100% represented in Christ. [Romans 3:21-24].)*

3:11 Because there seems to be no sincere craving and desire to know God there is no spiritual [1]insight. *(While a person remains casual and indifferent about God, their heart remains calloused; the word, [1]suinemi, means a joint-seeing.)*

3:12 Their distraction has [1]bankrupted their lives; that goes for the mass of mankind, without any exception. *(This word, [1]נאלחו neelachu 'unprofitable' in Hebrew/Aramaic means to become 'putrid' and 'offensive,' like fruit that is spoiled. In Arabic, it is applied to 'milk' that becomes sour.)*

3:13 When they open their mouths to speak they bury one another with destructive words. They snake each other with lies and corruption. *(Albert Barnes comments, Their throat is an open sepulchre - This and all the following verses to the end of the 18th are found in the Septuagint, but not in the Hebrew text; and it is most evident that it was from this version that the apostle quoted, as the verses cannot be found in any other place with so near an approximation to the apostle's meaning and words. The verses in question, however, are not found in the Alexandrian manuscript. But they exist in the Vulgate, the Ethiopic, and the Arabic. As the most ancient copies of the Septuagint do not contain these verses, some contend that the apostle has quoted them from different parts of Scripture; and later transcribers of the Septuagint, finding that the 10th, 11th, and 12th, verses were quoted from the 14th Psalm, imagined that the rest were found originally there too, and so incorporated them in their copies, from the apostle's text.*

Their throat is an open sepulchre - By their malicious and wicked words they bury, as it were, the reputation of all men. The whole of this verse appears to belong to their habit of lying, defamation, slandering, etc., by which they wounded, blasted, and poisoned the reputation of others.)

3:14 With sharp tongues they [1]cut one another to pieces, cursing and cheating; their every word is inspired by the [2]wearisome effort to survive in a dog-eat- dog world. *(Taken direct from the Hebrew text in Psalm 10:7 in Hebrew, [1]tok tok תך תך from tavek, תוך to cut to pieces. In Hebrew [2] עמל amal and און aven, to exert oneself in wearisome effort.)*

3:15 Murder has become a regular ritual; without any regard for another's life.

3:16 Their path is littered with broken lives.

3:17 They have lost the art of friendship.

3:18 They have completely lost sight of God. *(3:13-18 are quotations from Psalm 10 and Psalm 14.)*

3:19 The fact that all these quotations are from Jewish writings, confirms that their law of moral conduct did not free them from the very same sins the rest of the world was trapped in. The entire human race is now confronted with the [1]righteousness of God. *(The word [1]upodikos, from upo under and dikē, suggesting to be judged equal; it implies the idea of two parties finding likeness in each other; the stem of the word dikaiosunē, righteousness. See Romans 1:17; also 3:21 and Acts 17:31, Romans 4:25.)*

3:20 The law proves all of mankind equally guilty and confirms that their most sincere duty-driven decisions and 'self-help' programs within the confines of the flesh could not give them any sense of improved confidence in their standing before God.

3:21 We are now talking a completely different language: the gospel unveils what God did right not what we did wrong! Both the law and all the prophetic writings pointed to this moment! *(This brings me back to the theme of my ministry, chapter 1:1, 2, 5, 16, 17. There is no point in telling people how condemned they are! Tell them how loved they are! God's dealing with mankind is based on the fact that their conscience continues to bear witness to their original design. Romans 7:22.)*

3:22 Jesus is what God believes about you! In him the righteousness of God is on display in such a way [1]that everyone may be equally persuaded about what God believes about them, regardless of who they are; there is [2]no distinction. *(The Preposition, [1]eis, indicates a point reached in conclusion. The Greek, ou gar estin diastolē means [2]there is no exception - this includes every single person, Jew and Gentile alike!)*

3:23 Mankind is in the same boat; their [1]distorted behavior is proof of a [2]lost [3]blueprint. *(The word sin, is the word [1]hamartia, from ha, negative or without and meros, portion or form, thus to be without your allotted portion or without form, pointing to a disoriented, distorted, bankrupt identity; the word meros, is the stem of morphē, as in 2 Corinthians 3:18 the word metamorphē, with form, which is the opposite of hamartia - without form. Sin is to live out of context with the blueprint of one's design; to behave out of tune with God's original harmony. See Deuteronomy 32:18, You have forgotten the Rock that begot you and have gotten out of step with the God who danced with you! Hebrew, חול khul, also means to dance, as in Judges 21:21. See Romans 9:33 in the Mirror! The word [2]hustereō, to fall short, to be inferior, [3]doxa, glory, blueprint, from dokeō, opinion or intent.)*

3:24 While the law proves mankind's dilemma, the grace of God announces the same mankind's redemption in Jesus Christ! Their blameless innocence is a free gift! The gift-principle puts the idea of reward out of business! There is no exception - this belongs to every single person, Jew and Gentile alike! *(v 22)* Mankind's righteousness is now redeemed. Jesus Christ is proof of God's grace gift; he redeemed the glory of God in human life; mankind condemned in the language of religion, is now mankind justified in the language of the gospel! *(The man Jesus Christ proved that God did not make a mistake when they made humankind in their image and likeness! Sadly the evangelical world proclaimed verse 23 completely out of context! There is no good news in verse 23, the gospel is in verse 24! All fell short because of Adam; the same 'all' are equally declared innocent because of Christ! The law reveals what happened to mankind in Adam; grace reveals what happened to the same mankind in Christ. There is no distinction - all have sinned and fallen short of the glory of God - now they are all justified freely as a gift through the redemption [the liberating action] of Jesus Christ!)*

3:25 Jesus exhibits God's mercy. In his blood conciliation God's faith persuades mankind of his righteousness and the fact that he has brought closure to the historic record of their sins. *(Not by demanding a sacrifice but providing the sacrifice of himself.)* **Jesus is the unveiling of the Father's heart towards us.** *(See note to Hebrews 8:12; also 1 John 2:2.)*

3:26 All along God [1]refused to let go of mankind. At this very moment God's act of [2]righteousness is [3]pointing them to the evidence of their innocence, with Jesus as the [4]fountainhead of faith. *(God's tolerance, [1]anochē, to echo upward; God continues to hear the echo of his likeness in us. [See Romans 2:4. If we are able to invent tracking devices to find stolen property via satellite, God has every person on the planet covered.*

*In both these verses [25+26] Paul uses the word, [3]**endeixis**, where we get the word indicate from. It is also part of the stem of the word translated, righteousness, [2]**dikaiosunē**. To point out, to show, to convince with proof. Then follows, [4]**ek pisteos iesou; ek,** source or origin and **iesou** is in the Genitive case, the owner of faith is Jesus. He is both the source and substance of faith. Hebrews 11:1, 12:2*

The Incarnation means that God Himself condescended to enter into our alienated human existence, to lay hold of it, to bind it in union with Himself; and the consummation of the Incarnation in the death and resurrection means the Son of God died for all men, and so once and for all constituted men as men upon whom God had poured out His life and love, so that men are forever laid hold of by God and affirmed in their being as His creatures. They can no more escape from His love and sink into non-being than they can constitute themselves men for whom Christ has not died. How can God go back upon the death of His dear Son? How can God undo the Incarnation and go back upon Himself? How can God who is Love go back upon the pouring out of His love once and for all and so cease to be Himself? That is the decisive, final thing about the whole Incarnation including the death of Christ, that it affects all men, indeed the whole of creation, for the whole of creation is now put on a new basis with God, the basis of a Love that does not withhold itself but only overflows in our unending Love. That is why creation still continues in being, and that is why man still exists, for God has not given him up, but on the contrary poured out His love upon him unreservedly once and forever, decidedly and finally affirming man as His child, eternally confirming the creation as His own handiwork. God does not say Yes, and No, for all He has done is Yes and Amen in Christ. That applies to every man, whether he will or not. He owes his very being to Christ and belongs to Christ, and in that he belongs to Christ he has his being only from Him and in relation to Him. Thomas F. Torrance courtesy Baxter Kruger's study notes.)

3:27 The law of faith cancels the law of works; which means there is suddenly nothing left for anyone to boast about. No one is superior to another. *(Bragging only makes sense if there is someone to compete with or impress. While we compete with one another and compare ourselves with one another we are without understanding. [2 Corinthians 10:12]. Through the righteousness of God we have received a faith of equal standing. [See 2 Peter 1:1 RSV] The OS (operating system) of the law of works is willpower; the OS of the law of faith is love. Galatians 5:6 Love sets faith in motion. The law presented one with choices; grace awakens belief. Willpower exhausts, love ignites. If choices could save us we would be our own Saviors. Willpower is the language of the law, love is the language of grace and it ignites faith that leads to romance; falling in love beats making a decision to believe in love by far. See Romans 7:19 Willpower has failed me; this is how embarrassing it is, the most diligent decision that I make to do good, disappoints.)*

3:28 This leaves us with only one logical conclusion, mankind is justified by God's faith and not by their ability to keep the law.

3:29 Which means that God is not the private property of the Jews but belongs equally to all the nations. *(While the law excludes the non-Jewish nations, faith includes us all on level terms.)*

3:30 There is only one God, he deals with everyone, circumcised or uncircumcised exclusively on the basis of faith.

3:31 No, faith does not re-write the rules; instead it confirms that the original life-quality meant for mankind as mirrored and documented in the 10 commandments, is now realized in the Gospel. *(Jesus brought closure to the old in his death and introduced the new dimension in his resurrection.)*

In the following chapters, Paul further embroiders his powerful logic and revelation of mankind's redemption. *[As highlighted in Romans 1:16,17 & 2:24-29 and here in chapter 3, especially verses 20-31]*

He now continues in Chapter 4, reminding his audience of their ancestor Abraham.

Faith-righteousness was not Abram's idea or invention. He was simply overwhelmed by his Maker's belief and favor, in his God-encounters! See Genesis 12-17 to begin with. Only then *[in chapter 17]*, he became Abra*ham*; when God added the *hey* of their own name יהוה Jahweh in his name. The letter ה *hey*, in Ancient Hebrew is, ⚲ the man with raised hands pictures a sigh of wonder, behold, as when looking at a great sight; thus, meaning, breath or sigh, as one does when seeing something wonderful and pointing it out. The ה *[hey]* is also the number 5, which is the number for grace.

No, it was not Abram's faith that rewarded him with righteousness! Faith is not something we do; it is what happens to us when we encounter the Agapē of God! There is only ONE faith! Ephesians 4:5. Jesus is both the Source and sustenance of this faith! Hebrews 12:2. Also Romans 1:17 & 2:21,22.

In my book, Divine Embrace, I have a chapter on Incarnate Faith which addresses the statement of Jesus, Let it be to you according to <u>your faith</u>.

Also here, https://mirrorword.net/what-does-the-mirror-say-about/

4:1 If we look at our father Abraham as an example and scrutinize his life, would you say that he discovered any reason for placing confidence in the flesh through personal contribution?

4:2 If he felt that his friendship with God was a reward for good behavior, then surely he would have reason to recommend the recipe; yet it is plain to see that it was all God's initiative from start to finish.

4:3 Scripture is clear, Abraham reflected God's belief in him; this is the basis of the [1]rediscovery of [2]righteousness. *([1]One must remember that in Adam & Eve's communion with Elohim, something was lost which would be redeemed - there would be a return to the consciousness of this union. [2]This most significant, relational term, righteousness, points to a shared likeness; this includes one's authentic identity and innocence. The word [2]dikaiosunē, righteousness is from the stem dikē, suggesting to be judged equal; it implies the idea of two parties finding likeness in each other. Also, note that the name of the Greek goddess of Justice is Dikē [pronounced, Dikey]; she is always pictured holding a scale of balances in her hand.)*

4:4 There is a large difference between a reward and a gift: if you have earned something through hard work, then what you receive in return is your due and certainly not a gift.

4:5 Righteousness as God's free gift, takes the idea of reward out of the equation - faith and not our toil celebrates the innocence of the ungodly!

4:6 David confirms this principle when he speaks of the blessedness of the one who discovers God's approval without any reference to something specific that they had done to qualify themselves.

4:7 Oh what [1]happy progress one makes with the weight of sin and guilt removed and one's slate wiped clean. *(The Greek, μακάριος makarios, means extremely blessed/happy. The Aramaic/Hebrew word [1]ashar, אשר blessed, means to advance, to make progress.)*

4:8 How blessed is the one who receives a [1]receipt instead of an invoice for their sins. *([1]logitzomai, to make a calculation to which there can only be one logical conclusion, to take an inventory. LXX-Psalm 31:1, 2; Masoretic Hebrew Text -Psalm 32:1, 2)*

4:9 Now, is the blessedness that we are talking about restricted exclusively to the circumcised, or are those who have never even heard about the cut equally included? Remember we are looking at Abraham *[in whom all nations are blessed]*, as our example of a righteousness that is purely based upon the principle of a faith sourced in God's persuasion. *(Note, ἡ πίστις, he pistis, the faith. There is only one valid source of faith, not what we believe about God or about ourselves, but what God believes about us. Romans 1:17; 2:22)*

4:10 So, the question is, was he reckoned righteous before or after he was circumcised? It is clear that Abraham's faith-encounters *[as recorded in Genesis 12 through 15]*, happened long before circumcision was mentioned! *(The symbolic circumcision covenant was only introduced years later in Genesis 17, when he was already 99 years old. [Isaac's birth is only recorded in Genesis 21.]*

*See my **notes on circumcision** at the end of this chapter.)*

4:11 Thus, Abraham received circumcision as an external, symbolic [1]seal to remind him of what God had already [2]declared many years ago, when he was first introduced to the concept of the [3]righteousness of God. Since Abraham's supernatural fatherhood is celebrated in circumcision, it infers that he is both the father of Jew and Gentile alike - God already engaged him in covenant as an uncircumcised Gentile - he thus represents them in all that was predicted concerning the blessing of every nation in the Seed of faith!

*([1] A [1]seal of the righteousness of the faith - **sphragida tēs dikaiosunēs tēs pisteōs**. The [1]seal of circumcision was not meant to be a distraction but rather a prophetic confirmation to the only valid basis to the righteousness [of God] by the principle of the faith [of God]. Just like a receipt is only a reference to, and not the actual transaction. Note, <u>the</u> faith and <u>the</u> righteousness. See 2 Corinthians 13:5. Also here in Romans 4:25.*

*[2] Circumcision did not introduce an adjusted or new covenant - it was simply added as a symbolic seal in [2]confirmation to God's resolve, as recorded in Genesis 12:2,3 and Genesis 15:5. In the meantime, Abraham's moments of unbelief, delays and detours did not distract from God's determined destiny for the prophetic Messianic Seed. **Galatians 3:16** It is on record that the promise [of the blessing of righteousness by God's faith] was made to Abraham and to his Seed, singular, [thus excluding his effort to produce Ishmael.] Isaac, the child of promise, and not of the flesh, mirrors the Messiah. [Genesis 3:15])*

4:12 At the same time he also represents all Jews as their father; especially those, for whom circumcision is not merely a skin deep religious ritual, but who engages the same principle of the faith that ignited Abraham's belief.

4:13 [1]Righteousness by faith and not righteousness by law prompted the promise when God announced to Abraham that he would father those who would inherit the world. It is again a matter of embracing a gift rather than receiving a reward for keeping the law.

*Look away [from the law of works] unto Jesus; he is the Author and finisher of faith. [Hebrews 12:2]. It is God's faith to begin with; it is **from faith to faith**, and not our good or bad behavior; we are not defined by our performance or circumstances. The Greek word translated from is the Preposition, **ek**, which always denotes source or origin. The language of the old written code was, Do in order to become. The language of the new is, Be, because of what was done. Instead of do, do, do, it's done, done, done. Paul refers here to **Habakkuk 2:4, The just shall live by his [God's] faith.** Habakkuk sees a complete new basis to mankind's standing before God. Instead of reading the curse when disaster strikes, he realizes that the Promise out-dates performance as the basis to mankind's acquittal. The curse is taken out of the equation. Galatians 3:13.*

4:14 Faith would be emptied of its substance and the principle of promise would be meaningless if the law of personal performance was still in

play, to qualify the heirs. *(Faith is not in competition with the law. The life quality that faith reveals is consistent with mankind's original design and mirrors the very life that the law promotes.)*

4:15 The law system is bound to bring about disappointment, regret and anger; if there is no law there is nothing to break; no contract, no breach.

4:16 Therefore since faith sponsors the gift of grace, the promise is equally secured for all the children. The law has no exclusive claim on anyone *[the reward system cannot match the gift principle].* Faith is our source, and this makes Abraham our father.

4:17 When God changed Abram's name to Abraham, he made a public statement that he would be the father of all nations. *[Genesis 17]* Here we see Abraham faced with God's faith; the kind of faith that resurrects the dead and calls things which are not *[yet visible in planet earth's time-zone],* as though they were. *(See my extended notes at the end of this chapter.)*

4:18 Faith gave substance to hope when everything seemed hopeless; the words, so shall your seed be conceived in him the faith of fatherhood. *(Abraham's case here pictures the hopelessness of fallen mankind, having lost their identity, and faced with the impossibility to redeem themselves.)*

4:19 Abraham's faith would have been nullified if he were to take his own age and the deadness of Sarah's womb into account. His hundred year old body and Sarah's barren womb did not distract him in the least. He finally knew that no contribution from their side could possibly assist God in fulfilling the promise.

4:20 While he had every reason to doubt, he did not hesitate for a moment but instead, empowered by faith's persuasion, he continued to communicate God's opinion. *(His name was his confession: in the Hebrew language, Abraham* אברהם *was not a mere familiar sounding name, but a meaningful sentence, a confession of faith's authority, against the odds. He did not become embarrassed about his name; he did not change his name to Abe for short when there seemed to be no change in his circumstances. Every time he introduced himself or someone called him by his name, it was a bold declaration and repetition of God's promise, calling things that were not as though they were. I would imagine that Sarah spoke his name the most. In fact, every time they addressed one another they spoke the promise, Mother of nations, kings of peoples shall come from you. [Genesis 17:5, 16]. Abraham, the father of the multitudes.)*

4:21 Abraham's confidence was his [1]dress-code; he knew beyond doubt that the power of God to perform was equal to his promise. *([1]plerophoreō, from plerō to be completely covered in every part, + phoreo, to wear garments or armor; traditionally translated to be completely persuaded. His faith was his visible identity and armor; he wore his persuasion like he would his daily garments.)*

4:22 The persuasion of God rubbed off on Abraham and became his personal conviction. This is the [1]basis of righteousness. *(Righteousness was [1]reckoned to him, this means that God's faith pointed Abraham to an invisible future where mankind's innocence and identity would be redeemed again. Greek, [1]logitsomai, logical conclusion.)*

4:23 Here is the Good News: the recorded words, It was reckoned to him were not written for his sake alone.

4:24 Scripture was written with us in mind. We are audience to the same faith in the face of death. The same [1]conclusion is now equally relevant in our realizing the significance of Jesus' resurrection from the dead. *(By raising Jesus from the dead God proclaims his belief in our redeemed innocence. Isaac's birth from Sarah's barren womb prophetically declared the resurrection of Jesus from the tomb. Abraham's best efforts could not produce Isaac. Sarah's dead womb is a picture of the impossibility of the flesh to produce a child. This underlines mankind's inability to redeem themselves under the performance-based law of willpower.*

Jesus said, Abraham saw my day. Mankind's most extreme self-sacrifice offered in an attempt to win the favorable attention of their deity could never match the sacrifice of God's Lamb to win the attention of mankind. When Isaac questioned his father about the sacrifice, then Abraham announced, Jahweh jireh. יהוה יראה *Jahweh sees. And he lifted up his eyes and behold **behind him** was a ram caught in the thorn bush by its horns. Note, Behind him. Faith sees the future in past tense-mode.*

*The resurrection is the ultimate proof and trophy of righteousness by God's faith. [See Romans 6:11] [1]**logitsomai** - logical conclusion. Consider [**logitsomai**] yourself dead indeed, compared with 4:19, Abraham considered his own body dead. We can only study Scripture in the context of Christ as representing the human race; God had us in mind all along [John 5:39].)*

4:25 While our [1]sins [2]resulted in his death; our righteousness and redeemed innocence is [2]celebrated in his resurrection!

*([1] The word [1]**parapiptō** has two components, **para**, closest possible proximity of union, and **piptō**, to descend from a higher place to a lower; to fall; to be thrust down; from **petomai**, to fly. Thus to stop flying. Losing altitude. This speaks of mankind's short falling, or their fallen mindset. Romans 3:23,24; Also, Colossians 3:1-3. See **Philippians 3:10**, Oh to comprehend the dynamic of his resurrection. His resurrection is evidence of our righteousness.*

[2] It is most wonderful to discover that his resurrection does not include us only once we believe! If something is not true to begin with, our belief will not make it true!

*Paul uses the word, **dia** twice in this verse! Unfortunately most translations in most languages only translate the 1st **dia** correctly!*

*He was handed over <u>BECAUSE of</u> [**dia**] our sins - why was he raised?*

NOT so that some small portion of the elite Christian group may stand a dim chance to be justified!!!

*NO! Hallelujah! The same word, **dia** is used again!*

*He was raised <u>BECAUSE of</u> [**dia**] our righteousness!*

Here is the equation: His cross = our sins,

His resurrection = our innocence.

His resurrection is the official receipt to our acquittal. This is one of the most important statements in the entire Bible. His death brought closure to our short falling; his resurrection is proof of our redeemed righteousness.

His resurrection reveals our righteousness. If mankind was still guilty after Jesus died, his resurrection would be irrelevant. This explains Acts 10:28 and 2 Corinthians 5:14 and 16.

See Young's Literal Translation, Romans 4:25 who was delivered up because of our offenses, and was raised up because of our being declared righteous.

In Acts 17:31, Paul explains to the Greek philosophers that according to the Jewish prophetic word, God had fixed a day on which he would judge the world in righteousness by a man whom he has appointed, and of this he has given proof to all mankind by raising him from the dead. God's declaration of your redeemed innocence is his most urgent invitation to you[manity] to encounter intimate oneness.

See also 1 Peter 1:10-12 This salvation which you now know as your own, is the theme of the prophetic thought; this is what captured the Prophets' attention for generations and became the object of their most diligent inquiry and scrutiny. They knew all along that mankind's salvation was a grace revelation, sustained in their prophetic utterance. [Salvation would never be by personal achievement or a reward to willpower-driven initiative. The law of works would never replace grace.]

1 Peter 1:11 In all of their conversation there was a constant quest to determine who the Messiah would be, and exactly when this would happen. They knew with certainty that it was the spirit of Christ within them pointing prophetically and giving testimony to the sufferings of the Christ and the subsequent glory. [Whatever glory was lost in Adam, would be redeemed again in Jesus Christ.]

1 Peter 1:12 It was revealed to them that this glorious grace message that they were communicating pointed to a specific day and person beyond their own horizon and generation; they saw you in their prophetic view. This heavenly announcement had you in mind all along. They proclaimed glad tidings to you in advance, in the Holy Spirit, commissioned from heaven; the celestial messengers themselves longed to gaze deeply into its complete fulfillment.)

Romans Chapter 4 Extended Notes:
The Prophetic Significance of Circumcision

The Prophetic Significance of Circumcision

In symbolic-language, circumcision communicates that the son of man is the son of God, and not the fruit of his natural father's seed. There is only ONE Father of the human race. Malachi 2:10 & Ephesians 3:15.

So, what makes childless, pagan Abram, such a key candidate to be the carrier of the Seed of Promise?

Consider the meaning of his grandfather and father's names:

Abram's grandfather is **Nahor** נחור, *meaning nose, inhaling the breath of life; in Ancient Hebrew [also reading from right to left] , ৭* **ᴨ**ᶺ *a picture of a seed sprout, representing the idea of continuing into a new generation;* **ᴨ** *for the letter* ח *ch, like in the sound, ch in the word, Bach - it is a picture of a tent wall, to protect the occupants from the elements outside; the head of a person,* ৭ *can also represent the mind; thus, to see an offspring, protected in the tent walls of a person's mind. As Abraham's grandfather, Nahor's name carries the prophetic word in-spite of the seeming delay in both of the births of his son* **Terah** תרח *[meaning delay!], as well as his grandson Abram!*

Abram אברם; *the first two letters Aleph and Bet,* **Ab** אב *means father, and* **ram**, רם *in Hebrew is exalted; above, as in the heavenly dimension. In Ancient Hebrew,* ᴨᶺ *the head of a young bull - strength and* ᴨ *tent, house; strength of the house; thus, meaning father or head of the house. Then follows the word,* רם *ram, The letter r, is the head of a person,* ৭ *which also represents the mind, and the letter m,* ᴧᴧ *as a picture of water or the sea representing mass, also the heavenly dimension*

Note that most of Abram's ancestors were already fathers at the ages of 29 or 35; yet his own father, **Terah** תרח *[meaning,* **delay!***] was 70 years old before he had* **Abram**; אברם *his name suggests that Terah acknowledged that he could not claim parenthood of this son, he was 'fathered from above'! [Genesis 11:12-26]*

Now imagine how nervous Abram was, when he was 75 [In Haran] and still without a child.

Abram's early life

Abram's first 70 years are rooted in Babylonian culture, most of which represents man's failed attempts to reach beyond their earthbound horizon; as in the tower of Babel, which then spiraled out into a confusion of languages, philosophies and religions. Their quest continued to be expressed in the many **Zigurrats**, which were a type of rectangular, very high temple tower or tiered mound erected by the Sumerians, Akkadians, and Babylonians in Mesopotamia. *[Like the Great Ziggurat of Ur, the capital of the ancient Chaldean Empire where Abram stems from.]*

The Chaldeans were the learned class; they were farmers, traders, priests, magicians and astronomers.

The Greek word Χαλδαῖος **Chaldaios**, *referring to a native of the region of the lower Euphrates bordering on the Persian Gulf. In Hebrew,* **kaśdty** - כַּשְׂדִּי *meaning,* **clod breakers** *- from the root, keśed* כֶּשֶׂד *Chesed,* **increase**.

The extraordinary fertility of the Chaldaean soil has been noticed by various writers. It is said to be the only country in the world where wheat grows wild.

*The etymology of Babel is associated with the Hebrew verb **balal**, to confuse or confound. The word **Bab-ilu** Gate of God in Akkadian language, **bab**, gate + **ilu**, god; or its Sumerian name, **E-temen-an-ki** means, house of the foundation of heaven on earth.*

An amazing prophetic mirror unfolds 1500 years later! Israel is taken captive into Babylon for 70 years! They have metaphorically returned to the dormant womb of Abram's 70 years in Babylon before Jahweh broke the silence! *[Representing the failure of the entire religious Jewish-Levitical and institutionalized Christian-order! Which would sadly be the repeat-cycle of their own blindfolds until the ends of the earth return to the Lord in their realizing and re-discovering their redeemed sonship. Psalm 22:27; Psalm 110:4; Hebrews 6:20 & chapter 7]*

Jeremiah 29:10 For thus says the LORD: After seventy years are completed at Babylon, I will visit you and perform My good word toward you, and cause you to return to this place. *[The Promised land - symbolically pointing to the entire human person, both individually, as well as globally]*

Jeremiah 29:11 For I know the thoughts that I think toward you, says the LORD, thoughts of peace and not of evil, to give you a future and a hope.

Meanwhile, Abram is stuck in a conversation that has, instead of leading him through the Gate of God, entangled him in a cul-de-sac, pagan religion. His accumulated wealth wouldn't buy him and Sarai a child! Yet, he held on to a fragile thread of hope, since his father Terah only conceived him when he was 70 years old.

Abram's God-encounters

It was at this time that he encounters God, who conceives in him *a new conversation* - the seed theme of the promise to Eve, is revived.

Genesis 3:15 Your seed shall crush the head of the serpent! [Representing the mindset of the I am not-Tree; I have to strive to be.]

God, very intentionally and at various intervals, continues to meet with landless, and childless Abram, for the next 30 years, from Ur in ancient Macedonia to Haran; then, at various locations, in Shechem, Mamre, Bethel, Canaan and Valley of Shaveh *(that is, the King's Valley)*.

In *Genesis 15:5*, God engages Abraham with a larger dimension than his present circumstantial horizon - Lift up your eyes! - Realize how impossible it is to count the stars! So shall your seed be!

At that point, faith happened! The very next verse reads, *Genesis 15:6* Abraham believed what God believed about him and that concluded his righteousness.

Time and again God confirms to him that in his Seed, all the families of the earth shall be blessed! See Genesis 12:1-3; Genesis 13-17 & Acts 7:2-5. *Genesis 15:7*, I am the LORD, who led you out of Ur in Babylonia...

A glimpse of Abram's wealth, fortitude and strategic skills. None of which would succeed in fulfilling the promise of his own offspring.

Genesis 14 describes the battle of nine kings, but then, while living in Mamre, Abram the Hebrew, hears that his brother's son Lot's is taken captive. *[This is the 1st time the word Hebrew is used עבר Heyber is connected with crossing over and the beyond. Abram by now, has this reputation of traveling beyond boundaries and difficulties.]*

He then mustered 318 of his servants, skilled in warfare - all of them born in his household - and pursued the captors for a hundred and twenty miles, all the way to Dan. There, he and his men split into small groups and attacked by night. They chased them as far as Hobah, and defeated them just north of Damascus. Thus they recovered all the loot, along with nephew Lot and his possessions, including the women and the people. Genesis 14:14-16

Melchizedek and the Covenant meal

And now on his victorious return, he encounters *a tenth king*, Melchizedek, King of Righteousness, the King of Salem *[the king of peace]*, who did not partake in the Canaanite warfare but, in his King/Priestly capacity, blesses Abram and shares with him the covenant meal of bread and wine. *(See my notes on* **Understanding the significance of meals in Covenant context** *at the end of Luke 11.)*

Furthermore, the king of Sodom desires to reward Abram with the spoils of war - but, he refuses to take even a shoestring, so that you may not say, I have made Abram rich! Instead, he gives a tenth of the spoils to the tenth King, Melchizedek!

Genesis 15:1 in the Septuagint LXX reads, **Immediately after Abram meets Melchizedek, Jahweh speaks to him and addresses his fears** *[no land; no child]* **Fear not! Beyond all comparison** *[υπερασπιζω from ὑπεράνω* **huperanō***; uper + ano - over and above],* **I am your priceless reward***; exceedingly surpassing any possible reward you could wish for, as achieved in by your own efforts!*

See **Hebrews 7:3 There exists no record that can link Melchizedek to a natural father or mother; no birth certificate neither any account of his death, nor is there any record of his age. He resembles exactly the Son of God: his priesthood abides without beginning or end.** *[This was at a time where detailed records were kept of every genealogy. This encounter greatly boosts Abram's faith!]*

Hebrews 7:10 When Melchizedek and Abraham met, Levi was already present in the loins of his father. *[By the time Levi was born, Melchizedek was still alive; since he has no beginning of time nor end of life,* **in him time and eternity meet.***]*

In **Psalm 110:4** *[***109** *in LXX] David announces the Messianic priesthood after the order of Melchizedek; which will eclipse the Levitical order [of natural birth].*

Bread and wine points to the ultimate covenant.

The cutting of covenants involved the shedding of blood, which was a familiar practice between two parties in those times. *In Hebrew,* כרת ברית *karat berit literally means to cut a covenant. [Even our modern day handshake still reminds of the symbolic mingling of blood between two parties]*

In Ancient Hebrew, also reading from right to left, ‪†⅃ᕊ⊡ †ᕊ⸦*the letter* ⸦*, or* כ *k-sound, pictures a open palm presenting a free-will offering; then the r,* ᕊ *the head or mind; followed by the letter t, Tau* † *the cross! Karat translates to cut. Then the word, covenant* ברית *berit, or in Ancient Hebrew,* ‪†⅃ᕊ⊡ *the letter B is the house; then the person's head* ᕊ *- the head of the house; then the i* ⅃ *Jod,* ⅃ *is an outstretched arm reaching into our lostness [our out of homeness] in order to rescue us. Then the Tau* † *which is the last letter of the Hebrew alphabet - the fulfillment of the conversation. This is a powerful picture of the Cross of Christ - the covenant of salvation. Philippians 2:8-11.*

In Genesis 15:13-17, God instructs him to cut the animals in half; with the two halves representing and mirroring the two parties; both parties would typically walk between these pieces and declare their mutual covenant commitment, based on various conditions. Yet, in Abram's case, he fell into a deep sleep. *[This reminds of Adam - Eve was not an afterthought! Adam was put into a deep sleep; then God took her out of the Word that was already made flesh! Mankind redeemed, the Bride, began the same way! Co-quickened, co-raised we are!]* And, while Abram was fast asleep, Jahweh spoke to him about future generations of his seed. Then, God moved between the mirror-pieces in a smoking fire pot and a flaming torch. *[The prophetic pointer to God's act of redemption in the Messiah. [Also the trinity of 3 animals - three years old - representing the 3 years of Jesus ministry of Salvation.]*

Jesus crucified between two criminals is the ultimate **Mirror Covenant.**

1 Corinthians 11:23-25, The night in which the Lord Jesus was betrayed, he took bread and gave thanks; breaking the bread into portions, he said, Realize your association with my death, every time you eat, remember my body that was broken for you. He did exactly the same with the cup after supper and said, This cup holds the wine of the New Covenant in my blood; you celebrate me every time you drink ¹with this understanding. *(From now on our meals are meaningful. We celebrate the fact that the incarnation reveals our redemption; the promise became a person. The word,* ¹αναμνησιν **ana,** *upwards, and* **mnesin,** *remembrance - to bring something from memory into the here and now!)*

Romans 4:2... it is plain to see that it was all God's initiative from start to finish. Romans 4:3 Scripture is clear, Abraham reflected God's belief in him; this is the basis of the rediscovery of righteousness.

Also, **Hebrews 6:13 Since God had no one greater by whom to swear, he swore by himself. He could give Abraham no greater guarantee but the integrity of his own Being; this makes the promise as sure as God is.**

Abram awakens to an unconditional covenant. *[James, the younger brother of Jesus, calls it the perfect law of liberty, ἐλεύθερος **eleutheros**, unrestrained; exempt from obligation or liability!]*

Circumcision follows a game-changer Name Change!

Finally, at the age of 99 *[Genesis 17]*, when everything still seems rather hopeless, God introduces Abram to **Abraham**! He adds the letter 'ה *he'*, the breath of life, of יהוה Jahweh's own name into Abram's name and he becomes, *Abra<u>ha</u>m* אברהם the father of the multitudes of nations.

And, in Ancient Hebrew, ᴍ𐤔𐤀𐤌𐤏 *The letter* ה h, *in Ancient Hebrew is* 𐤔 *man with the raised hands pictures a sigh of wonder.behold, as when looking at a great sight; thus, meaning, breath or sigh, as one does when seeing something wonderful and pointing it out. The* ה *[he] is also the number 5, which is the number for grace!*

*There is no Hebrew word, -**raham** but, in Arabic the word means drizzling and lasting rain. The innumerable drops of water in the rain are like the stars mentioned in* **Genesis 15:5 Look toward heaven, and number the stars, if you are able to number them - so shall your seed be! Now, imagine those innumerable stars raining down upon the earth and each one becomes a grain of sand!**

> **Genesis 22:17 I will indeed bless you, and I will multiply your Seed as the stars of heaven and as the sand which is on the seashore.**

In **Genesis 17:4-5** *God announces him as the father of the masses of nations* אב המון *גוים, **ab hamon goyim**; The word* המון, **hamon**, *does not express simply a large number, but the rain-like noise that emerges from a unified, seething throng of people!*

Abraham's identity, his name, was the echo of God's faith and his bold confession in the absence of Isaac.

> *This significant name change reminds of* **Matthew 16:17** *Blessed are you, Simon, son of Jonah! [Bar Jonah, his surname identity] Flesh and blood did not reveal this to you, but My Father! I say, you are Rock, a chip [**petros**] of the old Block [**petra**]! And upon this revelation, that the son of man is the son of God, I will build my **ekklesia** and the gates of **Hadēs** will not prevail against it.*

> *The **ekklesia** from ek, source/origin and **kaleō**, to surname; original identity. **Hadēs**, from **ha**, negative particle, and **eidō** to see. In a walled city, the gates are the most strategic point - if the gates are disengaged, the city is taken! Thus, the blindfold mode of mankind's forgotten identity, will not prevail against you!*

Also See **Deuteronomy 32:4, Ascribe greatness to our God, the Rock! His work is perfect and all his ways are just! A God of faithfulness, righteous and upright is he.**

Deuteronomy 32:18, But you were unmindful of the Rock that begot you, and forgot the God who gave you birth.

Also **Isaiah 51:1,2 Look to the Rock from which you were hewn, the quarry from which you were dug!**

66

Look to Abraham your father and to Sarah who bore you; for when he was but one I called him, and I blessed him and made him many.

<u>Now God introduces Abraham to the covenant of circumcision</u>.

We have said that circumcision symbolically communicates that **the son of man is the son of God**, and not the fruit of his natural father's seed! There is only ONE Father of the human race. Malachi 2:10 & Ephesians 3:15; Ephesians 4:6.

While this circumcision-mirror-covenant does not involve an animal or bird [*as in Genesis 15*]; it will engage Abram in a most personal way; perhaps, the most sensitive and very significant member of the male human body, the foreskin of the penis! Here is the profound connection, not only does this member feature prominently in sexual intimacy, but entire future generations are represented in it.

In this circumcision-cut, God is saying to Abraham that the very member of his body which failed to produce the promised Seed, will now remind him of the covenant of promise. That, in the prophetic Seed of the Promise, all the nations of the earth will be blessed with their redeemed, restored identity and innocence. [*Righteousness*] The authentic life of their design will be rebooted in resurrected hope!

In **Genesis 17:10,11**, we have the first mention of the words connected with circumcision. God again repeats the fact that the fruit of his seed, [τοῦ σπέρματός σου] **sperma** *in Greek, and* זרע *zera, in Hebrew; will be exceedingly multiplied...* [*Which reminds of* **John 12:24**, *The single grain of wheat will not abide alone - it will bear much fruit*]

[1] *The term, translated* [1]**circumcision** περιτέμνω **peritemno**, *is from* **peri***, around, and* τομώτερος **tomōteros** *a derivative of* τέμνω **temno** *to cut with precision; and in Hebrew* מול **mul**, *to cut off.*

[2] *Then the term,* ἀκροβυστία [2]**akrobustia** *from* ἄκρον **akron** *the tip, and* πόσθη **posthē** *- the penis. In the Tanach [Jewish Bible] the Hebrew word for* [2]*foreskin is,* עורלה *'orlá.*

This significant covenant-cut is intended to symbolically remind every circumcised male, that the son of man is the son of God! Both our eternal Genesis, as well as our eternal Destiny are endorsed. The Father of creation, in whom we live and move and have our being, is metaphorically communicated in this covenant of remembrance.

Everyday, the circumcised penis would represent this profound, and figurative token; whether the man reliefs his bladder or enjoys intimacy - the reminder is evident!

I bless the Lord for [1]**bringing understanding to me. Also in the nights, when my** [2]**kidneys prompt me** [*to get up and go for a leak*], **they instruct me. Psalm 16:7.** (*The word,* συνετίσαντά, *Aorist Participle of* [1]συνετίζω *to bring to an awareness. The word,* νεφροι [2]**nephroi** *refers to kidneys; also, one's inner promptings/thoughts.*)

67

So shall your Seed be...

Galatians 3:16 It is on record that the promise *[of the blessing of righteousness by God's faith]* **was made to Abraham and to his Seed, singular,** *[thus excluding his effort to produce Ishmael.]* **Isaac, the child of promise, and not of the flesh, mirrors the Messiah.**

Romans 4:18 Faith gave substance to hope when everything seemed hopeless; the words, so shall your seed be conceived in Abraham the faith of fatherhood. *(Abraham's case here pictures the hopelessness of fallen mankind, having lost their identity, and faced with the impossibility to redeem themselves.)*

Romans 4:19 Abraham's faith would have been nullified if he were to take his own age and the deadness of Sarah's womb into account. His hundred year old body and Sarah's barren womb did not distract him in the least. He finally knew that no contribution from their side could possibly assist God in fulfilling his promise.

Romans 4:20 While he had every reason to doubt the promise, he did not hesitate for a moment but instead, empowered by faith confidence, he continued to communicate God's opinion. *(His name was his confession: in the Hebrew language, Abraham* אברהם *was not a mere familiar sounding name, but a meaningful sentence, a confession of faith's authority, against the odds. He was not embarrassed about his name; he did not change his name to Abe for short, when there seemed to be no change in his circumstances. Every time he introduced himself, or someone called him by his name, it was a bold declaration and repetition of God's promise, calling things that were not as though they were. I would imagine that Sarah spoke his name the most. In fact, every time they addressed one another they spoke the promise, Mother of nations, kings of peoples shall come from you. [Genesis 17:5, 16]. Abraham, the father of the multitudes.)*

The Seed of David

Jesus' grandfather, from his mother's side, was Eli, עלי *- meaning, elevation; to raise above; ascension. In Luke 3:23, Luke records the genealogy of Jesus, beginning with Mary's father, Eli. He confirms the prophetic word pointing to the virgin birth, Ask a sign of the LORD your God; let it be deep as Sheol or high as heaven. But you would not, therefore the Lord himself will give you a sign. Behold, a virgin shall conceive and bear a Son, and shall call his name Immanuel. Isaiah 7:11-14.*

Luke 1:27 Gabriel was to visit Mary, a [1]**young, virgin girl, engaged to marry Joseph, a descendant of David.** *(The word* [1]*parthenos, literally, from Athens - an epithet meaning Virgin, applied by the Greeks to several goddesses, especially Athena. Always associated with a virgin girl - as in LXX Isaiah 7:14. [The LXX was the Jewish Scriptures of the time. The Septuagint, from the Latin: septuāgintā literally seventy; often abbreviated as 70 in Roman numerals, i.e., LXX; sometimes called the Greek Old Testament. It is the earliest extant Koine Greek translation of the Hebrew Scriptures. [It was at the request of Ptolemy II Philadelphus (285–247 BCE) by 70 Jewish scholars or, according to later tradition, 72, with six scholars from each of the Twelve Tribes of Israel.] The discovery of the Qumran scrolls reveal that the LXX represents much older manuscripts than our OT, which used the*

1000 years later Masoretic text.] **In the Masoretic text the word virgin was changed to, an unmarried girl.)**

This also endorses the earliest prophetic reference to the Messiah's triumph over the serpent mindset - The seed of the woman shall crush the serpent's head! Genesis 3:15.

Matthew writes the genealogy of Joseph, descended from David via Solomon, while Luke connects Jesus with David via Nathan! See, 2 Samuel 5:14, David's children, born in Jerusalem: Shammua, Shobab, Nathan, Solomon.

Also **Romans 1:3 The Son of God has his natural lineage from the seed of David.**

The prophet **Micah**, מיכה *[meaning, who is like God], wrote,* **And you, Bethlehem, belonging to the house of Ephrathah; you are the least among the thousands of Judah; yet, my ruler in Israel will emerge out of you; this One's origin is from the beginning, whose lineage can be traced to the Ancient of Days. Micah 5:2.**

Jesus quotes a very prominent Messianic Psalm in, **Luke 20:42-44 David himself says, Jahweh said to my Lord, sit at my right hand, until I have subdued your enemies under your feet.** *[Psalm 109:1 LXX - Psalm 110 Masoretic Text]* **So, if David calls him my Lord, how can he be his son?**

Jesus, knowing that prophetic scripture is all about him [Luke 24:27], now engages this Psalm of David; every Jew and especially their Scribes would recognize it as a most significant Messianic prophecy. Imagine the courage flooding Jesus' spirit as he mirrored this crucial moment in Scripture. By quoting the opening verse of a Psalm; every Scribe immediately knows that the entire Psalm is intended. See my commentary on Psalm 109 [Psalm 110] at the end of Luke 20.

No wonder then that he says in **Matthew 23:9 You must not call** *[μὴ καλέσητε]* **anyone here on earth Father, because you have only the one Father in heaven.**

1 Corinthians 8:6 There is only one God, the Father, who is the Creator of all things and for whom we live; and there is only one Lord, Jesus Christ, through whom all things were created and through whom we live.

Before Abraham was, I am.

John 1:1 To go back to the very [1]beginning, is to find the [2]Word already [3]present there; [4]face to face with God. The one mirrors the other. The Word is [3]I am; God's [2]eloquence echoes and [4]concludes in him. The Word equals God.

In the beginning, [1]archē, to be first in order, time, place or rank.

The Word, [2]logos, [intelligence as an interconnected network of things known; the sum total of logic] was with God; here and again in verse 2, John uses the Greek Preposition [4]pros, towards; face-to-face.

Three times in this sentence John uses the Active Indicative Imperfect form of the verb [3]eimi, namely aēn [ἧν] to continue to be, [in the beginning 'was' the Word etc...], which conveys no idea of origin for God or for the Logos, but simply continuous existence, I am.

*Quite a different verb **egeneto**, became, appears in John 1:14 for the beginning of the Incarnation of the Logos. The Word 'became' flesh. **The incarnation is not the origin of Jesus.** See the distinction sharply drawn in **John 8:58**, before Abraham was [born, **genesthai** from **ginomai** - to become], I am. The word **eimi**, I am; the essence of being, suggesting timeless existence. See also John 1:15, John the Baptists said, He was, before I was born.*

1 Peter 1:16 On the very account that what is [1]written in prophetic Scripture, *[and echoes in your innermost being]*, already mirrors the life of your design, you are free to [2]be who you are. As it is written, I am, therefore you are. I am wholly separated unto you, and invite you to explore the same completeness of your being in me.

*[1] The word, [1]**graphō**, to engrave, often refers to the prophetic writings, Old Testament Scripture. The appeal of truth is confirmed in the resonance within us due to the echo of that which is already written in our innermost being by design. Did not our hearts ignite within us while he opened to us the Scriptures. Luke 24:27,32,44,45.*

*[2] The Textus Receptus [KJV] uses the word **genēsthe**, from **ginomai**, to become; instead of [2]**esesthe**, from **eimi**, I am, as in the Westtcott & Hort text. This makes a massive difference.*

You did not begin in your mother's womb. You began in God's I-am-ness. You are the most magnificent idea that the Engineer of the Universe has ever had. **I knew you before I formed you in your mother's womb. Jeremiah 1:5.**

In him we live and move and have our being; we are indeed his offspring! Acts 17:28.

Sonship and Innocence Redeemed

Hebrews 1:1 Throughout [1]ancient times God spoke in many fragments and glimpses of prophetic thought to our fathers. Now, this entire conversation has [2]finally dawned in sonship. Suddenly, what seemed to be an ancient language falls fresh and new like the dew on the tender grass. He is the sum total of every utterance of God. He is whom the Prophets pointed to and we are his immediate audience. *(The word [1]palai, meaning, of old, ancient; from **palin** through the idea of oscillatory repetition or retrocession; anew, afresh. Like in James 1:24, we have forgotten what manner of people we are - we have forgotten the face of our birth. Jesus successfully rescued the real you, not the pseudo, make-belief you. God has never believed less of you than what he was able to communicate in the sonship that Jesus mirrored and redeemed.*
The word [2]eschatos means extreme; last in time or in space; the uttermost part, the final conclusion. What God said about 'you-manity' in Jesus defines eschatology.)

Hebrews 1:2 In a son, God declares the Incarnate Word to be the heir of all things. He is, after all, the author of the ages.

Hebrews 1:3 The Messiah-message is what has been on the tip of the Father's tongue all along. Now he is the crescendo of God's conversation with us and gives context and content to the authentic, prophetic thought. Everything that God has in mind for mankind is voiced in him. Jesus is God's language. He is the [1]radiant and flawless mirror expression of the person of God. He makes the [2]glorious intent of God visible and exhibits the [3]character and every attribute of Elohim in human form. His being announces our redeemed innocence; having accomplished purification for sins, he sat down, enthroned in the boundless measure of his majesty in the right and of God as his executive authority. He is the force of the universe, [4]upholding everything that exists. This conversation is the dynamic that sustains the entire cosmos. *(The word* $\alpha\pi\alpha\upsilon\gamma\alpha\sigma\mu\alpha$ [1]***apaugasma***, *only occurs here, and once only in the Greek Septuagint, LXX, in the book of Wisdom 7:26, For she is the brightness of the everlasting light, the unspotted mirror of the power of God, and the image of his goodness. [The Book of Wisdom 7:26.] The word,* $\delta\delta\xi\alpha$ [2]***doxa*** *glory is the expression of the divine attributes collectively. It is the unfolded fullness of the divine perfections. Vincent. The word* $\chi\alpha\rho\alpha\kappa\tau\eta\rho$ [3]***charakter*** *from* $\chi\alpha\rho\alpha\gamma\mu\alpha$ **charagma** *- to engrave - translated mark of the beast, in Revelation 13:16,17. Either the character of the Father or the character of the fallen mind will influence our actions (hand) because it is what engages our thoughts (forehead).*

Having accomplished purification of sins, he sat down ... *His throne is the very endorsement of mankind's redeemed innocence. See Ephesians 1:20-23; LXX Psalm 109:1.*

The words, $\phi\epsilon\rho\omega\nu$ $\tau\epsilon$ $\tau\grave{\alpha}$ $\pi\acute{\alpha}\nu\tau\alpha$ - [4]*upholding all things, are not static, but They imply sustaining, but also movement. It deals with a burden, not as a dead weight, but as in continual movement; as Weiss puts it, with the all in all its changes and transformations throughout the aeons. Vincent.*

More than two thousand years ago the conversation that had begun before time was recorded—sustained in fragments of thought throughout the ages, whispered in prophetic language, chiseled in stone and inscribed in human conscience and memory—became a man. Beyond the tablet of stone, the papyrus scroll or parchment roll, human life has become the articulate voice of God. Jesus is the crescendo of God's conversation with mankind; he gives context and content to the authentic thought. His name declares his mission. As Savior of the world he truly redeemed the image and likeness of the invisible God and made him apparent again in human form as in a mirror.)

1 Peter 1:19 but you were redeemed with the priceless blood of Christ. He is the ultimate sacrifice; spotless and without blemish. Jesus completes the prophetic picture.

In him God speaks the most radical scapegoat language of the law of judgment and brings final closure to a dead and redundant system.

In **Psalm 40:6,7**, *it is clearly stated that God does not require sacrifices or offerings. Jesus is the Lamb of God. He collides victoriously with the futile sacrificial system whereby offerings are constantly made to the pseudo, moody, monster gods of our imagination. This is the scandal of the cross. God does not demand a sacrifice that would change the way he thinks about mankind; he provides the sacrifice of himself in Christ in order to forever eradicate sin-consciousness from our minds and radically change the way we think about our Maker, one another and ourselves.*

Sin is singular - its symptoms are plural - its been a sonship thing from the beginning - no wonder Jesus says freedom indeed is found in the truth of our authentic and redeemed sonship - even the other brother has the Father pleading with him, My son you have always been with me and all that I have is yours!! Sin is not about things you do or don't do - sin is missing out on sonship!

It was God's initiative from start to finish

Romans 4:1 If we look at our father Abraham as an example and scrutinize his life, would you say that he discovered any reason for placing confidence in the flesh through personal contribution?

Romans 4:2 If he felt that his friendship with God was a reward for good behavior, then surely he would have reason to recommend the recipe; yet it is plain to see that it was all God's initiative from start to finish.

Romans 4:3 Scripture is clear, Abraham reflected God's belief in him; this is the basis of the [1]rediscovery of [2]righteousness.

> *([1] [1]One must remember that in Adam & Eve's communion with Elohim, something was lost which would be redeemed - there would be a return to the consciousness of this union.*
>
> *[2] [2]This most significant, relational term, righteousness, points to a shared likeness; this includes one's authentic identity and innocence.*
>
> *The word [2]dikaiosunē, righteousness is from the stem dikē, suggesting to be judged equal; it implies the idea of two parties finding likeness in each other. Also, note that the name of the Greek goddess of Justice is Dikē [pronounced, Dikey]; she is always pictured holding a scale of balances in her hand.)*

This thought is powerfully emphasized in Abram's encounter with Melchizedek in Genesis 14, on the threshold of Genesis 15 where God cuts covenant with Abraham and introduces him to righteousness based on faith, and not one's natural lineage, heritage or performance.

Who am I?

In **Mirror-language**, Jesus asks the most important, two-in-one question, in Matthew 16:13, **Who is the Son of Man? Who am I?** In this question, Jesus mirror-echoes the universal quest of the human race.

> Upon the rock of this revelation, that the son of man is the son of God, he builds his ekklesia, *[authentic identity]* and the gates of the blindfold-mode *[Hadēs; ha, not and eidō, to see]* will not prevail against it! See Revelation 1:18.
>
> Also, **Revelation 3:7 And to the messenger of the ekklesia of Philadelphia write: I am the Holy and True One. I hold the key of David as prophesied in Isaiah 22:22. Yes, I unlock the mysteries of the heavenly dimension and no one can shut the door. And I lock the entrance and none of the old mindsets can access it.**
>
> Simon, son of Jonah, flesh and blood did not reveal this to you! Now that you know who I am, allow me to introduce you to you, Mr Rock! *[Petros]* You're a chip off the old Block! *[Petra]*
>
> See Isaiah 51:1,2 and Deuteronomy 18:4,18. Also my extended notes at the end of Revelation 2. https://www.mirrorword.net/books/revelation-the-apocalypse-uncovered-msb

The younger biological brother of Jesus, James, like his other siblings, did not believe that their brother was indeed the Messiah...

John 7:5 Yet none of his immediate family believed that he really was the Christ. It was only after his resurrection when Jesus also appeared to James, that his brother's eyes were opened, *1 Corinthians 15:7, and Galatians 1:19.* This prompted James to write about seeing the face of your birth when you hear the authentic word of our co-begotteness by the Father of lights. *James 1:17,23.*

James 1:17 Without exception God's [1]gifts are only good; its perfection cannot be flawed. They come from [2]above *(where we originate from)*; **proceeding like light rays from its source, the Father of lights, with whom there is no distortion, or even a shadow of shifting to obstruct, or intercept the light; nor any hint of a hidden agenda.**

> *[1] The principle of a [1]gift, puts reward-language out of business.*
>
> *[2] The word, [2]anouthen, means, from above. John 3:3, 13.*

James 1:18 We are God's idea to begin with! Our true origin is preserved in God's resolve. It was according to the Father's delight that he birthed us; giving authentic, incarnate expression to the Word. *[The face to face-ness of the Logos that was before time was. John 1:1]* **Just like the first-fruits mirror the harvest, so we mirror the conclusion of his workmanship in the core of our being.**

James 1:23 Anyone who hears the word, sees the face of their birth, as in a mirror. The difference between a mere spectator and a participator is that both of them hear the same voice and perceive in its message the face of their own genesis reflected there;

James 1:24 they realize that they are looking at themselves, but for the one it seems just too good to be true; this person departs *[back to the old way of seeing themselves],* **and immediately forgets what manner of person they are; never giving another thought to the one they saw there in the mirror.**

James 1:25 The other is [1]mesmerized by what they see; [2]captivated by the effect of a law that frees them from the obligation to the old written code that restricted them to their own efforts and willpower. No distraction or contradiction can dim the impact of what is seen in the mirror concerning the law of perfect [3]liberty *[the law of faith]* **that now frees one to get on with the act of living the life** *[of their original design.]* **They find a new [3]spontaneous lifestyle; the poetry of practical living.**

Romans 8:29, He pre-designed and engineered us from the start to be jointly fashioned in the same mold and image of his Son according to the exact blueprint of his thought. We see the original and intended pattern of our lives preserved in his Son. He is the firstborn from the same womb that reveals our genesis. He confirms that we are the invention of God. Also, John 1:1-18; 1 Peter. 2:9,10.

John 1:13 These are the ones who discover their genesis in God, beyond their natural conception. This is not about our blood lineage

or whether we were a wanted- or unwanted-child; this is about our God-begotteness. We are his dream come true and not the invention of our parents. You are indeed the greatest idea that God has ever had. *[See Jeremiah 1:5; 29:11 & John 3:2-7]*

Also 2 Corinthians 3:18 Now, we all, with new understanding, see ourselves in him as in a mirror... We suddenly realize that we are looking into a mirror, where every feature of his image, articulated in Christ, is reflected within us. The Spirit of the Lord engineers this radical transformation; we are led from an inferior mind-set to the revealed endorsement of our authentic identity. From the fading glory of our own making, to the discovering of the most amazing reality, that **we are his glory!** *(We've got our masks off and God's brilliance is bouncing off our faces. We're glowing from knowing. 2 Corinthians. 3:18 [Rob Lacey]*

Abraham saw My Day

Genesis 22:7 Then Isaac said to Abraham, My father; and he said, Here am I, my son. And he said, We have wood and fire here, but where is the lamb for the burnt offering?

Genesis 22:13 And Abraham lifted up his eyes and looked. And behold! A ram <u>behind him</u> was entangled in a thicket by its horns. And Abraham went and took the ram and offered it for a burnt offering instead of his son. *(This reminds of **Revelation 1:10** I was in a spiritual trance where I witnessed the [1]Day of the Lord. <u>I heard a loud voice [2]behind me</u>, clear and distinct, like the sound of a trumpet. (The [1]Day of the Lord is the very day to which the prophetic voice of the Spirit of Christ pointed - Jesus the Messiah, is the fulfillment of this day. The word [2]opisō points to that which is behind in place and time. The fact that John hears a word **behind him** is so significant. It means that what he hears already happened within its prophetic context.*

Genesis 22:14 And Abraham called the name of that place Jahweh Sees; so that it is said until this day, In the mount of Jahweh, it will be seen!

יהוה יראה *Jahweh Jireh Jahweh sees!*

Genesis 22:17 that blessing I will bless you, and multiplying I will multiply your seed as the stars of the heavens, and as the sand which is on the shore of the sea. And your Seed shall possess the gate of His enemies.

Genesis 22:18 And in your Seed shall all the nations of the earth be blessed.

John 8:56 Your father Abraham was leaping with joy to see my day. What he saw made him exceedingly glad.

John Then the Jews said, Ha. You're not even fifty years old and you claim to have seen Abraham.

John 8:58 Most certainly do I say unto you that before Abraham was born, I am. *(Before Abraham was [born, **genesthai** from **ginomai** - to become] I am. The word **eimi**, I am; the essence of being, suggesting timeless existence.)*

Slave or Son?

Jacob, the son of Isaac...

Luke 3:34 son of Jacob, son of Isaac, son of Abraham, son of Terah, son of Nahor, *(The name,* יעקב *Jacob means, the heel-holder.* **Hosea 12:3** *In the womb he took his brother by the heel, And by his strength he was a prince with God.*

Also, **Genesis 25:23 And the Lord said to her, Two nations are in your womb, and the two peoples, born of you, shall be divided; the one shall be stronger than the other; the elder shall serve the younger.**

> *The two come out of the same mold; yet they represent two types of people: one who understands their true identity by faith [authentic value] and one who seeks to identify themselves after the flesh [performance-based].*
>
> *Again, the law of performance versus the law of faith is emphasized in order to prepare the ground for the promise-principle.*
>
> *Mankind's salvation would be by promise and not by performance; i.e. it would not be a reward for good behavior. No one will be justified by the tree of the knowledge of good and evil;* **poneros,** *evil, full of hardships, annoyances and labor. The Tree of Life is our true Family-tree.*

Galatians 3:6 Abraham had no other claim to righteousness but simply believing what God declared concerning him. Isaac confirmed God's faith, not Abraham's efforts. This is all we have in common with Abraham.

Galatians 3:7 The conclusion is clear; faith and not flesh relates us to Abraham. *(Grace rather than law is our true lineage. Ishmael represents so much more than the Muslim religion. Ishmael represents the clumsy effort of the flesh to compete with faith; the preaching of a mixed message of law and grace.)*

John 8:32 In this abiding you will fully know the truth about who you are and this knowing will be your freedom.

John 8:33 They answered him, We are the seed of Abraham; we have never been anybody's slaves. Why do you suggest that we are not free?

John 8:34 Jesus answered and said, I say unto you with absolute certainty that everyone engaging in the distorted mindset of sin is a slave to it. *(Sin is not about things you do or don't do - sin is missing out on sonship. Their failing to see Jesus as their Messiah, and him as the mirror image Redeemer of their true sonship, is their sin. Religion is enslaved to the fruit of the wrong tree.*

The sin-system is governed by the idea of justification by personal effort, performance and pretense; which is the typical fruit of the 'I am-not-mindset' which Peter refers to as the futile ways we inherited from our fathers. 1 Peter 1:18.)

John 8:35 The difference between the slave and the son is that the slave only works there; for the son the father's house is home.

John 8:36 With the freedom found in sonship there is [1]no pretense. *(Free indeed. The word,* [1]*ontoos, indeed is the opposite to what is pretended.)*

Galatians 4:22 The law records the fact that Abraham had two sons: one by a slave girl, the other by a free woman.

Galatians 4:23 The one is produced by the flesh *[the Do It Yourself-tree],* **the other by faith** *[the promise].*

Galatians 4:24 There is a parallel meaning in the story of the two sons: they represent two systems, works and grace.

Galatians 4:25 Sinai is an Arabian rocky mountain named after Hagar, *[outside the land of promise]*. Its association with the law of Moses mirrors Jerusalem as the capital of Jewish legalism. Hagar is the mother of the law of works. *[DIY-religion Do it Yourself]*

Galatians 4:26 But the mother from above, the true mother of mankind is grace, the free Jerusalem; she is the mother of the promise.

Galatians 4:27 For it is written, Rejoice, Oh childless one. Erupt in jubilee. For though you have never known travail before, your children will greatly outnumber her who was married. *(Married to the law; Isaiah 54:1; see also Romans 7:1-6.)*

Galatians 4:28 We resemble Isaac: we are begotten of faith; the promise is our parent.

Galatians 4:29 Just as when the flesh child persecuted the faith child, so now these Jerusalem Jews in their Christian disguise seek to harass you.

Galatians 4:30 However, Scripture is clear: Expel the slave mother and her son; the slave son cannot inherit with the free son.

(In exactly the same way, rid your minds radically from the slave mother and child mentality. Light dispels darkness effortlessly.)

Galatians 4:31 Realize whose children we are my Brothers and Sisters: we are not children of the slave-mother, the law, but children of the free mother; we are begotten of grace.

The symbolic nature of circumcision is further emphasized here,

See **Deuteronomy 10:16**, Circumcise therefore the foreskin of your heart, and be no longer stubborn.

Romans 4:10 So, the question is, was he reckoned righteous before or after he was circumcised? It is clear that Abraham's faith-encounters *[as recorded in Genesis 12 through 15]*, **happened long before circumcision was mentioned!** *(The symbolic circumcision covenant was only introduced years later in Genesis 17, when he was already 99 years old. [Isaac's birth is only recorded in Genesis 21.])*

Romans 4:11 Thus, Abraham received circumcision as an external, symbolic [1]seal to remind him of what God had already [2]declared many years ago, when he was first introduced to the concept of the [3]righteousness of God. Since Abraham's supernatural fatherhood is celebrated in circumcision, it infers that he is both the father of Jew and Gentile alike - God already engaged him in covenant as an uncircumcised Gentile - he thus represents them in all that was predicted concerning the blessing of every nation in the Seed of faith!

*([1] A [1]seal of the righteousness of the faith - **sphragida tēs dikaiosunēs tēs pisteōs**. The [1]seal of circumcision, was not meant to be a distraction but rather a prophetic confirmation to the only valid basis to the righteousness [of God] by the principle of the faith [of God].*

Just like a receipt is only a reference to, and not the actual transaction. Note, the faith and the righteousness. See 2 Corinthians 13:5. Also here in Romans 4:25.

[2] Circumcision did not introduce an adjusted or new covenant - it was simply added as a symbolic seal in ²confirmation to God's resolve, as recorded in Genesis 12:2,3 and Genesis 15:5.

In the meantime, Abraham's moments of unbelief, delays and detours did not distract from God's determined destiny for the prophetic Messianic Seed.

Galatians 3:16 **It is on record that the promise** [*of the blessing of righteousness by God's faith*] **was made to Abraham and to his seed, singular,** [*thus excluding his effort to produce Ishmael.*] **Isaac, the child of promise, and not of the flesh, mirrors the Messiah.** [*Genesis 3:15*]

Galatians 5:11 **Would I compromise the message of the cross and preach circumcision just to avoid persecution. How insane would that be?** (*This whole matter boils down to thinking that justification is the result of something we still have to do, or knowing that it is the result of something that God has already done.*)

Galatians 5:12 **These people who are so keen to cut off things should ¹chop off their legalistic influence in your lives altogether.** (ἀποκόπτω **apokoptō** *with Preposition,* **apo**, *away from, and* **kopto**, *to chop off, mutilate/dismember/castrate*)

Just as Paul's noble birth was not his claim to fame - **God separated me from my mother's womb! Grace defines me! Not my natural lineage and identity as a son of Benjamin. Galatians 1:15.**

John 7:22 Lets take one of those rules: Moses represents circumcision as the tradition of the fathers and you are okay with performing the cut on the Sabbath;

John 7:23 now in order not to disappoint Moses you have made your circumcision rule superior to the Sabbath; when a boy is eight days old you have no problem with performing circumcision even when it coincides with the Sabbath and here I am making a man's entire body well on the Sabbath and you're ready to kill me and break another one of the ten commandments. (*See Genesis 17:12, He that is eight days old among you shall be circumcised.*)

John 7:24 Do not cloud righteous judgment with your biased opinions and traditions.

There is no magical power in circumcision

Romans 2:25 The real value of circumcision is tested by your ability to keep the law. If you break the law you might as well not be circumcised.

Romans 2:26 The fact that you are circumcised does not distinguish you from the rest of the world; it does not give you super-human power to keep the commandments.

Romans 2:27 If it is not about who is circumcised or not, but rather who keeps the law or not, then in that case even uncircumcised people can judge the ones who claim to know it all and have it all. On the one hand you have those who feel naturally inclined to do what is right, yet none of them are circumcised, then you have the circumcised who know the letter of the law but fail to keep it.

Romans 2:28 So it is not about who you appear to be on the outside that makes you a real Jew, but who you really are on the inside.

Romans 2:29 For you to know who you are in your heart is the secret of your spirit identity; this is your true circumcision, it is not the literal outward appearance that distinguishes you. After all it is God's approval and not another's opinion that matters most. People see skin-deep; God knows the heart.

1 Corinthians 7:18 Circumcision or the lack of it does not [1]define you. In Christ your Jewish or Gentile heritage is irrelevant and can never again [1]label you. *(The word, [1]kaleō, means to identify by name; to surname.)*

1 Corinthians 7:19 You couldn't keep the commandments anyway, whether you were circumcised or not. *(So if circumcision did not contribute anything while you were seeking to be justified under the law, how can it possibly now advantage you in your understanding of righteousness by faith?)*

Circumcision controversy

Galatians 2:2 I especially wanted the most senior leadership of the ekklesia-church to hear what I teach in the Gentile nations as my revelation and specific emphasis of the Gospel. We decided to meet in private to avoid any possible public controversy. In this way they could best judge for themselves whether, according to their opinion, my ministry had credibility or not.

Galatians 2:3 Our Greek companion, Titus, survived the circumcision scrutiny and wasn't forced to go for the cut.

Galatians 5:1 Christ defines your faith; he is your freedom from anything from which the law could never free you. Find your firm footing in this freedom. Do not let religion trip you up again and harness you to a system of rules and obligations. *(In this parallel, Christ represents Sarah, the faith-mother who birthed you in the resurrection. The rock-hewn tomb represents Sarah's dead womb. 1 Peter 1:3.)*

Galatians 5:2 I, Paul, am of the opinion, and you can quote me: If you would again consider circumcision as necessary to improve your standing before God, then you make Christ of no relevance to yourselves. Then you might as well delete him from your life altogether. *(By still holding on to any Jewish sentiment like keeping the Sabbath, etc., has the same effect.)*

Galatians 5:3 I will state it categorically, that if you endorse circumcision as a means to obtain righteousness, you are immediately obliged to keep the whole law. *(In for a penny, in for a pound.)*

Galatians 5:4 Law-righteousness has nothing in common with grace-righteousness; they are opposites. As impossible as it is for anyone to travel in two opposite directions at the same time, equally irrelevant Christ becomes to anyone who continues to pursue righteousness under the law.

Galatians 5:5 Our minds are made up; there is absolutely no advantage for anyone to pursue righteousness in the flesh; righteousness is a spirit-dimension reality and can only be [1]embraced by faith. What God believes is our exclusive reference. *(Any other basis for righteousness leaves mankind falling hopelessly short. The word, [1]apekdechomai is often translated, to wait for; the components however, point to a favorable embrace; apo, from, ek out of, and dechomai to grasp, to welcome hospitably, to embrace.)*

Galatians 5:6 God believes that we are fully represented in Christ, which takes circumcision or any contribution of the flesh out of the equation. Love fuels belief and sets faith in motion. *(It is easy for love to believe.)*

Galatians 5:7 You started off like an athlete on a mission, who distracted you? You seemed so completely persuaded about the truth.

Galatians 5:8 God is not confused about you. He surnamed you.

Galatians 5:9 It is impossible to hide the effect of the smallest amount of yeast; the process of fermentation is immediately triggered. *(A little bit of legalism corrupts a person's whole life.)*

Galatians 6:14 May my boasting be in nothing but the cross of our Lord Jesus Christ, through whom the world has been crucified to me and I to the world. The religious-systems and applause of this world have no appeal to me. As far as they are concerned, I am like a dead person.

Galatians 6:15 The new creation in Christ steals the show; not whether someone is circumcised or not. *(God associated us in Christ; when he died we died, when he was raised we were raised together with him in newness of life.)*

Galatians 6:16 Our union with Christ sets the pace and makes us the true Israel, not whether we are Jew or Gentile, circumcised or not. Oh, what peace we discover in his mercy. This rule is the new law we submit ourselves to as the principle of our daily walk.

Galatians 6:17 I will not be troubled anymore. I already bear enough scars in my body that brand me as being under the ownership of Jesus. *(Those scars that I carry from being persecuted for this Gospel are more significant to me than the scar of circumcision.)*

Ephesians 2:11 Remember where you came from; *[not only were you spiritually dead but]* it wasn't long ago when you were still classified as non-Jewish, judging on the surface you had nothing that linked you to them. They sneered at you because you didn't share their distinguishing mark of circumcision, which was their claim to fame.

Ephesians 2:12 During that time you were distanced from the Messianic hope; you had nothing in common with Israel. You felt foreign to the covenants of prophetic promise, living a life with nothing to look forward to in a world where God seemed absent.

Ephesians 2:13 But now, wow. Everything has changed; you have discovered yourselves to be located in Christ. What once seemed so distant is now so near; his blood reveals your redeemed innocence and authentic genesis.

Ephesians 2:14 It is in him that we are one and at peace with everyone; he dissolved every definition of division. *(What we know will put war and divorce out of business.)*

Ephesians 2:15 In his incarnation, he rendered the entire Jewish system of ceremonial laws and regulations useless as a measure to justify human life and conduct. In that he died mankind's death all grounds for tension and hostility were entirely removed. The peace he proclaims reveals one new human race, created and defined in Christ, instead of two groups of people separated by their ethnic identity and differences.

Ephesians 2:16 Both parties are fully represented and equally reconciled to God in one human body through the cross. He reinstated the former harmony; all opposing elements were thus utterly defeated.

Ephesians 2:17 On that basis he made his public appearance, proclaiming the Good News of peace to the entire human race; both those who felt left out in the cold *[as far as the promises and covenants were concerned]*, as well as to those who were near all along *[because of their Jewish identity]*.

Ephesians 2:18 Because of Christ both Jew and Gentile now enjoy equal access to the Father in one Spirit.

Ephesians 2:19 The conclusion is clear; you are no longer frowned upon as a foreigner; you are where you belong and part of an intimate family.

<u>Brood of Vipers</u>

In Luke 3:7 John the baptist calls the people an [1]offspring of serpents!

Brood of Vipers - [1]begotten of a mindset, poisoned by the serpent that snared mankind in the garden of Eden and abandoned them in the wilderness of a lost identity.

John 8:37 I know you are the seed of Abraham, yet you are seeking opportunity to kill me because my word finds no [1]resonance in you. *(The word χορός - **choros** relates to a [1]**chorus**, harmony in song or dance.)*

John 8:38 I observe my Father's voice with close attention; this inspires my every expression. You hear a different father's voice and behave accordingly.

John 8:39 They immediately responded with, But Abraham is our father. To which Jesus replied, If you were conceived by Abraham's faith, you would mirror his persuasion. *(Jesus said in John 6:29 This is the work of God; your belief in the One whom he has sent.)*

John 8:40 But here you are, desiring to destroy me because I declare to you the truth which I heard from a place of intimate acquaintance with God; this certainly does not reflect Abraham's faith.

John 8:41 Your actions clearly show who your father is. They said unto him, We are not conceived in fornication, God is our only Father.

John 8:42 Jesus said, If you were convinced that God was your Father, you would love me. Look, here I am. I did not arrive here by my own doing; I proceeded from him who sent me.

John 8:43 You do not understand my [1]language because you do not hear my logic. (*My dialect seems foreign to you because you are not familiar with the Logic of God. You might be acquainted with the letter of the law in Scripture but you are not acquainted with the Word. See John 5:39,40 also John 8:31. The word [1]lalia means dialect or language.*)

John 8:44 You are the offspring of a perverse mindset and you prove its [1]diabolical parenthood in your willingness to execute its cravings. The intention was to [2]murder humanity's awareness of their god-identity [3]from the beginning since it is in violent opposition to the idea of the image and likeness of God in human form. It cannot abide the truth. Lying is the typical [4]language of the distorted desire of the father of deception. (*The word, [1]diabolos, Devil, has two components, dia, because of, or through and ballō, to cast down; thus referring a cast down condition and warped mentality that mankind inherited in their association with Adam's fall.*

The diabolos is a man-slayer, [2]anthrōpoktonos from anthropos and kteinoo to kill. The word for the human species, male or female is anthropos, from ana, upward, and tropos, manner of life; character; in like manner. See John 1:51, 2:25. [3]Just like Eve was deceived to believe a lie about herself, which is the fruit of the I-am-not-tree. The word [4]lalia means dialect or language.

Your True Circumcision!

Luke 3:8 [1]Now, [2]bear fruit that matches the [3]awakening of your authentic identity and your redeemed innocence. Quit seeking your origin in Abraham - your true lineage is found in God's faith; not in Abraham's efforts to bear children. See beyond mere flesh and discover God's power [4]raising the offspring of Abraham out of these stones.

(*[1] Again, the [1]Aorist Imperative is used; ποιησατε from [1]poieō, Get on with it. Stressing the urgency and priority of the matter.*

[2 & 3] [2]Let this [3]metanoia-moment conceive your offspring. Cease bearing the viper-fruit of a lost identity. [See notes on Luke 3:3]

[4] The word εγειραι [4]egeirai, from egeirō, to arouse from sleep; to raise the dead. Here in the Aorist Infinitive which presents the action expressed by the verb as a completed unit with a beginning and end. In this parallel, Christ represents Sarah, the faith-mother who re-birthed you in the resurrection. The rock-hewn tomb represents Sarah's dead womb. 1 Peter 1:3. See Deuteronomy. 32:18, You were unmindful of the Rock that begot you, and you forgot the God who gave you birth..

I love John the Baptist's father, Zechariah's song recorded in Luke 1 ... here is just a glimpse...

Luke 1:73 **As in the face to face oath which he gave to Abraham our father.**

Luke 1:74 **This was his resolve and gift to us all along - he undertook to rescue us out of the grip of everything contrary to us, freeing us to worship him without fear,**

Luke 1:75 **in [1]spontaneous innocence and righteousness, every day of our lives.** *The word, ὁσιότης* **hosiotēs** *suggests an innocence beyond the written code.*

Colossians 2:11 **You were in Christ when he died; which means that his death is your true circumcision. This is [1]not hypothetical; this is the real deal. Thus, sin's authority in the human body was stripped of its control over you.** *(ἀχειροποίητος [1]acheiropoiētos; meaning, not made with hands.)*

Colossians 2:12 **In the same parallel** *[your co-circumcision in his death]***, your co-burial and joint-resurrection is now demonstrated in baptism; your co-inclusion in Christ is what God's faith knew when he powerfully raised him from the dead.** *(Hosea 6:2.)*

He is the Desire of the Nations

John 12:19 The Pharisees were perplexed about this and said, Look, we are gaining no ground against him. The entire world is running after him.

John 12:20 There were also a number of Greeks who came to worship at the feast because of the rumors they have heard.

John 12:21 They approached Philip who was from Bethsaida in Galilee and asked him, Sir, we would be delighted to see Jesus. Is there perhaps any chance that you could introduce us to him? *(He had a Greek name and the Greeks may have seen Philip in Galilee where there were many Greeks.)*

John 12:22 Philip went and told Andrew and the two of them told Jesus.

John 12:23 Jesus, immediately understanding the prophetic significance of the moment, knew that he, the Messiah, was who all the nations were longing for and answered, The hour is here for the Son of man to be glorified. *(Jesus studied Scripture as in a mirror - he knew that in the book, it is written about me. Haggai 2:7 and the desire of the nations shall come...See Colossians 1:27.)*

John 12:24 Most certainly shall the single grain of wheat fall into the earth and die - if it doesn't die it remains alone - but in its death it produces much fruit.

Your word saturates the earth of hardened hearts and minds, to then extend that the hidden mystery within the incorruptible seed, germinates and sprouts, and bears much fruit!

Isaiah 55:10,11 For as the rain and the snow come down from heaven, and return not there without saturating the earth [all flesh], so shall my word be that goes forth from my mouth; it shall not return to me empty, but it shall accomplish that which I purpose, and prosper in the thing for which I sent it.

In him every definition of separation and distance is canceled. The prophetic word was destined to become flesh; every nook and cranny of human life is saturated in the incarnation.

And in your Seed shall all the nations of the earth be blessed!

John 12:25 To hold on desperately to a mere life defined by the soul realm is to lose it; but to abandon the soul substitute for the real deal is to observe your spiritual life which is the life of the ages.

While sin means a missing out on sonship; righteousness and redemption means a celebration of sonship!

<u>Can these bones live?</u>

One wonders why God showed Ezekiel a valley of bleached bones? Zero sign of life left! And then asks the question, Can these bones live? Ezekiel 37

And why God waited till Sarah's womb was dead!

And why God only created Adam on the 6th day when all his work was already done? No help needed from Adam!

2 Corinthians 5:14 The love of Christ constrains us and [1]resonates within us; leaving us with only one [2]conclusion: when Jesus died, every individual simultaneously died. In God's logic, one has died for all, [2]thus all have died.

*([1] The word, [1]sunechō, to press together; to squeeze; from **sun**, meaning together with and **echō**, meaning to echo; to embrace; to hold; also, to resonate.*

*[2] The word αρα [2]ara, means conclusion. Jesus didn't die 99% or for 99%. He one hundred percent died humanity's death. If Paul had to compromise the last part of verse 14 to read: one died for all therefore only those who follow the prescriptions to qualify, have also died, then he would have had to change the first half of the verse as well. Only the **agapē** of Christ can make a calculation of such enormous proportions. The religious mind would question the extremity of God's love and perhaps prefer to add a condition or two to a statement like that.)*

The good news unveils the love of God spectacularly! And the dimensions of his love exceed any concept we could possibly have of length or breadth, *(the horizontal extent of agapē which includes the entire planet)* - neither the depth of darkness and hell he descended to nor the heights of heaven he raised us to!

Something happened to mankind, **while we were still dead in our trespasses and sins!** We were co-quickened and co raised without our permission! Ephesians 2:5,6

Romans 4:23 Here is the Good News: the recorded words, It was reckoned to him were not written for his sake alone.

Romans 4:24 **Scripture was written with us in mind. We are audience to the same faith in the face of death. The same ¹conclusion is now equally relevant in our realizing the significance of Jesus' resurrection from the dead.**

(By raising Jesus from the dead God proclaims our redeemed innocence.

Isaac's birth from Sarah's barren womb prophetically declared the resurrection of Jesus from the tomb. Abraham's best efforts could not produce Isaac. Sarah's dead womb is a picture of the impossibility of the flesh to produce a child.

This underlines mankind's inability to redeem themselves under the performance-based law of willpower.

Jesus said, Abraham saw my day. Mankind's most extreme self-sacrifice offered in an attempt to win the favorable attention of their deity could never match the sacrifice of God's Lamb to win the attention of mankind.

Faith sees the future in past tense-mode.

*The resurrection is the ultimate proof and trophy of righteousness by God's faith. [See Romans 6:11] ¹**logitsomai** - logical conclusion. Consider [**logitsomai**] yourself dead indeed, compared with Romans 4:19, Abraham considered his own body dead. We can only study Scripture in the context of Christ as representing the human race; God had us in mind all along [John 5:39].)*

Romans 4:25 **While our sins resulted in his death; our righteousness and redeemed innocence is celebrated in his resurrection!**

(It is most wonderful to discover that his resurrection does not include us only once we believe!

*Paul uses the word, **dia** twice in this verse! Unfortunately most translations in most languages only translate the 1st **dia** correctly!*

*He was handed over <u>BECAUSE of</u> [**dia**] our sins - why was he raised?*

*NOT so that some small portion of the elite christian group may stand a dim chance to be justified!!! NO! Hallelujah! The same word, **dia** is used again!*

*He was raised <u>BECAUSE of</u> [**dia**] our righteousness!*

His cross = our sins,

His resurrection = our innocence.

Romans 4:3 **Scripture is clear, Abraham reflected God's belief in him; this is the basis of the ¹rediscovery of ²righteousness.**

([1] ¹One must remember that in Adam & Eve's communion with Elohim, something was lost which would be redeemed - there would be a return to the consciousness of this union.

*[2] ²This most significant, relational term, righteousness, points to a shared likeness; this includes one's authentic identity and innocence. The word ²**dikaiosunē**, righteousness is from the stem **dikē**, suggesting to be judged equal; it implies the idea of two parties finding likeness in each other.*

Also, note that the name of the Greek goddess of Justice is Dikē [pronounced, Dikey]; she is always pictured holding a scale of balances in her hand.)

Hebrews 11:12 **Faith brought into reality an offspring beyond calculation; from one, as good as dead, children would be born, more numerous than**

the stars and as impossible to count as the grains of sand on every distant sea shore. *(The uttermost parts of the earth, bordered by the sea shore, will know the blessing of righteousness by faith which is the blessing of Abraham, meant for the entire world. 1 Peter 1:3.)*

Hebrews 11:13 These heroes of faith all died believing. Although they did not witness the promise in their lifetime, they saw its fulfillment in the future and by faith embraced the promise. Convinced of its reality; they declared by their way of living that they were mere sojourners and pilgrims in a shadow land whose geography could neither confine nor define their true inheritance.

Hebrews 11:14 They clearly declared by faith a hinterland beyond their immediate horizon. *(A place of promise where God and mankind would be one again.)*

Hebrews 11:15 They did not regret the country they had left behind. Their faith took them beyond the point of no return. *(Do not allow the contradictions in your past or present to become your reference once again. James says that the person who goes back into an old mindset immediately forgets what manner of person they are. James 1:24, 25. The old things have passed away [in his death]. Behold, everything has become new. In his resurrection we were born anew. 2 Corinthians 5:14-17, 1 Peter 1:3.)*

Hebrews 11:16 Their faith saw a greater reality in the spiritual realm than that which they experienced in their present situation; they reached for their true native city designed by God where he himself is proud to be their permanent address. *(The fulfillment of the promise is Christ. He is both our native land and our eternal city.)*

Hebrews 11:17 Faith became a more tangible evidence of the promise than even Isaac could ever be to Abraham. Isaac neither fulfilled nor replaced the promise. Inspired by what faith saw, Abraham was ready to do the ridiculous; to sacrifice his only son, convinced that not even Isaac's death could nullify the promise that God had made to him. *(If Isaac was not the substance of Abraham's faith then who was? Abraham saw beyond Isaac. Jesus said, Abraham saw my day. [John 8:56-58] Before Abraham was, I am.)*

Hebrews 11:18 Yet Abraham knew that God had said that his lineage of faith would be traced through Isaac.

Hebrews 11:19 He made a prophetic [1]calculation by faith to which there could only be one logical conclusion based on the word he had received: that God would raise the promise from the dead. *(In the context of Abraham's vision, this was an analogy pointing to the parable of the death and resurrection of Christ. A calculation, logical conclusion, from the word, [1]logitzomai, from logos; God's faith is God's logic.)*

Hebrews 11:20 By the same faith Isaac extended the future of the promise in the blessing he pronounced over his sons, Esau and Jacob.

5:1 The [1]conclusion is clear: our blameless innocence has absolutely nothing to do with something we did to qualify ourselves; it is what happened to us, solely because of our Lord Jesus Christ's doing. Faith, and not reward, is the only valid [2]basis for righteousness. Let us now fully [2]engage this seamless union in our [3]face to face [4]friendship with God. *(In one sentence Paul sums up the previous four chapters. Standing then acquitted as the result of faith, let us enjoy peace with God through our Lord Jesus Christ. Weymouth NT. The word [1]dikaiōthentes is an Aorist Participle, which translates, having been justified by faith. See previous verse, Romans 4:25 ...who was delivered up because of our offenses, and was raised up because of our being declared righteous. Young's Literal Translation. The Preposition [2]ek confirms that faith is the source or basis of our righteousness. Let us have [[2]echō, engage/resonate] peace with God - eirēnēn echomen pros ton theon. This is the correct text beyond a doubt, the Present Active Subjunctive, not echomen (Present Indicative) of the Textus Receptus. One has only to observe the force of the tense to see Paul's meaning clearly. The mode is the volitive subjunctive and the Present tense expresses linear action. [Robertson] The Preposition [3]pros means face to face; see John 1:1. The word, [4]eirēnē, means peace, from eirō, to join, to be set at one again, in carpentry it is referred to as the dovetail joint, which is the strongest joint. Peace is a place of unhindered enjoyment of friendship beyond guilt, suspicion, blame or inferiority.)*

5:2 Jesus is God's face to face grace [1]embrace of the entire human race. So here we are, [2]standing tall in the joyful bliss of our redeemed innocence. We are God's [3]dream come true. This was God's [4]idea all along. *(To be welcomed with wide-open arms, [1]prosagoge, from pros, face to face and agō, to lead as a shepherd leads his sheep. The words, 'by faith' are in brackets in the Greek text and are not supported by the best Greek manuscripts. Joy is not an occasional happy feeling; we are [2]positioned there, [2]histēmi, in an immovable, unthreatened union. Hope, [2]elpis from elpo, to anticipate, usually with pleasure. The word [4]doxa, often translated, glory, is from dokeō, to form an idea, opinion.)*

5:3 Our blissful boasting in him remains uninterrupted in times of trouble; we know that pressure reveals patience. Tribulation does not have what it takes to nullify what hope knows we have.

5:4 Patience provides [1]proof of every positive expectation. *([1]dokimos, proof. Thayer Definition: scrutinized and accepted, particularly of coins and money.)*

5:5 This kind of hope does not disappoint; the gift of the Holy Spirit completes our every expectation and ignites the love of God within us like an artesian well. *(ekxeo, to pour out. The Holy Spirit is an outpouring not an in-pouring. See John 7:37-39, also Titus 3:6.)*

5:6 God's timing was absolutely perfect; mankind was at their weakest when Christ died their death. *(We were bankrupt in our efforts to save ourselves.)*

5:7 It is most unlikely that someone will die for another person, even if they are righteous; yet it is remotely possible that someone can brave such devotion that one would actually lay down one's own life in an effort to save the life of an extraordinary good person.

5:8 Herein is the extremity of God's love gift: mankind was rotten to the core when Christ died their death.

5:9 If God could love us that much when we were ungodly and guilty, how much more are we free to realize his love now that we are declared innocent by his blood? *(God does not love us more now that we are reconciled to him; we are now free to realize how much he loved us all along. [Colossians 2:14, Romans 4:25].)*

5:10 Our hostility and indifference towards God did not reduce his love for us; in his death our minds were [1]rescued from our sense of unworthiness and separation. Now that this act of reconciliation is complete, his life in us saves us from the gutter-most to the uttermost. *(Reconciliation, from καταλλάσσω [1]katallassō, meaning a mutual exchange of equal value. Thayer Definition: to exchange, as coins for others of equivalent value.)*

5:11 Thus, our joyful boasting in God continues; Jesus Christ has made reconciliation a reality.

5:12 One person opened the door to [1]sin. Sin introduced *(spiritual)* death. Both sin and death had a global impact. No one escaped its tyranny. *(The word translated sin, is the word [1]hamartia, from ha, negative and meros, portion or form, thus to be without your allotted portion or without form, pointing to a disoriented, distorted identity; the word meros, is the stem of morphē, as in 2 Corinthians 3:18 the word metamorphē, with form, is the opposite of hamartia - without form. Sin is to live out of context with the blueprint of one's design; to behave out of tune with God's original harmony.)*

5:13 The law did not introduce sin; it was just not pointed out yet.

5:14 In the meantime death dominated everyone's lifestyle, from Adam till Moses, *[2500 years before the law was given]* no one was excluded; even those whose sins were different from Adam's. The fact is that Adam's [1]deviation set sin into motion - what happened to mankind because of one man, Adam, is in principle typical of what was about to happen to the same mankind because of the one man, Jesus. *(Paul now employs a word that only he uses in his epistles [7 times] parabasis instead of the usual word for sin, hamartia - parabasis has two components, para, which points to a close proximity/union and bainos, step, footprint - in this sense, a deviation; out of step - out of sync. In Adam mankind became out of sync with their true identity but didn't know it until the law revealed it - in Christ the same mankind became exceedingly righteous, but do not realize it until the gospel reveals it.)*

5:15 The only similarity in the comparison between the [1]crash-landing and the gift, is that both Adam and Christ represent the masses. However, the grace gift lavished upon mankind in the one man Jesus Christ supersedes the effect of Adam's failure by far and is beyond comparison in significance to the idea of [2]death and separation. *(Now Paul introduces the word [1]paraptōma, from para closest possible proximity and piptō, to descend from a higher place to a lower – to stop flying. No wonder he urges us in Colossians 3:1-3 to engage our thoughts with the things that are above, where we are co-elevated and jointly enthroned in the heavenlies together with Christ. The word [2]apothnēskō, death, suggests a separation; from apo, meaning any kind of separation of one thing* *from another by which the union or fellowship of the two is destroyed; also of a state of separation and distance. The word, **thnēskō** means death.*

But God's free gift immeasurably outweighs the transgression. For if through the transgression of the one individual the mass of mankind have died, infinitely greater is the generosity wherewith God's grace, and the gift given in his grace which found expression in the one man Jesus Christ, have been bestowed on the mass of mankind. — Weymouth, 1912.)

5:16 The principle of the gift speaks a different language and brings a radically different equation to the table. Whereas a single sin resulted in a judgment that concluded in condemnation; grace translates countless deviations into acquittal and innocence.

5:17 Death no longer has the final say. Life rules. If the effect of one man's crash-landing engaged mankind in a death-dominated lifestyle how much more advantaged is the very same mankind now that they are the recipients of the boundless reservoirs of grace, empowering them to enjoy the dominion of life through the gift of righteousness because of that one man, Jesus Christ. Grace is out of all proportion in superiority to transgression. *(No, grace is not something you qualify for by receiving it. Grace already belongs to mankind without their permission. The words οἱ λαμβάνοντες - [1]oi lambanontes do not mean, to believingly accept, but simply the recipients. [The Present Active Participle Nominative] The word [2]perisseia περισσεία means super abundantly; that which exceeds all boundaries. Of course it doesn't take faith out of the equation. It gives context to faith. See verse 1&2. Faith isn't what you do in order to; it's what happens to you because of.)*

5:18 The conclusion is clear: if one offense condemns the entire human race; then in principle, the righteousness of one vindicates the entire human race. *(Phillips translation: We see then, that as one act of sin exposed the whole race of humanity to condemnation, so one act of perfect righteousness presents all humanity freely acquitted in the sight of God.)*

5:19 The disobedience of one [1]exhibits mankind as sinners; the obedience of another exhibits mankind as righteous. *(The word, [1]kathistēmi, means to cause to be, to set up, to exhibit. We were not made sinners by our own disobedience; neither were we made righteous by our own obedience.)*

5:20 The presence of the law made no difference, instead it merely highlighted the offense; but where sin increased, grace superseded it.

5:21 Death provided sin its platform and power to reign from; now grace has taken over sovereignty through righteousness to introduce unthreatened life under the Lordship of Jesus Christ over us.

(A simple equation: We were not made sinners by our own disobedience; neither were we made righteous by our own obedience.

The same humanity represented in the one man Adam, is triumphantly represented in the one man Jesus Christ.

Adam's transgression no longer holds the human race hostage.)

6:1 It is not possible to interpret grace as a cheap excuse to continue in sin. It sounds to some that we are saying, Let's carry on sinning then so that grace may abound. *(In the previous chapter Paul expounds the heart of the gospel by giving us a glimpse of the far-reaching faith of God; even at the risk of being misunderstood by the legalistic mind he does not compromise the message.)*

6:2 How ridiculous is that. How can we be dead and alive to sin at the same time?

6:3 What are we saying then in baptism, if we are not declaring that we understand our union with Christ in his death?

6:4 Baptism pictures how we were co-buried together with Christ in his death; then it powerfully illustrates how in God's mind we were co-raised with Christ into a new lifestyle. *(Hosea 6:2.)*

6:5 We were like seeds planted together in the same soil, to be co-quickened to life. If we were included in his death we are equally included in his resurrection. *(2 Corinthians 5:14 - 17.)*

6:6 We perceive that our old lifestyle was co-crucified together with him; this concludes that the vehicle that accommodated sin in us, was scrapped and rendered entirely useless. Our slavery to sin has come to an end.

6:7 If nothing else stops you from doing something wrong, death certainly does.

6:8 Faith sees us joined in his death and alive with him in his resurrection.

6:9 It is plain for all to see that death lost its dominion over Christ in his resurrection; he need not ever die again to prove a further point.

6:10 His appointment with death was [1]once-off. As far as sin is concerned, he is dead. The reason for his death was to take away the sin of the world; his life now exhibits our union with the life of God. *(The Lamb of God took away the sin of the world; [1]efapax, once and for all, a final testimony, used of what is so done to be of perpetual validity and never needs repetition. This is the final testimony of the fact that sin's power over us is destroyed. See Hebrews 9:26, But Jesus did not have to suffer again and again since the fall (or since the foundation) of the world; the single sacrifice of himself in the fulfillment of history now reveals how he has brought sin to naught. Thus, in this context [of everyone's appointment with death], Jesus is the ultimate sacrifice. What the first, shadow-dispensation merely prophetically pointed to, he fulfilled once and for all, when he was presented as an offering, to take upon himself the sins of the entire human race. Now, with sin no longer on the agenda, he appears a second time, out of this death, to be clearly seen in everyone's whole-hearted embrace of him as Savior. [Hebrews 9:28].)*

6:11 This reasoning is equally relevant to you. [1]Calculate the cross; there can only be one logical conclusion: he died your death; that means you died to sin, and are now alive to God. Sin-consciousness can never again feature in your future. You are in Christ Jesus; his Lordship is the authority of this union. *(We are not being presumptuous to reason that we are in Christian.* [1]*Reckon yourselves therefore dead to sin The word,* [1]**logitsomai**, *means to make a calculation to which there can only be one logical conclusion. [See Ephesians 1:4 and 1 Corinthians 1:30].*

From now on, think of it this way: Sin speaks a dead language that means nothing to you; God speaks your mother tongue, and you hang on every word. You are dead to sin and alive to God. That's what Jesus did.— The Message.)

6:12 You are under no obligation to sin; it has no further rights to dominate your dead declared body. Therefore let it not entice you to obey its lusts. *(Your union with his death broke the association with sin [Colossians 3:3].)*

6:13 Do not let the members of your body lie around loose and unguarded in the vicinity of unrighteousness, where sin can seize it and use it as a destructive weapon against you; rather place yourself in [1]**readiness to God, like someone resurrected from the dead and present your whole person as a weapon of righteousness.** *(Thus you are reinforcing God's grace claim on mankind in Christ;* [1]***paristēmi****, to place in readiness, in the vicinity of.)*

6:14 Sin was your master while the law was your measure; now grace rules. *(The law revealed your slavery to sin, now grace reveals your freedom from it.)*

6:15 Being under grace and not under the law most certainly does not mean that you now have a license to sin.

6:16 As much as you once gave permission to sin to trap you in its spiral of spiritual death and enslave you to its dictates, the obedience that faith ignites now, introduces a new rule, rightness with God; to this we willingly yield ourselves. *(Righteousness represents everything that God restored us to—in Christ.)*

6:17 The content of teaching that your heart embraced has set a new [1]**standard to become the** [1]**pattern of your life; the grace of God ended sin's dominance.** *(The word,* [1]***tupos****, means form, mold. The Doddrich translation translates it as, the model of doctrine instructs you as in a mold.)*

6:18 Sin once called the shots; now righteousness rules.

6:19 I want to say it as plainly as possible: you willingly offered your faculties to obey sin, you stained your body with unclean acts and allowed lawlessness to gain supremacy in all of your conduct; in exactly the same way, I now encourage you to present your faculties and person to the supremacy of righteousness to find unrestricted expression in your lifestyle.

6:20 You were sins' slaves without any obligation to righteousness.

6:21 I know you are embarrassed now about the things you used to do with your body; I mean was it worth it? What reward or return did you get but spiritual death? Sin is a cul-de-sac. *(Sin is the worst thing you can ever do with your life.)*

6:22 Consider your life now; there are no outstanding debts; you owe sin nothing. A life bonded to God yields the sacred expression of his character,

and completes in your experience [1]what life was always meant to be. *(Lit. The life of the ages, [1]aionios; traditionally translated, and the end, eternal life.)*

6:23 The reward of the law is death the gift of grace is life. The bottom line is this: sin employs you like a soldier for its cause and rewards you with death; God gifts you with the highest quality of life all wrapped up in Christ Jesus our Leader. *(A soldier puts his life on the line and all he gets in the meantime is a meager ration of dried fish for his effort. opsonion, a soldier's wage, from opsarion, a piece of dried fish.)*

7:1 I write to you in the context of your acquaintance with the law; you would agree with me that laws are only relevant in this life.

7:2 A wife is only bound by law to her husband while he lives; any further legal claim he has on her ends with his death.

7:3 The law would call her an adulteress should she give herself to another man while the first husband is still alive. Yet, once he's dead, she is free to be another's wife.

7:4 The very same finality in principle is applicable to you, my brothers and sisters. In the incarnate Christ you died to the system of the law; your inclusion in his resurrection brought about a new union. Out of this marriage, [faith] now bears children unto God. (*Where the first marriage produced sin [a forgotten identity]; righteousness [rediscovered sonship] is the child of the new union. In the previous chapter Paul deals with the fact that our inclusion in Christ in his death broke the association with sin; now he reveals that it also broke the association with the system of the law of works as a reference to righteousness.*)

7:5 At the time when the flesh ruled our lives, the subtle influences of sins which were ignited by the law, conceived actions within us that were consistent in character with their [1]parent and produced spiritual death. (*[1]The parent Paul refers to is the law-system of self-effort based on the fruit of the I am not Tree. See my notes in 1 John 3:12.*)

7:6 But now we are fully released from any further association with a life directed by the rule of the law, we are dead to that which once held us captive, free to be slaves to the newness of spirit-spontaneity rather than age old religious rituals, imitating the mere face value of the written code. (*The moment you exchange spontaneity with rules, you've lost the edge of romance.*)

7:7 The law in itself is not sinful; I am not suggesting that at all. Yet in pointing out sin, the law was in a sense the catalyst for sinful actions to manifest. Had the law not said, Thou shall not covet, I would not have had a problem with lust.

7:8 But the commandment triggered sin into action, suddenly an array of sinful appetites were awakened in me. The law broke sin's dormancy.

7:9 Without the law I was alive; the law was introduced, sin revived and I died.

7:10 Instead of being my guide to life, the commandment proved to be a death sentence.

7:11 Sin took advantage of the law and employed the commandment to seduce and murder me.

7:12 I stress again that the law as principle is holy and so are the ten commandments; it consistently promotes that which is just and good.

7:13 How then could I accuse something that is that good to have killed me? I say again, it was not the law, but sin that caused my spiritual death.

The purpose of the law was to expose sin as the culprit. The individual commandment ultimately serves to show the exceeding extent of sin's effect on mankind.

7:14 We agree that the law is spiritual, but because I am [1]sold like a slave to sin, I am reduced to a mere carnal life. *(Spiritual death. The word, [1]piprasko comes from perao, meaning to transport into a distant land in order to sell as a slave. Sin is a foreign land.)*

7:15 This is how the sell-out to sin affects my life: I find myself doing things my conscience does not allow. My dilemma is that even though I sincerely desire to do that which is good, I don't, and the things I despise, I do.

7:16 It is obvious that my conscience sides with the law;

7:17 which confirms then that it is not really I who do these things but sin manifesting its symptoms in me. It has taken my body hostage. *(Sin is similar to a dormant virus that suddenly breaks out in very visible symptoms.)*

7:18 The total extent and ugliness of sin that inhabits me, reduced my life to good intentions that could not be followed through.

7:19 Willpower has failed me; this is how embarrassing it is, the most diligent decision that I make to do good, disappoints; the very evil I try to avoid, is what I do. *(If mere quality decisions could rescue mankind, the law would have been enough. Good intentions cannot save someone. The revelation of what happened to us in Christ's death is what brings faith into motion to liberate from within. Faith is not a decision we make to give God a chance, faith is realizing our inclusion in what happened on the Cross and in the resurrection of Christ. See Romans 3:27.)*

7:20 If I do the things I do not want to do, then it is clear that I am not evil, but that I host sin in my body against my will.

7:21 It has become a predictable principle; I desire to do well, but my mere desire cannot escape the evil presence that dictates my actions.

7:22 The real person that I am on the inside delights in the law of God. *(The law proves to be consistent with my inner make-up.)*

7:23 There is another law though, *(foreign to my design)* the law of sin, activating and enrolling the members of my body as weapons of war against the law of my mind. I am held captive like a prisoner of war in my own body.

7:24 It doesn't matter how I [1]weigh myself by my own efforts, I just do not measure up to expectations. The situation is absolutely desperate for mankind; is there anyone who can deliver them from this death trap? *(The word [1]talaiporos occurs only twice in the New Testament - Romans 7:24, Revelation 3:17 - and both times it is translated wretched!? It has two components, talanton, which is the word for a scale of balance; that which is weighed, a talent [of gold]; and poros from peira, to examine closely, to pierce; a test to determine the hidden value of something. You cannot measure temperature with a ruler. See 2 Corinthians 3:15 In the meantime nothing seems to have changed; the same veil continues to blindfold the hearts of people whenever Moses is read. (Moses symbolizes the futility of self righteousness as the global blindfold of the religious world. [John 1:17] Against the stark backdrop of the law; with Moses representing the condemned state of mankind, Jesus Christ unveils grace and truth. He is the life of our design redeemed in human form.)*

2 Corinthians 3:16 The moment anyone [1]returns to the Lord the veil is gone. (The word, [1]epistrephō means to return to where we've wandered from; we all like sheep have gone astray. Jesus is God unveiled in human form. [Colossians 1:15] Also 1 Peter 2:25 You were completely vulnerable, just like sheep roaming astray without direction or protection, but now you have returned and are restored to the shepherd and Guardian of your souls. And 1 Peter 1:17. Then, Hebrews 8:1, The conclusion of all that has been said points us to an exceptional Person, who towers far above the rest in the highest office of heavenly greatness. He is the executive authority of the majesty of God. 8:2 The office he now occupies is the one which the Moses-model resembled prophetically. He ministers in the holiest place in God's true tabernacle of worship. Nothing of the old man-made structure can match its perfection. Hebrews 8:10 Now, instead of documenting my laws on stone, I will chisel them into your mind and engrave them in your inner consciousness; it will no longer be a one-sided affair. I will be your God and you will be my people, not by compulsion but by mutual desire. See James 1:25, Those who gaze into the mirror reflection of the face of their birth are captivated by the effect of a law that frees them from the obligation to the old written code that restricted them to their own efforts and willpower. No distraction or contradiction can dim the impact of what they see in that mirror concerning the law of perfect liberty [the law of faith] that now frees them to get on with the act of living the life [of their original design]. They find a new spontaneous lifestyle; the poetry of practical living. [The law of perfect liberty is the image and likeness of God revealed in Christ, now redeemed in human life as in a mirror.])

7:25 Thank God, this is exactly what he has done through Jesus Christ our Leader; he has come to our rescue. I am finally freed from this conflict between the law of my mind and the law of sin in my body. *(In the Incarnation, in a human body exactly like ours, Jesus balanced the scales. He is the true measure of the life of our design - he revealed and redeemed the image and likeness of God in us as in a mirror. See Romans 1:16,17 and 3:24 and 27.*

Note, Paul speaks of the letter of the law in 2 Corinthians 3:6, which he elsewhere also calls the law of works; or the law of the flesh; or the law of sin; these willpower-driven, performance-based systems enslave the masses and are only conquered by the Agapē-driven law of faith [Romans 3:27] which he also calls the law of God [Romans 7:22], in which my inner man delights and my conscience embraces. [Here in verse 25 he calls it the law of my mind]. And now two verses further, in Romans 8:2 Paul calls the same law the law of the Spirit of life in Christ - James calls it the law of eleutherios [liberty or spontaneity - without obligation! James 1:25] See also its reference in Romans 6:18, Romans 6:22, Romans 8:2, Romans 8:21, Romans 8:2, Galatians 2:4, Galatians 5:1, Galatians 5:13, 1Corinthians 7:39, 1Corinthians 10:29, 2Corinthians 3:17, John 8:32, John 8:36, James 2:12, 1Peter 2:16, 2Peter 2:19

2 Corinthians 3:6 *... The letter [of the law] is the administration of death; it is the Spirit [of grace] that quickens life.)*

8:1 Now the decisive conclusion is this: in Christ, every bit of condemning evidence against us is canceled. *(Who walk not after the flesh but after the spirit. This sentence was not in the original text, but later copied from verse 4. The person who added this most probably felt that the fact of Paul's declaration of mankind's innocence had to be made subject again to a person's conduct. Religion under the law felt more comfortable with the condition of personal contribution rather than the conclusion of what faith reveals. The in Christ revelation is key to God's dealing with mankind. It is the PIN-code of the Bible. [See 1 Corinthians 1:30 and Ephesians 1:4].)*

8:2 The law of the Spirit is the liberating force of life in Christ. This leaves me with no further obligation to the law of sin and death. Spirit has superseded the sin enslaved senses as the principle law of our lives. *(The law of the spirit is righteousness by faith vs. the law of personal effort and self righteousness which produces condemnation and spiritual death which is the fruit of the DIY tree.)*

8:3 The law *[of Moses - John 1:17]* **failed to be anything more than an instruction manual; it had no power to deliver us from the strong influence of sin holding us hostage in our own bodies. God disguised himself in his Son in this very domain where sin ruled us, in flesh. The body he lived and conquered in, was no different to ours. Thus sin's authority in the human body was condemned.** *(Hebrews 4:15, As High Priest he fully identifies with us in the context of our frail human life. Having subjected it to close scrutiny, he proved that the human frame was master over sin. His sympathy with us is not to be seen as excusing weaknesses that are the result of a faulty design, but rather as a trophy to mankind. He is not an example for us but of us.)*

8:4 The very righteousness promoted by the law is now realized in us. Our practical day-to-day life bears witness to spirit inspiration and not flesh domination.

8:5 Sin's symptoms are sponsored by the senses, a mind dominated by the sensual. Thoughts betray source; spirit life attracts spirit thoughts.

8:6 Thinking patterns are formed by reference; either the sensual appetites of the flesh and spiritual death, or zoe-life and total tranquillity flowing from a mind addicted to spirit *[faith]* **realities.**

8:7 A mind focused on flesh *(the sensual domain where sin held me captive)* **is distracted from God with no inclination to his life-laws. Flesh** *[self-righteousness]* **and spirit** *[faith righteousness]* **are opposing forces.** *(Flesh no longer defines you; faith does.)*

8:8 It is impossible for those immersed in flesh to at the same time [1]accommodate themselves to the opinion, desire and interest of God. *(The word ἀρέσκω [1]areskō means to accommodate oneself to the opinions desires and interests of others.)*

8:9 But you are not ruled by flesh-consciousness, *(law of works)*, **but by spirit-consciousness** *[faith]*, **[1]since God's Spirit is permanently [2]at home in you. Anyone who does not [3]embrace the at-homeness of the Spirit of Christ, cannot be [4]themselves.**

*([1] The conditional particle [1]**eiper** with the Indicative Mood [οἰκέω] assumes the fact; thus, since.*

*[2] The word, οικει is the Present Active Indicative of οἰκέω [2]**oikeō**, thus Holy Spirit is permanently residing within.*

*[3] The word [3]**echō** means to have in hand, to hold, in the sense of wearing like a garment, to possess in mind, to be closely joined to a person.*

*[4] Then, the word αὐτοῦ [4]**hautou** G848 contracted for G1438, **heauto**, reflexive relation, himself, herself, themselves. In James 1:24, for they go away from what the mirror reveals, and immediately forget what manner of person they are. Also in Romans 1:23, Losing sight of God, made them lose sight of who they really were. In their calculation the image and likeness of God became reduced to a corrupted and distorted pattern of themselves. See also Luke 15:17, The prodigal son came to himself ... [same word used here, [4]**heauto**]. This is a very important clarification to explain why the Mirror is so different here than any other translation! Other translations use αυτου G846 which is the same spelling, but G846 is from the root, **autos** and not **hautou** [G848])*

8:10 The revelation of [1]Christ in you [1]declares that your body is as good as dead to sin's demands; sin cannot find any expression in a corpse. You co-died together with him. Yet your spirit is alive because of what righteousness reveals. *(The word traditionally translated, if [1]**de ei**, as in if Christ is in you ... can either be a condition or a conclusion, which makes a vast difference. [1]If God be for us (v 31) is most certainly a conclusion of the revelation of the Gospel; all of God's action in Christ confirms the fact that he is for us and not against us. Thus, [1]because God is for us ... in the same context this verse reveals that Christ is in us. See Galatians 1:16, it pleased the Father to reveal his Son in me, in order that I might proclaim him in the nations. See also Romans 10:6-8, Righteousness by faith says ... .)*

8:11 Our union with Christ further reveals that because the same Spirit who awakened the body of Jesus from the dead inhabits us, we equally participate in his resurrection. In this act of authority whereby God raised Jesus from the dead, he co-restores your body to life by his indwelling Spirit. *(Your body need never again be an excuse for an inferior expression of the Christ-life, just as it was reckoned dead in Christ's death, it is now reckoned alive in his resurrection. See Ephesians 2:5.)*

8:12 We owe flesh nothing.

8:13 In the light of all this, to now continue to live under the sinful influences of the senses, is to reinstate the dominion of spiritual death. Instead, we are indebted to now exhibit the highest expression of life inspired by the Spirit. This life demonstrates zero tolerance to the habits and sinful patterns of the flesh.

8:14 The original life of the Father revealed in his Son is the life the Spirit now [1]conducts within us. *(The word, [1]**agō**, means to conduct or to lead as a shepherd leads his sheep.)*

8:15 Slavery is such a poor substitute for sonship. They are opposites; the one leads forcefully through fear while sonship responds fondly to Abba Father. We are not slaves to a cruel taskmaster but gifted with the spirit of sonship; engaging the tender affection of Papa without any reserve.

8:16 Holy Spirit [1]personally entwines our spirit; resonating [2]ceaselessly within, endorsing Abba's parenthood. *(The words, αὐτὸ τὸ Πνεῦμα, with* [1]***auto*** *being the reflexive Personal Pronoun Nominative - thus Holy Spirit self...*

Then, the word, συμμαρτυρει [2]***summarturei*** *is the Present Active tense, suggesting a seamless, ceaseless endorsement; a joint-testimony. Thus, sonship is not something we imagine, but it is the very theme of God's mystery unveiled in us!* **1 John 5:9,** *If we receive the testimony of men, the testimony of God is greater.* **Hebrews 1:1-3.**

The Holy Spirit endorses in us what happened to us when Jesus died and was raised [**Titus 3:7**]*, and now echoes from within our spirits, Abba Father.*

There is concurrent testimony of the human spirit with God's Spirit. [Vincent]

See **Galatians 4:6** *To seal our sonship God has commissioned the Spirit of sonship to resonate the Abba echo in our hearts.)*

8:17 The fact that we are God's offspring, [1]certainly also means that we are equal heirs of God. Not only is God our portion, but we are his. We are co-heirs in Christ. [2]So, whatever we may suffer, at any time could never separate us from our inclusion in his sufferings. Thus, every reminder of this mystery, also reinforces the fact that [3]we have been made equal participants in the glory of his resurrection. *(See Ephesians 1:18 I pray that your thoughts will be flooded with light and inspired insight; that you will clearly picture his intent in identifying you in him so that you may know how precious you are to him. What God possesses in your redeemed innocence is his treasure and the glorious trophy of his inheritance. You are God's portion. You are the sum total of his assets and the measure of his wealth.*

[1] Paul uses the primary particle, **μέν** [1]***men,*** *truly, certainly, surely, indeed.*

[2] Then, the conditional particle [2]***eiper*** *with the Indicative Mood assumes the fact; So ...*

Paul is fond of compounds of **sun,** *together with/in union with - 3 in this verse -* **sunklēronomoi,** *co-heirs;* **sun***paschōmen, included in his suffering;* **sun***doxas thōmen; sharing in his glory; continuing from the previous verse,* **summartureō,** *bearing joint witness.*

[3] The verb συνδοξασθωμεν [3]***sundoxasthōmen*** *is the Aorist Passive Subjunctive of* **sundoxazō** *with* **hina** *[purpose], late and rare, here only in NT. The Aorist Passive Subjunctive suggests inevitable fulfillment. Therefore, our equal participation in his glory is a given.)*

8:18 Thus, my most logical conclusion is this, he has taken the sting out of our suffering; what seems burdensome at the time, becomes insignificant in comparison to the glory which is about to be [1]fully uncovered [2]in us.
(See 2 Corinthians 4:8,16-18. The verb, αποκαλυφθηναι is [1]*the Aorist Infinitive which describes the action expressed by the verb as a completed unit with a beginning and end; to be fully uncovered. Then, the preposition εἰς* [2]***eis,*** *points to a final conclusion - in us.)*

8:19 This reflects the deepest longing of every created being - the one event, which [1]captivates their attention. Picture creation standing on tip-toe with held breath as it were, to [2]mirror-witness for themselves, the unveiling of the sons of God; can you hear the drum roll?

([1] The word, ἀποκαραδοκία [1]apokaradokia, is only used here and Philippians 1:20. From ἀπό apo, away κάρα kara, the head, δοκεῖν dokein, to watch.

A watching with the head erect or outstretched. Hence, waiting in suspense. The Preposition απο apo, away from, implies abstraction; the attention turned from other objects.

[2] Then the word which I translated, to mirror-witness, απεκδεχεται [2]apekdechetai, which is the Present Middle Indicative, of apodechomai - it is the timeless Present tense and in the Middle Voice, giving a personal touch to it all; it also has a reflexive quality. The word, apekdechomai, means to fully embrace, from apo, away from [that which defined me before] and ek, out of, source; and dechomai, to take into one's hands; to accept wholeheartedly.)

8:20 Every creature became subject to a frustrating life of [1]vanity and futility, because of a [2]lost identity. Creation [3]involuntarily fell prey to a mindset [4]imposed upon everyone. Yet within this stark setting, [5]hope prevails.

[1] The word, [1]mataiotes from mataios, describes futility; vanity.

> *See Ephesians 4:17 My most urgent appeal to you in the Lord is this: you have nothing in common with the folly of the empty-minded masses; the days of conducting your lives and affairs in a meaningless way are over. (The Gentiles, ethnos, the masses of people who are walking in the vanity of their minds.)*

> *Also 1 Corinthians 3:20 The Lord is familiar with the unfruitful search for meaning in mankind's empty debates and dialogue. (The word, dialogismos, translates as someone deliberating with themselves. Psalm 94:11 says, The Lord knows the thoughts of a person; that they are vanity. The word, μάταιος mataios, translates as fruitless.)*

> *Then, Titus 3:9 Avoid confusing speculations and debates about genealogies and quarrelsome controversies about the law; it is folly to engage in such useless conversation. It is like chewing chewing-gum that has long lost its flavor. (The word, mataios, translates as folly, of no purpose, from maten, which is the accusative case of a derivative from the base of massō, to chew, to gnaw, like eating food with zero nutritional value.*

[2] See my comment on Romans 7:24 It doesn't matter how I weigh myself by my own efforts, I just do not measure up to expectations. The situation is absolutely desperate for mankind; is there anyone who can deliver them from this death trap?

[3] The words, οὐχ ἑκοῦσα [ouk, not and ἑκών hekōn, willingly] translate, [3]involuntarily.

This reminds of the context of this conversation where Paul states in chapter 7 that his best intention to consistently do that which is good, fails him! Alas, his own willpower cannot save him. This is the crux of mankind's dilemma! The duty-driven law of performance had to be rendered redundant and entirely useless. This is now eclipsed by the Agapē-driven law of the Spirit of Christ, unveiling mankind's redeemed innocence and freedom! Romans 3:27

*[4] The verb, υπεταγη [4]**hupetagē**, is the Aorist Passive of **hupotassō**, imposed upon - forced into subjection. [Not by God!] See **Romans 5:12-21** ...Adam's deviation set sin into motion - what happened to mankind because of one man, Adam, is in principle typical of what was about to happen to the same mankind because of the one man, Jesus.*

*[5] Hope prevails! Jesus is the fulfillment of the prophetic word in **Genesis 3:15**. The seed of the woman would crush the serpent's head [Ophis- the mindset of accusation based upon the deception of an inferior identity. See my notes on **Ophis, the old Serpent** at the end of Revelation chapter 12.])*

8:21 With eager expectation, every creature yearns to be released from its slavery to this [1]wearisome, perishable existence; trapped within a fragile time frame of fading glory, into the glorious freedom of discovering their true [2]sonship. They are indeed children, and not mere creatures of God.

*([1] The word, φθορας [1]**phthoras**, from **phtheirō**, means to pine or waste away, to wither .*

> *See **2 Corinthians 11:3** I am concerned for you that you might [1]pine away through the illusion of separation from Christ and that, just like Eve, you might become blurry-eyed and deceived into believing a lie about yourselves. The temptation was to exchange the truth about our completeness [I am] with the idea of incompleteness [I am not] and shame; thinking that perfection required your toil and all manner of wearisome labor. [The word, [1]phteirō, means to pine or waste away, to wither . Any idea of separation causes one to wither away in loneliness.]*

> *See **2 Corinthians 3:18** ... The Spirit of the Lord engineers this radical transformation; we are led from an inferior mind-set to the revealed endorsement of our authentic identity. [Changed 'from glory to glory', **apo doxes eis doxan; eis**, a point reached in conclusion; **apo**, away from, meaning away from the glory that previously defined us, i.e. our own achievements or disappointments, to the glory of our original design that now defines us; then the word **doxa**, glory, translates as mindset, or opinion from **dokeō**, authentic, blueprint-thought. Two glories are mentioned in this chapter; the glory of the flesh, which is the veiled, fading kind represented by Moses, and the unfading, unveiled glory of God's image and likeness, mirrored in the face of Christ and now redeemed in us.*

[2] Note a few verses back Romans 8:15 Slavery is such a poor substitute for sonship!

This is exactly what Jesus redeemed! He mirrors the Father's parenthood of the human race.

> *See **Hebrews 1:1** Throughout ancient times God spoke in many fragments and glimpses of prophetic thought to our fathers. Now, this entire conversation has finally dawned in sonship. Suddenly, what seemed to be an ancient language falls fresh and new like the dew on the tender grass. He is the sum total of every utterance of God. He is whom the Prophets pointed to and we are his immediate audience.*

> ***Hebrews 1:2** In a Son, God declares the Incarnate Word to be the heir of all things. He is, after all, the author of the ages. (See John 1:2 The beginning mirrors the Word face to face with God. [The beginning declares the destiny of the Word, image and likeness would be mirrored and redeemed in incarnate human form.] Also John 1:3, All things came into being through him, and apart from him nothing that exists came into being. Sonship endorses heirship. See Hebrews 6:16-18.)*

Hebrews 1:3 *The Messiah-message is what has been on the tip of the Father's tongue all along. Now he is the crescendo of God's conversation with us and gives context and content to the authentic, prophetic thought. Everything that God has in mind for mankind is voiced in him. Jesus is God's language. He is the radiant and flawless mirror expression of the person of God. He makes the glorious intent of God visible and exhibits the character and every attribute of Elohim in human form. His being announces our redeemed innocence; having accomplished purification for sins, he sat down, enthroned in the boundless measure of his majesty in the right and of God as his executive authority. He is the force of the universe, upholding everything that exists. This conversation is the dynamic that sustains the entire cosmos.*

Also, ***Galatians 4:1*** *Infant heirs have no more say than a slave, even though they own everything. (The best deal the law could possibly broker confirmed mankind's slavery to sin.)*

Galatians 4:2 *He would remain under domestic supervision and house rules until the date fixed by his father for his official graduation to the status of sonship.*

Galatians 4:3 *This is exactly how it was with us; we were kidnapped as if in infancy and confined to that state through the law. (An inferior mindset as a result of Adam's fall.)*

Galatians 4:4 *But then the day dawned; the most complete culmination of time. (Everything predicted was concluded in Christ.) The Son arrived, commissioned by the Father; his legal passport to the planet was his mother's womb. In a human body exactly like ours he lived his life subject to the same scrutiny of the law.*

Galatians 4:5 *His mandate was to rescue the human race from the regime of the law of performance and announce the revelation of their true sonship in God. (Now our true state of sonship is again realized. [John 1:12; see John 1:11-14] It was not as though he arrived on a foreign planet, he came to his own, yet his own did not recognize him. [Psalm 24:1] But to everyone who realizes their association in him, convinced that he is their original life, in them he confirms that we are his offspring. These are they who discover their genesis in God beyond their natural conception. Man began in God. We are not the invention of our parents. Suddenly the invisible eternal Word takes on visible form. The Incarnation. In him, in us. The most accurate tangible display of God's eternal thought finds expression in human life. The Word became a human being; we are his address; he resides in us. He captivates our gaze. The glory we see there is not a religious replica; he is the authentic* ***monogenes*** *begotten only of God. In him we recognize our true beginning. The Glory that Adam lost, returns. In fullness. Only Grace can communicate truth in such a complete context.)*

Galatians 4:6 *To seal our sonship God has commissioned the Spirit of sonship to resonate the Abba echo in our hearts; and now, in our innermost being we recognize him as our true and very dear Father.)*

8:22 We sense a global groaning of birth pangs; witnessed throughout history until this very moment. The world is pregnant with expectation.

8:23 We ourselves echo their groaning within us while we are ready to embrace the original blueprint also of our physical stature to the full consequence of sonship. What we already now participate in as first fruits of the spirit, will bloom into a full gathering of the harvest. *(The glorified physical body [Matthew 17]. Also the full realization of everything reconciled in Christ. In James 1:18, It was his delightful resolve to give birth to us; we were conceived by the unveiled logic of God, the Word of truth. We lead the exhibition of his handiwork, like first fruits introducing the rest of the harvest he anticipates.)*

8:24 For what we already experience confirms our hope and continues to fuel our expectation for what we still cannot see. In the final visible completeness of the harvest, hope has fulfilled its function.

8:25 In the meantime our expectation takes us beyond visual confirmation into a place of patient contentment.

8:26 Likewise, the Spirit also sighs within us with words too deep for articulation, and [1]mirrors our prayers when we struggle to find words. When we're not sure how to pray properly, Holy Spirit supersedes our clumsy efforts and [2]hits bullseye every time.

*([1] Again a word only Luke uses, συναντιλαμβανεται, [1]**sunantilambanomai**, which is compounded of συν, together, αντι, against, and λαμβανομαι, to support or help, and signifies such assistance as is afforded by any two persons to each other, who mutually bear the same load or carry it between them. Adam Clark*

*[2] The Spirit υπερεντυγχανει, [2]**huperentugchano** means to strike, hit the bullseye [spot on]. Accordingly, it is used in classical Greek as the antonym of **harmartia** [to miss the mark, sin - literally, to be out of sync with one's true from.])*

8:27 He who has always known us, mirrors the mind of the Spirit within us and brings our conversation back to the point. *(See the Message Bible, He knows us far better than we know ourselves, knows our pregnant condition, and keeps us present before God.*

*I knew you before I fashioned you in your mother's womb [Jeremiah 1:5]. Then you will know, even as you have always been known. [1 Corinthians 13:12]. Again the word, [1]**entungchano**, which means to hit the target with an arrow or javelin. This word is often translated intercession, yet, Holy Spirit is not trying to persuade God about us, but persuades us about the Father and the finished work of the cross!)*

8:28 Meanwhile we know that the love of God causes everything to mutually contribute to our advantage. His Master Plan is announced in our authentic identity. *(Called according to his purpose, **kaleō**, meaning to surname, to identify by name.)*

8:29 He [1]has always known us face to face, and [2]engineered us upon the mirror-horizon of his faith, to be [3]jointly fashioned in the same mold and image of his Son. We see the authentic pattern of our lives preserved in the Incarnate One. He is the firstborn from [4]the same womb that reveals our genesis. *(The word, προεγνω [1]**proegnoō**, is the Aorist Active of **proginōskō**, to have always been known, face to face. Then again he uses the Aorist Active Indicative προωρισεν [2]**prohorisen** of **prohoritsō**, I've translated, engineered us upon the mirror-horizon of his faith. Then the adjective, συμμορφός [3]**summorphos** the exact same form of his image [eikon]. We come from above [See John 1:13; also John 3:3-13] We were also born anew when he was raised from the dead. [1 Peter 1:3] His resurrection co-reveals our common genesis as well our redeemed innocence. [Romans 4:25 and Acts 17:31] No wonder then that he is not ashamed to call us his siblings. The word, [5]**adelphous**, with **a** as a connective particle and **delphus**, the womb. We share the same origin [Hebrews 2:11 **eks** [origin; source] **henos** [one] **pantes** [everyone], and, In him we live and move and have our being, we are indeed his offspring. [Acts 17:28].)*

8:30 Jesus reveals that we [1]pre-existed in God; he [2]defined us. He [3]rendered us innocent and also [4]adorned us with splendor and esteem. *(The word [1]prohorisen from prohoritsō, pre-defined, like when an architect draws up a detailed plan. Then [2]ekalesen from kaleō, to surname, identify by name. The verb, [3]edikaiosen is in the Aorist Active form from dikaioo, to declare righteous and innocent. All the verbs in this verse are in the Aorist tense. The Aorist presents an occurrence in summary, viewed as a whole from the outside, almost like a snapshot of the action. Also [4]edoxasen from doxazō; we have been adorned with splendor and glory. He redeemed our innocence and restored the glory we lost in Adam. See Romans 3:23, 24.)*

8:31 All these things point to one conclusion, God is for us. Who can prevail against us?

8:32 The [1]gift of his Son is the irrefutable evidence of God's heart towards us. He [2]held nothing in reserve; but freely [3]gave everything we could ever wish to have; this is what our [4]joint sonship is all about. *(The word [1]paradidomi, reflects the source of the gift, the very bosom of the Father. Without reserve, ouk [strong negative] epheisato from [2]pheidōmai, means to treat leniently or sparingly. To show oneself gracious, kind, benevolent, is the word [3]charizomai. The word [4]sun (pronounced soon) suggests complete union. Everything we lost in Adam is again restored to us in Christ. Sin left mankind with an enormous shortfall; grace restores mankind to excellence. [Romans 3:21-24, 1Corinthians 2:7].)*

8:33 God has [1]identified us, who can disqualify us? His [2]word is our origin. No-one can point a finger; he declared us innocent. *(The word [1]kaleō, means to identify by name, to surname. The word [2]eklektos suggests that we have our origin in God's thought; from ek, source, and legō, to communicate. He has placed us beyond the reach of blame and shame, guilt and gossip.)*

8:34 What further ground can there possibly be to condemn mankind? In his death he faced our judgment; in his resurrection he reveals our righteousness; the implications cannot be undone. He now occupies the highest seat of authority as the executive of our redemption in the throne room of God. *(See Romans 8: 1, also Romans 4:25.)*

8:35 What will it take to distance us from the love of Christ? You name any potential calamity: intense pressure of the worst possible kind, claustrophobia, persecution, destitution, loneliness, extreme exposure, life-threatening danger, or war?

8:36 Let me quote Scripture to remind you, Because of our association with you, we were [1]reckoned as sheep to be slaughtered; we have been [2]jointly slain on that day. *(The word [1]logitsomai, to take an inventory; to conclude. The word [2]thanatoumetha is only used once in this form - Paul quotes the LXX in Psalm 43:23 [44:22 in Hebrew text] The Preposition meta, together with, is combined with thanatos, to kill, to emphasize the idea of our joint crucifixion. Psalm 44:22. See also Ephesians 2:5,6; 4:8,9; Hosea 6:2, After two days he will revive us, on the third day he will raise us up. We have been co-crucified, co-raised and are now co-seated together with Christ.)*

8:37 On the contrary, in the thick of these things our triumph remains beyond dispute. His love has placed us above the reach of any onslaught.

8:38 This is my conviction; no threat whether it be in death or life; be it celestial messengers, demon powers or political principalities, nothing known to us at this time, or even in the unknown future;

8:39 no dimension of any calculation in time or space, nor any device yet to be invented, has what it takes to separate us from the love of God unveiled in our Lord, Jesus Christ.

9:1 What I am about to say is my honest persuasion; I am convinced beyond doubt of our inseparable union in Christ; my own conscience bears witness to this in the Holy Spirit.

9:2 In the light of mankind's inclusion and redeemed innocence, I feel such sorrow and painful longing for my fellow Jews. *(They are all equally included but they just do not see it.)*

9:3 If it could in any way profit them I would prefer myself to rather be excluded from the blessing of Christ. If my exclusion could possibly help them understand their inclusion, I would gladly offer my body as a sacrifice.

9:4 Sonship is the natural heritage of Israel; they historically witnessed the glory and covenants and the dramatic endorsement of the law; the prophetic rituals of worship and the Messianic promises belong to them.

9:5 They are the physical family of the Messiah. Yet he supersedes all our definitions; he is God, the [1]source of blessing and the ultimate announcement of everything good, for all ages. Amen. *(The word, [1]eulogetos, means blessed, from eulogeō, good word, good news, or well done announcement; normally translated, blessing. The Word of God reaches far beyond the boundaries of Israel, it includes every nation.)*

9:6 It is not as though their unbelief neutralized the Word of God in its effect; Israel is no longer restricted to a physical family and geographic location.

9:7 It is not the natural seed of Abraham that gives them their [1]identity, but Isaac, the faith-child. God said, Your children's [1]identity is revealed in Isaac. *([Genesis 21:12]; [1]kaleō, to surname, or to identify by name. Mankind's original identity was not preserved in the flesh, but in the Promise.)*

9:8 By this God clearly indicates that mankind's true spirit identity is revealed in faith and not in flesh. The Promise is the fuel of faith. *(The promise ignites faith. Faith gives substance to what hope sees.)*

9:9 Remember God's pledge, In nine months time, Sarah shall have a son. *(Genesis 18:10, according to the time of life, thus nine months; Galatians 4:4, Jesus is the fullness of time; the promise is a Person.)*

9:10 Rebecca and Isaac also conceived, consistent with the promise, to further prove the point of faith versus performance.

9:11 God spoke to Rebecca while the twins were still in the womb. Nothing distinguished them in terms of good looks or performance. *[Except the fact that the one would be born minutes before the other, which would give him 1st born preference, according to human tradition.]* It was recorded to emphasize the principle of [1]faith-identity as the ultimate value above any preference according to the flesh. *(The word often translated as election is the word [1]ekloge, from ek, origin, source and legō from logos, the Word, see John 1:1,14. Faith nullifies any ground the flesh has to boast in. Romans 3:27.)*

9:12 She was told, the elder shall serve the younger.

9:13 We would say that Esau had the raw deal; he was disliked while Jacob was favored. *(And the Lord said to her, Two nations are in your womb, and two peoples, born of you, shall be divided; the one shall be stronger than the other; the elder shall serve the younger. [Genesis 25:23].*

The two come out of the same mold; yet they represent two types of people: one who understands his true identity by faith and one who seeks to identify himself after the flesh. Again, the law of performance versus the law of faith is emphasized in order to prepare the ground for the promise-principle. Mankind's salvation would be by promise and not by performance; i.e. it would not be a reward for good behavior. No one will be justified by the tree of the knowledge of good and evil; **ponēros***, evil, full of hardships, annoyances and labor.)*

9:14 To say that God is unfair, is to miss the point.

9:15 Moses saw the glory of God's goodness; he saw God's mercy and the kindness of his compassion. *(Even when Israel deserved his absence he promised them his presence. Moses saw the glory and goodness of God, while he hid in the cleft of the rock. [Exodus 33:18, 19]. Throughout Scripture the Rock represents the blueprint of mankind's original identity [Isaiah 51:1, Deuteronomy 32:18, Matthew 16:15-18].)*

9:16 God's mercy is not a reward for good behavior; it is not a wreath given to the fastest athlete.

9:17 God employed Pharaoh as a prophetic figure to demonstrate the drama of mankind's salvation from their slavery to an inferior identity. Scripture records God's conversation with Pharaoh, (Exodus 9:16) But to show you my power working in you, I raised you up so that my Name *(revealing mankind's authentic and original identity)* **might be declared throughout all the earth.** *(Mankind's identity is not in Pharaoh's claim or some political leader's influence, but in their Maker.)*

9:18 The same act of mercy that he willingly bestows on everyone, may bless the one and harden the heart of the other.

9:19 This just doesn't sound reasonable at all. What gives God the right then to still blame anyone? Who can resist his will?

9:20 Who can dispute with God? The mold dictates the shape. *(There is only one true mold of mankind's design: the image and likeness of God.)*

9:21 The Potter sets the pace; same Potter, same clay; one vessel understands its value and another not; one realizes that it is priceless, the other seems worthless to itself.

9:22 Their sense of worthlessness has labelled them for destruction, yet God's power and passion prevail in patient endurance. *(God is not schizophrenic, having to balance out a seemingly unstable character by creating a nice guy and a bad guy: one for blessing and one for wrath. He cannot be both the Author of light and darkness; there is in him no shadow of compromise or change; no inconsistency or distortion whatsoever. [James 1:17, 18]. Mankind deceive themselves when their knowledge of their true identity becomes blurred by the flesh. They go away and immediately forget what manner of person they are.*

Paul's noble birth carried no further significance when he discovered his spirit identity revealed in Christ. The recorded history of Israel prepares the prophetic stage of God's dealing with global mankind. Faith and not flesh would be the medium of God's dealing with man. Flesh reduces man to the senses and the soul realm, while faith's substance reveals mankind's true spirit identity. Truth immersed in agapē, ignites faith. His patience is shown in Pharaoh: So get your livestock under roof, everything exposed in the open fields, people and animals, will die when the hail comes down. All of Pharaoh's servants who had respect for God's word got their workers and animals under cover as fast as they could, but those who didn't take God's word seriously left their workers and animals out in the field [Exodus 9:19-21]. For good news came to us just as to them; but the message which they heard did not benefit them, because it did not meet with faith in the hearers. [Hebrews 4:2 RSV].)

9:23 He has set the stage to exhibit the wealth of his mercy upon the vessels of value. He desires to confirm in them his original intent. *(His glory, doxa, opinion, intent.)*

9:24 Being Jewish or Gentile no longer defines us; God's faith defines us. *(He called us; kaleō, to identify by name, to surname.)*

9:25 Hosea voiced the heart of God when he said, I will call a people without identity, my people, and her who was unloved, my Darling. *(Even Esau whom you said that I hated. [See v 13]. It was common among the Hebrews to use the terms love and hatred in this comparative sense, where the former implied strong positive attachment, and the latter, not positive hatred, but merely a lesser love, or the withholding of the expressions of affection [compare Genesis 29:30-31; Luke 14:26].)*

9:26 He prophesies that the very same people who were told that they are not God's people, will be told that they are indeed the children of the living God.

9:27 Isaiah weeps for Israel: You might feel lost in the crowd, because your numbers equal the grains of the sand of the sea, but God does not abandon the individual. Numbers do not distract God's attention from the value of the one. *(Isaiah maintained this same emphasis: If each grain of sand on the seashore were numbered and the sum labelled 'chosen of God,' They'd be numbers still, not names; salvation comes by individual realization. God doesn't just count us; he calls us by name. Arithmetic is not his focus. — The Message.)*

9:28 For his Word will perfect his righteousness without delay; his Word is poetry upon the earth. *(John 1:1,14; Romans 1:16,17.)*

9:29 The Lord of the ¹multitudes preserved for us a Seed, to rescue us from the destruction of Sodom and Gomorrah. *(From Hebrew, אבא tzaba [Strongs H6635], a host/mass of people. [See note on Romans 3:10] In Genesis 18, Abraham intercedes for Sodom and Gomorrah, If there perhaps are 50 righteous people, will you save the city on their behalf? He continues to negotiate with God, until he's down to, perhaps ten? But, alas! There was none righteous, no not one!*

The remnant represents the one Seed that would rescue the mass of mankind.

*See **Romans** 5:17 Death no longer has the final say. Life rules. If the effect of one man's crash-landing engaged mankind in a death-dominated lifestyle how much more advantaged is the very same mankind now that they are the recipients of the boundless reservoirs of grace, empowering them to enjoy the dominion of life* *through the gift of righteousness because of that one man, Jesus Christ. Grace is out of all proportion in superiority to transgression. (No, grace is not something you qualify for by receiving it. Grace already belongs to mankind without their permission. The words οἱ λαμβάνοντες - [1]oi lambanontes do not mean, to believingly accept, but simply the recipients. [The Present Active Participle Nominative] The word [2]perisseia περισσεία means super abundantly; that which exceeds all boundaries. Of course it doesn't take faith out of the equation. It gives context to faith. See verse 1&2. Faith isn't what you do in order to; it's what happens to you because of.)*

Romans 5:18-19 states, The conclusion is clear: it took just one offense to condemn mankind; one act of righteousness declares the same mankind innocent. The disobedience of one exhibits mankind as sinners; the obedience of another exhibits mankind as righteous.)

9:30 This means that the nations that stood outside and excluded, the very Gentiles who did not pursue righteousness through religious discipline of any kind, have stumbled upon this treasure of faith.

9:31 Yet Israel who sought to achieve righteousness through keeping the law, based upon their own discipline and willpower, have failed to do so.

9:32 How did they fail? Faith seemed just too good to be true. They were more familiar and felt more comfortable with their own futile efforts than what they did with faith. Their faith identity *[reflected in Christ]* **was a stone of offense.**

9:33 The conclusion of the prophetic reference pointed towards the rock as the spirit identity of human life. In Messiah, God has placed his testimony of mankind's identity in front of their eyes, in Zion, the center of their religious focus, yet, blinded by their own efforts to justify themselves, they tripped over him. But those who recognized him by faith, as the Rock from which they were hewn, are freed from the shame of their sense of failure and inferiority. *(See Deuteronomy 32:18, you have forgotten the Rock that birthed you…, and in Isaiah 51:1, Look to the Rock from which you were hewn. It is only in him that mankind will discover what they are looking for. Who is the Son of Man? Mankind's physical identity is defined by their spiritual origin, the image and likeness of God, I say you are Petros; you are Mr. Rock, a chip off the old block. [See Matthew 16:13-19]. Mankind's origin and true identity is preserved and revealed again in the Rock of ages. The term, rock, in those days represented what we call the hard drive in computer language; the place where data is securely preserved for a long time. Also interesting to note that rock fossils carry the oldest data and evidence of life. See 1 Peter 2:6.)*

9:30 This means that the nations that stood outside and excluded, the very Gentiles who did not pursue righteousness through religious discipline of any kind, have stumbled upon this treasure of faith.

9:31 Yet Israel who sought to achieve righteousness through keeping the law, based upon their own discipline and willpower, have failed to do so.

9:32 How did they fail? Faith seemed just too good to be true. They were more familiar and felt more comfortable with their own futile efforts than what they did with faith. Their faith identity *[reflected in Christ]* **was a stone of offense.**

9:33 The conclusion of the prophetic reference pointed towards the rock as the spirit identity of human life. In Messiah, God has placed his testimony of mankind's identity in front of their eyes, in Zion, the center of their religious focus, yet, blinded by their own efforts to justify themselves, they tripped over him. But those who recognized him by faith, as the Rock from which they were hewn, are freed from the shame of their sense of failure and inferiority. *(See Deuteronomy 32:18, you have forgotten the Rock that birthed you..., and in Isaiah 51:1, Look to the Rock from which you were hewn. It is only in him that mankind will discover what they are looking for. Who is the son of man? Mankind's physical identity is defined by their spiritual origin, the image and likeness of God, I say you are Petros; you are Mr. Rock, a chip off the old block. [See Matthew 16:13-19]. Mankind's origin and true identity is preserved and revealed again in the Rock of ages. The term, rock in those days represented what we call the hard drive in computer language; the place where data is securely preserved for a long time. Also interesting to note that rock fossils carry the oldest data and evidence of life. See 1 Peter 2:6.)*

10:1 God knows how my heart aches with deep and prayerful longing for Israel to realize their salvation.

10:2 I have been there myself. I know their zeal and devotion; their problem is not their passion, but their ignorance.

10:3 They are tirelessly busy with their own efforts to justify themselves while blatantly ignoring the fact that God already justified them in Christ.

10:4 Christ is the conclusion of the law, everything the law required of mankind was fulfilled in him; he thus represents the righteousness of the human race, based upon faith *[and not personal performance]*.

10:5 Moses is the voice of the law; he says that a person's life is only justified in doing what the law requires.

10:6 Faith finds its voice in something much closer to a person than their most disciplined efforts to obey the law. Faith announces that the Messiah is no longer a distant promise; neither is he reduced to a mere historic hero. He is mankind's righteousness now. The revelation of what God accomplished in Christ, births a new conversation. The old type of guess-and pretense-talk has become totally irrelevant; Christ is not hiding somewhere in the realm of heaven as a future hope; so, to continue to say, Who will ascend into heaven, to bring Christ down, makes no sense at all.

(The nearness of the Word in incarnation-language is the new conversation. The word made flesh so that all flesh may witness the glory of God reflected in the radiance of their own illuminated understanding. 2 Corinthians 3:18; Isaiah 40:5.

See my notes on The Voice of Faith at the end of the chapter.)

10:7 **Faith-conversation understands the resurrection-revelation** *[and mankind's co-inclusion in it. Hosea 6:]).* **The Messiah is not roaming around somewhere in the region of the dead. Someone asks, Oh, but what about the pit? Where does the abyss fit into this? Who will descend into the abyss to bring Christ back from the dead? This revelation takes the abyss out of the equation.** *(Those who deny the resurrection of Jesus would wish they could send someone down there and confirm their doubts, and bring back final proof that Jesus was not the Messiah. Faith announces a righteousness that reveals that mankind has indeed been co-raised together with Christ.*

See Ephesians 4:8 Scripture confirms that he arrested every possible threat that held mankind hostage. [he took captivity captive] And in his resurrection, he led us as trophies in his triumphant procession on high. Consider the genius of God, in the incarnate Christ, he repossessed what belonged to us by design, [4]in human form; this is his grace-gift to us.

Ephesians 4:9 The fact that he ascended confirms his victorious descent into the deepest pits of human despair.

*See Luke 9:27 You don't have to wait till you're dead to see the kingdom of God; some of you standing here with me right now, are about to dramatically witness the kingdom of God with your own eyes. [The word, ὁράω **horaō**, to stare; to gaze with wonder; to encounter; to see for yourselves.*

*Then, in the next verse, [**Luke 9:28**], Peter James and John join Jesus in prayer on the mountain, where his appearance is spectacularly changed by the radiance of God's glory bursting through his skin; even his clothes became dazzling white like light. Then, the voice of his Father confirms that his beloved son is the conclusion of the conversation represented in both Moses, [the law] and Elijah, [the prophets] - Hear him. - Jesus is the conversation of God - he is the Logos.*

*See **John 1:1,2,5,9** To go back to the very beginning, is to find the Word already present there; face to face with God.*

The Word is I am; God's eloquence echoes and concludes in him.

The Word equals God. The beginning mirrors the Word face to face with God. [Nothing that is witnessed in the Word distracts from who God is. If you have seen me, you have seen the Father.]

The darkness was pierced and could not comprehend or diminish this light. A new day for mankind has come.

The authentic light of life that illuminates everyone was about to dawn in the world.

*At the end of his life Peter reminds us that, **2 Peter 1:16** We are not con-artists, fabricating fictions and fables to add weight to our account of his majestic appearance; with our own eyes we witnessed the powerful display of the illuminate presence of Jesus the Master of the Christ-life.*

***2 Peter 1:17** He was spectacularly endorsed by God the Father in the highest honor and glory. God's majestic voice announced, This is the Son of my delight; he completely pleases me.*

***2 Peter 1:18** For John, James, and I, the prophetic word is fulfilled beyond doubt; we heard this voice loud and clear from the heavenly realm while we were with Jesus in that sacred moment on the mountain.*

***2 Peter 1:19** For us the appearance of the Messiah is no longer a future promise but a fulfilled reality. Now it is your turn to have more than a second-hand, hearsay testimony. Take my word as one would take a lamp at night; the day is about to dawn within you, in your own understanding. When the Morning Star appears, you no longer need the lamp; this will happen shortly on the horizon of your own hearts.*

***2 Peter 1:20** It is most important to understand that the prophetic word recorded in Scripture does not need our interpretation or opinion to make it valid.*

***2 Peter 1:21** The holy men who first spoke these words of old did not invent these thoughts, they simply voiced God's oracles as they were individually inspired by the Holy Spirit.)*

10:8 Righteousness announced by God's faith, is the authentic conversation. Here, every definition of distance in time, space, or even indifference and hostility, is canceled. The word is no longer a distant prophetic pointer in the mouths of Moses and Elijah. They announced its destiny to be mirrored in the incarnation. The Word is extremely close to you. It spills over from your heart and becomes a dynamic conversation in your mouth. [*Deuteronomy 30:11-14.*] We publicly announce this message, since we are convinced that it belongs to everyone.

*(Lxx Greek OT - ἔστιν σου ἐγγὺς τὸ ῥῆμα σφόδρα [**extremely near**] ἐν τῷ στόματί [**in your mouth**] σου καὶ ἐν τῇ καρδία σου [**in your heart**] καὶ ἐν ταῖς χερσίν σου [**in your hands.**])*

10:9 Now your salvation is realized. Your own [1]words echo God's voice. The unveiling of the masterful act of Jesus forms the words in your mouth, inspired by the conviction in your heart that God indeed raised him from the dead.

(In his resurrection, God co-raised us [Hosea 6:2]. His resurrection declares our innocence [Romans 4:25]. Salvation is not reduced to a recipe or a sinners prayer formula; it is the spontaneous inevitable conversation of a persuaded heart. To confess, [1]homologeō, homo, the same thing + logeō, to say.)

10:10 This is where believing happens spontaneously, in the heart. The revelation of mankind's redeemed righteousness ignites a new conversation, announcing salvation.

*(The word **pisteuetai** is the impersonal construction, it is believed; believing takes place. [Present Passive Indicative of **pisteuō**] Faith is not something we do - faith is what happens to us when we realize what God had done for us. Isaiah 26:12 O LORD, you have wrought for us all our works. RSV. Of God's doing are we in Christ. 1 Corinthians 1:30.*

He restored us to blameless innocence. It is impossible not to boldly announce news of such global consequence [Isaiah 40:9])

10:11 Scripture declares that, whosoever believes in Christ *[to be the fulfillment of the promise of God to redeem mankind]*, will [1]not be ashamed.

*(See Isaiah 28:16. These two Hebrew words, חוש **chush**, to make haste, and [Isaiah 49:23] בוש **bush**, to be[1] ashamed, look and sound very similar and were obviously confused in some translations—the Septuagint [LXX], was the text that Paul was familiar with and there the Greek word, καταισχύνω **kataischunō** to be ashamed; thus, it was clearly translated from the word בוש **bush**.)*

10:12 Nothing distinguishes the Jew from the Greek when it comes to the generosity of God. He responds with equal benevolence to everyone who sees themselves identified in him.

(They realize that God defines them and not their cultural identity.)

10:13 Salvation is to understand that every person's [1]true identity is revealed in Christ.

(Whosoever shall [1]call upon the Name of the Lord shall be saved; [1]epikaleōmai, to entitle; to identify by name, to surname.)

10:14 How is it possible to convince people of [1]their identity in him while they do not believe that he represents them? How will they believe if they remain ignorant about who they really are? How will they understand if the Good News of their inclusion is not announced?

*(The word, [1]epikaleōmai, traditionally translates as to call upon, from **kaleō**, which literally means to surname, or to identify by name. This is also the stem in **ekklesia**, with **ek** being a Preposition that denotes origin, and **kaleō**. In the context of Matthew 16*

where Jesus introduces this word, he reveals that the son of man is indeed the son of God,
I say to you Simon, son of Jonah, you are Petros [Rock] and upon this petra I will build
my ekklesia. [See Romans 9:33])

10:15 What gives someone the urgency to declare these things? It is recorded
in prophetic Scripture, How lovely on the mountains *[where the watchmen*
were stationed to witness the outcome of a war] **are the feet of them leaping with**
the exciting news of victory. Because of their eyewitness encounter they
are qualified to run with the Gospel of peace and announce the consequent
glad tidings of good things that will benefit everyone.

10:16 It is hard to imagine that there can yet be a people who struggle
to hear and understand the Good News. Isaiah says, Lord, who has
believed our report?

10:17 So, ¹this faith is ²sourced in discerned hearing; the kind of hearing
that recognizes the authentic unveiling of Christ as the ²fountainhead
of faith.

*(Note, ¹**this faith**; see 2 Corinthians. 13:5, also, Ephesians 4:5. There is only*
one faith that matters - not what we, or a million others believe, but what God
believes. Jesus is what God believes about you-manity. We are God's audience;
*Jesus is God's language. The Greek, ²**ek**, is a Preposition that denotes origin; thus,*
faith emerges out of the word that reveals Christ. Hearing this dynamic message,
both in the mouths of the prophets and now unveiled in the incarnate Christ, ignites
persuasion.

*The word [rhema] of Christ, **not**, of God appears in the best manuscripts. It's not*
the mere quoting of the Scriptures that brings faith. It is the unveiling of Christ
within, that does. See Luke 24:27 And beginning with Moses and all the prophets,
he interpreted to them in all the Scriptures the things concerning himself. They
later testified, Did not our hearts ignite within us while he explained the Scriptures
to us?)

10:18 Has God not given mankind a fair chance to hear? Psalm 19 says,
His words touch the entire world like the rays of the sun; nothing is hid
from its heat; yes, truly their resonance resounded in all the earth, and
their voice unto the ends of the earth.

*(**Romans 1:19** God is not a stranger to anyone; whatever can be known of God*
is ¹manifest in man. God has revealed it in the very core of their being which bears
witness within their own conscience. [Note Romans 2:14 & 15 ...The law is so
much more than a mere written code; its presence in human conscience even in
the absence of the written instruction is obvious. See also 2 Corinthians 4:4 & 7
and Colossians 1:27. Blindfold-mode does not remove the treasure from where it
was hidden all along. Every time we love, encounter joy, or experience beauty,
a hint of the nature of our Maker reflects within us; even in the experience of the
unbeliever. In the incarnation Jesus unveils God's likeness, not his otherness, in
*human form as in a mirror. The word ¹**phaneros** from **phaino**, means to shine like*
light. Colossians 2:9,10 It is in Christ that God finds an accurate and complete
expression of himself, in a human body. Jesus mirrors our completeness. While

the expanse cannot measure or define God, his exact likeness is displayed in human form. Jesus proves that human life is tailor-made for God. See also Ephesians 4:8 And James 3:9 We can say beautiful things about God the Father but with the same mouth curse a fellow human made in his mirror likeness. The point is not what the person did to deserve the insult. The point is that people are image and likeness bearers of God by design.] **Romans 1:20** *God is on display in creation; the very fabric of visible cosmos appeals to reason. It clearly bears witness to the ever present sustaining power and intelligence of the invisible God, leaving mankind without any valid excuse to ignore him.* **[Psalm 19:1-4**, *God's glory is on tour in the skies, God-craft on exhibit across the horizon. Madame Day holds classes every morning, Professor Night lectures each evening. Their words aren't heard, their voices aren't recorded, But their silence fills the earth: unspoken truth is spoken everywhere. The Message.])*

10:19 I cannot understand how Israel could be so blind as to miss the Messiah in their midst. First it was Moses who predicted that God would provoke them to jealousy with a mass of people who are the nobodies in their estimation; a seemingly senseless bunch of people will steal the show to the disgust of Israel.

(They have stirred me to jealousy with what is no god; they have provoked me with their idols. So I will stir them to jealousy with those who are no people; I will provoke them with a foolish nation. [Deuteronomy 32:21 RSV].)

10:20 Then Isaiah in no uncertain terms hears God say, I was stumbled upon by them who did not even bother to seek me, I became obvious to a people who did not pursue me.

10:21 Yet My hands were continually hovering over Israel in broad daylight beckoning them, while their [1]unbelief and negative and [2]contradictory conversation caused them to blatantly ignore me.

*(The word, [1]**apetheo**, [apathy] means refusal to believe; and [2]**antilego** means contradictory conversation. See Isaiah 65:1 I was ready to be sought by those who did not ask for me; I was ready to be found by those who did not seek me. I said, Here am I, here am I, [mirror-language] to a nation that did not call on my name. Isaiah 65:2 I spread out my hands all the day to rebellious people, who walk in a way that is not good, following their own devices.)*

Romans Chapter 10 Extended Notes:
The Voice of Faith - Romans 10:6,7

The Voice of Faith - Romans 10:6,7

Romans 10:5 Moses is the voice of the law; he says that a person's life is only justified in doing what the law requires.

Romans 10:6 Faith finds its voice in something much closer to a person than their most disciplined efforts to obey the law. Faith announces that the Messiah is no longer a distant promise; neither is he reduced to a mere historic hero. He is mankind's righteousness now. The revelation of what God accomplished in Christ, births a new conversation. The old type of guess-and pretense-talk has become totally irrelevant; Christ is not hiding somewhere in the realm of heaven as a future hope; so, to continue to say, Who will ascend into heaven, to bring Christ down, makes no sense at all.

(The nearness of the Word in incarnation-language is the new conversation. The word made flesh so that all flesh may witness the glory of God reflected in the radiance of their own illuminated understanding. 2 Corinthians 3:18; Isaiah 40:5.)

Romans 10:7 Faith-conversation understands the resurrection-revelation *[and mankind's co-inclusion in it. Hosea 6:2].* **The Messiah is not roaming around somewhere in the region of the dead. Someone asks, Oh, but what about the pit? Where does the abyss fit into this? Who will descend into the abyss to bring Christ back from the dead? This revelation takes the abyss out of the equation.** *(Those who deny the resurrection of Jesus would wish they could send someone down there and confirm their doubts, and bring back final proof that Jesus was not the Messiah. Faith announces a righteousness that reveals that mankind has indeed been co-raised together with Christ.*

*See **Ephesians 4:8** Scripture confirms that he arrested every possible threat that held mankind hostage. [He took captivity captive] And in his resurrection, he led us as trophies in his triumphant procession on high. Consider the genius of God, in the incarnate Christ, he repossessed what belonged to us by design, [4]in human form; this is his grace-gift to us.*

***Ephesians 4:9** The fact that he ascended confirms his victorious descent into the deepest pits of human despair.*

*See **Luke 9:27** You don't have to wait till you're dead to see the kingdom of God; some of you standing here with me right now, are about to dramatically witness the kingdom of God with your own eyes. [The word, ὁράω **horaō**, to stare; to gaze with wonder; to encounter; to see for yourselves.*

*Then, in the next verse, [**Luke 9:28**], Peter James and John join Jesus in prayer on the mountain, where his appearance is spectacularly changed by the radiance of God's glory bursting through his skin; even his clothes became dazzling white like light. Then, the voice of his Father confirms that his beloved son is the conclusion of the conversation represented in both Moses, [the law] and Elijah, [the prophets] - Hear him. - Jesus is the conversation of God - he is the Logos.*

*See **John 1:1,2,5,9** To go back to the very beginning, is to find the Word already present there; face to face with God.*

The Word is I am; God's eloquence echoes and concludes in him.

The Word equals God. The beginning mirrors the Word face to face with God.

[Nothing that is witnessed in the Word distracts from who God is. If you have seen me, you have seen the Father.]

The darkness was pierced and could not comprehend or diminish this light. A new day for mankind has come.

The authentic light of life that illuminates everyone was about to dawn in the world.

At the end of his life Peter reminds us that, **2 Peter 1:16** *We are not con-artists, fabricating fictions and fables to add weight to our account of his majestic appearance; with our own eyes we witnessed the powerful display of the illuminate presence of Jesus the Master of the Christ-life.*

2 Peter 1:17 *He was spectacularly endorsed by God the Father in the highest honor and glory. God's majestic voice announced, This is the Son of my delight; he completely pleases me.*

2 Peter 1:18 *For John, James, and I, the prophetic word is fulfilled beyond doubt; we heard this voice loud and clear from the heavenly realm while we were with Jesus in that sacred moment on the mountain.*

2 Peter 1:19 *For us the appearance of the Messiah is no longer a future promise but a fulfilled reality. Now it is your turn to have more than a second-hand, hearsay testimony. Take my word as one would take a lamp at night; the day is about to dawn within you, in your own understanding. When the Morning Star appears, you no longer need the lamp; this will happen shortly on the horizon of your own hearts.*

2 Peter 1:20 *It is most important to understand that the prophetic word recorded in Scripture does not need our interpretation or opinion to make it valid.*

2 Peter 1:21 *The holy men who first spoke these words of old did not invent these thoughts, they simply voiced God's oracles as they were individually inspired by the Holy Spirit.)*

11:1 I want to make it clear that I am not saying that God rejected Israel, my own life bears witness to that, and I am as Jewish as you can get; you can trace me back to Benjamin and Abraham.

11:2 God did not push his people aside; his reference is his knowledge of them before they rejected him. Scripture accounts for occasions where God had abundant reason to abandon Israel. Elijah hits out against them and lists their sins to persuade God to utterly cast them off.

(proginōskō - to know in advance.)

11:3 Lord, they butchered your Prophets, and undermined your provision through the sacrificial altar; I am the only one left and scared to death.

(1 Kings 19:14.)

11:4 Yet God answers him in a completely different tone, You are counting wrong, you are not alone; I have seven times a thousand on reserve who have not bowed the knee to Baal. They have not exchanged me for a foreign owner.

(Seven times a thousand refers to an innumerable amount and not to an exact 7000 people. The Hebrew word Baal בעל means owner, husband or master [1 Kings 19:18].)

11:5 Thus even in today's context, God's original word of grace has preserved a remnant of much larger proportion than what we can number.

(The word, ekloge, from ek, a Preposition denoting source or origin, + logos, word or logic, thus translated as the original word. Traditionally this is translated as election.)

11:6 Grace cannot suggest debt or obligation at the same time. The word grace can only mean what it says. The same argument goes for mankind's good works; if salvation or any advantage for that matter is to be obtained according to prescribed regulations of conduct, then that's it. No amount of grace can change the rules. Grace means grace and work means work.

11:7 The very thing Israel sought to obtain through their diligent labor they failed to get; yet those who embraced grace as God's [1]original intent hit the bull's eye every time, leaving the rest groping around in the dark like blindfolded archers. *([1]eklegō: the original reasoning, logic, word.)*

11:8 Isaiah said that God has given them a spirit of slumber, causing their eyes and ears not to function. This drowsiness seems to prevail even to this day.

(Unbelief and religious ritual are blindfolds. And the Lord said, these people draw near to me with their mouth and honor me with their lips but remove their hearts and minds far from me, and their fear and reverence for me are a commandment of men that is learned by repetition ... [Isaiah 29:10, 13].)

11:9 David sees how the very table of blessing has become a stumbling block to them through their ignorance. The table of the Lord is the prophetic celebration of the sacrificed Lamb, where God himself provides redemption according to the promise; yet therein they were trapped and snared and they stumbled by their own unbelief. Now their only reward is the table they set for themselves.

(Commentary by John Gill: ... the table may be called an altar. 'You put unclean bread on my altar. And you say, 'How have we made it unclean?' By your saying, the table of the Lord is of no value [Malachi 1:7].

The sacrifices offered up upon the table; their meat offerings and drink offerings, and all others, likewise the laws concerning the differences of meats and indeed the whole ceremonial law which lay in meats and drinks and such like things; now the Jews are placing their justifying righteousness before God, in the observance of these rites and ceremonies, and imagining that by these sacrifices their sins are really expiated and atoned for; they neglected and submitted not to the righteousness of Christ, but went about to establish their own so that which should have led them to Christ became a handwriting of ordinances against them, and rendered Christ of no effect to them. Moreover, the sacred writings, which are full of spiritual food and divine refreshment, the prophecies of the Old Testament which clearly pointed out Christ, are not understood but misapplied by them, and proved a trap, a snare, and a stumbling block to them.)

11:10 This is the penalty of their disbelief; eyes that constantly fail to focus on the fact that Christ took their burdens and now their backs are still bending to the point of breaking under the strain of their own burdens.

11:11 Does this mean that the Jews are beyond redemption? Is their stumbling permanent? No, not at all! Their failure emphasized the inclusion of the Gentile nations. May it only prove to be their wake-up call.

11:12 If their stumbling enriched the rest of the world and their lack empowered the Gentiles, how much more significant will their realizing their completeness be?

11:13 In my capacity as a representative of the Good News to the Gentiles, I will speak in such a way that the clarity of my conclusion

11:14 will provoke my own flesh-and-blood family to jealousy. I know that my words will rescue many of them.

11:15 The Gentile nations realized their inclusion in Christ in a sense at the expense of the Jews; to now also embrace the Jews in the welcome of God is to raise them from the dead.

11:16 The seed sets the pace; it sanctifies what sprouts from it. Seed produces after its kind. If the invisible root is holy so are the visible branches.

11:17 And if some of the original branches were broken off, and you Gentiles like a wild olive were grafted in to partake of the same nourishing fatness of the roots,

11:18 then there is no cause for boasting against the ignorance of the Jews because you are now suddenly better off than they are. Remember, the roots sustain the branches, and not the other way round.

11:19 There is no point in thinking that in order to accommodate you, God had to first break off the Jewish branches.

11:20 Their unbelief was their loss; your faith is your gain.

11:21 God could do them no favors just because they were the natural branches; neither does God now owe you any special privileges.

11:22 Both God's goodness as well as his decisiveness are based on his integrity; unbelief is not tolerated, not in them, neither will it be tolerated in you. His favor is not to be taken for granted; instead, continue to embrace and appreciate his goodness with gratitude.

11:23 The moment Israel turns from their unbelief, God is ready to immediately graft them back into the tree.

11:24 You were cut out of the unfruitful olive tree and were grafted into the stock of the original tree. How much more will these natural branches be grafted again into their original identity.

11:25 Do not be ignorant then, of the [1]mystery of their temporal exclusion; their blindness opened your eyes to the fullness of God's plan for the whole world. *(In Paul's reference to the gospel, he often uses the word mystery to emphasize the genius of God in hiding the treasure of the gospel from view. See 1 Corinthians 2:1-16. Also see Matthew 13:44, the man who found the treasure, hid it again! See Further notes on,* **Why the Mystery***, at the end of the chapter)*

11:26 Once the nations realize the full extent of their inclusion, then all Israel shall also be saved. Just as it is written prophetically, There shall come a Deliverer out of Zion; he shall turn ungodliness away from Jacob.

11:27 For this is my covenant with them that I shall take away their sins. *(And as a Savior he will come to Zion, turning away sin from Jacob, says the Lord. [Isaiah 59:20] And as for me, this is my agreement with them, says the Lord: my spirit which is on you, and my words which I have put in your mouth will not depart from your mouth, or from the mouth of your children, or from the mouth of your children's children, says the Lord, from now and for the ages to come. [Isaiah 59:21].)*

11:28 In your estimation they appear to be enemies of the gospel, but their Father's love for them has not changed. He knows their original worth.

11:29 For God's grace gifts and his persuasion of mankind's original identity are irrevocable. *(kaleō - to surname, to identify by name.)*

11:30 In days gone by, you did not believe God; yet in a sense Israel's unbelief opened the door for you to realize God's mercy.

11:31 Now you are returning the favor as it were; your testimony of his mercy extends an opportunity to them to turn from their unbelief and embrace mercy.

11:32 In God's calculation the mass of mankind is trapped in unbelief. This qualifies all mankind for his mercy.

11:33 Oh, how amazing is the depth of the wealth of God's wisdom and knowledge. The understanding of his judgements can only be sourced in a conversation that originates from above; his ways are only accessible in the footprints of his thoughts. *(The word ἀνεξερεύνητος **anexereunētos***

from **ana**, *upward and* **exereunaō**, *to search out [1 Peter 1:10] from* **ek**, *source, and* **ereō**, *to utter to speak - [only here and in Ephesians 3:8] Again the next word begins with the Preposition* **ana** - ἀνεξιχνίαστος **anexichniastos** *from* **ana**, *upward and* **ek**, *source and* **ichnos**, *a footprint. Sadly, both these words have been wrongly translated to suggest that it is impossible to explain God's decisions or to understand his ways. Sounds like Isaiah 55:8,9 until verse 10 comes to the rescue. BUT, just as the rain and the snow come down from heaven [from above] and saturate the soil, SO shall my Word be! The Incarnation is the key to understanding God's thoughts and his ways.)*

11:34 Who inspired his thought? Who sat in council with him?

11:35 Is God indebted to anyone?

11:36 Everything originates in him; finds both its authentic expression and ultimate conclusion in him. His opinion rules the ages. We cannot but agree with our yes and awe. Amen.

Romans Chapter 11 Extended Notes:

Why the Mystery? Romans 11:25 & Matthew 13:44

Why the Mystery? Romans 11:25 & Matthew 13:44
Also, Colossians 1:26 & 27 and 1 Corinthians 2:1-16.

In **Matthew 13:44,** Jesus tells one of my most favorite parables. The kingdom of heaven is like a treasure hidden in a field, which a man found and covered up; then in his joy he went and sold all that he had and bought the entire field. *(Greek,* **agros***; an agricultural field.)*

The fact that it is an agricultural field means that it already has a calculated, historical value. It has been cultivated for many years and valued accordingly.

But now, the presence of a hidden treasure immediately brings a new dynamic to the table - there is so much more to the field than what meets the eye.

Imagine how intrigued his Jewish audience was. They themselves were farmers and business men - and here's a man, who has discovered something that no one else knew about.

This puts him in a most unique position to buy a farm, holding a priceless hidden treasure, for a ridiculous bargain.

And if, in this narrative, the field represents the world, then it is in a bad shape. Overgrown with thorns and thistles, and certainly one could point to many flaws that should influence the seller to settle for a much reduced price; they must have reasoned.

But, Jesus shocks them out of their wits when he reveals that the man who found the treasure, hid it again, and goes away and sells all he has, and buys the entire field.

This doesn't make any sense. Why would this man be prepared to pay such a ridiculous and most extreme price, knowing that no one else had a clue about the treasure? Who did he it buy from?

I mean, a thief surely never gets ownership; so, God did not buy us back from no devil.

The man who discovered the treasure is also the original owner of the field. *Psalm 24:1* The earth is the LORD's and the fullness thereof, the world and those who dwell therein.

There is only one legitimate Father.

Herein lies the crux of the story. Jesus very intentionally tells this in a language that will awaken us to the most amazing discovery about ourselves.

The mystery, that was hidden for ages and generations, is now unveiled. *Colossians 1:26 & 27.*

He was about to ransom us from our own ignorance; our fallen mindsets [[1]***diabolos***, *through the fall; from* **dia** *and* **ballō***, a mindset defined by the fall - I am not who God says I am*], and the lies that we believed about ourselves.

See *Hebrews 6:17*; He desired to show more convincingly to the heirs of the promise the unchangeable, non-negotiable character of his resolve - so he swore by himself.

How was it possible to interpret Matthew 13:44 any other way? Who bought who from whom?

Law-language cannot comprehend gift language. He sold all he had and bought the entire field to persuade mankind that they belonged to him all along.

The field is all he has. God has no other interest in the universe but you.

The whole of the gospel is to persuade us of our original, and now redeemed value.

1 Peter 1:18 It is clear to see that you were ransomed from the futile, fallen mindset that you inherited from your fathers. This was not concluded by the currency of your own labor, represented by the fluctuating values of gold and silver, and the economy of your religious efforts;

1 Peter 1:19 but you were redeemed with the priceless blood of Christ. He is the ultimate sacrifice; spotless and without blemish. Jesus completes the prophetic picture. *(In him God speaks the most radical scapegoat language of the law of judgment and brings final closure to a dead and redundant system. In Psalm 40:6,7, it is clearly stated that God does not require sacrifices or offerings. Jesus is the Lamb of God. He collides victoriously with the futile sacrificial system whereby offerings are constantly made to the pseudo, moody, monster gods of our imagination. This is the scandal of the cross. God does not demand a sacrifice that would change the way he thinks about mankind; he provides the sacrifice of himself in Christ in order to forever eradicate sin-consciousness from our minds and radically change the way we think about our Maker, one another and ourselves. [Sin-consciousness is in essence a works-based consciousness.] God did not clothe Adam with the skin of an animal because of a divine need to be appeased, but because of their unconditional love for Adam; they spoke the language of Adam's own judgment: Adam, not God, was embarrassed about his nakedness. The clothing was not to make God look at Adam differently, but to make Adam feel better about himself. And ultimately it was to prophetically prepare Adam for the unveiling of the mystery of mankind's redemption in the incarnation. Here Deity would clothe themselves in human skin, in a Son; and the Lion of Judah would become the Lamb of God in order to free our minds to re-discover his image and likeness in our skin. See 1 Peter 1:2.)*

12:1 Live consistent with [1]who you really are, inspired by the loving kindness of God. My [2]brothers, the most practical expression of worship is to [3]make your bodies available to him as a living sacrifice; this pleases him more than any religious routine. He desires to find visible, individual expression in your person. *(The word, [1]parakaleō, comes from para, a Preposition indicating close proximity; a thing proceeding from a sphere of union; to have sprung from its author and giver; originating from a place of intimate connection; and the word kaleō, meaning to identify by name, to surname. Jesus introduces the Holy Spirit in the same capacity: paraklētos, meaning close companion, kinsman [John 14:16]. The word, [2]adelphos, comes from a, as a connective particle, and delphos, meaning womb. Commonly translated as brother. [See Hebrews 2:11] The word, [3]paristēmi, means to exhibit, to present. In the context of the New Testament, the sacrificial system no longer involves dead animals, but living people. You died in his death and are now alive to God. [Romans 6:11])*

12:2 Do not allow [1]current religious tradition to mold you into its pattern of reasoning. Like an inspired artist, give attention to the detail of God's desire to find expression in you. Become acquainted with perfection. To [2]accommodate yourself to the delight and good pleasure of him will transform your thoughts afresh from within. *(The word, [1]aion, is traditionally translated as do not be conformed to this world. Actually aion points to a period of time of specific influence. In the context of this writing, Paul refers to the religious traditional influence of his day. The word [2]euarestos, comes from eu, praiseworthy, well done + arestos, meaning to accommodate oneself to the opinions, desires, and interests of others.)*

12:3 His grace gift inspires me to say to you that your thinking must be consistent with everything that is within you according to the measure of faith that God has apportioned to every individual. [1]Let the revelation of redemption shape your thoughts. *(The word [1]sōphrōn means a saved mind.)*

12:4 The parallel is clear. There are many different members in one body, yet not one competes with the other in function. Instead every individual member co-compliments the other.

12:5 In Christ, the many individuals are all part of the same body and members of one another.

12:6 Our gifts may differ in function, but his grace is the same. If it is your turn to prophesy, let faith and not a title be your inspiration.

12:7 The same goes for every aspect of ministry, whether it be serving or to give instruction,

12:8 or to just be there [1]alongside someone to remind them of their true identity; always let faith set the pace. You are [3]intertwined with your [2]gift, wrapped up in the same parcel. Lead with passion; minister mercy cheerfully. *([1]parakaleō, alongside, closest possible proximity of nearness; [2]metadidomi [see note on Romans 1:11], and [3]haplous from ha, a particle of union and plekō, to plait, braid or weave together. You cannot distance yourself from your giving. What God now has in us is gift-wrapped to the world. [Ephesians 4:11])*

12:9 Love without any hidden agenda. Utterly detest evil; be glued to good.

12:10 Take tender care of one another with fondness and affection; esteem one another's unique value.

12:11 Do not allow any hesitation to interrupt the rhythm of your zeal; capture the moment; maintain the boiling-point intensity of spirit devotion to the Lord.

12:12 Delight yourself in the pleasure of [1]expectation; prayer prevails victoriously under pressure. *([1]elpis, to anticipate, usually with pleasure.)*

12:13 Purpose with resolve to treat strangers as saints; pursue and embrace them with fondness as friends on equal terms of fellowship. Make yourself useful in the most practical way possible. *(See Hebrews 13:2)*

12:14 Continue to speak well even if someone wants to take advantage of you; bless and do not blame when you feel exploited.

12:15 Do not merely act the role in someone else's gladness or grief; feel with them in genuine joy and compassion.

12:16 Esteem everyone with the same respect; no one is more important than the other. Associate yourself rather with the lowly than with the lofty. Do not distance yourself from others in your own mind. *(Take a real interest in ordinary people.— JB Phillips.)*

12:17 Two wrongs do not make a right. Never retaliate; instead, cultivate the attitude to [1]anticipate only beauty and value in every person you encounter. *([1]pronoeō, to know in advance.)*

12:18 You have within you what it takes to be everyone's friend, regardless of how they treat you. *(See Romans 1:16, 17. Also Matthew 5:44, 45.)*

12:19 Do not bother yourselves to get even, dear ones. Do not let anger or irritation distract you; [1]that which we have in common with one another *(righteousness)* sets the pace. Scripture confirms that the Lord himself is the [1]revealer of righteousness. *([1]ekdikeō, from ek, a Preposition denoting origin, and dikeō, two parties finding likeness in one another. That which originates in righteousness sets the pace in every relationship. The word dikē is the stem word for the word, righteousness, dikaiosunē. It is interesting to note that the Greek goddess of Justice is Dikē [pronounced, dikay] and she is always pictured holding a scale of balances in her hand.)*

12:20 If your enemy is hungry, feed him; if he is thirsty, give him something to drink. These acts of kindness will be like heaping coals of fire on his head and certainly rid him of the dross in his mind and win him as a friend. *(A refiner would melt metal in a crucible and intensify the process by heaping coals of fire on it [Proverbs 25:21,22]. This is a good strategy, be sensitive to the needs of your enemies. God sees gold in every person. Hostility cannot hide our true value. He won us while we were hostile towards him [see also Romans 5:8, 10]. His kindness led us to the radical awakening of our minds. [Romans 2:4].)*

12:21 Do not let evil be an excuse for you to feel defeated; rather seize the opportunity to turn the situation into a victory for good.

13:1 Submit to the authorities with your whole heart. Any authority only has its relevance in God. God is a God of order.

13:2 To rebel against a God ordained structure of authority is a criminal offense.

13:3 Rulers are there to encourage good behavior and frighten off any evil intention.

13:4 They represent God's desire to protect you and to do you good. The sword they carry is not for decoration; they know how to use it against evil.

13:5 Do not let fear of punishment be your motivation, rather embrace a good conscience.

13:6 The taxes you pay is to show the government that you support what they represent on God's behalf.

13:7 Fulfill all your obligations to the government, whatever the tax is that they require of you. Give them their due honor and respect.

13:8 Remain debt free; the only thing we owe the world is our love. This is the essence of the law.

13:9 Love makes it impossible for you to commit adultery, or to kill someone, or to steal from someone, speak evil of anyone, or to covet anything that belongs to someone else. Your only option is to esteem a fellow human with equal value to yourself.

13:10 Everything love does is to the advantage of another; therefore, love is the most complete expression of what the law requires.

13:11 You must understand the urgency and context of time; it is most certainly now the hour to wake up at once out of the hypnotic state of slumber and unbelief. Salvation has come.

13:12 It was [1]night for long enough; the day has arrived. Cease immediately with any action associated with the darkness of ignorance. [2]Clothe yourselves in the radiance of light as soldiers would wear their full weaponry. *(The night is far spent, [1]prokoptō, as a smith forges a piece of metal until he has hammered it into its maximum length. The verb, ενδυσωμεθα is the Aorist Middle Subjunctive. From [2]enduō to sink into clothing; to clothe oneself. See Luke 24:49.)*

13:13 Our lives exhibit the kind of conduct consistent with the day, in contrast to the [1]parade of the night of intoxicated licentiousness and lust, with all the quarrels and jealousy it ignites. *(The word, [1]komos, refers to a nocturnal and riotous procession of half drunken and frolicsome fellows who after supper parade through the streets with torches and music in honor of Bacchus or some other deity, and sing and play before houses of male and female friends; hence used generally to describe feasts and drinking parties that are protracted late into the night and indulge in revelry.)*

13:14 By being fully [1]clothed in Christ makes it impossible for the flesh to even imagine to find any further expression or fulfillment in lust. Jesus is Lord of your life. *(The word, [1]enduō, clothed; to be fully immersed in the consciousness of the Christ-life as defining you.)*

14:1 ¹Welcome those who are young in their faith with warm hospitality. Avoid controversial conversation. (¹*proslambanō, to take somebody as one's companion.*)

14:2 One may feel free to eat anything, while another believes one should only eat vegetables.

14:3 By having faith to eat anything does not qualify you to judge the one who abstains; God doesn't treat the vegetarian any differently.

14:4 You are in no position to criticize the hospitality of God; he invited both to the same table and he is well capable to uphold and establish someone who still stumbles and seems weak in faith.

14:5 One person may see more religious importance in some days while another values every day the same. Let everyone come to the full conclusion of what the day means in their own understanding.

14:6 Whoever esteems the specific importance of a certain day does so to the Lord, so does he who values every day equally. One eats while another abstains; both honor God in gratitude.

14:7 No one can live or die in isolation; our life and death touch others.

14:8 Neither can our life or death distance us from him; we remain his property.

14:9 The death Jesus died and his resurrection and the conclusion of his life now in us is the only relevance of life and death.

14:10 What qualifies you to be your brother's judge? On what grounds do you condemn your brother? All of us stand in the footprint of Christ. (*We are equally represented in him.*)

14:11 The Prophet recorded what he heard God say, My own life is the guarantee of my conviction, says the Lord, every knee shall freely bow to me in worship, and every tongue shall spontaneously ¹speak with the same certainty mirrored in me. (*The word ¹exomologeō, from ek, source, origin, homo, the same and logeō, to speak, thus to speak from the same source, the same inspired persuasion, to fully agree. Paul, here quotes Isaiah 45:23 See verse 20,22,& 23 Face me and be saved all the ends of the earth. [Note, 'Be saved.' Not 'become saved.'] I am God; your idols are figments of your invention and imagination. Isaiah 45:23 I have sworn by myself; the word of my mouth has begotten righteousness; this cannot be reversed. (See Romans 1:17. The Hebrew word Yatsa יצא can be translated, begotten like in Judges 8:30) Every knee shall bow to me and every tongue shall echo my oath. (Thus, speak with the same certainty that is sourced in me. The Hebrew word, שבע Shaba means to seven oneself, that is, swear - thus in the Hebrew mind, by repeating a declaration seven times one brings an end to all dispute. See Hebrews 6:13.16,17.) See also Philippians 2:10, 11.*)

This echoes what John heard in Revelation 5:13, Then I heard the voice of everything created in heaven, upon earth, under the earth and in the sea, all living beings in the universe, and they were singing: To him who sits upon the throne and to the Lamb, be praise and honor, glory and might, for timeless ages. And in Colossians

1:15-17, Now Christ is the visible expression of the invisible God. He existed before creation began, for it was through him that everything was made, whether spiritual or material, seen or unseen. Through him, and for him, also, were created power and dominion, ownership and authority. In fact, every single thing was created through, and for him. He is both the first principle and the upholding principle of the whole scheme of creation ... . [Phillips] Colossians 1:20, And God purposed through him to reconcile the universe to himself, making peace through his blood, which was shed upon the Cross, in order to reconcile to himself through him all things on earth and in heaven. [Weymouth Translation] In Ephesians 1:9, 10, For God had allowed us to know the secret of his plan, and it is this: he purposed in his sovereign will that all human history shall be consummated in Christ, that everything that exists in heaven or earth shall find its perfection and fulfillment in him. [Phillips Translation].)

14:12 Thus the logic of God will find its personal expression in every person.

14:13 There remains no further cause for judging anyone. Rather determine that you will not allow suspicion or prejudice to snare your brother into a trap.

14:14 I am completely persuaded that in the Lord Jesus nothing is unclean in itself; it only seems unclean in someone's own religious reasoning.

14:15 But to walk in love is more important than to feed your appetite with your favorite food. Much rather lose out on a meal than lose a brother for whom Christ died. I mean Jesus sacrificed his life; for you to sacrifice a meal is no big deal.

14:16 Do not let your right to eat bring shame on Christ.

14:17 God's royal dominion is not based on food and drink regulations, but righteousness, *[likeness]* friendship *[peace]* and joy in the Holy Spirit.

14:18 This is definitely a win-win situation; God is pleased and people respect you.

14:19 Pursue whatever promotes peace and mutual encouragement.

14:20 Do not let a diet issue undo the work that God has done in someone's life. All foods are good in essence; it only becomes evil if someone causes or takes offense.

14:21 For your brother's sake, in order not to offend or tempt his weakness, it is better to not eat meat or drink wine in his presence.

14:22 At the end of the day, it is your own belief that matters most before God; do what your heart approves of without allowing guilt to interfere with your joy.

14:23 Don't let principle and prejudice spoil your meals. Whatever is law- rather than faith-inspired is [1]out of sync with the celebration of life. *(Whatever is not sourced in faith is sin [1]hamartia, a distorted form; out of sync.)*

15:1 We who are strong in faith are obliged to lift up those who are weak, to seek their advantage and not our own.

15:2 We are to please others and consider their good and benefit.

15:3 For Christ was not in it for himself, but for us. It is written about him, that he took the full blow of the reproach and insults directed at us.

(The curses of those cursing you fell on Me. LXX-Psalm. 68:10; Matthew-Psalm. 69:9)

15:4 Whatever was written about him includes and represents us. We take instruction and encouragement from his patience, while Scripture is our close companion to remind us of our true spiritual identity. We anticipate the future with delight.

15:5 God's patience and reflection of who we really are transmits in us like-mindedness toward one another according to the pattern of Christ Jesus.

15:6 The opinion of God, the Father of our Lord Jesus Christ, speaks one global language in us inspired by the same passion.

15:7 This gives us all the more reason to embrace one another in friendship with the same warmth wherewith Christ embraced us into the welcome of God.

15:8 I am convinced that the ministry of Jesus Christ was confirmation to the circumcised Jews of the truth of God's promises to their fathers.

15:9 So also will the Gentile nations glorify God for his mercy towards them. David prophesied the resonance and echo of praise in the Gentile nations who would discover their true identity in his name. *(See also Psalm 22:27.)*

15:10 Again Scripture reveals in Deuteronomy 32:43 that the Gentiles will join in celebration as they too are co-revealed as his people. *(See context of Deuteronomy 32.)*

15:11 Yet again in Psalm 117:1 the Gentiles are exhorted to give God praise and to join in the global applause of all the peoples of the earth.

15:12 The Prophet Isaiah sees the root of Jesse who shall rise out of the ground where it was cut off, to reign over the Gentiles; he will win their trust. *(Isaiah 11:1,10)*

15:13 God who is the engineer of expectation [1]fills you to the brim with tranquil delight. The dynamic of the Holy Spirit causes your believing to increasingly exceed any possible hesitation in hope.

([1] The word, πληρωσαι fills you (¹plērōsai humas) is the Aorist Optative - the Optative often expresses a wish. But here, when the Aorist Optative is used, it implies that the first action took place and was completed before the second one πιστευειν, [to be increasingly persuaded] began.

*[2] **Pisteuein** is the Present Infinitive, which expresses progressive or imperfective aspect. It pictures the action expressed by the verb as being in progress.*

Paul desires that this expectation, which is now announced in the gospel of how fully every prophetic pointer was fulfilled in Christ, in us - will flood our minds to the brim and engage the dynamic of a belief that never grows stale - but ever increasingly impacts our lives to live from fullness and not from lack.)

15:14 I am completely persuaded about you, my friends, that you are able to mutually instruct one another in the full measure of the knowledge of everything that is good in you.

15:15 God's gift of grace is the motivation of my writing to you; I urge you to remember your [1]allotted portion in life. *(The word, [1]meros, means form or allotted portion; note the word translated as sin is **hameros**, which means to be without form, without your allotted portion. Every sin springs thus from someone's sense of unfulfillment and lack, due to ignorance concerning those things which rightfully belong to them, their true spiritual identity, their redeemed innocence, and their participating in the Divine nature which is their inheritance in Christ.)*

15:16 It is because of Jesus Christ that I am in the people business. I occupy this priestly office representing the goodness of God to [1]the masses of mankind persuading them to see how presentable and approved they are to God in the Holy Spirit. *(The word [1]ethnos, means the masses of non-Jewish people, gentiles.)*

15:17 Because of who I am in Christ Jesus, I have taken a bold stand before God.

15:18 I could entertain you with all the detail of my personal adventures, yet all I desire to communicate is how actively Christ worked through my words to grab the attention of the nations.

15:19 The message was confirmed in every sign and miracle in the power of the Holy Spirit. Thus, I went full circle from Jerusalem to Illyricum proclaiming the glad tidings of Christ in its most complete context. *(Taking Jerusalem as a center, Paul preached not only in Damascus and Arabia, but in Syria, in Asia Minor, in all of Greece, in the Grecian Islands, and in Thessaly and Macedonia. Illyricum was a country of Europe extending from the Adriatic Gulf to Pannonia; it extended from the river Arsia to the river Drinius thus including Liburnia on the west and Dalmatia on the east. It now forms part of Croatia, Bosnia, Istria, and Slavonia.)*

15:20 I have placed such fond value on the fact that I could pioneer the glad tidings in many of these areas without building on someone else's interpretation of Christ.

15:21 Isaiah prophesied that, Those who have never been told about him, will be startled to see him clearly; even though they have never heard of him, they will understand his message. *(The message of truth speaks a global language. Paul says that the open statement of the truth, which is the Word made flesh in us in the mirror reflection of Christ, appeals to everyone's conscience [2 Corinthians 4:2]. Our lives are letters known and read by all. [2 Corinthians 3:2].)*

15:22 Now you know why it took me so long to finally get to you.

15:23   There seems to be no more room for pioneering work in these regions, after these many years I can finally fulfill my dream.

15:24   I purpose to journey all the way through Italy to Spain, but it is with great delight that I look forward to meeting with you first and enjoy a rich measure of fellowship that will again propel me onward.

15:25   I am on my way to Jerusalem to encourage the saints.

15:26   The believers in Greece, all the way from Macedonia as well as those in Achaia, have prepared a gift with great delight to bring relief to their Jewish friends in Jerusalem who are struggling financially.

15:27   They feel indebted to them since they share freely in their spiritual wealth.

15:28 As soon as I have delivered their harvest officially, I will depart to Spain via you.

15:29   I know that my coming to you will be like a cargo ship [1]filled to the brim with the blessing of everything that the Gospel of Christ communicates. (*[1]pleroma means those things wherewith a ship is filled, freight, merchandise, etc.*)

15:30 Being co-identified with you as members of a godly family through our Lord Jesus Christ and feeling the same spiritual love-bond toward one another, we are prayer partners before God joined in urgent passion.

15:31   Labor fervently in prayer with me that I will be rescued from the unbelievers in Judea, and also that my service to the saints in Jerusalem will be favorably received.

15:32 Through the pleasure of God's purpose I will arrive in Rome in joy so that we may be mutually refreshed in one another's company.

15:33   God who sustains us in oneness and [1]peace is with everyone of you. Amen. (*The word, [1]eirēnē, means peace, from eirō, to join, to be set at one again, in carpentry it is the strongest joint,referred to as the dovetail joint.*)

The names of 37 individual believers are personally honored in this chapter of salutation. Seven home churches are also specifically mentioned, five in Rome and two in Corinth. Since Paul never visited Rome before, these people were all acquaintances, converts, fellow prisoners, or travel companions of his before they moved to Rome.

Since Prisca and Aquilla originally came from Rome [Acts 18:2, 26 and 1 Corinthians 16:19], they possibly purposefully returned there to start or strengthen the ekklesia together with a strong team of believers. Their strategy was to scatter several home-fellowships throughout the city. This is reflected in Paul's letter to the Corinthians where he says, Our expectation is that as your faith increases, our field amongst you will be greatly enlarged so that we may preach the gospel also in lands beyond you. 2 Corinthians 10:15, 16.)

16:1 I would like to introduce Phoebe to you, she is our sister and serves the ekklesia in Corinth located in the port of Cenchreae.

16:2 Welcome her with appropriate saintly hospitality in the Lord. Support her and her business in every possible way you can. I am one of many who have greatly benefitted from her care and practical help.

16:3 Warmly embrace Prisca and Aquilla, my business partners in the Lord.

16:4 They are respected in all the Gentile churches for their unselfish lives. They have risked their own necks for me.

16:5 Salute the ekklesia in their house. Give my dear friend Epaenetus a warm hug from me. He represents the whole of Asia to me since he was my first convert there.

16:6 Miriam must also be mentioned; I remember how relentlessly she exhausted herself for others.

16:7 Embrace my cousins Andronicus and June who were in prison with me. I hold them in high regard as ambassadors for Christ; they are my seniors in him.

16:8 Hug Amliatus, my lovely friend in the Lord.

16:9 Then there is Urbanos, my co-worker in Christ, as well as my dear friend Stachys.

16:10 Acknowledge Apelles, a true veteran in Christ; honor the household of believers in the home of Aristobulus.

16:11 Say a big hello to cousin Herodian; greet the believers in the Narcissus home.

16:12 Salute Tryphena and Tryphosa whose work in the Lord bears testimony to their diligence; also my dear friend Persis who works so tirelessly.

16:13 I also remember Rufus as an outstanding worker in the Lord, and salute his mother who has become a mother to me.

16:14 I embrace Asyncritus, Phlegon, Herman, Patrobas, Hermes and all the family in fellowship with them.

16:15 Warmly greet Philologus and Julia, Nereus and his sister, as well as Olympas and all the saints in their fellowship.

16:16 Our friendship is sacred. The ekklesia of Christ here in Corinth salutes you.

16:17 Consistent with who you really are my friends, be alert to avoid anything that causes disunion or offense, contrary to the teaching that you have become acquainted with. *(Galatians 1:7 There is no other gospel in spite of the many so-called Christian products branded gospel. If any hint of the law remains, it is not good news but merely religious people's ideas, detracting from the gospel of Christ. [Some seek to unsettle your minds by perverting the Gospel to accommodate their own opinion.])*

16:18 For there are those who are not addicted to our Lord Jesus Christ but, prompted rather by the hidden agenda of their own fleshly appetites, they use their clever manipulation of words and eloquent speech to deceive the emotionally unstable.

16:19 Your ¹obedience *[faith-focus]* has become known everywhere. I am so happy for you; still, I desire for you to be wisely and exclusively acquainted with that which is good and ²innocent *[unmixed]* of evil. *(Paul's mission is to bring about the obedience prompted by faith [Romans 1:5, 16:26]. The word, ¹upoakouo, is translated as obedience or accurate hearing; and ²akeraios as unmixed, innocent.)*

16:20 God who is the author of our peace shall quickly and utterly trample ¹Satan, doing it with your feet. Your victory is realized in the revelation of the grace of our Lord Jesus Christ, and echoed *[personalized]* in your amen. *(We are the body of Christ. God desires to demonstrate his reign of peace in us by confirming satan's defeat in our practical day to day experience. The defeat of ¹accusation is celebrated in what grace communicates. The word, ¹satanas, means accuser. The law of faith defeated the law of works.)*

16:21 Timothy my co-laborer greets you affectionately; also Luke, and Jason and Sosipater who are fellow Jews, salute you kindly.

16:22 I, Tertius, who wrote this epistle, acknowledge you in the Lord.

16:23 My host, Gaius, in whose house the ekklesia meets, sends you his greetings. Then there is Erastus, the city chief who greets you, so does Brother Quartos. *(See Acts 19:29: Gaius was a travel companion of Paul, and he also mentions him in 1 Corinthians 1:14.)*

16:24 The grace of our Lord Jesus Christ belongs to you.

16:25 I am not talking hearsay-theory; I own the gospel I proclaim. This is my message. I salute God who empowers you dynamically and establishes you to be strong and immovable in the face of contradiction. Jesus Christ is the disclosure of the very mystery that was concealed in silence before ¹time or human ²history were recorded. *(Titus 1:2 This is the life of the ages which was anticipated for generations; the life of our original design announced by the infallible resolve of God before ²time or space existed. [Mankind's union with God is the original thought that inspired creation. The word, ²aionios, speaks of ages.] Paul speaks of*

*God's mind made up about us, before the ages, which is a concept in which eternity is divided up into various periods, the shorter of which are comprehended in the longer. The word, [1]xronos, means a measured duration or length of time; [**kairos** is a due, or specific moment of time.] This was before the ages or any measure of calendar time existed, before the creation of the galaxies and constellations. There exists a greater dimension to eternity than what we are capable of defining within the confines of space and time. God's faith anticipated the exact moment of our redeemed union with him for all eternity. This life was made certain before eternal time. [BBE 1949, Bible in Basic English] Paul's gospel does not merely proclaim Christ in history; he announces Christ unveiled in human life; Christ in you. Colossians 1:27.)*

16:26 The mystery mirrored in [1]prophetic Scripture is now unveiled. The God of the ages determined to make this mystery known in such a way that all the nations of the earth will hear and realize the [2]lifestyle that faith ignites. *(This gospel breaks the silence of the ages and reveals how God succeeded to redeem his image and likeness in mankind. [1]Isa 53:4, 5. See note on 16:19, Faith inspires an [2]obedience of spontaneity beyond guilt and obligation.)*

16:27 Jesus Christ [1]uniquely [2]articulates the [3]wisdom of God; he is the [4]conclusion of the ages. *(Uniquely, [1]monos, alone, Jesus has no competition; this one man represents the entire human race; this is the mystery of the ages. 1 Corinthians 2:7 We voice words of wisdom that were hidden in silence for timeless ages; a mystery unfolding God's Masterful plan whereby he would redeem his glory in man. Our glorification has always been God's agenda, even before time was. 1 Corinthians 2:8 Neither the politicians nor the theologians of the day had a clue about this mystery [of mankind's association in Christ]; if they did, they would never have crucified the Lord whose death redeemed our glory. The word, [3]sophos, means clarity, wisdom. He forever broke the silence of the ages. The words, [4]eis aion, eis indicates a point reached in conclusion, thus the conclusion of the ages. He is the [2]doxa, opinion; the logos that was before time was; the Word that became flesh and dwells within us [John 1:1, 14]. The incarnation [Latin, in carne, in the body] is the final trophy of the eternal logos and doxa of God.*

Colossians 1:15 In him the image and likeness of God is made visible in human life in order that everyone may recognize their true origin in him. He is the firstborn of every creature. [What darkness veiled from us he unveiled. In him we clearly see the mirror reflection of our original life. The Son of his love gives accurate evidence of his image in human form. God can never again be invisible.]

Colossians 2:3 In Christ the complete treasure of all wisdom and knowledge is sourced.

Colossians 2:9 It is in Christ that God finds an accurate and complete expression of himself, in a human body. [While the expanse cannot measure or define God, his exact likeness is displayed in human form. Jesus proves that human life is tailor-made for God.]

Colossians 2:10 Jesus mirrors our completeness and endorses our true identity. He is I am in us. The days are over where our lives were dictated to under the rule of the law of performance and an inferior identity. [See Colossians 1:19] The full measure of everything God has in mind for a person, indwells him.)

Paul's persuasion is firmly founded in his understanding of the success of the cross. In the economy of God, Jesus represents the human race. Every possible contradiction is filtered through this perspective.

In this letter Paul addresses several concerns regarding reports of divisions amongst the believers, a sexual scandal in their ranks and questions regarding marriage, diets and money.

In the first four chapters he takes his time to reinforce their faith in the finished work of the cross as the only valid reference to their lives.

In chapters 12 and 14, he brings clarity regarding the charismatic gifts.

Then he highlights the essence of the gospel in the most beautiful love poem in chapter 13. For many years this chapter was read and preached in a typical window-shopping frame of mind.

In Paul's gospel this mindset is completely reversed; he proclaims that, what God has done in Christ actually unveils the life of our design. Love celebrates the completeness of all that God has always had in mind for us. Love is not some prize one has to labor for; love mirrors who you are. What we perceived in prophetic glimpses is now concluded in completeness. (1 Corinthians 13:9, 10.)

In chapter 15, he emphasizes that the resurrection revelation is the theme and conclusion of the message he preaches.

Then he concludes in chapter 16:14 with, Agapē is your genesis. Loving everyone around you is what you are all about. (Our love for one another is awakened by God's love for us.) And in verse 22, he makes this final powerful statement: Anyone who prefers the law above grace remains under the curse mentality. Jesus Christ has come; grace is the authority of his Lordship; we are so fond of him. He is the Messiah the world has been waiting for. (The Aramaic word, **maranatha,** מרן אתא *maran ata*, means, Our Lord has come.

See **Luke 1:31 For behold, you will be [1]mystically captured in your womb and conceive and bear a son. And you shall name him Jesus.** *(The word, συλλαμβάνω [1]sullambanō, means to capture/arrest; thus to conceive - the male sperm is captured in the womb [en gastri]. Now, since the spoken language of the day was Aramaic, Gabriel obviously spoke Aramaic to Mary and instructed her, that the name of this wonder child is to be* יהושׁיע *Yehoshia, Jahweh rescued. Iēsoús is the Greek translation of the Hebrew/Aramaic word,* יהושׁיע *Yehoshia, Jahweh rescued. This verb is the Hif'il 3rd person Past tense. Moses changed Joshua's name from* הושע *Hoshea, meaning he rescued - to* יהושע *Yehoshua - Jahweh rescued. In prophetic endorsement of God's salvation unveiled in Jesus. Numbers 13:16. These are the names of the men whom Moses sent to spy the land; and Moses called Hoshea [he saved] son of Nun, Yehoshua -* Ἰησοῦς *- Iēsous in the LXX Septuagint [H3091] See John 12:13)*

1:1 My name is Paul, the ministry of Jesus Christ is the mandate of my life according to God's delightful purpose. Brother Sosthenes is my colleague. (*[1]He was formerly the chief ruler of the synagogue at Corinth. [Acts 18:17].*)

1:2 I address this writing to the [1]Ekklesia of God in Corinth. You have been restored to the harmony of your original design, made holy in Christ Jesus; no wonder then that you are surnamed saints. You are in association with all those who have discovered their true identity in Jesus Christ everywhere in every location; he is the head of this union; his name relates us to one another in a global family. (*Ephesians 3:15 ... from whom every family in heaven and on earth is named. [1]Church, **ekklesia**, those who have discovered their original identity; from **ek**, source, origin + **kaleō**, to surname, identify by name.*)

1:3 Grace and peace is your portion, proceeding from God our Father and our Lord, Jesus Christ. (*Grace and peace express the sum total of every beneficial purpose of God towards us. Paul brands his gospel with these words in order to distinguish the message of the revelation of the finished work of Christ as the basis to faith, from the law of Moses, which restricted a person to their own efforts to justify themselves. It is a matter of gift vs. reward and peace vs. striving.*)

1:4 I am always so happy for you when I consider how greatly advantaged you are because of God's grace unveiled in Jesus Christ.

1:5 Your knowledge of Christ is based on so much more than hearsay; every aspect of your life gives eloquent expression to the rich reservoir of your union in him.

1:6 You certainly have the testimony of Christ evidenced in you. (*You possess full knowledge and give full expression because in you the evidence for the truth of Christ has found confirmation. − NEB.*)

1:7 In [1]receiving the [2]revelation of Jesus Christ as the principal influence in your life (*his Lordship*), **you prove that you lack nothing and that his grace gifts fully compliment you.** (*This is in such contrast to those days when under-achievement was the rule; when you felt that you were never good enough and always lagging behind. Note: [1]**apekdechomai** is not eagerly waiting for, but eagerly accepting or to welcome with hospitality; [2]**apokalupsis** is the unveiling, disclosure. I don't know why most translations always want to postpone what God has already unveiled.*)

1:8 He establishes you from start to finish; to stand [1]vindicated in your identity in the light of day as evidenced in the Lord Jesus Christ. (*The word, [1]**anegkletos**,from **ana**, upward, **en**, in and **kaleō**, to identify by name. Jesus gives evidence to our original identity. Compare **anochē** from **ana** + **echō** in Romans 3:26.*)

1:9 We are [1]surnamed by God; this is our true lineage; he is faithful and fully persuaded about our joint participation in the fellowship of sonship; we are included in everything that our Lord Jesus Christ and the Father enjoys. God's faithfulness is the basis of this union. (*The word [1]**kaleō**, means to call or identify by name, to surname.*)

1:10 Friends, because we are surnamed and identified in the name of our master Jesus Christ, I [1]urge you to speak with one voice; we share the same source as our reference; the idea of division is an illusion. We are a perfect match; accurately joined in the same thought and communicating the same resolve. *(The word, [1]parakaleō, is from para, a Preposition indicating close proximity, and kaleō, to surname.)*

1:11 Some of the believers in Chleo's fellowship told me about the controversy in your ranks; this is most disturbing.

1:12 What I was told is that you are divided into groups, where some side with Paul, others with Apollos, still others with Cephas, and even some who say, we are the Messianic group.

1:13 This is really ridiculous: can Christ be cut up into little relics? Was Paul crucified for you? Were you baptized into Paul's name?

1:14 Baptism is not my business or emphasis; I am glad that I only baptized Crispus and Gaius amongst you. *(Crispus was his neighbor and leader of the synagogue [see Acts 18:8]. Gaius resided at Corinth. Paul stayed with him when he wrote the Epistle to the Romans [Romans 16:23]; he was also a travel companion of Paul's [Acts 19:29].)*

1:15 I distance myself from the idea of employing baptism as a means of branding my ministry with my name. Somehow baptism has become a snare to some who wish to win members to their denomination.

1:16 Oh yes. Now I remember that I also baptized the family of Stephanus. *(In 1 Corinthians 16:15, the family (young and old) of Stephanus were the first converts in Achaia.)*

1:17 My mandate was not about winning members for some 'Christian club' through baptism. I am commissioned to declare the Good News without any strings attached; nothing to distract from the powerful effect of the revelation of the cross of Christ. *(The mystery of the cross is the revelation of mankind's inclusion in his death and resurrection [see 1 Corinthians 2:2,7].)*

1:18 To their own loss the message of the cross seems foolish to some; but to us who discover our salvation there, it is the dynamic of God.

1:19 Isaiah wrote: I will confuse the wisdom of the so-called wise and prove their experts wrong. *(Isaiah 29:14.)*

1:20 God's wisdom puts the rest out of business. They have all closed shop; the philosophers, the academics, the smooth-talkers, the lot. *(When it comes to real answers to the dilemma of mankind, God's wisdom, revealed in the foolishness of the cross, is the currency of the Gospel.)*

1:21 By suspicious scrutiny the sense-ruled world surveys the works of God in creation and still do not recognize or acknowledge him; in sharp contrast to this, the foolishness of the message we proclaim brings God's work of redeeming his image in us into faith's focus. *(What we preach cancels every basis for boasting in personal contribution, which seems folly to the DIY systems of this world. [DIY - Do It Yourself])*

1:22 **The Jews crave signs** *[to confirm their doubts]* **while the Greeks revel in philosophical debate.** *(Both groups are addicted to the same soul realm.)*

1:23 **The crucified Christ is the message we publicly proclaim, to the disgust of the Jews while the Greeks think we are wacky.**

1:24 **The dynamic of God's wisdom is the fact that both Jew and Greek are equally included and defined in Christ.**

1:25 **It seems so foolish that God should die mankind's death on the cross; it seems so weak of God to suffer such insult; yet their wisest schemes and most powerful display of genius cannot even begin to comprehend or compete with God in his weakest moment on the cross.**

1:26 **You might as well admit it, my friends; it was not your academic qualifications or your good looks or social connections that influenced God to represent you in Christ.**

1:27 **It is almost as if God deliberately handpicked the wacky of this world to embarrass the wise, the rejects to put to shame the noble.**

1:28 **The ones with no pedigree of any prominence, the nobodies in society, attracted God's initiative to unveil his blueprint opinion in order to redefine mankind. Thus he rendered any other social standard entirely irrelevant, redundant and inappropriate.** *(Blueprint opinion, **eklegomai**, from **ek**, meaning origin, source, and **legomai** from **logos**, the logic of God; traditionally translated as elect.)*

1:29 **Every reason for someone's boasting in themselves dwindles into insignificance before God.**

1:30 **[1]Of God's doing are we in Christ. He is both the genesis and genius of our wisdom; a wisdom that reveals how righteous, sanctified and redeemed we already are in him.** *(The Preposition, [1]ek, always denotes origin, source. Mankind's association in Jesus is God's doing. In God's economy, Jesus Christ represents us; what mankind could never achieve through personal discipline and willpower as taught in every religion, God's faith accomplished in Christ. Of his design we are in Christ; we are associated in oneness with him. Our wisdom is sourced in this union. Also, our righteousness and holiness originate from him. Holiness equals wholeness and harmony of a person's spirit, soul, and body. Our redemption is sanctioned in him. He redeemed our identity, our sanity, our health, our joy, our peace, our innocence, and our complete well-being. [See Ephesians 1:4]. The Knox Translation reads, It is from him that we take our [1]origin.)*

1:31 **He is our claim to fame.** *(This is what Jeremiah meant when he wrote: Let not the wise glory in their wisdom, let not the mighty glory in their might, let not the rich glory in their riches; but let the one who glories glory in this, that they understand and know me, that I am the Lord who practice steadfast love, justice, and righteousness in the earth; for in these things do I delight, says the Lord. Jeremiah 9:23, 24.)*

2:1 My intention in visiting you was not to engage with you in theological debate or to impress you with clever philosophical words guessing about the [1]mystery of God. *(The words μαρτύριον marturion, testimony and μυστήριον musterion, mystery, look similar. The Alexandrian copy, and others, read, the mystery of God: also the Syriac version רזא דאלהא, the mystery of God. The Alexandrian text-type is the form of the Greek New Testament that predominates in the earliest surviving documents. The Syriac version of the New Testament, dates back to the second century A.D. Syria was the country in which the Greek language intersected with the Syriac, which was closely related to the Aramaic dialect used by Jesus and the Apostles. That is why Syriac versions are highly esteemed by textual critics. The context of this chapter beautifully unfolds the mystery of the Gospel. See my notes on,* **Why the Mystery? Romans 11:25**)

2:2 My [1]mind is fully made up about you. The only possible way in which I can truly [2]know you, is in the light of God's mystery, which is [3]Christ in you. Jesus died mankind's death on the cross and thus brought final closure to any other basis of [1]judgment. *(The word, [1]krino, to judge, to determine, to deem in a forensic sense, here, in the Aorist tense, ekrina, which suggests a once and for all completed act. The Aorist tense presents an occurrence in summary, viewed as a whole from the outside, almost like a snapshot of the action. Paul makes a very bold and radical statement, confining his ministry focus to know the full scope and consequence of the revelation of mankind's redeemed innocence as communicated in the cross of Jesus Christ. This is the essence of the mystery of God. For I am determined to [2]know [[2]eidō, to see, to perceive] nothing in you except Jesus Christ and him crucified. Nothing else. Not the latest gossip or popular news events. He says in 2 Corinthians 5:14,16, The love of Christ leads to this conclusion, one has died for all - therefore all have died. From now on therefore, I no longer know ANYONE from a human point of view.*

Paul continues to unfold the mystery of our redeemed oneness. In the previous chapter, he concludes that we are **in Christ** *by God's doing; here he clearly points to [3]***Christ in us***. [As Jesus declared in John 14:20]*

See 2 Corinthians 3:4 Christ is proof of our persuasion about you before God. Also 2 Corinthians 1:18 God's certainty is our persuasion; there is no maybe in him. 2 Corinthians 1:19 The Son of God, Jesus Christ, whom I, Paul, Sylvanus and Timothy boldly announced in you is God's ultimate yes to mankind. Human life is associated in all that he is. In God's mind, there exists not even a hint of hesitation about this. Also Galatians 1:16 and Colossians 1:27.)

2:3 I felt completely inadequate; you know that it was not my eloquent speech that persuaded you. I was so nervous that my whole body was trembling with stage fright.

2:4 My message was not with persuasive arguments based on secular wisdom, since my aim was [1]not to point people to me but rather to the powerful working of the Spirit in them. *(Thayer's Greek definition of [1]apodeiknumi is to point away from oneself. Previous translations of this word have often given the impression that the great, miracle-working man of God would steal the show and entertain the crowds. This was so unlike Jesus and Paul. Paul* *never writes about how many people he had healed and brought to faith, etc. His all-consuming concern was that the eyes of our understanding would be illuminated with the revelation of Christ in us.*

Note 2 Corinthians 10:10 [RSV], For they say, 'His letters are weighty and strong, but his bodily presence is weak, and his speech of no account.' Also, 2 Corinthians 11:6, Even if I am unskilled in speaking, I am not in knowledge. — RSV.)

2:5 Mankind's wise schemes of influence could never match the power of God as reference to your faith.

2:6 The words we speak resonate revelation wisdom in those who understand how perfectly redeemed they are in Christ, this wisdom supersedes every secular kind; suddenly what once seemed wise and good advice has become useless information. *(All popular programs towards improved moral behavior are now outdated. Of God's doing are we in Christ. He is both the genesis and genius of our wisdom; a wisdom that reveals how righteous, sanctified, and redeemed we already are in him. In God's economy, Christ represents us; what mankind could never achieve through personal discipline and willpower as taught in every religion, God's faith accomplished in Christ [1 Corinthians 1:30].)*

2:7 We voice words of wisdom that were hidden in silence for timeless ages; a mystery unfolding God's ¹Masterful plan whereby he would redeem his glory in man. Our glorification has always been God's agenda, even ²before time was. *(Paul employs the words, ¹prohoritso, predesigned and ²pro aion before the ages, in order to emphasize the certainty of God's persuasion concerning their determined intent to rescue and restore their image and likeness in us. Our redemption existed upon the inner-horizons of God before the ages. The word, prohoritsō, from pro, before and horitsō, horizon; means pre-defined, like when an architect draws up a detailed plan. See Romans 8:30 Jesus reveals that we pre-existed in God; he defines us. He justified us and also glorified us. He redeemed our innocence and restored the glory that we lost in Adam.)*

2:8 Neither the politicians nor the religious leaders of the day had a clue about this mystery; if they did, they would never have crucified the Lord whose death redeemed our glory. *(Time witnessed and recorded the death and resurrection of an individual; eternity witnessed and recorded the death and resurrection of the entire human race.)*

2:9 It is written: What has been concealed for ages in a realm inaccessible to the senses; what no human eye could catch a glimpse of, nor their ear could even hear a whisper of, neither could the inquiring mind decipher the code of that mystery which God has already ¹fully accomplished and prepared as a royal highway ²imprinted in the hearts of his lovers. *(The exact detail of his plan, to rescue his image and likeness in man, was in place. How Jesus would represent mankind to die their death was the wisdom of God concealed. In the mind of God we were associated in Christ before the ages; this was according to God's eternal resolve. The things that God has prepared or ¹hetoimatzo, from the oriental custom of sending people ahead to level the roads and make them passable before a king's journey. What seemed a cul-de-sac for the flesh is a royal highway for faith.*

*The redemption of mankind was not to be the product of human philosophy or speculation. In the Hebrew text it is a quote from Isaiah 64:3 [In our English translations it is v 64] the Hebrew [2]word חכה **ghaka**, is used, which means to carve an image; to show by drawing or description, piercing, traditionally also translated as those who wait upon the Lord. [In Psalm 130:5 and also in Isaiah 40:31, a different word is used for those who wait upon the Lord, קוה **kawa** means to intertwine.] Paul writes in Greek and most probably from the Septuagint when he quotes Isaiah 64 (verse 3 in the Septuagint) and uses the phrase, for those who love him. The Septuagint uses the word, **eleos**, tender compassion. Thus, faith opens the horizon of love's mystery. It is a place where thoughts [2]carve an impression; a place not accessible to the scrutiny of a suspicious, academic or a religious, guilt and a performance-based approach. [see 1 Corinthians 3:20].)*

2:10 These profound [1]mysteries of God's eternal resolve are now unveiled in us; nothing is hidden from Holy Spirit, who explores the innermost thoughts of God. *(In early ecclesiastical Latin [1]**mustērion** was rendered by **sacramentum**, which in classical Latin means the military oath. The explanation of the word sacrament, which is so often founded on this etymology, is therefore mistaken, since the meaning of sacrament belongs to **mustērion** and not to sacramentum in the classical sense Vincent).*

2:11 Just as a person's spirit knows their own thoughts beyond the public eye, even so the Spirit of God is our faith decoder to access the thoughts of God. *(In modern technology it would be impossible to access information from a source that is not compatible with your device; or without a decoder.)*

2:12 The Spirit proceeding from God unveils the gifts of his generosity. He has graced us with understanding so that we may know what he has always had in mind for us; this is so unlike the secular spirit of the wisdom of the world where everything has a price tag. *(Christ is the unveiling of the mystery of God's wisdom: now we know how God redeemed our righteousness and our wholeness in Christ. In God's economy, Christ represents us; what mankind could never achieve through personal discipline and willpower as taught in every religion, God's faith accomplished in Christ. Of his design are we in Christ; we are associated in oneness with him. Our wisdom is sourced in this union. Also our righteousness and holiness originate from him.*

Holiness equals wholeness and harmony of someone's spirit, soul and body. Our redemption is sanctioned in him. He redeemed our identity, our sanity, our health, our joy, our peace, our innocence and our complete well-being. [See note on 1 Corinthians 1:30] Secular religion is the product of the spirit of this world where everything is performance based; only the heroes of the moment are acclaimed; the rest are reduced to spectators and audience.)

2:13 The impact of our words are not confined to the familiar wisdom of the world taught by human experience and tradition, but communicated by seamless spirit resonance, [1]combining spirit with spirit. *(The word* **sugkrinō**, *suggests a spirit compatibility; joint together fitly, compound, combine, to interpret, to compare: thus, a joining of spirit with spirit.)*

2:14 The soulish person has no capacity to comprehend the language of the Spirit of God; spiritual things seem meaningless to them; they are

incapable to discern that which can only be spiritually appreciated. *(A performance-based mindset cannot access what grace communicates. It would be as impossible as trying to get airborne with a motor car. Law cannot compete with grace.)*

2:15 Those who are spiritually awakened are immediately compatible to discern all things from a spiritual *[grace]* perspective, while they themselves are free from anyone's critical scrutiny.

2:16 There is no other basis to teach from but to echo the mind of Christ; he is the Mastermind personified within us.

3:1 This is ridiculous. Who am I talking to here? Are you mere spiritual infants stuck in the soul-ruled mode of the flesh, reduced to baby-talk? *(Cooing sentimental gibberish about who your favorite preacher is instead of discovering who you are in Christ.)*

3:2 I fed you with milk and now after all this time it seems that you have no appetite nor capacity for the meat of the gospel. While you remain on the milk diet of the soul-ruled realm of the flesh *(knowing Christ merely from a human point of view [see 2 Corinthians 5:16]),* you are unable to digest the meat message of what has been concluded and revealed in your union with Christ. *(There is a huge difference between seeing Christ historically and sentimentally and realizing the revelation of the Gospel. This is the mystery of grace: God reveals us in Christ. He associated us in Christ before time began. Jesus did not die as an individual. He died our death and we were raised together with him.)*

3:3 Your heated debates and divisions prove that you are completely missing the point of the Gospel. You behave like any other spiritually unenlightened person, religiously obsessed with petty party politics while missing the essence of the message.

3:4 Can you not see that it is not about Paul or Apollos or any teacher you wish to associate with? We are not here to play the one off against the other, in a desperate attempt to win your vote to join our group. *(Acts 19:1.)*

3:5 Both Apollos and I are on the same assignment: we are here for you, to influence your faith to discover yourself in Christ. Every individual is equally gifted in him. *(See verses 21 and 22.)*

3:6 I have planted, by bringing the gospel to you in the first place, then Apollos watered the seed in his ministry to you; but God causes the Christ-life to ignite and expand in you.

3:7 If all we succeeded to do was to attach you to us as individuals, then we have failed you; the one who plants is not more important than the one who waters; it is not about us, it is about you realizing God's work within you. *(Our ministry has only one objective: to reveal Christ in you. See Paul's urgency in Philippians 2:12, not only in my presence but much more in my absence, discover the full extent of your own salvation: it is God working in you both to will and to do. This working out your own salvation has nothing in common with the guilt, willpower-restricted law of works system. It is discovering his working in you; energizing you with both the desire and capacity to give expression to him.)*

3:8 Our individual assignment does not place the one above the other; we have exactly the same mission; how we succeed or fail in that is to our own account.

3:9 We are co-employed by God. You are God's agricultural field; or in another context, you are his building and he is the architect and engineer of the life of your design.

3:10 His grace is the only reference for my skill; his gift qualifies me. The faith foundation that I have laid in your lives gives evidence to that. So let the next person take extra caution to build consistent with what grace communicates. *(I did not earn my certificate as Master Builder at a university as a reward for my excellence. Grace alone defines and inspires New Testament ministry.)*

3:11 Jesus Christ is the only foundation; nothing that anyone else can possibly teach you can replace him.

3:12 Imagine the contrast in building materials, one builds with gold, silver and precious stones, while another uses wood, hay and stubble. *(By comparison, the teaching of the cross and its glorious effect in the believer's life is like building with gold, silver, and precious stones, whereas the wisdom of this world system based upon religious good works and not faith is like building with wood, hay, and stubble which is fuel for fire.)*

3:13 Everyone's work shall be tested in the scrutiny of real life; it shall be made apparent as in broad daylight just as gold is tested in fire: what you live will either burn like stubble or shine like gold. *(The revelation of mankind's co-crucifixion and co-resurrection with Christ is the gold of the gospel.)*

3:14 If what you teach is based on the revelation of the success of the cross it will certainly be confirmed in the heat of contradiction.

3:15 Obviously to witness the fruit of one's labor go up in smoke would be devastating, even though you escape with your own life.

3:16 Realize that your life is God's building; his sanctuary, designed for his permanent abode. His Spirit inhabits you. *(He designed every cell in your body to accommodate and express him.)*

3:17 Just like fire would burn away the dross, any defilement of God's temple would be destroyed in order to preserve human life as his permanent sanctuary. *(See verse 15.)*

3:18 Why fool yourself? What is esteemed as wise according to popular Jewish sentiment is folly. There is no compromise when it comes to wisdom; the only wisdom that matters is what God deems wise, even if it seems foolishness to the reasoning of typical religion. Much rather be ridiculed by religion than esteemed as wise by them. *(The dynamic of God's wisdom is the fact that both Jew and Greek are equally represented and defined in Christ. It seems so foolish that God should die mankind's death on the cross; it seems so weak of God to suffer such insult; yet mankind's wisest schemes and most powerful display of genius cannot even begin to comprehend or compete with God in his weakest moment on the cross [1 Corinthians 1:24-25]. [See also 1 Corinthians 1:30, 2:7, 8].)*

3:19 God's wisdom proves the foolishness of secular wisdom. It is on record in Scripture how God outwits the wise of this world. *(In The Message Translation, Job 5:13 reads, He catches the know-it-alls in their conspiracies - all that intricate intrigue swept out with the trash.)*

3:20 The Lord is familiar with the [2]fruitless search for meaning in mankind's empty [1]debates and dialogue. *(The word, [1]dialogismos, translates as someone deliberating with themselves. Psalm 94:11 says, The Lord knows the thoughts of a person; that they are vanity. The word, [2]maten, translates as fruitless.)*

3:21 Therefore no one has any reason to boast about themselves, as if they gained anything that does not already belong to them. For all things you wish to gain already belong to you. *([See 1 Corinthians 4:7] Thus says the Lord: Let not the wise glory in their wisdom, let not the mighty glory in their might, let not the rich glory in their riches; but let the one who glories glory in this, that they understand and know me, that I am the Lord who practice steadfast love, justice, and righteousness in the earth; for in these things I delight, says the Lord. [Jeremiah 9:23, 24].)*

3:22 You are not winning any competition by picking your favorite teacher amongst Paul, Apollos or Kefas; they all belong to you anyway. The world belongs to you. Life and death are yours; in what you now have in this present moment you already possess the future. *(Not even death can threaten what you have in life. See Romans 8:38, 39.)*

3:23 As much as Christ is inseparably God's own, you are the property of Christ. You are one with him. *(Jesus endorsed God's ownership of the human race. See Psalm 24:1, Matthew 13:44 and Luke 15 where all three parables celebrate ownership - you cannot be lost unless you belong.)*

4:1 This is how one should regard us *(so-called, Apostles)*: **we are the ¹under-rowers of Captain Christ; responsible for the engine room as it were. We are entrusted with the administration of the mysteries of God.** *(The unveiling of the mystery of the gospel of mankind's association in Christ is the driving force of the Ekklesia. The word, ¹**hupērétēs**, means an under-rower, who was one who was in the trireme, quadrireme, or quinquereme galleys and rowed in one of the undermost benches; those who were the lowest ranked slaves and often the most invisible part of the whole operation. We are not hiding behind fancy titles or impressive CV's to try and win your applause or financial support. We are not here to impress you with us; our mandate is to impress you with how complete you are in Christ because of God's doing. [See 1 Corinthians 1:30, 2:6-9].)*

4:2 *(Our title might be unimpressive, but our job is most significant.)* **For this reason our ministry is of unquestionable integrity.**

4:3 The authority of my ministry is not based upon your scrutiny of my life or even any cross examination by a human court. Neither is it by my own assumption;

4:4 even though I know of nothing against my conscience, I am not thereby acquitted. The point is not how self righteous I appear in my own eyes; the Lord's judgment is the only valid reference to our innocence.

4:5 Any judgment prior to the Lord's coming *[prior to the cross]* **is out of context.** *[The days of performance-based judgment are over.]* **His coming illuminates all the hidden mysteries** *[concerning mankind's inclusion in the death and resurrection of Christ. See 1 Corinthians 2:7, 8])* **and unveils the ¹deepest desire of the heart of a person. In his appearance** *[through the proclamation of this gospel [see 1 Corinthians 5:4]* **shall everyone be ²commended by God.** *(Not contaminated by an inferior judgment; ²**apo** means away from the influence of mankind's judgment. ¹He is the desire of all nations. All nations long for the redemption of their true identity and their true innocence. [See Haggai 2:7; also 1 Corinthians 1:7 and 1 Corinthians 2:7.] We voice words of wisdom that were hidden in silence for timeless ages; a mystery unfolding God's Masterful plan whereby he would redeem his glory in man.)*

4:6 I have deliberately applied this to myself and Apollos to show you the futility of hero-worshipping; to put us in a contest would be completely out of context of what I have written to you *(Both Apollos and I are on the same assignment: we are here for you, to influence your faith to discover yourself in Christ. Every individual is equally gifted in him. [See 1 Corinthians 3:5] Therefore no one has any reason to boast about themselves, as if they gained anything that does not already belong to them. For all things you wish to gain already belongs to you. [See 1 Corinthians 3:21].)*

4:7 How can there possibly be any ground left for dispute or discrimination if there is nothing in us that we did not freely receive? Now if who you are and what you have is a gift and not a reward for good behavior, then boasting makes no sense. *(See Romans 3:27.)*

4:8 You are already saturated, literally jam-packed to capacity; you cannot get any wealthier than what you are. You are royalty *[because of what* *happened to you in Christ]* **not because of Apollos or Paul. Oh, that you might know this so that we may co-reign together with you.** *(We are not ranked any differently because we taught you the Good News. So do not try to make heroes of us while you reduce yourselves to mere supporters and spectators [see also 1 Corinthians 1:30 and 2 Corinthians 10:12]. Paul is reinforcing the message of how complete we already are in Christ as our only reference. We are no longer striving towards completeness; we are living from completeness. The language of the Old Covenant was towards; the language of the New is from. The old said, Do. The new says, Done.)*

4:9 If you really want to know, there is nothing glamorous about being an Apostle. It seems to some that God has us on exhibition as it were, as clowns in the circus; the laughing stock of the religious world. We are the latest gossip in town. Even the celestial messengers pity us. And you want to idolize us, think again. We are not handing out autographs. Neither are we your latest brand of Christianity. We have a death-sentence hanging over our heads.

4:10 Because of Christ we are considered fools *(in the eyes of the religious society.)* **Our foolishness serves only one purpose though: to prove to you that Christ is your wisdom. Our weakness serves to convince you of your source of strength in Christ; our ill repute in the eyes of popular opinion is to persuade you of your honored standing in Christ.** *(Do not allow what we are suffering for you to distract you from realizing how wise, strong, and honored you really are in Christ. See 2 Corinthians 13:5,8)*

4:11 While writing this to you my life would seem such a contradiction. I mean here I am telling you how complete and without shortcoming you already are, and I can hardly remember when last I have had a decent meal. As I am writing this my mouth is dry with thirst, I'm stripped of my clothing; I have been beaten black and blue, and have nowhere to go.

4:12 I feel fatigue from my physical labor. When people insult us we make sure that we speak well of them. We are harassed, but bear with it.

4:13 Hurtful rumors do the rounds but we find refuge and [1]**comfort in our true identity. We are reckoned as** [2]**scapegoats, the scum of society. This is what we are faced with on a daily basis.** *(The word,* [1]*parakaleō, comes from* **para**, *a Preposition indicating close proximity, with a suggestion of union, and* **kaleō**, *to identify by name, to surname. The Greeks used to apply the term* [2]**katharmata** *as scapegoats, to victims sacrificed to make expiation for the people, and even to criminals who were maintained at the public expense, that on the outbreak of a pestilence or other calamity they might be offered as sacrifices to make expiation for the state.)*

4:14 My intention is not to embarrass you. I bring these things to your attention because you are my very dear children.

4:15 While you may have countless mentors supervising your lives, you do not have many fathers; for in Christ Jesus I have begotten you through the Gospel.

4:16 I therefore summon you urgently to mirror my message.

4:17 This is why I send my beloved son Timothy to you. He is rock-solid in his faith. He shall remind you of me and reinforce my specific message and emphasis in every place and every ekklesia I visit. *(Paul's emphasis is unique in the way he teaches the 'in Christ', and the 'Christ in you', and his finished work-message. There is no other gospel in spite of the many so-called Christian products branded 'gospel.' If any hint of the law remains, it is not good news but merely religious people's ideas, distracting from the gospel of Christ. [See Galatians 1:7] This is the heart of the gospel that I proclaim; it began with an unveiling of sonship in me, freeing me to announce the same sonship in the masses of non-Jewish people. I felt no immediate urgency to compare notes with those who were familiar with Christ from a mere historical point of view. [Galatians 1:16] The Greek text is quite clear, It pleased the Father to reveal his Son in me in order that I may proclaim him in the nations. The words, **en emoi**, translate as in me, and **en ethnos** translates as in the Gentile nations, or the masses of non Jewish people. Not among the Gentiles as most translations have it. Later when Barnabas is sent to investigate the conversion of the Greeks in Acts 11, instead of reporting his findings to HQ in Jerusalem, he immediately finds Paul, knowing that Paul's gospel is the revelation of the mystery of Christ in the nations [see Colossians 1:27]. No wonder then that those believers were the first to be called Christians, or Christ-like. For the Son of God, Jesus Christ, whom we proclaimed in you, Silvanus and Timothy and I, was not Yes and No; but in him it is always Yes. [2 Corinthians 1:19].)*

4:18 I know some of you have the vaunted idea that my message and I will just vanish off the face of the earth. You cannot wish me away.

4:19 In the Lord's purpose I might show up sooner than what you think; then we will know if there is any dynamic in their inflated talk.

4:20 The kingdom of God *[the dominion of the Christ-life]* is about an empowered life and not just a matter of quoting your favorite teacher or Scripture.

4:21 Would you prefer it if I come to you with a whip-in-hand approach or with a loving, gentle spirit?

5:1 The sexual scandal in your ranks has become public news: someone is said to have slept with his stepmother. This kind of behavior is not even tolerated in society in general, let alone among believers.

5:2   And you are engaged in discussing doctrine and organizing denominations. *(Chapter 1:10-13)* This is heartbreaking. This shameful situation should have been dealt with in the most urgent manner by clearly distancing yourselves from such behavior and even going as far as disassociating yourselves from this person. *(In the first four chapters Paul makes it very clear that this gospel is not an excuse to disguise sin but to remove it. Anyone who suggests that grace is a license to sin is fuel for fire. [See 1 Corinthians 3:12-15].)*

5:3 Even though I am not physically with you, my spirit is present in this reading of my letter; and I assure you as solemnly as if actually present in your gathering, that I have already concluded my verdict in the Name of the Lord Jesus Christ:

5:4 As you meet together and I meet with you in my spirit by the power of our Lord Jesus Christ present with us,

5:5 such a person is to be released from your midst and handed over to the [1]Accuser; let the accusation consume his flesh until the light of day, the revelation of Jesus Christ rise for him again to rescue his spirit from the deceit of his sin.

(The word [1]satanas means accuser and [2]nous refers to mind or strategy, agenda, schemes.

Consider Paul's heart in 2 Corinthians 2:6-11 This person has been amply taxed by all. It is due time now to offer him your forgiveness and closeness lest he be completely swamped with regret. I implore you to make your love for him very clear. (The word, kuroo, translates as officially; publicly confirm your love for him.) The intent and urgency of my first letter was to prove your loyalty to my ministry and message in its full context. I am joined to you [geographic distance does not separate us]; your forgiveness is my forgiveness. The favor reflected in the face of Christ is our only valid reference to true forgiveness anyway. The agenda of any accusation is to divide and dominate. We are not ignorant about that.)

Also Ephesians 4:26 Even if you think you have a valid excuse, do not let anger dominate your day. By not dealing with it promptly [in the light of your authentic likeness, redeemed in Christ], the sun seems to set for you, and your day becomes one of lost opportunities, where darkness employs anger to snare you into sin. (Many interpretations of this verse have left one with the idea that, in order to get maximum mileage out of anger, one should get angry as early as possible in the day as long as you get over it by nightfall!)

Ephesians 4:27 Engaging the energy of anger in any prolonged time-slot, typically sets up the [1]stage for the [2]Diabolos, giving opportunity for a destructive and out of sync-mindset to take mean advantage of you and others. (The word, τόπος [1]topos suggests a place specially marked off; a platform to operate from. The word,

[2]*diabolos, has two components, the Preposition **dia** through; by means of, and **ballō**, to cast down; to put in a lower place or order. Pointing to the root of deception and temptation, engaging a mindset, defined by the fall - I am not who God says I am.)*

5:6 By ignoring the presence of even a small amount of leaven the whole lump of dough will soon be permeated; thus all ground for boasting in how good things seemed to have been will be lost. *(See my Notes on Luke 22:1 The Pascha & The Unleavened Bread)*

5:7 Because Christ our Paschal Lamb has already been sacrificed once and for all, the old leaven of sin-consciousness, which was upheld by the law, has already been thoroughly removed. On that basis alone are you able to now permanently rid yourselves of the old leaven mindset of tolerating sin, which was our reasoning under the law-system. *(We are talking a brand new language: the new covenant is the new lump of dough without a trace of the leaven of the old system that was done away with in Christ. A mindset introduced and sustained by the law. In the very repetition of these ritual sacrifices the awareness of guilt is reinforced rather than removed. [Hebrews 10:3] The testimony of God is my only persuasion concerning you: Jesus Christ died your death on the cross. I can see you in no other light. I have determined to know nothing in you except Jesus Christ and him crucified. [1 Corinthians 2:2]*

Hebrews 9:11-12 says, But now Christ has made his public appearance as High Priest of a perfect tabernacle. The good things that were predicted have arrived. This new tabernacle does not derive from its shadow type, the previous man-made one. It is the reality. (The restoration of God's original dwelling place in human life is again revealed.) As High Priest, his permission to enter the Holy Place was not secured by the blood of beasts. By his own blood he obtained access on behalf of the human race. Only one act was needed for him to enter the most sacred place of grace and there to institute a ransom of perpetual consequence.

[The perfection of the redemption he secured needs no further sacrifice. There are no outstanding debts; there is nothing we need do to add weight to what he has accomplished once and for all. The only possible priesthood activity we can now engage in is to continually bring a sacrifice of the fruit of our lips, giving thanks to his Name; no blood, just fruit, even our acts of self-sacrifice, giving of time and money, etcetera are all just the fruit of our constant gratitude.])

5:8 Our daily life is now the extension of the Passover celebration; feasting on sustained innocence. The old sin conscious-system, the leaven-mind set *(always anticipating and tolerating sin),* **is replaced with an understanding of our unleavened innocence, just like when a diamond is [1]scrutinized in the rays of the sun to confirm its flawless integrity.** *(The word, [1]elikrineia, translates as scrutinized in the rays of the sun.)*

5:9 When I wrote to you about not associating with fornicators,

5:10 I certainly did not mean that you should distance yourself from the people of the world. If you had to avoid contact with the immoral, the greedy, the thieves, and the idol worshippers *[those worshipping a distorted image of themselves],* **then you would have to leave the planet.**

5:11 What I am saying is that anyone who acts like a brother while he continues his old typical lifestyle of fornication, greed, idolatry, abusing people, drunkenness, and stealing is obviously not sitting around the same table of fellowship with you.

5:12 It is none of my business to speak about the behavior of those outside the ekklesia-church; we are giving a responsible opinion regarding the behavior of those within our ranks.

5:13 We know God's judgment regarding the world [*the cross of Christ brought closure to every inferior reference*]; but in this case I am saying that you have to deal decisively with the troublemakers in your midst. *(The sinners were attracted to Jesus not because he introduced a compromised set of rules; something like, it's all right to sin just don't get caught or, try and do it less. Instead, he revealed in his person the mirror-reflection of their true origin, their original identity and the integrity of their authentic innocence.*

They knew that the lie they lived as their identity had no power against the resonance of their own conscience. Jesus didn't say to the prostitute, Go and sin less, he said to her, Go and sin no more. Jesus knew something about the life of our design that we had lost sight of. What he revealed, he also redeemed.)

6:1 It alarms me that you even consider to have law-people decide on disputes within your fellowship, while these so-called judges have no clue of the basis of our righteousness in Christ. (*Now keep Paul's introduction in mind from 1 Corinthians 1:2, I address this writing to the ekklesia of God in Corinth. You have been restored to the harmony of your original design; made holy in Christ Jesus; no wonder then that you are surnamed saints. His name relates us to one another in a global family. See Revelation 14:10 and 1 Corinthians 1:30.*)

6:2 Having discovered how thoroughly God sanctified us in Christ [*1 Corinthians 1:30*], we now represent the principle of righteous judgment wherewith the whole world is to be judged; how can we possibly shrink from deciding a trivial matters within our own ranks?

6:3 If the judgment we are entrusted with extends even into the spiritual realm where we are to judge celestial messengers, how much more relevant is our judgment now in deciding on day-to-day matters.

6:4 Since you are fully competent to judge such matters in the light of the gospel of grace, why bother to involve people who judge according to the standards of this world?

6:5 I mean this is most embarrassing. Are you expecting more justice from the world than from your own family? Is there not even one wise person in your midst that is able to settle in-house disputes?

6:6 Do you see how foolish it would be for friends to sue one another and reduce justice to a system that is founded in unbelief. (*A system based on the law of works and personal performance and not faith in the finished work of the cross.*)

6:7 Even if one wins the case, it is a defeat for the ekklesia. Why not suffer wrong; it is a far greater victory if you rather be cheated and accept it joyfully, than what it would be to fight for the right to prove your point.

6:8 By allowing the wisdom of this world to be your judge nothing will change; the injustice and fraud will merely continue to spread like cancer in your ranks.

6:9 To live [1]out of sync with one another does not mirror your participation as fellow-heirs in God's kingdom. The entire business of abusing people is foreign to our design and does not become you. Why live a [2]lie? Seeing people as [3]sex objects for sale, is just another form of [4]idolatry. [5]Having a secret lover is the same deception. Why pretend that you're someone you're not, by deceitfully [6]dressing up [*like an actor playing a role*] in wearing fine, royal clothing, only to [7]exploit others financially or sexually.

(*[1] The word ἄδικος [1]adikos, from a, negative and δίκη dike, suggesting to be judged equal; it implies the idea of two parties finding likeness in each other - the stem for the word, righteousness, dikaiosune - where Dike reminds of the Greek goddess of Justice by the same name, typically portrayed holding a scale of balances in her hand. Thus - out of sync with another.*

[2] The word, πλανάω [2]planaō, from πλάνη deceit - to live a lie.

[3] The word πόρνος [3]pornos from πέρνημι pernēmi means to sell as merchandize [especially in the porn/sex-industry].

*[4] The word for idolatry, ειδωλολατραι [4]**eidōolotarai**, points to exactly what mankind lost in the garden - their awareness of the mirror image and likeness of Elohim. Idolatry represents mankind's futile search for a substitute image of their own making. [See Acts 17:29]*

*[5] The word, μοιχός [5]**moichos**, adultery - having a secret lover.*

*[6] The word, [6]**malakos** fine clothing, is again a word only used here, and in two references which both point to the contrasting garments of John the Baptist. See Matthew 11:8 and Luke 7:25 The apparel of John the Baptist was certainly not the latest, fine fashion, worn in a king's palace or any place representing the opulence of someone's importance and success.*

*[7] Then, the word, [7]**arsenokoites** is a word only Paul uses in the NT, and in the context of this statement recorded in verses 9 and 10, he is not speaking about homosexuality, but sexual exploitation. The word arsenokoitai shows up in only two different verses in the bible, but it was not translated to mean homosexual until 1946.)*

6:10 The list continues, people [1]who lust after money are dangerous. They think nothing of [2]cheating in business, *[or marriage for that matter].* **They have done it for so long that it has become an [3]addiction. It's like being a chronic drinker. Then there are those who would typically hurl [4]abusive insults - injuring another's reputation by denigrating. They are like [5]predators out on the hunt. These things are not reflecting the kingdom of God-society at all.**

*([1] The word, κλέπτης [1]**kleptes**, is where our English word, kleptomaniac derives from.*

*[2] Also the word πλεονέκτης [2]**pleonektes** someone whose greed is never satisfied. [See 1 Corinthians 5:10-11]*

*[3] Then the word, μέθυσος [3]**methusos** a chronic drinker - addicted to strong drink.*

*[4] The word, λοίδορος [4]**loidoros** means abusive language.*

*[5] The word ἅρπαξ [5]**harpax** means a ravenous predator. See Rev 17:18 The woman you saw is the great city which dominated the kings of the earth. [The Prostitute city-society of Babylon stands in contrast to the Bride of Christ as the New Jerusalem. Just like Babylon is not a city in the symbolic language of Revelation, it is a fallen, distorted-mindset-society; so the New Jerusalem is not a city but the redeemed society of mankind. The Bride of Christ.])*

6:11 Some of you can relate to that lifestyle, but look at you now. You have been cleansed, restored to total harmony *[holiness]* **and made righteous. The name of the Lord Jesus declares your salvation; the Spirit of our God realizes salvation in you.** *(1 Corinthians 1:30, 1 Corinthians 2:2. Also Ephesians 4:22,23, ... Just like an actor who wore a cloak for a specific role he had to interpret; the fake identity is no longer relevant.)*

6:12 I am free to do what I want, but if what I do is inappropriate, I refrain from doing it and will not be snared by sudden notions.

6:13 Your appetite for food and sex does not define you. Your life is tailor-made for God; you fit him like a glove; he fulfills your deepest longings. *(You know the old saying, First you eat to live, and then you live to eat? Well, it may be true that the body is only a temporary thing, but that's no excuse for stuffing your body with food, or indulging it with sex. Since the Master honors you with a body, honor him with your body. — The Message. But you cannot say that our physical body was made for sexual promiscuity; it was made for God, and God is the answer to our deepest longings. — Phillips.)*

6:14 God reveals in dramatic fashion the value he places on the human body by our joint resurrection with Jesus from the dead. *(Faith sees us joined in his death and alive with him in his resurrection. It is plain for all to see that death lost its dominion over Christ in his resurrection; he need not ever die again to prove a further point [Romans 6:8, 9].)*

6:15 This means that your bodies are co-members of his; which makes it absurd to even consider engaging his body in sexual promiscuity.

6:16 Sex involves so much more than two bodies joining together; Scripture speaks of a sacred union of two lives becoming one. How can we reduce this sacred union to harlotry? *(There's more to sex than mere skin on skin. Sex is as much spiritual mystery as physical fact. — The Message.)*

6:17 In our union with him we are one spirit with the Lord.

6:18 Flee fornication. Every sexual sin is a violation of the sacredness of the human body and scars the conscience of the individual like no other sin does. *(The best way to escape temptation is to remember who you are.)*

6:19 Do you not realize that your body by design is the sacred shrine of the Spirit of God, echoing within you. You are not the sole owner of your life.

6:20 You are bought and paid for. All of you are his. Live your life conscious of how irreplaceably priceless you are. You host God in your skin. *(See 1 Peter 1:18 It is clear to see that you were ransomed from the futile, fallen mindset that you inherited from your fathers, not by the currency of your own labor, represented by the fluctuating values of gold and silver, and the economy of your religious efforts; 1 Peter 1:19 but you were redeemed with the priceless blood of Christ; he is the ultimate sacrifice; spotless and without blemish. He completes the prophetic picture. (In him God speaks the most radical scapegoat language of the law of judgment, and brings final closure to a dead and redundant system. In Psalm 40:6,7, it is clearly stated that God does not require sacrifices or offerings. Jesus is the Lamb of God.) See rest of Mirror Commentary 1 Peter 1:19-21.*

Also Matthew 13:44; Hebrews 6:16,17.)

7:1 In your writing to me you asked questions about marriage.

7:2 *(The fact that I am not married does not mean that I am against marriage.)* Where a man is attached to his wife and she to him they are sexually secure.

7:3 Marriage provides the ideal environment for both husband and wife to mutually esteem one another.

7:4 The wife belongs to her husband and he belongs to her. Their bodies are no longer their own.

7:5 By mutual agreement they may decide to abstain from physical contact for a specific period of time for prayer and fasting; not for prolonged times since this might give occasion for temptation.

7:6 I am not making rules about marriage; this is simply my advice to you in response to your request.

7:7 I could recommend my own life to everyone; yet I am convinced that life is a gift whether you are single or married.

7:8 My advice to the unmarried as well as to those who have lost their partner: it might be to your best interest to remain single even as I am.

7:9 Again, I am not laying down a law; much rather face the challenges of marriage than be consumed with desire.

7:10 Concerning your questions about divorce, I am strongly opposed to the idea; and this is not merely my advice, this is the Lord's instruction.

7:11 If the wife leaves her husband she is not to get re-married; her only option would be to be reconciled to her husband. In that case the husband may not resist her.

7:12 The brother who asked about his unbelieving wife: my advice is to remain committed to her as long as she is prepared to remain with you. *(Unbelief: not believing the truth about themselves as revealed in the gospel of the grace of God [1 Corinthians 1:30].)*

7:13 The same goes for the lady with the unbelieving husband; if he is pleased to be with you then you have no reason to divorce him.

7:14 In principle the unbelieving husband is sanctified by his wife's faith, and the unbelieving wife, by her husband's faith. If that was not true then your children would be contaminated by the unbelieving partner; yet they are pure because of the one parent's faith. The individual's faith blesses the whole family. *(Faith does not exclude; God's faith includes.)*

7:15 Yet if the unbelieving partner desires to divorce, then let it be. Pursue peace rather than forced friendship.

7:16 To fake friendship is not worth it; not even for the sake of possibly winning your partner to the Lord.

7:17 God dealt with each one of us uniquely and individually and connected with us regardless of our circumstances. He defines and completes your life, not your partner or lack of one. I am not just saying this in response to your questions about your specific challenges; I am equally persuaded about this in principle in all the churches.

7:18 Circumcision or the lack of it does not [1]define you. In Christ your Jewish or Gentile heritage is irrelevant and can never again [1]label you. *(The word, [1]**kaleō**, means to identify by name; to surname.)*

7:19 You couldn't keep the commandments anyway, whether you were circumcised or not. *(So if circumcision did not contribute anything while you were seeking to be justified under the law, how can it possibly now advantage you in your understanding of righteousness by faith?)*

7:20 You are not what your career or job description say you are.

7:21 Even if you were the lowest ranked slave before, it makes no difference to the dignity of your true identity. I am not saying that you should not go for promotion; by all means take it if it comes your way. The point that I am making is that in Christ you are equally free, whether you are a slave or free in society, a boss or an employee.

7:22 Society might label you as a slave, but Christ reveals how free you really are. Then again you might be a so-called, free person in society but in Christ you are a bond slave.

7:23 You are not for sale. The ransom God paid for your freedom now binds you to the lordship of his love. The sign over your life says, SOLD. *(You are not for sale to the religious system of the law of works and performance based approval.)*

7:24 We belong to the same [1]household. Every individual originates from God and is [2]surnamed in him; this is our true lineage, [3]abide herein without compromise. *([1]Brothers, **adelphos**, meaning from the same womb. The word, [2]**kaleō**, means to surname, and [3]**para**, is a Preposition indicating close proximity, a thing proceeding from a sphere of influence, with a suggestion of union of place of residence, to have sprung from its author and giver, originating from, denoting the point from which an action originates, intimate connection.)*

7:25 With regards to your question whether it was proper that the young unmarried people refrain from marriage because of the times we are facing, I have no specific direction from the Lord, but again you can trust my good advice. By the mercy of God I personally have no plans to get married.

7:26 Especially in these stressful times I would say that it is a good thing to remain single and unattached.

7:27 So my advice is, if you are already in a relationship with someone, don't quit; and if you are unattached, don't get involved.

7:28 It is certainly not wrong to get married. All I am saying is that marriage brings extra challenges in already difficult times.

7:29 The urgency of these times might demand mutual sacrifices from those who are married, such as sacrificing their time together for other priorities.

7:30 Even our most personal space for grief or joy is invaded; that leaves you with no time to indulge in your own interests and possessions. If you are in the process of buying something, buy as if you will never own it.

7:31 Do not lean too hard upon the fragile [economic] structures of this world; they are here today and gone tomorrow.

7:32 In my opinion the unmarried person lives an uncomplicated life; fully devoted to the Lord without any distractions;

7:33 while the married person is confronted with all the typical domestic challenges absorbing his attention in his commitment to his wife and her delights and demands.

7:34 The same goes for the ladies; the unmarried woman can give her undivided attention to the Lord without any emotional or physical marital obligations.

7:35 I really have your focused devotion to the Lord at heart and desire for you to live a beautiful life without any distractions that could possibly snare you.

7:36 If a man is engaged to a young girl and feels that he doesn't want to wait until she is older before they marry, let them go ahead and marry, there is nothing wrong with that.

7:37 Yet if he decides to rather wait, he is free to do as he has determined in his heart.

7:38 My personal conviction is to remain single, but I am not at all against marriage.

7:39 As long as the husband is alive, his wife is bound by law to remain with him; if he dies, then obviously she is free to marry another as she is led by the Lord.

7:40 Of course in my opinion she should not marry again.

(Obviously Paul's advice is typically that of a bachelor who has to feel justified in his decision to remain single. Lydia and I are now together for more than 40 years and certainly do not find our commitment to one another a distraction from the Lord at all. On the contrary it is the most recommendable, wonderful life. August, 2014)

Paul addresses the same issues he writes about here in Chapters 7 and 8 in his letter to Timothy, warning him against those who forbid marriage and enjoin abstinence from foods which God created to be received with thanksgiving by those who believe and know the truth. For everything created by God is good, and nothing is to be rejected if it is received with thanksgiving. [1 Timothy 4:3, 4] These issues were obviously controversial at the time.

8:1 You have also asked me questions about whether believers are free to eat food offered to idols. We are free to hold to our own convictions about what to eat and what not to eat; but ultimately it is not about who wins the diet debate, but about sincerely loving people.

8:2 Let love define your convictions and not mere head knowledge.

8:3 Loving God *[and your fellow human]* **is so easy when you understand that he knows you. Let God's knowledge of you inspire your love for him and your fellow human.**

8:4 By making a fuss about eating food offered to idols gives idols undue prominence; they are nothing so why make something out of nothing. We know that there is only one God and that he has no competition.

8:5 There is a lot of talk about other gods and demonic powers operating on earth as well as in the heavenly realm; obviously they seem to be empowered by people's belief in them and conversation about them; so there seem to be many gods lording it over people.

8:6 This does not make them competition to God; we know that there is only one God, the Father, who is the Creator of all things and for whom we live; and there is only one Lord, Jesus Christ, through whom all things were created and through whom we live. All things exist because of him; we owe our very being to him. He alone gives context and reference to our lives.

8:7 However not everyone realizes this; there are some believers who are convinced that idols are real, so for them to hear that we say that it's okay to eat food offered to idols presents a massive problem to their conscience.

8:8 Your diet preference certainly does not improve your standing before God; whether you eat meat or not.

8:9 The point is not about how justified you feel in your freedom to eat what you like, but how considerate you are not to be a stumbling block to someone else.

8:10 If someone who looks up to you as an example sees you eat at a banquet in a temple where the meat has obviously been sacrificed to idols, your liberty might give occasion for this person to be snared into idol worship.

8:11 So your superior knowledge is actually causing the ruin of someone for whom Christ died. *(You are influencing someone to exchange their new found* *belief in the sacrifice of Christ, to become involved again in an outdated and redundant system of Jewish laws and in pagan worship in the sacrifice of animals.)*

8:12 You might think you have a valid argument to justify your position, but in the process you are beating your brother's conscience black-and-blue without realizing that you are injuring the cause of Christ.

8:13 I will much rather abstain from eating meat altogether than run the risk of offending my brother.

9:1-6 There seems to be different criteria whereby our ministries are judged; some Apostles seem to have liberties that others don't; in terms of their diets, financial benefits, plus the luxury to be accompanied by their wives. Would the brothers of Jesus and Kefas be rated higher than Barnabas and I amongst you? What would you say qualifies my commission to you? The fact that I have had a face-to-face encounter with our Master Jesus Christ followed by the impact and fruit of my ministry to you can surely not count against me?

9:7 Imagine a soldier goes to war at his own expense. I mean how absurd. Yet it is almost taken for granted that Barnabas and I have to earn our own living not to burden the very people we established and daily feed in their faith.

9:8 Anyone who plants a vineyard eats its fruit for free; the shepherd likewise is not expected to pay for a drink of milk.

9:9 Or is this just my own idea? If you insist on scriptural evidence, even the law of Moses says that the bull's treading out the grain shall not be muzzled.

9:10 If God so cares for the oxen imagine how much more he cares for you. Moses certainly had more than oxen in mind in writing this; the farmer would be wasting his time plowing his field without participating in the harvest. While the oxen were still treading out the corn the farmer joyfully anticipates the bread.

9:11 Spiritual seed also translates into a material harvest.

9:12 While others enjoy this privilege why would it seem wrong that we share the same? We have not taken any advantage of you; we would rather suffer lack than insisting on our rights and in the process cause you to be distracted from the gospel of Christ.

9:13 It is common knowledge that the people engaged in temple ministry eat what is sacrificed there.

9:14 The same principle goes for those who proclaim the Gospel; and this is not just someone's good idea it is endorsed by the Lord.

9:15 The reason for my writing about these issues is not to bring you under any kind of obligation; on the contrary, I want to be very clear about this, the fact that I do things differently by not expecting anyone to pay me for my ministry is to emphasize my urgency to remove any possible excuse from anyone's mind that I might have ulterior motives. I am dead serious about this Gospel.

9:16 I live to preach; it consumes my total being. Your money is not going to make any difference since this Gospel has my arm twisted and locked behind my back. [anagkē] In fact, my life would be reduced to utter misery if it were not possible for me to preach the Good News.

9:17 If this was a mere career choice, then surely you could hire or fire me. But I am not for sale; I am employed by the economy of persuasion.

9:18 So what's in it for me, you may ask? The pleasure of declaring the Gospel of Christ at no expense is priceless. No, I am not cheating anyone or myself by foregoing the rights I might have as a preacher.

9:19 So in a sense I am free from everyone's expectation or management; yet I have voluntarily enslaved myself to all people. This beats any other motivation to influence people.

9:20 I am like a Jew to the Jew to win them; I am disguised as a legalist to win those stuck under the law.

9:21 To the Gentiles who have no regard for Jewish sentiment, I became like one without any obligation to Jewish laws to win them. Don't get me wrong; I am not sinning to identify with the sinners. I am in the law of Christ. *(The agapē law.)*

9:22 I am so persuaded about every person's inclusion in Christ that I desire to be everything I need to be in order to win everyone's understanding of their union with Christ. I do not present myself as super strong to the weak, but rather expose myself to their weakness in order to win them. I do not distance myself from anyone. My mission is to be exactly what is required of me in every possible situation to awaken every kind of person, whoever they are, to own their salvation. I have no other agenda. *(Traditionally translated, in order to save some; I do not believe that this is what Paul is saying here. The word, ¹tis, can also suggest every single kind.)*

9:23 The gospel explains my lifestyle; it is so much more than a pulpit ministry to me. My life is inseparably joined to you in the fellowship of the Good News.

9:24 Athletes run a race to win; their aim is to receive the prize not just to compete. This is why I preach, to persuade you and not just to entertain you. *(A soccer player can do magic with his footwork and ball skills, but it is no good if he cannot take the gap and score the goal.)*

9:25 The athlete knows how to draw from focused inner strength in order to win the crown; for them all their effort translates into a mere moment celebrated by a fading wreath of honor. For us to win your faith is of imperishable value.

9:26 I run with certain victory in my every step. I am not shadow boxing when I preach.

9:27 I deliberately compare myself to the sacrifice and dedication of a champion athlete; in similar fashion I would pummel my body and subdue it. I would deny myself many things in my pursuit to win your faith so that you will not have any excuse to reject my message. I want you, not your money. *(Paul is not saying this because he is worried about God's approval. It is his audience's approval that he is after: becoming all things to all types of people in order to win every single one of them. 1 Corinthians 9:12, we would rather suffer lack than insisting on our rights and in the process cause you to be distracted from the gospel of Christ. [See also Paul's urgency in Colossians 1:25-28].)*

10:1 Now remember how the people of Israel were all delivered from slavery; the cloud of God's presence, protection, and provision included everyone equally. They were all miraculously led through the Red Sea on dry land and witnessed how their oppressors were completely defeated. *(These Egyptians whom you see today you will never see again. [Exodus 14:13]. Pharaoh was not to be blamed for their forty-year detour in the desert.)*

10:2 The cloud and sea was a type of baptism that they underwent to identify with the leadership of Moses. *(This was all a prophetic picture of Christ leading us out of bondage and slavery in his death and resurrection.)*

10:3 All of them daily partook of the same miraculous food.

10:4 They drank the same supernatural water from the Rock that accompanied them in all their travels; the Rock was the Messiah. *(Their experience was saturated in spirit dimension and the miraculous, yet they died through unbelief. The supernatural is not proof of faith. Their unbelief was rooted in their believing a lie about themselves. [Numbers 13:33]. Yet Christ was there even in their unbelief, the Rock accompanied them.)*

10:5 The vast majority of them completely disappointed God and died in the desert. *(Israel never entered into their inheritance. The desert was not their destiny. Hebrews 4:1 admonishes, What a foolish thing it would be for us if we should now fail in a similar fashion to enter into the full consequences of our redemption. And in Hebrews 4:6, They failed because of unbelief; they underestimated their deliverance and believed a lie about themselves; and in Hebrews 2:3, No one can afford to underestimate and be blasé about this final message, a salvation of such magnificent proportions. There is no alternative escape. Salvation as it is articulated in Christ is the message that God spoke from the beginning, and it was confirmed again and again by those who heard him. We cannot afford to delay the promise to a future event yet again.)*

10:6 We are clearly reminded not to follow their example; instead of feasting on God's merciful provision they had a craving appetite for evil.

10:7 Their idolatry snared them further. They were infatuated with a distorted pattern of themselves. *(This all started with them believing a lie about themselves [Numbers 13:33]. This was the same sin that snared Eve in paradise.)*

10:8 They became completely disoriented and indulged in sexual sins which killed countless thousands of them. *(What a foolish alternative to embracing and possessing the promise: Jesus redeemed the life of our design.)*

10:9 Remember also how Israel spoke against God and Moses and were snared by their own unbelief, suspiciously scrutinizing the Messiah who is the promise of God. *(They blamed God for what they brought upon themselves. [See Numbers 13:33 and Numbers 21:5, 6, 8] Even though God mercifully provided for them, they remained unfulfilled in their own miserable unbelief. Grumbling sets up the stage for the enemy to snare you. God's mercy prevailed in spite of their sins and here we see another dramatic prophetic picture of the judgment that was our due, taken by the scapegoat, Jesus. [John 3:14, 15; Galatians 3:13; see notes in Mirror Translation on 2 Corinthians 5:21]. Jesus says in John 12:32, When I am lifted up [on the cross], I will draw all of mankind and every definition of judgment unto me.)*

10:10 Grumbling is a killer.

10:11 Now these prophetic pictures were written to alert us to the fact that they pointed to what we are now witnessing in the gospel; we are confronted with the completeness of everything that was promised.

10:12 If you reckon that you have it altogether, make sure that you are standing strong *[in your true identity]* when temptation strikes. How foolish it would be for us to now fall into the same unbelief that killed Israel. *(They believed a lie about themselves [Numbers 13:33].)*

10:13 Your situation is not unique. Every human life faces contradictions. Here is the Good News: God believes in your freedom. He has made it possible for you to triumph in every situation that you will ever encounter.

10:14 My [1]dearly loved friends. Escape into his image and likeness in you where the [2]distorted image *[[2]idolatry]* loses its attraction. *(Dearly loved friends, translated as [1]agapētos; to know the agapē love of God is to know our true identity. The word, agapaō, comes from agō, meaning to lead as a shepherd guides his sheep, and paō, to rest, like in Psalm 23, he leads me beside still waters where my soul is restored; by the waters of reflection my soul remembers who I am. Now I can face the valley of the shadow of death and fear no evil.)*

10:15 I appeal to your common sense. Do not underestimate what I am saying to you.

10:16 When we share a meal together we declare our association in Christ. Every time we drink from the same cup, we communicate the language of the covenant of grace, which is what our fellowship is all about. The wine we drink is our participation in what the blood of Christ represents. The bread we break celebrates our participation in the incarnation. The prophetic promise became flesh in his person; we are jointly declaring that in the revelation of our inclusion in his death and resurrection we are now the visible body of Christ. *(You know that you were ransomed from the futile ways inherited from your fathers, not with perishable things such as silver or gold, but with the precious blood of Christ, like that of a lamb without blemish or spot [1 Peter 1:18, 19]. He redeemed our original value and transparent innocence.)*

10:17 The single loaf of bread that we all partake of represents the fact that although there are many of us, there is only one Christ. By eating together from that one bread we are declaring that we are one body in Christ and that he is incarnated in each one of us. *(Our many-ness becomes one-ness; Christ doesn't become fragmented in us. Rather, we become unified in him. — The Message.)*

10:18 Let us consider the context of the prophetic type of the sacrificial system of Israel; those who ate the sacrificed animals were partners in the same altar.

10:19 Now by this I am not saying that there is any magical power in a sacrifice made to an idol; an idol is nothing more than a mere figment of the imagination. The meat offered to an idol is just meat like any other barbecue.

10:20 The difference between Israel and the Gentile nations is in the prophetic type that Israel's sacrifices pointed to; a sacrifice offered to demons points to nothing and holds no advantage to you. I mean why would you associate with anything that reduces you to less than what you are. *(The only significance in the Jewish sacrificial system was in its pointing to the Messiah; both the promise and the person of the Messiah points to the redemption of mankind's original identity and innocence.)*

10:21 You cannot celebrate the Lord in one meal and then devote yourselves to pagan worship the next time you eat. Every time you drink and eat you [1]co-echo your union in Christ. *(In our every communion, even in our daily meals, we co-echo I am. To partake comes from [1]metechō; with meta meaning together with, and echō meaning to echo what God spoke to us in Christ; like the word metanous, NOT repentance [re-penance]; but to join thoughts about something; to co-know with God; to agree with God about you.)*

10:22 God is not in a tug of war with demons or our obsession with religious rituals. He has no competition. He is I am. *(Even the Jews, who continued their sacrificial rituals after Christ was sacrificed as God's Passover Lamb, were presenting their offerings to pagan gods and not to God. There remains no further spiritual relevance in the practice of Jewish rituals, including the Sabbaths and the annual feasts.)*

10:23 Everything is [1]endorsed in I am. Everything originates and [2]concludes in I am. Now that the prophetic picture is completed in Christ, Jewish rituals can no longer be [3]accommodated under the same roof. Christ is the relevance, not the historic ritual. *(Everything begins in I am. This comes from the Greek, exesti, from [1]exousia, which is ek + eimi. The word ek always denotes origin and eimi, I am. This word is often translated as authority, or in this case, endorsed; traditional translations read, everything is lawful. The word, [2]sumpherō, means to bear together, to conclude. The image and likeness of God revealed and redeemed in human form is the substance of the prophetic picture. The word, [3]oikodomē, comes from oikos, meaning dwelling or family and domē, meaning roof. Paul is urging the ekklesia to find their fellowship in the revelation of Christ and not in a mixture of Jewish and pagan religious rituals.)*

10:24 Even though I am free in my own persuasion, I do not pursue my freedom at someone else's expense. So even though we might feel perfectly justified in our own convictions, let each one of us consider how to benefit one another instead. *(The good news of what happened to every single person in Christ is all that matters.)*

10:25 Do not think twice about eating meat bought from the local market; why bother to ask questions about whether or not it was sacrificed at a Jewish or heathen temple. Such questions are completely irrelevant. To continue to live in a right or wrong consciousness is to injure yourself and others.

10:26 In Psalm 24:1, David declares categorically that the earth is the Lord's and the fullness thereof. *(That should settle your conscience once and* *for all about diet debates. In mankind's mind an animal is sacrificed to a demon or deity of choice but the Creator owns everything anyway and he needs no one's permission to endorse his ownership, neither is he influenced by what a person believes.)*

10:27 Should you get a personal invitation to a banquet hosted by unbelievers and you desire to go, then be at liberty to eat whatever they prepare. Please do not embarrass them by asking sensitive questions about whether the food was sacrificed to idols or not. Leave your religious sentiment behind and enjoy the feast.

10:28 However if someone specifically mentions to you that the meat was indeed sacrificed to idols, then for that person's conscience sake rather refrain from eating the item in question in order to avoid giving the impression that you approve of idol worship.

10:29 No, I am not compromising my freedom by being sensitive to someone else's conscience. *(But, except for these special cases, I'm not going to walk around on eggshells worrying about what small-minded people might say; I'm going to stride free and easy, knowing what our large-minded Master has already said. — The Message.)*

10:30 Grace sets the pace in my conscience, not people's suspicious scrutiny. Every meal to me is a celebration of what grace reveals.

10:31 Live your life overwhelmed by God's [1]opinion of you. Your eating and drinking is certainly a constant reminder that you are his glory. Every meal proclaims the fact that the life of your design is redeemed again in Christ; salute life. *([1]Glory, doxa from dokeō, a good opinion.)*

10:32 So live your life in freedom and wisdom. Thus the Jews, the Gentiles and the ekklesia will all witness the attraction of your life without taking any offense.

10:33 I am so persuaded about every person's inclusion in Christ that I desire to be everything I need to be in order to win everyone's understanding of their union with Christ; my mission is to be exactly what is required of me in every possible situation to awaken every kind of person, whoever they are, to own their salvation. I have no other agenda. *(See 1 Corinthians 9:22.)*

11:1 Mirror me as I mirror Christ. *(Jesus is not an example for us but of us.)*

11:2 I commend you for giving such attention to detail concerning the heart of the gospel that I communicate.

11: 3-17 *(I did not translate 1 Corinthians 11:3-17 since my opinion is that they are certainly not in the context of the gospel that Paul preached. Paul understood that when Jesus died, all died; he therefore no longer knew people from a human point of view [see 2 Corinthians 5:14,16]. He declares in Galatians 3:28 [RSV], There is neither Jew nor Greek, there is neither slave nor free, there is neither male nor female; for you are all one in Christ Jesus. These thoughts seem to have been added by a scribe to justify the tradition of the day where women had to show their submission to their husbands by wearing a head covering. Our eldest son, Renaldo, once attended a church with Lydia and I, where the women wore head coverings. One of the ladies brought a napkin and placed it on Lydia's head. Renaldo started giggling and when I asked him what was so funny, he said, Dad, this is a crazy church, women are not allowed to show their hair but it's okay to show their breasts. All around us there were mothers feeding their babies. This is Africa, lol!)*

11:18 My priority concern is that you are divided into different and distracting opinions when you gather as a fellowship. Our focus is the nitty-gritty essence of the gospel. I believe in oneness not divisions.

11:19 The only advantage of any controversy is that the authentic becomes even more apparent in you.

11:20 What I heard is most disturbing: when you get together for a fellowship meal, instead of celebrating what the Lord's communion introduced,

11:21 some behave like gluttons while others are starving; then there are those who get wasted on the wine.

11:22 If you want to over indulge then do so in the privacy of your own homes. Why despise the assembly and insult the poor in the process. This is most disgusting. I am disappointed in you.

11:23 Let me remind you then what we are actually celebrating in our fellowship meal: The night in which the Lord Jesus was betrayed, he took bread

11:24 and gave thanks; breaking the bread into portions, he said, [1]Realize your association with my death, every time you eat, remember my body that was broken for you. *(Meaning [1]take, grasp, lambanō, to take what is one's own, to associate with oneself.)*

11:25 He did exactly the same with the cup after supper and said, This cup holds the wine of the New Covenant in my blood; you celebrate me every time you drink [1]with this understanding. *(From now on our meals are meaningful. We celebrate the fact that the incarnation reveals our redemption; the promise became a person. The word, [1]αναμνησιν ana, upwards, and mnesin, remembrance - to bring something from memory into the here and now!*

He redeemed our original value, identity, and innocence; he died our death and defines the life we now live. He fulfills the theme of Scripture: the sufferings of the Messiah and the subsequent glory. [1 Peter 1:10, 11].)

11:26 Your every meal makes the ¹mandate of his ²coming relevant and communicates the meaning of the New Covenant. *(Whether you eat or drink, you are declaring your joint inclusion in his death and resurrection, confirming your redeemed innocence. Some translations read, until I come... The word translated until is, ¹**achri**, from **akmen**, which means extremity, conclusion, the present time; Jesus is the conclusion of prophetic time. The word ²**erchomai**, to come is in the Aorist Subjunctive Mood, **elthē**, which is similar to the Optative expressing a wish. The Mood of the Greek verb expresses the mode in which the idea of the verb is employed. Thus, we are communicating the desire to have all people realize the meaning of the New Covenant. See 2 Peter 1:19 For us the appearance of the Messiah is no longer a future promise but a fulfilled reality. Now it is your turn to have more than a second-hand, hearsay testimony. Take my word as one would take a lamp at night; the day is about to dawn for you in your own understanding. When the Morning Star appears, you no longer need the lamp; this will happen shortly on the horizon of your own hearts.)*

11:27 So whoever does not value the meaning of the bread and the wine, keep themselves in condemnation.

11:28 To see oneself associated in Christ's death and declared innocent in his blood is the only worthy manner in which to examine one's own life in the context of the new covenant meal. *(Self examination according to the Old Covenant, i.e. Deuteronomy 28 is no longer relevant. Examine yourselves to see whether you are holding to the faith, test yourselves, do you not realize that Jesus Christ is within you. [2 Corinthians 13:5 — RSV.])*

11:29 Anyone who partakes of this meal in an indifferent manner, either because of religious sentiment or merely being blasé about the meaning of the meal, eats and drinks judgment upon themselves. The human body of Jesus represents the judgment of every single human life; to fail to acknowledge this is to deliberately exclude yourself from the blessing of the New Covenant. *(Isaiah 53:3-8, He was despised and rejected by men; a man of sorrows, and acquainted with grief, and we esteemed him not. Surely he has borne our griefs and carried our sorrows; yet we esteemed him stricken, smitten by God, and afflicted. But he was wounded by our transgressions, he was bruised by our iniquities; upon him was the chastisement that made us whole, and with his stripes we are healed. All we like sheep have gone astray; we have turned everyone to his own way; and the Lord has laid on him the iniquity of us all. Like a lamb that is led to the slaughter, and like a sheep that before its shearers is dumb, so he opened not his mouth. By oppression and judgment he was taken away; and as for his generation, who considered that he was cut off out of the land of the living, stricken by the transgression of my people? [RSV] No one can afford to underestimate what happened to us on the cross. To discern the Lord's body is to grasp what God's faith saw when Jesus died.)*

11:30 This is the reason why many of you are suffering unnecessarily with weaknesses and illnesses, and many have already died.

11:31 By judging that we indeed co-died in his death we are free from any kind of judgment. *(John 5:22, The Father judges no one, but has given all judgment to the Son. [RSV] John 12:31-33, Now is the judgment of this world, now shall the ruler of this world be cast out; and I, when I am lifted up from the earth, will draw all judgment to myself. He said this to show by what death he was to die.)*

11:32 By discerning the broken body of Christ we can only conclude that he suffered our brokenness and distortion. This is the instruction of the Lord; what foolishness it would be to continue to place yourself and the rest of the world under judgment when Jesus already took all judgment upon himself.

11:33 So when you come together to eat the covenant meal, embrace one another with utmost courtesy;

11:34 there is no point in getting together to see who can eat or drink the most. Eat at home if you are hungry; why turn a celebration into condemnation? *(Our feast celebrates the success of the cross and has nothing in common with a pagan banquet.*

The prophetic picture of the table was most significant. Every Sabbath the priests were to place fresh bread on the table in the sanctuary. It was called Showbread; in Hebrew, לחם הפנים lechem haPānīm, literally: Face-bread; Bread of the Presence. The Hebrew word for presence means face to face. While Jesus spoke to the two disciples on their way to Emmaus in Luke 24, they did not recognize him, even though their hearts ignited while he was pointing to himself in Scripture, explaining the prophetic promise of mankind's redemption, from Moses through the Psalms and the Prophets. In Luke's interview, he pressed them for the detail; he wanted to know exactly at what point in their meeting with Jesus they recognized him in person. He writes in verse 28, So they drew near to the village to which they were going and Jesus appeared to be going further... Wow. Should Jesus not at this point have given them an opportunity to make a commitment or at least say a sinners prayer? Not even the best Rabbi could take them any further. Luke 24:29 But they constrained him, saying, Sir, stay with us, for it is toward evening and the day is now far spent. So he went in to stay with them. Luke 24:30 When he was at table with them, he took the bread and blessed, and broke it, and gave it to them.

Luke 24:31 And their eyes were opened and they recognized him; and he vanished from their sight. Instead of disappointment, a great excitement arrested their hearts and they took off in the night desiring to tell the others back in Jerusalem. Nothing mobilizes one more than realizing the relevance of the revelation of the incarnation. They knew that Jesus could no longer be any more present in his person than what he is present in the Word incarnate in us.

The moment we discover Jesus in Scripture as in a mirror, our hearts ignite and our very next meal becomes a celebration of the incarnation. Every time you eat or drink, remember me. Every meal celebrates the temple. Your body is God's address on planet earth. He does not dwell in buildings made by human hands. You will never again need to employ your willpower to diet and get into shape.

Willpower is the language of the law. Love and value-consciousness ignites belief. The revelation of the truth sets you free to be free indeed. The days of fast food and junk-food are over. The Table is sacred and celebrates your body as the sanctuary of your redeemed life, the life of your authentic design. Sitting around the table is a feast of friendship and delightful conversation. Eat food that blesses the temple. Most diseases are diet-related. Study nutrition. We have this treasure in earthen vessels. The vessel takes its value from the treasure it holds.

Knowing now, that our bodies are God's temple, we daily feast as we remember that every meal celebrates the incarnation [Jesus said, ...as often as you do this, remember me!]

Just as food is spontaneously digested and becomes flesh in skin and bone, so the word was destined to become flesh in Living Epistle language, known and read by all!)

12:1 Spiritual manifestations are supernatural, yet often very natural. Just because it is spirit dimension does not mean that you cannot understand what God's Spirit is saying to you.

12:2 Remember how, when you were still practicing pagan worship, you got carried away by dead and dumb idols into doing many weird things. *(Then you were snared by voiceless idols, now you are empowered by the voice God finds in ordinary people who amplify what he spoke to mankind in Christ.)*

12:3 Holy Spirit will never distract from Jesus or prompt anyone to dishonor Christ; Holy Spirit will always magnify Jesus. *(See John 16:13 But when she is come, the Spirit of truth, she will take you by the hand and guide you into the path of all truth. She will not draw attention to herself but will communicate and unveil everything she hears and discerns from a heavenly perspective about the things that is about to happen within you. John 16:14 Holy Spirit will endorse my opinion of you by taking that which is mine and interpreting it in you. See commentary notes in Mirror Bible. In Hebrew the word, Ruach, רוח Spirit, is Feminine.)*

12:4 There may be different manifestations of the grace gifts but they will not confuse, since the same Spirit is speaking.

12:5 Also ministries may appear to be different in their function but the same Lord endorses his purpose and management in everyone.

12:6 We might be doing things differently but we are drawing from the same source. God energizes each and everyone for their particular purpose.

12:7 Every expression of the Spirit is given to bring that which God has accomplished in Christ, ¹into full focus. *(The word, ¹sumphero, means to gather together for our advantage.)*

12:8 To one is given a word that clears the air and wisdom prevails; to another a word of knowledge, where something that could not be known in any other way comes to light. The same Spirit is the source.

12:9 Yet another person is inspired with a gift of faith in the same Spirit and another with gifts of healing of specific diseases in the same Spirit.

12:10 And to another the working of mighty acts of miracles, and to another enlightened speech *[prophecy]*; to another the ability to discern the difference between God's Spirit and a foreign spirit; to someone else the ability to communicate in many different languages; another has a gift to interpret these languages.

12:11 All these various gifts are inspired by the same Spirit who individually works in every person as Holy Spirit desires. *(See 1 Corinthians 14:1.)*

12:12 The many members of the same body do not divide the oneness of the individual. The various gifts and workings of the Spirit of Christ find a beautiful similitude taken from the mutual dependence of the numerous parts of the human body. All the parts unite harmoniously into one whole. The Spirit of Christ is one Spirit; although their workings in each one of us may seem different there is no distraction from their oneness in us.

12:13 For in one spirit we are all immersed into one body; Jew and Gentile alike, whether we were slave or free is no longer relevant, we are all saturated in one spirit. We are drinking from the same fountain.

12:14 The individual member and its function do not define the body; the body gives context to the individual member. Your specific gifting does not define you; Christ defines you.

12:15 The different members co-compliment each other. The hand is not a more valid member of the body than the foot. How silly it would be for the foot to feel inferior to the hand simply because it does not look the same. They fulfill completely different roles but are equally part of the same body.

12:16 Should the ear say, Because I am not the eye I am not part of the same body; does that mean that the ear is right?

12:17 If the body was just one huge eye, then everything would be silent; if it was all ears, then how could it smell the fragrance of the flowers.

12:18 God engineered every individual part of the body according to his deliberate design.*(The hearing ear and the seeing eye, the Lord has made them both. Proverbs 20:12.)*

12:19 Our individual significance only finds context in relationship to others.

12:20 The sum total of the members equals one body.

12:21 The eye perceives and the hand touches; they do not compete for importance. The head will never make the feet feel inferior. In the body there is no sense of, I am positioned higher than you and therefore I do not need you.

12:22 The members are not rated in importance with how visible and prominent they seem to be. The less visible parts are indispensable; it is impossible for the body to function without them.

12:23 Those members that seem to be of lesser visible value deserve the greater and more personal care. There is so much more to a person than a pretty face.

12:24 God so structured the body that every single part is equally valued; the less visible parts are often treated with even greater honor and more specific care.

12:25 Because of the delicate interdependence of the various parts of the body it is natural that no schism can be tolerated; instead every member considers the other with affectionate care.

12:26 It is impossible for one part of the body to suffer injury without the rest of the body being immediately alerted to it; the pain of the one is the pain of all. In the same way the complete person is honored, not just the fingers that skillfully play the harp. Everyone is equally included in the same joy. *(This parallel explains perfectly mankind's inclusion in the horror of Christ's death and the glory of his resurrection; one has died for all, therefore all have died. 2 Corinthians 5:14-17.)*

12:27 You are the body of Christ; individually as much as you are his body corporately. Everyone of you mirrors him. [1]He defines your [2]form. The individual member does not give context to the body; the body gives context to the member. *(Members in particular or individually comes from [1]ek, a Preposition that always denotes origin and [2]meros, meaning a part or portion.)*

12:28 Wherever God places you in the body is to co-compliment the full function of the ekklesia. The seemingly most prominent and visible gifts are the apostolic, then the prophetic, the teachers, the workers of miracles, those gifted with healing various diseases. Then there are those who can fulfill any role required of them for the moment; they are the ones who can [1]stand in full support to assist any of the other gifts. The administrators are gifted to [2]manage the various functions of the ekklesia with great skill. Then there are those gifted in languages. *(The word, [1]antilepsis, means to lay hold of together; the word [2]kubernesis comes from kubernaō, Latin for to steer. No one is more important than the other. An apostle is not a title. To be apostolic simply explains that you are gifted with a specific function, which includes your commission to pioneer new frontiers as well as to take leadership initiative with wisdom and passion. A gift can never be mistaken with reward. Your gift does not define you; so don't let people call you Mr. Prophet. [See Ephesians 4:11]*

What God now has in us is gift-wrapped to the world; some are commissioned to pioneer; others are gifted prophetically; some gifted as announcers of good news; some are shepherds with a real gift to care and nurture, and others have a gift to ignite instruction through revelation knowledge.

[Couriers, communicators, counselors and coaches —Rob Lacey]

Each expression of his gift is to fully equip and enable the saints for the work of the ministry so that they may mutually contribute in their specific function to give definition to the visible body of Christ. Ephesians 4:12.)

12:29 Everyone is not an apostle, or a Prophet, or a teacher, or a miracle worker. *(Your gift does not exalt you above anyone else; it is clear then, that there can be neither competition nor any ground for boasting. The gifts do not compete with the each other; instead each gift compliments the other.)*

12:30 All are not specifically gifted as healers. All do not necessarily speak in tongues. Are all equally accurate in their interpretation of what was said in a foreign tongue? *(The point is not how gifted you are in yourself, but how effective you are to equip others to discover themselves in the full stature of Christ.)*

12:31 While you are keen to discover which are your favorite gifts, allow me to introduce you to the *summum bonum* of life. This transcends all. *(summum bonum - the highest good - Latin.)*

LOVE IS WHO YOU ARE.

The days of window-shopping are over! 2 Corinthians 3:18

13:1 Speaking in tongues is not the point; [1]love is. It is neither celestial-angelic eloquence, nor the mastery of human language that persuades. It doesn't matter how poetic, prophetic, or profound I may sound; my conversation is reduced to the hollow noise of clanging brass cymbals if love's echo is absent. *(The Greek noun, [1]agapē, or its verb form, agapaō has 2 components, agō, meaning to lead like a shepherd guides his sheep, and paō, meaning to rest, i.e. he leads me beside still waters. By the waters of reflection my soul remembers who I am. [Psalm 23]. God's rest is established upon his image and likeness redeemed in us. Thus, to encounter agapē is to remember who I am. Jesus the Savior of mankind rescued God's image and likeness in human form. The grace of God shines as bright as day making the salvation of mankind undeniably visible [Titus 2:11].)*

13:2 I could predict the future in detail and have a word of knowledge for everyone. I could possess amazing faith, and prove it by moving mountains. It doesn't make me any more important than anyone else. Love is who you are. You are not defined by your gift or deeds. *(Love gives context to faith. Moving mountains is not the point, love is.)*

13:3 Love is not about defending a point of view; even if I am prepared to give away everything I have and die a martyr's death; love does not have to prove itself by acts of supreme devotion or self sacrifice.

13:4 Love is large in being passionate about life and relentlessly patient in bearing the offenses and injuries of others with kindness. Love is completely content and strives for nothing. Love has no desire to make others feel inferior and has no need to sing its own praises.

13:5 Love is predictable and does not behave out of character. Love is not ambitious. Love is not [1]spiteful and gets no mileage out of another's mistakes; it bears no record of wrongs. *(The word, [1]paroxunō, translates as spiteful, it has no sharp edges.)*

13:6 Love sees no joy in injustice. Love's delight is in everything that truth celebrates.

13:7 Love is a fortress where everyone feels protected rather than exposed. Love's persuasion is persistent. Love believes. Love never loses hope and always remains constant in contradiction.

13:8 Love never loses its altitude. *[The word, ekpiptō, means to lose height, to stop soaring.]* **Prophecies will cease.** *[Just like when a placenta is discarded after a baby is born.]* **Tongues will pause.** *[In order for that which was spoken in shadow-language to be fully interpreted.]* **The quest for knowledge will be inappropriate when perfection is grasped.**

13:9 What we perceived in prophetic glimpses,

13:10 is now concluded in completeness.

13:11 When I was an [1]infant I spoke infant gibberish with the mind of an infant; my reasoning also was typical of an infant; how it all changed when I became a grown-up. I am an infant no more. *(The word, [1]nepios, means without any command of speech.)*

13:12 There was a time of [1]suspense, when everything we saw was merely mirrored in the prophetic word, like in an enigma; but then *[when I became an adult in the revelation of Christ]*, **I gaze face-to-face that I may know me, even as I have always been known.** *(The word, [1]arti, comes from airō, meaning to keep in suspense. I knew you before I formed you in your mother's womb. Jeremiah 1:5.)*

13:13 [1]**Now persuasion and every pleasurable** [2]**expectation is** [3]**completed in agapē.** *(Here, in agapē, my soul remembers who I am. Psalm 23)* **Faith, hope and love are in** [3]**seamless union. Agapē is the superlative of everything faith and** [2]**hope always knew to be true about me. Love defines my** [3]**eternal moment.** *(Where the word, [1]nun, means now, at this very moment, arti, [v 12] means until now, a time of suspense; [2]elpis, means hope, pleasant expectation; and [3]menō, means to continue to be present. To continue in a seamless union.)*

Note on the Etymology of Agapē

The Greek verb ἀγαπάω **agapaō** to love, or noun, **Agapē**, has two components, **agō**, meaning to lead as a shepherd guides his sheep, and **paō**, to rest, like in Psalm 23, he leads me beside still waters where my soul is restored; by the waters of reflection my soul remembers who I am. Now I can face the valley of the shadow of death and fear no evil.

It does not derive from the Hebrew עֲגַב **Agab** as the dictionaries would imply – *Agab* is a word that Ezekiel uses 6 times and Jeremiah only once; and every time it is used for lust as in whoredom! The Hebrew word for love, closest to Agapē is the word, אהב **Ahab** which is used 207 times.

See my use of the word agapē here,

John 14:23 Jesus answered him, This is so much more than a mere casual, distant and suspicious, or indifferent observation of me; this is about someone's [1]**passionate, loving desire, finding its rest in me; they will treasure my words and encounter my Father's love reflecting in them, and my Father and I will** [2]**appear** [3]**face to face to them, and make our** [4]**abode** [5]**with each one individually.** *(To love passionately, [1]agapaō from agō and paō, to lead to rest [Psalm 23 in one word] – this word also links to the Hebrew word for love, אהב Ahab, to love with passionate desire; like a beating heart or breathing chest. Genesis 22;2 Abraham's love for Isaac. Jeremiah 31:3 I have loved you with an everlasting love: therefore, with lovingkindness have I drawn you.*

14:1 Agapē is God's only agenda. Be love driven in your pursuit of spiritual gifts; love awakens your most earnest desire to speak with [1]**inspired revelation.** *(The best way to pursue love and spiritual gifts is to realize how pursued you are by love. The word, [1]προφήτης prophētēs, from pro[s] before, also face to face, and phainō, to bring forth into the light, cause to shine, shed light; translates as enlightened speech. In Greek writings, a prophet is an interpreter of oracles or of other hidden things. The prophetic foretelling of the Old Testament pointed to Christ. [Luke 24:27, & 44; John 5:39]. In the New Testament, the profoundness of the prophetic ministry, including words of knowledge and amazing insights into future events, has its reference and relevance in a redemption which unveils the mystery that was hidden for ages and generations - no longer as a future Messiah on the horizon, but as the incarnate Christ mirrored in you!) See commentary note on the prophetic at the end of this chapter.)*

14:2 For the one who speaks in a strange tongue speaks intimate spirit mysteries between him and God but no one else can understand him.

14:3 But those who prophesy inspire their audience constructively and comfort them with [1]**companionship** and [2]**instruction.**

([1] The word [1]parakaleō; to accompany; to affiliate; to associate; from para, a Preposition indicating close proximity, a thing proceeding from a sphere of influence, with a suggestion of union of place of residence; to have sprung from its author and giver; originating from; denoting the point from which an action originates; intimate connection; and kaleō, to identify by name; to surname. See my note on paraklesis in Acts 4:36.

[2] Instruction is translated from [2]paramutheō, from para and muthos from mueō, meaning to teach with narratives.)

14:4 While speaking in tongues is primarily for personal edification, prophetic instruction inspires the ekklesia.

14:5 I am happy for all of you to speak in tongues, but I desire even more that each one of you will also speak revelation knowledge for the benefit of the whole ekklesia. So please do not speak in tongues in the ekklesia unless you can also interpret what you have just said.

14:6 Imagine how confusing it would be if I visit you and all I do is impress you with my spirituality by speaking in tongues; how could I possibly benefit you unless I speak with revelation, insight and inspired prophetic instruction.

14:7 Any musical instrument like a flute or guitar would irritate the audience if all it did was repeating indistinct sounds without any melody. Play music that everyone will appreciate. *(The Greek word for harp is kithara.)*

14:8 If the bugle gives an uncertain sound, the soldiers will miss the moment to prepare themselves to advance in battle. *(Do you realize the importance of what I am saying? Do not misinterpret strategic instruction for personal edification.)*

14:9 [1]**Make every word count in order to bring maximum benefit to your audience; weigh your words then you will not be wasting your breath.** *(The words [1]eusemos logos translate as a well marked word.)*

14:10 In nature every voice vibrates with meaning; even animal and bird sounds are distinct and significant.

14:11 There is no point in having a conversation with someone if you do not understand one another's language.

14:12 Let me make it very clear, while speaking in tongues has its personal benefits, do not make it the thing everybody wants to do. Then you miss the whole point of spiritual gifts. What is the value if a million people can speak in tongues but they are completely incapable of bringing a word of inspired instruction? Tongues are most certainly not a mark of spirituality. The greater blessing is not in getting the blessing but in being a blessing to others.

14:13 Do not even attempt to speak in tongues in the congregation if you are unable to also unfold and explain the meaning of what was said.

14:14 Why pray in tongues without understanding? Then there is no point in it.

14:15 Even in worship the two go hand in hand: I will pray with the spirit and continue with understanding; I will worship God in spiritual songs and then conclude by singing with inspired understanding. *(Remember Paul's introduction to the spiritual gifts in chapter 12:1, Spiritual manifestations are supernatural, yet often very natural. Just because it is spirit dimension does not mean that you cannot understand what God's Spirit is saying to you. Paul's passion is to make all men see what God saw when Jesus died and was raised; the spiritual gifts are not to add confusion but clarity to the gospel.)*

14:16 If all you do is speak blessings in tongues, how can anyone else in the same room, especially those who are completely ignorant of spiritual things, feel included and resonate with what you are saying? *(See verse 25)*

14:17 There is nothing wrong with your thanksgiving as such; it is just a pity that you should exclude someone in your immediate audience.

14:18 Am I against speaking in tongues? Not at all. I am so grateful to God that I speak in tongues; I do so perhaps more than all of you.

14:19 But when we gather together I would rather speak five words with my understanding in order to inspire someone with mutual [1]resonance than waste a thousand words in tongues. *(The word, [1]katēcheō, is where the word catechism comes from, kata, downward and echō, to hold or echo; thus, to resonate. Resonance instructs truth and defeats debate.)*

14:20 Brothers and sisters, the days of being children in our understanding of spiritual matters are over. Be innocent as [1]infants concerning evil but in [2]understanding be perfectly articulate. *(The word, [1]nepios, translates as without the command of language, babyish, gibberish. The word Paul uses here for understanding is the word [2]phren where we get the word diaphragm; it refers to an inner knowing, a deeper knowledge than mere academic consent.)*

14:21 In the law it is written, In foreign tongues and strange sounds I will speak to these people, and still they will not understand, says the Lord. *(The law refers to the Old Covenant Scriptures, including the Psalm and the Prophets. [In Isaiah 28:9-11, Isaiah writes: You say, Who are you to lord it over us? We're not babies in diapers to be talked down to by such as you — 'Da, da, da, da, blah, blah, blah, blah. That's a good little girl, that's a good little boy.' But that's exactly how you will be addressed. God will speak to these people in baby talk, one syllable at a time — But they won't listen. — The Message.]*

*By now you [Jews] should have been professors, able to teach the rest of the world, but you are still struggling with the ABC of God's language in Christ [**Hebrews 5:12**]. The difference between the prophetic shadow and the real is like that between milk and meat in your diet. You cannot live on baby food for the rest of your lives. [**Hebrews 1:1-3**] The revelation of righteousness is the meat of God's word. [Babes live on milk, the prophetic shadow of the real, which was to come.] So does everyone who is not ¹pierced in the ear of his heart by the revelation of Christ. [**Romans 1:17**, God's act of righteousness in Christ restored mankind to blameless innocence.] The word, ¹apeiros, translates as not pierced, tested by piercing.*

***Hebrews 5:14**, This is the nourishment of the mature. They are those who have their faculties of perception trained as by gymnastic precision to distinguish the relevant from the irrelevant. [The mature are those who know the difference between the shadow and the substance; between the futility of the law of works and willpower to work righteousness, and righteousness revealed by the faith of God in the finished work of Christ.])*

14:22 In a certain sense, tongues are also a prophetic sign pointing towards the revelation of Christ; thus unbelievers are brought to faith. Prophetic instruction is often used specifically to edify the believers. *(It can also be used to convince an unbeliever, e.g., through a word of knowledge. [See **John 4:18, 19, 29**]*

Acts 2:4 And everyone was infused and permeated in Holy Spirit and spontaneously began to speak in a language they have never learned before. They uttered the exact words the Spirit prompted within them.

Acts 2:5 Residing in Jerusalem at the time, there were ¹devout Pilgrims, who embraced the goodness of God. They were from many different and distant lands.

*([1] The word ευλαβής ¹**eulabēs**, [devout] one who embraces/grasps goodness.*

> *See **Luke 2:25 And significantly so, there happened to be a man Simeon, in Jerusalem; he was a righteous man who embraced the goodness of God.** This is again unique to Luke - he alone uses this word here in Luke, then twice in the book of Acts.)*

Acts 2:6 Hearing the sound of this orchestra of voices speaking different languages, the multitudes rushed together. They were ¹baffled to hear their own mother tongue dialect spoken fluently by the disciples of Jesus.

*([1] The word, συνεχύνθη ¹**sugcheō** from σύν **sun** [together] and χέω **cheō** [to pour], again a word unique to Luke; precisely like the Latin **confundo**, to confound.)*

Acts 2:7 They were totally blown away with wonder and kept saying to one another how completely odd it was, especially since the people speaking, were all Galileans.

Acts 2:8 And yet, they were clearly communicating in the native language and specific dialect of every nation represented in the crowd.

Acts 2:9 Parthians, and Medes, and Elamites, Parthians, Medes, [north-eastern Iranians and north-western Iranians - each with their own dialect and Elamites: All 3 representing portions of the Persian empire]; also the Judeans living in Mesopotamia,

[Judea seems to be in strange sequence here, it is possibly an adjective; or an erroneous addition by copyists. Also, possibly since the dialect in Judea was different to that of Galilee], and Cappadocia, Pontus and Asia; [Asia: In the time of the apostles the term was commonly understood of the proconsular province of Asia, principally of the kingdom of Pergamus left by Attalus III to the Romans, and including Lydia, Mysia, Caria, and at times parts of Phrygia. The name Asia Minor did not come into use until the fourth century of our era. [East central Turkey, the coastal areas of the Black Sea, Asia]

Acts 2:10 Then, Phrygia and Pamphylia, [North central Turkey and southern Turkey], Egypt [two-fifths of the population of Alexandria were said to have been Jews] and the regions of Libya, neighbors of Cyrene, as well as visitors from all over the Roman Empire, both Jews and proselytes;

Acts 2:11 also Cretans and Arabians; we hear them proclaiming the magnificent works of God in our mother tongue!)

14:23 If an unbeliever or someone completely ignorant of spiritual things happens to walk into one of your meetings while everyone is going off in tongues they will think that you are crazy and nothing will attract them to your faith.

14:24 However if all speak with inspired revelation, the newcomer will feel drawn by the message that brings conviction and light.

14:25 By witnessing the gift of the word of knowledge, where something that could not be known in any other way comes to light, the visitor will be struck with awe and acknowledge God in you and will yield himself to God in worship.

14:26 I would encourage you to conduct your meetings in such a way that everyone is mutually edified. Each one in turn may contribute in music, in a teaching; another may bring a tongue with a revelation and interpretation.

14:27 I want to be very clear on the issue of tongues and its practice in the assembly: if someone insists on speaking in tongues; keep it short, let it be only two or at the most three in turn, definitely not all three at the same time, and let one interpret what was said.

14:28 If there is no interpretation, let the one who wants to talk in tongues rather be quiet; he can have his own private conversation with God when he is alone.

14:29 Let only two or three Prophets speak while the others weigh what was said.

14:30 If someone picks up something that is not consistent with the revelation of the gospel, they should bring the conversation back to order while the first person keeps quiet. *(Which is exactly what I have done with verses 34-38. I do not consider them legitimate Scriptures from Paul.)*

14:31 The two or three people prophesying should take turns to speak; if more than one speaks at the same time the objective is lost and no one can gain any insight or encouragement from the prophetic word.

14:32 The spirit of the Prophet is subject to the Prophet.

14:33 Confusion is not of God; peace and harmony sets the pace in every ekklesia of the saints.

14:34-35 *(Women should keep quiet in the church; they should know their place of submission just as they are taught in the law. If they need to know anything their husbands can instruct them at home. The church is certainly not a place where women should voice their opinion; they also do not qualify to operate in any of the gifts of the spirit.*

Hee hee hee. This sounds like a grumpy scribe of the day, voicing his opinion.

This is certainly not consistent with Paul's revelation that in Christ there is neither male nor female. [See 2 Corinthians 5:14,16, Galatians 3:28, also 1 Corinthians 11:3-17].)

14:36-38 *(Also verses 36-38, Now to add insult to injury, the same author of the previous verses lashes out against anyone who would not share his sentiment concerning women.*

Luke clearly mentions Philip the Evangelist who had 4 daughters who prophesied! They were hosting Paul and Agabus the prophet also visited Acts 21:8,9. Where did they prophesy if not in the church? The ekklesia was a fellowship, not a building!)

14:39 To conclude the tongues and prophecy debate; encourage prophecy with greater enthusiasm than tongues. However do not forbid tongues altogether,

14:40 but let it all happen with discretion and dignity.

1 Corinthians Chapter 14 Extended Notes:
The Prophetic

The Prophetic

The purpose of the prophetic, just like with every other ministry gift, is to engage, encourage and edify the ekklesia - even an unbelieving newcomer would feel magnetically drawn, and not shunned, shamed or excluded in your company. [1 Corinthians 14:23-25].

Remember, 1 Corinthians 13 precedes chapter 14! Love is who you are!

1 Corinthians 14:1 Agapē is God's only agenda. Be love driven in your pursuit of spiritual gifts; love awakens your most earnest desire to speak with [1]inspired revelation. *(The best way to pursue love and spiritual gifts is to realize how pursued you are by love. The word, [1]προφήτης prophētēs, from pro[s] before, also face to face, and phaino, to bring forth into the light, cause to shine, shed light; translates as enlightened speech. In Greek writings, a prophet is an interpreter of oracles or of other hidden things. In the context of Scripture, Jesus is both the theme as well as the completeness of the prophetic word.)*

1 Corinthians 14:3 But those who prophesy inspire their audience constructively and comfort them with [1]companionship and [2]instruction.

([1] The word [1]parakaleō; to accompany; to affiliate; to associate; from para, a Preposition indicating close proximity, a thing proceeding from a sphere of influence, with a suggestion of union of place of residence; to have sprung from its author and giver; originating from; denoting the point from which an action originates; intimate connection; and kaleō, to identify by name; to surname. See my note on paraklesis in Acts 4:36.

[2] Instruction is translated from [2]paramutheo, from para and muthos from mueō, meaning to teach with narratives.)

The entire prophetic, foretelling of the **Old Testament** pointed to the Messiah-Christ. *[Luke 24:27, & 44; John 5:39].* Now, in the **New Testament**, the profoundness of the prophetic ministry, including words of knowledge and amazing insights into future events, has its reference and relevance in a redemption which unveils the mystery that was hidden for ages and generations - no longer as a future Messiah on the horizon, but as the incarnate Christ mirrored in you! You are the subsequent glory that Peter speaks of in 1 Peter 1:10-11. *[Also 2 Corinthians 3:18; Isaiah 40:5]*

Some modern day prophetic ministries have brought confusion rather than clarity and freedom by a wrong emphasis on the prophetic. Many sincere believers became addicted to the prophetic and began to attach more value to yet another future prediction than what they saw in the completed work of Christ, now unveiled in them. This became a snare and made the prophetic a type of Christian fortune telling. The key here is in the difference between window-shopping and mirror-gazing - living FROM, rather than towards! We have wasted so much time trying to get there, when there is where we are to begin with! *Colossians 3:1-3* and *Ephesians 2:5,6.* While knowledge about future happenings can be exciting and often strategic, if it does not celebrate Christ incarnate in you as its point of reference it can become a distraction.

See my *Notes on The Five-fold Ministry* - at the end of Acts chapter 11.

Foretelling an event - a strategic opportunity unfolds...

Acts 11:27 During that time there were prophets from Jerusalem, who visited Antioch.

Acts 11:28 One of them, Agabus, prompted by the Spirit, foretold that a severe famine was about to devastate the country. *(This happened in the reign of Claudius.)*

Acts 11:29 This prophetic word gave these new Greek disciples a strategic opportunity to bless their suspicious Judean brethren. They determined to set a plan in motion, where each one of them, according to the measure of their own means and prosperity, would administer their support to be sent to the brethren in Judea.

Antioch was the first community of believers to be called Christian, and they were non-Jewish; this caused a measure of suspicion amongst the believers in Judea; but here was their opportunity to take the initiative to break down any such barriers. When your enemy is hungry, feed him.

> **Romans 12:20 If your enemy is hungry, feed him; if he is thirsty, give him something to drink. These acts of kindness will be like heaping coals of fire on his head and certainly rid him of the dross in his mind and win him as a friend.**
>
> *(A refiner would melt metal in a crucible and intensify the process by heaping coals of fire on it [Proverbs 25:21,22]. This is a good strategy, be sensitive to the needs of your enemies. God sees gold in every person. Hostility cannot hide our true value. He won us while we were hostile towards him [see also Romans 5:8, 10]. His kindness led us to the radical awakening of our minds. [Romans 2:4].)*

The OT prophetic word concludes in God's Fullness of Time. Jesus is God's eschatology. *Hebrews 1:1-3.*

In one act of righteousness, God removed every possible definition of distance and delay. Every excuse that we could have to feel separated or abandoned, was canceled on the cross. **Every valley shall be lifted up, and every mountain and hill be made low; every crooked place shall be made straight and the rough places, smooth. And the glory of the Lord shall be revealed and ALL flesh shall see it together!** *[Isaiah 40:4,5]*

Now, the incarnate Christ unveiled in us, the Living Epistles, continues to speak a global, mother tongue language - known and read by all!

The hour that was to come has come; Jesus is the fullness of time. God can never get any closer to mankind than what he already did in the incarnation. He cannot say more to the human race than what he did in Jesus.

In the New Testament the profoundness of the prophetic ministry, including words of knowledge and amazing insights into future events, has its reference and relevance in a redemption which unveils the mystery that was hidden for ages and generations - no longer as a future Messiah on the horizon, but as the incarnate Christ mirrored in you!

1 Peter 1:10 This salvation which you now know as your own, is the theme of the prophetic thought; this is what intrigued the Prophets' minds for generations and became the object of their most diligent inquiry and scrutiny. They knew all along that mankind's salvation was a grace revelation, sustained in their prophetic utterance. *(Salvation would never be by personal achievement or a reward to willpower-driven initiative. The law of works would never replace grace.)*

1 Peter 1:11 In all of their conversation there was a [1]constant quest to determine who the Messiah would be, and exactly when this would

happen. They knew with certainty that it was the spirit of Christ within them, pointing prophetically and giving testimony to the sufferings of the Christ and the subsequent glory. *(The [1]big question was, Who and When? In Acts 17:31 Paul addresses the Greek Philosophers and reminds them of their own ancient writings and he quotes two of their well-known philosophers: in 600BC Epimenedes wrote a song saying, We live and move and have our being in God; and Aratus wrote in 300BC that we are indeed God's offspring. Paul then announces to them that the God whom they worship in ignorance is not far from each one of us. He is not more Immanuel to the Jew than what he is to the Gentile. Now follows the punch line of the gospel: in the context of his Jewish background and personal encounter with Jesus Christ, Paul declares to them the Good News of mankind's redeemed innocence. God has overlooked the times of ignorance, and is now urging all of mankind, whoever and wherever they are, to a radical mind-shift, since he has prophetically **fixed a day** on which he would judge the world in righteousness **by a man whom he has appointed**, and of this [righteous judgment] he has given proof to all by raising him from the dead. Acts 17:30,31. See also Romans 4:25 where, in Paul's understanding, the resurrection of Jesus from the dead includes mankind's co-resurrection and seals their acquittal and redeemed innocence. **This is the predicted subsequent glory that was to follow the cross.** Hosea 6:2, After two days he will revive us; on the third day, he will raise us up. Whatever glory was lost in Adam, would be redeemed again in Jesus Christ.)*

1 Peter 1:12 It was revealed to them that this glorious grace message that they were communicating pointed to a specific day and person beyond their own horizon and generation; they saw you in their prophetic view. This [1]heavenly announcement had you in mind all along. They proclaimed glad tidings to you in advance, in the Holy Spirit, commissioned from heaven; the prophetic messengers themselves longed to gaze deeply into its complete fulfillment. *(Peter uses the word, [1]anaggellō, where the Preposition, **ana**, points upward to the source of the announcement.)*

1 Peter 1:13 How amazing is that. Jesus is what the Scriptures are all about; and you are what Jesus is all about. Now wrap your minds around that. This unveiling is [1]what tied up all the loose ends that would trip you and frustrate your seamless transition from the old to the new. The revelation of Jesus is no longer a future expectation. Do not allow the old mindset of a future tense glory to intoxicate you and distract you from the relevance of this moment. Stop pointing to a future Messiah. Jesus is who the Prophets pointed to. You are the fruit of his sufferings; you are the glorious resurrection generation. Fully engage your [2]minds with the consequence of this grace in the revelation of Jesus Christ. He [3]completes your every [4]expectation. *(The word [1]anazōsamenoi, to gird up, is an Aorist Participle, which translates, having girded up the loins of your mind, be sober. The word [2]dianoia, suggests deep contemplation, thinking something thoroughly through in order to reach a sober conclusion. Then Peter writes, [3]teleios [4]elpisate, this is the completeness of every expectation. See Colossians 1:27.)*

Hebrews 1:1 Throughout [1]ancient times God spoke in many fragments and glimpses of prophetic thought to our fathers. Now, this entire conversation has [2]finally dawned in sonship. Suddenly, what seemed to be an ancient language falls fresh and new like the dew on the tender grass. He is the sum total of every utterance of God. He is whom the Prophets pointed to and we are his immediate audience.

([1] The word [1]palai, meaning, of old, ancient; from palin through the idea of oscillatory repetition or retrocession; anew, afresh.

> *Deuteronomy 32:1 Give ear, Oh heavens, and I will speak; and let the earth hear the words of my mouth.*

> *Deuteronomy 32:2 May my teaching drop as the rain, my speech distil as the dew, as the gentle rain upon the tender grass, and as the showers upon the herb....*

> *Deuteronomy 32:18 You were unmindful of the Rock that begot you, and you forgot the God who gave you birth.*

> *Like in James 1:24, we have forgotten what manner of people we are - we have forgotten the face of our birth.*

> *Jesus successfully rescued the real you, not the pseudo, make-belief you. God has never believed less of you than what he was able to communicate in the sonship that Jesus mirrored and redeemed.*

[2] The word [2]eschatos means extreme; last in time or in space; the uttermost part, the final conclusion. What God said about 'you-manity' in Jesus defines eschatology.)

Hebrews 1:2 In a son, God declares the Incarnate Word to be the heir of all things. He is, after all, the author of the ages.

*(See John 1:2 **The beginning mirrors the Word face to face with God.** [The beginning declares the destiny of the Word, image and likeness would be mirrored and redeemed in incarnate human form.] Also John 1:3, All things came into being through him, and apart from him nothing that exists came into being. Sonship endorses heirship. See Hebrews 6:16-18.)*

Hebrews 1:3 The Messiah-message is what has been on the tip of the Father's tongue all along. Now he is the crescendo of God's conversation with us and gives context and content to the authentic, prophetic thought. Everything that God has in mind for mankind is voiced in him. Jesus is God's language. He is the radiant and flawless mirror expression of the person of God. He makes the glorious intent of God visible and exhibits the character and every attribute of Elohim in human form. His being announces our redeemed innocence; having accomplished purification for sins, he sat down, enthroned in the boundless measure of his majesty in the right hand of God as his executive authority. He is the force of the universe, upholding everything that exists. This conversation is the dynamic that sustains the entire cosmos.

Women - Luke clearly mentions Philip the Evangelist who had 4 daughters who prophesied! They were hosting Paul, while Agabus the prophet also visited. Acts 21:8,9. Where did they prophesy if not in the ekklesia? The ekklesia was a fellowship, not a building!

Also, Priscilla, wife of Aquila, held a position of tremendous honor as teacher in the early church. There is also a strong possibility that she could have been the author or co-author of the book of Hebrews. *[See my introduction to Hebrews]*

15:1 Brothers and sisters, herewith a summary of the Good News that I endorse; I announced to you with glad confidence how greatly advantaged you are in Christ; you immediately associated yourselves with this message in which you are now firmly established.

15:2 In this gospel you realized your salvation; the words I spoke echoed in your hearts; I now desire to reinforce your faith in order to erase any possible grounds for doubt.

15:3 I fully included you in the message I embrace with my whole being. Of first importance is the fact that the death that Jesus died for our sins was in exact fulfillment of the promise recorded in Scripture. *(Isaiah 53:4, 5, Psalm 22.)*

15:4 Also his burial and third day resurrection were accurately foretold. *(Hosea 6:2.)*

15:5 Then there are the many eyewitnesses; Kefas, as well as all the other disciples who saw him after his resurrection.

15:6 He then appeared to more than five hundred followers of whom most are still alive at the time of this writing.

15:7 After that he was seen by James *[Jesus' brother; Galatians 1:19]*, then again by all the Apostles *[at the Mount of Olives]*,

15:8 and finally he also appeared to me; certainly not as a reward for my spirituality or good behavior. It was like an unexpected traumatic birth. *(The word, **ektroma**, means out of trauma.)*

15:9 Because I persecuted the ekklesia of God, I cannot even begin to rate myself along with the Apostles. I am the least of the least and unworthy to even be called an Apostle.

15:10 While my own doing completely disqualified me; his doing now defines me. I am what I am by the grace of God. I am because he is. His grace was not wasted on me; instead I am inspired to labor beyond the point of exhaustion, more than anything I ever did under the law of performance; whatever it is that I accomplish now, has grace written all over it. I take no credit for it.

15:11 Whether you came to faith through my preaching or someone else's is not important.

15:12 What is important though, is that you understand the revelation of his resurrection. The resurrection of Christ from the dead is the theme of preaching; for some to say that he is not also raised within you is to miss the whole point of the message.

15:13 If our co-resurrection is not proclaimed then the resurrection of Jesus from the dead is no longer relevant.

15:14 If Christ is not raised from the dead there is nothing left for us to preach and nothing left for you to believe.

15:15 We would be misrepresenting God since we declared that he raised Christ from the dead; when in fact he did not, so it would be man's word against God's.

15:16 If there is no global resurrection from the dead then there can be no individual resurrection from the dead; then Jesus did not really rise from the dead.

15:17 And if Jesus is still dead your faith has no relevance and you are still in your sins. *(In Paul's understanding the body of Christ on the cross was the document of mankind's guilt and the resurrection was the receipt of their acquittal [Colossians 2:14, 15 and Romans 4:25]. If mankind was still guilty after Jesus died, his resurrection would neither be possible nor relevant. This explains Acts 10:28 and 2 Corinthians 5:14 and 16. Acts 17:31 says, because God had fixed a day on which he would judge the world in righteousness by a man whom he has appointed, and of this he has given assurance to all men by raising him from the dead.*

It's when we see what Peter saw when God dramatically challenged his paradigms in Acts 10; I mean the man's hungry, and when a Jew gets hungry he's supposed to see favorite food pop-ups! But instead God shows him every unclean animal alive in their skins, feathers, warts and scales! Not neatly chopped up into a Gumbo or stew, and flavored with favorite spices! Alive, dirty and ugly! And three times later, after Peter tried his best take on a favorite scripture (Don't eat anything unclean, remember!) God shows him in v 28 that he may no longer call anyone unclean or unholy!! Haha! We've so underestimated what God did when Jesus died humanity's death! Behold the Lamb OF GOD who takes away the sin of the world! He did it once and for all long before anyone but God believed it! And without our permission!)

15:18 No resurrection implies no hope for anyone beyond the grave; it makes no difference whether you believed that you were included in Christ's death or not.

15:19 If our hope in Christ was restricted to only benefit us in this life then imagine the severity of our disappointment if it all had to come to an abrupt end when we died.

15:20 However this very moment the risen Christ represents everyone who has ever died; exactly like the first fruit represents the complete harvest.

15:21 The same mankind who died in a man was raised again in a man. *(Eve was not an afterthought! Adam was put into a deep sleep; then God took her out of the Word that was already made flesh! Mankind redeemed, the Bride, began the same way! Co-quickened, co-raised we are! When Adam awoke from his sleep, Eve was there! Behold! Flesh of my flesh!)*

15:22 In Adam all died; in Christ all are made alive.

15:23 Each and everyone are individually awakened to life in succession to the order, mirrored in Christ, who is the first fruit. In [1]his unveiled, immediate presence we are personally endorsed as his own. *The word [1]parousia was often translated to mean the coming of the Lord; however, the two components of the word are, para, a Preposition indicating close proximity, a* *thing proceeding from a sphere of influence, with a suggestion of union of place of residence, to have sprung from its author and giver, originating from, denoting the point from which an action originates, intimate connection; and **eimi**, I am: thus, his immediate presence realized in me. This word occurs 24 times in the NT and only twice it is translated correctly - I was so blessed to discover that Robert Young's Literal translation published in 1862, has it correct every time!)*

15:24 The complete conclusion of his work of redemption is [1]repeatedly celebrated in every individual discovering that they too are part and parcel of the full harvest of his resurrection. This is the extent of his reign that he yielded to God the Father, having [2]brought to naught every definition of dominion, including all [3]principalities, all [4]authority and every [5]dynamic influence in society.

*([1] The Conjunctive Particle, [1]otan, often translated as when is better translated as every time. See Colossians 3:3, Thus, Every time Christ is revealed we are being co-revealed in his glory. According to the Walter Bauer Lexicon, **otan** is often used for an action that is repeated. Referring to the previous verse, all are individually made alive in the order of Christ. Mankind's co-resurrection with Christ is repeatedly celebrated in every individual throughout time - whenever this truth is discovered in human history. Colossians 3:1-3.*

*[2] He brought to naught the law of works; καταργηση [2]katargēsē, is the Aorist Subjunctive of **katargeō**, which indicates a definite outcome that happens as a result of another stated action, [in Christ all are made alive]. The word **katargeō**, with **kata**, down, and **argos**, rendered useless; from **a**, as a negative particle and **ergon**, toil, labor; thus, inactive, that is, unemployed; useless; thus the entire system of performance, to improve what God has already perfected in Christ, is brought to naught.*

[3] All principalities, [3]archē, or chief ranks, i.e. kings or governors; this includes any governing system whereby one is ranked above the other on the basis of their performance or preference.

*[4] All authority, [4]exousia, comes from **ek**, denoting origin and **eimi**, I am; in this case, because of what I can do I am defined by what I can do better than you; therefore, I have authority over you.*

*[5] Every dynamic influence in society, [5]**dunamis**, means power, in this case, willpower. Every government structure in society will be brought under the dominion of grace where the Christ-life rules.*

See 1 Corinthians 2:7-8, We voice words of wisdom that were hidden in silence for timeless ages; a mystery unfolding God's Masterful plan whereby he would redeem his glory in man. Neither the politicians nor the theologians of the day had a clue about this mystery [of mankind's association in Christ]; if they did, they would never have crucified the Lord whose death redeemed our glory.

The kingdom of God is the authority of the Christ-life in ordinary, day to day life, where righteousness is based on who we are and not on who we are trying to impress. The law of works is duty and guilt driven, whereas the law of faith is love driven. Romans 3:27, Galatians 5:6. Also 2 Corinthians 10:12 When they measure themselves by one another, competing and comparing, they are without understanding.)

15:25 His dominion is destined to subdue all hostility and contradiction under his feet. *(The Lord said to my Lord, Sit at my right hand until I make your enemies your footstool. [Psalm 110:1] Jesus is Lord of Lords; in his victory mankind is restored to lordship; I say you are gods, all of you are sons of the Most High [Psalm 82:6 RSV].)*

15:26 Resurrection life will finally triumph over every definition of death.

15:27 When David says in Psalm 8 that human life is destined to reign over all things he obviously does not mean that they will also rule over their Maker.

*(**Psalm 8:4** What is man that you are mindful of him, and the son of man that you care so much for him?*

***Psalm 8:5** Yet you made him little less than God, [Elohim] and crowns him with glory and honor.*

***Psalm 8:6** You have given him dominion over the works of your hands; you have put all things under his feet.*

*Also **Philippians 2:8** And so we have the drama of the cross in context: the man Jesus Christ who is fully God, becomes fully man to the extent of willingly dying humanity's death at the hands of his own creation. He embraced the curse and shame of the lowest kind in dying a criminal's death. [Thus, through the doorway of death, he descended into our hellish darkness. **Revelation 1:18** I am also the Living One; I died and now, see, here I am alive unto the ages of the ages and I have the keys wherewith I have disengaged the gates of Hadēs and death.]*

***Philippians 2:9** From this place of utter humiliation, God exalted him to the highest rank. God graced Jesus with a Name that is far above every other name. [**Ephesians 1:20** Do you want to measure the mind and muscle of God? Consider the force which he unleashed in Jesus Christ when he raised him from the dead and forever seated him enthroned as his executive authority in the realm of the heavens. Jesus is God's right hand of power. He was raised up from the deepest dungeons of human despair to the highest region of heavenly bliss. **Ephesians 1:21** Infinitely above all the combined forces of rule, authority, dominion or governments; he is ranked superior to any name that could ever be given to anyone of this age or any age still to come in the eternal future. The name of Jesus endorses his mission as fully accomplished. He is the Savior of the world.]*

***Ephesians 4:8** Scripture confirms that [in his death], he arrested every possible threat that held mankind hostage [He took captivity captive]. And in his resurrection, he led humanity as prisoners of war trophies in his triumphant procession on high. Consider the genius of God how, in the incarnate Christ, he repossessed and redeemed what belonged to us by design, in a man. [Mankind's co-in-Christness is the crux of the Gospel!]*

*Quote from Psalm 67:19 LXX Septuagint, ἔλαβες δόματα ἐν ἀνθρώπῳ, **elabes domata en** [in] **anthrōpō** - You have repossessed gifts in human form. The word **elabes** from **lambanō** means to take what is one's own. The word for the human species, male or female is **anthropos**, from **ana**, upward, and **tropos**, manner of life; character; in like manner. [Hebrew text, Psalm 68:18,19 לקחת מתנות באדם **lakachat mattanoth ba adam** - You have taken gifts in Adam. **The gifts which Jesus Christ distributes to us he has received in***

185

us, in and by virtue of his incarnation. Adam Clarke.] We were born anew in his resurrection. 1 Peter 1:3, Hosea 6:2, and Ephesians 2:6, We are also elevated in his ascension to be equally welcome in the throne room of the heavenly realm where we are now seated together with him in his authority.]

Ephesians 4:9 The fact that he ascended confirms his victorious descent into the deepest pits of human despair. (See John 3:13, No one has ascended into heaven but he who descended from heaven, even the son of man. All mankind originates from above; we are anouthen, from above [see James 1:17, 18].)

Ephesians 4:10 He now occupies the ultimate rank of authority, from the lowest regions of our darkness, into which he reached in order to rescue us, to the highest authority in the heavens, having triumphantly executed his mission. He fills the entire universe with himself! [Fallen mankind is fully restored to the authority of the authentic life of their design. Psalm 139:7,8 Whither shall I go from thy Spirit? Or Whither shall I flee from thy presence? If I ascend to heaven, You. If I make my bed in Sheol, You. Hebrews 2:10 He towers in conspicuous prominence far above all things. He is both their author and their conclusion.])

15:28 In subduing all things under him, the Son himself in his own submission to the Father will confirm that God is all and in all.

(John 14:20, In that day you will know that we are in seamless union with one another. I am in my Father, you are in me and I am in you. The day Jesus refers to here happened when he died and was raised again; the day for us dawns the moment we realize our co-inclusion in his death and resurrection.)

15:29 *(Now here's a novel idea: if someone died who didn't get baptized then you can baptize someone else in their stead. Hah! That should convince God to raise that person from the dead one day; this way you don't have to worry about anything, just remember to charge a decent fee so that you can build an Olympic size pool in your church.*

There is no doubt that this passage was squeezed in here by some heretic copyist; since the practice referred to only existed in some churches 200 years later and is in total contradiction to Paul's message; as were other practices that later evolved in churches, such as buying indulgences to shorten a deceased loved one's time in the church's idea of purgatory.

Here is Paul's take on baptism: 1 Corinthians 1:17, My mandate was not about winning members for some Christian club through baptism. I am commissioned to declare the Good News without any strings attached; nothing to distract from the powerful effect of the revelation of the cross of Christ. [The mystery of the cross is the revelation of mankind's inclusion in his death and resurrection. See 1 Corinthians 2:7])

15:30 Why would we bother to constantly put ourselves in life threatening situations by preaching this gospel if it is all coming to nothing in the end anyway?

15:31 My passion for your joy in Christ Jesus our Lord puts my life at frequent risk. As [1]certain as I am of your salvation, so certain am I of the resurrection; therefore, I am more than confident to daily live dangerously

close to death. *(This ¹ne is a particle of swearing. People swear or affirm by their objects of dearest affection and desire; our salvation and joy was Paul's dearest affection.)*

15:32 If I like many other prisoners had to fight wild beasts in the amphitheater of Ephesus, what would be my gain if the dead are not raised; then we might as well live by the philosophy, let us eat and drink as much as we can today for tomorrow we die.

15:33 Do not be distracted by a message that excludes the revelation of the resurrection; yielding yourselves to the persuasive conversation of others, their negative influence in your lives would be inevitable.

15:34 Awake to righteousness, and the distortion of sin will have no further effect on you. God is not confused. What a shame that anyone should exchange what God knows to be true about us to someone else's inferior opinion.

15:35 There might be many skeptics who would say, How are the dead raised and what does the resurrected body look like?

15:36 Think about it this way, a seed that is sown has to first die before it lives again.

15:37 And the plant that grows from the seed does not even resemble the grain that was sown. If you only know what wheat looks like in its seed form you might not be able to recognize the plant.

15:38 God has designed a unique body for every plant species.

15:39 The human body differs from the bodies of animals and so do the bodies of fish and birds differ from all other bodies.

15:40 There are celestial bodies as well as terrestrial bodies. The glory of the one differs from the other. There are skin-bodies and spirit-bodies. *(Our skin-bodies have a sell by date; our spirit-bodies are eternal. 2 Corinthians 5:1.)*

15:41 The glory of the sun differs from the glory of the moon; *[while the one radiates light, the other reflects light.]* Also the stars differ from one another. Each one occupies its own unique place in space.

15:42 So also with the resurrection from the dead, the body that was sown into the earth decays, but the risen person is immortal.

15:43 It is sown in sadness but raised in honor; it is sown in frailty but raised in power.

15:44 It is sown as a physical body and raised as a spiritual body. The fact that there is a physical body confirms that there is also a spiritual body.

15:45 It is recorded in Scripture how the first Adam became a living soul; the last Adam is a life radiating spirit. *(In partaking of resurrection life now, we radiate the Christ-life. No wonder then that Peter's shadow healed people. Jesus is the last Adam; when he died mankind's Adamic reference died. Jesus is the head of the human race. Human life is not defined by Adam but defined in Christ.)*

15:46 Physical life is the platform for spiritual life.

15:47 Human life was reduced to slavery and the soul-ruled earthly realm through Adam's fall but is now awakened to lordship in the heavenly realm of spiritual realities through the knowledge of our co-resurrection with Christ. *([See Colossians 3:1-11.] We theologically created the idea of mankind being sinful by nature as if humans are flawed by design. In fact it is a distorted mindset that we inherited from Adam that Jesus had to free us from. Your indifferent mindset alienated you from God into a lifestyle of annoyances, hardships, and labors, sponsored by the law of sin and death that lodged in your bodies hosting a foreign influence, foreign to your design; just like a virus that would attach itself to a person. Colossians 1:21 There is nothing wrong with our design or salvation, we were thinking wrong. [See Isaiah 55:8-11, Ephesians 4:17, 18 and also Ephesians 2:1-11.])*

15:48 The reduced state of the individual left its mark on mankind as being earthly; now the redeemed state of mankind confirms their origin in God and marks their new heavenly life.

15:49 Just as we were once defined by the flesh *[our performance-based mindset & image]* **we are now defined by our spirit image** *[our Agapē-based mindset & likeness].*

15:50 Flesh and blood has a sell-by date; the bodies you live in now will not last forever.

15:51 [1]Ponder this mystery, I want to show you something that you have never seen before: [2]everyone will be awakened out of sleep; we will [3]all experience exactly the same change. *(In other words, [1]idou musterion, Look. A Mystery. And [2]**pantes ou koimethesometha, means** no one will be left sleeping; and [3]**pantes de allangesometha**; everyone will be changed. Both verbs are in the Future Passive tense. See 1 Thessalonians 4:13-18*

If our hope in Christ was restricted to only benefit us in this life then imagine the severity of our disappointment if it all had to come to an abrupt end when we died. However this very moment the risen Christ represents everyone who has ever died; exactly like the first fruit would represent the complete harvest [1 Corinthians 15:19-22].

*The same mankind who died in a man was raised again in a man. In Adam all died; in Christ all were made alive. [See 2 Corinthians 5:14] The love of Christ resonates within us and leaves us with only one conclusion: Jesus died mankind's death; therefore, in God's logic every individual simultaneously died. [See also Hebrews 9:27 So, every person's [1]once-off appointment with death is mirrored in the full consequence of [1]this very judgment, which Jesus now disengaged. [[1]hapax as in once-off; μετὰ with δὲ [1]τουτο this κρίσις judgment. See John 12:31 Now is the judgment of this world; this is the moment where the ruler of the world-system is [1]conclusively cast out. The serpent's head is about to be crushed. Genesis 3:15; Colossians 2:14,15. This is what the Holy Spirit will convince the world of. John 16:11. John uses a double-barrel word here, **ekballō eksō** - completely thrown out. Thus, taken out of the equation. Luke 10:18. John 12:32 When I am lifted up from the earth, I will draw all of mankind and every definition of judgment unto me.]*

Hebrews 9:28 Thus, in this context [of everyone's appointment with death], Jesus is the ultimate sacrifice. What the first, shadow-dispensation merely prophetically pointed to, he fulfilled once and for all, when he was presented as an offering, to take upon himself the sins of the entire human race. Now, with sin no longer on the agenda, he appears a second time, out of this death, to be clearly seen in everyone's whole-hearted embrace of him as Savior. [See my extended notes after Hebrews chapter 9]

Eve was not an afterthought! Adam was put into a deep sleep; then God took her out of the Word that was already made flesh! Mankind redeemed, the Bride, began the same way! Co-quickened, co-raised we are! When Adam awoke from his sleep, Eve was there! Behold! Flesh of my flesh! When Adam awoke from his sleep, Eve was there! Behold, Bone of my bone, flesh of my flesh! She shall be called woman...

See Isaiah 11:1 Then a shoot will come out from the stump of Jesse, and a branch from its roots will bear fruit. See notes on Jesse in **Luke 3:32** *Son of* **Jesse** ישי *Jahweh is my husband - from* יאיש *from* יֵ *yêsh/yaysh. From an unused root meaning to stand out, or exist; entity; used adverbially or as a copula for the substantive verb* 𐤄𐤉𐤄 היה *hâyâh H1961 to breathe; to be; to exist; from the core of the name of Jahweh,* יהוה *existing. Thus, the root word for Jesse,* היה **hajah,** *in the Ancient Hebrew is,* 𐤄𐤉𐤄 *- the pictograph* 𐤄 *represents one who is looking at a great sight with his hands raised. In David's father, Jesse, it is the one looking at the other in mirror likeness. See Acts 13:22, Romans 15:12, And further Isaiah says, The root of Jesse shall come, he who rises to rule the Gentiles; in him shall the Gentiles hope. Also, hidden in the name Jesse is the prophetic picture of the incarnation - Jahweh embracing man. The word for man,* איש **ish** *and woman, adding the* ה *breath-sound, hey,* **ishah** אשה *- Thus, Jesse also includes the jod connecting Jahweh with* **ish***, man - Jahweh, the incarnate man.)*

15:52 This will happen in an instant, in a blink of the eye: the final trumpet will sound, then the dead shall be woken out of their sleep and we, who are still alive, shall be instantly changed into a different kind of body.

15:53 For this corruptible must be clothed with incorruption and this mortal must be clothed with immortality.

15:54 What was spoken in Isaiah 25:8 is finally realized even in our physical death: Death is swallowed up in victory.

15:55 Oh death where is your sting? Oh grave, where is your victory?

15:56 The sting of death is sin; the strength of sin is the law. *(It was sin that made death so frightening and law-code guilt that gave sin its leverage. — The Message.)*

15:57 Your victory is not a maybe; because of the magnanimous doing of Jesus Christ, it is a given. *(But now in a single victorious stroke of Life, all three—sin, guilt, death—are gone, the gift of our Master, Jesus Christ. Thank God. — The Message.)*

15:58 For this reason you can afford to be absolutely settled and rock-solid in faith's persuasion and always ready to go beyond where you would have gone before. Your doing now is inspired by your knowing that you are in him. If his resurrection is yours then his victory over sin and death is equally yours.

16:1 With regards your financial contributions to the saints, I have the following arrangement with all the churches in Galatia:

16:2 I encourage you to prepare your individual gifts in advance on a [1]week-by-week basis to whatever extent each one has prospered. This should be kept in treasury; this way there will be no delays or distractions regarding money matters when I visit you. *(Romans 15:25-27, I am on my way to Jerusalem to encourage the saints. The believers in Greece, all the way from Macedonia as well as those in Achaia have prepared a gift with great delight to bring relief to their Jewish brothers and sisters in Jerusalem who are struggling financially. They feel indebted to them since they share freely in their spiritual wealth.*

In Greek, [1]On one of the Sabbaths. The Jews, however, used the word Sabbath to denote the week; the period of seven days [See Matthew 28:1, Mk 16:9, Luke 18:12, Luke 24:1, John 20:1, and John 20:19; compare with Lev 23:15 and Deuteronomy 16:9.] In the Christian tradition, the first day of the week celebrates the resurrection of Jesus as the new beginning of every week.)

16:3 Upon my arrival I will endorse by letter those whom you delegate to take your grace gifts to Jerusalem.

16:4 Should there be any merit in my joining them, then they can travel with me.

16:5 It is my intent to visit you via a brief visit to the province of Macedonia. *(Northern Greece.)*

16:6 I will probably stay for a while and might even spend the winter with you; then you can help me prepare for my next destination wherever that might be. Some of you may even join me.

16:7 Even though I am not far from you presently, I would prefer not to just see you now in passing but would rather enjoy an extended stay with you in the Lord's purpose. *(The trip from Ephesus to Corinth was merely across the Aegean Sea, and comparatively a short passage en-route to Macedonia. He eventually stayed three months. See Acts 20:2,3.)*

16:8 I am presently in Ephesus and will not begin my journey before Pentecost. *(Which was in the latter part of spring.)*

16:9 A massive door of opportunity to establish a powerful and effective ministry in Ephesus has opened for me, but since there are also many who dispute this message, I do not want to leave here too soon. *(In Acts 19:9, 10: but when some were stubborn and disbelieved, speaking evil of the Way before the congregation, he withdrew from them, taking the disciples with him, and dialogued daily in the school of Tyrannus. This continued for two years, so that all the residents of Asia heard the word of the Lord, both Jews and Greeks. Luke does not mention the size of the building but much can be said about the impact of the message. In Acts 19:20-22, So the word of the Lord grew and prevailed mightily. Now after these events Paul resolved in the Spirit to pass through Macedonia and Achaia and go to Jerusalem, saying, 'After I have been there, I must also see Rome.'*

And having sent into Macedonia two of his helpers, Timothy and Erastus, he himself stayed in Asia for a while' RSV.)

16:10 My colleague in ministry, Timothy, should arrive in Corinth shortly; ensure that he feels absolutely at home with you. *(In 1 Corinthians 4:17, This is why I send my beloved son Timothy to you. He is rock-solid in his faith. He shall remind you of me and re-enforce my specific message and emphasis; [the way I teach the 'in Christ' and 'the Christ in you' and his finished work message] in every place and every ekklesia I visit.)*

16:11 No one should underrate him; honor him by providing for him and even accompanying him on his journey to join me again in Ephesus. I am eagerly anticipating to welcome him and his team on their arrival from you.

16:12 I strongly urged Apollos to join the team visiting you at present, but he did not feel at liberty to do so. I am sure that he will come in due time. *(Apparently Apollos had left Corinth in disgust over the strife there, which involved him and Paul. He had enough of partisan strife over preachers. See Acts 19:1 and 1 Corinthians 1-4.)*

16:13 Be wide awake and constant in your faith, courageous and invincible.

16:14 Agapē is your genesis. Loving everyone around you is what you are all about. *(Our love for one another is awakened by God's love for us.)*

16:15 Here is my urgent appeal to you: take the household of Stephanos as an example; this family was my first fruit of Greece and have taken the initiative to position themselves in ministering to the needs of the saints.

16:16 Give yourselves in the same way to them and to everyone laboring tirelessly in team ministry.

16:17 I want you to know my delight in having Stephanus, Fortunatus and Achaius here with me in Ephesus. They certainly represent you and have made up for your absence.

16:18 Because of them I have such peace about you. They are a real credit to you.

16:19 The churches in all of Asia salute you; also Aquila and Priscilla and the ekklesia in their home greet you fondly in the Lord.

16:20 The whole ekklesia family sends you big hugs from here; greet one another with a sacred kiss.

16:21 This letter carries my personal signature.

16:22 Anyone who prefers the law above grace remains under the curse mentality. [1]Jesus Christ has come; grace is the authority of his Lordship; we are so fond of him. He is the Messiah the world was waiting for.

(The Aramaic word, [1]maranatha, מרן אתא maran ata, means, Our Lord has come. **See Luke 1:31 For behold, you will be [1]mystically captured in your womb and conceive and bear a son. And you shall name him Jesus.** *(The word, συλλαμβάνω [1]sullambanō, means to capture/arrest; thus to conceive - the male sperm is captured in the womb [en gastri]. Now, since the spoken language of the day was Aramaic, Gabriel obviously spoke Aramaic to Mary and instructed her, that the name of this wonder child is to be יהושיע Yehoshia, Jahweh rescued.*

Iēsoús *is the Greek translation of the Hebrew/Aramaic word, יהושיע Yehoshia, Jahweh rescued. This verb is the Hif'il 3rd person Past tense. Moses changed Joshua's name from הושע Hoshea, meaning he rescued - to יהושע Yehoshua - Jahweh rescued. In prophetic endorsement of God's salvation unveiled in Jesus. Numbers 13:16. These are the names of the men whom Moses sent to spy the land; and Moses called Hoshea [he saved] son of Nun, Yehoshua - Ἰησοῦς - Iēsous in the LXX Septuagint [H3091] See John 12:13.*

The Apostolic bible's rendering, reads, For a child has been born to us; a Son was given to us, of whom the sovereignty became upon his shoulders; and his name is called, Messenger of great counsel, wonderful, mighty God, potentate, ruler of peace, father of the Ages.

The coming One, who shall bruise the serpent's head, shall be the woman's seed - the son of woman, that so he may become more truly, the son of man; while later a strange expression finds its way into the sacred prophecy, how a Virgin shall conceive, and bear a son. The Expositor's Bible Commentary.)

Instead of reading the curse when disaster strikes, Habakkuk realizes that the Promise out-dates performance as the basis to mankind's acquittal. Deuteronomy 28 would no longer be the motivation or the measure of right or wrong behavior. Though the fig tree do not blossom, nor fruit be on the vines, the produce of the olive fail and the fields yield no food, the flock be cut off from the fold and there be no herd in the stalls, yet I will rejoice in the Lord, I will joy in the God of my salvation. God, the Lord, is my strength; he makes my feet like hinds' feet, he makes me tread upon my high places. [Habakkuk 3:17–19. RSV.])

16:23 His grace is with you; you are highly favored.

16:24 My love is with you; our lives are intertwined in Christ Jesus. I salute him with a bold Yes and Amen. Paul.

In defense of his personal integrity and the content of his message, Paul writes with utmost clarity and confidence in chapter 1:18, 19, God's certainty is our persuasion; there is no maybe in him. The Son of God, Jesus Christ whom I, Paul, Sylvanus, and Timothy boldly announced in you is God's ultimate yes to mankind; human life is associated in all that he is. In God's mind there exists not even a hint of hesitation about this.

The two passages of Scripture that impacted my own life and message perhaps more than anything else are recorded in this Epistle. They are 2 Corinthians 3:18, Now we all with new understanding see ourselves in him as in a mirror; thus, we are changed from an inferior mindset to the revealed opinion of our true Origin.. Then there are these verses in 2 Corinthians 5:14-17, The love of Christ resonates within us and leaves us with only one conclusion: Jesus died mankind's death; therefore, in God's logic every individual simultaneously died.

Now if all were included in his death they were equally included in his resurrection. This unveiling of his love redefines human life. Whatever reference we could have of ourselves outside of our association with Christ is no longer relevant.

This is radical. No label that could possibly previously define someone carries any further significance. Even our pet-doctrines of Christ are redefined. Whatever we knew about him historically or sentimentally is challenged by this conclusion.

(By discovering Christ from God's point of view, we discover ourselves and every other human life from God's point of view.)

Now whoever you thought you were before, in Christ you are a brand new person. The old ways of seeing yourself and everyone else are over. Look. The resurrection of Jesus has made everything new

Scofield's Reference Bible notes the following on 2 Corinthians

DATE: A.D. 60; probably from Philippi, after the events of Acts 19:23 to 20:1-21.

THEME: This Epistle discloses the touching state of the great apostle at this time. It was one of physical weakness, weariness and pain. Also his emotional burdens. These were two kinds: solicitude for the maintenance of the churches in grace as against the law-teachers, and anguish of heart over the distrust felt toward him by Jews and Jewish Christians. The chilling doctrines of the legalizers were accompanied by detraction, and by denial of his Apostleship.

It is evident that the really dangerous sect in Corinth was that which said, and I of the Messiah [1 Corinthians 1:12]. They rejected the new revelation through Paul of the doctrines of grace; grounding themselves, probably, on the kingdom teachings of our Lord as a minister of circumcision [Romans 15.8]; seemingly oblivious that a new dispensation had been introduced by Christ's death. This made necessary a defense of the origin and extent of Paul's apostolic message. — *Scofield's*

1:1 I, Paul, am overwhelmed with the sense of God's commission on my life; Jesus Christ is the compelling urgency of my ministry. My brother Timothy and I address this writing to the [1]Ekklesia of God in Corinth, including all the saints in the whole of Greece. *(Meaning [1]church; from the Preposition ek, which always denotes origin, and kaleō, which means to identify by name; to surname.)*

1:2 The Lordship of Jesus the Messiah endorses the fact that you are the object of God's favor and friendship.

1:3 [1]Well done, God. You are the Father of our Master Jesus Christ; you are the Father of [2]compassion and the God in whom everyone is equally esteemed. *(The word, [1]eulogeō, is the well done announcement; [2]parakaleō, comes from para, a Preposition indicating close proximity, a thing proceeding from a sphere of influence, with a suggestion of union of place of residence, to have sprung from its author and giver, originating from, denoting the point from which an action originates, intimate connection and kaleō, to surname.)*

1:4 There is no contradiction of any proportion that we can possibly face that has what it takes to exasperate us or distance us from God. Our consciousness of his inseparable nearness immediately reinforces us to extend the same tangible [1]closeness to you in your difficult times, and together we snuggle up in the [1]comfort of his intimate embrace. *(Paul uses the word, [1]parakaleō, which comes from para, close proximity, and kaleō, to identify by name; often translated, to comfort.)*

1:5 This bliss and closeness we now participate in was made possible through the enormous [1]consequence of the sufferings of Christ. The overwhelming extent of his sufferings brought about this equally overwhelming sense of inseparable oneness. *(Paul uses [1]eis, which is a primary Preposition indicating the point reached in conclusion. The theme of Scripture is the sufferings of Christ and the subsequent glory. This is why no form of suffering can interfere with my joy. Every suffering on your behalf is just another opportunity to reinforce that which might still be lacking [in your understanding] of the affliction of Christ on behalf of his body which is the ekklesia. [1 Peter 1:10 and Colossians 1:24]*

The inconvenience that Paul might be suffering on behalf of the believers is not to add to the sufferings of Christ—as though the sufferings of Christ on our behalf were insufficient, but it is to further emphasize and confirm the principle of unselfish love that constrains New Testament ministry.)

1:6 Our afflictions and testimony of his closeness in the midst of it all is to spark you with courage whenever you might be facing similar contradictions. We all participate in the same salvation and enjoy equal closeness.

1:7 We are so confident about you, knowing that there is nothing you could possibly face or suffer that can separate you from his nearness.

1:8 We want you to know that we are not exaggerating the extreme contradictions and sufferings we faced in Asia. We were weighed down with enormous persecution beyond any measure of endurance; we really thought that we were going to die.

1:9 We came to terms within ourselves with the fact that we were on death row; there was no escape except our belief that God could raise us from the dead.

1:10 In the resurrection of Jesus from the dead he already delivered us from death's greatest threat; now he continues to make our victory over death's claim a daily reality. We are confident that he will raise us again. *(See 2 Corinthians 11:24-28 and Acts 14:19. 2 Timothy 1:10)*

1:11 We value your prayers. The more people partner with us in prayer the greater the gratitude shared in our testimony.

1:12 The testimony of our [1]conscience is the source of our joy. We are [2]intertwined together in [3]transparent innocence; there is no trace of a hidden agenda for the flesh to glory in. God's grace is our [4]conversation in the world and is amplified in our oneness with you. Grace abounds. *(What we are able to see together gives me so much reason for boasting in our salvation. The word, [1]suneidō, translates as conscience, joint-seeing; and [2]haplous comes from hama, a particle of union, and the word, plekō, which means to intertwine. The word [3]heilikrine translates as scrutinized in the rays of the sun to prove its flawlessness. The word [4]anastrephō from ana, upward and strephō, to turn back again. See James 1:5.)*

1:13 There is nothing to be read between the lines but only that which you will be able to [1]recognize with [2]immediate resonance. I am convinced that you will see the full intent and conclusion of our testimony from start to finish, and that you will never find any reason to think otherwise. *(The word, [1]anaginōskō, from ana, upward and ginōskō; means to know again by recognition, and [2]epiginōskō, where the Preposition epi suggests a continuous influence upon; means to become fully acquainted with.)*

1:14 To some extent you have already understood that our joy is [1]mirrored in one another. The [2]day of the Lord Jesus Christ is no longer a distant promise but a fulfilled reality. *(The word, [1]kathaper, often translated, exactly as, comes from kata, meaning according to and per, which is an enclitic particle significant of abundance and thoroughness which comes from the word, peirō, meaning to pierce. The use of the Latin enclitic relates to a word that throws an accent back onto the preceding word, which is here translated as mirrored.*

The day of the Lord Jesus Christ, is [2]hemera, which is a specific and measured period. Eastern usage of this term differs from our western usage. Any part of a day is counted as a whole day, hence the expression, three days and three nights, does not mean literally three whole days, but at least one whole day plus part of two other days.

The day of the Lord Jesus is the theme of Scripture as in 1 Peter 1:10; this was what the Prophets were studying and desiring to know. The content of their message always pointed to the day and the person where the promise of redemption would be realized. The sufferings of the Messiah would redeem and release the glory of God's image and likeness in human life; the glory that Adam lost on behalf of the human race, returns. In Acts 17:31, In the resurrection, God gave proof to the redeemed innocence of mankind; the day and the person prophesied was fulfilled in Jesus. Jesus gives context to this day in John 14:20, In that day you will know that we are in seamless union with one another. I am in my Father, you are in me and I am in you.)

1:15 Looking forward to celebrate our mutual joy, my initial plan was to come to you first before going anywhere else. We wanted you to enjoy the double blessing of our visit.

1:16 We were really looking forward to seeing you again on our return from Macedonia and then to be escorted by you on our trip to Judea.

1:17 It is not our style to hesitate between two opinions. We have no desire to make promises that we cannot keep. When we said yes to you we did not mean, no.

1:18 God's certainty is our persuasion; there is no maybe in him.

1:19 The Son of God, Jesus Christ, whom I, Paul, Sylvanus and Timothy boldly announced in you, is God's ultimate yes to you-manity. Jesus is God's Yes to you. Human life is associated in all that he is. In God's mind there exists not even a hint of hesitation about this. *(Note, Paul and his team proclaimed Christ in them, not, tothem. See Galatians 1:16; and Colossians. 1:27. Also 2 Corinthians 3:4.)*

1:20 In him the detail of every single promise of God is fulfilled; Jesus is God's yes to your entire well being. In our union with him the Amen that echoes in us gives evidence to his glorious intent through us.

1:21 God himself authorizes our oneness with you in Christ. He is our anointing. *(The word, χρίω **chriō** means to smear or rub with oil, to anoint.)*

1:22 His personal signet signature is the official stamp that sanctions the integrity of our ministry to you; this is the seal of the Spirit in our hearts.

1:23 So God is my witness in this; I did not break my promise to you. The only reason I did not come to Corinth was to spare you the embarrassment.

1:24 I am not your faith-monitor. I am your co-worker and I am jealous for your joy. You stand on your own feet in your faith.

2:1 I came to the following conclusion that paying you another painful visit *[on my return trip]* would be of no advantage to you.

2:2 My visit would only put you in an awkward position; since you knew that you caused me grief, you would feel under obligation to cheer me up.

2:3 I wrote to you instead; not risking the embarrassment of facing you and then having to deal with sorrow when all I really desired from you was joy. I am convinced that my joy is also your joy.

2:4 There was nothing blasé about my writing. I was in tears with painful distress and deep-felt anguish, certainly not to upset you but that you would know the intensity of my love for you.

2:5 I am not exaggerating the issue by saying that the man whose behavior caused such alarm in me did not merely grieve me but in a sense everyone of you.

2:6 This person has been amply taxed by all.

2:7 It is due time now to offer him your forgiveness and closeness lest he be completely swamped with regret.

2:8 I implore you to make your love for him [1]very clear. *(The word, [1]kuroō, translates as officially; publicly confirm your love for him.)*

2:9 The intent and urgency of my first letter was to prove your loyalty to my ministry and message in its full context.

2:10 I am joined to you *[geographic distance does not separate us]*; your forgiveness is my forgiveness. The favor reflected in the face of Christ is our only valid reference to true forgiveness anyway.

2:11 The [2]agenda of any [1]accusation is to divide and dominate. We are not ignorant about that. *(The word [1]satanas means accuser and [2]nous refers to mind or strategy, agenda, schemes.)*

2:12 So instead of coming to you I went to Troas where again a great ministry opportunity in the Good News of Christ was opened for me in the Lord. *(There is not a place on this planet that is not an open door for this gospel.)*

2:13 I expected to find Titus in Troas and was hoping to hear from him refreshing news concerning you. I felt so urgent to meet with Titus that I took leave from Troas and hastened on to look for him in Macedonia. *(See 2 Corinthians 7:4-8.)*

2:14 I am overwhelmed with gratitude. Wherever my travels take me I am so aware that God leads us as trophies in his victory parade. What he knows to be true about us diffuses through us like a perfume of sweet aroma everywhere we go, celebrating the success of the cross. *(In ancient triumphs, abundance of perfumes and wreaths of sweet smelling flowers were used in victory celebrations.)*

2:15 We are a sweet savor of Christ to God evident in everyone we meet. The fragrance of Christ is recognized in all to salvation. The same gospel that announces the fragrant victory of Christ declares the odor of death; the [1]defeat of destruction in everyone. (*This parade of victory is a public announcement of the defeat of the religious systems and structures based on the law of works. Just like it is in any public game where the victory celebration of the winning team is an embarrassment for the losing team. The death of evil is announced in resurrection life. The word,* [1]**apollumi**, *is derived from* **apo**, *away from, and* **luō**, *to loosen, to undo, to dissolve. See 1 John 3:8.*)

2:16 The message we communicate is a fragrance with an immediate association; to darkness, it is the smell of doom [*the death of death*]; to life it is the familiar fragrance of life itself.

2:17 We are not competing with those who have added their [1]price tag to the gospel. Our conversation has its source in Christ; we communicate from the transparent innocence of a face to face encounter with God. (*The law of personal performance or* [1]**kapeleuō**, *meaning retail, which I translated here as a gospel with a price tag.*)

3:1 The days when I needed letters to endorse my authority are over. *(See Acts 9:2)* We are not in a competition showing off our credentials. Some insist on certificates; I do not see any relevance in it. Neither do I require a note of recommendation to you or from you.

3:2 Instead of an impressive certificate framed on my wall I have you framed in my heart. You are our Epistle written within us, an open letter speaking a global language; one that everyone can [1]read and recognize as their mother tongue. *(The word [1]anaginōskō, from ana, upward and ginōskō, to know upward; thus to draw knowledge from a higher reference; from above; to recognize; to read with recognition.)*

3:3 The fact that you are a Christ-Epistle shines as bright as day. This is what our ministry is all about. The Spirit of God is the living ink. Every trace of the Spirit's influence on the heart is what gives permanence to this conversation. We are not talking law-language here; this is more dynamic and permanent than letters chiseled in stone. This conversation is embroidered in your inner consciousness. *(It is the life of your design that grace echoes within you.)*

3:4 Christ is proof of our persuasion about you [1]before God. *(The Greek Preposition [1]pros, means towards; face-to-face. Also 2 Corinthians 1:18,19,20.)*

3:5 We have not [1]reached this conclusion by any merit of our own. Of God's doing are we made competent. *(The word, [1]logitsomai, means to reckon; making a calculation to which there can only be one logical conclusion.)*

3:6 It is God's signature in our spirit that authorizes New Testament ministry. We are not qualified by a legal document endorsed by a fellow human. The letter *[of the law]* is the administration of death; it is the Spirit *[of grace]* that quickens life.

3:7 Because of its prophetic purpose, even the old administration of death, carved in stone, evidenced a glimpse of glory; for a brief moment the face of Moses shone with such brilliance that the people of Israel could not even look at his face. The fact that the glory reflected in Moses was brief and fading, confirmed that the ministry of the letter had a sell by date and that it was destined [1]to be brought to naught. *(It served merely to emphasize the failure of the flesh to access the glory that Adam had lost on mankind's behalf. The word, [1]katargeō, derives from kata, meaning intensity, and argos, meaning labor, denotes that the law of works would be rendered entirely useless; thus, the new arrangement would free us from all self-effort to attempt to improve what God has already perfected in Christ. Consider the contrast in verse 18; from a mere glimpse of a veiled and fading glory to unveiled gazing into the face of glory as in a mirror and a transformed life radiating the same glory.)*

3:8 How much more radiant would the ministry of the Spirit be.

3:9 If the ministry of condemnation had a glimpse of glory, the glory that the ministry of righteousness now communicates is beyond comparison. *(There are two administrations: the one confirms mankind's guilt because of Adam; the other confirms mankind's innocence because of Christ. The one was upheld by the letter of the law; the other is sustained by the life of the Spirit. Mankind's standing before God is*

199

restored; righteousness by the merit of the cross far outweighs any attempt of the flesh to compete. Nothing that anyone can do can improve their standing before God.)

3:10 What seemed glorious and important at the time has been reduced to total obscurity and irrelevance.

3:11 The fragile and fading glory of the flesh is dwarfed into insignificance by the unfading glory of the Spirit. *(The ministry of the New Testament reveals oneness and permanence. In Christ the idea of distance and delay is canceled.)*

3:12 Our every expectation is fulfilled; therefore, we speak with clarity and conviction. *(Every definition of veil is removed from our conversation. We have no hidden agenda. This is what we say as plainly as possible: Jesus mirrors you! The image and likeness of God is no longer a future promise of possibilities and potential; it is our reality and reference now. See Colossians 1:27.)*

3:13 What we say is so unlike Moses who had to keep Israel in suspense with a veiled face; they did not realize that this arrangement would never suffice to secure their standing before God. In essence the letters on stone confirmed their death. All that they could see was the futility of the law of works; how entirely useless their best attempts would be to match the life of their design. *(In Adam all are represented in the I am not-illusion of the Performance-based Tree; they did not realize it until the law revealed it. In Christ all are equally mirrored in their redeemed innocence and identity, but do not realize it until the Gospel reveals it! Romans 3:23,24; & Romans 10:17; Romans 7:4-25.)*

3:14 Since the time of Moses until this very day their minds remain calloused and veiled. They are kept in suspense without realizing that there is no glory left in the law: *(whatever glory there was, carried merely a fading, prophetic glimmer)* **reading the Old Covenant without understanding that Christ is the fulfillment of Scripture is a complete waste of time. Only in discovering our union with Christ is the veil removed and do we realize that the old system is [1]rendered entirely useless.** *(The word [1]katergeō comes from kata, meaning intensity, and argos, meaning labor, the law of works is rendered entirely useless; thus the new arrangement frees us from all self-effort to attempt to improve what God has already perfected in Christ.)*

3:15 In the meantime nothing seems to have changed; the same veil continues to blindfold the hearts of people whenever Moses is read. *(Moses symbolizes the futility of self righteousness as the global blindfold of the religious world. [John 1:17] Against the stark backdrop of the law; with Moses representing the condemned state of mankind, Jesus Christ unveils grace and truth. He is the life of our design redeemed in human form.)*

3:16 The moment anyone [1]returns to the Lord the veil is gone. *(The word, [1]epistrephō means to return to where we've wandered from; we all like sheep have gone astray. Jesus is God unveiled in human form. [Colossians 1:15] Also 1 Peter 2:25 You were completely vulnerable, just like sheep roaming astray without direction or protection, but now you have returned and are restored to the shepherd and Guardian of your souls. And 1 Peter 1:17. Then, Hebrews 8:1, The conclusion of all that has been said points us to an exceptional Person, who towers far above the rest in the highest office of heavenly greatness. He is the executive authority of the majesty of God.*

Hebrews 8:2 The office he now occupies is the one which the Moses-model resembled prophetically. He ministers in the holiest place in God's true tabernacle of worship. Nothing of the old man-made structure can match its perfection. Hebrews 8:10 Now, instead of documenting my laws on stone, I will chisel them into your mind and engrave them in your inner consciousness; it will no longer be a one-sided affair. I will be your God and you will be my people, not by compulsion but by mutual desire. See James 1:25, Those who gaze into the mirror reflection of the face of their birth are captivated by the effect of a law that frees them from the obligation to the old written code that restricted them to their own efforts and willpower. No distraction or contradiction can dim the impact of what they see in that mirror concerning the law of perfect liberty [the law of faith] that now frees them to get on with the act of living the life [of their original design]. They find a new spontaneous lifestyle; the poetry of practical living. [The law of perfect liberty is the image and likeness of God revealed in Christ, now redeemed in human life as in a mirror.])

3:17 The Lord and the Spirit are one; his Lordship sanctions our freedom. A freedom from rules chiseled in stone to the voice of our redeemed design echoing in our hearts.

3:18 [1]Now, we all, with [2]new understanding, see ourselves in him [3]as in a mirror. The days of window-shopping are over. In him every face is [2]unveiled. In [3]gazing with wonder at the [4]likeness of Elohim displayed in human form, we suddenly realize that we are looking into a mirror, where every feature of their image, articulated in the Lord, is reflected within us. The Spirit of the Lord engineers this radical [5]transformation; we are led from an inferior [6]mind-set to the revealed [6]endorsement of our authentic identity. [7]From the fading glory of our own achievement, to the discovery of the most amazing reality, that we are God's glory!

([1] This is the fulfillment of Isaiah 40:5 [1]Then the glory of the Lord shall be revealed, and all flesh shall see it together, for the mouth of the Lord has spoken!

We've got our masks off and God's brilliance is bouncing off our faces. We're glowing from knowing. 2 Corinthians. 3:18 [Rob Lacey]

[2] The word, [2]anakaluptō; from ana, a Preposition denoting upward, to return again, and kaluptō, to uncover, unveil.

[3] The word, [3]katoptrizomai, means to gaze into a reflection, to mirror oneself.

[4] Let Us make man in Our image, according to Our likeness. [Genesis 1:26] The word, [4]eikon, translates as exact resemblance, image and likeness; eikon always assumes a prototype, that which it not merely resembles, but from that which it is drawn.

[5] Then Paul uses [5]metamorphumetha as a Present Passive Indicative from metamorphoō; meta, together with, and morphoō, form. [The word commonly translated sin, hamartia, from ha, negative, or without and meros, allotted portion or form; thus, a distorted form, which is the opposite of metamorphē; with form. The word meros is the stem of morphē, [from the base of G3313 meros, through the idea of adjustment of parts; shape; form. As in Mark 16:12] Now, with unveiled faces we are gazing at the glory of the Lord as in a mirror and metamorphosis happens - image and likeness awakens within us.

[6] The word *⁶doxa, glory, translates here as mindset. It is an ancient Greek term from the verb,* **dokein** δοκεῖν, *to appear like something, to seem to be, to think, to form an opinion; to evaluate; reputation, credit, honor. Between the 3rd and 1st centuries BCE, the term picked up additional meanings when the Biblical Hebrew word for 'glory'* כבוד, *kavod -weight, was translated by the Septuagint as* **doxa**. *See 2 Corinthians 4:17 where Paul uses both meanings: the weight of glory. The extended meaning of doxa now includes the following meanings, splendor, majesty, magnificence, brilliance, beauty.*

[7] Note the word translated from *glory to glory', apo doxes eis doxan; eis, a point reached in conclusion; the Preposition ⁷apo, here points away from, meaning away from the glory that previously defined us, i.e. our own achievements or disappointments, to the glory of our original design that now defines us.* **Two glories are mentioned in this chapter:** *the* **glory of the flesh,** *which is the veiled, fading kind represented by Moses,* **and the unfading, unveiled glory of God's image and likeness,** *mirrored in the face of the Lord Jesus, the Incarnate Christ, and now redeemed in us. See also 2 Corinthians 4:4 -7.*

[The Greek word translated from in this verse is not the same as the word translated from in Romans 1:17. Paul says the unveiling of God's righteousness is **from** *faith to faith, where he does not use the word* **apo**, *away from, but the Preposition,* **ek**, *which always denotes source or origin.]*

Some translations of this Scripture read, we are being changed from glory to glory. This would suggest that change is gradual and will more than likely take a lifetime, which was the typical thinking that trapped Israel for forty years in the wilderness of unbelief. We cannot become more than what we already are in Christ. We do not grow more complete; we simply grow in the knowledge and awareness of our completeness. [See Colossians 3:10]

How long does it take the beautiful swan to awaken to the truth of its design? The ugly duckling was an illusion. Whatever it was that endorsed the 'ugly duckling' mindset, co-died together with Christ. In the death and resurrection of Jesus Christ, God did not redeem a compromised replica of you; he rescued the original, blueprint you, created in his radiant mirror likeness. Any other 'self' you're trying to find or esteem will disappoint. See Romans 6:11, Reckon your 'DIY-law of works-self' dead, and your redeemed self co-raised and co-seated together with Christ. This is freedom indeed. Galatians 2:19,20; Galatians 2:20 So here I am dead and alive at the same time. I'm dead to the old me I was trying to be and alive to the real me which is Christ in me. Co-crucified, now co-alive. What a glorious entanglement. I was in him in his death; now he is in me in my life. For the first time I'm free to be me in my skin, immersed in his faith in our joint-sonship. He loves me and believes in me. He is God's gift to me. (The verb συνεσταύρωμαι from **suntauroō**, *is in the Perfect tense, indicating that not only was I crucified with Christ in the past, but I am existing now in that present condition. How can any human effort improve on this. See Hosea 6:2 and Ephesians 2:5 also Romans 7:6 But now we are fully released from any further association with a life directed by the rule of the law, we are dead to that which once held us captive, free to be slaves to the newness of spirit-spontaneity rather than age old religious rituals, imitating the mere face value of the written code. The moment one exchanges spontaneity with rules, the edge of romance is compromised.))*

4:1 Since we are employed by the mercy of God, and not by our own qualifications, quitting is not an option. (*Having this ministry by the mercy of God, we do not lose heart. RSV.*)

4:2 We have renounced hidden agendas [*employing a little bit of the law in an attempt to balance out grace*]; we have distanced ourselves from any obscure [1]craftiness to manipulate God's word to make it mean what it does not say. With truth on open display in us, we highly recommend our lives to everyone's [2]conscience. Truth finds its most authentic and articulate expression in human life, [3]mirrored in the face of God. (*It is our passion for all to see what is so completely obvious in the mirror of our redeemed likeness and innocence; this beats any doctrinal debate. The word translated craftiness, is the word* [1]**panourgia** *from* **pas** *and* **ergon**, *all manner of wearisome labor.* [2]*Conscience in Latin means to know together; in the Greek,* [2]**suneidō**, *translates as joint seeing; which is the opposite of* **Hadēs**, *from* **ha** + **eidō**, *not to see.* πρὸς πᾶσαν [*every individual*] συνείδησιν [*seamless-seeing*] ἀνθρώπων ἐνώπιον τοῦ Θεοῦ *pros* [*face to face*] *The word for the human species, male or female is* **anthropos**, *from* **ana**, *upward, and* **tropos**, *manner of life; character; in like manner.*)

4:3 If our message seems vague to anyone, it is not because we are withholding something from certain people. It is just because some are so stubborn in their efforts to uphold an outdated system that they don't see it. They are all equally found in Christ but they prefer to remain lost in the cul-de-sac language of the law.

4:4 The survival and self-improvement programs of the [1]religious systems of this world veil the minds of the unbelievers; exploiting their ignorance about their true origin and their redeemed innocence. The veil of unbelief obstructs a person's view and keeps them from seeing what the light of the gospel so clearly reveals: the [2]glory of God is the image and likeness of our Maker redeemed in human form; this is what the gospel of Christ is all about. (*The god of this* [1]**aion**, *age, refers to the religious systems and governing structures of this world. The unbelief that neutralized Israel in the wilderness was the lie that they believed about themselves; We are grasshoppers, and the 'enemy' is a giant beyond any proportion. [Numbers 13:33, Joshua 2:11, Hebrews 4:6.] They failed to possess the promise due to unbelief. The blueprint* [2]**doxa**, *glory of God, is what Adam lost on mankind's behalf. See Ephesians 4:18.*)

4:5 Even though we recommend ourselves with great confidence, it is not with arrogance; we do not preach ourselves. We preach Christ Jesus the Lord; we are addicted to this gospel; employed by Jesus for your sakes.

4:6 The light source is founded in the same God who said, Light, be. And light shone out of darkness. He lit the lamp in our understanding so that we may clearly recognize the features of his likeness in the face of Jesus Christ reflected within us. (*The same God who bade light shine out of darkness has kindled a light in our hearts, whose shining is to make known his glory as he has revealed it in the features of Jesus Christ. — Knox Translation.*)

4:7 And now, in the glow of this glorious light and with unveiled faces we discover this treasure where it was hidden all along, in these frail skin-suits made of [1]clay. We did not invent ourselves; we are God's idea to begin with

and the dynamic of his doing and amazing engineering. *(The word translated earthen vessel or clay jar is the word [1]ostrakinos from ostrakon oyster. It is a great visual picture of how we carry a very valuable pearl within us. The cosmetic value of the clay pot can never compete with the treasure it holds. There is so much more to you than what meets the eye. The kingdom of heaven is like treasure hidden in an agricultural field, which a man found and covered up; then in his joy he goes and sells all that he has and buys the entire field. [Matthew 13:44] In order to redeem our minds from the lies that we believed about us, God invested all that he has in the redeeming of our original value. See 1 Peter 1:18,19. He rescued the life of our design. Our inner life hosts this treasure. Jesus said in John 7:37,38, In your realizing that I am what the Scriptures are all about, you will discover uniquely for yourself, face to face with me, that I am what you are all about and rivers of living waters will gush out of **your innermost being.**)*

4:8 We often feel completely hemmed in on every side but our inner space remains unrestricted; when there seems to be no way out, we escape within.

4:9 At times we are persecuted to the extreme but we are never abandoned. We are knocked down but not knocked out.

4:10 Wherever we go, whatever we encounter in our bodies, we bear witness within us of the fact that Jesus died our death; in this same body, we now exhibit his life. The fact that we co-died in his death confirms that we now co-live in his resurrection.

4:11 Our day-to-day experience continues to exhibit that even in the face of death, our association with the death Jesus already died remains the inspiration of his life made so clearly visible within us. This is in such contrast to the circumstances that we are often faced with.

4:12 Our persuasion of our co-crucifixion with Christ in the face of death threatening circumstances [1]inspires life in you. *(The word, [1]energeo, translates as energy trigger.)*

4:13 We [1]echō the exact same spirit of faith David had when he wrote: I [2]believe and so I speak. We too believe and so we speak. Our persuasion is our conversation. *(The word, [1]echō, means to hold or to embrace. Paul quotes David here in Psalm 116; sometimes one's soul wants to gallop away into distraction like a wild horse; then, David reminds himself, Return to your rest, oh my soul, for the Lord has dealt bountifully with you. I believe, and so I speak. God's bountiful dealings with us in Christ is our only valid rest; Sabbath celebrates perfection. Behold, it is very good. Genesis 1:31,2:2 And remember God does not employ circumstances to teach us something. The finished work of Christ teaches us; his work on the cross rescued us. Psalm 116:7,10 I [2]believe; I am sure, אמן aw-man, with the root meaning, to build up, or support; to foster as a parent or nurse; figuratively to render [or be] firm or faithful, to trust or believe, to be permanent or quiet; to be true or certain; to go to the right hand: - hence assurance, [relocate yourself mentally where you are co-seated together with Christ in God's right hand.] Also, the word, amen, so it be.)*

Hebrew word to speak, דבר dabar, to arrange words in such a way that their effect is to subdue. [Like a lawyer's letter; using legal language.]

Then David uses the word, עֶנָה *anah, which was translated, 'afflicted', but the same word is also used to respond; by extension to begin to speak; specifically to sing, shout, testify, announce: - give account, which is a much more appropriate rendering of this word in context. The Hebrew actually says: I will sing loudly. Remember Paul sang in prison.*

Let faith speak. Let faith break out in song.)

4:14 **This resurrection life we enjoy in Jesus fully includes you.**

4:15 **Whatever we go through in the gospel is to advantage you. We live for you. As grace abounds in more and more people, so does the volume of gratitude in the accomplished mission of Jesus - breaking through the sound barrier to exhibit the [1]heart dream of God.** (*The word, [1]doxa, means glory, from dokeō, meaning intent, opinion, the heart dream of God. [Their image and likeness redeemed and revealed in incarnate human life.])*

4:16 **We have much reason to be brave. There might be a lot of wear and tear on the outside; but don't be distracted by that. On the inside we are celebrating daily revival.**

4:17 **We are fully engaged in an exceedingly superior reality; the extent and [1]weight of this glory make any degree of suffering vanish into insignificance. The suffering is fleeting and ever so slight by comparison to the weight and enduring effect of this glory we participate in for all eternity.** *(In Hebrew the word* כבד *Kabod, means weight - this is also the word for glory - Paul reflects on this weight as the standard measure of everything that defines the glory of God. According to 2 Corinthians 3:18 mankind is his glory. This glory is the true currency of life. Paul reasons that by comparison, any size contradiction is dwarfed into insignificance and appears ever so slight when positioned against the enormity of the weight of glory that dwells within us.)*

4:18 **We are not keeping any score of what seems so obvious to the senses on the surface; it is fleeting and irrelevant; it is the unseen eternal realm within us which has our full attention and captivates our gaze.** *(See John 1:18 Until this moment God remained invisible to mankind; now the [1]authentic begotten Son, ([1]monogenes, begotten only of God) the blueprint of mankind's design who represents the innermost being of God, the Son who is in the bosom of the Father, brings him into full view. He is the [2]official authority qualified to announce God. He is our guide who accurately declares and interprets the invisible God within us. (Official guide, [2]eksegesato, from ek, Preposition denoting source, and hegeomai, the strengthened form of agō, to lead as a shepherd leads his sheep; thus hegeomai means to be officially appointed in a position of authority.*

2 Corinthians 3:18 The days of window-shopping are over. In him every face is unveiled. In gazing with wonder at the likeness of God displayed in human form, we suddenly realize that we are looking at ourselves. Every feature of their image is mirrored in us. This is the most radical transformation engineered by the Spirit of the Lord; we are led from an inferior mindset to the revealed endorsement of our authentic identity.)

5:1 Our [1]skin-suits have a [2]sell by date; our spirit-bodies are eternal. The same God who fashioned these skin-bodies in our mother's womb, engineered our spirit-bodies to be our permanent dwelling. *(The word, [1]skēnos, reminds of the English word skin and translates, tabernacle. The word, [2]kataluō means to be loosed because it has completed its function - like on a journey of travelers, when they halt to put up lodge for the night; the straps and packs of the beasts of burden are unbound and taken off or, more correctly, from the fact that a traveller's garments were tied up when they were on a journey to be loosed at its end.)*

5:2 Facing pressure times the way we often do, makes us sigh with longing to exchange our skin-suit with the permanent splendor of the heavenly-body.

5:3 In the meantime, whatever challenges we are facing in the meat-box, we know that we shall never be found naked; since we are already fully clothed with our heavenly identity in Christ in our inner person.

5:4 We are not complaining about our bodies, even though we are often aware of its frailties; instead we yearn to be overwhelmed with life. We know that every evidence of death, even in our bodies, will dissolve into life.

5:5 God wired us this way; his Spirit already confirms within us the present evidence of eternity. We are eternal beings by design.

5:6 We are cheerfully courageous, knowing that our immediate address in our earthly bodies cannot distance us from the Lord, since we originate from him.

5:7 Faith is to our spirit what our senses are to our bodies; while the one engages with the fading and the fragile, the other celebrates perfection. *(Faith is not blindly believing what you don't understand; faith sees. The eye through the lens of the law cannot see what faith sees. Faith is seeing through Father's eyes.)*

5:8 Our [1]confidence stems from [2]knowing that even though it might feel at times that we are merely [4]reduced to flesh, our [3]greater reality is that we are [5]entwined in the Lord. He is our permanent abode. *(The word, [1]tharreō, means confident courage; [2]eudokeō, means well done opinion; [3]mallon, means prefer or rather; and [4]ekdēmeō, from ek, is a Preposition that always denotes origin or source and dēmeō from deō, to bind, to wind, to tie, to knit; originating out of the body (we were knitted together in our mother's womb). In severe affliction one feels at times reduced to mere physical identity; but [2]our persuasion is anchored in a greater [2]opinion; the reality of our genesis in God and our union in him. The word, [5]endēmeō, means entwined, knitted together, tied in oneness. Yet at times it almost feels strange to be trapped in this body especially when we are exposed to such abuse and suffering; one longs to then do the exchange and relocate to our permanent address, where our hearts already are; in the immediate embrace of the Lord.)*

5:9 We are [1]completely engaged in the loveliness of that which is of exceedingly great value; whether we are [2]in a physical union with our bodies or a [3]spiritual union with our source; it makes no difference to God's esteem of us. We are highly favored by the Lord. *(The word, [1]philotimeomai, comes from phileō, meaning dear, fondness; timay, meaning value, esteem; and einai from eimi, I am. The word, [2]endēmeō, means in union with, entwined; and [3]ekdēmeō means tied to our source.)*

5:10 For we have all been [1]thoroughly scrutinized in the [2]judgment of Jesus. We are [3]taken care of and restored to the life of our design, regardless of what happened to us in our individual lives, whatever amazing or meaningless things we encountered in the body. *(See 2 Corinthians 5:14,16. We are mirrored in his life; his life reflects ours, not as an example for us but of us. Also, 2 Corinthians 3:18. The word, [1]phaneroō, means to render apparent; to openly declare; to manifest. Paul uses the Aorist Passive Infinitive tense phanerōthēnai, not referring to a future event. The Present Infinitive expresses progressive or imperfective aspect. It pictures the action expressed by the verb as being in progress. The Aorist Infinitive, however, does not express progressive aspect. It presents the action expressed by the verb as a completed unit with a beginning and end. The word, bematos, comes from [2]bayma, which means footprint, also referring to a raised place mounted by steps, or a tribunal, the official seat of a judge. The word, κομισηται komisētai is the Aorist Subjunctive of [3]kolumbaō, means to tend, to take care of, to provide for, to carry off from harm. Paul's reference was not about how much abuse and affliction he suffered, nor was it the many good times he remembered that defined him; I am what I am by the grace of God. If we are still to be judged for good or bad deeds that we performed in the body, then the judgment that Jesus faced on mankind's behalf was irrelevant. Sadly this verse has been grossly misrepresented in most other translations - For we must all appear before the judgment seat of Christ, so that each one may receive good or evil, according to what he has **done** in the body. Note the word done is in italics in the Authorised Versions - it's not in the original text.*

*For more context on the word, **kolumbaō**, see 1 Peter 1:8 So even though you have never seen Jesus in the flesh, you love him; even at times where he seems remote and invisible, your awareness of your union in him continues to ignite belief. You are leaping with indescribable and exuberant joy as you hold him in high esteem. 1 Peter 1:9 In this place of joy, you are [1]**beyond the reach of any harm**. Joy gives your faith a voice announcing the perfection of your soul's salvation. (Joy celebrates the fulfillment of Scripture. Belief gives evidence of everything the Prophets pointed to. The word, [1]**kolumbaō**, to carry off from harm.) 1 Peter 1:10 This salvation which you now know as your own, is the theme of the prophetic thought; this is what intrigued the Prophets' minds for generations and became the object of their most diligent inquiry and scrutiny. They knew all along that mankind's salvation was a grace revelation, sustained in their prophetic utterance. (Salvation would never be by personal achievement or a reward to willpower-driven initiative. The law of works would never replace grace.)*

5:11 We persuade people in the [1]radiance of the Lord. His visible glory is mirrored in us. Our lives are transparent before God; we anticipate that you will witness the same transparency in your [2]conscience. *(The word, [2]suneidō, translates as conscience, joint seeing. In 2 Corinthians 4:2, with the open statement of the truth we commend ourselves to everyone's conscience. The word, **phobe**, speaks of* *dread terror and fear. I would prefer to use the word, [1]phoibe, which means radiant. Because of images and idols of our own imagination of a schizophrenic, monster god, we have Bible translations to endorse that. If 2 Corinthians 5:10 points to a future judgment of condemnation, then verse 11 makes sense. We persuade people by the terror of God. Wow. And 3 verses later in verse 14, Paul is constrained by the love of Christ? Jesus is the express image of God, the radiance of his beauty. He has made the invisible God visible. He is the Father of lights with whom there is no shadow due to compromise; there is no dark side to God. Paul is not one day motivated by the terror of God and the next day by his love.)*

5:12 We do not want you to pity us, but rather to be proud of us for your own sakes. We are not into window-dressing because we are not into window-shopping. Neither are we here to impress you with us but to impress you with you.

5:13 We are [1]blissfully out of our minds with pleasure before our Maker; he delights in our ecstasy. Our insane mode is between us and God; we promise to behave ourselves sane and sober before you. *(The word, [1]ekstase, is to be blissfully out of one's mind with pleasure.)*

5:14 The love of Christ constrains us and [1]resonates within us; leaving us with only one [2]conclusion: when Jesus died, every individual simultaneously died. In God's logic, one has died for all, [2]thus all have died. *(The word, [1]sunechō, to press together; to squeeze; from sun, meaning together with and echō, meaning to echo; to embrace; to hold; also, to resonate. The word αρα [2]ara, means conclusion. Jesus didn't die 99% or for 99%. He one hundred percent died humanity's death. If Paul had to compromise the last part of verse 14 to read: one died for all therefore only those who follow the prescriptions to qualify, have also died, then he would have had to change the first half of the verse as well. Only the agapē of Christ can make a calculation of such enormous proportions. The religious mind would question the extremity of God's love and perhaps prefer to add a condition or two to a statement like that.)*

5:15 Now if all were included in his death they were equally included in his resurrection. This unveiling of his love redefines human life. Whatever reference we could have of ourselves outside of our association with Christ is no longer relevant.

5:16 Therefore, from now on, I no longer know anyone according to the flesh. I no longer see people from a human point of view. This is a radical and most defining moment. No label that could possibly previously identify someone carries any further significance. Even our pet-doctrines of Christ are redefined. Whatever we knew about him historically or sentimentally is challenged by this conclusion. *(By discovering Christ from God's point of view we discover ourselves and every other human life from God's point of view. Paul sees by revelation that, what Jesus redeemed in every person, brings final closure and death to any other reasoning and judgment we may have had of ourselves or anyone else for that matter. This is Paul's 'metanoia' moment. Note, the Greek word, metanoia, from meta, together with and voιέω noieō, to perceive with the mind. It describes the awakening of the mind to that which is true;*

a re-alignment of one's reasoning; it is a gathering of one's thoughts, a co-knowing. Faith is not a decision; it is a discovery. It has nothing in common with the Latin word **paenitentia** *- where the idea of penance and repentance stems from.)*

5:17 Now, in the light of your co-inclusion in his death and resurrection, whoever you thought you were before, in Christ you are a brand new person. The old ways of seeing yourself and everyone else are over. Acquaint yourself with the new. *(Just imagine this. Whoever a person was as a Jew, Greek, slave or freeman, Boer, Zulu, Xhosa, British, Indian, Muslim or American, Chinese, Japanese or Congolese; is now dead and gone. They all died when Jesus died. Remember we are not talking law language here. The 'If' in, If anyone is in Christ is not a condition, it is the conclusion of the revelation of the gospel. Mankind is in Christ by God's doing [1 Corinthians 1:30 and Ephesians 1:4]. The verses of 2 Corinthians 5:14-16 give context to verse 17. For so long we studied verse 17 on its own and interpreted the 'if' as a condition. Paul did not say, If anyone is in Christ, he said THEREFORE if anyone is in Christ ... The therefore immediately includes verses 14 to 16. If God's faith sees everyone in Christ in his death, then they were certainly also in Christ in his resurrection. Jesus did not reveal a potential you, he revealed the truth about you so that you may know the truth about yourself and be free indeed. In the death and resurrection of Jesus Christ, God did not redeem a compromised replica of you; he rescued the original, blueprint you, created in his radiant mirror likeness. Any other 'self' you're trying to find or esteem will disappoint. Reckon your 'DIY-law of works-self' dead, and your redeemed self co-raised and co-seated together with Christ. This is freedom indeed. Galatians 2:19,20; Romans 6:11. See 1 Peter 1::3 We are reconnected with our original genesis through the resurrection of Jesus from the dead. This new birth endorses and celebrates the hope of the ages; God's eternal love dream concludes in life.)*

5:18 The idea of mankind's co-inclusion in the death and resurrection of Jesus Christ is entirely God's doing. To now realize that God has indeed brought final closure to the old and for us to see everything and everyone in this new light is to simply see what God has always known to be true about us in Christ; we are not debating human experience, opinion, or their contribution; this is exactly what God believes. In Jesus Christ, God [1]exchanged equivalent value to redeem us to himself. He went to the highest extreme in this act of reconciliation to persuade us of our original worth. This, God has given us as the mandate of our ministry. *(The word, καταλλάσσω [1]katallassō, translates as reconciliation; meaning a mutual exchange of equal value. Thayer Definition: to exchange, as coins for others of equivalent value. This transaction was not to buy us back from the Devil; a thief never becomes an owner; it was God redeeming our minds from the lies that we believed about ourselves - reconciliation is the bold unveiling of the value of the hidden treasure in everyone. See 2 Corinthians 4:7 and Matthew 13:44.)*

5:19 Jesus [1]did not act independently of his Father. God was present in Christ when they [2]reconciled the total [3]cosmos to themselves. Deity and humanity embraced. God's act of reconciliation takes every other conclusion out of the equation! [4]No amount of trespasses can match

God's evaluation of the human race. Redeemed friendship is now announced from within us! *(The ¹incarnation did not separate the Father from the Son and the Spirit. In him dwells the fullness of Deity in a human body. Colossians 2:9. As a human person, Jesus felt the agony of mankind on the cross when he echoed Psalm 22, My God, my God, why have you forsaken me. Why are you so far from helping me, from the words of my groaning? But then in verse 24, David declares triumphantly: He has not despised or abhorred the affliction of the afflicted; and he has not hid his face from him.*

The word translated reconciliation, is καταλλάσσω ²katallassō, meaning a mutual exchange of equal value. The word, ³kosmos in the NT refers to the entire human family. The words, μὴ λογιζόμενος from, μὴ me, negative and ⁴logitsomai to make a calculation to which there can only be one logical conclusion. Thus, there is no possible calculation that can outweigh the extremity of God's act of reconciliation.)

5:20 The voice God has in Christ he now has in us; we are God's ambassadors. Our lives exhibit the urgency of God to ¹persuade everyone to realize the reconciliation of their redeemed identity. *(The word, ¹parakaleō, comes from para, a Preposition indicating close proximity, a thing proceeding from a sphere of influence, with a suggestion of union of place of residence, to have sprung from its author and giver, originating from, denoting the point from which an action originates, intimate connection, and kaleō, to identify by name, to surname. In Luke 15:28, 31, His father pleaded with him, My child, you are always with me, and all that I have is yours. Be reconciled could not be translated, Become reconciled. Do in order to become is the language of the Old Testament; the language of the New Testament is, Be, because of what was done.)*

5:21 This is the divine exchange: he who knew no ¹sin embraced our perversion; he appeared to be without form; this was the mystery of God's prophetic ²poetry. He was disguised in our distorted image and marred with our iniquities; he took our sorrows, our pain and our shame and ³birthed his righteousness in us. He took our sins and we ³became his innocence. *(The word sin, is the word ¹hamartia, from ha, negative or without and meros, portion or form, thus to be without your allotted portion or without form, pointing to a disoriented, distorted, bankrupt identity; the word meros, is the stem of morphē, as in 2 Corinthians 3:18 the word metamorphē, with form, which is the opposite of hamartia - without form. Sin is to live out of context with the blueprint of one's design; to behave out of tune with God's original harmony. The word, ²poema, often translated made like in, he was made to be sin. However, because of its context here I have translated poema to read prophetic poetry. As the scapegoat of the human race, he took on the distorted image of fallen mankind, he did not become a sinner, but the official representative of mankind's sin. Then Paul uses the word ³ginomai, he birthed his righteousness in us since we were born anew in his resurrection from the dead. Hosea 6:2, Ephesians 2:5, 1 Peter 1:3.*

Isaiah 52:10 The Lord has bared his holy arm before the eyes of all the nations, and all the ends of the earth shall see the salvation of our God. Isaiah 52:14-15 Just as many were astonished at you—so was he marred in his appearance, more than any human and his form beyond that of human semblance—so will he startle many nations. Kings will shut their mouths because of him; for what had not been told them, they will see and what they had not heard, they will understand. Isaiah 53:4-5 Surely he has borne our griefs and carried our sorrows; yet we esteemed him stricken, smitten of God, and afflicted. But surely he was wounded by our transgressions; he was bruised by our iniquities; the chastisement of our peace was on him and by his stripes we ourselves are healed.

*Note: He was not bruised by God but by the very mankind he was about to redeem. You may ask, But what about Isaiah 53:10? [It pleased the Lord to crush him.] Translators of the New Revised Standard Version say in their footnotes to this verse: Meaning of Hebrew uncertain. The Septuagint - Greek version of this verse - written between 300BC and 250BC, by 72 Hebrew scholars, with access to older manuscripts than what we have today, have rendered the Hebrew text as follows: and the Lord desires to purify him of **the plague**. Also translated, The Lord desires to cleanse his wounds. The word, πληγή **plēgē** means a wound.*

Deuteronomy 32:5, 6 They have corrupted themselves; they did not behave as his children, they have become a distorted generation of people, twisted out of their true pattern; they are a crooked and perverse generation.[Paul quotes this verse in Philippians 2:15.]

*Deuteronomy 32:18 You were unmindful of the Rock that begot you and have forgotten the God who danced with you. [Hebrew, חול **khul**, also means to dance, as in Judges 21:21.]*

Romans 8:29 He pre-designed and engineered us from the start to be jointly fashioned in the same mold and image of his Son according to the exact blueprint of his thought. We see the original and intended pattern of our lives preserved in his Son. He is the firstborn from the same womb that reveals our genesis. He confirms that we are the idea and invention of God. (We were born anew when he was raised from the dead. [1 Peter 1:3] His resurrection co-reveals our common genesis as well as our redeemed innocence. [Romans 4:25 and Acts 17:31, 2 Timothy 1:9] No wonder then that he is not ashamed to call us his family. We indeed share the same origin [Hebrews 2:11], and, In him we live and move and have our being; we are indeed his offspring. [Acts 17:28].)

*Romans 8:30 Jesus reveals that mankind pre-existed in God; he defined us. He justified us and also glorified us. He redeemed our innocence and restored the glory we lost in Adam. [Romans 3:23, 24: the word, **prohoritsō**, means pre defined, like when an architect draws up a detailed plan; and the word, **kaleō**, to surname, identify by name.]*

Titus 2:11 The grace of God shines as bright as day making the salvation of mankind undeniably visible.)

6:1 I want you to hear the urgency of our appeal: we are co-employed and implore you not to take God's grace for granted; what a waste it is to see less in grace than what God does. The danger is not to exaggerate what happened to mankind in Christ, but rather to underestimate it. *(Jesus did not warn his disciples not to see him in too many people, but certainly cautioned them not to miss him in the most unlikely. How you treat the least is how you treat me. See 2 Corinthians 1:19, The Son of God, Jesus Christ, whom I Paul, Sylvanus, and Timothy boldly announced in you, is God's ultimate yes to mankind. Human life is associated in all that he is. In God's mind there exists not even a hint of hesitation about this.)*

6:2 God declared his ¹delight to do you good. I have heard the ³cry of the human race echo within ²you *[Jesus; Psalm 22:1]* **and immediately ³ran to your rescue. ⁴Now this is mankind's defining moment. See it for yourself. This is your time; this is your salvation.** *(Already in the previous chapter Paul shares his own from-now-on-therefore moment in 2 Corinthians 5:16. Now he encourages us to come to the same conclusion. There is no need to wait any longer for that which was written to be fulfilled. God spoke of a specific time and person when he announced salvation. Jesus is the day of salvation [Jeshua] that Isaiah foretold. This day has fully come. Even though Isaiah spoke these words 700 years BC they were already recorded in the past tense. Isaiah 49:8 in the LXX Greek Septuagint. Also in the Hebrew text,* בעת רצון *be eth [⁴now] ratson, now is the time of God's pleasure or benevolence. The Hebrew word, ¹**ratson,** means pleasure, delight, favor, goodwill, acceptance. The Greek word, ³**boētheō,** from **boaō,** a boisterous, most urgent cry for help, and **theō,** to run to the rescue. This is so typical of God; the Greek for God is **theos,** which is so similar to **theō.** God heard the cry of the human race echo in Christ. My God my God, why have you forsaken me. Psalm 22:1, and in verse 24 he says, For he has not despised nor distanced himself from the affliction of the afflicted; and he has not hid his face from him, but has heard, when he cried to him. Note the ²singular, **soi,** thus pointing to the Messiah, the one who died for all, as in 2 Corinthians 5:14. Isaiah saw the human race fully represented in the one act of righteousness completed in the one man. [Isaiah 53:4,5.] See also Hebrews 4:16, For this reason we can approach the authoritative throne of grace with bold utterance. We are welcome there in his embrace, and are reinforced with immediate effect in times of trouble. (The word, **boetheia,** means to be reinforced, specifically a rope or chain for frapping a vessel in a storm.))*

6:3 See to it that you do not give offense or allow any kind of casual indifference to discredit this message.

6:4 In every circumstance we commend ourselves to be jointly positioned as ¹deacons of God; we co-exhibit incarnate grace, regardless of the degree of the contradictions that we might be facing. We remain constant in a fortress of patience, in situations of extreme pressure; even at times where it seems like we have our arms locked behind our backs and we feel squeezed into claustrophobic spaces. *(The Greek word, ¹**diakonos,** from **dia,** a primary Preposition denoting the channel of an act, and **konos,** dust; thus, we ¹co-exhibit incarnate grace.)*

6:5 In physical abuse; beaten up and bruised; caged in prison cells; often in chaotic circumstances; exasperating toil, with little sleep and nothing to eat.

6:6 While abiding constantly in bliss knowing what our innocence is founded in; we remain absolutely unmoved by any of these severe contradictions. We are in Christ; in Holy Spirit; in agapē without a hint of hypocrisy.

6:7 We are sheltered in the word, entwined in unveiled truth, in the dynamic of God's power, because righteousness empowers us with every necessary weapon in our right and left hand to daily live undefeated by any of these onslaughts and contradictions. (*Righteousness by God's faith frees us from anything more we could do to prove or defend ourselves through our own efforts. See Habakkuk 2:4; 17-19 and Romans 1:17, also Hebrews 12:1.*)

6:8 Whether people esteem us or despise us; whether we are ridiculed or recognized, we may even be accused of misleading people we are in actual fact freeing people.

6:9 Some would say that we are vague and ambiguous and yet who we are is an open letter to everyone's conscience. Some would wish us dead; but hey, here we are, fully alive. (*2 Corinthians 4:2.*)

6:10 Our joy exceeds any reason for sadness; to enrich countless others by far outweighs the expense. It may appear that we are empty handed, yet we have everything in a firm grasp.

6:11 Precious Corinthians. Our bold words flow from hearts where you are embraced in a wide-open space.

6:12 Any sense of inadequacy you might feel comes from having an inferior perception about yourselves; the gospel we communicate esteems you highly.

6:13 We invite you in the most affectionate terms to respond to us without hesitation or restraint. See yourselves [1]mirrored in the same boundless space. (*The word [1]antimisthia, means requital, or correspondence, which I translated here, mirrored.*)

6:14 Faith-righteousness has nothing in common with the philosophies of karma and performance-based approval; they could never [1]balance the scales or be evenly yoked together in any context. (*The word [1]heterozugeō, an unequal or different yoke; from the Hebrew word, zugot, זוגות indicates pairs of two identical objects; a yoke or a teaching; the yoke of a rabbi or philosopher represented their doctrine; reminds of the Hebrew word for righteousness, tzedek, צדק which also includes the idea of the wooden beam in a scale of balances. He who judges his neighbor according to the balance of righteousness, or innocence, judges him according to righteousness. [T. Bab. Sabbat, fol. 127. 2.] The Greek stem for righteousness is dikē - it is interesting to note that the Greek goddess of Justice is Dikē [pronounced, dikay] and she is always pictured holding a scale of balances in her hand.*)

213

6:15 There is no [1]symphony between the value that Christ reveals in people and the worthlessness that [2]Belial represents. Faith-righteousness and work based-righteousness are two opposites; they are conflicting systems that can never match. *(Paul uses the word [1]sumphonēsis from sun, denoting union and phonay, voice. Faith-righteousness is to know the truth about the redeemed life of your design; whereas a works-based righteousness is to believe a lie about yourself. The Hebrew word, [2]beliya'al בליעל literally means without profit; worthlessness. The etymology of this word has been variously given. The Talmud [Sanh. 111b] regards it as a compound word, made up of beli and 'ol, without a yoke, which is very interesting in this context. Jesus says, My yoke is easy and my burden is light. Peterson renders it, Walk with me and work with me--watch how I do it. Learn the unforced rhythms of grace. I won't lay anything heavy or ill-fitting on you. Keep company with me and you'll learn to live freely and lightly. Matthew 11:29,30. The Message.)*

6:16 How can the tangible, physical address of the living God [1]compare with a phantom image that people host in their minds? Mankind is God's idea - we did not invent God or ourselves; he invented us. He said, In you will I reside and move and have my being; we belong together; I am yours and you are mine. *(Ezekiel 37:27 My dwelling place shall be with them; and I will be their God, and they shall be my people. The word, [1]sugkatathesis means, a putting together or joint deposit [of votes], hence approval, assent, agreement; you cannot vote for both systems, they are opposites.)*

6:17 Consequently, escape the snare of these phantom ideas; do not reduce your horizon to become [1]attached to anything that is not equally [2]elevated. *(Continue to engage your joint-seatedness in heavenly places, in your co-resurrection and co-ascension with Christ. The word [1]haptomai means to fasten to oneself; to adhere to; to cling to. The word [2]akathartos, from ha, which is a negative particle, and kathairō, from kata, intensive and airō, to lift up. The same word is used in John 15 where it was translated, to prune, or cut off the branches that do not bear fruit; yet the word would rather mean to lift up those branches so that they may bear more fruit.)*

6:18 Then you will know the embrace of your Father to simply enjoy being my sons and daughters, says the Almighty.

7:1 Dearly beloved, these promises engage us with elevated thoughts and free us from the frustrating efforts of the flesh to compete with the innocence of the spirit in our divine devotion. *(Paul contrasts the futile efforts of the flesh to the spirit of grace, which is celebrated in the bliss of righteousness by faith.)*

7:2 You will have to admit it, we have judged no-one in an unworthy manner, or made anyone feel inferior, neither have we taken advantage of anyone.

7:3 There is no hint of condemnation in my message; I have always maintained that our hearts are joined with you in death and in life.

7:4 I am absolutely convinced about you and take great pride in you; we are [1]seamlessly one; therefore my joy rises [2]above all sense of [3]claustrophobia. *(The word, [1]parakaleō, comes from para, a Preposition indicating close proximity, a thing proceeding from a sphere of influence, with a suggestion of union of place of residence, to have sprung from its author and giver, originating from, denoting the point from which an action originates, intimate connection; and kaleō, meaning to identify by name, to surname. The word [2]epi, is a Preposition of position, over or against. The word [3]thlipsis means a pressing, to be under severe pressure; from thlibō, to crowd (literally or figuratively): - afflict, narrow, throng.)*

7:5 When we first arrived in Macedonia we had no chance to relax for a moment; we were literally thronged by trouble; we faced conflict on every side and felt deeply alarmed.

7:6 How wonderful it is to discover God's [1]comforting closeness when one feels like a bird that [2]cannot rise in flight to escape the fowler; this time God's closeness was reinforced in the arrival of Titus. *(The word, [1]parakaleō, comes from para, a Preposition indicating close proximity, and kaleō, meaning to identify by name, to surname. The word, [2]tapeinos, means, not rising far from the ground.)*

7:7 Oh, and what a joy it was to hear personally from him how greatly encouraged he was by all of you. He told us how deeply you missed me and how you grieved with sincere concern for me. I immediately went from feeling a little sorry for myself into a happy-dance-mode.

7:8 For a brief moment I felt a little bad that I had perhaps saddened you with my previous letter yet I have no regrets now.

7:9 I rejoice in knowing that your sadness caused you to realize my sincere concern for you. The grief you felt brought God's heart into clear view and confirmed in you that I have always only had your best interest in mind.

7:10 To [1]anchor one's thoughts in God's thoughts when faced with difficult or painful experiences, brings escape from sorrow and leaves one with no [2]regrets; but oh, what a dreadful contrast is the religious system *(of the law of karma and performance)* which adds [2]regret upon sorrow. Whereas the one brings such immediate relief, the other seems to be an inescapable deathtrap. *(The word [1]metanoia means to realize God's thoughts. Like most Greek words,* *μετάνοια **metanoia** is a compound word, from **meta**, together with and νοιέω* **noieō**, *to perceive with the mind. It describes the awakening of the mind to that which is true; a re-alignment of one's reasoning; it is a gathering of one's thoughts, a co-knowing. Faith is not a decision; it is a discovery. It has nothing in common with the Latin word **paenitentia** - where the idea of penance and repentance stems from. Sadly the word repentance became the popular English translation of **metanoia**. The word [2]**ametamelētos**, has 3 components, **a**, negative and **meta**, with and **melō**, to regret; thus, with no regret.)*

7:11 Consider how this very thing that caused you such initial grief has turned your attention to God. It revived an [1]immediate sense of urgency to [2]realize your position in grace; almost [3]like when your arm is twisted and locked behind your back, and your own efforts to clear or save yourselves were completely neutralized. You were greatly alarmed with an intense desire and burning zeal to [4]re-endorse the basis of your righteousness. And so in everything your blameless innocence is vindicated. *(The word [1]**spoudē** suggests speed, immediate, urgent. The word [2]**apologia** means to answer with reason, to apologize, to defend one's case. The word [3]**aganaktēsis**, from **agō**, to lead and **anagkē** to bend the arm. The word [4]**ekdikeō**, is a compound word from **ek**, a Preposition denoting origin, and **dikeō**, two parties finding likeness in one another; which is the basis of the word for righteousness, **dikaios**. That which originates in righteousness. See Romans 12:19, Do not bother yourselves to get even, dear ones. Do not let anger or irritation distract you; that which we have in common with one another (righteousness) must set the pace. Scripture confirms that the Lord himself is the revealer of righteousness.)*

7:12 The object of my writing was not to debate the detail of who was wrong and who was wronged, but you, discovering the heart of God [1]mirrored in our urgent appeal to you. *(The word, [1]**enōpion**, in the face or gaze of God.)*

7:13 We are so [1]inspired to know that you [1]are acquainted your true identity and are overjoyed by the way you have gladdened the heart of Titus; he is so happy and completely blessed and refreshed by all of you. *(The word, [1]**parakaleō**, comes from **para**, a Preposition indicating close proximity, with a suggestion of union, originating from, and **kaleō**, meaning to identify by name, to surname. Jesus introduces the Holy Spirit in the same capacity: **paraklētos**, meaning close companion, kinsman [John 14:16].)*

7:14 It is a wonderful thing to brag about one another and to know that we can never exaggerate the truth. Titus has confirmed our boasting about you.

7:15 He is absolutely overwhelmed with deep affection for you and reminded of the way you have accurately heard and the warm hospitality that all of you have shown him.

7:16 This pleases me so much. I am so proud of you.

8:1 Allow me to encourage you with the striking testimony of the grace of God evidenced in the churches of [1]**Macedonia**. *(The Romans had lacerated [1]Macedonia economically. (Livy, XLV. 30)[30] The churches in Macedonia included Philippi, Thessalonica and Berea.)*

8:2 Their mental mettle was [1]tested to the extreme; they found themselves squeezed into a very [2]narrow space. Yet, in the depth of their poverty, their ecstatic joy led them into extravagant generosity. They had discovered the conclusion of grace: no degree of poverty can separate us from our [3]seamless oneness with one another. Grace translates within us a wealth of liberality. *([1]Proof, dokimē, a test proving the true character of metal. The word [2]thipsis from thlibō, to be thronged, hemmed into a very narrow space. The word [3]haplotēs, from hama, which is a particle of union and plekō, braided; quality or state of unmixed motivation, without mental reservation, no hidden agenda, undivided heart.)*

8:3 I salute them for intentionally giving themselves beyond their means.

8:4 We had nothing to do with this - they were the ones who insisted with utmost sincerity and urgency that we mediate their [1]tangible grace-gift to their fellow saints. *(For they gave according to their means, and beyond their means, of their own free will, begging us earnestly for the favor of partaking in the relief of the saints. In modern churches it is often the preacher begging his congregation to give! The word, [1]diakonos, deacon or minister from dia + konis etymologically, through dust [Liddell, Scott & Jones], which I translated here as tangible, practical or incarnate; this word commonly translates as ministry, service, running errands. I believe that the ultimate service is the expression of the heart of God in tangible human form. In essence, New Testament ministry is a celebration of the incarnation.)*

8:5 No-one expected this from them. They simply demonstrated how completely sold out they were to the Lord and to us. This explains their generous giving. The delightful pleasure of God compelled them.

8:6 Inspired by their enthusiasm, we [1]prompted Titus to complete his initiative in this grace gift that you yourselves were keen to participate in. *(Here I have used the word, 'prompted', for [1]parakaleō, which etymologically means to draw from the source of your identity. The Preposition para, indicates close proximity, a thing proceeding from a sphere of influence, with a suggestion of union of place of residence, to have sprung from its author and giver, originating from, denoting the point from which an action originates, intimate connection; and kaleō, to surname; to identify by name. Thus, they gave themselves wrapped up in Titus and the gift he would administer on their behalf!)*

8:7 Now everything about you already shines with extravagant evidence of your faith, your conversation, your knowledge, your enthusiasm. All bear witness to the affection that we have awakened in you. This is your opportunity to now equally excel in the grace of giving. *(See 1 Corinthians 1:4, Every aspect of your life already gives eloquent expression to the rich reservoir of your union in him. 1:6 You certainly have the testimony of Christ evidenced in you.)*

8:8 I am not laying out rules on giving to bring you back into bondage and duty-driven legalism. Your sincere love, encouraged by the enthusiasm of fellow believers, is what distinguishes your giving *[from the old written code of tithing.]*

8:9 You are acquainted with what the grace of our Lord Jesus Christ communicates: He exchanged his riches for our poverty; the extremities of his identifying with our poverty became the reference to our wealth. Everything he has is ours. *(We are his wealth. See Matthew 13:44, He sold all he had and bought the entire field; in this parable Jesus persuades us that we are all he has. Also, Ephesians 1:18)*

8:10 Here is my advice: since you originally came up with the idea a year ago.

8:11 It can only be to your own advantage if you would now also complete your willingness by reaching into your resources and giving liberally according to your means.

8:12 The willingness of heart is matched by what someone is able to give. I mean it is one thing to be willing to give a million dollars, but if you haven't got a million dollars then at least give the $10 you do have.

8:13 I am not suggesting that others must be eased at your expense.

8:14 The idea is that everyone should always have enough; your abundance can now bring immediate relief to them and vice versa.

8:15 The principle of share and share alike is as old as the Scriptures. *(See Exodus 16:18)*

8:16 I thank God for Titus; he feels entrusted with an equal urgency about you.

8:17 He readily responded to our prompting and immediately volunteered to go.

8:18 A brother who is very gifted in the gospel and popular with every ekklesia-church will accompany Titus.

8:19 He was also [1]handpicked by all the churches to join us on this journey of grace in the administration of the gifts to the glory of the Lord. We know that this will meet with your approval since it is what you really wanted to do all along. *(The word [1]cheirotoneō means to handpick or to vote by a show of hands. See 1 Corinthians 16:3.)*

8:20 We understand how sensitive money matters are and have taken the utmost precaution to secure the transparency of the administration of your bountiful gift.

8:21 We [1]anticipate this to be a [2]beautiful testimony to the Lord and to everyone. *(The word [1]pronoeō means to know in advance, to anticipate; the word [2]kalon means beautiful.)*

8:22 Along with these two men we are also sending a brother in whom we have great confidence; he has often proven himself trustworthy in many different situations and is now even more eager than ever since he knows how urgent we feel about you.

8:23 As for Titus, he is my close companion and represents my heart to you. The brothers who accompany him are commissioned by the churches to the glory of Christ.

8:24 Give these churches proof of your love and confirm the good reason we have to be proud of you.

9:1 Our commitment to administer this relief fund to assist our fellow saints is obvious. It shouldn't even be necessary for me to write to you about this.

9:2 When I witnessed your enthusiasm a year ago, I bragged about you before the churches in Macedonia and your zeal greatly inspired many of them.

9:3 So now I am sending these brothers in response to your readiness to confirm our boasting about you. *(If you see them, you see me!)*

9:4 I just want to make sure that, should some of the Macedonians perhaps join me when I visit you, that it won't turn out to be an embarrassment to all of us.

9:5 This is the reason why I have recruited this team, to go in advance and give you the necessary time to arrange for the blessing that you have promised. I want it to remain the blessing that you originally intended and not something that you now feel pressured to give.

9:6 We are all familiar with the natural law that says, Stingy sowing will always reflect in the harvest; so does liberal sowing.

9:7 Every individual must [1]thoroughly think this through in their own heart, not with thoughts of possible regret or out of a legalistic sense of duty. The agapē-love of God inspires extravagance of [2]hilarious proportions. *(The word* [1]*proaireomai means to take full inventory; the Greek word* [2]*hilaros is from the stem hileōs which means cheerful, attractive. Where we get our word, hilarious from!)*

9:8 It is impossible to exaggerate the [1]dimensions and detail of the grace of God. Plunge into the [2]extravagance of grace where he exhibits the extreme [3]dynamics of his bountiful dealing with us. We are already advantaged far beyond any calculation of personal merit to be completely [4]self sufficient at all times in every possible situation that we might face. The overflow thereof amply supplies the needs of others in many creative ways to do good.

([1] In Paul's estimate, grace cannot be exaggerated. He bursts forth in eloquent grace language in an attempt to explain the extremities of God's goodness. He strings together one superlative after the other in order to reinforce the all-inclusive and conclusive work of grace evidenced within us. With the word [1]**dunatei**, *he speaks of* **the powerful dynamic of God**, *which is a word and a late tense that Paul invents from the word* **dunamos**. *Only he uses it and repeats it 3 times in his Epistles.*

[2] In the words, [2]**pasan charin**, *Paul includes every detailed aspect of grace;*

[3] then he uses the verb, [3]**perisseuō** *which means to exceed some number, measure, rank or need; to go over the limits, beyond and above, more than is necessary. Paul employs this verb in* **the Aorist Infinitive** *tense,* **perisseusai**, *which indicates prior completion of an action in relationship to a point in time. Greek Infinitives could have either a Present or Aorist form. The contrast between the two forms has nothing to do with time. It is a difference of aspect. The Present Infinitive was used to express progressive or Imperfective Aspect. It pictures the action expressed by the verb as being in progress. The Aorist Infinitive however does not express progressive aspect. It presents the action expressed by the verb as a completed unit with a beginning and end.* **This is an important point since many translations of this verse suggest that God's ability to make all grace abound towards us can only be in response to something we must first do**

in order to trigger God into action. Our doing good is simply the overflow of his good work within us.

[4] The word [4]autarkēs, is translated as self sufficient; it is the feeling you have when you are completely satisfied with yourself. This word is only used here, in Philippians 4:11 and in 1 Timothy 6:6, There is great gain in godliness with contentment. The use of this word shows Paul's acquaintance with Stoicism. He takes this word from Greek philosophy and applies it to the revelation of the completeness of the life of our design restored in us. Paul lived his life in touch with this place within himself. He discovered that the same I-amness that Jesus walked in, was mirrored in him. I am what I am by the grace of God.)

9:9 Here is David's take on liberal and extravagant giving: in Psalm 112:9 he says, He has distributed freely, he has given to the poor; his righteousness consistently triumphs even in challenging times.

9:10 The inventor of seed and bread is also the one who supplies and multiplies your resources and increases the harvest of your righteousness.

(Here Paul reminds them of Isaiah 55:10 & 11 For as the rain and the snow come down from heaven, and do not return there until the earth is saturated, [incarnation]; awakening the incorruptible seed in it to bring forth and sprout, giving seed to the sower and bread to the eater, so shall my word be that goes forth from my mouth; it shall not return to me empty, but accomplish that which I purpose, and prosper in the thing for which I sent it. The incarnation is the reality of this prophecy! John 1:14. Now we are Living Epistles, known and read by all! See 2 Corinthians 3:2-3.)

9:11 You are mutually enriched in every possible sense of the word and [1]inseparably joined to one another in an undivided heart, without any hidden agenda. And together we, the conduit of your gifts, will set the stage for a joyous grace celebration to God. *(The word [1]haplotēs, from hama, which is a particle of union and plekō, meaning to plait, braid or weave together; it suggests an undivided heart. See Luke 11:34 The eye is the lamp of the body; if the eye is single [entwined with light], the whole body is full of light. Entwining our eyes with Papa's eyes is what enlightens our entire being. Which is exactly what the word קוה Kawa in Hebrew means in Isaiah 40:31, they that entwine with the Lord's thoughts mount up with wings like eagles. We are wired by design to entwine.)*

9:12 This is such a win-win situation: not only are the saints endorsed in their I-am-ness through this most practical translation of your generosity, but it also causes an abundant overflow of great gratitude to God as the testimony of his goodness finds tangible expression in your gifts.

9:13 And so the ripple effect continues. The gospel you communicate has found a very articulate voice in your giving and produces a rich harvest of glory to God. Your union with them further communicates the all-inclusive nature of the [1]koinonia we all participate in. *(The word [1]koinonia means to participate in; to fellowship. See Philemon 1:6)*

9:14 Can you imagine how your abundant generosity to them has tied them to you with deep affection in their prayers for you.

9:15 Gratitude is the language of grace. Your giving has given a voice to his gift, beyond words.

10:1 So here I am, Paul, somewhat shy when I am face to face with you, but, according to some rumors, my courage borders on arrogance in my absence. I ¹address you from this place where there is no distance; our authentic identity is referenced in gentleness and ²Christlikeness. *(The word, ¹parakaleō, comes from para, a Preposition indicating close proximity, a thing proceeding from a sphere of influence, and kaleō, meaning to identify by name, to surname. The word ²epeikeia, from epi, continuous influence upon, and eiko, to be like, to resemble.)*

10:2 I am ¹cautious not to come across arrogantly when I am ²present with you. Yet I am extremely confident before those who accuse me of conducting myself in a mere carnal manner. *(The word ¹deomai, to desire, from deō, to bind; the word ²pareimi refers to the closest proximity of the source of my I-am-ness.)*

10:3 The fact that we are living in a physical world in human bodies of flesh does not mean that we engage ourselves in a combat dictated to by the typical tit-for-tat strategies of religion and the politics of the day.

10:4 The dynamic of our strategy is revealed in God's ability to disengage mindsets and perceptions that have held people captive in pseudo fortresses for centuries.

10:5 Every lofty idea and argument positioned against God's knowledge of us, is cast down and exposed to be a mere invention of our own imagination. We ¹arrest every thought at spear point - anything that could possibly trigger an opposing threat to our redeemed identity and innocence is taken captive. The caliber of our weapon is empowered by the revelation of the ultimate consequence of the obedience of Christ. *(The obedience of Christ dwarfs the effect of the disobedience of Adam into insignificance! See Romans 5:12-21.*

The word ¹aichmalōtizō from aichmē, spear and halōsis, to capture, thus, to arrest at spear point. Note, while the sword is for close combat as in Hebrews 4:12, a spear is used long distance. Arresting thoughts that would wish to sneak up on you, in advance, while they are still hovering on the horizon.)

10:6 Our ears are fine tuned to ¹echō the voice of ³likeness that resonates within us. We are ²acquainted with the articulate detail of the ⁴authentic language of our origin. *(The word ¹echō, means to hold or embrace; the word ²hetoimos, is from an old noun heteos (fitness) which means adjusted, ready, prepared. The word ³ekdikeō from ek, denoting origin + dikē, suggesting to be judged equal; it implies the idea of two parties finding likeness in each other. The word ⁴parakoē from para, originating from, + akouō, to hear.)*

10:7 Do you form your perceptions on mere face value? No one has a secret advantage in his or her claim of Christ; think again: each one belongs equally to him, despite appearances or whether they realize it or not.

10:8 There is nothing superior in my confidence in who I am. God's gift to you wrapped up in me is not to intimidate you but to edify you.

10:9 The intention of my letters is not to daunt you with eloquent words.

10:10 Some are of the opinion that my letters are forceful, but my physical appearance is feeble and I am not much of a public speaker.

10:11 I assure you that the words my Epistles communicate in my absence, are confirmed in my day to day lifestyle.

10:12 We are not contesting with those who desire to commend themselves. While they compete and compare with one another they completely miss the point; they fail to [1]comprehend our joint I-am-ness. *(The word, [1]suniemi, means a joining together like that of two streams; a fusion of thought.)*

10:13 Why boast in something you can take absolutely no credit for. The only valid measure that defines our lives and explains why we have [1]arrived on your doorstep with the gospel, is the one wherewith God has measured us in Christ. *(One cannot measure temperature with a ruler. The word [1]ephikneomai, from epi, continuous influence upon, and hēkō, to have come, to have arrived, to be present. See Romans 6:14, Sin was your master while the law was your measure; now grace rules. [The law revealed your slavery to sin; now grace reveals your freedom from it.] Also Romans 3:27 The law of faith cancels the law of works, which means there is suddenly nothing left for mankind to boast about. No one is superior to another. Bragging only makes sense if there is someone to compete with or impress. Through the righteousness of God we have received a faith of equal standing. See 2 Peter 1:1 RSV The OS (operating system) of the law of works is willpower; the OS of the law of faith is love. Galatians 5:6 Love sets faith in motion. The law presented mankind with choices; grace awakens belief. Willpower exhausts, love ignites. If choices could save us we would be our own Saviors. Willpower is the language of the law, love is the language of grace and it ignites faith that leads to romance; falling in love beats making a decision to believe in love. See Romans 7:19.)*

10:14 Our ministry to you is proof that there are no geographic limitations that could possibly exclude you from the gospel of Jesus Christ.

10:15 We are not competing with others for your membership; our vision for you is to see your faith mature into a full harvest; this is our standard rule, we have no other expectation. To the same degree that your faith matures, our field among you is greatly increased.

10:16 You become the extension of our sphere of influence as we together reach neighboring regions beyond yourselves. The gospel is the key role-player here, not hidden agendas of man-made ministries.

10:17 So if you desire to boast about anything, boast in the Lord. *(Even as Jeremiah writes in Jeremiah 9:23 & 24 The LORD says: Let not the wise glory in their wisdom, let not the mighty glory in their might, let not the rich glory in their riches; but let the one who glories glory in this, that they understand and know me, that I am the LORD who practice steadfast love, a [favorable] verdict, and righteousness in the earth; for in these things I delight, says the LORD.)*

10:18 The true [1]recipe for authentic ministry is not in clever marketing schemes; let the Lord promote you, he beats the best. *(The word [1]dokimos means test, proof, accepted, particularly of coins and money.)*

11:1 This might sound a little foolish, but please bear with me.

11:2 I feel a divine jealousy for you; like a grooms-man who wooed you to belong solely to your one husband and presented you as a pure bride to Christ.

11:3 I am concerned for you that you might [1]pine away through the [2]illusion of separation from Christ and that, just like Eve, you might become [3]blurry-eyed and [4]deceived into believing a lie about yourselves. The temptation was to exchange the truth about our completeness *(I am)* with the idea of incompleteness *(I am not)* and shame; thinking that perfection required your [5]toil and all manner of wearisome labor.

([1] The word, [1]phteirō, means to pine or waste away, to wither . Any idea of separation causes one to wither away in loneliness.

*[2] The word [2]haplotēs from **hama**, a particle of union, and **plekō**, to braid or plait together; sometimes translated, simplicity or unmixed. See commentary in James 1:5 on entwined eyes.*

[3] The Greek word, [3]ophis is translated serpent and comes from optomai, to gaze, in this case, to present a visual idea through illusion.

*[4] The word [4]exapataō from **ek**, source + **apateō**, apathy is the source of deception, to be without faith, believing a lie about yourself. Hebrews 4:6 Israel died in the wilderness because of their unbelief. [Both Adam and Israel believed a lie about themselves. Numbers 13:33, Joshua 2:11, 2 Corinthians 4:4.]*

*[5] The word [5]panourgia, from the words, **pas**, all, and **ergon**, work or toil, where your entire existence is reduced to wearisome labor. This word is often translated, cunning or craftiness. See also 2 Corinthians 4:2 We have renounced hidden agendas [employing a little bit of the law in an attempt to balance out grace]; we have distanced ourselves from any obscure craftiness to manipulate God's word to make it mean what it does not say.)*

11:4 You will know by the echo within you whether the Jesus someone else preaches is the same Jesus we proclaim to you. You will recognize the same spirit; if it is a different spirit, it is not the same gospel. Why would you politely put up with deception, even if it comes packaged in prominent names and titles.

11:5 I am not inferior by any calculation to those Apostles so highly ranked in your estimate.

11:6 I am not here to entertain you with my public speaking skills, or to impress you with [1]me, but to impress you with you. It is not in the plausible sounding words of my conversation, it is in what I know to be true about you. This is clearly evident in all of our dealings with you. *(See 1Corinthians 2:4 My message was not with persuasive arguments based on secular wisdom, since my aim was not to point people to me but rather to the powerful working of the Spirit in them. Thayer's Greek definition of [1]apodeiknumi is to point away from oneself. Previous translations of this word have often given the impression that the great, miracle-working man of God would steal the show and entertain the crowds. This was so unlike Jesus and Paul. Paul never writes about how many people he had healed and brought to faith, etc. His all-consuming concern was that the eyes of our understanding would be illuminated with the revelation of our own salvation. Note 2 Corinthians 10:10 [RSV], For they say, 'Paul's letters are weighty and strong, but his bodily presence is weak, and his speech of no account.')*

11:7 Something doesn't seem to match here – am I humbling myself in order to elevate you by not putting a price tag on my preaching of God's gospel? Am I presenting a distorted picture?

11:8 It seems to me that you are taking it for granted that other churches sponsored my ministry to you.

11:9 Even while I was with you I did not burden you with my personal needs, but received provision from my Macedonian friends. I have no intent to ever be a burden to you.

11:10 The integrity of my ministry is [1]endorsed by Christ in me and not by human opinion; the same goes for my confident joy even in the regions of Achaia. *(The word [1]sphragizō, to set a mark upon by the impress of a seal or a stamp. Achaia was that part of Greece of which Corinth was the capital.)*

11:11 How is it possible for you to think that I do not love you? God knows my heart.

11:12 The way I do things exposes the agendas of others who claim that we are in the same team.

11:13 They are obviously operating under the deceitful disguise of an Apostleship with a hidden agenda. They are certainly not Apostles of Christ.

11:14 It shouldn't be a surprise since the [1]Accuser often comes camouflaged as a bearer of light. *(The word [1]satanos means the accuser. The dispensation of the law is the ministry of accusation.)*

11:15 Therefore it is no big deal if his associates in ministry would claim to also teach righteousness under the disguise of grace, while their message clearly promotes a righteousness based on their own works *(and not upon the finished work of Christ.)*

11:16 Let me put it to you plainly, if I am already behaving foolishly in your opinion, would you please bear with me in the foolishness of my boasting.

11:17 I am not saying the Lord says, but allow me to say a few foolish things in my own defense.

11:18 Since there are so many who are boasting according to the flesh, I might as well enroll in the competition.

11:19 Your wisdom certainly equips you to grin and bear with the foolishness of others.

11:20 The ability to perceive things from an elevated place of wisdom already gives you the advantage to bear with their insults. Their intent is obvious: all they wish to achieve is to bring you back into the bondage of their own Jewish legalism. They wish to abuse and devour you; their apparent attempts to raise themselves to your level are only to slap you in the face.

11:21 Since Timothy and I did not take any part in their bravado at the time, it perhaps appeared to you as a weakness on our part. I know this might not make sense to you, but whatever extreme measures they pride themselves in, I can match.

11:22 Every possible advantage they claim through their natural lineage, whether it be their Hebrew language, their Jewish identity or their connection to the patriarch Abraham himself, I can equal that.

11:23 If you want to compare notes, I eclipse their claims as ministers of Christ. I speak from personal experience; none of them could compete with me when it comes to the extremities of wearisome labors endured: I was beaten up many times, frequently jailed, often face to face with death.

11:24 To be more specific, I received the infamous forty lashes less one, five times from the Jews.

11:25 Three times the Romans beat me up with sticks; once I was stoned and left for dead. Three times on my journeys I have been shipwrecked. I have been adrift at sea for a night and a day.

11:26 My frequent travels have kept me on the road more than most people I know; I faced flooded rivers, I was attacked by robbers and encountered life threatening dangers from both Jew and Gentile. Everywhere I turned I was confronted with great danger, whether in the city, countryside or at sea. It seemed that there was no safe place left for me on the planet. Even amongst fellow Christians I was snared into controversy and betrayal.

11:27 I was often extremely exhausted with a burdensome workload. The list goes on and on: I had many a sleepless night; I was frequently forced to fast since I had nothing to eat or drink; I suffered extreme exposure in bitterly cold conditions with nothing warm to wear.

11:28 Beside the many external challenges I face daily, I continuously care for the churches in every place with all my heart.

11:29 Don't talk to me about weaknesses and scandalous insults. I have been there and bought the T-shirt. The scandal of the cross ignites me with fervor.

11:30 My frailties are my claim to fame.

11:31 God, the Father of our Lord Jesus Christ, has the full panorama of my life and testimony. In Jesus the ages conclude in beautiful logic. He is the ultimate reason of the universe. (The word [1]*eulogētos* often translated, blessing, is from *eu*, beautiful or well done, and *logos*, word, thought or logic.)

11:32 Oh yes, and here is another bit of adventure: while in Damascus the governor under King Aretas set up a military guard in the city of Damascenes to hunt me down and arrest me.

11:33 I escaped through a window in the city wall, having been let down in a basket. (Acts 9:25.)

12:1 It would be inappropriate for me to boast about anything as though I achieved it by my own doing. My confident persuasion in what I have received by revelation of the Lord is not to be confused with arrogance.

12:2 I know of an encounter in Christ fourteen years ago, where a person was translated into the third heaven.

12:3 Only God knows whether it was in or out of the body; it does not really matter to me.

12:4 This person was caught up into paradise. There he heard words that could not be articulated into language; he understood a conversation that did not [1]originate in human thought. *(The word [1]exousia, has two components, ek, a Preposition pointing to the origin of something, and eimi, I am, in this case Paul refers to who I am as a human being.)*

12:5 Of this encounter I will confidently boast because it has nothing to do with anything that I did to promote myself. I would rather glory in that which emphasizes my failure to get it right by myself. Divine revelation is a gift, not a reward.

12:6 Even though I have legitimate reasons to boast, I prefer not to. My life speaks for itself and I have nothing to hide. *(See also 1 Corinthians 4:10-14 & 2 Corinthians 6:4-8.)*

12:7 In sharp contrast to these spiritual revelations, the physical pain that I suffered and my severe discomfort momentarily distracted me. It was as if the old mindset of accusation [Satan] persuaded me that this affliction was actually God's way of keeping me humble. *(Note that it was not a messenger from God, but from Satan. The word, satanas means accuser. By these revelations of extreme proportions and consequence Paul understood that we are indeed co-seated together with Christ in heavenly places. In his resurrection he already elevated us beyond any claim of accusation. See Hosea 6:2 and Ephesians 2:5,6. We cannot get any more elevated into the bliss of our redeemed innocence than discovering our joint-seatedness with Christ in the throne room . Colossians 3:1-3.)*

12:8 I almost believed this lie and even implored the Lord three times to remove the thorn from my flesh.

12:9 Finally it dawned on me that grace is God's language; he doesn't speak thorn-langauge. He said to me, My grace [1]elevates you, to be fully content. And now, instead of being overwhelmed with a sense of my own weakness, he overwhelms me with an awareness of his strength. Oh what [2]bliss to rejoice in the fact that in the midst of my frailties I encounter the dynamic of the grace of God to be my [3]habitation. *(The word [1]arkeō, content, stems from the word airō which means to elevate. The word [2]hedista from hedeos, means pleasure. The word [3]episkēnoō has two components: epi, continuous influence upon and skēnoō, to encamp, to reside in a tent; the noun, skēnos reminds of the English word skin. Paul suggests that God's grace fits you like a skin. One feels most at home in the consciousness of his grace.)*

12:10 I now enjoy a [1]delightfully different frame of mind when I encounter things that would normally make me feel frail, whether it be from insults or when I am in situations where [2]I'm forced to do things with my arms twisted behind my back; whether I am persecuted or feel squeezed into [3]claustrophobic spaces. Because of Christ, every time that I encounter weakness I escape into the strength of my [4]I am-ness. *(The word, [1]eudokeō is a compound word from, eu, well done, beautiful, and dokeō, to form an opinion. The word [2]anagkē to bend the arm like when your arm is locked behind your back, where your own efforts to clear or save yourself are completely neutralized. The word [3]stenochōria, means a narrowness of place. The word [4]eimi, is the verb, I am.)*

12:11 It is not my style to talk so much about myself, but here I am foolishly defending my reputation against your esteemed Apostles. Hey, I was hoping that you would rather defend me.

12:12 All the signs that confirmed my commission and Apostleship were evidenced in you. These signs and miracles and mighty works consistently accompany my ministry.

12:13 How can you possibly feel neglected? The only way in which you were treated differently from the other churches is that I did not burden you with any financial obligations to me.

12:14 This will be my third visit to you and again I have no intent to burden you in any way. Your money cannot enrich me but your friendship surely does. It is the parent's job to look after their children and not the other way around.

12:15 It is my pleasure to go to any expense, even to the extreme of bankrupting myself for your sakes. Yet it seems to me that the more I show my love the less I am loved.

12:16 Did I have a hidden agenda, tricking you with guile?

12:17 Did anyone that I sent to serve you perhaps abuse you?

12:18 I entreated Titus to encourage you in our [1]joint-affiliation and co-assigned our brother *[Luke]* with him; did Titus take any advantage of you? Did we not conduct ourselves in the same spirit and leave the same impression? *(The word, [1]parakaleō, comes from para, a Preposition indicating close proximity, with a suggestion of union, originating from, and kaleō, meaning to identify by name, to surname. Jesus introduces the Holy Spirit in the same capacity: paraklētos, meaning close companion, kinsman. John 14:16.)*

12:19 My intent is not to justify myself at your expense. God knows that our sincere desire in everything we say is to edify you in Christ, dearly beloved.

12:20 I do not desire that my coming to you will disappoint any of your or my expectations. Contentious debates, petty jealousies, flaring emotions, divisions, bad-mouthing, rumorous gossip, inflated selfish ambitions and disharmony can certainly not be justified and should not be allowed to replace the rich and edifying fellowship which we can anticipate.

12:21 I certainly have no desire to be humiliated again facing the same old mindsets and sins of immorality, adultery and licentiousness . This will break my heart. God knows.

13:1 In getting ready to visit you now for the third time, I am reminded of the Scripture that says that at the mouth of two or three witnesses every word shall be established.

13:2 I addressed this issue during my second visit and do so again now, in my absence, with this letter: when I arrive I will not tolerate the stubborn attitude of those who wish to continue in their [1]**old distorted deeds.** *(The word,* [1]***prohamartia**, translate, old sins or previous sins, from **pro**, previous, and the word **ha**, without and **meros**, allotted portion or form; suggesting the distorted patterns of judgments we have had of ourselves, thus justifying the lies that we believed about ourselves and one another.)*

13:3 The frailties that I testify to in myself, do not distract from the powerful impact that the word of Christ in me, has in you. This should be enough proof to you of the integrity of my ministry.

13:4 It seems such a paradox when one considers the frailty of Christ's frame, how he suffered such a dreadful death on the cross, compared to the power of God so evident in him as his source of life. Our own lives often mirror the same contrasting paradox that we have witnessed in Christ, where our times of weakness become a platform for the power of God to be displayed as the secret source of the life we participate in together with Christ, to encourage you.

13:5 I implore you to [1]**examine faith for yourselves in order to test what it is that you really believe. Faith is so much more than the mere veneer of a superstitious belief in a historical Christ; faith is about realizing Jesus Christ in you, in the midst of contradiction. Just** [2]**as ore is placed into a crucible, where the dross is separated from the gold in a furnace, come to the conclusion for yourselves of his indwelling. Should it appear to you that he is absent in your life, look again, you have obviously done the test wrong.** *(You cannot measure temperature with a ruler. Paul uses the word,* [1]*peiratzō, to examine closely, from **peira,** to pierce; a test to determine the hidden value of something; also from the word **peras**, which speaks of extremity or the furthest boundary. Faith is not a veneer to cover up potential depression or disappointment when faced with trying times. Note that Paul is not speaking about you putting your beliefs to the test; but you testing **the** faith for yourself. There is only one valid faith, not what we believe about God or about ourselves, but what God believes about us. Paul wants you to discover for yourselves what God believes about you. God is persuaded about Christ indwelling you, now he wants you to be equally persuaded. Then he uses the word,* [2]*dokimatzō, as in the testing of metals. <u>Self-examination has nothing to do with finding hidden sins and flaws in you; it is all about realizing Christ in you.</u> The object of the furnace is not to reveal the dross, but the gold. Christ himself is the proof of faith, he is the substance of things hoped for, the evidence of things not seen. Hebrews 11:1. The test of truth is foolproof. See verse 8. Truth is not threatened by our scrutiny. See also 2 Corinthians 4:18 We are not keeping any score of what seems so obvious to the senses on the surface, it is fleeting and irrelevant; it is the unseen eternal realm within us that has our full attention and captivates our gaze. 2 Corinthians 4:7 We have discovered this* *treasure where it was hidden all along, in these frail skin-suits made of clay. 1 Corinthians 1:6 You certainly have the testimony of Christ evidenced in you. [You possess full knowledge and give full expression because in you the evidence for the truth of Christ has found confirmation. — NEB.])*

13:6 I really hope that in your discovery of Christ's indwelling, you will realize that we ourselves are equally found to have passed the test.

13:7 My sincere prayer is that, even if you cannot see us as meeting the requirements in your estimate, you do not use our apparent failure as an excuse to disqualify yourselves.

13:8 Someone's indifference to the truth has no power whatsoever to compromise it ever so slightly, to be what it's not. We can do nothing against the truth, only for the truth. *(Romans 3:3 The question is, how does someone's failure to believe God affect what God believes? Can their unbelief cancel God's faith? [What we believe about God does not define him; God's faith defines us. See the RSV translation, What if some were unfaithful? Does their faithlessness nullify the faithfulness of God? By no means.] Romans 3:4 God's word is not under threat. In fact, if all of mankind fails, truth remains intact. Truth is defined in God; it is neither challenged nor vindicated by human experience. Contradiction does not intimidate or diminish God's belief. Scripture records that God stands justified in his own word; it confirms that God's promise and purpose are not compromised through mankind's failure; neither is God's reputation threatened by our behavior. [Truth does not become true by popular vote. We were convinced for many generations that the earth was flat; yet, our belief does not make something true.])*

13:9 We rejoice in the fact that our weakness serves to prove you strong. We pray that you will find all the evidence you need to persuade yourself of your own perfection.

13:10 Somehow it seems better for me to write my thoughts to you; I think that, if I was physically present with you now, I might have been more abrupt. Yet [1]who I am in the Lord is a gift to you; I only wish to edify you; there is nothing in me that could possibly do you any harm. *(The word [1]exousia, from ek, source, and eimi, I am, is often translated, authority. Thus it would read, according to the authority which the Lord has given me to build you up and not to disappoint you.)*

13:11 And now, dear friends, we wish you joy; to be fully established, living your lives [1]within the immediate proximity of your true identity; with your minds made up about the fact that we are one, [2]fitly joined together in perfect harmony; and knowing that God is your constant companion and that he himself is the source of love and peace. *(The word, [1]parakaleō, comes from para, a Preposition indicating close proximity, a thing proceeding from a sphere of influence, with a suggestion of union of place of residence, to have sprung from its author and giver, originating from, denoting the point from which an action originates, intimate connection; and kaleō, meaning to identify by name, to surname. The word καταρτίζω katartizō means, to be fully restored.)*

13:12 Embrace one another with godly affection.

13:13 All the saints enfold you in their hearts.

13:14 The grace of the Lord Jesus Christ and the love of God and the fellowship of the Holy Spirit abide with all of you.

In this amazing book, Paul endorses the gospel he owns and proclaims as a gift by the revelation of Christ within him.

Galatians 1:12 This message is not invented by a man; my source was not my formal religious education; I received it by the revelation of Jesus Christ.

Galatians 1:15-16 God's eternal love dream separated me from my mother's womb; his grace became my identity. This is the heart of the gospel that I proclaim; it began with an unveiling of sonship in me, freeing me to announce the same sonship in the masses of non-Jewish people. I felt no immediate urgency to compare notes with those who were familiar with Christ from a mere historical point of view.

Paul contrasts the futility of the law of works in its clumsy effort to improve human behavior with the amazing revelation of the life of our design redeemed in us, in Christ. He uses the words, law, flesh and works vs. grace, spirit and faith to give reference to the dynamic of the success of the cross.

The promise is concluded in the person of Christ; unveiled in human life.

Galatians 3:21 No, the law does not oppose God's promise; it emphasizes the desperate need for a Redeemer to release righteousness in mankind as their life; something the law would certainly not be capable of. Had it been possible for the human race to be justified by the law, the promise would be unnecessary.

Galatians 3:22 Scripture concludes that all mankind without exception are in the same predicament; they are imprisoned to sin. Now faith brings the promise of immediate release within everyone's reach. Jesus Christ makes it possible for all to believe what God believes concerning their righteousness and restored innocence.

Galatians 4:5 Jesus' mandate was to rescue the human race from the regime of the law of performance and announce the revelation of their true sonship in God.

Galatians 4:6 To seal our sonship God has commissioned the Spirit of sonship to resonate the Abba echo in our hearts; and now, in our innermost being we recognize him as our true and very dear Father.

Galatians 5:1 Christ defines your faith; he is your freedom from anything the law could never free you of. Find your firm footing in this freedom. Do not let religion trip you up again and harness you to a system of rules and obligations.

Galatians 5:6 Love sets faith in motion. *(It is easy for love to believe.)*

1:1 My name is Paul, my ministry and message are neither accredited to a theological education, nor am I sponsored by a religious institution. I am sanctioned by Jesus the Messiah and God the Father who raised him from the dead. *(Apostle, compelled to go, commissioned. [2 Corinthians. 5:14, 20 and Romans. 1:5] Rather than a title, Apostleship defines the compelling urgency that prompts the spreading of the gospel. The resurrection revelation inspires the commission. Paul saw that mankind was co-raised together with Christ. Hosea 6:2 and Ephesians 2:5, 6.)*

1:2 I and my team of fellow believers here in Rome address this letter to all the churches in Galatia.

1:3 We greet you with [1]grace and the [2]peace that comes from knowing God as your Father, and Jesus who heads up the Christ-life. *(Paul's regular greeting - [1]Grace and [2]peace! The word, χάρις [1]charis, the divine influence upon the heart; that which affords joy, pleasure, delight, sweetness, charm, loveliness.*

Then, the word [2]eirēnē, means peace, from eirō, to join, to be set at one again; in carpentry it is the strongest joint, referred to as the dovetail joint. Peace is a place of unhindered enjoyment of friendship beyond guilt, suspicion, blame or inferiority. See 1 Corinthians 1:3)

1:4 Grace and peace have their reference in the fact that Jesus gave himself as the scapegoat for our sins and plucked us out from the [1]evil of this present religious age that encroached on us. This was exactly what the Father had planned in his love for mankind. *(The word, [1]ponēros, means full of labors, hardships and annoyances; the fruit of the tree of the knowledge of good and labor ponēros. This concludes in a judgment based on performance. Which is the opposite to an opinion of approval based on value.)*

1:5 His glorious reputation is ageless; it extends beyond all times and seasons. We salute him with our amen. *(Nothing that religion communicates in any age or context can match him.)*

1:6 I am amazed that you can so easily be fooled into swapping the Gospel for a gimmick. The Gospel reveals the integrity of your original identity rescued in Christ; the gimmick is a conglomeration of grace and legalism. This mixture boils down to a do-it-yourself plan of salvation. *(Which is a recipe for disaster.)*

1:7 There is no other gospel in spite of the many so-called Christian products branded gospel. If any hint of the law remains, it is not good news but merely religious people's ideas, detracting from the gospel of Christ. *(Some seek to unsettle your minds by perverting the Gospel to accommodate their own opinion.)*

1:8 I and any of my team would stand equally disqualified, even if we claim to have had a celestial messenger visitation, if what we preach were to stray ever so slightly from the Gospel of the finished work of Christ.

1:9 Let me be blatant and clear about this: any gospel that does not emphasize the success of the cross is counterfeit and produces nothing but the curse.

1:10 *(In sharp contrast to the time when I needed letters of authority from the religious institutions of the day, endorsing my mission)* **God is my complete persuasion. I answer to him alone, not anyone else. Christ employs me; I am addicted to his grace. Popular religious opinion will not influence me to compromise my message.** *(What is the point of an impressive CV, when your Maker is not even asking for it?)*

1:11 I want to make it very clear to you my friends that the message I proclaim is not mere speculation or the product of philosophical or religious debate.

1:12 This is not my own invention, neither was I spoon-fed by human tuition; my source of reference is the unveiled mystery of Christ in me. *(Even though we once knew Christ from a human point of view, we know him thus no longer. 2 Corinthians 5:16.)*

1:13 Everyone knows what a zealous Jew I was when I savagely persecuted God's ekklesia.

1:14 And how I progressed in the Jewish faith beyond many of my peers in my excessive eagerness to preserve the traditions of my ancestors.

1:15 God's eternal [1]love dream separated me from my mother's womb; his grace became my [2]identity. *(The word, [1]eudokeō, means his beautiful intention; the well done opinion. [My mother's womb, my natural lineage and identity as a son of Benjamin.] The word, [2]kaleō, means to surname, to summon by name.)*

1:16 This is the heart of the gospel that I proclaim; it began with the unveiling of his Son [1]in me, freeing me to announce the same sonship [2]in the masses of non-Jewish people. I felt no immediate urgency to compare notes with those who were familiar with Christ from a mere historical point of view.

(Paul uses the verb, ἀποκαλύψαι apokalupsai which is the Aorist Infinitive of apokaluptō, to uncover. The Aorist Infinitive, indicates prior completion of an action in relationship to a point in time. Greek Infinitives could have either a present or Aorist form. The contrast between the two forms has more to do with aspect than with time. The Present Infinitive is used to express progressive or imperfective aspect. It pictures the action expressed by the verb as being in progress. The Aorist Infinitive however, does not express progressive aspect. It presents the action expressed by the verb as a completed unit with a beginning and end.

The Greek text is quite clear: It pleased the Father to reveal his Son in me in order that I may proclaim him in the nations. The words, ἐν ἐμοὶ en emoi, translate as in me, and ἐν τοῖς ἔθνεσι en tois ethnesi translate as in the nations, or the masses of non Jewish people. The use of the Dative together with the preposition en - en tois ethnesi [from ethnos], further emphasizes location in. Some translations would correctly translate the first part of the sentence, the Father was pleased to reveal his Son in me; but then sadly, all translations would translate the same word, in the very next line to say among the nations.

Later, when Barnabas is sent to investigate the conversion of the Greeks in Acts 11, instead of reporting his findings to HQ in Jerusalem, he immediately finds Paul, knowing that Paul's gospel is the revelation of the mystery of Christ in the nations [see Colossians 1:27]. No wonder then that those believers were the first to be called Christians, or Christ-like Anointed ones.

Jesus Christ confirms that the son of man is the son of God. Call no man your father on earth, for you have one Father who is in heaven. [Matthew 23:9] Paul reminds the Greek philosophers in Acts 17 that we live and move and have our being in God; mankind is indeed the offspring of God. He is quoting from their own writings, Epimenedes 600 BC and Aratus, 300 BC. The incorruptible seed of sonship is as much present in every person as the seed is already in all soil, even in the desert, waiting for the rain to awaken and ignite its life.

For as the rain and the snow come down from heaven and water the earth, making it bring forth and sprout, so shall my word be that proceeds from my mouth, it shall not disappoint my purpose, it shall saturate the soil and cause it to bring forth and sprout. Instead of the thorn the cypress and instead of the brier the myrtle. [Isaiah 55:8-11, 13]

In Matthew 13:44, Jesus says that the kingdom of heaven is like a treasure hidden in an agricultural field. There is more to the field than what meets the eye.

In 2 Corinthians 4:4, 7 Paul says that we have this treasure in earthen vessels. But the god of this world has blindfolded our minds through unbelief [believing a lie about ourselves, Numbers 13:33] to keep us from seeing the light of the gospel revealing the glory of God in the face of Christ who is the image of God, as in a mirror.

When Jesus speaks of the sinner he speaks of him as the lost sheep, coin, or son. [Luke 15] You cannot be lost unless you belong. The inscription and image did not disappear from the coin when it was lost. How can we praise God and with the same mouth curse a person made in his image? [James 3:9 and Luke 20:20-26] Mankind has forgotten what manner of people they are by design; we are the image and likeness bearer of our Maker; this is exactly what Jesus came to reveal and redeem.

We may now behold him with unveiled faces as in a mirror and be immediately transformed [in our understanding] into his likeness. From the glory [opinion] of the flesh to the glory [opinion] of God. Legalistic religion kept the veil in place; the proclamation of the liberating truth of the Good News, removes the veil. The ugly duckling didn't need a face-lift or lessons on how to fake the swan life. It only needed to know the truth about itself to be free indeed.

John 14:20 In that day you will know that we are in seamless union with one another. I am in my Father, you are in me and I am in you. (The incarnation does not divide the Trinity; the incarnation celebrates the redeemed inclusion of humanity. Picture 4 circles with the one fitting into the other - The outer circle is the Father, then Jesus in the Father, then us in Jesus and the Holy Spirit in us. This spells inseparable, intimate oneness. Note that it is not our knowing that positions Jesus in the Father or us in them or the Spirit of Christ in us. Our knowing simply awakens us to the reality of our redeemed oneness. Gold does not become gold when it is discovered but it certainly becomes currency.))

1:17 This is radical. I deliberately distanced myself from Jerusalem and the disciples of Jesus. I landed up in Arabia before I returned again to

Damascus. *(The weight of this revelation left me no choice; instead of finding out more about Christ in history, I desire to discover him more in me. Also 2 Corinthians 5:16.)*

1:18 Then three years later I ventured into Jerusalem, specifically to meet with [1]Kefas. I ended up staying with him for two weeks. *(In [1]Aramaic the word rock is **kefas**, and in Greek it is **petros**. Here Paul calls Peter, Kefas, in order to emphasize the meaning of his name rather than the familiar sound of Peter. Jesus said that the revelation of mankind's true identity and origin is the rock foundation of the **ekklesia**, lit. original identity from **ek**, the Preposition denoting origin and **kaleō**, to surname. [Matthew 16:13-18; see also Isaiah 51:1; Deuteronomy 32:18; 1 Peter 2:5 and 1 Kings 6:7.])*

1:19 During this time I did not see any of the other Apostles except James, the younger brother of Jesus. *(Saul [Paul], Peter [Kefas] and James shared a vital revelation; all three of them discovered their original identity beyond their natural birth: From now on, we no longer know anyone according to the flesh, says Paul in 2 Corinthians 5:16. Simon son of Jonah, flesh and blood did not reveal to you that as the son of man, I am the Christ, the Son of God; now that you know who I am, allow me to introduce you to you. I say that you are Mr Rock; a Chip off the old Block. [Matthew 16:17, 18] James speaks about the effect of the Word as discovering the reflection of the face of our birth as in a mirror there. Rescuing us from our forgetfulness. We have forgotten what manner of people we are.*

During the three years of Jesus' ministry none of his brothers believed in him. [John 7:5] But in 1 Corinthians 15:7, Paul specifically mentions the fact that Jesus also appeared to James after his resurrection. Suddenly it dawns on James that the Father of light birthed mankind by the eternal Word of truth; the word that became flesh and died mankind's death and who co-raised mankind into newness of life in his resurrection. If anyone hears this word they see the face of their birth as in a mirror. As Peter later admitted We were born anew when Jesus was raised from the dead. [1 Peter 1:3] The word that was before time was, is our genesis. James 1:17, 18, 23, 24.)

1:20 I'm not writing this to trick you into anything; this is really how I started off preaching this gospel.

1:21 After my brief visit to Jerusalem, I traveled to the regions of Syria and Cilicia.

1:22 None of the Judean communities in Christ, knew me face to face.

1:23 They only heard the rumor that the fierce opponent of their cause was now proclaiming the very Gospel he once endeavored to eradicate.

1:24 Consequently, they were celebrating God for what they now witnessed in me. *(The verb εδοξαζον is the Imperfect Active of **doxazō;** thus, to continue to magnify & celebrate God.)*

2:1 It was fourteen years after that first visit that I went on a special mission to Jerusalem with Barnabas; we deliberately took Titus with us. *(Titus was one of Paul's first fruits in Greece. Remember Barnabas was sent by HQ in Jerusalem to investigate the rumor of Greek converts; instead of returning to Jerusalem to give feedback to the senior Apostles, he went to fetch Paul, knowing his gift as a teacher and revelation of the mystery of Christ in you. Colossians 1:26 and Acts 11:25,26.)*

2:2 I especially wanted the most senior leadership of the ekklesia-church to hear what I teach in the Gentile nations as my revelation and specific emphasis of the Gospel. We decided to meet in private to avoid any possible public controversy. In this way they could best judge for themselves whether, according to their opinion, my ministry had credibility or not.

2:3 Our Greek companion, Titus, survived the circumcision scrutiny and wasn't forced to go for the cut.

2:4 Some disguised Jewish friends secretly sneaked in on us to spy out whether he was circumcised or not. Our liberty in Christ offended them; these spies had one agenda; to enslave us to their legalistic bondage.

2:5 We want you to know that we are sold out to keep the Gospel undiluted for your sake; had we compromised the message ever so slightly to accommodate their opinion, the whole Gentile world would have felt cheated. We see such a future for the pure gospel in you.

2:6 The high ranked leaders had nothing to add to my message. I must say that their seniority did not intimidate me in the least. God does not judge people on face value. *(The important ones and the unimportant ones are equally esteemed and loved by him. 2 Corinthians 5:14, 16.)*

2:7 From what I shared with them they acknowledged the accuracy of my message and felt that while Peter's ministry was more directed to the Jews, mine is tailor-made for the Gentile world.

2:8 They acknowledged that as much as Peter's ministry was sanctioned by God to preach to the Jews, my assignment was to evangelize the Gentiles.

2:9 The so-called pillars of the ekklesia, James *[the Lord's brother. Galatians 1:19]*, Kefas, and John acknowledged my gift in the revelation of the message of grace, and extended their blessing on my work by giving us the right hand of fellowship. While they concentrated on converting the Jews I was recognized as the one with a message for the Gentiles.

2:10 Their only request was that we give something to the poor amongst them which we were keen to do since we already came prepared with gifts. *(Acts 11:29, 30.)*

2:11 But when Kefas in turn visited Antioch I had to take him to task for his hypocrisy.

2:12 His fellowship with the Greek believers seemed so sincere, he even ate with them until James's group arrived from Jerusalem. Then his loyalty to the law showed its true colors. His pretense was an embarrassment.

2:13 Because of his senior position, the other Jewish believers were swept along with his hypocrisy; they even seduced Barnabas. What a shame.

2:14 Their interpretation of the Gospel was clearly compromised. I confronted Peter publicly about this. Behind your colleagues' backs you pretend to live just like a Gentile as if your Jewish customs were no longer relevant; now suddenly you're imposing out-dated Jewish rules on these Gentile believers, to impress your Jewish friends.

2:15 Sin is not a respecter of persons. Sin is sin whether you're Jew or Gentile.

2:16 As Jews we should be the first to know that righteousness is not a reward for good behavior according to the requirements of the Law. We have pursued righteousness for generations under the system of personal performance but failed miserably. Jesus Christ embodies [1]God's belief concerning mankind's redeemed righteousness; this is the only valid basis of our belief. Our best intentions to do good cannot add any weight to our righteousness. We have no advantage over any other person. Jew and Gentile alike were equally disqualified by the law; now we are equally justified because of Jesus and for no other reason. *(Paul uses the [1]objective Genitive - faith of. He is the author and finisher of faith; he is both the origin and conclusion of faith [Hebrews. 12:2]; from faith to faith [Romans 1:17]. It is God's persuasion in the merit of his Son's achievement that awakens faith in mankind. Romans 4:25.)*

2:17 However, if in our quest to discover righteousness by faith in what Christ did for us, we find that it is still possible to stumble; do not now label yourself a sinner yet again. The fact that you sinned does not cancel the cross of Christ and gives you no reason to abandon justification by faith as if Christ is to be blamed for your distraction. That would be absurd. *(Now all of a sudden you want to keep the law again to further add to your righteousness as if Christ did not achieve enough. Do not let your experience deceive you to invent a new doctrine.)*

2:18 Only a con artist will try to be a law-man and a grace-man at the same time.

2:19 The law [1]demanded my death; grace reveals that in God's mind Jesus died that death. So as far as the law is concerned, I'm a dead man but as far as God is concerned I'm alive. *(The word [1]dia means because of; suggesting here that the law was what demanded my death. But in the mystery of God's genius, Jesus died mankind's death; which means, in God's belief, I died to the old system of trying to please him with my own good behavior. We might as well admit it. Our most sincere beliefs as well as our best attempts to attain to a righteousness based on us getting ten out of ten all the time, failed. There is no ways to get around this. See Romans chapter 7 in the Mirror Bible.)*

2:20 So here I am dead and alive at the same time. I'm dead to the old me I was trying to be and alive to the real me which is Christ in me. Co-crucified, now co-alive. What a glorious entanglement. I was in him in his death; now I discover that he is infused in me, in my life. For the first time, I'm free to be me in my skin, immersed in his faith in our joint-sonship. He loves me and believes in me. He is God's gift to me.

(The verb συνεσταυρωμαι **sunestaurōmai** *from* **sustauroō**, *is in the Perfect tense, indicating that not only was I crucified with Christ in the past, but I am existing now in that present condition. How can any human effort improve on this. See Hosea 6:2 and Ephesians 2:5 also Romans 7:6 But now we are fully released from any further association with a life directed by the rule of the law, we are dead to that which once held us captive, free to be slaves to the newness of spirit-spontaneity rather than age old religious rituals, imitating the mere face value of the written code. The moment one exchanges spontaneity with rules, the edge of romance is compromised.)*

2:21 It is an insult to the grace of God to prefer Moses to Jesus. If the law could justify you then Jesus wasted his time dying your death. *(That would reduce salvation to a ludicrous contest between your obedience and the obedience of Christ. Romans 5:19.)*

Notes on Galatians 2:20

See **1 Thessalonians 5:10** *The fact that he died our death is equally valid to those who are awake to its effect or still fast asleep in their indifference to it; we are together destined to live entwined in the [1]closest possible association with him.*

*(The word [1]***hama** *is a particle of union denoting close association.)*

Also **Ephesians 4:21** *[1]Truth is defined in Jesus. It is not possible to study him in any other context; he is the incarnation; hear him resonate within you. The truth about you has its ultimate reference in Jesus.*

(Lit. [1]The truth, as it is in Jesus. See **1 John 2:7,8**, *Whatever is true of him, is equally true of you. He did not come to introduce a new compromised set of rules; he is not an example for us but of us.)*

Ephesians 4:22 *For in the truth of your union in him [in his death and resurrection], [1]you have stripped off that old identity like a filthy worn-out garment. Ignorance and lust [v18] corrupted you and cheated you into wearing it in the first place.*

*(The verb, απoθεσθαι [1]***apothesthai**, *is the Aorist Middle Infinitive which presents the action expressed by the verb as a completed unit with a beginning and end. Just like an actor who wore a cloak for a specific role he had to interpret; the fake identity is no longer relevant. See* **Colossians 3:1-3,9**. **Colossians 3:9** *That old life was a lie, foreign to our design. Those garments of disguise are now thoroughly stripped off us in our understanding of our union with Christ in his death and resurrection. We are no longer obliged to live under the identity and rule of the robes we wore before, neither are we cheating anyone through false pretensions. [The garments an actor would wear define his part in the play but do not define him.])*

Ephesians 4:23 *Thus [1]you are habitually renewed in your innermost mind. This will cause you to be completely re-booted in the way you think about yourself.*

*(Ponder the truth about you, as it is displayed in Christ; begin with the fact of your co-seatedness. You can never be more co-raised and co-elevated than what you already are. [***Ephesians 2:5,6***] You can only grow in your awareness of your redeemed oneness. Notice that Paul does not say, Renew your minds. But,* **to be habitually renewed...** *He uses the* **Present Passive Infinitive** *ανανεουσθαι*

[1]*ananeosthai*, from *ana*, upwards [by setting your mind on the things that are above where you are co-seated together with Christ] and νεώτερος *neoteros*, renovated; renewed. Greek Infinitives could have either a Present or Aorist form. The contrast between the two forms has more to do with aspect than with time. The Present Infinitive is used to express progressive or imperfective aspect. It pictures the action expressed by the verb as being in progress. The Aorist Infinitive however, does not express progressive aspect. It presents the action expressed by the verb as a completed unit with a beginning and end.

This transformation happens in the spirit of your mind, awakened by truth on a much deeper level than a mere intellectual or academic consent. We often thought that we had to get information to drop from the head to the heart; but it is the other way around.

Jesus says in **John 7:37**, When you believe that I am what the Scriptures are all about, then you will discover that you are what I am all about, and rivers of living waters will gush out of your innermost being. The spirit of mankind was never contaminated; just like the watermark in a paper note.

The lost coin never lost its original inscription and image [see also James 3:9]; it was the mind that was veiled by darkness; we were darkened in our understanding. Our thoughts were reduced to the soul realm reference, knowing ourselves, and one another merely after the flesh. **Isaiah 55:8-13**

There is nothing wrong with our design or our redemption; we were thinking wrong. In order for our thoughts to be rescued from the dominion of darkness, Jesus as the incarnate image and likeness of God, has gone into our darkest hellish nightmare, and faced our cruelest judgment and fears, and died our death.

This is the mystery that was hidden for ages and generations, for our glorification. We were co-crucified, to bring absolute closure to every reference we have had of ourselves as a result of Adam's fall. And while we were dead in our sins and trespasses, God co-quickened us and co-raised us, and co-seated us in Christ. Now, we all with unveiled faces may behold the glory of the Lord as in a mirror. And be radically transformed in our thinking in order to rediscover his image and likeness fully redeemed in us.

Ephesians 4:24 [1]Remain fully [2]immersed in this God-shaped new person from above. You are created in the image and likeness of God. This is what righteousness and true holiness are all about.

(The copulative Particle [1]*kai*, as in καὶ ἐνδύσασθαι, continues the thought expressed in the previous 3 sentences. Again, the verb, ενδυσασθαι *endusasthai* [as in verse 22], is the Aorist Middle Infinitive which presents the action expressed by the verb as a completed unit with a beginning and end.)

Also **Luke 9:24** Trying to keep the self of your own making intact, is a lost cause to begin with. Losing yourself in me, is realizing that I am the source of who you are by design. This is your saving grace.

[See my notes on Luke 24:49, your Dress-code.]

3:1 Oh, Galatians, Galatians! Have you completely lost your common sense? Can't you see how the law bewitched you and blurred your vision to distort the revelation of what the cross of Christ accomplished in you? This was so clearly predicted in Scripture. How can you not be persuaded by the truth? *(He did not die as an individual, he died your death. Isaiah 53:4, 5.)*

3:2 Please would you reason with me on this one issue; on what basis did you receive the Holy Spirit? Are we talking gift or reward here? What kind of message ignites faith? What a condemned sinner and failure you are as revealed in the law, or what God believes to be true about you as revealed in the Gospel. Let's not confuse Law with Grace.

3:3 Can you see how stupid it would be to start in the spirit *(believing in the success of the cross)* and then for some crazy reason to switch modes back to DIY again. As if your own works could add anything to what God has already done in Christ. *([DIY - Do It Yourself.] It would be suicidal. It's like deliberately jumping out of the boat to try and swim across the ocean. There are two trees: the DIY tree or the Life tree. They represent two laws or systems: the law of works and the law of faith; the one represents what you have to do in order to become; the other tree reveals who you are by design and what Christ has done. Because of the Calvary-tree we are free to be. Spirit = faith; flesh = works.)*

3:4 Remember how you felt when you first encountered faith; are you prepared to exchange that for religious sentiment? All the ground you've gained would be lost. *(The law does not complete faith, it nullifies it.)*

3:5 Would you accredit what you have received from God to something you did or something you have heard? Did God reward you for your high moral standards when he worked extravagant miracles in you and lavished his Spirit upon you; or did it perhaps have anything to do with the content of the revelation of the message of grace that you have heard? Faith is the source of God's action on mankind's behalf; our hearing is the conduit of what God's faith reveals.

3:6 Abraham had no other claim to righteousness but simply believing what God declared concerning him. Isaac confirmed God's faith, not Abraham's efforts. This is all we have in common with Abraham. *(Righteousness reveals God's faith as responsible for mankind's salvation in direct contrast their own ability to be righteous.)*

3:7 The conclusion is clear; faith and not flesh relates us to Abraham. *(Grace rather than law is our true lineage. Ishmael represents so much more than the Muslim religion. Ishmael represents the clumsy effort of the flesh to compete with faith; the preaching of a mixed message of law and grace.)*

3:8 Scripture records prophetically that the mass of non-Jewish nations would be justified by faith and not by their own ability to be righteous. This announcement by God over Abraham is the gospel in advance. God saw every nation included in the same principle of the faith that

Abraham pioneered. In you all the nations of the earth are equally represented in the blessing of faith. *([Genesis 22:17] I will indeed bless you, and I will multiply your seed as the stars of heaven and as the sand which is on the seashore. And your seed shall possess the gate of their enemies, Genesis 22:18 and by your seed shall all the nations of the earth bless themselves. Righteousness by faith is the revelation of the gospel; [Romans 1:17 and Habakkuk 2:4] the just shall live by his (God's) faith Righteousness by God's belief defines your life.)*

3:9 As did Abraham so do we now find our source in the blessing of faith.

3:10 In clear contrast to faith, the law is the authority of the curse. As it is written, Everyone who fails to perform the detailed requirements of the law, even in the least, is condemned. *(Deuteronomy 27:26.)*

3:11 Habakkuk confirms conclusively that righteousness by God's faith is the only basis to life; this terminates any possible justification before God based on moral behavior. *(Habakkuk 2:4, 3:17-19.)*

3:12 Law and faith have nothing in common. Law measures a person's doing and experience as defining their life. *(Faith measures God's doing in redeeming his design in us, as defining our lives.)*

3:13 Christ redeemed us from the curse as consequence of our failure to keep the law. In his cross he concentrated the total curse of the human race upon himself. In his abandoning himself to death, he absorbed and dissolved the horror of the curse in his own person. Scripture declares that anyone hanging on a tree embodies the curse. *(Deuteronomy 21:23.)*

3:14 This act of Christ released [1]the blessing of Abraham upon the [2]Gentiles. Now we are free to receive [1]the blessing of the Spirit. *([1]Righteousness by God's faith in the achievement of Christ, and not as a reward for our behavior. In the obedience of Christ Deuteronomy 28 is out-dated. [Romans 5:19, Ephesians 1:3] [2]The mass of non-Jewish nations.)*

3:15 We are familiar with the fact that in civil affairs a testament, once endorsed, is authoritative and cannot be tampered with at a later stage.

3:16 It is on record that the promise *[of the blessing of righteousness by God's faith]* was made to Abraham and to his seed, singular, *[thus excluding his effort to produce Ishmael.]* Isaac, the child of promise, and not of the flesh, mirrors the Messiah.

3:17 This is my reasoning: God endorsed the covenant of promise in Christ 430 years before the law was given. The law did not later replace the promise. *(God's faith, as embodied in Christ, is the only basis to mankind's acquittal and could never be replaced by their own ability to justify themselves. See Romans 4:25.)*

3:18 The law and the promise are not compatible; the one system nullifies the other. God gifts Abraham with an heir-ship by promise *(and not by reward for his behavior.)*

3:19 So what is the use of the law then? The law was doing you a ¹favor, in that it was ²positioned as a ³mirror-measuring rod as an intermediary arrangement to make people aware of the extent of their out of sync-ness with the life of their design and at the same time point them to the promise of a Redeemer, the Messianic seed. It was given by celestial messengers to Moses. *(Paul uses the word ¹charin here - God graced us with the law as a mirror-reminder of our original identity. The word, ²prostithēmi means to be positioned in the face of; like a mirror. The word ³parabasis suggests a standard/ measuring stick; from para, close proximity and basis, footprint; thus compared to the standard rule, mankind's out of sync-ness with their default settings became obvious.]*

3:20 With Abraham there was no middleman; it was just God. *(The Mosaic law sopke the language of the fallen mind and required mediators - the Levitical priesthood - because it was an arrangement whereby mankind had a part and God had a part. God's covenant with Abraham was a grace covenant pointing to the man Jesus Christ, in whom God himself would fulfil mankind's part and therefore needed no mediator apart from himself. See Hebrews 6:17*

In the incarnation Jesus fulfills both the proposal and the I do. Melissa Perez)

3:21 No, the law does not oppose God's promise; it emphasizes the desperate need for a Redeemer to release righteousness in mankind as their life; something the law would certainly be incapable of. Had it been possible for a person to be justified by the law, the promise would be unnecessary. *(For if any kind of rule-keeping had power to create life in us, we would certainly have gotten it by this time. — The Message.*

Romans 5:6 God's timing was absolutely perfect; mankind was at their weakest when Christ died their death—we were bankrupt in our efforts to save ourselves.)

3:22 Scripture concludes that all men without exception are in the same predicament; they are imprisoned to sin; now faith brings the promise of immediate release within everyone's reach. Jesus Christ makes it possible for all to believe what God believes concerning their righteousness and restored innocence. *(Jesus is the embodiment of God's faith in mankind. The righteousness of God is now on display in such a way that all may believe, regardless of who they are, there is no distinction. The same mass of mankind that was once reduced to an inferior identity through their sin, is now gifted with acquittal on the basis of the ransom paid by Jesus Christ for their liberation. [Romans 3:22-24])*

3:23 We were confined to the law, kept in custody to its constraining influence until the revelation of faith would come to our rescue.

3:24 The law was acting just like a slave appointed to be the guardian of his master's children, until they would be of age to go to the proper school of Christ to find in faith their righteousness revealed and endorsed.

3:25 Now that we have arrived at our destination, the prophetic road signs and pointers are of no further use. Faith replaced the Custodian. Now that faith has come the law is no longer relevant.

3:26 What Jesus Christ believes to be true about you is the final confirmation of mankind's redeemed sonship. His faith is the only valid reference to your belief.

3:27 To be immersed in Christ is to be fully clothed with him. He is your brand new wardrobe confirming your sonship. *(From now on, the diaper days are over. Our own righteousness, measured by our efforts to keep the law, compares to filthy rags. Isaiah 64:6.)*

3:28 Nothing resembles your previous identity as Jew or Gentile, bond or free, male or female, Billabong or Gucci, now you are all defined in oneness with Christ. He is your significance and makes you beautiful. *(Galatians 3:28 In Him the distinctions between Jew and Gentile, slave and free man, male and female, disappear; you are all one in Christ Jesus. Weymouth Translation)*

3:29 Since Christ is the seed of promise, it is only in our realizing our union with him *[in the incarnation]* that we are equally related to Abraham and heirs of the promise. Faith and not flesh relates us to Abraham. *(We inherit his righteousness by the same faith.)*

4:1 Infant heirs have no more say than a slave, even though they own everything. *(The best deal the law could possibly broker confirmed mankind's slavery to sin.)*

4:2 He would remain under domestic supervision and house rules until the date fixed by his father for his official graduation to the status of sonship.

4:3 This is exactly how it was with us; we were kidnapped as if in infancy and confined to that state through the law. *(An inferior mindset as a result of Adam's fall.)*

4:4 But then the day dawned; the most complete culmination of time. *(Everything predicted was concluded in Christ.)* **The Son arrived, commissioned by the Father; his legal passport to the planet was his mother's womb. In a human body exactly like ours he lived his life subject to the same scrutiny of the law.**

4:5 His mandate was to rescue the human race from the regime of the law of performance and announce the revelation of their true sonship in God. *(Now our true state of sonship is again realized. [John 1:12; see John 1:11-14] It was not as though he arrived on a foreign planet, he came to his own, yet his own did not recognize him. [Psalm 24:1] But to everyone who realizes their association in him, convinced that he is their original life, in them he confirms that we are his offspring. These are they who discover their genesis in God beyond their natural conception. Man began in God. We are not the invention of our parents. Suddenly the invisible eternal Word takes on visible form. The Incarnation. In him, in us. The most accurate tangible display of God's eternal thought finds expression in human life. The Word became a human being; we are his address; he resides in us. He captivates our gaze. The glory we see there is not a religious replica; he is the authentic* **monogenes** *begotten only of God. In him we recognize our true beginning. The Glory that Adam lost, returns. In fullness. Only Grace can communicate truth in such a complete context.)*

4:6 To seal our sonship God has commissioned the Spirit of sonship to resonate the Abba echo in our hearts; and now, in our innermost being we recognize him as our true and very dear Father. *(The original life of the Father revealed in his Son is the life the Spirit now conducts within us. [Romans 8:14] Slavery is such a poor substitute for sonship. They are opposites; the one leads forcefully through fear; sonship responds fondly to Abba Father. [Romans 8:15] His Spirit resonates within our spirit to confirm the fact that we originate in God. [Romans 8:16] Because we are his offspring, we qualify to be his heirs, God himself is our portion, we co-inherit with Christ. Romans 8:17.)*

4:7 Can you see how foolish it would be for a son to continue to live his life with a slave mentality? Your sonship qualifies you to immediately participate in all the wealth of God's inheritance which is yours because of Christ. *(Legalism in its every disguise contradicts sonship. Sonship is not for sale.)*

4:8 What really amazes me is how gullible you Gentile believers are to get yourselves all tangled up again in oppressive Jewish rites. I mean you know all about your BC days of slavery to imaginary gods under your pagan beliefs.

4:9 In the meantime, you have come to know the real God; *[quite unlike the god of your imagination]* what is most significant however, is to discover that he knew you all along. After all, how could you possibly feel attracted again to the pathetic principles of religious deception? It does not matter in what disguise legalism comes, whether pagan or Jewish, it brings the same bondage.

4:10 All of a sudden there are special days, months, seasonal, and annual festivities that are scrupulously celebrated; this is nothing more than superstitious religious sentiment.

4:11 I am alarmed that all my passion seems wasted on you.

4:12 I urge you to imitate me *[in my conviction about the fact that Jewish customs and their shadow-sentiments are out-dated.].* We are exactly in the same boat, it is really not about me; it is about you. *(Our Jewish or Gentile background makes absolutely no difference. I'm not into winning or losing votes for my ministry or me. It's this Gospel that is my concern and urgency.)*

4:13 I have never compromised the Gospel, from the first day I met you, even though I was physically challenged at the time it did not distract from the message.

4:14 Remember how hospitable and sensitive you were towards me in spite of my frail condition. Instead of feeling embarrassed or repelled you treated me like a celestial messenger with the same courtesy you would have shown Christ Jesus.

4:15 At that time you were so overwhelmed with gratitude towards me that you would have gladly given me what is most precious to you, even your own eyes, to give me relief for my discomfort. What tenderness of affection you showed.

4:16 Alas. How is it possible that the same truth that then bonded you to me now turns me into your enemy?

4:17 The people who make me out to be your enemy do that to your disadvantage: they are very eager to isolate you from me, so that your zeal for their Jewish sentiments will boost their religious ego. *(Can you not see it; the Law and its followers do not like you for you; their only desire is for themselves.)*

4:18 If you want to be zealous for the best possible cause, be zealous for grace. You are fooling yourselves to be nice to me when I'm with you but zealous for them behind my back. It is not about me, I am jealous for you. It is the message that matters most, not someone's private agenda.

4:19 My darling little children, my jealousy for you compares to a mother over her newly born. I gave birth to you once through my gospel; now I feel those same labor pains all over again. I travail for the full realization of Christ to be [1]formed within you. *(The word, [1]**morphoō**, means to mold, from **meros**, form or portion; note the word translated, sin, **hameros**, to be without form or without your allotted portion; **metamorphoō**, together with form.)*

4:20 I long to be with you right now; I want you to hear the urgency in my voice. I wish I could convince you that the law is a cul-de-sac. *(Any effort of your own to add to what God has already perfected in you in Christ is a waste of time. It is like trying to re-invent the wheel.)*

4:21 Since you are so intrigued by the law, would you please, also understand its prophetic message:

4:22 The law records the fact that Abraham had two sons: one by a slave girl, the other by a free woman.

4:23 The one is produced by the flesh *[the Do It Yourself-tree]*, the other by faith *[the promise]*.

4:24 There is a parallel meaning in the story of the two sons: they represent two systems, works and grace.

4:25 Sinai is an Arabian rocky mountain named after Hagar, *[outside the land of promise]*. Its association with the law of Moses mirrors Jerusalem as the capital of Jewish legalism. Hagar is the mother of the law of works. *[DIY-religion]*

*(See **Galatians 3:7** The conclusion is clear; faith and not flesh relates us to Abraham. [Grace rather than law is our true lineage. Ishmael represents so much more than the Muslim religion. Ishmael represents the clumsy effort of the flesh to compete with faith; the preaching of a mixed message of law and grace.])*

4:26 But the mother from above, the true mother of mankind is grace, the free Jerusalem; she is the mother of the promise.

4:27 For it is written, Rejoice, Oh childless one. Erupt in jubilee. For though you have never known travail before, your children will greatly outnumber her who was married. *(Married to the law; Isaiah 54:1; see also Romans 7:1-6.)*

4:28 We resemble Isaac: we are begotten of faith; the promise is our parent.

4:29 Just as when the flesh child persecuted the faith child, so now these Jerusalem Jews in their Christian disguise seek to harass you.

4:30 However, Scripture is clear: Expel the slave mother and her son; the slave son cannot inherit with the free son. *(In exactly the same way, rid your minds radically from the slave mother and child mentality. Light dispels darkness effortlessly.)*

4:31 Realize whose children we are my Brothers and Sisters: we are not children of the slave-mother, the law, but children of the free mother; we are begotten of grace.

5:1 Christ defines your faith; he is your freedom from anything from which the law could never free you. Find your firm footing in this freedom. Do not let religion trip you up again and harness you to a system of rules and obligations. *(In this parallel, Christ represents Sarah, the faith-mother who birthed you in the resurrection. The rock-hewn tomb represents Sarah's dead womb. 1 Peter 1:3.)*

5:2 I, Paul, am of the opinion, and you can quote me: If you would again consider circumcision as necessary to improve your standing before God, then you make Christ of no relevance to yourselves. Then you might as well delete him from your life altogether. *(By still holding on to any Jewish sentiment like keeping the Sabbath, etc., has the same effect.)*

5:3 I will state it categorically, that if you endorse circumcision as a means to obtain righteousness, you are immediately obliged to keep the whole law. *(In for a penny, in for a pound.)*

5:4 Law-righteousness has nothing in common with grace-righteousness; they are opposites. As impossible as it is for anyone to travel in two opposite directions at the same time, equally irrelevant Christ becomes to anyone who continues to pursue righteousness under the law.

5:5 Our minds are made up; there is absolutely no advantage for anyone to pursue righteousness in the flesh; righteousness is a spirit-dimension reality and can only be ¹embraced by faith. What God believes is our exclusive reference. *(Any other basis for righteousness leaves mankind falling hopelessly short. The word, ¹apekdechomai is often translated, to wait for; the components however, point to a favorable embrace; apo, from, ek out of, and dechomai to grasp, to welcome hospitably, to embrace.)*

5:6 God believes that we are fully represented in Christ, which takes circumcision or any contribution of the flesh out of the equation. Love fuels belief and sets faith in motion. *(It is easy for love to believe.*

In Christ Jesus neither circumcision nor uncircumcision is of any avail, but faith working through love. RSV.)

5:7 You started off like an athlete on a mission, who distracted you? You seemed so completely persuaded about the truth.

5:8 God is not confused about you. He surnamed you.

5:9 It is impossible to hide the effect of the smallest amount of yeast; the process of fermentation is immediately triggered. *(A little bit of legalism corrupts a person's whole life.)*

5:10 In spite of the interference of those law-loving people, I remain convinced about our like-mindedness in the Lord. It does not matter what high profile position anyone may occupy, do not let their title disturb you. The very law they promote is their judgment. *(The fermentation process is unavoidable when you host a legalistic mindset.)*

5:11 Would I compromise the message of the cross and preach circumcision just to avoid persecution. How insane would that be? *(This whole matter boils down to, either thinking that justification is the result of something we still have to do, or knowing that it is the result of something that God has already done.)*

5:12 These people who are so keen to cut off things should cut off their legalistic influence in your lives altogether.

5:13 Your redeemed identity defines your freedom, my friends. But freedom does not mean that you are now free to again employ the law. On the contrary, your freedom finds its most complete expression in a love that serves one another. As free as you are to the law, so enslaved you are now to love. *(You are at last free to live the life of your original design.)*

5:14 Love already completes the law: this is the nitty-gritty of the law; to value your fellow human as equal to yourself. *(Which was again and again proved to be completely impossible to achieve by employing the DIY tree-principle.)*

5:15 The best efforts under the legalistic mindset sooner or later ended up in strife: back-biting, tearing one another apart, devouring and consuming one another. *(It gets ugly. See how divorce destroyed love dreams; Exodus-business partners fighting one another in court; consider how worthless life becomes in war.)*

5:16 I conclude: engage your spirit to be the dominant influence in your daily walk and see how it defeats the cravings of flesh. *(Spirit is satisfied by the love-law, the revelation of grace; flesh craves to prove and gratify itself by the DIY law. Faith defeats flesh.)*

5:17 While the law of works still features in your mind, it is a catalyst to disaster; you are caught in the middle of a war zone, wanting to do the things that you desire by design, but finding the flesh in strong resistance to what the spirit desires. *(The two trees, the flesh and the spirit, represent two opposing systems or forces of influence, two separate mind-sets; while the tree of life represents the inner-life of our design, the I-am-not-tree, or what I call the DIY-Tree, is not the real you. Just like the flu. You can host the virus but the flu is not you. Paul compares the fruit of righteousness by faith working through love versus the works of the flesh and guilt performance based on obligation, guilt and willpower. See Romans 3:27, also Romans 7. And remember, the war is over. It's already won. Engage your thoughts with throne room realities. Colossians 3:1-3. Your victory rests in the triumph of Jesus. See Ephesians 6 and 2 Corinthians 10:3-6 also 2 Corinthians 12:7-10 in the Mirror.)*

5:18 To be [1]acquainted with the prompting of your spirit [faith] is to be free from the law [of personal performance.] *(The word **agesthe**, from **agō**, is in the Present Passive tense - continual prompting. See Galatians 3:3.)*

5:19 The typical lifestyle wherever a legalistic judgmental attitude prevails is one where sexual sins are rampant. Anything goes: adultery, filth, and outrageous licentiousness.

5:20 Then there is the worshipping of a distorted image of oneself, which is what idolatry is all about; drugs, hatred, constant conflict, jealous suspicion, violent outbursts of rage, everyone for himself in a cut-throat competitive world, trampling on others to get to the top, dissension, heresy, and manipulating people's minds with false teachings. *(The flesh* *is not your lower nature; it is the fruit of the I-am-not tree system ; it is a mindset governed by a sense of lack and desperately trying to do life by sheer willpower, independent of your Source.)*

5:21 This is such a sad picture of a life consumed with envious self pity, murder, drunken stupor, intoxicated licentiousness and lust, with all the quarrels and jealousies it ignites. As I have stated before: those who are practicing this kind of lifestyle have nothing in common with the Kingdom of God. *(The authority of the Christ-life opposes and defeats the dominance of the flesh.)*

5:22 Your spirit effortlessly bears the rich harvest of love, joy, peace, patience, kindness, goodness, integrity, gentleness and self control; all these individually reveal the irresistible attraction of the inner-life of our design. *(They are not fading, fragile emotions produced by willpower. This is the fruit of what you know in your spirit to be true about you. Fruit is the effortless, spontaneous expression of the character of the tree. Rest in the awareness and assurance of who you really are.)*

5:23 Legalism can neither match nor contradict this. There is no law against love. *(Love does not compete with law; love is extravagant in its exhibition of the Christ-life.)*

5:24 Those who understand that their righteousness is of Christ and that it does not come as a reward for their ability to keep the law, have discovered that their flesh with its dictates and lusts were co-crucified with Christ. *(Galatians 2:20; see also Galatians 5:18.)*

5:25 Because faith defines us and not flesh, we take our lead from the spirit in our daily conduct. There is an authority in our step; we are marching in rank like soldiers. *(The Christ-life is the dominant authority in the universe.)*

5:26 Quit your efforts to try and impress one another. The law of works reduces your life to envious comparison and petty competition, while love only always seeks the advantage of the other. *(This means total freedom from any external law.)*

6:1 Brothers and sisters, if it seems that someone continues to [1]anticipate their next [2]failure *[by carrying just too much load, see verse 2]*, from your position in faith restore such a person in a spirit of courtesy and grace, keeping your own attitude in check; a legalistic approach would want to suspiciously probe into problems. *(The word, [1]prolambanō, means to anticipate, take in advance; [2]paraptōma, comes from para, close proximity, proceeding from a sphere of influence, and piptō, means to lose height, stop flying, to fail. Remember you represent grace not law.)*

6:2 **Taking the weight off someone's shoulder is fulfilling the law of Christ.** *(The message of grace removes all law-related burdens such as guilt, suspicion, inferiority, shame and a sin-consciousness.)*

6:3 **Anyone who imagines to be someone they are not, lives a lie.** *(The law system sponsors pretense; grace reveals your true identity redeemed in Christ.)*

6:4 **Now, without the pressure of pretense, you are free to give expression to your individual self and not some phony life you're trying to fake. Evaluate your own conduct in such a way that you do not need another's approval to confirm your joy.**

6:5 **Everyone ultimately lives their own life.** *(Even though we share our lives with one another.)*

6:6 **Both student and teacher draw from the same source; they equally participate in every good thing. The word they share echoes its distinct resonance within them.**

6:7 **Show-business does not deceive God. Do not be led astray and then pull your nose up at God, as if it was God who let you down. The harvest always reveals the seed.**

6:8 **The flesh cannot compete with the spirit; just like with Adam, the fruit of the DIY tree still produces death, while faith produces the spirit fruit of the life of the ages, the God-kind of life.**

6:9 **Every good deed has a predictable harvest. Let's not get discouraged in the in-between times.** *(Make sure your good deeds are love-driven rather than duty-driven. Faith works by love, duty by willpower.)*

6:10 **Let us take advantage of every opportunity to be a blessing to everyone we meet, without neglecting our fellow faith family.**

6:11 To raise the urgency in my voice, I will write the following in my own hand and in large letters:

6:12 Those who urge you to be circumcised are only trying to avoid persecution for the cross of Christ. They prefer to be popular with their fellow Jewish colleagues and thus compromise the message of the cross. To them it is only the outward sign in the flesh that matters.

6:13 It is not even so much for the law that they are concerned, they just want to boast about your flesh, as a sign that they successfully recruited you for their cause.

6:14 May my boasting be in nothing but the cross of our Lord Jesus Christ, through whom the world has been crucified to me and I to the world. The religious-systems and applause of this world have no appeal to me. As far as they are concerned, I am like a dead person.

6:15 The new creation in Christ steals the show; not whether someone is circumcised or not. *(God associated us in Christ; when he died we died, when he was raised we were raised together with him in newness of life.)*

6:16 Our union with Christ sets the pace and makes us the true Israel, not whether we are Jew or Gentile, circumcised or not. Oh, what peace we discover in his mercy. This rule is the new law we submit ourselves to as the principle of our daily walk.

6:17 I will not be troubled anymore. I already bear enough scars in my body that brand me as being under the ownership of Jesus. *(Those scars that I carry from being persecuted for this Gospel are more significant to me than the scar of circumcision.)*

6:18 Brothers and sisters, may the revelation of the grace of our Lord Jesus Christ be the rule of your spirit.

Amen

In poetic articulation Paul unfolds the message of the mystery of Christ as representing mankind. He is absolutely passionate in his prayers and desires for everyone to see how completely associated they are in Christ. We were found in Christ before we were lost in Adam.

Ephesians 1:10 In the economy of the fullness of time, everything culminates in Christ; all that is in heaven and all that is on earth is reconciled in him.

He sees heaven not as a distant goal for us to strive towards, but how completely God has already lavished upon us every blessing heaven has in Christ. This is our point of departure. We are co-raised and co-seated together with Christ in heavenly places to begin with. Long before anyone but God believed it we were made alive together with Christ; I desire that you know by revelation what he has known about you all along. I pray that your thoughts will be flooded with light and inspired insight.

Ephesians 2:10 We are engineered by his design; he molded and manufactured us in Christ. We are his workmanship, his poetry. We are fully fit to do good, equipped to give attractive evidence of his likeness in us in everything we do.

Ephesians 3:4 In reading these words you will perceive my insight into the mystery of Christ.

Ephesians 3:20 We celebrate him who supercharges us powerfully from within. Our biggest request or most amazing dream cannot match the extravagant proportion of his thoughts towards us.

Ephesians 4:7 The gift of Christ measures the extravagant dimensions of grace; where everyone is equally advantaged.

Ephesians 4:23 Be renewed in your innermost mind. It will cause you to be completely reprogrammed in the way you think about yourself.

Ephesians 4:15 Love gives truth its voice. The conversation that truth inspires creates the atmosphere wherein growth is both spontaneous and inevitable. The whole person is addressed in Christ who is the head of the body; he is the conclusion of God's communication with mankind.

Ephesians 4:16 From him flows the original composition and detail of our design. Like words entwined in poetry, they connect layer upon layer to complete the harmony, following the rhythm of his thoughts like footprints. Meanwhile the body thrives and pulsates with the energy of love. Each individual expression finds its complete measure there.

Ephesians 4:21 It is not possible to study Christ in any other context; he is the incarnation; hear him resonate within you. The truth about you has its ultimate reference in Jesus.

He did not come to introduce a new compromised set of rules; he is not an example for us but of us.

Ephesians 5:14 This is the message of light; Christ awakens you from your intoxicated slumber and resurrects you out of the death trap of enslaved thought patterns.

1:1 Paul, employed by the delightful resolve of God and commissioned to represent Jesus Christ to the saints in Ephesus and also to every believer in Christ Jesus.

1:2 I greet you with the grace and peace that proceed from God the Father and the Lord Jesus Christ. *(Paul's regular greeting - [1]Grace and [2]peace! The word, χάρις [1]charis, the divine influence upon the heart; that which affords joy, pleasure, delight, sweetness, charm, loveliness.*

Then, the word [2]eirēnē, means peace, from eirō, to join, to be set at one again; in carpentry it is the strongest joint, referred to as the dovetail joint. Peace is a place of unhindered enjoyment of friendship beyond guilt, suspicion, blame or inferiority. See 1 Corinthians 1:3)

1:3 Let's celebrate God. He lavished every blessing heaven has upon us in Christ.

1:4 He associated us in Christ before [1]the fall of the world. Jesus is God's mind made up about us. He always knew in his love that he would present us again [2]face-to-face before him in blameless innocence. *(The implications of the fall are completely canceled. Paul uses the word, [1]kataballō, meaning to fall away, to put in a lower place, instead of themelios, meaning foundation [see Ephesians 2:20]; thus, translated the fall of the world, instead of the foundation of the world. The entire Fall was a falling away in our minds from our true identity as image and likeness bearers of Elohim. Just like Eve, were we all deceived to believe a lie about ourselves, which is the fruit of the I-am-not-tree. We all, like sheep, have gone astray. [Isaiah 53:6]) We were found in Christ before we were lost in Adam. We are presented in blameless innocence before him. The word, [2]katenopion, suggests the closest possible proximity, face-to-face.*

Your in-Christness is not the result of a lucky draw. Calvinism lied to you. Neither is it the result of your choice to follow Jesus. Something doesn't become true by popular vote. Or by our beliefs. If it wasn't true to begin with, we're wasting our time trying to believe it true. Faith happens to you when you encounter the good announcement. Of God's doing are we IN CHRIST... (1 Corinthians 1:30) For evangelical theology to miss the meaning of mankind's inclusion IN CHRIST before they knew it or believed it, is to completely miss the point of the death, descent into hell, resurrection and ascension of Jesus. This would make Jesus irrelevant and reduce the salvation of the human race to their own fate managed by institutionalized religion, attaching mere sentimental value to a historical Jesus who died and rose again. By dying our death as fully God and fully man, once and for all (not for a select few.), death became the doorway, whereby Jesus would enter into our hell and deepest darkness and sense of lostness and loneliness as a result of the lies we believed about ourselves - to triumphantly lead us out as his trophies and relocate us face to face with the Father of the universe. Ephesians 4:7,8 and 9 See Mirror Bible. All this happened while we were still dead in our trespasses and sins. Ephesians 2:5,6 Co-quickened, co-raised, co-seated in his Executive authority [his right hand] Now ponder Colossians 3:1-3 and engage your thoughts with throne room realities.)

1:5 He is the architect of our design; his heart dream realized our [1]coming of age in Christ. *(Adoption here is not what it means in our Western society. It* *is a coming of age, like the typical Jewish Barmitsva. See Galatians 4:1-6, ... and to seal our sonship the spirit of his Son echoes Abba Father in our hearts. This is [1]huiothesia.)*

1:6 His grace-plan is to be celebrated: he [1]greatly endeared us and highly favored us in Christ. His love for his Son is his love for us. *(The Gospel is not about telling people how lost they are but reminding them of how loved they are. See Luke 1:28 only other use of the word, χαριτόω [1]charitoō.)*

1:7 Since we are *[fully represented]* **in him, his blood is the ransom that secures our redemption. His forgiving our sins measures the wealth of his grace.**

1:8 This grace shown towards us communicates a wisdom and discernment of our worth that completely surpasses any definition.

1:9 The secret is out. His cherished love dream now unfolds in front of our very eyes.

1:10 In the [1]economy of the fullness of time, everything culminates in Christ. All that is in heaven and all that is on earth is reconciled in him. Jesus is the [2]consummation of the ages. *(The word,[1]oikonomia, translates as administration. The word, ανακεφαλαιωσασθαι is the Aorist Infinitive of anakephalaiomai, which has two components, ana, upward and kephalē, head, pointing to a condition where no separation exists - the return to our Source. The Aorist Infinitive presents the action expressed by the verb as a completed unit with a beginning and end.*

All human history consummates in Christ; everything that exists in heaven or earth shall find its perfection and fulfillment in him.   — Phillips. All that is in heaven, all that is on earth, summed up in him. — Knox.)

1:11 This is how we fit into God's picture: Christ is the measure of our portion, we are in him, invented and defined in him. God's blueprint intention is on exhibition in us. Everything he accomplishes is inspired by the energy and intent of his affection. *(See Romans 8:29, He engineered us from the start to fit the mold of sonship and likeness according to the exact blueprint of his design. We see the original and intended shape of our lives preserved in his Son; he is the firstborn from the same womb that reveals our genesis. He confirms that we are the invention of God.)*

1:12 It was our initial privilege *(as Jews)* **to cherish the Messianic hope; our lives in Christ were destined to prophetically promote the celebration of his [1]glorious plan with mankind** *([1]doxa, intention, opinion.)*

1:13 Now you *[Gentiles]* **also have discovered yourselves to be equally included in him having witnessed [1]the unveiled [2]logic of God. What exciting news. Your salvation is publicly announced. Consistent with the promise of God, the Holy Spirit gives guarantee to the fact of your faith, like the stamp of a signet ring that certifies a document. You are in him.** *([1]The Word, logic, from logos, of truth. The word, [2]alethea, comes from a + lanthanō, meaning not hidden.)*

1:14 The Holy Spirit now [1]tangibly intertwines us to the inheritance that was ransomed and preserved for us. God's glorious plan for mankind is the theme of our celebration. *(The word, ἀῤῥαβών, arrhabōn, [1]guarantee, or earnest comes from the Hebrew word, ערבון arabon, meaning to braid, as two parties intertwine in an inseparable union. Holy Spirit completes the full reality of our redemption. See 2 Corinthians 5:5 where the same word is used.)*

1:15 I am sure you can appreciate how the news of your faith and love greatly inspires me.

1:16 I am so happy for you; my thoughts and prayers are full of you.

1:17 I desire that you will draw directly [1]from the Source; the God whom our Lord Jesus Christ exhibits as the Father of glory. Who [2]kindles within you the Spirit of wisdom and of revelation in the unveiling of [3]their Master Plan. I long for you to know by revelation, [4]what God has known about you all along.

*([1] **The God** of our **Lord Jesus Christ** is ὁ Θεὸς [Nominative] τοῦ Κυρίου ἡμῶν Ἰησοῦ Χριστοῦ [Genitive] , ὁ πατὴρ [Nominative] τῆς δόξης, [Genitive] **ho [1]Pater tēs doxēs, the Father of glory**. I believe the use of the Genitive case here is both **Relational** as well as **Epexegetic** - defining, explaining, clarifying. Thus, on exhibit in! See **Isaiah 9:6** ...unto us a child is born...**the Everlasting Father!**... **John 14:7 -9** To see me is to see the Father. See also **Hebrews 1:1-3***

> *See **2 Corinthians 4:6** The light source is founded in the same God who said, Light, be, and light shone out of darkness. He lit the lamp in our understanding so that we may clearly recognize the features of their likeness in the face of Jesus Christ reflected within us. [Elohim as in Genesis 1:26 Let US make man in OUR image and according to OUR likeness...]*

> *Also, **2 Corinthians 3:16** The moment anyone returns to the Lord [from the blindfold of the law], the veil is gone. **3:17 The Lord and the Spirit are one**; his Lordship sanctions our freedom. A freedom from rules chiseled in stone to the voice of our redeemed design echoing in our hearts. **3:18** Now, we all, with new understanding, see ourselves in him [the Incarnate One] as in a mirror. The days of window-shopping are over. In him every face is unveiled. In gazing with wonder at the blueprint of God displayed in human form, we suddenly realize that we are looking into a mirror, where every feature of their image, articulated in Christ, is reflected within us. The Spirit of the Lord engineers this radical transformation; we are led from an inferior mind-set to the revealed endorsement of our authentic identity. From the fading glory of our own making, to the discovering of the most amazing reality that we are their glory!*

> *We've got our masks off and God's brilliance is bouncing off our faces. We're glowing from knowing. 2 Corinthians. 3:18 [Rob Lacey]*

*[2] The word, [2]**didomi**, to endue as a gift [I translated, kindles within you], is here in the Aorist Subjunctive form, δωη **doē**, which expresses a wish with emphatic assertion; which indicates a definite outcome that happens as a result of another stated action. [As stated in verses 13 &14.]*

*[3] Paul employs the words, πνεῦμα σοφίας [3]**pneuma sophias**, Spirit of wisdom, again, endorsing the Trinity in Holy Spirit along with the Father and the Lord Jesus Christ - thus, **Their** Master plan - Father , Son and Spirit. **Colossians 2:9,10**.*

[4] In the words, ⁴en epignosei auto, Paul suggests that we might find our source in God's knowledge - in what it is that 'they' know. See 1 Corinthians 13:12 - to know even as we have always been known.)

1:18 Now, with the eyes of ¹your inner-mind ²illuminated and flooded with light, you may encounter an ³endless unfolding in knowing, in order to fully grasp the fact that you are ⁴the pleasure of God's delight; you are their dream come true; ⁵defined and mirrored in the incarnate Christ. What God possesses ⁶in your redeemed innocence is ⁷their treasure and the glorious trophy of their inheritance. You are God's portion, the sum total of their assets and the measure of their wealth.

*([1] The word, διάνοια **dianoia** suggests the deepest level of the mind. One's innermost thoughts and imagination. Ephesians 4:23. See its use in 1 John 5:20.*

*[2] The the Perfect Passive Participle, πεφωτισμενους **pephotismenous** of, φωτίζω ²**phōtizō**; flooded with light; thus, **having been illuminated** [as a result of the enduement of the Spirit of wisdom, verse 17. The Perfect tense always suggests an action which is completed in the past, but the effects of which are regarded as continuing into the present.*

*[3] εἰς τὸ εἰδέναι - the verb, ειδεναι **eidenai**, is the Perfect Active Infinitive of ³**eidō**, to see/know; thus suggesting an endless unfolding in knowing. The infinitive is used to complete the thought of a finite verb.*

*[4] The word ἐλπίς ⁴**elpis**, to anticipate; to dream, with pleasure and persuasion [pistis].*

*[5] Then, ⁵**klesis** from **kaleō**, to identify by name; to surname. See Ephesians 3:15. Also Isaiah 43:1 I have called you by name—you are mine.*

*[6] I have translated the words, **in the saints** ἐν τοῖς ἁγίοις, ⁶in your redeemed innocence. See Hebrews 1:3, he announces our redeemed innocence; having accomplished purification for sins, he sat down, enthroned in the boundless measure of his majesty.*

*[7] ὁ πλοῦτος **the wealth** τῆς δόξης τῆς κληρονομίας αὐτοῦ of ⁷**his glorious inheritance** - Matthew 13:44 & 2 Corinthians 4:7. For the LORD'S portion is his people, Jacob his allotted heritage. Deuteronomy 32:9)*

1:19 I pray that you will be ¹overwhelmed with the unequalled greatness and magnitude of his power, ²which he has wrought in us, in Christ; according to the working of his great might! This is the ³conclusion and dynamic of ⁴faith.

*[1] Paul loves his superlatives, as in this next phrase, ὑπερβάλλον μέγεθος **huperballon megethos** the surpassing, unequalled greatness of his power.*

*[2] The word, ενεργειαν pointing to ενηργηκεν ²**energeken**, which he has wrought... [see v 20] is the Perfect tense of **energeo**, to energize; to work dynamically. The Perfect tense denotes an action which is completed in the past, but the effects of which are regarded as continuing into the present.*

*[3] The Preposition ³**eis**, speaks of a point reached in conclusion.*

*[4] The word πιστευοντας ⁴**pisteuontas** is the Present Participle in the Accusative case of **pisteuō** [to continue to be certain/persuaded] which describes an action thought*

*of as simultaneous with the action of the main verb, **energeken** [v20]. **Paul is desiring to establish a basis for our faith that exceeds our attempts to believe**.)*

1:20 Do you want to measure the mind and muscle of God? Consider the [1]force which he unleashed in Jesus Christ when he raised him from the dead and forever seated him enthroned as his executive authority in the realm of the heavens. Jesus is God's right hand of power. He was raised up from the deepest dungeons of human despair to the highest region of heavenly bliss.

([1] Even in modern times, we still speak of horse power and candle power, which are common parallels of past centuries, whereby engine power or spotlights compare.

*The verb ενηργηκεν is the The Perfect Indicative of ἐνεργέω **energeō** energy/ force - The Perfect tense realizes the completeness of the act in the past, but the effects of which are regarded as continuing into the present without any compromise.*

See Ephesians 2:5,6 & 4:8,9.)

1:21 Infinitely above all the combined forces of rule, authority, dominion or governments; he is ranked superior to any name that could ever be given to anyone of this age or any age still to come in the eternal future.

1:22 I want you to see this: he subjected all these powers under his feet. He towers head and shoulders above everything. He is the head;

1:23 the [1]Ekklesia is his body. The completeness of his being that fills all in all resides in us. God cannot make himself more visible or exhibit himself more accurately. *(The word, [1]**Ekklesia**, comes from **ek**, a Preposition always denoting origin, and **klesia** from **kaleō**, to identify by name, to surname; thus the ekklesia-church is his redeemed image and likeness in human form.)*

2:1 Picture where God found us. We were in a death trap of an inferior lifestyle, constantly living below the [1]blueprint measure of our lives. *(The word sin, is the word [1]hamartia, from ha, negative or without and meros, portion or form, thus to be without your allotted portion or without form, pointing to a disoriented, distorted, bankrupt identity; the word meros, is the stem of morphē, as in 2 Corinthians 3:18 the word metamorphē, with form, which is the opposite of hamartia - without form. Sin is to live out of context with the blueprint of one's design; to behave out of tune with God's original harmony. See Deuteronomy. 32:18, You have forgotten the Rock that begot you and have gotten out of step with the God who danced with you. Hebrew, חול khul, also means to dance, as in Judges 21:21.)*

2:2 We were all part of a common pattern, swept along under a powerful invisible influence, a spirit-energy that adopted us as sons to its dictates through [1]unbelief. *(The words, ἐν τοῖς υἱοῖς τῆς ἀπειθείας· children of unbelief - ἀπειθείας [1]apetheias, unbelief, from the negative particle, a, and πείθω peithō, to believe, - have often been wrongly translated as children of disobedience.)*

2:3 Throughout that time everyone of us were warped and corrupted in our conduct; snared in a jumble of forbidden lusts, driven by the desires of the senses, completely engaged in an expression of a life ruled by mind games; it was as if a twisted passion parented a global breed of people.

2:4 None of this could distract from the extravagant love of God; he continued to love us with the exact same intensity.

2:5 This is how grace rescued us: while we were yet in that state of deadness and indifference in our [1]deviations, we were [2]co-quickened together with Christ. We had nothing to do with it. Grace [3]freed us, once and for all from the lies that we believed about ourselves under the performance-driven system, and now [4]defines our authentic identity. *(The word often translated, trespasses, παράπτωμα [1]paraptōma, deviation; from para close proximity and piptō, to descend from a higher place to a lower; to stop flying, petomai, to fly. Losing altitude speaks of mankind's fallen mindset. Colossians 3:1-3. The verb συνεζωοποιησεν [2]sunetzōopoiēsen [co-quickened] is the Aorist Active Indicative, describing an action that was completed in the past. The sentence, χάριτί [2]ἐστε [3]σεσωσμένοι - literally translates, By grace you are - having been saved. The verb, [4]este is the Present Active Indicative of eimi, I am - indicating the continuous state of your being which celebrates an [3]unstoppable freedom that happened in your favor. The verb [3]sesōsmenoi, having been rescued; is the Perfect Passive Participle, describing a state that exists, as a result of something that happened previously. The basic thought of the Perfect tense is that the progress of an action has been completed and the results of the action are continuing on, in full effect. In other words, the progress of the action has reached its culmination and the finished results are now in existence. We had no contribution to our salvation. God's Masterplan unfolded in the mystery of the gospel declaring our joint inclusion in Christ's death and resurrection. This is the mystery of grace, God reveals us in Christ. Now we may know, even as we have always been known. 1 Corinthians 13:12. Of God's doing are we in Christ. 1 Corinthians 1:30. God saw us in Christ, in his death and resurrection before we saw ourselves there. He declared mankind's co-resurrection with Christ 800 BC. This is* *the only scripture in the entire Old Testament that specifically mentions the third day resurrection and it includes us. After two days he will revive us, on the third day, he will raise us up. Hosea 6:2.)*

2:6 We are co-included in his resurrection. We are also co-elevated in his ascension to be equally present in the throne room of the heavenly realm where we are co-seated with him in his executive authority. We are fully represented in Christ Jesus. *(We have wasted so much time trying to get there, when there is where we are to begin with. Our joint position in Christ defines us; this can never again be a distant goal to reach through religious devotion or striving, but our immediate location. See Ephesians 4:8-10; Colossians 3:1-3.)*

2:7 *(In a single triumphant act of righteousness God saved us from the guttermost to the uttermost. Here we are now, revealed in Christ, in the highest possible elevation of bliss. Humanity's sad history could not distract from the extravagant love of God.)* **Imagine how God is now able for timeless perpetuity to exhibit the trophy of the wealth of his grace demonstrated in his kindness towards us in Christ Jesus. Grace exhibits excessive evidence of the success of the cross.**

2:8 Your salvation is not a reward for good behavior. It was a grace-thing from start to finish; you had no hand in it. Even the gift to believe simply reflects his faith. *(Again, as in Ephesians 2:5 Paul says, χάριτί ἐστε σεσωσμένοι chariti este sesōsmenoi, By grace you are, having been saved from the I am not-lie by the gift of faith; grace reveals who we are and the faith of God persuades us of it. We did not invent faith; it was God's faith to begin with. It is from faith to faith, says Paul in Romans 1:17. Jesus is both the source and conclusion of faith. Hebrews 12:2.)*

2:9 If this could be accomplished through any action of yours then there would be ground for boasting.

2:10 We are engineered by his design; he molded and manufactured us in Christ. We are his workmanship, his ¹poetry. We are ²fully fit to do good, equipped to give attractive evidence of his likeness in us in everything we do. *(God finds inspired expression of Christ in us. The Greek word for workmanship is ¹poeima. God has done everything possible to find spontaneous and effortless expression of his character in us in our everyday lifestyle. The word, ²proetoimatsō, translates a notion that God has prepared a highway for us to lead us out like kings, just like the Oriental custom, where people would go before a king to level the roads to make it possible for the king to journey with ease and comfort. Isaiah 40:3-5.)*

2:11 Remember where you came from; *[not only were you spiritually dead but]* **it wasn't long ago when you were still classified as non-Jewish, judging on the surface you had nothing that linked you to them. They sneered at you because you didn't share their distinguishing mark of circumcision, which was their claim to fame.**

2:12 During that time you were distanced from the Messianic hope; you had nothing in common with Israel. You felt foreign to the covenants of prophetic promise, living a life with nothing to look forward to in a world where God seemed absent.

2:13   But now, wow. Everything has changed; you have discovered yourselves to be located in Christ. What once seemed so distant is now so near; his blood reveals your redeemed innocence and authentic genesis.

2:14 It is in him that we are one and at peace with everyone; he dissolved every definition of division. *(What we know will put war and divorce out of business.)*

2:15 In his incarnation, he rendered the entire Jewish system of ceremonial laws and regulations useless as a measure to justify human life and conduct. In that he died mankind's death all grounds for tension and hostility were entirely removed. The peace he proclaims reveals one new human race, created and defined in Christ, instead of two groups of people separated by their ethnic identity and differences.

2:16 Both parties are fully represented and equally reconciled to God in one human body through the cross. He reinstated the former harmony; all opposing elements were thus utterly defeated.

2:17   On that basis he made his public appearance, proclaiming the Good News of peace to the entire human race; both those who felt left out in the cold *[as far as the promises and covenants were concerned]*, as well as to those who were near all along *[because of their Jewish identity]*.

2:18 Because of Christ both Jew and Gentile now enjoy equal access to the Father in one Spirit.

2:19   The conclusion is clear; you are no longer frowned upon as a foreigner; you are where you belong and part of an intimate family.

2:20 Your lives now give tangible definition to the spiritual structure, having been built into it by God upon the foundation of the Prophets and Apostles. Jesus Christ himself is the [1]chief cornerstone. *(The word, ακρογωνιαιον [1]akrogooniaioo occurs only in the LXX [first in Isaiah 28:16] and in the NT here, and in 1Peter 2:6.*

The cornerstone is the foundation stone, which is the setting stone. It is the first stone set in the construction of a masonry foundation. All other stones will be set in reference to this stone, thus determining the position of the entire structure. See 1 Kings 6:7 Not a sound of a hammer or chisel while the temple was built. Every stone was perfectly cut in the quarry [the cross], to exactly mirror the pattern of the chief cornerstone. Also Isaiah 51:1. And, Romans 9:30-33, Isaiah 8:14, Isaiah 28:16. It is the primary foundation-stone at the angle of the structure by which the architect fixes a standard for the bearings of the walls and cross-walls throughout. [W. W. Lloyd])

2:21   In him everyone of us are like [1]living Lego blocks fitted together of the same fabric *[[1]conversation]*, giving ever [2]increasing articulation to a global mobile [3]sanctuary intertwined in the Lord. *(The word, [1]sunarmologeō, from sun, meaning union, and harmos meaning harmony, then, logeō meaning conversation. The word, [2]auxanō, means expanding with growth. The word, [3]naos, inner sanctuary; is translated as the most sacred dwelling space.)*

2:22 In him you are co-constructed together as God's permanent spiritual residence. You are God's address.

3:1 My ministry is not measured by the size of my prison cell. I am confined by his grace; Christ Jesus is the prison keeper. You are why I am here. *(Grace measures my ministry; this prison cell cannot contain or hide my message from you.)*

3:2 It is common knowledge that I have been entrusted with a message that reveals how included you Gentiles are in the grace gift of God.

3:3 You must have heard how this mystery was revealed to me, in a dramatic disclosure that broke the silence of a long kept secret. I have previously written briefly about this.

3:4 In [1]pondering these words you will [2]perceive my [3]insight into the mystery of Christ. *(The word, [1]anaginōskō, suggests an upward knowledge; to know again, to recognize, to read with recognition. You will comprehend, νοιέω [2]noeō, to perceive; thoughtful understanding. [Also the word connected with the preposition meta [with] in μετανοέω metanoeō, to awaken in your understanding. It does NOT mean, to repent. See Luke 5:32]. Paul anticipates the impact of his own insight in his audience. The word, insight, [3]sunesis, from συνίημι suniemi - sun + eimi, together with my I am-ness, to resonate; which means a flowing together as of two streams - a seamless merging; a fusion of thought; a joint-seeing; to sync together in order to form a mental picture. It suggests the grasp and comprehension that happens from comparing and combining things. A word only Paul uses; also his colleague Dr Luke , in Luke 2:47, as well as another disciple of Paul, Mark who uses it in Mark 12:33, To love him with all your heart, with all your understanding, with all your strength, and to love your neighbor as you love yourself; this is more important than all the burnt offerings and sacrifices.)*

3:5 In no previous generation has there been a more comprehensive and detailed knowledge *[of the full consequence of grace]* as it has now been uncovered in the Spirit to his ambassadors who brought the prophetic promise into full view. Mankind *[the sons of men]* may now realize that the prophetic word is fulfilled in them. Everything the Prophets saw is now declared. Both the Prophets *[who saw this in advance]* and the Apostles *[who now proclaim this]* are sanctioned in Christ.

3:6 The essence of what I see reveals the fact that the multitude of humanity are joint participants in the same inheritance. We are all part of one and the same body in Christ. The Good news is that God's promise is equally relevant and applicable to all.

3:7 This Gospel defines my ministry; I am supercharged by the gift of his grace.

3:8 I am the lowest ranked saint by far and qualified purely by his grace to declare this unexplored treasure of Christ in the nations. *(My claim to fame emphasizes the fact that grace is a gift and certainly not a reward for good behavior.)*

3:9 The mandate of my message is to make all men see. The unveiling of this eternal secret is to bring into public view an association that has always been hidden in God; Jesus Christ is the blueprint of creation. *(Ephesians 1:4.)*

3:10 Every invisible authority and government in the arena of the heavenlies were confronted with the display of God's genius. The ekklesia disperses the varied magnitude of God like a prism, in human form. *(See Matthew 16:18, Upon this rock, I will build my ekklesia [authentic identity] and the gates of Hadēs [from ha, negative and eidō, to see; the blindfold] will not prevail. Also, Revelation 12: 8 and Revelation 17:14, These join forces in that hour to wage war against the Lamb, but the Lamb defeats them since he is the Lord of lords and the King of kings. And sharing with him in his victory are his kindred. They recognize their origin in this conversation and are now of the same persuasion. The Lamb led them into freedom from their lost identity, and their doubts. Also, 1 Corinthians 15:24 and Colossians 2:14,15.)*

3:11 This is [1]mirrored in Jesus Christ our Master, who is the [2]face-bread of the ages. He is the [3]eloquent exhibit of God's prophetic thought. *(The Preposition, [1]kata gives intensity as well as the idea of before, as in a mirror. Predetermined, prophetic thought; from the prophetic significance of the face-bread in the temple, [2]prothesis which is the Greek word for the show bread. The Hebrew word is לחם הפנים lechem haPānīm,, face bread, or bread of the presence. The word, εποιησεν [3]epoiēsen from poieō, to fashion; to poetically articulate.)*

3:12 His faith in us gives our lives integrity. We echo and articulate the [1]original conversation publicly. He is our platform to a global audience. *(The word [1]parrhesia, from para, a Preposition indicating close proximity, a thing proceeding from a sphere of influence, with a suggestion of union of place of residence, to have sprung from its author and giver, originating from, denoting the point from which an action originates, intimate connection; and rhesia, conversation. In him we express ourselves freely and openly.)*

3:13 You have no reason to feel embarrassed or responsible because of what I am suffering; rather feel honored.

3:14 Overwhelmed by what grace communicates, I bow my knees in awe before the Father.

3:15 Every family in heaven and on earth originates in him; his is mankind's family name and he remains the authentic identity of every nation.

3:16 I desire for you to realize what the Father has always envisaged for you, so that you may know the magnitude of his [1]intent and be dynamically reinforced in your inner being by the Spirit of God. *(The word, [1]doxa, opinion or intent.)*

3:17 This will ignite your faith to fully grasp the reality of the indwelling Christ. You are rooted and founded in love. Love is your invisible inner source, just like the root system of a tree and the foundation of a building. *(The dimensions of your inner person exceed any other capacity that could possibly define you.)*

3:18 Love is your reservoir of super human [1]strength which [2]causes you to see everyone equally sanctified in the context of the limitless extent

of love's breadth and length and the extremities of its dimensions in depth and height. *(The word, [1]exischuō means to be entirely competent, to be empowered to [2]comprehend. The word [2]katalambanō, kata, strengthened form; with lambanō, to grasp, thus to entirely grasp, means to come to terms with, to make one's own. Romans 12:13 Purpose with resolve to treat strangers as saints; pursue and embrace them with fondness as friends on equal terms of fellowship. Romans 12:16 Esteem everyone with the same respect; no one is more important than the other. Associate yourself rather with the lowly than with the lofty. Do not distance yourself from others in your own mind. [Take a real interest in ordinary people. — JB Phillips]*
If we go blurry eyed at the dimensions of outer space, how could we possibly underestimate the height, length, breadth and depth of the love of Christ, which surpasses knowledge. In the dimensions of its breadth and length, we see its geographic, horizontal extent; the complete inclusion of the human race. 2 Corinthians 5:14,16. The depth of his love reveals how his love rescued us from the deepest pits of hellish despair and led us as trophies in his triumphant procession on high. Ephesians. 1:20,21. Ephesians 2:5,6, Ephesians 4:8-10, Colossians 3:1-4.)

3:19 I desire for you to become intimately acquainted with the love of Christ on the deepest possible level; far beyond the reach of a mere academic, intellectual grasp. Within the scope of this equation God finds the ultimate expression of their image and likeness in you. *(So that you may be filled with all the fullness of God. Awaken to the consciousness of their closeness. Separation is an illusion. Oneness was God's idea all along. Father, Son and Spirit desire to express themselves through your touch, your voice, your presence; they are so happy to dwell in you. There is no place in the universe where God would rather be.)*

3:20 We celebrate Elohim who supercharges us powerfully from within. Our biggest request or most amazing dream cannot match the extravagant proportion of their thoughts towards us. *(Now to him that is able to do exceeding abundantly above all that we ask or think, according to the power that works in us...KJV*

Never doubt God's mighty power to work in you and accomplish all this. He will achieve infinitely more than your greatest request, your most unbelievable dream, and exceed your wildest imagination. He will outdo them all, for his miraculous power constantly energizes you. The Passion Translation.)

3:21 God is both the author and conclusion of the glory on display in the [1]Ekklesia, mirrored in Christ Jesus. The encore continues throughout every generation, not only in this age but also in the countless ages to come. Amen. *(The word, [1]Ekklesia, often translated church, comes from ek, a Preposition always denoting origin, and klesia from kaleō, to identify by name, to surname; the ekklesia is the expression of God's image and likeness redeemed in human life.)*

4:1 The fact that I am in prison does not in the least diminish my awareness of my in-Christ-ness. I am imprisoned in Christ. My complete existence is defined and confined in him. Let the detail of your day-to-day life ¹flow from the consciousness of your true ²identity and ³worth, as it is mirrored in him.

(See chapter 3:1 Paul writing from prison, but seeing himself co-seated together with Christ in heavenly places. Ephesians 2:6. No distraction or contradiction can reduce his life to any other reality. The sentence, Walking worthy of your calling, I have replaced with, Let the detail of your day-to-day life flow from the consciousness of your true identity and worth as defined in him. The word ¹parakaleō, inspired from within, to live the life of your design. Your calling or vocation, from ²kaleō, to surname, to identify by name. To ³walk worthy, axios, meaning having the weight of another thing of like value, worth as much.)

4:2 Meekness and tenderness are the fabric of your make-up; this enables you to show compassion even in seemingly impossible situations, eagerly bearing with one another in an environment where love rules.

4:3 Being alert to treasure our oneness in spirit; encapsulated in peace. *(The word sundesmos from sun, a primary Preposition denoting union and deō to bind in agreement like in a marriage. The word ¹eirēnē, means peace, from eirō, to join, to be set at one again; in carpentry it is referred to as the dovetail joint, which is the strongest of joints. Peace is a place of unhindered enjoyment of friendship.)*

4:4 There is only one body and one Spirit. We are inseparably one, in the same hope; there is no plan B. We bear the same ¹surname. *(Called, ¹kaleō, to identify by name, to surname. See Ephesians 3:15.)*

4:5 There is only one legitimate Lordship; one faith and one ¹baptism; we are all immersed in the same oneness. *(There is only one faith. Not what we believe about God but what God believes about us. Our faith does not invent God; God's faith defines us. Jesus is what God believes. See my commentary on John 1:33; John's baptism announces the incarnation; yet it communicates a mere prophetic picture of what Jesus' spirit baptism will fully interpret of mankind's co-inclusion and joint immersion into his death, resurrection and ascension. In the incarnation we have the prophetic word on exhibit, intercepting human history by assuming human form; thus we see divinity immersed into our humanity and declaring that there would be no stopping him from entering into our hell and deepest darkness. In dying our death, God would bring closure to every destructive mindset and futile fruit we inherited from Adam's fall. Just as he was raised out of the water in his baptism, we would be co-elevated together with him in his resurrection into newness of life. Hosea 6:2; Ephesians 2:5,6. The word ¹baptizō from baptō, to immerse, to overwhelm.)*

4:6 There is only one God. He remains the ultimate Father of the universe. We are because he is. He continues to hover over all; he infuses all, and indwells everyone. *(By three Prepositions, [epi, continuous influence upon; dia, permeates through, and en, in], Paul has endeavoured to express the universal sweep and power of God in everyone's lives; ὁ ἐπὶ πάντων, καὶ διὰ πάντων, καὶ ἐν πᾶσιν. [Robertson] The Textus Receptus has unfortunately added the word, ὑμῖν humin, at the end of the sentence in order to make this statement only relevant to the believers. See Bruce Metzger's Textual Commentary: The TR [Textus Receptus] and few miniscules are explanatory glosses, introduced to establish a personal reference of pasin to the Christians [ἐν πᾶσιν ὑμῖν en pasin humin - in all of you believers]; the older texts clearly read, en pasin IN ALL].*

Paul states to the pagan, philosophers in Acts 17:24-28 that, the Creator of the universe is not far from each one of us; in him we live and move and have our being. We are indeed his offspring. The father of lies is not the father of the human race. Immanuel is not more present in a Christian than what he is in a pagan! Psalm 24:1; Matthew 13:44 The multitudes don't have a clue! Be their clue! God's gift to the world is wrapped up in you! Nations shall come to your light and their kings to the brightness of your rising!)

4:7 The ¹gift of Christ measures the extravagant dimensions of grace. Every single individual is equally included and advantaged in this bountiful gift!

(Gift language puts reward language out of business! Grace was given to each one, according to the measure of the gift of Christ! Our universal, individual value is defined by his gift and not by anything we've done or failed to do.)

4:8 ¹Scripture confirms that *[in his death]*, **he arrested every possible threat that held mankind hostage** *[He took captivity captive]*. **And in his ²resurrection, he led humanity ³as prisoners of war trophies in his triumphant procession on high. Consider the genius of God how, in the incarnate Christ, he ⁴repossessed and redeemed what belonged to us by design, ⁵in a man.** *[Mankind's co-in-Christness is the crux of the Gospel!]*

(In this verse Paul continues to engage us with the extravagant extent and dimensions of the measure of the gift of Christ. Remember that he is writing from prison [3:1 & 4:1] He's not asking for prayers to get him out of jail. He is imprisoned in Christ - my complete existence is defined and confined in him. He was once a prisoner of the law of performance, held hostage in his own body, crying in desperation, Is there anyone who can deliver a person from this death trap? [Romans 7] Thus, as prisoner of Christ, he is reminded of, and obviously intrigued by, the entire context of **Psalm 67** *which celebrates God rescuing the prisoners from their captivity, even the wayward and stubborn, who already died and are stuck in their graves [mindsets]. See* **Psalm 67:6 & 7** *He is the father of the orphans, and protector of the widows. God settles the lonely in a home; leading forth prisoners mightily, also the stubborn, even them that dwell in tombs. [See* **Psalm 139:8**] *Paul sees Jesus dying our death and entering into our darkness and hell, on a rescue mission. 2 Corinthians 5:14-21.*

[1] Thus, διò **dio***, pointing to the gift of Christ as the theme and context of Scripture; Paul then uses the word λέγει* **legei** *which is the Present Indicative of* **legō** *- the prophetic word still speaks right now!*

The gift of Christ mentioned in verse 7, is now expanded in the resurrection conversation of David, who prophesied 1000 BC. Here Paul quotes **Psalm 67:19** *[from the LXX Septuagint - the Greek OT which is Psalm 68 in the Masoretic Hebrew text]...* **²anebes eis hupsos, ³ēchmaloteusas aichmalōsian, ⁴elabes domata ⁵en anthrōpō** *[καὶ γὰρ ἀπειθοῦντες τοῦ κατασκηνῶσαι. κύριος ὁ θεὸς εὐλογητός,* **⁶even the unbeliever is encamped in the Lord, the magnificent God!** *This last sentence points back to what Paul said in 4:6, There is only one God. He remains the ultimate Father of the universe. We are because he is. He continues to hover over all; he infuses all, and indwells everyone. Truth does not become true through man's belief, if it wasn't true to begin with!*

[2] Then follows resurrection language... ἀναβὰς εἰς ὕψος **²anabas eis** *[eis, points to a final conclusion]* **hupsō - anabainō** *to arise; to ascend; and* **hupsos***, elevation, You ascended on high... [Paul understands that in the incarnate Christ, humanity is encapsulated in Christ; we were co-quickened and co-raised together with Christ and co-elevated in him. Ephesians 2:5,6.]*

See **Psalm 139:7,8,12**, *Where shall I go from your Spirit? Or where shall I flee from your presence? If I ascend to heaven, you are there. If I make my bed in Hadēs, your presence already fills it. The night is bright as the day, for darkness is as light with you. When I awake, I am still with you! [There is no escape! Every eye shall see, every knee bow in worship and every tongue sing and celebrate mankind's redeemed innocence! Isaiah 40:5 & Philippians 2:8-11; Revelation 5:13]*

[3] Then, the verb, ³*ēchmalōteusas, the Aorist of* **aichmalōteuō - he arrested captive mankind at spearpoint** *as prisoners of war trophies, and led them out triumphantly on high! From* **aichmē**, *spear and* **halōsis**, *to capture. Note, the same word is now used as a noun in the Accusative Case,* **aichmalōsian** *[the ones held hostage]. Captive mankind is arrested at spearpoint! This points to the prophetic word, which is sharper than a two-edged sword, which has taken an already imprisoned [in their fallen mindset] mankind, 'captive' in Christ! Hebrews 4:12. This all happened in the death, descent into hell and the triumphant resurrection of the incarnate Word; the man Jesus Christ. Leading out captive mankind into a new 'captivity' that celebrates their freedom! They are captivated in the love of Christ.*

[4] The word **elabes** *from* **lambanō,** *means to take what is one's own;* ⁴*elabes - He repossessed what belonged to mankind all along! And* ⁴***repossessed mankind's gifts***.

[5] Then the words [in the LXX], ἔδωκε δόματα ἐν ἀνθρώπῳ **edōke** *[from* **didomi**, *to return something to someone that which already belongs to them];* **domata** *- He gave gifts;* **en anthrōpō in a man.** *[Singular in the LXX] The word for the* ⁵*human species, male or female is* **anthrōpō**, *from* **ana**, *upward, and* **tropos**, *manner of life; character; in like manner. Here, in the NT, τοῖς ἀνθρώποις* **tois anthrōpois** *[plural], which is the Dative Case - pointing to - IN humanity.*

[In the Masoretic Hebrew text it is in Psalm 68:18,19, לקחת מתנות באדם **lakachat mattanoth ba adam** - You have taken gifts in Adam. The gifts which Jesus Christ distributes to us, he has received in us, in and by virtue of his incarnation. *Adam Clarke.]*

[6] **Psalm 67:19** LXX continues: *καὶ γὰρ ἀπειθοῦντες τοῦ κατασκηνῶσαι -* **kai gar apeithountes tou kataskenōsai.** *In the incarnation he fully includes and represents even the unbelievers,* **apeithountes** *- the ones resisting persuasion, the indifferent, the backsliding, the headstrong, the wayward, the rebellious. Literally, In the incarnation he has gifted man, even those who do not realize that they too, are indwelt! The word,* **kataskēnosai** *- to encamp within - again this word emphasizes the significance of the incarnation -* **kata**, *down and* **skēnosai**, *from* **skēnos** *- skin. While their ignorance of Christ within, veils him from them, Elohim is never absent. See* **2 Corinthians 13:5.**

The eternal thoughts of God, the conversation that was before time was, is clothed in skin. John 1:1-3,14.

See **Revelation 13:10**, *Being taken captive by the spear and killed by the sword [John 18:3] made death a doorway into the very domain in which mankind was held prisoner, [to be led out triumphantly in the resurrection as the Lamb's trophies.] After two days he will revive us. On the third day he will raise us up.* **Hosea 6:2** *We were born anew in his resurrection.* **1 Peter 1:3.** *Also* **Ephesians 2:5,6.** *This is how grace rescued us: while we were yet in that state of deadness and indifference in our deviations, we were co-quickened together with Christ.)*

4:9 The fact that he ascended confirms his victorious descent into the deepest pits of human despair. *(See John 3:13, No one has ascended into heaven* *but he who* [1]*descended from heaven, even the son of man. All mankind originates from above; we are* [1]***anouthen***, *from above [see James 1:17, 18].)*

4:10 He now occupies the ultimate rank of authority, from the lowest regions of our darkness, into which he reached in order to rescue us, to the highest authority in the heavens, having triumphantly executed his mission. He fills the entire universe with himself! *(Fallen mankind is fully restored to the authority of the authentic life of their design. Psalm 139:7 Where shall I go from Your Spirit? Or where shall I flee from Your faces? Plural* מפניך ***mippaneycha*** *Faces of Elohim. The plurality of persons in the Godhead is intended. Psalm 139:8 If I go up to Heaven, You.* שמים שם אתה ***Shemayim Shem/ Sham Atah***. *The word* שמים ***shemayim***, *the heavens [which is the plural of the next word],* **Shem**, *meaning, name or renown; the identical adverb* **Sham** *meaning, here, there. In Ancient Hebrew,* ᛗᚳᛁᚲ *breath.*

Then the word, אתה *begins with* **Aleph** *and* **Tav** את *AT which are the first and last letters in the Hebrew Alphabet; the Rabbis interpret as the first matter out of which all things were formed, [see Genesis 1:1]. The particle AT [pronounced,* **et**], *is untranslatable in English; but, says Rabbi Aben Ezra, it signifies the substance of the thing. Then follows the letter* ה ***hey***, *in Ancient Hebrew, it is* ⚴, *the man with raised hands pictures a sigh of wonder, behold, as when looking at a great sight; thus, meaning, breath or sigh, as one does when seeing something wonderful and pointing it out. The* ה *[hey] is also the number 5, which is the number for grace. The union of* **Alpha** *and* **Omega** *[which are the first and last letters in Greek], makes the verb* αω *aō, I breathe. And in Hebrew the union of the first and last letter in their alphabet,* את *[in modern Hebrew] are written,* **Aleph** *[bull's head] and* **Tav** *[the cross]* ✝ᛣ *in Ancient Hebrew.*

If I make my bed in Hadēs, your presence already fills it. LXX - πάρειμι ***pareimi*** *your immediate presence - I am. In the LXX, which is the Greek Septuagint [250 BC] it is Psalm 138:8 [139 in the Hebrew text] See my notes on 1 Thessalonians 2:19.)*

4:11 What God has in us, is gift-wrapped to the world: some are commissioned to pioneer, others are gifted prophetically, some as announcers of good news, some as shepherds with a real gift to care and nurture, and others have a gift to ignite instruction through revelation knowledge. *(Couriers, communicators, counsellors and coaches. — Rob Lacey.*

It is impossible to really appreciate what the 5-fold ministry is all about [verse 11], unless one sees the build up to it in the preceding 10 verses!)

4:12 Each expression of his gift is to fully equip and enable you for the work of the ministry so that you may mutually contribute in your specific function to give definition to the visible body of Christ.

4:13 The purpose of these ministry gifts is to present everyone on par and in oneness of faith; believing exactly what the Son of God believes and knowing accurately what he knows concerning us. Standing face-to-face in equal stature to the measure of the [1]**completeness of Christ.** *(To bring everyone into the realization of the fullness of the measure of Christ in them. The word,* **xristos**, *the Anointed one, from* χρίω **chriō**, *to smear or rub with oil, to anoint; to draw the hand over, to measure; from* χείρ **cheir**, *hand. [We still measure the height of horses by hand - ie. A seventeen hand horse.] The word,* [1]**pleroma**, *means a life filled to the brim with Christ, like a freight ship carrying its cargo. He measures the full stature of our beingness as image bearers! In HIM, the fullness of the Godhead tabernacles in a human body! AND you are complete in him! Colossians 2:9,10.)*

4:14 The most dangerous life you can live is an ignorant one. You're left like an infant on a ship out of control in the waves and winds of the storms of life. The fall of the dice dictates while the deceptive teachings of men and their distracting tricks entertain.

4:15 [1]Love gives truth its voice. The conversation that [2]truth inspires creates the atmosphere wherein growth is both spontaneous and inevitable. The whole person is addressed in Christ who is the head of the body; he is the conclusion of God's communication with mankind. *(Speaking the truth in love is not only the preferred attitude in our every conversation, but the only option; where truth gives integrity to love, and love gives attraction to truth.*

[1] The Greek word, to love, agapaō, has two components, agō, to lead as a shepherd leads his sheep, and paō, to rest. [Which is Psalm 23 in one word!] God's rest celebrates our perfection; agapē is to see the same value that God sees in every person. Perfection is not defined by our perception, but by what God saw when he said, It is finished! [Now we may know, even as we have always been known! 1 Corinthians 13:12.]

[2] The truth is not the detail of the problem, but the truth about you, as it is mirrored in Christ [Ephesians 4:21].)

4:16 [1]From him flows the original composition and detail of our design. Like words entwined in poetry, *[[1]like a conductor of music, [1]epichoregeō]* they connect layer upon layer to complete the harmony, following the rhythm of his thoughts like footprints. Meanwhile the body thrives and pulsates with the energy of love. Each individual expression finds its complete measure there. *(The ekklesia is not a dismembered, dysfunctional body, but a fully functional, coordinated lover of people. — Rob Lacey.)*

4:17 My most urgent appeal to you in the Lord is this: you have nothing in common with the folly of the empty-minded [1]masses; the days of conducting your lives and affairs in a meaningless way are over. *(The Gentiles, [1]ethnos, the masses of people who are walking in the vanity of their minds.)*

4:18 The life of their design seems foreign to them because their minds are darkened through a hardened heart ruled by ignorance. They are blinded by the illusion of the senses as their only reference, stubbornly wearing a blindfold in broad daylight. *(Hardness of heart is the result of a darkened understanding; a mind veiled through unbelief. See 2 Corinthians 4:4.)*

4:19 Having become conditioned to a life distanced from God; they are calloused in spirit, and are lust and greed driven; they have completely abandoned themselves to outrageous, shameless living. *(See Romans 1:19-23.)*

4:20 Of what total contrast is Christ.

4:21 [1]Truth is defined in Jesus. It is not possible to study him in any other context; he is the incarnation; hear him resonate within you. The truth about you has its ultimate reference in Jesus. *(Lit. [1]The truth, as it is in Jesus. See 1 John 2:7,8, Whatever is true of him, is equally true of you. He did not come to introduce a new compromised set of rules; he is not an example for us but of us.)*

4:22 For in the truth of your union in him *[in his death and resurrection]*, [1]you have stripped off that old identity like a filthy worn-out garment. Ignorance and lust *[v18]* corrupted you and cheated you into wearing it in the first place. *(The verb, αποθεσθαι [1]apothesthai, is the Aorist Middle Infinitive which presents the action expressed by the verb as a completed unit with a beginning and end. Just like an actor who wore a cloak for a specific role he had to interpret; the fake identity is no longer relevant. See Colossians 3:1-3,9. Colossians 3:9 That old life was a lie, foreign to our design. Those garments of disguise are now thoroughly stripped off us in our understanding of our union with Christ in his death and resurrection. We are no longer obliged to live under the identity and rule of the robes we wore before, neither are we cheating anyone through false pretensions. [The garments an actor would wear define his part in the play but do not define him.])*

4:23 Thus ¹you are habitually renewed in your innermost mind. This will cause you to be completely re-booted in the way you think about yourself. *(Ponder the truth about you, as it is displayed in Christ; begin with the fact of your co-seatedness. You can never be more co-raised and co-elevated than what you already are. [Ephesians 2:5,6] You can only grow in your awareness of your redeemed oneness. Notice that Paul does not say, Renew your minds. But,* **to be habitually renewed...** *He uses the* **Present Passive Infinitive** *αναvεουσθαι* **¹ananeosthai**, *from* **ana**, *upwards [by setting your mind on the things that are above where you are co-seated together with Christ] and* νεώτερος **neoteros**, *renovated; renewed. Greek Infinitives could have either a Present or Aorist form. The contrast between the two forms has more to do with aspect than with time. The Present Infinitive is used to express progressive or imperfective aspect. It pictures the action expressed by the verb as being in progress. The Aorist Infinitive however, does not express progressive aspect. It presents the action expressed by the verb as a completed unit with a beginning and end.*

This transformation happens in the spirit of your mind, awakened by truth on a much deeper level than a mere intellectual or academic consent. We often thought that we had to get information to drop from the head to the heart; but it is the other way around. Jesus says in John 7:37, When you believe that I am what the Scriptures are all about, then you will discover that you are what I am all about, and rivers of living waters will gush out of your innermost being. The spirit of mankind was never contaminated; just like the watermark in a paper note. The lost coin never lost its original inscription and image [see also James 3:9]; it was the mind that was veiled by darkness; we were darkened in our understanding. Our thoughts were reduced to the soul realm reference, knowing ourselves, and one another merely after the flesh. Isaiah 55:8-11 There is nothing wrong with our design or our redemption; we were thinking wrong. In order for our thoughts to be rescued from the dominion of darkness, Jesus as the incarnate image and likeness of God, has gone into our darkest hellish nightmare, and faced our cruelest judgment and fears, and died our death. This is the mystery that was hidden for ages and generations, for our glorification. We were co-crucified, to bring absolute closure to every reference we have had of ourselves as a result of Adam's fall. And while we were dead in our sins and trespasses, God co-quickened us and co-raised us, and co-seated us in Christ. Now, we all with unveiled faces may behold the glory of the Lord as in a mirror. And be radically transformed in our thinking in order to rediscover his image and likeness fully redeemed in us.)

4:24 ¹Remain fully ²immersed in this God-shaped new person from above. You are created in the image and likeness of God. This is what righteousness and true holiness are all about. *(The copulative Particle ¹kai, as in* καὶ ἐνδύσασθαι, *continues the thought expressed in the previous 3 sentences. Again, the verb,* ενδυσασθαι **endusasthai** *[as in verse 22], is the Aorist Middle Infinitive which presents the action expressed by the verb as a completed unit with a beginning and end.*

Galatians 2:20 So here I am dead and alive at the same time. I'm dead to the old me I was trying to be and alive to the real me which is Christ in me. Co-crucified, now co-alive. What a glorious entanglement. I was in him in his death; now I discover that he is infused in me, in my life. For the first time, I'm free to be me in my skin, immersed in his faith in our joint-sonship. He loves me and believes in me. He is God's gift to me.

*Also **Luke 9:24** Trying to keep the self of your own making intact, is a lost cause to begin with. Losing yourself in me, is realizing that I am the source of who you are by design. This is your saving grace. Also my notes on Luke 24:49 your Dress-code.)*

4:25 Faking it and lying to one another was part of the old life; now truth remains the constant inspiration in your every conversation. We are related to one another like different parts in the same body. *(Which means that cheating one another would be cheating yourself. Truth only finds context in Christ [v 21].)*

4:26 Even if you think you have a valid excuse, do not let anger dominate your day. By not dealing with it promptly *[in the light of your authentic likeness, redeemed in Christ]*, **the sun seems to set for you, and your day becomes one of lost opportunities, where darkness employs anger to snare you into sin.** *(Many interpretations of this verse have left one with the idea that, in order to get maximum mileage out of anger, one should get angry as early as possible in the day as long as you get over it by nightfall! Lol)*

4:27 Engaging the energy of anger in any prolonged time-slot, typically sets up the [1]stage for the [2]Diabolos, giving opportunity for a destructive and out of sync-mindset to take mean advantage of you and others. *(The word, τόπος [1]topos suggests a place specially marked off; a platform to operate from. The word, [2]diabolos, has two components, the Preposition **dia** through; by means of, and **ballō**, to cast down; to put in a lower place or order. Pointing to the root of deception and temptation, engaging a mindset, defined by the fall - I am not who God says I am.)*

4:28 If you were a thief before, you are one no more. Find an honest job where the fruit of your labor can be a blessing to others.

4:29 Instead of cheap talk, your mouth is now a fountain of grace, giving encouragement and inspiration to everyone within earshot.

4:30 The Holy Spirit is your signet ring from God to confirm that you are redeemed to live your life in the light of day; any conduct that belongs to the night grieves him.

4:31 Take up the strongest possible position against every form of distorted behavior in your own life. Do not allow yourself to be spiteful; outbursts of violent emotion and rage do not become you. You don't have to shout in order to make your point. People must feel safe in your conversation; therefore, slander and hurtful words *[blasphemy]* **are out.**

4:32 Be inspired by kindness and compassion; your forgiving one another when you might feel irritated and frustrated demonstrates the way God graciously treated us in Christ.

5:1 Mirror God; you are his offspring. *(2 Corinthians 3:18.)*

5:2 This is how: let the love of Christ be your life; remember how he abandoned himself to us. His love is contagious, not reluctant but extravagant. Sacrificial love pleases God like the sweet aroma of worship. *(Resembling the holy anointing oil and the pure fragrant incense of spices, the work of a perfumer, to be burnt on the golden altar of incense in the inner court of the tent of meeting. Exodus 37:25-29.)*

5:3 Love has nothing in common with lust, immoral acts, or greed. The absence of these motives even in the way you talk sets a standard of excellence.

5:4 Any [1]distorted language, sarcasm, or below the belt jokes are uncalled for; much rather let gratitude grace your conversation. *(The word, [1]morologia, means disfigured, exaggerated speech.)*

5:5 The Christ-life gives distinct definition to the kingdom of God. You cannot live a double-standard life. Abusing people through adultery, lust, and greed is like worshipping a distorted image of yourself, which is what idolatry is all about.

5:6 Avoid any association with those who employ hollow words to entice you; [1]unbelief only produces a breed of people that distorts the pattern of their design as image bearers of God; this certainly does not [2]please God. *(The phrase, [1]uious tes apeitheias, translates as unbelief produces a breed of people; not sons of disobedience as most translations read here. The word, [2]orge, means excitement of mind, from the word, **oregomai**, meaning to stretch oneself out in order to touch or to grasp something, to reach after or desire something.)*

5:7 Do not allow their unbelief to include you in their company.

5:8 You were there once, trapped in the same darkness, but now you are light; your life confirms that light rules.

5:9 The spiritual harvest of light is evident in all that is excellent, innocent, and of impeccable integrity.

5:10 This gives certain evidence to the life of God's delight.

5:11 Do not tolerate anything in your life that associates you with darkness; there is no profit in it for you. Let light dispel any residue of darkness in you.

5:12 By gossiping about shameful acts that people do in secret, you are giving those things undue mileage.

5:13 Darkness loses its grip upon that which light manifests. Light displaces darkness.

5:14 This is the message of light: Christ awakens you from your intoxicated slumber and resurrects you out of the death trap of enslaved thought patterns.

5:15 Take accurate stock of your life; wise conduct defeats foolishness.

5:16 Wisdom converts time into opportunity and frees your day from slog.

5:17 Make his master plan your meditation.

5:18 While wine offers no lasting escape from the evil of the day, spirit certainly does. Indulge in spirit intoxication.

5:19 Speak Psalms to one another; burst out in spontaneous celebration songs and spirit-inspired resonance. In your heart do not let the music stop; continue to touch the Lord with whispers of worship.

5:20 Because you are identified in the Name of Jesus Christ, you can afford to always overflow in gratitude to the Father, [1]in spite of everything that happens to you. You are not under circumstances but above circumstances because you are in him. *(The word, [1]huper, translates as, in spite of, over and above, beyond the reach of circumstances. We are not grateful for everything like in many other translations, but in spite of everything.)*

5:21 Inspired by the selfless consideration you witnessed in Christ, show perfect courtesy to one another. *(The way he abandoned himself to the will of God and to us [verse 2]. See Colossians 1:24, This is why no form of suffering can interfere with my joy. Every suffering on your behalf is just another opportunity to reinforce that which might still be lacking [in your understanding] of the affliction of Christ on behalf of his body which is the ekklesia. [The inconvenience that Paul might be suffering on behalf of the believers is not to add to the sufferings of Christ—as though the sufferings of Christ on our behalf were insufficient but it is to further emphasize and confirm the principle of unselfish love that constrains New Testament ministry.])*

5:22 *(Marriage is a portrait of this mutual yielding to one another.)* **Wives give yourselves fully to your husbands as you would to the Lord.** *(Remember verse 2: love is contagious, not reluctant but extravagant. Sacrificial love pleases God like the sweet aroma of worship.)*

5:23 In the same way that Christ gives salvation, security and completeness to the ekklesia, as the head does to the body, the husband is all of that to his wife.

5:24 The ekklesia enjoys the full advantage of the complete package of salvation, by yielding themselves fully to Christ; even so the wife enjoys every benefit her husband represents in her abandonment to him.

5:25 The husband loving his wife pictures the parallel of Christ loving the ekklesia completely, and his unreserved giving of himself to us. *(This is what marriage is all about; it celebrates love's initiative, whether coming from the husband or the wife. This awakens a different level of commitment beyond any sense of duty or guilt.)*

5:26 Christ is the voice of God's language, immersed in this conversation, his love words bathe us and remove from us every stain of sin.

5:27 This intimate language presents the ekklesia-church *[his restored image and likeness]* to himself, to his delightful approval without any distraction or reminder of a blemished past; no wrinkle or scar of sin's abuse remains; she stands before him in immaculate innocence. *(1 Kings 6:7.)*

5:28 *(A man could go through many disciplines in life to make himself look good financially or even go to great expense to win the applause of others; he could* *diligently workout in the gym and trim his body to perfection,)* **but the most valuable thing a man can do to himself is to love his wife.**

5:29 Consider how abnormal it would be for a man to abhor and detest his own body; the opposite is true. He would much rather pamper it and [1]fuss over it with tender care. *[It's all you've got. You can't trade it in for a new one so take good care of it. Watch what you feed it, how you exercise it, and gently nurse it when it is in pain.]* **Now get the message, you are the body of Christ; he does not merely tolerate you politely; you are his joy and delight. He wants to spoil you and take good care of you.** *(The word [1]thalpei is a late and rare word; used once in a marriage contract in a papyrus. In NT only here and 1Thessalonians 2:7. 2. It means to cherish with tender love and warm affection; - Latin foveo; to foster with tender care.)*

5:30 We are his flesh and bone body; bearing his image and likeness. We give tangible expression of him.

5:31 Marriage reflects this union: a man would separate himself from his own parents to be glued to his wife; thus two separate people are now merged into one new identity. Two individuals become one flesh. *(In the same way he elevated us from our natural birth as our only identity to an understanding of our origin in him. This he confirmed again in our new birth, his resurrection, and our subsequent restored joint position together with him in heavenly places. Thus, he brought about a new union of intimate oneness; God and mankind revealed again in one person.)*

5:32 The secret of a successful marriage is reflected in this inseparable union between Christ and the ekklesia, as God's redeemed image and likeness in mankind. *(This union ultimately defines both marriage and ekklesia-church.)*

5:33 In conclusion then, no one has any excuse to love his wife less than what he loves himself; at the same time every wife is now free and fully empowered to honor her husband in the same context and devotion as the ekklesia would respond to the love initiative of Christ. *(We love him because he first loved us. 1 John 4:19.)*

6:1 *(This mutual yielding to one another continues in every social relationship we engage in and extends the attractive display of the Christ-life, beginning at home, cradled in the warm embrace of loving parents;)* **the way children respond to their parents give evidence to their righteousness in the Lord.** *(In essence the term righteousness speaks of two parties esteeming likeness in one another.)*

6:2 The first commandment that includes an immediate and long term incentive is in reference to children honoring their father and mother.

6:3 Both quality and duration of life on earth is impacted by the way children relate to their parents. *(Length of life is meaningless outside of closeness in relationship.)*

6:4 Fathers, your role is not to exasperate your children *[by giving them burdens and tasks too heavy to bear].* **You are rather to awaken their minds in an environment conducive to draw on every virtue that is in them in the Lord.**

6:5 The next level of relationship equally implicated includes the heart attitude of a slave towards their owner; because of your devotion to Christ, you are now able to give your boss the same undivided, sincere respect and devotion. *(Remember we are talking practical ekklesia-life; the Christ-life celebrates love's initiative in transforming society.)*

6:6 This is not a matter of merely trying to put up a front in order to impress your boss; you are in essence slaves of Christ, addicted to the desire of God to find expression in you; now slave life becomes the Christ-life. *(The so-called low life now mirrors the highest life.)*

6:7 However menial the task, put your heart and mind into it as you would to the Lord; he is your real boss, no-one else.

6:8 It is a well known fact that it is impossible for good deeds to go unnoticed. It makes no difference whether someone is free or a slave; every single good deed equally enjoys the favorable attention of the Lord. *(We already enjoy Gods favorable attention before we have done anything to deserve it. Our good works are now an expression of that and not an attempt to win his approval.)*

6:9 If you're the boss, love's initiative applies to you on exactly the same terms; the way you treat your slaves with respect rather than threats, even when they do stupid things clears the air immediately. Take it from your heavenly Master; he does not judge people or circumstances on face value.

6:10 In conclusion and with reference to the theme and context of this writing, I encourage you to realize your strength in the Master; your union with him is your limitless resource. *(Remember my prayer for you at the outset of this letter to the Ephesians: 1:19 I pray that you will understand beyond all comparison the magnitude of his mighty power towards us who believe. Faith reveals how enormously advantaged we are in Christ. Ephesians 1:20 It is the same dynamic energy that he unleashed in Christ when he raised him from the dead and forever established him in the power of his own right hand in the realm of the heavens. Ephesians 1:21 Infinitely above all the combined forces of rule, authority, dominion, or governments; he is ranked superior to any name that could* *ever be given to anyone of this age or any age still to come in the eternal future. Ephesians 1:22-23, I want you to see this: he subjected all these powers under his feet. He towers head and shoulders above everything. He is the head; the ekklesia (his redeemed image and likeness in mankind) is his body. The completeness of his being that fills all in all resides in us. God cannot make himself more visible or exhibit himself more accurately.)*

6:11 Fully immerse yourself in the detail and significance of every individual part of the armor of God. *[Acquaint yourself with all that God's victory in Christ represents.]* **Just like every aspect in a soldier's armor significantly completes their battle uniform to best equip them to face every [1]method and strategy that an [2]enemy could possibly employ against them.** *(The word, [1]methodeia, means strategy; [2]diabolos, comes from dia, because of, and ballō, cast down; thus referring to the fall of mankind or the fallen mindset of mankind, often translated Devil, the accuser. [See 1 Corinthians 15:47] Human life was reduced to slavery and the soul-ruled earthly realm through Adam's fall but is now awakened to lordship in the heavenly realm of spiritual realities through the knowledge of our co-resurrection with Christ. [See Colossians 3:1-11] We theologically created the idea of a person being sinful by nature as if humans are flawed by design. In fact it is a distorted mindset that we inherited from Adam that Jesus had to free us from. Peter says that we were redeemed from the futile ways we inherited from our fathers. [1 Peter 1:18] Your indifferent mindset alienated you from God into a lifestyle of annoyances, hardships, and labors, sponsored by the law of sin and death that lodged in your bodies hosting a foreign influence, foreign to your design; just like a virus that would attach itself to a person. Colossians 1:21. There is nothing wrong with our design or salvation, we were thinking wrong. [See Isaiah 55:8-11, Ephesians 4:17, 18 and also Ephesians 2:1-11.])*

6:12 People are not the enemy, *[whether they be husbands, wives, children, or parents, slaves, or bosses. They might host hostile, law inspired thought patterns through their unbelief or ignorance but,]* **to target one another is to engage in the wrong combat. We represent the authority of the victory of Christ in the spiritual realm. We are positioned there** *[in Christ]*; **we [1]confront the mind games and [2]structures of darkness, religious thought patterns, governing and conditioning human behavior.**

([1] The word, [1]pros, face to face; towards.

[2] The word, [2]ponēros is often translated as evil; this word is described in Thayer's Lexicon as full of annoyances, hardships and labor, which is exactly what the DIY law-system of works produces.

1 Corinthians 15:24 The complete conclusion of his work of redemption is [1]repeatedly celebrated in every individual discovering that they too are part and parcel of the full harvest of his resurrection. This is the extent of his reign that he yielded to God the Father, having [2]brought to naught every definition of dominion, including all [3]principalities, all [4]authority and every [5]dynamic influence in society.

([1] The Conjunctive Particle, [1]otan, often translated as when is better translated as every time. See Colossians 3:3, Thus, Every time Christ is revealed we are being co-revealed in his glory. According to the Walter Bauer Lexicon, otan is often used for

an action that is repeated. Referring to the previous verse, all are individually made alive in the order of Christ. Mankind's co-resurrection with Christ is repeatedly celebrated in every individual throughout time - whenever this truth is discovered in human history. Colossians 3:1-3.

*[2] He brought to naught the law of works; καταργηση [2]**katargēsē**, is the Aorist Subjunctive of **katargeō**, which indicates a definite outcome that happens as a result of another stated action, [in Christ all are made alive]. The word **katargeō**, with **kata**, down, and **argos**, rendered useless; from **a**, as a negative particle and **ergon**, toil, labor; thus, inactive, that is, unemployed; useless; thus the entire system of performance, to improve what God has already perfected in Christ, is brought to naught.*

*[3] All principalities, [3]**archē**, or chief ranks, i.e. kings or governors; this includes any governing system whereby one is ranked above the other on the basis of their performance or preference.*

*[4] All authority, [4]**exousia**, comes from **ek**, denoting origin and **eimi**, I am; in this case, because of what I can do I am defined by what I can do better than you; therefore, I have authority over you.*

*[5] Every dynamic influence in society, [5]**dunamis**, means power, in this case, willpower. Every government structure in society will be brought under the dominion of grace where the Christ-life rules.*

See 1 Corinthians 2:7-8, We voice words of wisdom that were hidden in silence for timeless ages; a mystery unfolding God's Masterful plan whereby he would redeem his glory in man. Neither the politicians nor the theologians of the day had a clue about this mystery [of mankind's association in Christ]; if they did, they would never have crucified the Lord whose death redeemed our glory.

The kingdom of God is the authority of the Christ-life in ordinary, day to day life, where righteousness is based on who we are and not on who we are trying to impress. The law of works is duty and guilt driven, whereas the law of faith is love driven. Romans 3:27, Galatians 5:6. Also 2 Corinthians 10:12 When they measure themselves by one another, competing and comparing, they are without understanding.)

6:13 It is most important therefore to acquaint yourself with every aspect of God's armor. You are fully fit to powerfully defeat any onslaught or contradiction on any day of confrontation, triumphantly standing your ground. The days where the law of [1]hardships, annoyances and labor dictated your life are over. *(God's armor represents his reputation; his victory defines you. Again the word, [1]**ponēros**, is used, to be full of hardships, annoyances, and labor; traditionally translated evil. [See 1 Corinthians 15:48] The reduced state of the individual left its mark on mankind as being earthly; now the redeemed state of mankind confirms their origin in God and marks their new heavenly life. [1 Corinthians 15:49] Just as we were once defined by the flesh [our performance-based mindset & image] we are now defined by our spirit image [our Agapē-based mindset & likeness].*

6:14 Take your position: you have the truth *[of who you are in Christ]* **wrapped around your hips like a soldier's belt, holding the complete body armor together.** *[Know that your loins are protected from all manner of* *lust, gluttony and sexual sins.]* **Righteousness covers your heart like a bulletproof breastplate.**

6:15 You wear your eagerness and passion to communicate the Good News like soldier's shoes. Announce peace; the battle has already been fought and won. *(Isaiah 52:7 How beautiful upon the mountains are the feet of him who brings good tidings, who publishes peace, who brings good tidings of good, who publishes salvation. Picture the body language of the messengers returning from the battlefield with the glad tidings of victory.)*

6:16 It is most important to engage your faith as a [1]**man-size shield that covers your whole person and empowers you to extinguish the flame in every arrow of contradiction that you might face. The only visible part of you is your faith.** *(The word,* [1]*thureos means a door-size shield. To co-believe with God protects your whole person, body, soul and spirit. See 2 Corinthians 5:7.)*

6:17 Pondering redemption realities is your headgear that protects your mind; inspired thoughts give voice to God's word—this is your spiritual sword.

6:18 Prayer is an ongoing conversation; praying in the spirit includes every form of prayer, whether it be a prayer of request or a prayer of thanksgiving, or worship or interceding for all to realize their saintly innocence. Oh, and remember, you do not have to do all the talking. Always be attentive to the voice of the Spirit. *(Prayer is so much more than a one-way conversation.)*

6:19 My most urgent request is for clarity of utterance every time I open my mouth to speak. I desire that my words will be gifted with inspiration, boldly articulating the mystery of the gospel.

6:20 I am an ambassador in bonds, chained to this task of confidently communicating the revelation of the Gospel with the accuracy it deserves.

6:21 I know this is not much of a newsletter. My urgency is not to talk about myself, but my dear friend and faithful helper Tychicus, will fill you in on the detail. *(He is also the scribe of this letter.)*

6:22 That is really why I sent him to you, that you may be well informed about our affairs and see yourselves fully identified with us.

6:23 My prayer for you is a relationship with one another of happy harmony, and love-entwined faith flowing from God the Father and the Lord Jesus Christ.

6:24 Grace greetings to all of you who share our undivided passion for our Master, Jesus Christ. He is echoed in your amen.

Thoughts on spiritual warfare:

Speak tenderly to Jerusalem; and cry to her, that her warfare is accomplished, that her iniquity is pardoned. [Isaiah 40:2.]

The Message translation: ... the slate wiped clean, that old arrest warrant canceled and nailed to Christ's Cross. He stripped all the spiritual tyrants in the universe of their sham authority at the Cross and marched them naked through the streets. [Colossians 2:14, 15.]

Spiritual warfare teachings are a popular distraction that many modern-day churches engage in. It preaches a defeated Devil back into business. Pharaoh was taken out of the equation when Israel was delivered out of Egypt. They then became their own worst enemy by continuing to believe a lie about themselves. [See Numbers 13:33 and Joshua 2:11.]

James says that a double-minded person deceives himself.

Neither Jesus or anyone of the Acts-church ever marched around towns to bind so-called strong men or poured oil over buildings or places.

Any teaching that distracts from the success of the cross is a waste of time to pursue. The only possible way we can delay the glory that follows the cross is by underestimating what happened there when Jesus died and cried: It is finished.

Jesus, grilled by the Pharisees on when the kingdom of God would come, answered; The kingdom of God doesn't come by counting the days on the calendar. [The Message.] -

The kingdom of God is within you. Luke 17:20. The kingdom of God is the authority of the Christ-life, the life of our design redeemed to reign in the most attractive practical lifestyle. The world is a ready audience. Your life is the message; Christ is your life.

Paul, Silas, Timothy and Luke visited Philippe and founded the first ekklesia-church in Europe on Paul's second missionary journey around A.D. 50 (Acts 16:11-40)

This letter was written in about 61 A.D. from Rome while Paul was under house arrest.

He writes from a place of strength and joy to encourage his dear friends in Philippi, who were also facing many contradictions.

Philippians 1:20 My immediate circumstances do not distract from my message. I am convinced that our conversation now and always will continue to give an accurate account of the magnificence of Christ. The message is incarnate in me; whether I live or die, it makes no difference.

Philippians 1:21 Christ defines my life; death cannot threaten or diminish that.

Philippians 2:12 Not only in my presence but much more in my absence... Paul knew that he would be more present in his message than in his person. Ministry success is not measured by how many partners you can congregate, but how absent you can preach yourself.

Philippians 3:1 The conclusion of your faith is extreme gladness in the Lord. He is your constant reference to bliss. I am not just saying this to be repetitive; joy is your fortress. There is no safer place to be, but to be ecstatically happy.

Paul encourages them not to allow religion to distract from the delight of romance.

Philippians 3:7 The sum total of my religious pedigree and sincere devotion amounts to zero. What we have been gifted with in Christ has reduced what once seemed so important, to meaningless information. To esteem the law is to your loss. Faith is your profit.

Philippians 3:8 In fact, I have come to the conclusion that every association I have had with that which defined me before as a devout Jew, is by far eclipsed by what I have gained in knowing the Messiah. Jesus Christ and his masterful redemption define me now. Religion is like dog pooh; and it stinks, avoid stepping in it.

Philippians 4:4 Joy is not a luxury option; joy is your constant. Your union in the Lord is your permanent source of delight; so I might as well say it again, rejoice in the Lord always.

Philippians 4:6 Let no anxiety about anything [1]distract you.

Philippians 4:11 I have discovered my I-am-ness and found that I am fully [1]self sufficient, whatever the circumstance. (*Self sufficient,* [1]*autarkēs, self complacent, the feeling you have when you are completely satisfied with yourself.*)

Philippians 4:13 In every situation I am strong in the one who empowers me from within to be who I am. (*Paul lived his life in touch with this place within himself. He discovered that the same I-am-ness that Jesus walked in, was mirrored in him. I am what I am by the grace of God. 1 Corinthians 15:10.*)

1:1 Paul and Timothy address all the saints in Christ Jesus in Philippi, including your leadership team, both the [1]overseers and the [2]deacons. *(Overseer, [1]episkopos, from epi, indicating continuous influence upon, and* **skopos,** *scope to see the overall picture, [2]diakonos, from* διώκω **dioko,** *to run errands, to pursue; see Philippians 3:14.)*

1:2 The Father's favor joins our lives inseparably in the Lordship of Jesus Christ.

1:3 The thought of you always inspires me with joy and gratitude to God.

1:4 Praying for you is certainly not a job - it is more like poetry; I joyfully anticipate the outcome of my prayers for you.

1:5 Our blissful participation in everything that the gospel communicates does not age. The freshness of our first encounter continues to this very day.

1:6 I possess an inward certainty about you, confident that he who is the [1]initiator of the good work within you is also the one who executes its completeness as mirrored in Jesus Christ, who is the light of day. He is the fullness of time. *(Initiator, [1]enarche, to rehearse from the beginning. See Ecclesiastes 3:15, that which has been is now; and that which is to be has already been.)*

1:7 I am not being presumptuous to be this persuaded about you. In the context of our redeemed innocence I cannot think of you any differently; I have you in my heart. Your committed friendship in my imprisonment is of great encouragement to me in our combined defense and confirmation of the gospel. We are in this together. We are joint participants in the same grace. My grace is your grace.

1:8 God knows my intense longing for you. It is with the tender affections of Jesus Christ.

1:9 It is my desire for each one of you, that the realization of [1]love's completeness in you will increasingly burst through all boundaries and that every sphere of your relationship with others will be greatly impacted by your intimate acquaintance with love. *(The word [1]agapao is a compound word from* **ago,** *which means to lead as a shepherd leads his sheep, and* **pao,** *which means rest. His love leads me into his rest; into the full realization of his finished work. Agape is Psalm 23 in one word. By the waters of reflection my soul remembers who I am.)*

1:10 I urge you to examine this agape-love with the utmost scrutiny, just like when a diamond is viewed in the full sunlight to prove its flawless perfection. I dare you to take love to its ultimate conclusion. There is no offense in love, as evidenced in Jesus Christ who is the light of day. *(If the diamond is flawless to begin with, every possible test will prove its perfection; how someone might respond to love's initiative is not the point. Love's ultimate test was concluded on the cross. Truth does not become true by popular vote; someone's ignorance or indifference cannot change the truth.)*

1:11 You have been fully furnished with the harvest of your redeemed innocence and righteousness for which Jesus Christ labored. This is what the glorious intent of God is all about. Celebrate him.

1:12 I wish to encourage you, dear friends, that the opposition I face, which was meant to defeat the gospel, has only served to advance it.

1:13 The prison has become my pulpit. All the soldiers in the Governor's guard and everyone involved in the palace have learnt about my message. They know that I am not their prisoner but that I am enclosed in Christ.

1:14 My imprisonment has also persuaded many believers in the Lord to speak the word with fearless courage.

1:15 Some slander the message and others speak with passion and delightful certainty.

1:16 There are those who wish to get mileage out of my predicament for their own agenda.

1:17 Others again are completely love inspired and in full support with me in my defense of the gospel.

1:18 I am thrilled. Christ is the topic of conversation everywhere. Even the negative publicity continues to advertise him.

1:19 I can just see how the Spirit of Jesus Christ, like a ¹conductor of music, takes all of this together with your prayers and turns it into a concert that celebrates salvation. (The word, ¹epichoregeō, comes from epi, a Preposition of position, over, in charge, + chorus, choir, orchestra, or dance + agō, meaning to lead as a shepherd leads his sheep; thus, the leader of a dance or the conductor of music.)

1:20 My ¹thoughts are not trapped in my head. They roam free in expectation that I will not be ashamed by any contradiction. My ²immediate circumstances do not distract from my message. I am convinced that our ²conversation now and always will continue to give an accurate account of the magnificence of Christ. The message is incarnate in me; whether I live or die, it makes no difference. (The word, ¹apokaradokia is a compound word with 3 parts, apo, away from, kara, head and dokeō, thought. The word ²parrhesia, from para, a Preposition indicating close proximity, a thing proceeding from a sphere of influence, with a suggestion of union of place of residence, to have sprung from its author and giver, originating from, denoting the point from which an action originates, intimate connection; and rhesia, conversation.)

1:21 Christ defines my life; death cannot threaten or diminish that.

1:22 To be alive now is to feast on the harvest of your faith. I cannot tell when I shall lift up the anchor of the flesh and sail away. It doesn't really matter to me. (The word, ¹aihreomai, from airō, to lift the anchor and sail away.)

1:23 I am often torn between these two thoughts. I have this strong yearning to step out of the confines of this body into the immediate embrace of Christ. Can you imagine the awesomeness of that?

1:24 Yet this gospel has my [1]arm twisted and locked behind my back; I am therefore determined to remain in the body for your sakes. *(The word, [1]anagkē, suggests to have the arm twisted and locked behind one's back. See 1 Corinthians 9:16.)*

1:25 I am certain that my time with you will inspire the happy progress of your pioneering faith.

1:26 The joy of our union in Christ knows no limits. We have so much reason to celebrate. I can just imagine the eruptions of bliss should I be there with you right now in person.

1:27 The [1]one essential thing that would fully engage the focus of your earthly citizenship is the fact that your daily conduct communicates [2]like value and gives context to the gospel of Christ. So whether I am present with you to witness your steadfastness with my own eyes, or absent, our spiritual [3]union and single mindedness will be equally evident. *(The word [1]monon, points to that which is singled out as most essential; the word [2]axios, means, having the weight of another thing of like value, worth as much. Psyche, Greek, pshuchē, suggests consciousness, mental attitude, awareness. Paul desires to express an inseparable togetherness; [3]sunathleō, athletic contest. Bicycle racing uses the term peloton; where the riders are strongest and fastest when they ride in the so-called peloton, which is a densely packed group of riders, sheltering in each others' draft. In a mass-start race, most of the competitors usually end up in one large peloton for most of the race. The word is French, from a term that means rolled up in a ball.)*

1:28 Your brave fearlessness in the face of every kind of obstacle is a sure sign to those who oppose you that their efforts are futile. Your triumphant attitude makes salvation even more apparent. *(There is no counterfeit; God has no competition. Religion's self-help programs of salvation do not threaten him.)*

1:29 Because of the grace that you are gifted with in Christ, whatever you might suffer on behalf of him can never distract from what faith knows to be true about you.

1:30 Our faith is on exhibit in the same public [1]arena; we are not spectators of one another's endurance, but co-witnesses thereof. We mirror one another triumphantly. *(The word, [1]agon, refers to the place of contest, the arena or stadium.)*

2:1 In Christ our [1]association is most intimate; we [2]articulate his love story; entwined in spirit communion and tender affections. *(The word* [1]*parakaleō, from* **para***, a Preposition indicating close proximity, a thing proceeding from a sphere of influence, with a suggestion of union of place of residence, to have sprung from its author and giver, originating from, denoting the point from which an action originates, intimate connection, and* **kaleō***, to identify by name, to surname. The word* [2]***paramuthion***, *is from* **para** *+* **muthos***, a myth or tale, a story of instruction, told in heart to heart language.)*

2:2 Your Christ mindedness completes my delight. You co-echo the same agapē; we are soul mates, resonating the same thoughts.

2:3 No hidden agenda with a compromised mixture of leaven or empty philosophical flattery can match a mind that genuinely values others above oneself.

2:4 To discover your own completeness in Christ frees you to turn your attention away from yourself to others.

2:5 The way Jesus saw himself is the only valid way to see yourself.

2:6 His being God's equal in form and likeness was official; his Sonship did not steal the limelight from his Father. Neither did his humanity distract from the deity of God.

2:7 His mission however, was not to prove his deity, but to embrace our humanity. Emptied of his reputation as God, he fully embraced our physical human form; born in our resemblance he identified himself as the servant of the human race. His love enslaved him to us.

2:8 And so we have the drama of the cross in context: the man Jesus Christ who is fully God, becomes fully man to the extent of willingly dying humanity's death at the hands of his own creation. He embraced the curse and shame of the lowest kind in dying a criminal's death. *(Thus, through the doorway of death, he descended into our hellish darkness. Revelation 9:1 When the fifth celestial messenger blew his trumpet, I saw a star that had fallen to earth from the sky. The star was given the key to the shaft into the fathomless depths of the Abyss. [In his death, Jesus conquered the underworld and he has the keys; no-one else does.] Revelation 1:18 I am also the Living One; I died and now, see, here I am alive unto the ages of the ages and I have the keys wherewith I have disengaged the gates of Hadēs and death. Also, Ephesians 4:8-10.)*

2:9 From this place of utter humiliation, God exalted him to the highest rank. God graced Jesus with a Name that is far above every other name. *(Ephesians 1:20 Do you want to measure the mind and muscle of God? Consider the force which he unleashed in Jesus Christ when he raised him from the dead and forever seated him enthroned as his executive authority in the realm of the heavens. Jesus is God's right hand of power. He was raised up from the deepest dungeons of human despair to the highest region of heavenly bliss. [See Ephesians 2:5,6 & 4:8,9] Ephesians 1:21 Infinitely above all the combined forces of rule, authority, dominion or governments; he is ranked superior to any name that could* *ever be given to anyone of this age or any age still to come in the eternal future. The name of Jesus endorses his mission as fully accomplished. He is the Savior of the world. Titus 2:11 The grace of God shines as bright as day making the salvation of mankind undeniably visible. See also Ephesians 3:15, Every family in heaven and on earth originates in him; his is mankind's family name and he remains the authentic identity of every nation.)*

2:10 What his name unveils will persuade every creature of their redemption. Every knee in heaven and upon the earth and under the earth shall bow in spontaneous worship. *(See Isaiah 45:23 My own life is the guarantee of my conviction, says the Lord, every knee shall freely bow to me in worship, and every tongue shall spontaneously speak from the same God-inspired source.)*

2:11 Also every tongue will voice and resonate the same devotion to his unquestionable Lordship as the Redeemer of life. Jesus Christ has glorified God as the Father of creation. This is the ultimate conclusion of the Father's [1]intent. *(The word [1]doxa, intent, opinion, often translated, glory. Revelation 5:13 And I heard every creature in heaven and on earth and under the earth and in the sea, and all therein, saying, To him who sits upon the throne and to the Lamb be blessing and honor and glory and might forever and ever. Also my commentary note on Romans 14:11. Paul, here quotes Isaiah 45:23 See verse 20,22,& 23 Face me and **be** saved all the ends of the earth. [Note, '**Be saved.**' Not 'become saved.'] I am God; your idols are figments of your invention and imagination. Isaiah 45:23 I have sworn by myself; the word of my mouth has begotten righteousness; this cannot be reversed. The Hebrew word, יצא Yatsa can be translated, begotten like in Judges 8:30 Every knee shall bow to me and every tongue shall echo my oath. [Thus, speak with the same certainty that is sourced in me.] The Hebrew word, שבע Shaba means to seven oneself, that is, swear - thus in the Hebrew mind, by repeating a declaration seven times one brings an end to all dispute. See Hebrews 6:13.16,17.)*

2:12 Considering this amazing outcome of what our faith sees and celebrates, I strongly urge you my darling friends to continue to have your [1]ears tuned to that which inspires your conduct to give full expression to the detail of your own salvation in a most personal and practical way. See salvation in its earth-shattering awesome and ultimate conclusion. I know that my personal presence encourages you greatly but now I want you to realize an inspiration in my absence that supersedes anything you've known before. This would mean that even if you were never to see my face again or receive another Epistle from me, it will make no difference at all to your faith. *(The success of Paul's ministry was not to enslave people to him but to his gospel. He knew that he would be more present in his message than in his person. Ministry success is not measured by how many partners you can congregate, but by how absent you can preach yourself. The word often translated, obedience, is the word [1]upoakoō, to be under the inspired influence of what you hear.)*

2:13 Discover God himself as your inexhaustible inner source; he ignites you with both the desire and energy that matches his own delight.

2:14 Your entire life is a poem; any undercurrent murmuring or argumentative debating would be completely out of place. Do not let such issues disrupt the rhythm of your conversation.

2:15 Your flawless innocence radiates attraction as beacons of light in the midst of a people who have forgotten their true sonship and whose lives have become distorted and perverse. *(In this verse Paul quotes Deuteronomy 32:5 from the Greek Septuagint translation of the Hebrew text, with reference to Deuteronomy 32:4,5 &18. In context God's perfect workmanship as Father of mankind is forgotten; people have become crooked and perverse twisted and distorted out of their true pattern of sonship. Deuteronomy 32:18 says, you have forgotten the Rock that begot you and have gotten out of step with the God who [1]danced with you. Hebrew, [1]khul חול)*

2:16 Your lives [1]echō-exhibit the [2]logic of the message of life. You are positioned like the stars in the night sky, superimposed and radiating light, which shining pierces the darkness. Thus you [3]confirm the day of the Lord and [3]complete my joy. You are my wreath of honor and [3]proof that I did not run my race in vain. *(The word, [1]epechō, is from epi, to superimpose, and echō, to hold, echo resonance. The word of life, [2]logos, embodies a conception or idea; it means intelligence as an interconnected network of things known; the sum total of logic. The verb form of the noun logos is legō, to point out with words; a gathering, linking and combining of thoughts in an intelligent manner; thus, it suggests a woven-together discourse. Its Hebrew equivalent is dabar רבד meaning word, [which is the vehicle that stores and carries thought]; in its feminine form, הרבד Deborah means honey bee! Imagine the honey bee at work; irresistibly attracted to flowers and spontaneously pollinating it, while gathering and converting the nectar into wholesome honey!*

The Preposition [3]eis, suggests a point reached in conclusion. See Colossians 1:29 Your completeness in Christ is not a remote goal, but your immediate reference. My labor now exceeds any zeal that I previously knew under the duty-driven law of willpower. I am laboring beyond the point of exhaustion, striving with intense resolve with all the energy that he mightily inspires within me.)

2:17 I want you to see my ministry to you as wine poured out upon the altar of your faith. I rejoice in the thought that we drink from the same source and therefore celebrate a mutual joy.

2:18 Whatever you may suffer only concludes in joy. *(Joy is a bold declaration, in the face of severe danger and suffering, that contradiction does not define us or have the final say in our lives. We know that whether we live or die, our message is unstoppable and that it is conquering the world.)*

2:19 I trust the Lord that I will be able to send Timothy to you soon; this will be to me as if I am there personally with you.

2:20 I have no one here that share my heart more fully; I know that he will take care of you with utmost concern.

2:21 Sadly there are many in ministry with a selfish agenda.

2:22 I do not need to tell you anything about Timothy because you already know his worth. We have labored together in the gospel in the closest possible association; we are like father and son in joint partnership.

2:23 I would like to send him to you immediately, but I am just waiting to see how things here turn out for me.

2:24 I obviously would be very keen to join him shortly. I trust in the Lord for a positive outcome in my trial.

2:25 I feel urgent about sending Epaphrodites to you immediately; he is my brother, fellow-worker and co-campaigner. You initially sent him to help me and now I am returning the favor.

2:26 He longs for you and really misses you. He felt quite distressed when he heard of your concern for him when he was so sick.

2:27 He nearly died but thank God for his mercy, not just for Epaphroditus' sake but for ours also. I cannot imagine the grief we would have suffered had we lost him.

2:28 I am sending him to you without delay; knowing what joy he will be to you is already such a comfort to me.

2:29 The immense value of his life is to be celebrated with a massive bliss-party when he arrives. Oh the joy to love one another in the Lord.

2:30 I honor his total commitment to the work of Christ; he had no problem risking his life to serve me on your behalf.

3:1 The conclusion of your faith is extreme gladness in the Lord. He is your constant reference to bliss. I am not just saying this to be repetitive; joy is your fortress. There is no safer place to be, but to be ecstatically happy. *(The joy of Jahweh is your fortress.* בי חדות יהוה היא מעזבם *Nehemiah 8:10.)*

3:2 The circumcision party is the enemy of your faith and freedom. They work with an evil agenda. Be on your guard for them just like you would avoid a vicious hound on the loose. They have their knives in for you.

3:3 We give circumcision its true spiritual meaning. Our worship is not defined by anything external that would even remotely resemble the law of works and religious rituals. We worship God in the certainty of our redeemed innocence and rejoice in the finished work of Jesus Christ. Faith-righteousness gives substance to spiritual worship; the flesh occupies the religious mind with its own futile efforts to attain righteousness. I am convinced that circumcision or any work of the law can add nothing to the righteousness that Jesus secured on our behalf.

3:4 I have more reason than anyone else to rely on my years of diligent and most sincere devotion to Jewish sentiment and rituals. If gaining God's approval had anything to do with striving and personal effort I would beat the best in the business. My pedigree is obvious:

3:5 I received the famous cut when I was 8 days old, exactly as the law prescribed. I am Israeli by birth; the head of my tribe is Benjamin. I am a Hebrew of the Hebrews. In my observance of the law I belonged to the strictest party; I was proud to be a Pharisee. *(Rachel was the darling wife of Jacob; she died while giving birth to Benjamin; also the two tribes that did not revolt were Benjamin and Judah. By saying that he is a Hebrew of the Hebrews Paul emphasizes that his lineage from both parents side was not mixed with any Gentile blood.)*

3:6 The extremities of my fervor were demonstrated in the way I fiercely opposed and persecuted anyone who identified themselves in Christ. *[The so-called ekklesia.]* If keeping the law and these credentials could possibly have given me a blameless standing before God, I had it made.

3:7 The sum total of my religious pedigree and sincere devotion amounts to zero. What we have been gifted with in Christ has reduced what once seemed so important, to meaningless information. To esteem the law is to your loss. Faith is your profit.

3:8 In fact, I have come to the conclusion that every association I have had with that which defined me before as a devout Jew, is by far eclipsed by what I have gained in knowing the Messiah. Jesus Christ and his masterful redemption define me now. Religion is like dog pooh; and it stinks, avoid stepping in it.

3:9 So here I am; found in Christ. I was looking in the wrong place all along. My own duty-and-guilt-driven religious endeavor snared me in the cul-de-sac maze of self-righteousness, sponsored by the law of works. The faith of Christ reveals my identity; righteousness defines who God believes that I really am. This righteousness is sourced in God and endorses the authority of faith. *(Faith is a fairy tale if Jesus is not the substance of it.)*

3:10 Oh to comprehend the dynamic of his resurrection. His resurrection is evidence of our righteousness. In the revelation of God's economy of inclusion, I actually co-suffered with him and co-died together with Christ. *(Because I was already fully represented in his sufferings, his death and resurrection, I am greatly inspired when faced with contradictions now. Romans 4:25.)*

3:11 When confronted with death, I actually come ¹face to face with my own resurrection. *(The word ¹katantaō, from kata + anti, to come to a place over against, opposite another, face to face. 1 Corinthians 15:18 No resurrection implies no hope for anyone beyond the grave; it makes no difference whether you believed that you were included in Christ's death or not. 1 Corinthians 15:19 If our hope in Christ was restricted to only benefit us in this life then imagine the severity of our disappointment if it all had to come to an abrupt end when we died. 1 Corinthians 15:20 However this very moment the risen Christ represents everyone who has ever died; exactly like the first fruit represents the complete harvest. 1 Corinthians 15:21 The same mankind who died in a man was raised again in a man. 1 Corinthians 15:22 In Adam all died; in Christ all are made alive.)*

3:12 There may be blurry edges to my ¹comprehending the full scope of resurrection life beyond the grave; but I pursue the complete conclusion of co-comprehending and ²fully grasping exactly that which Jesus Christ knew all along about me when he died my death; and to see me in his faith where I am so perfectly included when he rescued and raised me out of the grasp of death. *(The word, ¹lambanō, means to comprehend, to grasp, to identify with. 1 Corinthians 13:12 To know even as I have always been known. The word ²katalambanō, from kata, which here strengthens the verb lambanō, thus to entirely grasp; to come to terms with, to make one's own. The KJV reads, that I may apprehend that for which also I am apprehended of by Christ Jesus.)*

3:13 I am not boasting about this new-found-righteousness as if I came up with the idea; on the contrary, I have distanced myself from everything the DIY-system of the law of works and willpower previously represented in my reference; now I am fully engaged with that to which the prophetic pointed. Christ is whom we were reaching for all along. Here he is ¹in our face; within our immediate grasp. *(The DIY-system is the fruit of the 'do it yourself-tree'. The word ¹emprosthen, from en, in, and pros, that which is right in front of me. See John 4:26 Mirror, Jesus responded ... I am the One you were longing for.)*

3:14 I have the prize of mankind's redeemed innocence in full view; just like a champion athlete in the public games I refuse to be distracted by anything else. God has ¹invited us in Christ, to lift up our eyes and realize our identity in him. *(The word, ¹klesis, invitation, from kaleō, to surname, to identify by name. While the law engages one with that which is below, faith captivates our gaze to only see that which is above, where we are co-seated together with Christ in heavenly places. We are identified in him. Colossians 3:1.)*

3:15 We who have discovered our perfect righteousness have our thoughts anchored in Christ. If you still see yourself as imperfect, God will reveal to you that you are wasting your time to imagine that you can become more accepted and righteous than what you already are.

3:16 So then, let the message of grace set the pace. *(The law is a detour leading nowhere.)*

3:17 You are free to mimic me as we together impact the lives of many others to follow in our footsteps.

3:18 As you know I am often moved to tears talking about these things; I am so passionate about the revelation of mankind's redeemed innocence that it makes no sense to me that there can still be people who oppose this message. Many are openly hostile and indifferent to the cross of Christ.

3:19 Do they not realize that the DIY law-system leads to self-destruction? All their devotion to the god of their religious appetites endorses their shame; yet they seem to have no problem with it since their minds are seared with [1]sin-consciousness. *([1]Earthly things in this case refers to the fallen mindset ruled by a sin-consciousness. See Colossians 3:1-3, Hebrews 10:1,19-22.)*

3:20 Our [1]citizenship is referenced in our joint position with Christ in heavenly places. Heaven is not our goal, it is our [2]starting point. Our understanding is [3]sourced in a Savior; we [4]fully embrace the Lord Jesus Christ. *(The word, [1]politeuma, common wealth, our social identity. The word [2]uparcho, means to make a beginning, starting point. The word translated source, is the word, [3]ek. To fully embrace, [4]apekdechomai, from apo, away from [that which defined me before] and ek, out of, source; and dechomai, to take into one's hands to accept wholeheartedly, to fully embrace.)*

3:21 The salvation that Jesus is the author of, re-fashions these bodies of clay and elevates us to fully participate in the same pattern of his heavenly glory. The severe contradiction that we might often face in the frailty of the flesh, is by far surpassed by the glorious splendor displayed in his human body raised from the dead; according to the working of God's dynamic power he imprints the mirror pattern of his likeness in us. Thus he subdues all things to himself. *(Paul's quest to fully comprehend the power of the resurrection [Philippians 3:10] is consistent with his prayer in Ephesians 1:19, I pray that you will understand beyond all comparison the magnitude of his mighty power at work [1]in us who believe. Faith reveals how enormously advantaged we are in Christ. [The Preposition [1]eis, speaks of a point reached in conclusion.] Ephesians 1:20, It is the same dynamic energy which God unleashed in Christ when he raised him from the dead and forever established him in the power of his own right hand in the realm of the heavens. Ephesians 1:21, Infinitely above all the combined forces of rule, authority, dominion, or governments; he is ranked superior to any name that could ever be given to anyone of this age or any age still to come in the eternal future. Ephesians 1:22, I want you to see this: he subjected all these powers under his feet. He towers head and shoulders above everything. He is the head; Ephesians 1:23, the [1]ekklesia is his body. The completeness of his being that fills all in all resides in us. God cannot make himself more visible or exhibit himself more accurately. [The word, [1]Ekklesia, comes from ek, a Preposition always denoting origin, and klesia from kaleō, to identify by name, to surname; thus the ekklesia-church is his redeemed image and likeness in mankind.]*

See again Philippians 2:6, His being God's equal in form and likeness was official; his sonship did not steal the limelight from his Father. Neither did his humanity distract from the deity of God. Philippians 2:7, His mission however, was not to prove his deity but to embrace our humanity. He emptied himself into a physical human form; born in our resemblance he identified himself as the servant of the human race. His love enslaved him to us. Philippians 2:8, And so we have the drama of the cross in context: the man Jesus Christ who is fully God, becomes fully man to the extent of willingly dying mankind's death at the hands of his own creation. He embraced the curse and shame of the lowest kind in dying a criminal's death. Philippians 2:,9 From this place of utter humiliation, God exalted him to the highest rank. God graced Jesus with a Name that is far [1]above as well as equally representative of every other name; [The word, [1]uper, means above, also instead, or for the sake of. The name of Jesus endorses his mission as fully accomplished. He is the Savior of the world. See also Ephesians 3:15, Every family in heaven and on earth originates in him; his is mankind's family name and he remains the authentic identity of every nation.] Philippians 2:10, What his name unveils will persuade every creature of their redemption. Every knee in heaven and upon the earth and under the earth shall bow in spontaneous worship. Ephesians 4:8 Scripture confirms that he arrested every possible threat that held mankind hostage. [he took captivity captive] And in his resurrection, he led us as trophies in his triumphant procession on high. Consider the genius of God, in the incarnate Christ, he repossessed what belonged to us by design, in human form; this is his grace-gift to us. (Quote from Psalm 67:19 LXX Septuagint, [1]ἔλαβες δόματα ἐν ἀνθρώπῳ, elabes domata en [in] anthrōpō - You have repossessed gifts in human form. The word elabes from lambanō means to take what is one's own. The word for the human species, male or female is anthropos, from ana, upward, and tropos, manner of life; character; in like manner. [Hebrew text, Psalm 68:18,19 לקחת מתנות באדם lakachat mattanoth ba adam - You have taken gifts in Adam. The gifts which Jesus Christ distributes to us he has received in us, in and by virtue of his incarnation. Adam Clarke.] We were born anew in his resurrection. 1 Peter 1:3, Hosea 6:2, and Ephesians 2:6, We are also elevated in his ascension to be equally welcome in the throne room of the heavenly realm where we are now seated together with him in his authority.)

4:1 Now in the light of all this, I am sure that you can appreciate what enormous delight you are to me. My precious friends, you are my trophy and my joy. Just as you have been doing, continue to stand immovably strong in the Lord.

4:2 Your ¹source defines you by name. Dear ²Eodias and ³Syntyche, let me remind you of the meanings of your names. Engage your thoughts to follow the direct and easy way of grace; then you will together fulfill your mission in the Lord without distraction. *(The word, ¹parakaleō, comes from para, a Preposition indicating close proximity, a thing proceeding from a sphere of influence, with a suggestion of union of place of residence, to have sprung from its author and giver, originating from, denoting the point from which an action originates, intimate connection; and kaleō, meaning to identify by name, to surname. The word ²eudias, from eu, good, and odos, a road, thus a prosperous and expeditious journey, to lead by a direct and easy way; ³suntuchē, from sun, together with, and tugchanō, to hit the mark; of one discharging a javelin or arrow.)*

4:3 Suzegos, you are the meaning of your name to me; my trustworthy yoke fellow. Associate yourself closely with these ladies who have been my fellow athletes in the gospel. Also Clement as well as all my other colleagues - I have their names on record in the book of life. *(Paul has all his friend's names on record. All who have discovered their redeemed identity in the Gospel. [See Romans 16:1-23.] See my notes on the Book of Life at the end of Revelation 17. Zoe life as defined in Christ has given such rich meaning to proper names. Suzugos, meaning yoke-fellow. At Philippi, women were the first hearers of the Gospel, and Lydia the first convert. Acts 16:13-15. Clement, clear skies, bright and sunny weather. Paul, whose own name was changed from, Sheol, meaning dark underworld, to Paō, rest, appreciates the meaning of proper names. He calls Peter, Kefas which is the Aramaic for Petros, to deliberately steer away from the more familiar sound of Petros, thus he specifically emphasizes the meaning of his name. The rock foundation of God's ekklesia. In Matthew 16 Jesus identifies Simon, the son of Jonah by a new name, Petros; and upon this revelation, that the son of man is the son of God the ekklesia is built.)*

4:4 Joy is not a luxury option; joy is your constant. Your union in the Lord is your permanent source of delight; so I might as well say it again, rejoice in the Lord always.

4:5 This kind of joy empowers you to show perfect ¹courtesy towards all people. The Lord is not nearer to some than what he is to others. *(The word, ¹epieikēs, from epi, indicating continuous influence upon, and eikos, reasonable, courteous. This is exactly Paul's attitude towards the idol worshipping Greek philosophers in Acts 17:27,28. See also Titus 3:3. Your joy makes the gospel visible and irresistible. Every definition of distance is canceled, as well as every excuse to feel miserable and neglected.)*

4:6 Let no anxiety about anything ¹distract you. Rather translate moments into prayerful worship, and soak your requests in gratitude

before God. *(The word* [1]***merimnaō****, anxiety, through the idea of distraction, from* **meritzō***, to divide. Your requests do not surprise God; he knows your thoughts from afar and is acquainted with all your ways; yet he delights in your conversation and childlike trust. Song of Songs 2:14; Matthew 6:8.)*

4:7 And in this place of worship and gratitude you will witness how the peace of God within you [1]**echoes the awareness of your oneness in Christ Jesus beyond the reach of any thought that could possibly unsettle you. Just like the** [2]**sentry guard secures a city, watching out in advance for the first signs of any possible threat, your deepest feelings and the tranquillity of your thoughts are fully guarded there.** *(The word,* [1]***uperechō*** *translates, echoes ...beyond the reach of. And, φρουρέω* [2]***phroureō*** *guarding the gates of the city. This peace is not measured by external circumstances, it is residing deeply in the innermost parts of your being. We are not talking about a fragile sense of peace that can easily be disturbed; one that we have to fabricate ourselves; this is God's peace; the peace that God himself enjoys. This peace surpasses all the confines of our own reasonings, and floods our hearts and minds with a tranquillity that takes charge of our emotions and wellbeing in fragile times.)*

4:8 Now let this be your conclusive [1]**reasoning: consider that which is** [2]**true about everyone as evidenced in Christ. Live** [3]**overwhelmed by God's opinion of you. Acquaint yourselves with the revelation of** [4]**righteousness; realize God's likeness in you. Make it your business to declare mankind's redeemed** [5]**innocence. Think** [6]**friendship. Discover how** [7]**famous everyone is in the light of the gospel; mankind is in God's limelight. Ponder how** [8]**elevated you are in Christ. Study** [9]**stories that celebrate life.** *(See Colossians 3:3, Engage your thoughts with throne room realities where we are co-seated together with Christ. The word* [1]***logitsomai*** *suggests a logical reasoning by taking everything into account;* [2]***alēthes****, means that which was hidden, but is now uncovered; In Ephesians 3:21 Paul speaks about the truth as it is embodied in Jesus. The word overwhelmed is,* [3]***semnos****, from* **sebomai***, to revere, to adore. The word for righteousness is* [4]***dikaios****, from* **dikē***, suggesting to be judged equal; it implies the idea of two parties finding likeness in each other, where there is no sense of inferiority, suspicion, blame, regret or pressure to perform. The gospel is the revelation of the righteousness of God; it declares how God succeeded to put mankind right with himself. It is about what God did right, not what Adam did wrong. See Romans 1:17. The word* [5]***hagnos*** *speaks of blameless innocence. The word* [6]***prophileō,*** *is exactly what it says, pro-friendship. The English word for famous is derived from the Greek word* [7]***euphemos****, from* **eu***, well done, good and* **phemos***; it means to be in the limelight, from* **phaō***, to shine; Jesus said, you are the light of the world. Just like a city set on a hill, your light cannot be hidden. The word* [8]***arete****, is often translated, virtue, from* **airō***, to raise up, to elevate;* [9]***epainos****, commendable, praise worthy, from* **epi***, indicating continuous influence upon, and* **ainos***, story.)*

4:9 These things are consistent with all that I teach and live; you can confidently practice what you hear and see in me. The peace that inevitably follows this lifestyle is more than a fuzzy feeling; this is God himself endorsing our seamless oneness.

4:10 I am so happy in the Lord that after all this time you have shown such revived concern in my well-being. It is refreshing to know your support, even though you did not recently have the opportunity to express it.

4:11 Hey, don't get me wrong, I am not hinting for funding. I have discovered my I-am-ness and found that I am fully ¹self sufficient, whatever the circumstance. *(Self sufficient, ¹autarkēs, self complacent, the feeling you have when you are completely satisfied with yourself.)*

4:12 I am not defined by abuse or abundance. It might be a different day and a different place, but the secret remains the same; whether I am facing a feast or a fast, a fountain or famine. *(Abundance is not a sign of God's goodness; neither is lack a sign of his absence. Righteousness by his (God's) faith defines life. The good news is the fact that the Cross of Christ was a success. God rescued the life of our design; he redeemed our innocence. Mankind would never again be judged righteous or unrighteous by their own ability to obey moral laws. It is not about what someone must or must not do but about what Jesus has done. It is from faith to faith, and not a person's good or bad behavior or circumstances interpreted as a blessing or a curse [Habakkuk 2:4]. Instead of reading the curse when disaster strikes, Habakkuk realizes that the Promise out-dates performance as the basis to mankind's acquittal. Deuteronomy 28 would no longer be the motivation or the measure of right or wrong behavior. Though the fig trees do not blossom, nor fruit be on the vines, the produce of the olive fail and the fields yield no food, the flock be cut off from the fold and there be no herd in the stalls, yet I will rejoice in the Lord, I will joy in the God of my salvation. God, the Lord, is my strength; he makes my feet like hinds' feet, he makes me tread upon my high places [Habakkuk 3:17-19 RSV]. Look away [from the law of works] to Jesus; he is the Author and finisher of faith. [Hebrews 12:1]. See Romans 1:17.)*

4:13 In every situation I am strong in the one who empowers me from within to be who I am. *(Paul lived his life in touch with this place within himself. He discovered that the same I-am-ness that Jesus walked in, was mirrored in him. I am what I am by the grace of God. Christ in me, mirrors Christ in you. Philippians 2:12, Not only in my presence but much more in my absence. Colossians 1:27 In us God desires to exhibit the priceless treasure of Christ's indwelling; every nation will recognize him as in a mirror. The unveiling of Christ in human life completes mankind's every expectation. He is not hiding in history, or in outer space nor in the future, neither in the pages of Scripture, he is merely mirrored there to be unveiled within you. Matthew 13:44, Galatians 1:15, 16.)*

4:14 Now I am not saying that I did not need or appreciate your help. Your joint participation in my difficult times was like beautiful poetry to me.

4:15 You and I know very well that your initial encounter with the gospel inspired you to partner with me in the wonderful rhythm of giving and receiving. Your generosity then financed my trip in and out of Macedonia. No other ekklesia-church did what you did. *(Paul visited Thessalonica and Berea, about 12 years before this epistle was written. Acts 17: 1-14.)*

4:16 You also helped me several times in Thessalonica.

4:17 I am not reminding you of your gifts for any other reason but to encourage you to realize the abundant harvest in the word that you are a living epistle of. *(Greek, the fruit of your word.)*

4:18 This letter is my official [1]receipt to you, proving that my capacity is filled to the brim. I am bursting at the seams indulging in your gifts that Epaphrodites brought. Your generosity celebrates God's pleasure like a sweet perfume poured out on the altar of your love for me. *(The word [1]**apechō** here is used as a commercial term meaning to receive a sum in full and give a receipt for it. From **apo** and **echō**, to hold; in this context the Preposition **apo** with the accusative denotes correspondence of the contents to the capacity; of the possession to the desire. J.B. Lightfoot.)*

4:19 My God shall also abundantly fill every nook and cranny to overflowing in all areas of your lives. The wealth of his dream come true in Christ Jesus measures his generosity towards you.

4:20 For countless ages upon ages God will be celebrated as our Father. We are his glory. Most certainly.

4:21 Embrace every saint in Christ Jesus on our behalf; the friends with me embrace you.

4:22 All the saints, especially those within the household of Caesar greet you dearly.

4:23 The grace that Jesus Christ embodies embraces you in your spirit.

In this marvelous work, Paul continues to eloquently celebrate the perfection of God's work in Christ in redeeming his likeness in us. His aim is to make the mystery of the gospel known in its most accurate context; the unveiling of Christ in us completes our every expectation. Paul sees the whole world as his audience. He has no other agenda but to reveal Christ in the nations.

Colossians 1:28 This is the essence and focus of our message; we awaken every person's mind, instructing every individual by bringing them into full understanding *(flawless clarity)* **in order that we may prove** *(present)* **everyone perfect in Christ.**

Colossians 1:15 In him the image and likeness of God is made visible in human life; in order that every individual may recognize their true origin in him; he is the firstborn of every creature. *(What darkness veiled from us he unveiled. In him we clearly see the mirror reflection of our original life. The Son of his love gives accurate evidence of his image in human form. The incarnation means that God can never again be invisible.)*

Colossians 2:9-10 Christ reveals that there is no place in the universe where God would rather be; his fullness physically resides in Christ. Jesus proves that human life is tailor-made for God. Jesus Christ mirrors our completeness; he is I am in us.

Any teaching that leaves you with a sense of lack and imperfection rather than completeness is a distraction from the truth.

Colossians 2:16 Do not let anyone therefore bring a restriction to your freedom by reviving religious rules and regulations pertaining to eating and drinking; also, all Jewish festivals, new moons, and Sabbaths have come to an end in Christ.

The religious facade that disguised the law of works as a means of defining a person's life, was openly defeated. The success of the cross will never be silenced.

Colossians 3:1 Since you are in fact raised together with Christ, relocate yourselves mentally; engage your thoughts with throne room realities.

Colossians 4:4 My sincere desire is that my message will accurately unveil the mystery of Christ in its most complete context. You. This is the mission of my life. *(Ephesians 3:9.)*

The city, *Colossae*, was in Phrygia, in the valley of the Lycus, about ten or twelve miles beyond Laodicaea and Hierapolis.

See my commentary note in Revelation 3:16.

1:1 My name is Paul. My colleague, Timothy and I, are together in this mission ordained by the resolve of God, representing the ministry of Jesus Christ.

1:2 The [1]favor and [2]friendship of our God and Father belongs to you. While you may be geographically [3]located in Colossae, your real location is in Christ! In him we are found in [4]blamelessness, persuasion and shared brotherhood.

(*Grace and peace express the sum total of every beneficial purpose of God towards us. Paul brands his gospel with these words in order to distinguish the message of the revelation of the finished work of Christ as the basis to faith, from the law of Moses, which restricts a person to their own efforts to justify themselves. It is a matter of gift vs. reward and tranquility vs. striving.*

[1] The word, χάρις [1]charis, refers to the divine influence upon the heart; that which affords joy, pleasure, delight, sweetness, charm, loveliness.

[2] Then, the word [2]eirēnē, which is a friendship word, meaning peace, from eirō, to join, to be set at one again; in carpentry it is the strongest joint, referred to as the dovetail joint. In Hebrew, שָׁלוֹם shalom peace, harmony, wholeness, completeness, prosperity, welfare and tranquility. Peace is a place of unhindered enjoyment of friendship beyond guilt, suspicion, blame or inferiority.

[3] ἐν Κολοσσαῖς en Kolossais and ἐν Χριστῷ - en Christō IN Christ; both words are with the Preposition en IN as well as in the Dative Case - which indicates indirect object or, location in.

[4] All these words ending in ois, are also in the Dative Case [plural], ἁγίοις [holiness/blameless] καὶ πιστοῖς [faith/ persuasion] ἀδελφοῖς [literally, sharing the same womb - brotherhood] See 1 Corinthians 1:30, Of God's doing are we...

[The longer text in the TR was later added by copyists. Bruce Metzger.])

1:3 Every time we pray for you we thank God for you. Together with our Lord Jesus Christ we enjoy a common origin in the Father.

1:4 The reports of your belief in Christ Jesus and your love for every devoted follower inspire us.

1:5 The heavenly dimension *[the spiritual realm]* is the limitless reservoir of your expectation. The announcement of the goodness of God is not far-fetched or too good to be true. The word you heard is absolutely true.

1:6 This word resonates within you and its appeal is prevailing in the whole world. The harvest is evident everywhere and gaining ground; as also witnessed in your own experience [1]from the moment you heard and understood the true implication and the relevance of his grace. (*My greatest joy is to realize that your faith is announced throughout the entire world. The total cosmos is our audience. [Romans 1:8] Paul always sees the larger audience when he addresses the individual.*

[1] While everything Jesus accomplished on humanity's behalf is already true before anyone but God believes it, the moment one realizes the truth, is life changing! Gold is already gold before it is discovered; but once discovered, it becomes currency!)

1:7 Your experience is consistent with the teaching you received from our dear co-worker Epafras. He is passionate about your well-being in Christ.

1:8 He told us how much you love us in the spirit;

1:9 and so we have become inseparably linked to you. Our constant desire for you is that you might be overwhelmed with the knowledge of God's dream for your lives. We pray that the pattern of his wisdom and thoughts will fall into place for you in all ¹spiritual understanding. *(The word, ¹sunesis from συνίημι suniemi - sun + eimi, together with my I am-ness, to resonate; which means a flowing together as of two streams - a seamless merging; a fusion of thought; a joint-seeing. It suggests the grasp and comprehension that happens from comparing and combining things. A word only Paul uses; also his colleague Dr Luke , in Luke 2:47, as well as another disciple of Paul, Mark who uses it in Mark 12:33, To love him with all your heart, with all your understanding, with all your strength, and to love your neighbor as you love yourself; this is more important than all the burnt offerings and sacrifices.)*

1:10 Go on a ¹walkabout tour to explore the extent of the land that is yours under his Lordship. Now you can conduct yourselves appropriately towards him, pleasing him in every harvest of good works that you bear. Meanwhile, you continue to increase in your intimate acquaintance with that which God knows to be true about you. This results in the most attractive and fulfilled life possible. *(The word, ¹peripateō, means to walk about everywhere. The knowledge of God is not our perception of him, but his knowledge of us; to know even as we have always been known. Jeremiah 1:5, 1 Corinthians 13:12.)*

1:11 You are empowered in the dynamic of God's strength; ¹his mind is made up about you. He enables you to be strong in endurance and steadfastness with joy. *(His glorious power, or ¹doxa, comes from dokeō, to recognize for what it really is, true opinion; God's intention—his mind made up.)*

1:12 We are grateful to the Father who qualified us to participate in the complete portion of the inheritance of the ¹saints in the light. *(The light of the Gospel reveals what God accomplished to transform the sinner into a saint; from hagos, an awful thing to ¹hagios, a consecrated object: call no-one unholy or unclean. Acts 10:28. It's when we see what Peter saw when God dramatically challenged his paradigms in Acts 10; I mean the man's hungry, and when a Jew gets hungry he's supposed to see favorite food pop-ups! But instead God shows him every unclean animal alive in their skins, feathers, warts and scales! Not neatly chopped up into a Gumbo or stew, and flavored with favorite spices! Alive, dirty and ugly! And three times later, after Peter tried his best take on a favorite scripture (Don't eat anything unclean, remember!) God shows him in v 28 that he may no longer call anyone unclean or unholy!! Haha! We've so underestimated what God did when Jesus died humanity's death! Behold the Lamb OF GOD who takes away the sin of the world! He did it once and for all long before anyone but God believed it! And without our permission! See Revelation 21:27.)*

1:13 He rescued us from the ¹dominion of darkness *(the sense-ruled world, dominated by the law of performance)* **and relocated us into the kingdom where the love of his Son rules.** *(Darkness is not a force, it is the absence of light. [See Ephesians 4:18] A darkened understanding veiled the truth of our redeemed design from us. 2 Corinthians 4:4. What empowered darkness was the* *lie that we believed about ourselves. The word, [1]exousia, sometimes translated as authority, is from ek, origin or source, and eimi, I am. Thus, I was confused about who I am until the day that I heard and understood the grace of God in truth, as in a mirror. See 2 Corinthians 3:18, John 1:12.)*

1:14 In God's mind mankind is associated in Christ; in his blood sacrifice we were ransomed; our redemption was secured; our [1]sins were completely done away with. *(The word sin, is the word [1]hamartia, from ha, negative or without and meros, portion or form, thus to be without your allotted portion or without form, pointing to a disoriented, distorted, bankrupt identity; the word meros, is the stem of morphē, as in 2 Corinthians 3:18 the word metamorphē, with form, which is the opposite of hamartia - without form. Sin is to live out of context with the blueprint of one's design; to behave out of tune with God's original harmony. See Deuteronomy 32:18, You have forgotten the Rock that begot you and have gotten out of step with the God who danced with you. Hebrew, חול khul, also means to dance, as in Judges 21:21. Sin distorts the life of our design. Jesus reveals and redeemed our true form.)*

1:15 In him the image and likeness of God is made visible in human form in order that everyone may recognize their true origin in him. He is the firstborn of every creature. *(What darkness veiled from us he unveiled. In him we clearly see the mirror reflection of our original life. The Son of his love gives accurate evidence of his image in human form. The incarnation means that God can never again be invisible.)*

1:16 Everything that is, begins in him; whether in the heavenly realm or upon the earth, visible or invisible, he is the original blueprint of every order of justice and every level of authority, be it kingdoms or governments, principalities or jurisdictions; the original form of all things were founded by him and created for him. *(Any order that does not mirror Christ is a distortion of man's own making.)*

1:17 He is the initiator of all things, therefore everything finds its relevance and its true pattern only in him.

1:18 The ekklesia-church is the bodily, incarnate expression of which Jesus is the head. He is the principal rank of authority who leads the triumphant procession of our new birth out of the region of the dead. His preeminent rank is beyond threat. *(... leading the resurrection parade — The Message. See also Revelation 1:5 and Ephesians 4:8,9; Colossians 2:9 & 10.)*

1:19 God is fully at home in him. Jesus exhibits God's [1]happy delight to be human. *(Delightful intent, [1]eudokeō. So spacious is he, so roomy, that everything of God finds its proper place in him without crowding. — The Message.)*

1:20 He initiated the reconciliation of all things to himself. Through the blood of the cross God restored the original harmony. His reign of peace now extends to every visible thing upon the earth as well as those invisible things which are in the [1]heavenly realm. *(The heavens, [1]ouranos, a place of elevation, from oros, a mountain, from airō, to lift, to raise, to elevate, Not only that, but all the broken and dislocated pieces of the universe, people and things, animals and atoms, get properly fixed and fit together in vibrant harmonies, all because of his death. — The Message.)*

1:21 Your indifferent mindset alienated you from God into a lifestyle of annoyances, hardships, and labors. Yet he has now fully [2]reconciled and restored you to your original design. *(The word, [1]ponēros, is described in Thayer's Lexicon to mean, annoyances, hardships, and labors, often translated as evil. [See Septuagint: tree of knowledge of good and hard labor.] To reconcile: [2]apokatallassō, fully restored to the original value. [In Thayer Definition: to change, exchange, as coins for others of equivalent value.])*

1:22 He accomplished this in dying our death in a human body; he fully represented us in order to fully present us again in blameless innocence, face-to-face with God; with no sense of guilt, suspicion, regret, or accusation; all charges against us are officially canceled.

1:23 Remain under the influence of what your faith knows to be true about you, firmly consolidated in the foundation of your belief so that nothing can distract you from the expectation of the Gospel; a hope that is consistent with what you have heard. Just as I, Paul, am in the ministry to proclaim the one and only message that rings true with resonance in all of creation under heaven. *(The dimension of the invisible spiritual realm. You stay grounded and steady in that bond of trust, constantly tuned in to the Message, careful not to be distracted or diverted. There is no other Message—just this one. Every creature under heaven gets this same Message. I, Paul, am a messenger of this Message. —The Message.)*

1:24 This is why no form of suffering can interfere with my joy. Every suffering on your behalf is just another opportunity to reinforce that which might still be lacking *(in your understanding)* of the affliction of Christ on behalf of his body which is the ekklesia-church. *(The inconvenience that Paul might be suffering on behalf of the believers is not to add to the sufferings of Christ—as though the sufferings of Christ on our behalf were insufficient but it is to further emphasize and confirm the principle of unselfish love that constrains New Testament ministry.)*

1:25 I am an administrator in God's economy; my mission is to make his word known to you with utmost clarity.

1:26 Mankind's most sought after quest, the mystery which has remained elusive and concealed for ages and generations, is now fully realized in our redeemed innocence. *(The word, ἁγνός hagnos, clean, blameless innocence.)*

1:27 Within us, God is delighted to exhibit the priceless treasure of this glorious unveiling of Christ's indwelling in order that every person on the planet, whoever they are, may now come to the greatest discovery of all time and recognize Christ in them as in a mirror. He is the [1]desire of the nations and completes their every expectation. *(He is not hiding in history, or in outer space nor in the future, neither in the pages of Scripture, he is merely mirrored there to be unveiled within you. Matthew 13:44, Galatians 1:15, 16, 2 Corinthians 3:18, 2 Corinthians 4:4,7. This is huge. What God was now able to disclose in the saints is immediately equally relevant in the nations. Christ in the nations is the hope of glory. This is the mystery of the ages. This is what we were waiting for. [1]Haggai 2:6,7.)*

1:28 This is the essence and focus of our message; we [1]awaken everyone's mind, instructing every individual by bringing them into [2]full understanding *[flawless clarity]* in order that we may [3]prove *(present)* everyone [4]perfect in Christ. *(Translating [1]vous + tithēmi as to re-align every mind with God's mind. The word, [2]sophos, comes from saphēs meaning clear, clarity. The word, [3]paristanō, comes from para, sphere of influence, closest possible association, and histēmi, meaning to stand, to exhibit with evidence. The word, [4]teleios, means perfect, without shortcoming and fully efficient.)*

1:29 [1]Your completeness in Christ is not a remote goal, but your immediate reference. My labor now exceeds any zeal that I previously knew under the duty-driven law of willpower. I am laboring beyond the point of exhaustion, striving with intense resolve with all the energy that he mightily inspires within me. *([1]eis, a point reached in conclusion.)*

2:1 Picture this: The stage is set; the game is on. And you are more than a mere spectator. We are ¹standing opposite each other in the ²arena like two athletes of exactly the same stature: the contest is to display Christ in you to the extent that all of you as well as those in Laodicea may witness what I know face-to-face and not just by hearsay. *(Christ is not more in Paul than what he is in his audience. The KJV reads, What ¹great ²conflict. The word, ¹helikos, from Thayers Definition translates as tall as; as old as; equal comrades. Two contestants weighing the exact same weight as well as being athletes of the exact same age. And arena or contest, ²**agon**, in Thayers Definition is an assembly met to see games within the arena or stadium.)*

2:2 The ¹mandate of my ministry is for everyone's heart to be awakened to their true identity, ²intertwined in love's tapestry. This will launch you into a life of knowing the wealth of every ³conclusion and joint witness hidden within the mystery of God who fathered us and co-revealed us in Christ. *(The word, ¹**parakaleō**, is often translated as comfort from **para**, a Preposition indicating close proximity, a thing proceeding from a sphere of influence, with a suggestion of union of place of residence, to have sprung from its author and giver, originating from, denoting the point from which an action originates, intimate connection; and **kaleō**, to surname, to identify by name, to call by name. The phrase, ²**sumbibatzō en agapē**, means intertwined in love's tapestry; and the word, σύνεσις ³**sunesis**, from **suniemi**, means joint seeing or understanding; a flowing together as of two streams - a seamless merging; a fusion of thought. It suggests the grasp and comprehension that happens from comparing and combining things.)*

2:3 Everything that could possibly define our wealth is ¹hidden in Christ. In this place of our union in him the complete ²treasure of all wisdom and knowledge is sourced. *(The word, ¹**apokriphos**, translates from **apo**, away from and **kruptō**, to conceal, to keep secret. The word, ²**thesaurus**, means treasure; the place in which precious things are collected and laid up; from **tithēmi**, to place and **theō**, God, the ultimate capacity of all things. Christ is the context of all wisdom and knowledge.)*

2:4 I want to say it with such clarity that no one will be able to lead you to an inferior conclusion by bending your mind with clever words. *(Any message that would divert from the revelation of the mystery of Christ in you is founded in error.)*

2:5 My physical absence does not distance me from you spiritually. I rejoice to witness that your disciplined and practical lifestyle does not distract from the simplicity of your faith and confidence in Christ.

2:6 Your daily walk is no different from that initial embrace when you first understood your divine association in him. *(As you have received Christ, so walk in him.)*

2:7 Just like the roots of a tree, draw your sustenance and strength from him. Like a building rising up out of its foundation your life makes the full stature of Christ visible; standing tall in his shoes, firm in your faith posture. The language of gratitude that overflows from your lips reflects the exact impression of what you were taught.

2:8   Make sure that you become no one's victim through empty philosophical intellectualism and meaningless speculations, molded in traditions and repetitions according to mankind's cosmic codes and superstitions and not consistent with Christ.

2:9 In him, all the fullness of [1]Deity [2]resides in a human body. He proves that human life is tailor-made for God. *(The word, [1]theotes, godhead/deity, is feminine. Jesus exhibits what the Father, Son and Spirit is like, in human form. The word [2]katoikeō means to dwell in, to inhabit. While the expanse cannot measure or define God, their detailed likeness is displayed in human skin. See Colossians 1:19, God is fully at home in him. Jesus is God's happy delight to be human.)*

2:10 We are complete in him. Jesus mirrors our wholeness and [1]endorses our true identity. He is I am in us. *(God packaged completeness in I am, mirrored in you. The word, [1]exousia, is often translated as authority; from, ek + eimi, originating out of I am. The days are over where our lives were dictated to under the rule of the law of performance and an inferior identity. It's not about who I used to be or who I'm striving to become; we are celebrating who I am. Any teaching that leaves one with a sense of lack and imperfection rather than completeness is a distraction from the truth. Jesus is the author and finisher of faith's capacity within us to mirror and celebrate completeness.)*

2:11   You were in Christ when he died; which means that his death is your true circumcision. This is [1]not hypothetical; this is the real deal. Thus, sin's authority in the human body was stripped of its control over you. *(ἀχειροποίητος [1]acheiropoiētos; not made with hands.)*

2:12   In the same parallel *[your co-circumcision in his death]*, your co-burial and joint-resurrection is now demonstrated in baptism; your co-inclusion in Christ is what God's faith knew when he powerfully raised him from the dead. *(Hosea 6:2.)*

2:13 You were once spiritually dead, as confirmed in your constant failure, being bound to a lifestyle ruled by the [1]distorted desires of the flesh; but now God made you alive together with him and thus [2]graciously restored our innocence and dignity, having forgiven us all our [3]short falling. *([1]The uncircumcision of the flesh, i.e., in the Greek, a life controlled by the sexual organs. God [2]graced us in Christ. The word translated, forgiven, [2]charisamenos from charizomai means he graciously restored our innocence and dignity. The word, [3]paraptōma, comes from, para, close proximity, sphere of influence and piptō, to stop flying, from petomai, to fly; thus, to fall from flight or to lose altitude.)*

2:14 His body nailed to the cross hung there as the [3]document of mankind's guilt; in dying our death he [1]canceled the detailed [2]hand-written [3]record which testified against us. Every [1]stain on our conscience, reminding of the sense of failure and guilt, was thus fully blotted out. *(The word, [1]exaleiphō, comes from ek, out of, and aleiphō, with a, as a particle of union, and liparos, to grease, to leave a stain; guilt, as well as all hurtful memories were like grease stains upon the conscience. In NT only here and Revelation 3:5; 7:17; 21:4 and in Acts 3:19 Be awakened in your minds and fully converted to face the fact of your redeemed innocence - your sins have been thoroughly blotted out. Plato used it of blotting out something that was written. The word, [2]cheirographon, translates as hand-written. The word, [3]dogma, comes from dokeō, a thought pattern; thus thought patterns engraved by human experience of constant failure to do what the law required. In his personal handwriting mankind endorsed their own death sentence. The hands of fallen mankind struck the body of Jesus with the blows of their religious hatred and fury when they nailed his bloodied body to the tree; they did not realize that in the mystery of God's economy, Jesus became the scapegoat of the entire human race. [Isaiah 53:4, 5] See my notes on Hebrews 8:12.)*

2:15   He thus ¹defused and brought closure to every possible claim of accusation against the human race. He turned the scandal and shame of the cross into an eternal trophy, celebrating the genius of God. Every principality and power was stripped naked and ²publicly paraded through the streets. The ⁴voice of the cross will never be silenced! *(The success of the cross is the crux of the gospel. Its horror is now the eternal trophy of God's triumph over sin. It is what stripped religion of its assumed role to control people with guilt. Every accusation lost its leverage to blackmail the human race with condemnation and shame.*

*[1] The word, ¹apekduomai, is translated from **apo**, away from, and **ekduō**, to be stripped of clothing; to disarm; the religious facade that disguised the law of works as a means of defining a person's life, was openly defeated. Same word used in Colossians 3:9. The dominance of the tree of the knowledge of good and evil [**ponēros**, hard work and labor] was ended.*

[2] The word, ²deikmatizō, means to exhibit in public.

*[3] See ³commentary below of the words **archē**, rule and **exousia**, authority.*

*[4] The word, ⁴parresia, comes from **pas**, all and **rheō**, outspokenness, pouring forth speech.*

He stripped all the spiritual tyrants in the universe of their sham authority at the Cross and marched them naked through the streets. — The Message

> *See **1 Corinthians 15:24** The complete conclusion of his work of redemption is ¹repeatedly celebrated in every individual discovering that they too are part and parcel of the full harvest of his resurrection. This is the extent of his reign that he yielded to God the Father, having ²brought to naught every definition of dominion, including all ³principalities, all ⁴authority and every ⁵dynamic influence in society.*

> *([1] The Conjunctive Particle, ¹otan, often translated as when is better translated as every time. See Colossians 3:3, Thus, Every time Christ is revealed we are being co-revealed in his glory. According to the Walter Bauer Lexicon, **otan** is often used for an action that is repeated. Referring to the previous verse, all are individually made alive in the order of Christ. Mankind's co-resurrection with Christ is repeatedly celebrated in every individual throughout time - whenever this truth is discovered in human history. Colossians 3:1-3.*

> *[2] He brought to naught the law of works; καταργηση ²katargēsē, is the Aorist Subjunctive of **katargeō**, which indicates a definite outcome that happens as a result of another stated action, [in Christ all are made alive]. The word **katargeō**, with **kata**, down, and **argos**, rendered useless; from **a**, as a negative particle and **ergon**, toil, labor; thus, inactive, that is, unemployed; useless; thus the entire system of performance, to improve what God has already perfected in Christ, is brought to naught.*

*[3] All principalities, ³**archē**, or chief ranks, i.e. kings or governors; this includes any governing system whereby one is ranked above the other on the basis of their performance or preference.*

*[4] All authority, ⁴**exousia**, comes from ek, denoting origin and **eimi**, I am; in this case, because of what I can do I am defined by what I can do better than you; therefore, I have authority over you.*

*[5] Every dynamic influence in society, ⁵**dunamis**, means power, in this case, willpower. Every government structure in society will be brought under the dominion of grace where the Christ-life rules.*

See 1 Corinthians 2:7-8, We voice words of wisdom that were hidden in silence for timeless ages; a mystery unfolding God's Masterful plan whereby he would redeem his glory in man. Neither the politicians nor the theologians of the day had a clue about this mystery [of mankind's association in Christ]; if they did, they would never have crucified the Lord whose death redeemed our glory.

The kingdom of God is the authority of the Christ-life in ordinary, day to day life, where righteousness is based on who we are and not on who we are trying to impress. The law of works is duty and guilt driven, whereas the law of faith is love driven. Romans 3:27, Galatians 5:6. Also 2 Corinthians 10:12 When they measure themselves by one another, competing and comparing, they are without understanding.)

2:16 Do not let anyone therefore bring a restriction to your freedom by reviving religious rules and regulations pertaining to eating and drinking; also, all Jewish festivals, new moons, and Sabbaths have come to an end in Christ. *(Their relevance only served to remind of the promise of Christ on an annual, monthly, and weekly basis. They carried the promise like a placenta would hold the unborn child, but became obsolete as soon as the child was born.)*

2:17 These things were only prophetic shadows; Christ is the substance.

2:18 A religious mentality of voluntary humility and obsession with pious observances of celestial 'beings' will bring you no further reward. So do not let anyone who tries to act as an umpire of your devotion insist on his own opinion, confined to a mind inflated by the sensational and spooky; his so-called visions are just a puff of hot air. *(In his judgment he fails to correctly interpret the legal implications of the Cross.*

Don't tolerate people who try to run your life, ordering you to bow and scrape, [in order to improve your standing before God] insisting that you join their obsession with angels and that you seek out visions. They're a lot of hot air, that's all they are. — The Message.)

2:19 Such religious jargon is completely out of rhythm with the head. You are directly connected to Christ who like a ¹choir conductor draws out the music in everyone like a tapestry of art that intertwines in harmony to reveal the full stature of divine inspiration. *(Which is Christ in you. The word, ¹**epichoregeō**, is choir director. [See 2 Peter 1:11] Thus, the great Conductor of music will draw your life into the full volume of the harmony of the ages.)*

2:20 If it is true that you were included in Christ's death, then the religious systems of this world with its rules and regulations no longer apply to you.

What further relevance would there be for you to continue to live under the influence of mankind's doctrines and ideas?

2:21 Things like: Do not associate with this one, or Do not taste that, or Do not even touch this with your finger.

2:22 These instructions are of no permanent value in any case since they refer to things that perish after it is consumed, thus they leave no lasting impact in your life. So do not let man-made menus cause you to major on minors. *(Jesus said it is not what goes into the mouth that matters, but what comes out of the heart.)*

2:23 Religious tradition appears to be very devout and its followers seem to be so humble and holy in their strict observance of rules that seek to control the behavior of the body. The only problem with this is that the flesh is never permanently satisfied. *(The Message translates verses 19-23 as: They're completely out of touch with the source of life, Christ, who puts us together in one piece, whose very breath and blood flow through us. He is the Head and we are the body. We can grow up healthy in God only as he nourishes us. So, then, if with Christ you've put all that pretentious and infantile religion behind you, why do you let yourselves be bullied by it? Don't touch this. Don't taste that. Don't go near this. Do you think things that are here today and gone tomorrow are worth that kind of attention? Such things sound impressive if said in a deep enough voice. They even give the illusion of being pious and humble and ascetic.)*

3:1 See yourselves co-raised with Christ. Now ponder with persuasion the consequence of your co-inclusion in him. Relocate yourselves mentally. Engage your thoughts with throne room realities where you are co-seated with Christ in the executive authority of God's right hand.

3:2 Becoming affectionately acquainted with throne room thoughts will keep you from being distracted again by the earthly [soul-ruled] realm. *(Set your minds upon the things that are above and not upon the things below. RSV. Whatever you face in your daily lives, acquaint yourselves with the greater reality. The things that are above. Do not engage the energy of the things that are below. Also note Romans 1:18, where the word **katechō** is used - to echo downwards is the opposite to **anochē**, to echo upward- Romans 2:4 and Romans 3:26. Also 2 Corinthians 4:18 We are not keeping any score of what seems so obvious to the senses on the surface; it is fleeting and irrelevant; it is the unseen eternal realm within us which has our full attention and captivates our gaze. A renewed mind conquers the space previously occupied by worthless pursuits and habits. See my notes on Earthbound vs. Heavenly Dimension Realities at the end of Revelation Chapter 16.)*

3:3 Your union with his death broke the association with that world; see yourselves located in a fortress where your life is hidden with Christ in God. *(In that day you will know that I am in my father, and you in me and I in you. [John 14:20] Occupy your mind with this new order of life; you died when Jesus died; whatever defined you before defines you no more. Christ, in whom the fullness of deity dwells, defines you now. The word, hidden can also be translated, secret; the secret of your life is your union with Christ in God. [See Colossians 2:9, 10]*

Risen, then, with Christ you must lift your thoughts above where Christ now sits at the right hand of God, you must be heavenly minded; not earthly minded, you have undergone death, and your life is hidden away now with Christ in God. Christ is your life, when he is made manifest you are made manifest in his glory. — Knox Translation.)

3:4 The unveiling of Christ, as defining our lives, [1]immediately implies that, what is evident in him, is equally mirrored in you. The exact life on exhibit in Christ is now repeated in us. We are included in the same bliss and joined-oneness with him; just as his life reveals you, your life reveals him. *(This verse was often translated to again delay the revelation of Christ to a future event. The word, [1]otan, often translated as when is better translated as every time. Thus, Every time Christ is revealed we are being co-revealed in his glory. According to the Walter Bauer Lexicon, **otan** is often used for an action that is repeated. Paul declares our joint-glorification in Christ. We are co-revealed in the same bliss. [See 1 Corinthians 2:7-8, Romans 3:23-24, Romans 8:30, 2 Peter 1:3.] In him we live and move and have our being; in us he lives and moves and has his being. Acts 17:28.)*

3:5 Consider the members of your body as dead and buried towards everything related to the porn industry, sensual uncleanness, longing for forbidden things, lust and greed, which are just another form of idol worship. *(Idol worship is worshipping a distorted image of yourself.)*

3:6 These distorted expressions are in total contradiction to God's design and [1]desire for your life. *(The word [1]orgē, associated with wrath or punishment* *is from **oregomai**, to stretch oneself out, to reach out, to long for, to desire. The sentence, upon the sons of unbelief [Greek word, ἀπείθεια Lit. without faith]; or as the KJV translates it, sons of disobedience, was added later in some manuscripts.)*

3:7 We were all once swept along into a lifestyle of lust and greed.

3:8 But now, because you realize that you co-died and were co-raised together with Christ, you can flush your thoughts with truth. Permanently put these things behind you: things such as violent outbursts of rage, depression, all manner of wickedness, ¹slander and every form of irregular conversation. *(The lifelong association with sin is broken; the dominion of the character of God is revealed again in ordinary life. The word ¹**blasphemos** means any attempt to belittle someone else and to cause someone to receive a bad reputation.)*

3:9 That old life was a lie, foreign to our design. Its ¹worn-out garments of disguise are now thoroughly stripped off us in our understanding of our union with Christ in his death and resurrection. We are no longer obliged to live under ²the identity and rule of the robes we wore before, nor are we cheating one another through false pretensions. *([1] The word, παλαιός **palaiós** means tattered with age; wear and tear. [2] The garments actors would wear define their part in the play but do not define them.)*

3:10 You are clothed in the knowledge of the authentic, yet brand new, you! Your thoughts are permeated in our co-resurrection and co-enthroned, royal life! Instead of the old, worn-out garments of pretense - there is a freshness about you which continues to sparkle with newness! Just like the beautiful blossoms on a tree, regardless of the age of the tree, so we continue to mirror the unfading, imperishable pattern of the exact image of our Creator. *(This was Caleb's secret, I am eighty-five years old. I am still as strong to this day as I was on the day that Moses sent me when I was forty years old; my strength now is as my strength was then. Give me this hill country with its giants and fortified cities! And Joshua gave him Hebron, which later became known as became the city of priests. Joshua 14:10,11; 21:11; - also, Isaiah 40:31, The young athletes become weary and exhausted, but they who **entwine** their eyes with Papa's eyes renew their strength; they mount up with wings like eagles! Which is exactly what the word קוה **Kawa** in Hebrew means See my comment in verse 22 here in Colossians 3.)*

3:11 The revelation of Christ in us gives identity to the individual beyond anything anyone could ever be as a Greek or a Jew, American or African, foreigner or famous, male or female, king or pawn. From now on everyone is defined by Christ; everyone is represented in him. *(In seeing him not just recorded in history but revealed in us, we re-discover the face of our birth as in a mirror. James 1:18.)*

3:12 You are the product of God's love; you are restored to their original thought. You are innocent and whole. It is like changing garments. The old person you thought you were is taken out of the equation. Sink into this beautiful new person, as into an exquisite, tailor-made garment, delicately embroidered with inner compassion, kindness, humility, gentleness and patience, *(Just like you were once identified by your apparel, the characteristics of these qualities now define you.)*

3:13 upholding one another in positive expectation. If anyone finds fault with another, restore that person to favor, remembering how the Lord's forgiveness has transformed our lives.

3:14 Wear love like a uniform; this is what completes the picture of our oneness.

3:15 Appoint the peace of Christ as umpire in your hearts. We are all identified in the same person; there is only one body. We are born to be a blessing and exhibit his benevolence.

3:16 [1]Welcome home the [2]clarity and genius of everything that God is saying to humanity in Christ. He is [3]the language of God's logic. The consciousness of our co-resurrection and joint-seatedness in the throne room have taken up permanent residence in you; allow its [4]magnificence to permeate your entire being. Celebrate God. Continue to [5]instruct one another with [6]inspired thoughts; making music on stringed instruments, [7]singing psalms, [8]celebration testimonies, poems and [9]spirit infused songs. This makes your fellowship an environment of edification in an atmosphere of music. Every lesson is a reminder, [10]echoing in the songs you sing. From this rich reservoir of the heart, the nuances of grace in the Lord are beautifully articulated.

([1] The word, [1]*enoikeitō* is the Present Active Imperative, welcome home; give the word of Christ permanent residence in you; the Present Stem of the Greek Verb has the sense of continuous action.

[2] Then, ἐν πάσῃ σοφία referring to the full effect of the indwelling word, in all [2]*sophia*, wisdom/clarity.

[3] The [3]*logos*; the word - see John 1:1 the eternal conversation; incarnate in Christ.

[4] The Adverb, πλουσίως [4]*plousiōs*, the permeating richness; overflowing abundance and magnificence.

[5] The Present Active Participle form of the verbs διδάσκω, to teach [[5]*didaskontes*] to emphasize a continual or habitual teaching;

[6] and νουθετέω [6]*noutheteō* to engage thought; also in the Present Active [*nouthetountes*] thus, to continually bring to mind.

[7] The word [7]*psalmos*, here refers to the prophetic Psalms celebrating the Messiah. Its verb form, ψάλλω *psallō*, means to touch; as in touching or plucking the strings; thus raving about the Messiah in praise and worship accompanied by musical instruments.

[8] The word [8]*humnos* suggests a celebration in song - a testimony song. In the Greek tradition, it is a song in the praise of gods, heroes and conquerors, from hudeō - to celebrate.

[9] An [9]*ōdē en pneumatikos* is a spirit infused chant or song. According to Jewish custom, as recorded in Nehemiah 8:8 "And they read from the book, from the law of God, clearly; and they gave the sense, so that the people understood the reading." Now, Paul connects the tradition of cantillation ["singing to speech"] with a new context: where you once chanted the Torah, now sing grace songs. "Cantillation serves to bring home to the listener the interrelation and coordination of the words used by the speaker. In order to appreciate the delicate shade of meaning conveyed. [Wickes]

[10] ἐν χάριτι ἄδοντες [10]*en chariti adontes* [grace inspired songs] ἐν τῇ καρδίᾳ ὑμῶν τῷ Κυρίῳ, making melody in your hearts to celebrate the grace of the Lord.)

3:17 Your every conversation and the detail of your daily conduct reflect him; his name and Lordship define your lives and inspire your deep gratitude to God the Father for his grace.

3:18 His peace is the umpire of your every relationship, especially in the family. Wives, place yourselves in the intimate care of your husbands, acknowledging the lordship of Christ in them.

3:19 Husbands, love your wives tenderly. Do not exasperate them.

3:20 Children, you display the Christ-life in the way you respond to your parents, keep them glowing with joy, they reflect God's delight in you.

3:21 Parents are responsible for the atmosphere at home; avoid vibes that dampen the child's spirit. *(Parents, don't come down too hard on your children or you'll crush their spirits. The Message.)*

3:22 If you are employed by someone, even having to work like a slave, remember your hearts are [1]intertwined in devotion to God. Don't just look busy when you are being watched, show the same diligence behind your boss's back. *(The word, [1]haplotēs, from ha, particle of union [hama], together with + plekō, meaning to plait, braid, weave together. See Luke 11:34 The eye is the lamp of the body; if the eye is single the whole body is full of light. Entwining our eyes with Papa's eyes is what enlightens our entire being. Which is exactly what the word קוה Kawa in Hebrew means in Isaiah 40:31 they that entwine with the Lord's thoughts mount up with wings like eagles. We are wired by design to entwine.)*

3:23 Whatever you do, picture Christ in the person you are doing it for; it makes such a difference when you put your heart into it.

3:24 God is no-one's debtor; you are employed under the Lordship of Christ.

3:25 Even those who live [1]contrary to their shared likeness, and in the process injure themselves and others; they are now taken care of and [2]shepherded away from their out of syncness. Everyone is equally valued; your job description does not define you; it doesn't matter who you are.

(See verse 13. If anyone finds fault with another, restore that person to favor, remembering how the Lord's forgiveness has transformed our lives.

[1] The word, [1]adikea meaning unrighteous; out of sync with likeness - the Particle a, negative/not, and the word, dikeo, two parties sharing likeness.

[2] The word, κομισηται [2]komisētai is the Aorist Subjunctive of kolumbaō, which means to tend, to take care of, to provide for, to carry off from harm. It indicates a definite outcome that happens as a result of another stated action, [in Christ all are made alive. 2 Corinthians 5:10]

See Ephesians chapters 2 as well as 6:1-12 in parallel to these thoughts of Paul in Colossians 3.

Ephesians 6:9 If you're the boss, love's initiative applies to you on exactly the same terms; the way you treat your slaves with respect rather than threats, even when they do stupid things clears the air immediately. Take it from your heavenly Master; he does not judge people or circumstances on face value.

4:1 If you are the boss, treat those who work for you in the light of their equality in Christ; he treats you like that and he is the big Boss in the spiritual realm. *(This verse concludes the thought in 3:25 and should rather be part of the previous chapter. Paul did not write in chapters and verses.)*

4:2 Persist in prevailing prayer. Be attentive and sensitive *[to the voice of the Spirit; do not be over-occupied with prayers for yourself and your own needs].* Grace and gratitude is the language of prayer.

4:3 At the same time remember me in your prayers. Pray that what God has in me would impact many with the revelation of the mystery of Christ far beyond the walls of this prison cell. The confines of this prison do not measure my ministry; the message of the mystery of Christ in me does. *(Colossians 1:25-29.)*

4:4 My sincere desire is that my message will accurately unveil the mystery of Christ in its most complete context. You. This is the mission of my life. *(Ephesians 3:9)*

4:5 Do not spoil your chances to touch others with the word through a lack of wisdom. Even though they may seem to be outside, your attitude towards them will reveal to them how inside they in fact are. Redeem the time by making the most of every opportunity. *(Time only finds its relevance in redemption-realities.)*

4:6 Season your conversation with grace. This remains the most attractive and appropriate option to respond in every situation.

4:7 Tychicus will tell you all the news about me. He is my colleague and such a lovely brother whose ministry is distinguished by integrity.

4:8 I commissioned him to come to you in this capacity, to cross-pollinate between us, so that you may also be encouraged and comforted by him.

4:9 Onēsimos, who originally comes from your area, will join him. He is a beloved and faithful brother. They will represent us with you.

4:10 Aristarchus, my fellow prisoner, greets you warmly; so does Mark, the son of Barnabas's sister. Remember I told you to give him a special welcome when he comes to you.

4:11 Then there is also Jesus, some call him Justus. These three brethren, originally Jews by faith, are my close companions and co-laborers for the Kingdom of God.

4:12 Epahras, who is also fruit of your ministry, salutes you. What a diligent worker of Christ he is, always laboring on your behalf with great intensity in his prayers. His desire for you is to stand strong in the full accomplishment of Christ and to be fully persuaded in God's purpose for your lives.

4:13 I can tell you that he has a real passion for your welfare, as well as for the believers in Laodicea and Hierapolis.

4:14 The dear doctor Luke greets you and so does Demas.

4:15 Please extend our greetings to the brethren in Laodicea and also to Nymphas and the ekklesia in her house.

4:16 Make sure that the ekklesia at Laodicea also gets the opportunity to read this epistle and that you again read the letter I wrote to them.

4:17 Archippus, I want you to be diligent to fulfill the ministry you have received in the Lord.

4:18 I, Paul, write this greeting with my own hand. You must remember my bonds. God's grace is yours.

This letter to the Thessalonians was probably the first of Paul's letters. It is not possible to say exactly when Paul appeared before Gallio, but Acts 18:12–18 suggests that this happened shortly after Gallio assumed office, probably towards the end of Paul's eighteen months in the city. It is likely that 1 Thessalonians was written shortly after Paul's arrival in Corinth. It may therefore be dated in the early part of 51 or 50 if the earlier dating of Gallio's assumption of office is preferred, making it *the first written book in the New Testament.*

Macedonia was organized as a Roman province in 146 B.C. Thessalonica was made the seat of government and was fondly called the Mother of all Macedon. Thessalonica, named after the stepsister of Alexander the Great, may have had as many as 200 000 people in Paul's day. It stood on the Via Egnatia, the Roman highway to the East and proved a very strategic location for an ekklesia-church. Also ideally situated for trade, Thessalonica attracted a community of Jews, which Luke notices by his reference to the synagogue Acts17:1

The following verses sum up Paul's heart toward the Thessalonians: For our appeal to you was from a place of union, a place of seamless oneness where distance or any definition of distraction of subtle hidden agendas were eliminated. *(The word, [1]parakaleō, comes from para, a Preposition indicating close proximity, a thing proceeding from a sphere of influence, with a suggestion of union of place of residence, to have sprung from its author and giver, originating from, denoting the point from which an action originates, intimate connection; and kaleō, meaning to identify by name, to surname.)* In God's [1]esteem of us, we were entrusted with this wonderful announcement: the gospel. Our conversation is prompted by God's approval of us which might not be very popular with the typical religious mindset. *(The word [1]dokimatsō, is from the word dokeō, to form an opinion, to estimate.)* Come on, you should know better than that. How could you possibly suspect us of setting you up with [1]smooth talk when all we were really after was your money and your vote? God knows that we would never disadvantage you. *(The Gospel does not flatter the religious ear because there is no ground left for boasting in personal achievement. Gift-language disarms reward-language. The word, [1]kolakeia means flattery.)* We were not even fishing for compliments from you or anyone else for that matter. We would never pull rank on you as commissioners of Christ. Instead we were fostering you with the tender care of a mother nursing her children. It is with this same motherly affection that we yearn for you and were delighted to present you God's gospel gift-wrapped in us, since you are so very dear to us. 1 Thessalonians 2:3-8

2 Thessalonians is the most doubted book in the Pauline Epistles. Some would argue that the linguistic features of this letter show far too much deviation from Paul's normal style. In particular, a few years back, Daryl D. Schmidt of Texas Christian University read a paper on the linguistic features of 2 Thessalonians at a Society of Biblical Literature meeting, arguing this very point. His conclusion was that this letter was not genuine.

1:1 Paul, Silvanus and Timothy greet the ekklesia-church in the region of Thessalonica with grace and peace from God our Father and the Lord Jesus Christ. *(The [1]Ekklesia-church, refers to those who have discovered their original identity, redeemed in Christ. From ek, origin and kaleō, to surname, to identify by name. The mission of Jesus through his ekklesia-church is to persuade the world of their true sonship: the son of man is the son of God. The gates of the Hadēs-blindfold will not prevail! Matthew 16:13-18. Also Psalm 22:27; Isaiah 40:5; 2Corinthians 3:18.)*

1:2 You feature so prominently in our prayers and conversation which is always marked with the gentle cheerfulness of a grateful heart to God.

1:3 We fondly remember the testimony of your faith which is so evident in your day to day lives in your love labor, even through many difficult times, and the cheerful constancy of the very hope that our Lord Jesus Christ personifies, in whom we enjoy the immediate presence of our Papa God. *(In sharp contrast to a duty-and guilt driven rule, Paul mentions their faith inspired work and their love inspired labor. Paul understands that love ignites faith. Galatians 5:6.)*

1:4 Beloved friends, you have come to understand that you are [1]God's idea to begin with. *(The word [1]ekloge has traditionally been translated and interpreted as election, which led to the illusion that some are in and some are out, by God's intent. However, the Preposition ek, always denotes source or origin and legō points to the authentic thought, the logos that John refers to in John 1:1 &14.)*

1:5 Our [1]gospel [2]birthed in you so much more than mere intellectual reasoning; your encounter bore witness to the dynamic of the Holy Spirit as you became thoroughly [3]permeated with [1]the well done announcement and [4]perceived within yourselves the full impact of our immediate influence. *(The gospel, [1]euaggellion, is the well done announcement. The word [2]ginomai, means to cause to be, to become. The word [3]plerophoria means to be permeated. The word [4]eidō means to see, to perceive. See Titus 3:5.)*

1:6 In [1]embracing the word as your own, even in the midst of great contradiction, the [2]mirror likeness of the Lord reflected in us was ignited in you with the joy of the Holy Spirit. *(The word [1]dechomai means to to receive favorably, give ear to, embrace, make one's own, approve. The word [2]mimetes, means to imitate or mirror.)*

1:7 And so the story unfolds; your lives came to be the very mirror, modeling the Christ-life and endorsing the faith of everyone throughout Macedonia and Achaia.

1:8 The word of the Lord found such an articulate voice in you and resounded forth to reach regions far beyond you. Not only in your immediate provinces, but in every place your faith concludes in a face to face encounter with God. You are the message. We need not say anything. *(The Greek Preposition pros, indicates direction, forward to; that is toward the destination of the relation. Face-to-face is the conclusion.)*

1:9 Others from these provinces testify of this; they recall how our visit to you has greatly influenced your lives to return to God and now, instead of being absorbed by the imaginary illusions of idolatry you are engaged with God unveiled in real life.

1:10 And all along you remain focused on the Son of God who reveals our joint-origin in the heavenlies. He endorsed our redeemed innocence in his resurrection. He has [1]drawn us to himself and rescued us from every definition of judgment. *(The word [1]rhuomai, means to draw to oneself, to rescue, to deliver.)*

2:1 I am sure that the [1]content of the gospel is clear to you ever since our first contact with you dear friends. *(The word [1]kenos, empty, means that our visit was not in vain.)*

2:2 As you know, the many things we suffered before, and even the way we were abused in Philippi, did not intimidate or distract us in any way. We were very bold in our God to communicate the news of what he has so wonderfully accomplished in Christ, in the face of much contradiction. *(The Greek word for the Good News is the word [1]euangelion, which is the well done announcement. It is the news of what God has so wonderfully accomplished. The gospel is a declaration. We have made it an 'if-then' proposition. But the 'if-then' proposition is a catch 22 situation; which is a 'no-win' dilemma or paradox. Often these situations are such that solving one part of a problem only creates another, which ultimately leads back to the original problem. A situation in which a desired outcome or solution is impossible to attain because of a set of inherently illogical rules or conditions. For so long evangelism has been beg, coerce, bribe or scare, now it is no longer telling people what they must do but what God has done and believes about them.)*

2:3 For our appeal to you was from a place of union, a place of seamless oneness where distance or any definition of distraction of subtle hidden agendas were eliminated. *(The word, [1]parakaleō, comes from para, a Preposition indicating close proximity, a thing proceeding from a sphere of influence, with a suggestion of union of place of residence, to have sprung from its author and giver, originating from, denoting the point from which an action originates, intimate connection; and kaleō, meaning to identify by name, to surname.)*

2:4 In God's [1]esteem of us, we were entrusted with this wonderful announcement: the gospel. Our conversation is prompted by God's approval of us which might not be very popular with the typical religious mindset. *(The word [1]dokimatsō, is from the word dokeō, to form an opinion, to estimate.)*

2:5 Come on, you should know better than that. How could you possibly suspect us of setting you up with [1]smooth talk when all we were really after was your money and your vote? God knows that we would never disadvantage you. *(The Gospel does not flatter the religious ear because there is no ground left for boasting in personal achievement. Gift-language disarms reward-language. The word, [1]kolakeia means flattery.)*

2:6 We were not even fishing for compliments from you or anyone else for that matter. We would never pull rank on you as commissioners of Christ.

2:7 Instead we were fostering you with the tender care of a mother nursing her children.

2:8 It is with this same motherly affection that we yearn for you and were delighted to present you God's gospel gift-wrapped in us, since you are so very dear to us. *(The word, [1]metadidomi, translates as the kind of giving where the giver is not distanced from the gift but wrapped up in it. The Apostles, Prophets, preachers, pastors, and teachers are gifts to the ekklesia to establish them in their faith and to present everyone in the full and mature stature of Christ*

[Ephesians 4:11-16]. There is such a vast difference between a gift and a reward. We are God's gifts to one another. What God now has in us is gift-wrapped to the world. What we are in our individual expression is a gift and not a reward for personal diligence or achievement. These gifts were never meant to establish one above the other, or to become mere formal titles, but rather to identify specific and dynamic functions with one defined purpose, to bring everyone into the realization of the fullness of the measure of Christ in them.)

2:9 I don't have to remind you to what extreme extent we were prepared to go in our efforts to bring you God's gospel at no expense to you at all. We kept going night and day, both teaching you as well as actively trading in the marketplace.

2:10 We behaved with utmost integrity and courtesy; making absolutely sure that we gave no offense to disappoint your faith. We have nothing to hide. God knows we had no ulterior motives.

2:11 Just like a father would instruct his children, so we engage ourselves with you to remind you of your origin in God,

2:12 ¹inspiring you to live in the ²daily awareness of your true value and ³identity. In God's opinion you are royalty. *(The word ¹paramutheomai, inspired from within to live the life of your design. To ²walk worthy, axios; having the weight of another thing of like value, to be worth as much. ³Your calling or vocation, from kaleō, to ²surname, to identify by name.)*

2:13 The way in which you joined yourselves to the word that we taught is such a constant source of gratitude to us; you immediately knew that this was not mere human opinion, but you took a hold of our message as the very logic of God, and so the truth energizes you from within, endorsing your faith.

2:14 You mirror those who have likewise discovered their original identity in Christ as God's ¹Ekklesia in Judea. You suffered persecution from your own people just as they did from the Jews. *(The traditions and cultures that defined people historically are challenged by the ¹church, the ekklesia of God which is the revelation of the original identity of mankind now declared and redeemed in Christ.)*

2:15 They killed their own Prophets as well as their Messiah, the Lord Jesus, and drove us out of their midst as if they were doing God a favor. Instead they have become enemies of the entire human race.

2:16 They sought to ¹intimidate us in order to dwarf our message into insignificance, hoping to prevent us from declaring to the nations their salvation. Their ²distorted behavior has come full circle. They have proved to themselves to be their own worst enemy. Their ³passion to oppose the message has become their judgment. *(¹kōluō , to prevent, from kolatzō, to dwarf. The word sin, is the word ²hamartia, from ha, negative or without and meros, portion or form, thus to be without your allotted portion or without form, pointing to a disoriented, distorted, bankrupt identity; the word meros, is the stem of morphē, as in 2 Corinthians 3:18 the word metamorphē, with form, which is the opposite of* **hamartia** *- without form. Sin is to live out of context with the blueprint of one's design; to behave out of tune with God's original harmony. Hamartia suggests anything that could possibly distract from the awareness of our likeness. See Deuteronomy 32:18, You have forgotten the Rock that begot you and have gotten out of step with the God who danced with you. Hebrew,* חול **khul**, *also means to dance, as in Judges 21:21. By killing their own Prophets and their Messiah and now seeking to prevent the spreading of the gospel to the nations, they are opposing the very promise of their patriarch Abraham in whom God has blessed all the nations of the earth. The word* [3]**orge**, *associated with wrath or punishment is from* **oregomai,** *to stretch oneself, to reach out, to long for, to desire, to experience the excitement of the mind.)*

2:17 We were only briefly separated from you in person but never in our hearts. This has caused us to yearn with greater expectancy to see you face to face again.

2:18 On two occasions I was restrained from coming to you. *(Luke mentions two occasions when they were restrained by the Holy Spirit not to go into an area for their own safety, Acts 16:6, Acts 16:7. Maybe the mention of Satan here in 1 Thessalonians 2:18 was in reference to the messenger of Satanas who frustrated Paul with the thorn in the flesh he mentions in 2 Corinthians 12 before he learned to deal with a defeated Devil by the understanding of his sufficiency and authority in grace. The thorns on Jesus' head broke the curse associated with the thorn in the flesh. I am also of the opinion that maybe the reference to Satan was added later when it became a popular excuse to blame the Devil when things did not seem to go according to plan.)*

2:19 We expect nothing less in the context of the gospel than you enjoying a face to face encounter in the [1]immediate presence of our Lord Jesus Christ. This is our delight and wreath of honor. *(The word* [1]**parousia** *speaks of the immediate presence of the Lord. From* **para**, *a Preposition indicating closest possible proximity; intimate connection; and* **eimi**, *I am. There is not even a hint of judgment or punishment in this word. While there are great and accurate definitions in Strongs, please do not believe everything you read there. G3952 parousia from the Present Participle of G3918 [**pareimi**]; a being near, that is, advent; often, return; specifically of Christ to punish Jerusalem, or finally the wicked.!?*

The Greek word **parousia**, *occurs 24 times in the NT, and 22 times it wrongly implies a 2nd coming or coming judgment. Only twice it is translated as presence. 2 Corinthians 10:10, Philippians 2:12. Of all the English translations that I have checked, only the Young's Literal has it correct. What a shame that this word has been so dramatically twisted over the years.*

In the Greek Septuagint Psalm 138:8 [in the Hebrew Psalm 139] reads, If I make my bed in Hadēs, your presence already fills it. LXX - πάρειμι **pareimi** *your immediate presence - I am.*

See Extended notes on **parousia** *at the end of Hebrews chapter 9.)*

2:20 You are our trophy and joy.

3:1 We could not bear being separated from you and since it did not seem possible for me to visit you personally any time soon, we determined to send Timothy to you in the meantime whilst I remained behind in Athens.

3:2 He is such a dear brother and minister of God; my colleague in the Good News of what Christ accomplished. His mission was to strengthen you and to establish you in your spirit identity and belief.

3:3 He was to make sure that none of you is shaken by these pressure times that somehow inevitably seem to lie in our way.

3:4 When we were with you, we told you that we were to often face fierce contradictions, just as you have indeed witnessed it for yourselves. *(The religious and traditional systems of this world will always feel threatened by what the gospel communicates, since your freedom means that they can no longer abuse you with fear and sin-consciousness.)*

3:5 It was most urgent then for me to get first-hand feedback from Timothy regarding your faith, since I know how temptation would scrutinize you and attempt to nullify what we have labored for in you.

3:6 So you can imagine how the wonderful news of your faith and love blessed us. Timothy returned with the happy tidings of how affectionately you remember me and also long to see me, even as I yearn for you.

3:7 We share such a constant bond in our oneness in Christ. Your faith greatly impacts and comforts us in our affliction and hard times.

3:8 Your strong standing in the Lord gives us such zest for life.

3:9 We cannot thank God enough for you. We dance with delight before him because of you.

3:10 You are constantly in our prayers, night and day; oh, how we long to see you face to face and thoroughly establish you in every area of your faith.

3:11 The God and Father of our Lord Jesus Christ will himself make a way for us to visit you.

3:12 We can already see how the Lord causes the love we have for you to dynamically impact each of you and burst its banks to flood the entire world.

3:13 The [1]dominion of the Christ-life establishes you in blameless innocence, face to face before our God and Father, in the constant awareness of his [2]presence in our mutual togetherness with all the saints. *(The subject of the sentence is the Lord Jesus Christ from the previous verse. His lordship endorses the reign of the Christ-life in us. Again the word **parousia** is translated in all other translations [Except YLT] as second coming. See my note in previous chapter, 2:19.)*

4:1 Finally then friends, we would earnestly implore you to mirror the walk which we share in this bond of oneness in the Lord Jesus. Live your lives fully in the delight of God.

4:2 For you are acquainted with the fact that Jesus Christ is the [1]source of our message. *(The word [1]paraggelia, from para, a Preposition indicating close proximity, a thing proceeding from a sphere of influence, with a suggestion of union of place of residence, to have sprung from its author and giver, originating from, denoting the point from which an action originates, intimate connection; and angellos, to announce.)*

4:3 The resolve of God declares you innocent; this announcement frees you from fornication. *(The resolve of God is declared in his accomplished redemption of the life of our design in Christ. Fornication is a form of idolatry, which is to be engaged with a distorted image of yourself. It is to be obsessed with something that you feel you must have in order to complete you. Just like Eve was attracted to eat the fruit of the I-am-not-tree.)*

4:4 Each of you marrying a wife should do so with the utmost dignity and intimate care. And remember, the vessel takes its value from the treasure it holds. *(The word timay means to highly esteem and honor. See 2 Corinthians 4:7.)*

4:5 To be lust-driven is typical of people who do not realize how complete they already are in God. *(The word, epithumia, means, to desire what is forbidden with an all-consuming longing.)*

4:6 In all of your dealings with one another, whether in business or the mere day-to-day domestic and social matters, live [1]from the persuasion of your mutual likeness, just as we have given testimony to and instructed you in the revelation of the Lord's righteousness. *(The word [1]ekdikē is traditionally, sadly, often associated with judgment and punishment. However the two components of this word are the Preposition ek, which always points to source or origin, and dikē, suggesting to be judged equal; it implies the idea of two parties finding likeness in each other. This is also the stem of the word for righteousness, dikaiosunē. The revelation of Paul's gospel declares how God succeeded in Christ to cancel all grounds for separation, hostility, inferiority and condemnation and how God's faith redeemed our blameless oneness. See Romans 1:17. The gospel is the happy announcement of the finished work of Christ and not a new compromised set of rules. Many traditional translations and interpretations do not distinguish between the deadly duty-driven law of self-effort and the life giving love-driven law of faith. Romans 3:27.)*

4:7 By design, God [1]defines you wholly separated unto him. Sin is not who you are. *(The word [1]kaleō means to surname, to identify by name.)*

4:8 This is not to be regarded lightly as mere good advice, since God has given us his Holy Spirit endorsing our holiness unto him, just as he has separated himself unto us.

4:9 I need not even write to you about your fondness for one another since the love of God is best taught by him within.

4:10 I know your affection for your fellow family throughout Macedonia. From this place of our close union in our [1]common origin we anticipate the ever [2]increasing impact of love's irresistible impression. *(Our common origin, [1]parakaleō; The word, [2]perisseuō means to super-abound.)*

4:11 Cultivate the [1]highest esteem for that which is of value and honor; [2]cease from striving; mind your own business and give whatever you do your personal touch. These practical instructions are all part and parcel of the same [3]source as our constant sphere of influence. *(The beautiful word [1]philotemeomai, means to have a fondness for value and honor. The word [2]hesuchatzo means to rest and to cease from striving. See commentary note on the word [3]paraggelia in verse 2.)*

4:12 Always maintain a good attitude towards those who still see themselves as outside of your company; do not hint for favors, echo completeness.

4:13 I do not want you to be ignorant concerning those who seem to be fast asleep in their indifference and unbelief. There is no need for you to grieve as if they are beyond hope. *(See 1 Corinthians 15:51 [1]Ponder this mystery, I want to show you something that you have never seen before: [2]everyone will awaken out of sleep; we will [3]all experience exactly the same change. Look. A Mystery - [1]idou musterion; [2]pantes ou koimethesometha, means no one will sleep; [3]pantes de allangesometha; everyone will be changed.)*

4:14 We believe that Jesus died and rose again, and that he fully represents and includes even those who have not awoken unto him yet. God will [1]lead them to realize that they are indeed in him. *(The word [1]agō means to lead as a shepherd leads his sheep. See 1 Corinthians 1:30, Ephesians 1:4.)*

4:15 We give voice to the word of the Lord; we are God's wake-up call to them that are asleep. We are exhibiting the [1]immediate tangible presence of the Lord and shall not [2]exclude them. *(The word [1]parousia means immediate presence. See my comment in 1 Thessalonians 2:19. See the use of the word [2]phthanō, to prevent, to hinder or exclude, also in 2 Corinthians 10:14, Our ministry to you is proof that there are no geographic limitations which could possibly exclude you from the gospel of Jesus Christ. See also 1 Thessalonians 3:12, We can already see how the Lord causes the love we have for you to dynamically impact each of you and burst its banks to flood the entire world. The people who dwelt in darkness have seen a great light. The true light that enlightens everyone has come. And the glory of the Lord shall be revealed and all flesh shall see it together.)*

4:16 *(There remains no disconnect between those who are dead and those who are alive; everyone will encounter the great awakening, where the invisible meets the visible.)* In their awakening, the dead will all, first-hand witness the Lord stepping out of the invisible heavenly realm into their immediate visible horizon with an inciting shout, announcing his triumphant reign in the trumpet-like billowing voice of God.

4:17 In the wake of their arising, we will all be gathered into a large dense multitude of an innumerable throng of people, united as one, like the particles of water in a cloud, and we will encounter the Lord in the very air we breathe and so shall we continually celebrate our I-am-ness in our union with him. *(All flesh shall see his glory together - ultimately every single one will realize that Deity and humanity are married - the Bride and her Groom are united.*

See Revelation 5:13 At that point the entire universe burst out in praise. I heard every created being in the heavenly realm and upon the earth and under the earth and upon the ocean and everything within all these spheres, declaring to the One seated upon the throne and to the Lamb: The most [1]articulate language, the admiration, the supreme magnificence, the might until the ages of the ages. [The word ¹eulogia, from eu, good, well done, and logos; thus, polished language; such language which is artfully adapted to captivate the hearer: fair speaking, fine speeches.]

Also, Revelation 7:9 At this moment I saw a massive throng of people, impossible to count, standing tall and innocent - all of them ¹dressed in white with palm branches in their hands; they had ²escaped everything that could possibly define them as a non-Jewish, Gentile world. In fact, every sphere of society was there - including the entire spectrum of people-groupings; all tribal identities with their unique language-specific dialect preferences, they were all present facing the throne and the Lamb as the people of the planet. [Amazing how, in the previous verses of this chapter, the tribes of Israel are associated with a very specific number, emphasizing the prophetic detail of the entire Jewish nation. But here, John sees a massive throng of people, impossible to count. In Israel there is a prophetic voice of God's intention to release the blessing of the single SEED of God's faith through Abraham and bless all the nations of the earth. Count the stars, count the sand.

The word ¹stolay, is the white outer garment worn by kings, priests, and persons of rank. The palm branches and the white robes are signs of the celebration of victory and joy. The Preposition ²ek, points to source or origin; mankind was delivered out of their national, geographical and historical identities. Seven times in the book of Revelation human society is addressed in the most all-inclusive fashion, with a similar grouping of words. Revelation 5:9, here in Revelation 7:9, Revelation 10:11, Revelation 11:9, Revelation 13:7, Revelation 14:6 and Revelation 17:15. Also note Revelation 5:13 and Revelation 11:15. See Extended Notes on Israel at the end of Revelation 20.

I looked again and saw a huge crowd, too huge to count. Everyone was there—all nations and tribes, all races and languages. And they were standing, dressed in white robes and waving palm branches, standing before the throne and the Lamb. The Message]

And, Revelation 19:6 Then I heard the voice of an innumerable mass of people exploding like a thunderous torrent of mighty cascading waterfalls, bellowing, Hallelujah. The Lord our God has claimed his kingdom and established his sovereign rule over everything.

Revelation 19:7 This is the climax of the ages. Celebrate his glory with ecstatic joy and extreme delight, for the wedding feast of the Lamb has come. The day didn't catch her by surprise. His bride has prepared herself appropriately. She is ready and fully ¹fit for the occasion. [The word, ¹hetoimasen, is in the Aorist Active Indicative tense pointing to what has already happened. This word derives from an old word, heteos, fitness. She has gotten herself ready. Verse 8 tells us how she did it. See my extended notes on the City-Bride at the end of this chapter.]

Revelation 19:8 She ¹was given the finest linen to clothe herself; there she stands, wrapped in radiant white - dressed in ²spotless, saintly innocence. [The verb, edothē from didomi, was given, Aorist Passive Indicative. The word innocence, ²dikaiōma stems from the word dikē, suggesting to be judged equal; it implies the idea of two parties finding likeness in each other. Dikē is also the root for the word dikaiosunē, righteousness. Sadly, many translations have it completely wrong here. This is not the righteous deeds of the saints. Our redeemed innocence gives testimony to the merits of the Redeemer.

Paul says in Philippians 3:9, And be found in him, not having my own righteousness, which is of the law, but what is through the faith of Christ, the righteousness which is of God by faith. Zechariah 3:4 And the celestial messenger said to those who were standing before him, Remove the filthy garments from him. And to him he said, Behold, I have taken your iniquity away from you, and I will clothe you with righteousness. Aramaic Targum. See my extended notes on **the City-Bride** *at the end of Revelation 3.]*

Revelation 19:9 And he instructed me to record this in writing: Oh the [1]blessedness of this bliss which is the supreme celebration of the union of the ages. You have individually been [2]identified by name and invited to the Lamb's supper, concluding in the ultimate wedding feast. This is the Grand Finale in the [3]unveiling of God's word. [This is not a wedding where you are invited simply because you're a friend of a friend of the Groom or the Bride - or a distant second cousin to a relative of a relative on someone's mother's side. No. You're the Bride.

The word, [1]makarios, usually translated, blessed, suggests a special intensity of delight. It is another beatitude [makarioi] like that in Revelation 14:13 [fourth of the seven in the book]

The verb, κεκλημενοι [2]kekelemenoi is a Perfect Passive Participle of kaleō, to identify by name, to surname. The Passive Participle describes a state that exists at the time coincident with that of the leading verb as a result of action completed prior to the time of the main verb, [in previous verse] edothē from didomi, was given [v8] which is in the Aorist Passive Indicative. The Perfect Participle endorses the fact that this is a standing invitation. See the extended notes on ekklesia at the end of chapter 1. The word, [3]alēthinos, from alēthes; from the negative particle, a and lanthanō, to lie hidden; thus, that which is unveiled truth.

Just like Babylon is not a city in the symbolic language of Revelation, it is a fallen, distorted-mindset-society; so the New Jerusalem is not a city but the redeemed society of humanity. The Bride of Christ. Revelation 17:18. See my extended notes on **the City-Bride** *at the end of this chapter.])*

4:18 The fact that we are all deeply connected in the same source of our 'beingness' causes us to be constantly engaged in this mirror conversation with one another. *(The word parakaleō, from para, a Preposition indicating close proximity, a thing proceeding from a sphere of influence, with a suggestion of union of place of residence, to have sprung from its author and giver, originating from, denoting the point from which an action originates, intimate connection; close association, and kaleō, to identify by name - to surname. The word ἀλλήλων allēlōn - one another; a Pronoun Genitive plural from allos - another; thus, reduplicated, reciprocally, mutually mirrored.)*

5:1 I do not need to speculate about [1]specific prophetic moments or even mention [2]significant dates. *(The word [1]xronos, speaks of a specific space or portion of time, an individual opportunity, or season; [2]kairos, a fixed and definite time, the decisive epoch waited for.)*

5:2 You know for yourselves from experience how the day of the Lord suddenly dawns like a thief in the night. *(Acts 9:3 Now as he journeyed he approached Damascus, and suddenly a light from heaven flashed about him. 2 Corinthians 4:6 For it is the God who said, Let light shine out of darkness, who has shone in our hearts to give the light of the knowledge of the glory of God in the face of Christ. Isaiah 9:2 The people who walked in darkness have seen a great light; those who dwelt in a land of deep darkness, have been illuminated with light. John 1:9 A new day for mankind has come. The authentic light of life that illuminates everyone was about to dawn in the world.)*

5:3 The systems of this world of darkness and unbelief, which held the masses under their pseudo-sway of make-belief peace and security shall suddenly be broken into, like travail upon a woman with child, and none of their captives shall remain under their claim. *(The gates of Hadēs shall not prevail. Hadēs from **ha + eidō**, not to see. In a walled city, the gates are the most strategic point - if the gates are disengaged, the city is taken. Thus, the blindfold mode of mankind's forgotten identity, will not prevail against you.)*

5:4 You are no longer in darkness; there are no daunting surprises waiting for you like a thief in the night.

5:5 All of you are begotten of light, the Day of the Lord is your true parent. Neither night nor darkness have any claim on you.

5:6 Live alert and you will not become intoxicated by the indifference of others.

5:7 Sleeping and drunkenness are typical things people do at night, but now the day of the Lord has dawned within us and has put an end to the slumbering effect and intoxication of the practices of darkness.

5:8 So let us clothe ourselves with day-garments, protecting our sober seeing by having our hearts fully guarded by the breastplate of love-inspired faith, and having our minds encircled, like a helmet, with an expectation which is consistent with what salvation declares.

5:9 For God did not set us up for disappointment; he is not teasing us with [1]desires that we desperately reach for but cannot attain. He has brought us to a place where we are surrounded by the poetry of what salvation communicates in the lordship of Jesus Christ. *(The word often translated, wrath, is the word [1]orgē, from **oregomai** which means to stretch oneself out with strong and passionate desire.)*

5:10 The fact that he died our death is equally valid to those who are awake to its effect or still fast asleep in their indifference to it; we are together destined to live entwined in the [1]closest possible association with him. *(The word [1]hama is a particle of union denoting close association. See Galatians 2:20.)*

5:11 Continue, as you so eloquently do, to edify one another by cultivating the environment of your [1]close association in your joint-genesis. *(The word [1]parakaleō is here translated as our joint-genesis.)*

5:12 We also entreat you as our fellow family, birthed from the same womb, that you recognize those whose toil is evidenced in you; those who are appointed to be your guides in the Lord and who re-align your thinking.

5:13 You can confidently lavish your esteem and extravagant love upon them because of your immense appreciation for their work. Be at peace within yourselves, joined into oneness, into a place of union, which cannot be disturbed.

5:14 And we remind you of our joint-genesis as our point of reference for you to re-align the thinking of those who seem to have lost life's rhythm; encourage the fainthearted; be the sounding board to them who feel weak; be super patient with one and all.

5:15 No-one is to requite evil with evil, regardless of how much someone may seem to deserve retaliation. Never allow the old law and judgment language to influence you again. At all times, under all circumstances, let that which is good set the pace in your dealing with every single person, both those who are in as well as the so-called outsiders. *(If we are to treat offenders like that, how could we possibly reason that God is about to strike the world with 'punishment' like a thief in the night? Are we to be more tolerant than God?)*

5:16 Be cheerfully happy at all times.

5:17 Constantly engage your thoughts in worshipful prayer.

5:18 Your gratitude is not based on anything fragile or fading, but secured in the fact that God's purpose for you was concluded in Christ Jesus.

5:19 Do not suffocate the flame of the Spirit within you.

5:20 The prophetic word is not to be underestimated.

5:21 Test everything like one would test gold to determine its true value, then treasure that which is precious with great care.

5:22 Distance yourselves immediately from every practice remotely related to the fruit of the I-am-not-tree , which is the typical exhausting [1]law of works system. *(The tree of the knowledge of good and evil [[1]ponēros] represents mankind's lost sense of identity and righteousness, where mankind's global pursuit would now be their constant effort to achieve righteousness by means of their own works. This inevitably leads to disappointment where shame replaces innocence, and union and fellowship are lost. The word evil, ponēros, suggests being full of hardships, labors and annoyances.)*

5:23 There, away from any effort of your own, discover how the God of perfect [1]peace, who fused you skillfully into oneness - just like a master craftsman would dovetail a carpentry joint - has personally perfected and sanctified the entire harmony of your being without your help. He has restored the detailed default settings. You were re-booted to fully participate in the life of your design, in your spirit, soul and body in blameless innocence in the [2]immediate presence of our Lord Jesus Christ. *(It is not in my I-used-to-be-ness or I'm-trying-to-become-ness, but in my I-am-ness. The word [1]eirēnē, translated peace, refers to the dovetail joint in carpentry. The word [2]parousia, suggests immediate presence; see my comment on 1 Thessalonians 2:19.)*

5:24 You are defined by the faith of God; you are his poetry.

5:25 Our precious family, continue to include us in your prayers.

5:26 Embrace one another with generous fondness.

5:27 I hereby solemnly implore you by the Lord's authority that this Epistle is read to everyone in every ekklesia-church. *(This was Paul's very first Epistle to the churches; written from Athens.)*

5:28 The grace of our Lord Jesus is your constant companion. Amen.

2 Thessalonians is the most doubted book in the Pauline Epistles. Some would argue that the linguistic features of this letter show far too much deviation from Paul's normal style. In particular, a few years back, Daryl D. Schmidt of Texas Christian University read a paper on the linguistic features of 2 Thessalonians at a Society of Biblical Literature meeting, arguing this very point. His conclusion was that this letter was not genuine.

I have therefore not yet included 2 Thessalonians into the Mirror Study Bible

Timothy is one of Paul's first disciples. His mother was a Jewess and a believer, and his father a Greek.

Paul wrote to Timothy from prison in Rome. This is his last writing, as he suffered martyrdom shortly thereafter; the tone of this letter is quite emotional and personal in character.

His love for Timothy is obvious: As my close associate and travel companion, you fully participate in everything that my teaching and life proclaims; you share my resolve, my belief, my fortitude, my love, my perseverance. 2 Timothy 3:10.

Paul says about Timothy in Philippians 2:19 I trust the Lord that I will be able to send Timothy to you soon, this will be to me as if I am there personally with you.

I am reminded of your tears and my heart takes such joyful courage at the thought of being with you soon. I rejoice in the pure faith that I see in you. Remember that you are the third generation of a strong lineage of faith. The same unwavering persuasion that indwelt your grandmother Lois also resides in your mother Eunice and is now abundantly evident in you. This gives me all the more reason to remind you to fan the flame of God's grace gift within you into a blazing hot fire. Your life and ministry mirrors mine; I endorsed the gift of God's boldness within you when I laid my hands on you. Become fully acquainted with his gift in you, there is nothing timid about it; the dynamic of a mind liberated in the spirit of love is fearless and unstoppable. Do not let my imprisonment make you feel embarrassed about the testimony of Christ or your association with me. We are partners in the afflictions of the gospel and also in the intensity of God's power. We experience a constant download of power in the midst of affliction. 2 Timothy 1:4-8.

He reminds Timothy that, Everything that grace pointed to is now realized in Jesus Christ and brought into clear view through the gospel: Jesus is what grace reveals. He took death out of the equation and re-defines life; this is good news indeed. Grace is my commission; it is my job and joy to proclaim this message and guide the nations into a full understanding of the love initiative of God. 2 Timothy 1:10,11.

He encourages him to, See the future of this gospel in everyone you influence; their persuasion is also their competence to instruct others in the same revelation. 2 Timothy 2:2.

Avoid foolish questions that do not educate anyone but only breed quarrels. In your position as someone completely dedicated to the Lord there is no virtue in winning an argument but losing the person. I would much rather have you exhibit a sensitive courtesy towards all people; skillfully educate them and keep your cool under pressure. Your gentle way of instructing those who oppose you will inevitably lead them to see what God believes concerning them and give them the best possible chance to acknowledge the truth. 2 Timothy 2:23-25.

1:1 The amazing news of [1]announcing this life which is unveiled in Christ Jesus is what my ministry is all about. The promise is a Person. I, Paul, am a man on a [2]mission; God's [3]delightful desire, sponsors me. *(The word [1]epangelia means the promise, announcement; [2]apostelo, a man with a mission; [3]thelema, delightful desire.)*

1:2 Dear Timothy, you are my son in everything that grace, mercy and peace communicate. This life has only one reference: God is our Father and Jesus is our Master; the Christ-life rules.

1:3 I love the [1]constant [2]thought of you; I am aware of our union in Christ 24/7. [3]Prayer is such a permanent thing when we discover God's [4]grace-echo in our [5]worship. Our [6]conscience celebrates our [7]pre-creation [8]innocence before God.

([1] The word [1]adialeiptos, means without interruption;

[2] The word, [2]mneia, remembrance; to bring something from memory into the here and now!

[3] Then [3]deeisis, prayer, from deō, to bind in agreement.

> *See reference to the root word in **Ephesians**. 4:3 Being alert to treasure our oneness in spirit; encapsulated in peace. [The word **sundesmos** from **sun**, a primary Preposition denoting union and **deō** to bind in agreement like in a marriage. The word **eirēnē**, means peace, from **eirō**, to join, to be set at one again; in carpentry it is referred to as the dovetail joint, which is the strongest of joints. Peace is a place of unhindered enjoyment of friendship.]*

[4] [4]charin echō, grace echo, sometimes translated as thanksgiving;

[5] [5]latreuō, to worship without obligation, not under compulsion;

[6] [6]suneidō, conscience, to see together [with God];

[7] [7]progonos, before birth;

[8] [8]katharos, innocent, clean, pure. We celebrate an innocence that pre-dates Adam's fall. We have allowed an illegitimate sin-consciousness to prevail in our theologies and worship. The prodigal son's father had no reference to, or remembrance of past sins; imagine how that would spoil the party.)

1:4 I am reminded of your tears and my heart takes such joyful courage at the thought of being with you soon.

1:5 I rejoice in the pure faith that I see in you. Remember that you are the third generation of a strong lineage of faith. The same unwavering persuasion that indwelt your grandmother Lois also resides in your mother Eunice and is now abundantly evident in you.

1:6 This gives me all the more reason to remind you to fan the flame of God's grace gift within you into a blazing hot fire. Your life and ministry mirrors mine; I endorsed the gift of God's boldness within you when I laid my hands on you.

1:7 Become fully acquainted with his gift in you, there is nothing timid about it; the dynamic of a [1]mind liberated in the spirit of love is fearless and unstoppable. *(The word [1]sophronismos means a saved mind, a mind saved from tolerating inferior thoughts. Isaiah 55:8-11.)*

1:8 Do not let my imprisonment make you feel embarrassed about the [1]testimony of Christ or your association with me. We are partners in the afflictions of the gospel and also in the [2]intensity of God's power. We experience a constant [2]download of power in the midst of affliction. *(The [1]testimony of Christ is what gives us great liberty. Jesus and his finished work is God's testimony of our redeemed innocence. [2]kata, down, also to emphasize intensity.)*

1:9 He rescued the [1]integrity of our authentic [2]identity and revealed that we have always been [3]his own from the beginning, even [4]before time was. This has nothing to do with anything we did to qualify or disqualify ourselves. We are not talking about religious good works or karma here. Jesus unveils grace to be the [5]eternal intent of God. Grace celebrates our pre-creation innocence and now declares our redeemed union with God in Christ Jesus.

([1] The word [1]hagios, means holiness, purity, integrity; hagios + kaleō is often translated, holy calling;

[2] [2]kaleō means to identify by name, to surname;

[3] The word, ἴδιος [3]idios meaning, pertaining to oneself - mankind is God's own idea before any of us participated in any way.

[4] The words, πρὸ χρόνων αἰωνίων [4a]pro [4b]xronōnion [4c]aioniōn;

[a]pro, before; [b]xronos, means a measured duration or length of time; [c]aionios, speaks of ages.

Paul speaks of God's mind made up about us, before the ages, which is a concept in which eternity is divided up into various periods, the shorter of which are comprehended in the longer; this was before calendar time existed, before the creation of the galaxies and constellations. With kairos meaning a due, or specific moment of time. So, aionios spans time in dimensions that includes specific seasons or eras, but expands it all from the immediate now as the focus, then zooms it out beyond boundaries without losing the now relevance.

Jesus defines it as, Before Abraham was, I am.

[5] What happened to us in Christ is according to God's eternal, [5]prophetic purpose. This is also the word for the Bread of the Presence, or showbread, in Greek, πρόθεσις [5]prothesis, pre-designed/prophetic purpose, which he has shown in every prophetic pointer and shadow.

In the Hebrew tradition the showbread [prothesis] pointed to the true bread from heaven, the authentic word that proceeds from the mouth of God - Jesus, the incarnate word - sustaining the life of our design.

> *See Hebrews 9:2 The first tented area was called the Holy Place; the only light here came from the lampstand illuminating the table upon which the showbread - prothesis - was presented. The Hebrew word is לחם הפנים lechem haPānīm, face bread, or bread of the presence.*

The lampstand was a beautifully crafted golden chandelier portraying budding and **blossoming almond branches**.

> *Remember, this is also what Jeremiah saw in* **Jeremiah 1:12**, *when God said, I am awake over my word to perform it. The same Hebrew word is used here,* שָׁקַד *shaqad, the* **almond** *was called* **'the awake tree'**, *because it blossomed first, while the other trees were still in their winter sleep.*

> *The showbread pointed towards the daily sustenance of life in the flesh as the ultimate tabernacle of God. This is beautifully realized in the account of Jesus with the two from Emmaus. Their hearts were burning with resonance while he opened the Scriptures to them, and then around the table, their eyes were opened to recognize him as the fulfillment of Scripture: their true meal incarnated within the tabernacle of their flesh!* Luke 24:27-31.

> *Mankind shall not live by bread alone, but by the authentic thought of God, the Word proceeding from his mouth, the original intent, his image and likeness incarnated, revealed and redeemed in human life.*

Titus 1:2 This is the life of the ages that was anticipated for generations; the life of our original design announced by the infallible resolve of God before time or space existed. [Mankind's union with God is the original thought that inspired creation. There exists a greater dimension to eternity than what we are capable of defining within the confines of space and time. God's faith anticipated the exact moment of our redeemed union with him for all eternity.]

This life was made certain before eternal time. [BBE 1949, Bible in Basic English])

1:10 Everything that grace pointed to is now realized in Jesus Christ and brought into clear view through the gospel: Jesus is what grace reveals. He [1]took death out of the equation *[in his resurrection, he entirely deprived death of its fearful force]* **and re-defines uninterrupted life; this is good news indeed.**

([1] The word καταργέω [1]**katargeō** *means to entirely deprive of force; to render it to be of no effect whatsoever. See* **2 Corinthians 1:10** *In the resurrection of Jesus from the dead he already delivered us from death's greatest threat; now he continues to make our victory over death's claim a daily reality.*

[2] The word, ἀφθαρσία **aphtharsia** *suggests uninterrupted, unending continuance. Death would never again be thought of as the ending of life! Living happily ever after is not a fairy-tale!)*

1:11 Grace is my commission; it is my job and joy to proclaim this message and guide the nations into a full understanding of the love initiative of God.

1:12 What I suffer because of this does not frighten me at all; faith has made him so [1]apparent. I am absolutely convinced that I am safe in him. We are no longer looking for a future event, or another day, the day has come. Death is not Doomsday; nothing can interrupt what he has done. *(Greek, [1]eidō, Latin, video, to see, to know.)*

1:13 Your conversation echoes what you have heard from me; you articulate the exact [1]drift of my thought. We are fully embraced in

the same persuasion of love, immersed in Christ Jesus. *(The word ¹para, is a Preposition indicating close proximity, a thing proceeding from a sphere of influence, with a suggestion of union of place of residence, to have sprung from its author and giver, originating from, denoting the point from which an action originates, intimate connection.)*

1:14 This priceless treasure is placed in your custody by the Holy Spirit who inhabits us.

1:15 I'm sure that you have heard by now that everyone in the province of Asia deserted me because of my chains, even Phygellus and Hermogenes.

1:16 Onesiphorus and his family have been a real gift from the Lord and a great encouragement to me. They have often taken tender care of me. The fact that I was jailed did not intimidate them at all.

1:17 When he was in Rome he immediately searched for me until he found me.

1:18 His visit meant so much to me that day in Rome; he made God's mercy tangible. No one knows better than you what a blessing he has been to us in Ephesus.

2:1 Timothy my son, grace is the source of your strength. It is so much more than a doctrine, it is the person of Jesus Christ; he embodies what grace reveals.

2:2 What you have learned from me is not a theory; you have witnessed ample evidence that confirms the integrity of my message. See the future of this gospel in everyone you influence; their persuasion is also their competence to instruct others in the same revelation. *(See Titus 1:9.)*

2:3 Picture yourself as a soldier who endures hardship for the cause of Christ.

2:4 A soldier does not get himself distracted by civilian pursuits; he fully engages himself with the job at hand.

2:5 An athlete stands no chance of winning the trophy if he cheats in his training.

2:6 A farmer understands how much hard work goes into a harvest. *(In all three examples, Paul reminds Timothy that our aim is to win the world with the gospel; the world is the trophy and the harvest of the cross; this is the motivation of our ministry.)*

2:7 Ponder my words; the Lord will give you insight which will inspire you in every contradiction that you face.

2:8 Make my gospel emphasis the focus of your thoughts: Jesus Christ is the seed of David, he is the promised Messiah; his resurrection from the dead is the proof. *(It is the evidence that he completed the salvation of mankind by defeating death. Hosea 6:2, Ephesians 2:5,6, Romans 4:25, Acts 17:31.)*

2:9 I might be in bonds, but the word of God is not. *(It might seem to some that my suffering contradicts what I preach, but it cannot. My ministry is measured by the word not by my circumstances. See Colossians 1:24.)*

2:10 This gives me more than enough reason not to quit. I desire for everyone to discover the fact that the life of their [1]design is redeemed in Christ Jesus; this is the timeless intent of God. *(The word [1]eklegomai, ek, source, origin, and **legomai** from **logos**, word, thus the life of our design.)*

2:11 The logic of God endorses our faith: we were included in his death and are therefore equally included in his resurrection.

2:12 Sufferings do not distract us; neither do they contradict our joint position with him in the throne room , the Christ-life rules. If we [1]contradict ourselves *(behave unlike ourselves)*, he will contradict us and prove us wrong. *(The word [1]**arneomai** means to contradict.)*

2:13 Our unbelief does not change what God believes; he cannot contradict himself. *(See Romans 3:3,4 What we believe about God does not define him; God's faith defines us. God cannot be untrue to himself.)*

2:14 Gently remind your audience of these things which focus on the fact that the life of your design is redeemed in Christ Jesus, because we were included in his death and are therefore equally included in his resurrection. This is the foundation of our faith and cannot be contradicted by any persecution, because God cannot be untrue to himself. Let your testimony in your face to face encounter with the Lord, speak for itself. You don't need to engage in a war of words to desperately try and defend doctrines and perceptions. Instead of proving profitable, these debates are catastrophic to the faith of your students.

To mix two systems will certainly confuse your audience. *(See verse 10, 11 and 2 Corinthians 5:14 & 15.)*

2:15 [1]Without any delay [2]live your life from a place where you are familiar with the complete approval of God; you do not need to apologize for the fact that your experience might be a contradiction to your faith. What God believes about you needs no defense. There is such an immediate authority in [3]clarity. Truth triumphs over every contradiction. It makes a clear-cut division between light and darkness; the word of truth shows distinctly that the duty-driven law of works and annoyances and the love-driven law of perfect liberty have nothing in common. *(The word [1]spoudazō means to use speed, to be prompt, immediately. The word [2]paristēmi from para, a Preposition indicating close proximity, a thing proceeding from a sphere of influence, with a suggestion of union of place of residence, to have sprung from its author and giver, originating from, denoting the point from which an action originates, intimate connection; and histēmi, to position. The word [2]alētheia means not concealed, truth, clarity.)*

2:16 Do not engage in any conversation that may sound pious but carries no content; it only leads to lengthy and meaningless ungodly debates.

2:17 Their conversation consumes like [1]gangrene; Hymenaeus and Philetus are typical examples. *(Greek, gaggraina.)*

2:18 They have completely lost track of the truth by arguing that the resurrection of Christ has no further relevance. Any teaching that distracts from mankind's joint-inclusion in Jesus' resurrection turns belief upside down. *(See verses 8 & 11. The inclusion of mankind in the death and resurrection of Christ is the focal point of the gospel. 1 Corinthians 2:8 Neither the politicians nor the theologians of the day had a clue about this mystery [of mankind's association in Christ]; if they did, they would never have crucified the Lord whose death redeemed our glory.)*

2:19 The foundation of what God believes about you stands immovable and beyond dispute regardless of human opinion or contradiction. The inscription and impression made by the signet ring of God is his signature in your innermost being; he knows you as his own. Let everyone see themselves defined by the name of Christ and depart from everything which does not reveal likeness.

2:20 Even in mega-rich households there are not only vessels of gold and silver but also of wood and clay; a vessel's usefulness defines its true value. Even though their functions differ, each vessel is equally important.

2:21 Realize your individual value and stop discrediting yourself. You are indispensable; the Lord knows exactly what he has in you; many amazing opportunities await you in giving beautiful and practical expression in helping others discover their value. *(See 2:12 If we contradict ourselves [behave unlike ourselves], he will contradict us and prove us wrong. Also 2:13 Our unbelief does not change what God believes; he cannot be untrue to himself.)*

2:22 The best way to consistently [1]escape the snare and distractions of youthful lusts, which are often typified by an all-consuming longing for forbidden pleasures, is to ²pursue and engage your life actively in everything that celebrates your ³redeemed oneness. Instead of a sin-consciousness, cultivate a ⁴righteousness-consciousness. *[This is a ¹righteousness based on God's belief and not a fake-righteousness - based on make-belief and self-effort. Romans 1:17/ Romans 3:27/ Romans 4:27]* **Become addicted to the adventures of ⁵faith; let the ⁶agapē-love of God romance you into his ⁷rest where you cease from striving and bask in completeness. Feast on ³peace; celebrate your ⁸joint togetherness with everyone who has mutually discovered their ⁹original identity in the Lord. Live your life from this place of ¹⁰innocence, ¹¹from your heart.** *(Linking with the previous verses, escaping contradictions. Pursuing a greater value and pleasure is the most effective way to flee temptation [contradictions] -*

*[1, 2] The words φευγε ¹**pheuge**, flee from, and διωκε ²**diōke**, pursue eagerly, earnestly; are both in the Present Active Imperative tense.*

*[3] The word, ειρηνη **eirēnē**, from ³**eirō** to join as in a dovetail joint in carpentry. Here translated, redeemed oneness.*

*[4] The word δικαιοσύνη - ⁴**dikaiosunē**, righteousness - from the root from δίκη [**dikē**], suggesting to be judged equal; it implies the idea of two parties finding likeness in each other, [where there is no sense of inferiority, suspicion, blame, regret or pressure to perform]. The gospel is the revelation of the righteousness of God as our blueprint identity. It is also interesting to note that the Greek goddess of Justice, Dikē [pronounced, dikay], is always pictured holding a scale of balances in her hand. Jesus balanced the scales when he redeemed our righteousness – see Romans 4:25.*

*[5] Linked to the word, πίστιν ⁵**pistin** - faith; persuasion; belief.*

*[6, 7] The word, ⁶**agapē** has 2 components, ἄγω to lead as a shepherd leads their sheep and παύω ⁷**pauō**, to rest - His love leads me into his rest; into the full realization of his finished work. Agapē is Psalm 23 in one word. By the waters of reflection my soul remembers who I am.*

*[8] The word, ⁸**meta**, a joint togetherness with those...*

*[9] Then the word, επικαλουμενων ⁹**epikaloumenōn**, - has two components, the Proposition **epi**, continual influence upon, and **kaleō**, to identify by name; to surname.*

*[10] The word, καθαρᾶς ¹⁰**katharas** blameless; clean; innocent.*

Note the following words are all in the Accusative Case; thus it is presented as the direct objects of your pursuit and engagement, δικαιοσύνην, [righteousness], πίστιν [faith], ἀγάπην [love], εἰρήνην [peace]. Then, μετὰ [together with] τῶν ἐπικαλουμένων [Present Middle, Participle Genitive - those who are owning their authentic identity] τὸν Κύριον [the Lord as object of our devotion]

*[11] The Preposition, ἐκ ¹¹**ek** [from out of; source] καρδίας **kardias** [heart].)*

2:23 Avoid foolish questions that do not educate anyone but only breed quarrels.

2:24 In your position as someone completely dedicated to the Lord there is no virtue in winning an argument but losing the person. I would much rather have you exhibit a sensitive courtesy towards all people; skillfully educate them and keep your cool under pressure.

2:25 Your gentle way of instructing those who oppose you will inevitably lead them to see what God believes concerning them and give them the best possible chance to acknowledge the truth.

2:26 And so they will escape the intoxicating influence of the fallen mindset and the enslaving dictates of the Devil.

3:1 Know also that there will be days where the [1]extremities of people's fallen mindsets will be very obvious; where the [2]gulf between heavenly grace-thinking and earthly legalism-thinking will be most pronounced. *(The word [1]escahtos, extreme, is the superlative form of the word echō, to hold or to resonate. The last days doctrine - eschatology, is associated with this word. The word [2]chalepos from chalao means to loosen, to slacken, to let down from a higher place to a lower. From 'I am' to 'I am not'; from finished to unfinished; from gift to reward; from love to judgment.)*

3:2 For people will be absorbed with their own selfish ambitions; in love with money and the illusion of how it could make their dreams come true; living a lie of pretense and vanity; loving the limelight; engaged in hurtful gossip and indifferent to their parents; taking everything for granted; ungrateful and having no genuine regard for that which is sacred.

3:3 Typically calloused and without affection; unforgiving, displaying the characteristic of an accusing diabolical mindset, they are without self-control; savage and cynical.

3:4 They easily betray friendship; are typically impulsive, living in pretense like a fire that is all smoke and no flame. Addicted to sensual pleasures but averse to God.

3:5 Their make-belief devotion denies the very dynamic of God. Avoid their hypocrisy.

3:6 They sneak into the homes of vulnerable women like wolves in sheep's clothing, and under the pretense of ministry they shepherd them into snares of exaggerated longings and the intoxicating lies of law-language.

3:7 These women are like sitting ducks, they never seem to learn. They fall for anything that remotely sounds like a Bible-study and fail to tell the difference between window-shopping the promises and mirror-gazing the truth.

3:8 These guys, with their deadly legalistic Jewish agendas, seem to be on par with the two Egyptian magicians, Jannes and Jambres, who tried their best tricks to compete with Moses. The supernatural is not proof of faith. These people oppose the truth *[of grace]*; their minds are fully engaged in selling their religious self-help programs, and they stubbornly refuse to acknowledge what God believes about them. *(Remember Israel died in the wilderness because of unbelief, which was believing a lie about themselves, not because of a lack of the supernatural. Numbers 13:33, Joshua 2:11)*

3:9 Enough is [1]enough. Their self-help systems are exhausted; their folly shall be on exhibit for all to realize, just like Jannes and Jambres. *(See Romans 13:12, It was [1]night for long enough; the day has arrived. Cease immediately with any action associated with the darkness of ignorance. Clothe yourself in the radiance of light [the night is far spent, [1]prokoptō, as a blacksmith forges a piece of metal until he has hammered it into its maximum length.])*

3:10 As my close associate and travel companion, you fully participate in everything that my teaching and life proclaims; you share my resolve, my belief, my fortitude, my love, my perseverance.

3:11 You have witnessed the persecutions and hardships that I endured in Antioch, Iconium and Lystra; at any time I could have been swept away by these, but the Lord dramatically rescued me out of every single situation.

3:12 Somehow, everyone who determines to live a life entwined in [1]beauty and worship in Christ Jesus will be persecuted. (The word [1]eusebos, from eu, good, well done, and sebomai, to adore, revere, worship, is born as the fruit of euaggelion, the well done announcement, the good of the Good News. The spontaneity of such worship often seems to offend those engaged in a system controlled by the legalistic rituals of institutional religion.)

3:13 People who are trapped in the mindset of [1]hardships, labors and annoyances will continue to desperately try to get mileage out of a dead and redundant system. The [2]lie that they believe is the very currency in which they trade. (The word, [1]poneros, means hardships, labors and annoyances. [2]Deceived and deceiving.)

3:14 In sharp contrast to this deceptive duty-driven system, continue to fully engage yourself in the certainty of what you have learned, knowing the integrity of your source.

3:15 The sacred Scriptures that you were raised with from your mother's womb dynamically pointed you to the [1]explicit clarity of salvation. God's [2]belief was always wrapped up in Christ Jesus. (The Greek word for wisdom, [1]sophos, from saphe, that which is clear. The words [2]tes pisteos are in the Genitive case which points to ownership, belonging to. Righteousness by his [God's] faith defines life. [Habakkuk 2:4; 3:17-19]. Instead of reading the curse when disaster strikes, Habakkuk realizes that the Promise out-dates performance as the basis to mankind's acquittal.)

3:16 Jesus Christ and his work of salvation is the theme of Scripture. The [1]value of [2]scripture in its most complete context is always found in [3]God's prophetic voice inspiring a [4]thorough education in the revelation of righteousness. This is what carries the [3]breath of God and gives substance and [5]proof to accurately [7]gauge what is being [6]taught. (Mankind's righteousness, lost in Adam, would be redeemed again in Christ. The breath of God, meaning [3]the words that proceed from his mouth, [4]educates us in the understanding of our original identity, likeness and innocence. The teaching of righteousness gives significance to Scripture. You search the Scriptures, because you think that in them you have eternal life; and it is they that bear witness to me; yet you refuse to come to me that you may have life. John 5:39,40. The promise will become a Person, and in his death he would be the Lamb of God laying down his life to die mankind's death. Throughout the writings of Moses and the Prophets and the Psalms, God speaks in Messianic language, revealing his resolve to redeem his image and likeness in human form. And beginning with Moses and all the Prophets, he interpreted to them in all the Scriptures the things concerning himself.

Luke 24:27 They said to each other, did not our hearts burn within us while he talked to us on the road, while he opened to us the Scriptures? Luke 24:32 Then he said to them, these are my words which I spoke to you, while I was still with you, that everything written about me in the law of Moses and the Prophets and the Psalms must be fulfilled. Then he opened their minds to understand the Scriptures, and said to them, it is written, that the Christ should suffer and on the third day rise from the dead. Luke 24:44-46

Ask a sign of the LORD your God; let it be deep as Sheol or high as heaven. But you would not, therefore the Lord himself will give you a sign. Behold, a virgin shall conceive and bear a Son, and shall call his name Immanuel. Isaiah 7:11-14. For unto us a child is born, to us a Son is given; and the government will be upon his shoulder, and his name will be called Wonderful Counselor, Mighty God, Everlasting Father, Prince of Peace. Of the increase of his government and of peace there will be no end. Isaiah 9:6,7. See also Psalm 22 and Isaiah 53. In his resurrection on the third day, God would co-quicken mankind and co-raise us together with him. Hosea 6:2, Ephesians 2:5,6. Human life will again be the tabernacle of God. Tear down this temple and in three days I will raise it up. John 2:19. For as Jonah was three days and three nights in the belly of the whale, so will the Son of man be three days and three nights in the heart of the earth. Matthew 12:40. On the third day Esther put on her royal robes and stood in the inner court of the king's palace, opposite the king's hall. The king was sitting on his royal throne inside the palace opposite the entrance to the palace; and when the king saw Queen Esther standing in the court, she found favor in his sight and he held out to Esther the golden scepter that was in his hand. Then Esther approached and touched the top of the scepter. Esther 5:1,2

*In many fragments of prophetic thought, God would [1]heap up the evidence as [5]proof of his purpose to raise fallen mankind up to be [7]co-elevated with him, standing tall like a mountain-monument. The little stone that was cut out by no human hand is destined to strike that image of vanity and piety on its feet of iron and clay, to remove every trace of the substitute, man-made self-image with its glorious head of golden glitter and its silvery bust and bronze body. The stone will become in its place a Rock that fills the whole earth; the true image and likeness of God, restored and revealed in ordinary human life. (Daniel 2:32-35) And the ends of the earth shall remember and return to the Lord. Psalm 22:27; The Prophets who prophesied of the grace that was to be yours, searched and inquired about this salvation; they inquired what person or time was indicated by the Spirit of Christ within them when predicting the sufferings of Christ and the subsequent glory. 1 Peter 1:10,11 See also Romans 4:25 Our sins [1]resulted in his death; our redeemed righteousness resulted in his resurrection. His resurrection is the receipt for our acquittal. This is one of the most important statements in the entire Bible. Why was Jesus handed over to die? Because of, **dia**, our sins. Why was he raised from the dead? Because of, **dia**, we were justified. His resurrection reveals our righteousness. Here is the equation: his cross = our sins; his resurrection = our innocence. If we were still guilty after Jesus died, his resurrection would neither be possible nor relevant. This explains Acts 10:28 and 2 Corinthians 5:14 and 16. Paul proclaims to a group of idol worshipping Greek philosophers, in Acts 17:31, that because human life is the offspring of God, and in the light of what happened to mankind in Christ, God now* *urgently implores all of mankind everywhere, to awaken in their understanding, because God had fixed a day on which he would judge the world righteous by a man whom he has appointed, and of this he has given proof to all by raising him from the dead. The resurrection of Jesus from the dead and mankind's mystical union with him, is the crux of the Gospel. This is God's receipt endorsing mankind's redeemed innocence and identity, which is what the Teaching of Righteousness is all about.*

The following words are highlighted: [1]***ōphelimos**, valuable, profitable, from* **ophellō***, to heap up, to accumulate benefit;* [2]***pasa graphe**, Scripture in completeness, context;* [3]***theopneustos** , God-breathed, Divine inspiration;* [4]***pros paideian ten en dikaiosunē**, for the purpose of a thorough education in the revelation of righteousness;* [5]***elegchos**, proof, evidence;* [6]***didaskalia**, teaching, instruction;* [7]***epanorthosis**, from* **epi***, continuous influence upon,* **ana,** *upward, and* **orthos** *from* **oros***, a mountain from* **airō***, to lift, to elevate, and* **ornis***, a bird, see Isaiah 40:3-5, & 31.)*

3:17 Being thoroughly schooled in the word of righteousness will equip you to be fully refreshed in the sparkling newness of life, giving you a fresh start to tackle every relevant and good task with renewed inspiration.

4:1 I give testimony to this word as one standing face to face with God and the Lord Jesus Christ, who is about to be equally visible to those who have died as well as those who are still alive; the dominion of the Christ-life has the final say.

4:2 Broadcast this word on every occasion, even when it doesn't seem to be convenient or appropriate; give evidence to this message; value every individual in your audience highly; esteem people's authentic identity passionately; teach tirelessly.

4:3 There will be times when people will not relate to their [1]inner resonance, when it comes to discerning [2]sound instruction. Instead they would prefer the familiar language of the [3]fallen mindset and [4]desperately chase after titles and teachers who [5]entertain rather than educate; they would [6]accumulate for themselves libraries of information without any revelation. *(I have translated [1]anechomai, our inner-resonance; from ana, upward and echō, to hold, to resonate, which suggests an upward echo. Our minds are redeemed to engage with the resonance of our inner witness - we are co-seated together with Christ in heavenly places - which is contrasted with a mindset engaged with the fallen soul realm below; from [3]kata, downward. See Colossians 3:1,2 Set your minds upon the things that are above and not upon the things below. Also note Romans 1:18, where the word katechō is used - to echo downwards, to suppress is the opposite to anochē, to echo upward- Romans 2:4 and Romans 3:26. Also 2 Corinthians 4:18 We are not keeping any score of what seems so obvious to the senses in the natural realm, it is fleeting and irrelevant. It is the unseen, eternal realm within us which has our full attention and captivates our gaze. A renewed mind conquers the space previously occupied by worthless pursuits and habits. The word [2]hugiainō, means sound, healthy, wholesome; the word [4]epithumia, means constant cravings, panting after in hot pursuit; [6]episōreuō means to heap up, to accumulate in piles; [5]knēthō from knaō, means to tickle the ear; it suggests to be entertained rather than educated. Seneca, a famous Greek philosopher in Paul's days, uses this word and says: Some come to hear, not to learn, just as we go to the theater, for pleasure, to delight our ears with the speaking or the voice or the plays. See Luke 7:31-34 in the Mirror Bible.)*

4:4 In their pursuit they would exchange the truth for man-made fictions and fables as their source of reference.

4:5 But be vigilant in all things, don't allow the devastating things that you suffer to get to you. Continue in the full persuasion of your ministry as herald of the Good News; you cannot have a more poetic job description.

4:6 So here I am, my life is poured out as a wine offering on the altar of ministry; I am ready to go. *(See also Philippians 2:17,18 I want you to see my ministry to you as wine poured out upon the altar of your faith. I rejoice in the thought that we drink from the same source and therefore celebrate a mutual joy. Whatever you may suffer only concludes in joy. - Joy is a bold declaration, in the face of severe danger and suffering, that contradiction does not define us or have the final say in our lives. We know that whether we live or die, our message is unstoppable and that it is conquering the world.)*

4:7 Like a champion athlete I have run my race and completed the course; I have carefully ¹attended to the faith. *(The word ¹tereō means to attend carefully, to guard.)*

4:8 My wreath of righteousness awaits me as testimony to the Lord's righteous judgment. He will crown me in that day, the moment I step out of this body. I will not be the only one receiving a wreath of honor; everyone, ¹loving the brilliance of his appearance will be jointly crowned. *(In seeing him, everyone will see themselves, mirrored in him. The word ¹agapaō, from ago, to lead as a shepherd leads his sheep, and paō, to rest. By the waters of reflection, my soul remembers who I am. Psalm 23:2,3. Note the 1st verse of chapter 4. See also 1 Corinthians 15:49-54 The reduced state of the individual left its mark on mankind as being earthly; now the redeemed state of mankind confirms their origin in God and marks their new heavenly life. Just as we were once defined by the flesh [our earthly image] we are now defined by our spirit [our heavenly] image. Flesh and blood has a sell-by date; the bodies you live in now will not last forever. Ponder this mystery, I want to show you something that you have never seen before: everyone will awaken out of sleep; we will all experience exactly the same change. This will happen in an instant, in a blink of the eye: the final trumpet will sound, then the dead shall be raised and we, who are still alive, shall be instantly changed into a different kind of body. For this corruptible must be clothed with incorruption and this mortal must be clothed with immortality. Also 1 Thessalonians 4:14-18 We believe that Jesus died and rose again, and that he fully represents and includes even those who have not awoken unto him yet. God will ¹lead them to realize that they are in Jesus. [The word ¹agō means to lead as a shepherd leads his sheep.] We give voice to the word of the Lord, we are God's wake-up call to them that are asleep. We are exhibiting the ¹immediate tangible presence of the Lord and shall not ²exclude those who are asleep. [The word ¹parousia means immediate presence. See the use of the word ²phthanō, to prevent, to hinder or exclude. The true light that enlightens everyone has come. And the glory of the Lord shall be revealed and all flesh shall see it together.] The Lord will personally step out of the invisible heavenly realm into our immediate visible horizon with an inciting shout, announcing his triumphant reign in the trumpet-like billowing voice of God; and even the dead will rise from their sleep. In the wake of their arising we will all be gathered into a large dense multitude of an innumerable throng of people, united as one, like the particles of water in a cloud, and we will encounter the Lord in the very air we breathe and so shall we continually celebrate our I-am-ness in our union with him. [All flesh shall see his glory together - ultimately every single one will realize that Deity and humanity are married - the Bride and her Groom are united.] The fact that we are all deeply connected in the same source of our 'beingness' causes us to be constantly engaged in this conversation with one another.*

Also Hebrews 12:1 So now the stage is set for us: all these faith-heroes cheer us on, as it were, like a great multitude of spectators in the amphitheater. This is our moment. As with an athlete who is determined to win, it would be silly to carry any baggage of the old law-system that would weigh one down. Make sure you do not get your feet clogged up with sin-consciousness. Become absolutely streamlined in faith. Run the race of your spiritual life with total persuasion, persuaded in the success of the cross. Hebrews 12:2 Look away from the shadow dispensation of the law and the Prophets and fix your eyes upon Jesus. He is the fountainhead and conclusion of faith. He saw the joy (of mankind's salvation) when he braved the cross and despised the shame of it. As the executive authority of God [the right hand of the throne of God] he now occupies the highest seat of dominion to endorse our innocence. [Having accomplished purification of sins, he sat down. Hebrews 1:3, Isaiah 53:11.])

4:9 I really need you with me right now; would you get over here as quickly as you can.

4:10 Demas abandoned me and left for Thessalonica; he has fallen in love with the current mindset of this philosophical religious age. Crescens is in Galatia province, Titus in Dalmatia.

4:11 Luke is the only one here with me. Make sure to bring Mark with you; he will be a great help in ministry.

4:12 I'm sending Tychicus to Ephesus.

4:13 Bring my winter coat that I left in Troas with Carpus; also the books and ¹parchments. *(The word ¹membranas, means skin, membrane, or parchment. Dressed skins were among the earliest materials for writing, and were in common use before the art of making paper from rags was discovered. These parchments seem to have been something different from books, and probably refer to some of his own writings. They may have contained notes, memorandums, journals, or unfinished letters.)*

4:14 Alexander the coppersmith has been a real pain in the butt. Is it not wonderful though to know that the Lord's work on the cross even includes him. He is equally forgiven. *(He will be rewarded according to his [the Lord's] work.)*

4:15 I do warn you however to be on the lookout for him, since he has greatly opposed our message.

4:16 No one dared associate themselves with me during my preliminary hearing, instead they all scattered; I hold nothing against them.

4:17 Throughout my trial, I was so aware of the Lord's tangible presence; he strengthened me with dynamic boldness and assured me that my life will be an accurate conduit of the message articulated in its most complete context, for all the nations to hear. And I was snatched from the very jaws of the lion.

4:18 I am so persuaded that the same Lord who delivered me out of the Lion's jaws, also safeguards me from getting snared by the subtle attempts of the ¹law-guys to break in on the effortless rhythm of grace that I am addicted to. Our salvation celebrates his heavenly kingdom. We live our lives from a dominion far superior to the systems of the world; there is no fading to the glory of his kingdom. His eternal intent spans the ages. *(The words, ¹ponēros ergon, refer to the law of works, hardships and annoyances.)*

4:19 Give Priscilla and Aquila a big hug from me. Also the family of Onesiphorus.

4:20 Erastus stayed behind in Corinth. I had to leave Trophimus in Miletus since he was sick.

4:21 Make sure you get here before winter. Eubulus, Pudens, Linus, Claudia, and all your friends send their greetings.

4:22 May your spirit continuously encounter his Lordship and grace. Grace rules.

Paul reminds Titus that mankind's union with God is the original thought that inspired creation. My mission is to persuade people of their origin in God; by bringing them into a complete understanding of the truth as the only valid reference to meaningful devotion.

Titus 2:11 The grace of God shines as bright as day making the salvation of mankind undeniably visible.

The following verses are some of the most profound in Paul's writings:

Titus 3:2 Gossip is out. Never have anything bad to say about anyone. You do not have to win every argument. Instead, avoid quarreling, be appropriate, always show perfect courtesy to one and all.

Titus 3:3 Do not be harsh on others. Remember that we too were typically foolish. We were stubborn and indifferent to spiritual things. Our addiction to the sensual and sexual kept us running around in circles. We were engaged in malice and spiteful jealousies. We were bored and lonely, often utterly disliking ourselves and hating one another.

Titus 3:4 But then, oh happy day. It was the generosity of God and his fondness for mankind that dawned on us like a shaft of light. Our days of darkness were over. Light shone everywhere, and we became aware: God rescued the human race.

1:1 Paul the bondman of God, on assignment by Jesus Christ; my mission is to persuade people of their [1]origin in God; by bringing them into a complete understanding of the truth as the only valid reference to [2]meaningful devotion.

([1] The word traditionally translated as 'elect' is [1]eklegō; ek is a Preposition that always denotes origin or source and legō, is the word or the logic of God as in John 1:1, To go back to the very beginning is to find the Word already present there. The Logic of God defines the only possible place where mankind can trace their genesis.

[2] Then, the word, [2]eusebeia, meaning beautiful worship, and adoration.)

1:2 This is the life of the [1]ages which was anticipated for generations; the life of our original design announced by the infallible resolve of God before [2]time or space existed.

(Mankind's union with God is the original thought that inspired creation.

[1] The word, [1]aionios, speaks of ages. Paul speaks of God's mind made up about us, before the ages, which is a concept in which eternity is divided up into various periods, the shorter of which are comprehended in the longer.

[2] The word, [2]xronos, means a measured duration or length of time; kairos is a due, or specific moment of time. This was before the ages or any measure of calendar time existed, before the creation of the galaxies and constellations. There exists a greater dimension to eternity than what we are capable of defining within the confines of space and time. God's faith anticipated the exact moment of our redeemed union with him for all eternity.

This life was made certain before eternal time. [BBE 1949, Bible in Basic English]

Hebrews 13:8 Take your lead from Jesus. He is your reference to the most complete life. In him yesterday is confirmed today and today mirrors tomorrow. What God spoke to us in Christ is as relevant now as it was in the prophetic past and will always be in the eternal future. [Jesus is the same yesterday, today, and forever; there is a history to our salvation that carries more authority and relevance than anything that ever happened in our past, or anything present in time or still to happen in the future. Imagine the enormity of eternity in his sameness before time was; and we were there in him all along. See Romans 8:34 What further ground can there possibly be to condemn mankind? In his death he faced our judgment; in his resurrection he declares our innocence; the implications cannot be undone. He now occupies the highest seat of authority as the executive of our redemption in the throne room of God. See Romans 8: 1, also Romans 4:25. The heavens declare his glory, night to night exhibits the giant solar testimony that is mathematically precise, revealing that God knew before time was the exact moment he would enter our history as a man, and the exact moment the Messiah would expire on the cross and be raised again from the dead.])

1:3 My message announces the completeness of time; God's eternal moment realized the logic of our salvation. *(But then the day dawned; the most complete culmination of time. [Galatians 4:4] Everything predicted was concluded in Christ.*

John 1:14   Suddenly the invisible eternal Word takes on visible form. The Incarnation. In him, and now confirmed in us. The most accurate tangible display of God's eternal thought finds expression in human life. The Word became a human being; we are his address; he resides in us. He captivates our gaze.

*Hebrews 1:1   Throughout ¹ancient times God spoke in many fragments and glimpses of prophetic thought to our fathers. Now, this entire conversation has ²finally dawned in sonship. Suddenly what seemed to be an ancient language, falls fresh and new like the dew on the tender grass. He is the sum total of every utterance of God in conversation with us. He is whom the Prophets pointed to and we are his immediate audience. [The word ¹***palai***, meaning, of old, ancient; from* ***palin*** *through the idea of oscillatory repetition or retrocession; anew, afresh. See Deuteronomy 32:1   Give ear, Oh heavens, and I will speak; and let the earth hear the words of my mouth. Deuteronomy 32:2   May my teaching drop as the rain, my speech distil as the dew, as the gentle rain upon the tender grass, and as the showers upon the herb.... Deuteronomy 32:18   You were unmindful of the Rock that begot you, and you forgot the God who gave you birth. Like in James 1: 24, we have forgotten what manner of people we are - we have forgotten the face of our birth.*

*The word ²**eschatos** means extreme; last in time or in space; the uttermost part, the final conclusion. Sonship revealed and redeemed defines eschatology.]*

Hebrews 1:2   In sonship, God declares the Incarnate Word to be the heir of all things. He is, after all, the author of the ages. We have our beginning and our being in him. [Sonship endorses heirship. See Hebrews 6:16-18.]

Hebrews 1:3 Jesus is the crescendo of God's conversation; he gives context and content to the authentic thought. Everything that God had in mind for mankind is voiced in him. Jesus is God's language. He is the radiant and flawless expression of the person of God. He makes the glorious intent of God visible and exhibits the character and every attribute of God in human form. He is God's voice, announcing our redeemed innocence. By his own doing he accomplished purification for sins and sat down, enthroned in the boundless measure of his majesty in the right and of God as the executive authority. He is the force of the universe, upholding everything that exists. This conversation is the dynamic that sustains the entire cosmos.

More than two thousand years ago the conversation that had begun before time was recorded—sustained in fragments of thought throughout the ages, whispered in prophetic language, chiseled in stone and inscribed in human conscience and memory—became a man. Beyond the tablet of stone, the papyrus scroll or parchment roll, human life has become the articulate voice of God. The name of Jesus defines his mission. As Savior of the world he truly redeemed the image and likeness of the invisible God and made him apparent again in human form, as in a mirror.)

1:4 Titus, you really are like a son to me in our mutual faith. The Father's favor, compassion, and tranquillity is yours; this is what our Master Jesus Christ restored us to through his great act of salvation.

1:5   There is still some unfinished business in Crete; I would like you to give it your undivided attention by appointing a leadership team in every city exactly as I have instructed you.

1:6 Here are some practical guidelines: appoint people with unquestionable integrity; consider what kind of husband and father your potential leader is. He must obviously be a man who is completely devoted to his wife and whose children are steadfast and are not troublemakers or unruly.

1:7 An overseer must be above reproach; if he has a bad reputation in the community you do not want him to be part of your leadership team. A leader administrates God's economy and must therefore be a competent manager of God's business. A person with his own selfish agenda, or one who loses his temper easily, or someone that is known to over indulge in food or wine, or a bully, or greedy for money is certainly not a candidate.

1:8 He must be [1]fond of strangers and able to make people feel immediately at home. Your leader must be a [2]caring person and one who shows [3]unselfish devotion to the welfare of others. Someone [3]sober-minded, whose thought-life is sorted out; one who walks in the [4]revelation of the finished work of Christ; a man of [5]mercy and who is strong in spirit. *(The word, [1]philoxenos, means fond of strangers. The word, [2]philagathos, translates as benevolent, good, kind, humane, generous, liberal, benign, philanthropic, altruistic. The word, [3]sōphrōn, means a saved mind. The word, [4]dikaion, translates as righteousness, the revelation of the finished work of Christ; and the word, [5]hosios, is translated as mercy as in Acts 13:44, which is a quote from Isaiah 55:3 from the Hebrew word, ghesed, חסד - mercy.)*

1:9 The overseer [1]mirrors the persuasion of the word he was taught and is competent to instruct with accuracy and to entreat and convince those who oppose the message. *(The word, [1]antechomai, comes from anti meaning against, standing opposite, and echo; thus one who mirrors the word.)*

1:10 There are many who engage in worthless debates about their Jewish sentiments and playing mind-games in order to snare new believers into legalism.

1:11 By entreating and persuading them with wisdom, their influence will be silenced. The rot must be stopped since they have already confused entire families with their teachings and robbed them financially in the process.

1:12 According to one of their own so-called enlightened leaders, the Cretans are known to be phony, lazy gluttons, and savage brutes.

1:13 This gives all the more reason that they need distinguished leaders who are capable of rebuking such behavior sharply and establish them in robust faith. *(We are not here to merely comment on people's behavioral trends; we are here to declare people free to live the life of their redeemed design. Faith sees that old life co-crucified with Christ and the new resurrected life emerge victoriously. Faith is not a mickey-mouse cover-up for sin; faith defeats sin.)*

1:14 Admonish them not to pay any attention to Jewish fiction and their man-made rules and regulations which achieve exactly the [1]opposite to what truth promotes. *(The word, [1]apostrephō, means to reverse).*

1:15 The truth proves everything to be pure but to those who are contaminated with unbelief in their minds and conscience everything seems to be equally stained with impurity. *(Unbelief is to believe a lie about yourselves. [Numbers 13:33 and 2 Corinthians 4:4.])*

1:16 They might even pretend that they know God by saying a few nice clichés, but when it comes to real life the veneer cracks and the stench is nauseating; the effects of unbelief cannot be camouflaged.

2:1 Your message is in its own class; you instruct with distinction.

2:2 Encourage the senior men to be established in their [1]I-am-ness; [2]focused in their faith; to be [3]distinguished with a [4]mind established in redemption realities and [5]comprehensive in their belief, their [6]love, and in their [7]fortitude. *([1]I-am-ness from **eimi**, I am; often translated, to be. The word, [2]**nephalios**, means sober, focused, not to compromise their belief with Jewish sentiment; [3]**semnos**, means eminent, distinguished; [4]**sophron**, means a saved mind; [5]**hugiainō te piste** translate as unmixed, comprehensive in their faith; [6]**agapē**, means to lead into rest, the love of God leads us to see in us and others what he sees in us; his rest celebrates our perfection, and [7]**hupomonē**, means fortitude, to be steadfast, to remain the same, from **hupo**, under the influence of, subject to + **menō**, to continue to be present.)*

2:3 Instruct the elderly women also to exhibit a consecrated character in all their conduct. Encourage them not to [1]slander, nor are they to get intoxicated with wine; their example makes [2]beauty irresistibly attractive. *(The word, [1]**diabolos**, means Devil, accuser, from **dia**, because of, and **ballō**, the fall; the Devil and the fall of mankind are no longer our reference in conversation. Gossip (to be double minded about someone) is a form of intoxication to be avoided at all costs. The word, [2]**kalodidaskalos**, means irresistibly beautiful teaching.)*

2:4 They are to radiate a conversation that flows from a mind radically transformed by redemption realities. Their instruction should inspire young women to treat their husbands and children with tender affection. *(The word, **philandros**, and **philoteknos**, connote fond affection for their husbands and children. Paul uses this same combination in chapter 3:4. It is the fondness of God for mankind that persuaded our hearts. [**philanthropos**])*

2:5 They are to be clear headed and innocent in heart, creative homemakers, gentle, exclusive in their devotion to their husbands *(not flirting with other men)*; nothing in their attitude or actions would distract from the word of God. Domestic life beautifully displays the fascination of the Incarnation.

2:6 In the same manner [1]incite the young men to become acquainted with their redeemed identity. *([1]Incite, arouse, being alongside, from the Greek [1]**parakaleō**, derived from **para**, a Preposition indicating close proximity, a thing proceeding from a sphere of influence, with a suggestion of union of place of residence, to have sprung from its author and giver, originating from, denoting the point from which an action originates, intimate connection, and **kaleō**, to identify by name, to surname.)*

2:7 Being a young man yourself, your day-to-day life mirror-echoes the typical mold into which your message translates [1]without any hint of the fallen mindset; you excel in distinguished eminence and innocence. *(The word, [1]**adiaphthoria**, means without any hint of the fallen mindset, from **a**, negative + **diaballō**, through the fall, cast down, Devil, accuser, + **phterō**, to waste away, to pine. Neither the Devil nor accusation feature in your conversation.)*

2:8 Your wholesome conversation will silence the opposition.

2:9 Employees are to give their undivided devotion to their bosses, making them proud of them in every respect. It is good advice never to give your boss any backchat, even if you think that you are in the right.

2:10 They are to exhibit their faith without any hidden agenda; thus making the message irresistibly attractive in everything they do.

2:11 The grace of God shines as bright as day making the salvation of mankind undeniably visible.

2:12 [1]The day and age we live in sets the stage for displaying the attraction of an [2]awe-inspired life; our [6]minds are rescued in the revelation of righteousness. We are in the [4]school of grace, instructed how to thoroughly [5]reverse the apathy and [3]indifference that erupts in a [5]wave of lust that would seek to dictate the day. *(The word, [1]aion, as in the day and age we live in; [2]eusebos, meaning godly, the attraction of devotion, awe; [3]asebeia, as in ungodliness, indifference; [4]paideou, training students; [5]arneomai, from a, negative, and rheō, pouring forth of utterance; [5]kosmikos epithumia, worldly lusts; [6]sophronos, saved minds; the revelation of righteousness shows how completely God redeemed mankind in Christ and empowers us to cultivate an innocence consciousness instead of a sin consciousness).*

2:13 Everyone must [1]welcome with open arms the outrageously blessed expectation; Jesus is what the world was waiting for. He radiates the brilliant intent of God, engineered by his greatness to rescue the world in him. *(The word, [1]prosdechomenoi, means to receive to oneself, to welcome with open arms.)*

2:14 He gave himself as sacrifice in [1]exchange for our freedom. We are [1]redeemed from every obligation and accusation under the law and declared absolutely innocent. He defines who we are. [2]Our brand name is I am. We are exclusively his. We are a [3]passionate people; we excel in doing everything we do beautifully. *(The word, [1]lutroō, means ransom, redemption price, to purchase from slavery; [2]periousios, comes from peri, for sphere, circuit, locality, pertaining to, and eimi, I am; [3]ζηλωτής zēlōtēs, translates as zealous, passionate; and [4]kalos, as beautiful.)*

2:15 Continue to communicate content in your every conversation; [1]inspire and entreat with conviction and assertiveness; you are not at the mercy of anyone's [2]suspicious scrutiny. *(Encourage everyone to become acquainted with their redeemed identity, [1]parakaleō; and the word, [2]periphroneō, translates as to think beyond what is obvious, suspicious scrutiny.)*

3:1 Remind the Christians in Crete to respect their Roman officials; they must be ready to volunteer for any beneficial service required of them.

3:2 Gossip is out. Never have anything bad to say about anyone. Don't try to be the [1]macho man, having to win every argument; instead, avoid quarreling, be appropriate, always show perfect courtesy to one and all. *(The word, [1]amachos from a as a negative particle and mache, a brawler, to be controversial, striving. You don't have to wait for people to change before you are nice to them. There is a big difference between fake politeness and perfect courtesy.)*

3:3 Do not be harsh on others. Remember that we too were typically foolish; we were stubborn and indifferent to spiritual things, our addiction to the sensual and sexual kept us running around in circles, we were engaged in malice and spiteful jealousies, we were bored and lonely, often utterly disliking ourselves and hating one another. *(The only difference in who we are now and who we were then is in what we now know to be true about ourselves.)*

3:4 But then, oh happy day. It was the generosity of God and his fondness for mankind that dawned on us like a shaft of light. Our days of darkness were over. Light shone everywhere and we became aware: God rescued the human race. *(See Titus 2:11.)*

3:5 Salvation is not a reward for good behavior. It has absolutely nothing to do with anything that we have done. God's mercy saved us. The Holy Spirit endorses in us what happened to us when Jesus Christ died and was raised. When we heard the glad announcement of salvation it was like taking a deep warm bath. Our minds were [1]thoroughly cleansed and re-booted into [2]newness of life. *(The word [1]paliggenesia suggests a complete restoration to the original, in modern terms, rebooted. The word [2]anakainosis, from ana, upward, and kainosis, newness, speaks of a fresh upward focus; a re-engaging with heavenly thoughts. See Colossians 3:1-3; also 1 Thessalonians 1:5. We realized that we were indeed co-included, co-crucified, and co-raised and are now co-seated together with Christ in heavenly places. [See 2 Corinthians 5:14-21; Hosea 6:2; Ephesians 2:5, 6; and 1 Peter 1:3.])*

3:6 Holy Spirit is the extravagant Administrator of the salvation of Jesus Christ; gushing forth within us like an artesian well. *(An artesian well is a well, sunk through solid strata of sedimentary rock into strata from an area of a higher altitude than that of the well, so that there is sufficient pressure to force water to flow upward. From the French word, artesian, referring to the old French province Artois, where such wells were common.*

In John 7:37-39, John records how Jesus witnessed the eighth day, the great and final day of the Feast of Tabernacles, when, according to custom, the High Priest would draw water from the Pool of Siloam with a golden jar, mix the water with wine, and then pour it over the altar while the people would sing with great joy from Psalm 118:25-26, and also Isaiah 12:3; Therefore with joy shall we draw water from the wells of salvation. Then, Jesus, knowing that he is the completeness of every prophetic picture and promise, cried out with a loud voice: If anyone is thirsty, let him come to me and drink. If you believe that I am what the Scriptures are all about, you will discover that you are what I am all about, and rivers of living waters will gush from your innermost being. See Romans 5:5.)

3:7 His grace [1]**vindicates our innocence. We have also** [2]**become heirs to the life that we have always longed for, the life of the ages.** *(God's gift has restored our relationship with him and given us back our lives. —The Message.*

Both verbs pointing to our righteousness, as well as the fact that by the same grace we have become heirs, are in the Aorist tense, [1]**dikaiōthentes,** *having been declared righteous, and* [2]**genēthōmen** *, having been begotten. The Aorist tense presents an occurrence in summary, viewed as a whole from the outside, almost like a snapshot of the action.*

Titus 1:2 This is the life of the ages that was anticipated for generations; the life of our original design announced by the infallible resolve of God before time or space existed.

This life was made certain before eternal time. (BBE). Mankind's union with God is the original thought that inspired creation.)

3:8 You can confidently lean the weight of your being on this word. I want you to be emphatic about this; encourage the believers to be conscious of the fact that they are the [1]**custodians of this message. In their day-to-day lifestyle they positively advertise its attraction and beauty.** *(The word,* [1]**proistemi,** *is protector, guardian.)*

3:9 Avoid confusing speculations and debates about genealogies and quarrelsome controversies about the law; it is folly to engage in such [1]**useless conversation. It is like chewing chewing-gum that has long lost its flavor.** *(The word,* [1]**mataios,** *translates as folly, of no purpose, from* **maten,** *which is the accusative case of a derivative from the base of* **massō,** *to chew, to gnaw, like eating food with zero nutritional value.*

Hebrews 13:9 Do not be swayed by distracting speculations. Any influence foreign to what grace communicates, even if it seems very entertaining and carries the Christian label, is to be shunned. Feast on grace; do not dilute your diet with legalism. There is no nourishment left in the law. What's the use of being busy but not blessed? [Legalism includes any form of self-sacrifice or self-effort with the illusion of gaining further favor from God or improving your spiritual standing before God.])

3:10 If a person continues to be argumentative and factious *[distracting from the essence of the gospel],* **and you have brought it to his attention several times, then it is better to avoid his company.—**

3:11 Such a person is obviously out of line and brings himself under condemnation by [1]**his own autocratic ruling.** *(*[1]*autokatakritos)*

3:12 I will send Artemas to you, or possibly Tychicus, and then I want you to join me as soon as possible in Nicopolis where I have decided to spend the winter.

3:13 Do whatever you can to assist Zenas the Scribe and Apollos with their trip. Make sure they lack nothing. *(Acts 18:24, 19:1, 1 Corinthians 16:12.)*

3:14 Encourage our people to be productive and generous.

3:15 We all send you our fond greetings; salute our friends in the faith. Grace.

Introduction to Philemon

For more than two years during his third missionary journey, Paul ministered in Asia Minor among the people of Ephesus. He led many gentiles to discover Christ.

One of the visitors to Ephesus, converted under Paul's teaching was a man named Philemon, a slave-owner from the nearby city of Colossae [Philemon 1:19].

A strong bond of friendship existed between Paul and Philemon, one that would serve a significant purpose in light of the circumstance that brought about the letter.

A slave named Onēsimos had escaped from his owner, Philemon, and had run away from Colossae to Rome in the hope that he could disappear into that populous, urban environment. Once in Rome, Onēsimos, either by accident or by his own design, came in contact with Paul, who promptly led the runaway slave to faith in Jesus Christ. Paul had already been planning to send a letter to the Colossian church by the hand of Tychicus. So in AD 60 or 61 from a prison cell in Rome, Paul wrote a personal letter to Philemon and sent Onēsimos the slave back to Colossae. [Charles R. Swindoll]

May this precious letter inspire a new day across the planet for slavery in its every definition to be dissolved!

Marvin Vincent writes in his commentary, *Here we have a picture of Paul as a Christian gentleman.*

It is also a powerful exhibition of his method of dealing with a great social evil.

Paul's dealing with the institution of slavery displayed the profoundest Christian sagacity [acuteness of mental discernment and soundness of judgment]. To have attacked the institution as such would have been worse than useless. To one who reads between the lines, Paul's silence means more than any amount of denunciation; for with his silence goes his faith in the power of Christian sentiment to settle finally the whole question. He knows that to bring slavery into contact with living Christianity is to obliterate slavery. He accepts the social condition as a fact, and even as a law. He sends Onēsimos back to his legal owner. He does not bid Philemon emancipate him, but he puts the Christian slave on his true footing of a Christian brother beside his master. As to the institution, he knows that the recognition of the slave as free in Christ will carry with it, ultimately, the recognition of his civil freedom.

History vindicated him in the Roman empire itself. Under Constantine the effects of Christian sentiment began to appear in the church and in legislation concerning slaves. Official freeing of slaves became common as an act of pious gratitude. In 312 AD a law was passed prohibiting all inhumane acts against slaves as well as the unlimited permission to emancipate slaves. Each new ruler enacted some measure which facilitated emancipation. Every obstacle was thrown by the law in the way of separating families. Under Justinian [527 – 565 AD] all presumptions were in favor of liberty.

Great and deserved praise has been bestowed on this letter. Bengel says: A familiar and exceedingly courteous epistle concerning a private affair is inserted among the New Testament books, intended to afford a specimen of the highest wisdom as to how civil affairs could be arranged on loftier principles.

Franke, quoted by Bengel, says: The single epistle to Philemon surpasses all the wisdom of the world.

Renan: A true little chef-d'oeuvre of the art of letter-writing.

Sabatier: This short epistle gleams like a pearl of the most exquisite purity in the rich treasure of the New Testament.

1:1 Paul, imprisoned in Christ Jesus! I am here with my companion Timothy, addressing this writing to you, beloved ¹Philemon; you are an essential part of our team.

*(φιλημα ¹**philema**, showing fondness and affection through a kiss or a heartfelt hug, from the adjective φιλος **philos**, fond, friend, love.)*

1:2 Including your wife, Aphia and Archippus our campaigner as well as the entire ekklesia in your house.

1:3 The Father's ¹favor ²joins our lives inseparably in the Lordship of Jesus Christ.

*(Paul's regular greeting - ¹Grace and ²peace! The word, χάρις ¹**charis**, the divine influence upon the heart; that which affords joy, pleasure, delight, sweetness, charm, loveliness.*

*The word ²**eirēnē**, means peace, from **eirō**, to join, to be set at one again; in carpentry it is the strongest joint, referred to as the dovetail joint. Peace is a place of unhindered enjoyment of friendship beyond guilt, suspicion, blame or inferiority.)*

1:4 The thought of you always fills my prayers with so much joy and gratitude to my God.

1:5 I am thrilled with the news I keep hearing, of how the love and belief, oozing out of you, in your face to faceness before the Lord Jesus, keep spilling over towards everyone as they discover their redeemed innocence.

1:6 The acknowledging of every good thing that is in us in Christ, ignites the energy of faith in our fellowship with one another! This kind of koinonia is addictive!

*(Literally, The word, ἐνεργής **energēs**, is where we get our English word energy from. Here's what fires up faith and fellowship - simply acknowledge and appreciate that every divine attribute on display in Jesus Christ - is equally present in another!)*

1:7 I have received so much joy and ¹companionship from your love - also the tender affections of the believers have been ²rejuvenated in your friendship.

*([1] παράκλησις **paraklēsis** close companionship The word **paraklētos** comes from **para**, a Preposition indicating close proximity, a thing proceeding from a sphere of influence, with a suggestion of union of place of residence, to have sprung from its author and giver, originating from, denoting the point from which an action originates, intimate connection; and **kaleō**, meaning to identify by name, to surname. Jesus introduces the Holy Spirit in the same capacity: **paraklētos**, meaning close companion, kinsman [John 14:16].*

*[2] ἀναπαύω **anapauō** - **ana**, upwards and **pauō** rest. Thus, refreshed; rejuvenated.*

*Here as a Perfect Passive, αναπεπαυτα - **anapepauta**, the effect of what has happened continues into this present moment.)*

1:8 Now, I could be ¹bluntly bold in the light of our co-in-Christness, and ²charge you with an assignment to do the proper thing.

([1] παῤῥησία [1]parrhēsia all outspokenness; frankness, bluntness.

[2] ἐπιτασσειν, [2]epitassein, Present Infinitive to charge you with an assignment.)

1:9 However, the agapē-factor is by far the [1]greater motivator in [2]this matter! So, here I am, Paul, an [3]ambassador in bonds, prisoner of Jesus Christ, appealing to you.

([1] μᾶλλον mallon Adverb, the comparative of; more in a greater degree, or rather; far more; so much the more.

[2] τοιοῦτος toioutos, this kind of thing/matter

[3] The word, πρεσβυτης presbutēs, an old man, could also be, presbeutēs ambassador, because of common confusion by the scribes between u and eu. In the LXX four times the two words are used interchangeably.

See Ephesians 6:20 I am an ambassador in bonds, chained to this task of confidently communicating the revelation of the Gospel with the accuracy it deserves.

1:10 I implore you concerning my child, Onēsimos, whom I have birthed in my bonds.

(The name means, valuable, profitable or useful.)

1:11 The very one who was previously useless to you will now live up to his name and be very valuable to both of us!

(ἄχρηστος achrēstos useless, unprofitable; now, εὔχρηστος euchrēstos very profitable.)

1:12 I have sent him back to you to deliver this letter to you in person. He represents my most tender affections.

(The word in the Textus Receptus, προσλαβου receive him was introduced by copyists later; also su [Nominative - subject - you must therefore receive him], instead of soi [Dative - I have sent him to you]. Bruce Metzger .)

1:13 My sincere wish was to keep him here with me, as representing you, ministering to my needs while I am in prison for the sake of the gospel.

1:14 However, I do not wish to pressurize you into making a decision that is not your desire as well.

1:15 Perhaps he was briefly removed from you, so that you may now be inseparable.

1:16 To us, he is no longer a slave, but beyond all comparison, a beloved brother! He is extremely dear to me, and I know he will be even more so to you! Both for the person he is in the flesh as well as who he is in the Lord.

1:17 So, in the context of the koinonia we participate in, embrace him as you would embrace me.

1:18 Whatever the damage he caused or debt he owes, charge it to my account.

1:19 I, Paul, personally sign as surety for this - not to mention that you owe your life to me!

1:20 Indeed, my Brother, my wish is that you may [1]benefit me in the Lord! Refresh my inner being in Christ.

*(Paul uses a play of words on the name **Onēsimos**: using the Aorist Optative verb form οναιμην of ὀνίνημι [1]**oninēmi** - valuable, benefit; advantage; profitable or useful.)*

1:21 I know that you have heard my heart in this writing and I am convinced that you will do even more than what I have requested!

1:22 In the meantime, get a guest room ready for me; I believe that, in answer to your prayer, I'll be seeing you soon!

1:23 Epaphras embraces you with fondness. He is equally arrested with me at the spear-point of the gospel of Christ Jesus.

*(συναιχμάλωτος **sunaichmalōtos**, **sun**, jointly, plus **aichmalōtos**, to be arrested at spearpoint! Consider where they are! Rome is 2 100 km [1300 miles] from Colossae. Paul sees their presence in Rome as a geographical spearpoint [long distance javelin] of the Gospel.)*

1:24 Along with Mark, Aristarchus, Demas, and Luke, my fellow workers.

1:25 The grace of our Lord Jesus Christ entwines your spirit; indeed, each and everyone of you are equally included!

*(χάρις **charis** is the loveliness of divine favor and its influence upon the heart, which then, most naturally reflects in one's life.)*

The Author

The fact that Paul's message, which is the revelation of our restored innocence, based on the finished work of the cross, as witnessed in all his Epistles, is evident throughout this magnificent study, overshadows the argument that his signature as probable author is absent.

If not Paul, then certainly someone close to him; both Luke as well as Priscilla come to mind. Several words that only Luke uses, occur. The earliest statement on the authorship of Hebrews comes from Clement of Alexandria, [150 AD - 215 AD] who said that Paul wrote it in Hebrew and Luke translated it into Greek (Eusebius, History 6.14.2).

The early commentator Tertullian *(who wrote in the early 200s)* said Barnabas wrote Hebrews.

A.J. Gordon ascribes the authorship of Hebrews to Priscilla, writing that It is evident that the Holy Spirit made this woman Priscilla a teacher of teachers. Later proposed by Adolf von Harnack in 1900; Harnack's reasoning won the support of prominent Bible scholars of the early twentieth century. Harnack believes the letter was written in Rome – not to the Church, but to the inner circle. In setting forth his evidence for Priscillan authorship, he finds it amazing that the name of the author was blotted out by the earliest tradition. Citing Chapter 13, he says it was written by a person of high standing and apostolic teacher of equal rank with Timothy. If Luke, Clemens, Barnabas, or Apollos had written it, Harnack believes their names would not have been obliterated.

Donald Guthrie's commentary The Letter to the Hebrews (1983) mentions Priscilla by name as a suggested author.

Believing the author to have been Priscilla, Ruth Hoppin posits that the name was omitted either to suppress its female authorship, or to protect the letter itself from suppression.

Also convinced that Priscilla was the author of Hebrews, Gilbert Bilezikian, professor of biblical studies at Wheaton College, remarks on the conspiracy of anonymity in the ancient church, and reasons: The lack of any firm data concerning the identity of the author in the extant writings of the church suggests a deliberate blackout re than a case of collective loss of memory.

The Sabbath Rest

In Christ the Sabbath Rest is no longer a shadow prefiguring the real, a token holy day in the week, but the celebration of a perfect redemption in which the exact image and likeness of God is revealed and redeemed in human form. Mankind's innocence is redeemed. Having made purification for sins, he sat down ...

The executive authority of his throne is established on the fact of our innocence. Sabbath is now a place of God's unhindered enjoyment of mankind, and mankind's unhindered enjoyment of God. Through the torn veil of his flesh, he has triumphantly opened a new and living way for everyone into the life of their design, in the loving embrace of their Maker.

The Sabbath is where the perfection of everything that God has ever contemplated is celebrated. It is where the artist touches the canvas with a final brush stroke, signs their Name and revels in its beauty. If you revel in something, you're not just pleased or even excited; you're overwhelmed with joy. *Revel means to take great pleasure; to bask in its reflection; which often results in a state of blissful silence or, extravagant merry-making.*

God is not in their rest because they are exhausted, but because they are satisfied with what they see and know concerning us.

We are now invited with urgent persuasion to enter into what they see.

Elohim's rest was never at risk.

Their works were finished from the foundation of the world. Hebrews 4:3

This letter has a Hebrew audience in mind

It is written to exhort the Jewish believer neither to underestimate such a great salvation, nor to clutter the message with redundant Jewish rituals and sentiments.

Under the dispensation of the law of performance, historic Israel failed to access the redemptive Sabbath of God and remained snared in an inferior slave-mentality, we are insignificant grasshoppers in our eyes. Numbers 13:33

Hebrews 4:10 God's rest celebrates his finished work; whoever enters into God's rest immediately abandons his own efforts to improve what God has already perfected. (The language of the law is do; the language of grace is done.)

Hebrews 4:11 Let us therefore be ¹prompt to understand and fully appropriate that rest and not fall again into the same trap that snared Israel in ²unbelief. (The word, ¹spoudatzo, from spoude, I translated prompt, not labor; this word also reminds of the English word, speed; immediately. The word, ²apeitheia [apathy] from a as a negative particle, not; and peithō, convince; is often, wrongly translated, disobedience.)

Hebrews 4:12 The message God spoke to us in Christ, is the most life giving and dynamic influence in us, cutting like a surgeon's scalpel, sharper than a soldier's sword, piercing to the deepest core of human conscience, to the dividing of soul and spirit; ending the dominance of the sense realm and its neutralizing effect upon the human spirit. In this way a person's spirit is freed to become the ruling influence again in the thoughts and intentions of their heart. The scrutiny of this living Sword-Logos detects every possible disease, discerning the body's deepest secrets where joint and bone-marrow meet. (The moment we cease from our own efforts to justify ourselves, by yielding to the integrity of the message that announces the success of the Cross, God's word is triggered into action. What God spoke to us in sonship (the incarnation), radiates his image and likeness in our redeemed innocence. [Hebrews 1:1-3] This word powerfully penetrates and impacts our whole being; body, soul and spirit. Psalm 139:2, You know the deepest impulse of my thoughts; engaging the secret longings of the heart. The Sword would always point back to mankind's original identity. The Hebrew word in Genesis 3:24, הפך hâpak is a primitive root; meaning to turn about; by implication to change, to return, to be converted, turn back. Also in the Septuagint the same thought is communicated in the Greek word, strephō, which is the strengthened from the base of tropay; to turn around or reverse: - convert, turn again, back again, to turn self about. In Luke 15 the prodigal son returns to himself - Plato is quoted by Ackerman [Christian Element in Plato] as thinking of redemption as coming to oneself. See Notes on the splendor of the Gates Revelation 21.)

Righteousness by God's faith. Habakkuk 2:4

Hebrews 10:38 Righteousness by God's faith defines life; reverting to the law of works ignores God's work of grace. (Instead of reading the curse when disaster strikes, Habakkuk realizes that the Promise out-dates performance as the basis to mankind's acquittal. Deuteronomy 28 would no longer be the motivation or the measure of right or wrong behavior. Though the fig trees do not blossom, nor fruit be on the vines, the produce of the olive fail and the fields yield no food, the flock be cut off from the fold and there be no herd in the stalls, yet I will rejoice in the Lord, I will joy in the God of my salvation. God, the Lord, is my strength; he makes my feet like hinds' feet, he makes me tread upon my high places. (Habakkuk 3:17-19 RSV)

In the Gospel, the righteousness of God is revealed, from faith to faith. [Romans 1:17] Herein lies the secret of the power of the Gospel; there is no good news in it until the righteousness of God is revealed. (The good news is the fact that the cross of Christ was a success. God rescued the life of our design; he redeemed our innocence. Mankind would never again be judged righteous or unrighteous by their own ability to obey moral laws. It is not about what a person must or must not do but about what Jesus has done.) God now persuades everyone to believe what he knows to be true about them. (It is from faith to faith.) The Prophets wrote in advance about the fact that God believes that righteousness unveils the life that he always had in mind for us. The just shall live by his (God's) faith. Righteousness by God's faith defines life.

Hebrews 12:1 Look away from the shadow dispensation of the law and the Prophets and fix your eyes upon Jesus. He is the fountainhead and conclusion of faith. He saw the joy (of mankind's salvation) when he braved the cross and despised the shame of it. As the executive authority of God (the right hand of the throne of God), he now occupies the highest seat of dominion to endorse mankind's innocence.

The Gospel is the revelation of the righteousness of God; it declares how God succeeded to put mankind right with him. It is about what God did right, not what Adam did wrong. The word righteousness comes from the Anglo Saxon word, *rightwiseness*, wise in that which is right. In Greek, the word for righteousness is *dikaiosunē*, from *dikē*, pronounced, dikay, suggesting to be judged equal; it implies the idea of two parties finding likeness in each other.

2 Corinthians 6:14 Faith-righteousness has nothing in common with the philosophies of karma and performance-based approval; they could never [1]balance the scales or be evenly yoked together in any context. (The word [1]*heterozugeō*, an unequal or different yoke; from the Hebrew word, **zugot**, זוגות indicates pairs of two identical objects; a yoke or a teaching; the yoke of a rabbi or philosopher represented their doctrine; reminds of the Hebrew word for righteousness, **tzedek,** צדק which also includes the idea of the wooden beam in a scale of balances. He that judges his neighbor according to the balance of righteousness, or innocence, they judge him according to righteousness. [T. Bab. Sabbat, fol. 127. 2.] The Greek stem for righteousness is **dikē** - it is interesting to note that the Greek goddess of Justice is Dikē [pronounced, **dikay**] and she is always pictured holding a scale of balances in her hand.)

Colossians 2:9 In him, all the fullness of [1]Deity [2]resides in a human body. He proves that human life is tailor-made for God. (The word, [1]**theotes**, godhead/ deity, is feminine. Jesus exhibits what the Father, Son and Spirit is like, in human form. The word [2]**katoikeō** means to dwell in, to inhabit. While the expanse cannot measure or define God, their detailed likeness is displayed in human skin. See Colossians 1:19, God is fully at home in him. Jesus is God's happy delight to be human.)

Colossians 2:10 We are complete in him. Jesus mirrors our wholeness and [1]endorses our true identity. He is I am in us. (God packaged completeness in I am, mirrored in you. The word, [1]**exousia**, is often translated as authority; from, **ek + eimi**, originating out of I am. The days are over where our lives were dictated to under the rule of the law of performance and an inferior identity. It's not about who I used to be or who I'm striving to become; we are celebrating who I am. Any teaching that leaves one with a sense of lack and imperfection rather than completeness is a distraction from the truth. Jesus is the author and finisher of faith's capacity within us to mirror and celebrate completeness.)

God desires to show more convincingly to the heirs of the promise the unchangeable character of his purpose. (Hebrews 6:17 — RSV)

If Christ is both the author and perfecter of faith, self-assessment by any other reference would be foolish. It would be just as impossible to attempt to measure temperature with a ruler. Christ defines our original design and our restored innocence. We find our identity and our destiny there.

We have obtained immediate and unrestricted access into the intimate fellowship and friendship of the Father, Son and Holy Spirit.

Nothing that we might personally sacrifice could ever add any virtue to our innocence.

A brand new way of life has been introduced.

Because of his torn flesh on the cross, our own flesh can no longer be made an excuse for veiling our experience of Abba's favor and presence.

We have a High Priest in the house.

We are free to engage Father Son and Spirit with absolute confidence, fully persuaded that nothing can ever separate us. We are invited to draw near now.

Hebrews 4:13 *The entire person is thoroughly exposed to his scrutinizing gaze.* *(The thought of you intrigues your Maker with delight. There is nothing about you that he doesn't know. He knows your deepest thoughts and understands the secret longings of your heart. Psalm 139:2)*

Hebrews 4:14 *In the message of the incarnation, we have Jesus the Son of God representing mankind in the highest place of spiritual authority. That which God has spoken to us in him is his final word. It is echoed now in our conversation.*

Hebrews 4:15 *As High Priest he fully identifies with us in the context of our frail human lives. Having subjected it to close scrutiny, he proved that the human frame was master over sin. His sympathy with us is not to be seen as excusing weaknesses which are the result of a faulty design, but rather as a trophy to mankind.* *(He is not an example for us but of us.)*

Hebrews 4:16 *For this reason we can approach the authoritative throne of grace with bold utterance. We are welcome there in his embrace, and are [1]reinforced with immediate effect in times of trouble.* *(The word, [1]boetheia, means to be reinforced, specifically a rope or chain for frapping a vessel in a storm. In his incarnate human body Jesus represents us on the deepest possible level of every detail of our lives, spirit, soul and body. He victoriously faced every onslaught and scrutiny that we would ever possibly encounter.)*

The Kruger National Park

Lydia and I love the Kruger National Park. It is our favorite holiday destination. *[We spent 5 weeks there at the end of 2010 doing most of the book of Hebrews.]*

While on a game drive early one morning, I was filled with such gratitude to be there, and to know that we have a valid entry permit; and how the gospel reveals our restored innocence through the successful accomplishment of Christ as the vehicle that gives access to the sanctuary encounter of God.

He secured our right of access to every imaginable blessing. Jesus gives definition to God's eternal love-dream of our unhindered union with him, forever free from the obstructive consciousness of sin.

This is what the theme of the book of Hebrews is all about.

When you visit the Game Reserve you are immediately aware that you are in a very special place. The glossy pictures in the official road map promise glimpses of the enormous variety of game on record. The stage is set; everything is in place. You do not bring anything but your own presence to this Reserve. All its magnificent plant, bird, animal, reptile, and insect species are already there and fully represented. They give unique context to the place. As you drive or sit quietly at your camp or some remote water hole, the sights, sounds and smells are powerful confirmations, complementing and confirming the attraction of the bush.

Here, the roar of the lion belongs to me, the fresh footprint in the sand, the call of the fish eagle, as well as the vastness of the landscape with its magnificent trees. Every sunrise and sunset continues to decorate the canvas of my horizon.

The entry permit gives every visitor equal access to the Reserve. Yet it takes the keen, observant eye to often encounter the most amazing sightings.

To visit the Reserve simply to tick off the next sighting on your list, certainly does not do justice to the awesome pleasure and thrill of being surrounded by such splendid beauty. The fact that these animals are not caged makes it even more exciting to track them down or be surprised by their sudden appearance in view.

This, by far, beats the glossy brochure and the most realistic zoo experience.

In traditional church-life we have often sought to confine the Holy Spirit within the narrow scope of predictable programs and routines.

In Christ, a new and exciting way for authentic encounter is opened, without hesitation or restriction. Christ is not caged in a historical prophetic picture, but unveiled in pulsating tangible human life.

This Epistle belongs to every believer.

It is a document of profound beauty, leading the student beyond insubstantial religious rituals and sentiments into tangible Divine intimacy.

In his book, Mind Aflame, James Arraj writes about Emile Merch, *It is the work of a guide to lead us to the top of a mountain and then to move aside to let us see the tremendous vistas on every side. What remains is our gratitude to the teacher for bringing us to such a place.*

But as splendid as this mystery is, it is meant to draw you into the mystery of Christ. The Word of God has become flesh, and by taking a human form in that very act has transformed it and transforms, as well, the universe and the human race. You have a new being in Christ in which you share through him in the very life of the Trinity.

1:1 Throughout [1]ancient times God spoke in many fragments and glimpses of prophetic thought to our fathers. Now, this entire conversation has [2]finally dawned in sonship. Suddenly, what seemed to be an ancient language falls fresh and new like the dew on the tender grass. He is the sum total of every utterance of God. He is whom the Prophets pointed to and we are his immediate audience.

([1] The word [1]palai, meaning, of old, ancient; from palin through the idea of oscillatory repetition or retrocession; anew, afresh.

Deuteronomy 32:1 Give ear, Oh heavens, and I will speak; and let the earth hear the words of my mouth.

Deuteronomy 32:2 May my teaching drop as the rain, my speech distil as the dew, as the gentle rain upon the tender grass, and as the showers upon the herb....

Deuteronomy 32:18 You were unmindful of the Rock that begot you, and you forgot the God who gave you birth.

Like in James 1:24, we have forgotten what manner of people we are - we have forgotten the face of our birth.

Jesus successfully rescued the real you, not the pseudo, make-belief you. God has never believed less of you than what he was able to communicate in the sonship that Jesus mirrored and redeemed.

[2] The word [2]eschatos means extreme; last in time or in space; the uttermost part, the final conclusion. What God said about 'you-manity' in Jesus defines eschatology.)

1:2 In a son, God declares the Incarnate Word to be the heir of all things. He is, after all, the author of the ages. *(See John 1:2 The beginning mirrors the Word face to face with God. [The beginning declares the destiny of the Word, image and likeness would be mirrored and redeemed in incarnate human form.] Also John 1:3, All things came into being through him, and apart from him nothing that exists came into being. Sonship endorses heirship. See Hebrews 6:16-18.)*

1:3 The Messiah-message is what has been on the tip of the Father's tongue all along. Now he is the crescendo of God's conversation with us and gives context and content to the authentic, prophetic thought. Everything that God has in mind for mankind is voiced in him. The incarnate Christ-Messiah, Jesus, is God's language. He is the [1]radiant and flawless mirror expression of the person of God. He makes the [2]glorious intent of God visible and exhibits the [3]character and every attribute of Elohim in human form. [4]Having accomplished the cleansing of our sins, he sat down, enthroned in the boundless measure of his majesty in the right hand of God. He is the force of the universe, [5]upholding everything that exists by the word of his power. This conversation is the dynamic that sustains the entire cosmos.

([1] The word απαυγασμα [1]apaugasma, only occurs here, and once only in the Greek Septuagint, LXX, in the book of Wisdom 7:26, For she is the brightness of the everlasting light, the unspotted mirror of the power of God, and the image of his goodness. [The Book of Wisdom 7:26.]

[2] The word, δόξα [2]doxa, intent, opinion, often translated, glory. See my comment on 2 Corinthians 3:18.

[3] The word χαρακτηρ [3]charakter from χάραγμα charagma - to engrave - translated mark of the beast, in Revelation 13:16,17. Either the character of the Father or the character of the fallen mind will influence our actions (hand) because it is what engages our thoughts (forehead).

[4] Having accomplished purification of sins, he sat down ... [4]His throne is the very endorsement of mankind's redeemed innocence. See Romans 4:25, also,

Colossians 2:14 His body nailed to the cross hung there as the document of mankind's guilt; in dying our death he canceled the detailed hand-written [3]record which testified against us. Every stain on our conscience, reminding of the sense of failure and guilt, was thus fully blotted out.

Colossians 2:15 He thus defused and brought closure to every possible claim of accusation against the human race. He turned the scandal and shame of the cross into an eternal trophy, celebrating the genius of God. Every principality and power was stripped naked and publicly paraded through the streets. The voice of the cross will never be silenced! *(The success of the cross is the crux of the gospel. Its horror is now the eternal trophy of God's triumph over sin. The cross stripped religion of its assumed role to control people with guilt. Every accusation lost its leverage to blackmail the human race with condemnation and shame.*

Also, Ephesians 1:20-23; LXX Psalm 109:1; Hosea 6:2; then, Ephesians 2:5,6 & Colossians 3:1-3, We were co-quicked, co-raised, co-elevated and co-seated!

[5] The words, φέρων τε τὰ πάντα - [5]upholding all things, are not static, but dynamic! They imply sustaining, but also movement. It deals with a burden, not as a dead weight, but as in continual movement; as Weiss puts it, with the all in all its changes and transformations throughout the aeons. Vincent.

More than two thousand years ago the conversation that had begun before time was recorded—sustained in fragments of thought throughout the ages, whispered in prophetic language, chiseled in stone and inscribed in human conscience and memory—became a man. Beyond the tablet of stone, the papyrus scroll or parchment roll, human life has become the articulate voice of God. Jesus is the crescendo of God's conversation with mankind; he gives context and content to the authentic thought. His name declares his mission. As Savior of the world he truly redeemed the image and likeness of the invisible God and made him apparent again in human form as in a mirror.)

1:4 He is beyond comparison in stature and significance to any prophetic messenger; his name spells mankind's salvation; the entire earth is his inheritance. *(Jesus says in* **John 5:39** *You scrutinize the Scriptures tirelessly, assuming that in them you embrace the life of the ages - yet I am what the Scriptures are all about.* **Psalm 2:7,8***...I have given you the ends of the earth as your inheritance. Also Psalm 24:1.)*

1:5 God did not address any of the prophetic messengers when he said, You are my Son, today I have [1]begotten you. I am to you all that a Father can be to a son, and you are to me all that a son can be to a Father.

([1] Psalm 2:7,8, 'You are my Son, today I have begotten you.' The word, γεγεννηκα [1]gegennēka, is the Perfect Active Indicative of gennaō which refers to the incarnation [John 1:1-3 and 14] as well as to the resurrection. It is important to note that the incarnation is not the origin of Jesus. See my commentary note on John 1:1. See Acts 13:30-33 But God raised him from the dead; and for many days he appeared to those who came up with him from Galilee to Jerusalem, who are now his witnesses to the people. And we bring you the Good News that what God promised to the fathers, he has fulfilled to us their children by raising Jesus; as also it is written in the 2nd Psalm, Today I have begotten you. The resurrection of Jesus represents our new birth and our redeemed sonship. See 1Peter 1:3. Also my notes on the day of the Lord, Revelation 1.)

1:6 And when he introduces his Son as his firstborn, to the whole inhabited world, he says, Let all God's messengers worship him in adoration.

(This quote is from the LXX Septuagint since this verse was not in the Hebrew text, **Deuteronomy 32:43** *Rejoice, oh heavens, with him, and let all the prophetic-messengers of God worship him; rejoice oh Gentiles together with his people, and let all the sons of God strengthen themselves in him. [Here the Gentiles are proclaimed as joint heirs in equal sonship.]*

> *This reminds of* **Ephesians 4:8, Scripture confirms that he led us as trophies in his triumphant procession on high; he [1]repossessed his gift** *[likeness]* **in mankind.** *Quote from Psalm 67:19 LXX Septuagint,* [1]ἔλαβες δόματα ἐν ἀνθρώπῳ, *elabes domata en [in] anthrōpō - You have repossessed gifts in human form. The word elabes from lambanō means to take what is one's own. The word for the human species, male or female is anthropos, from ana, upward, and tropos, manner of life; character; in like manner. [Hebrew text, Psalm 68:18,19* לקחת מתנות באדם *lakachat mattanoth ba adam - You have taken gifts in Adam.* **The gifts which Jesus Christ distributes to us he has received in us, in and by virtue of his incarnation.** *Adam Clarke.]*
>
> *We were born anew in his resurrection. [1 Peter 1:3, Hosea 6:2]*
>
> **Ephesians 4:9 The fact that he ascended confirms his victorious descent into the deepest pits of human despair** . *(See John 3:13 [RSV], No one has ascended into heaven but he who descended from heaven, even the son of man. All mankind originates from above; we are anouthen, from above.)*
>
> **Ephesians 4:10 He now occupies the ultimate rank of authority, from the lowest regions, wherein he stooped down to rescue us, to the highest authority in the heavens, having executed his mission to the fullest.** *(Fallen mankind is fully restored to the authority of the authentic life of their design. See Colossians 1:18... He is the principal rank of authority who leads the triumphant procession of our new birth out of the region of the dead. [... leading the resurrection parade — The Message.] See also Revelation 1:5,6.)*

1:7 Of the prophetic messengers he says, I inspire you to be swift like the wind and he fashions those who work his cause like a flash of lightning. *(LXX-Psalm 103:4)*

1:8 But when he addresses the Son he says, Your throne, Oh God, extends to the ages of the ages. The scepter of righteousness is the scepter of your kingdom. *(Psalm 45:6. His throne is established upon our redeemed innocence. Hebrews 1:3.)*

1:9 You love righteousness and [1]shield your seed from wickedness. Oh God, your God anointed you with the oil of joy; you stand head and shoulders above your associates. *(Psalm 45:7. The word, hate* שנא *sana the creation of distance between elements, often preceded by a breaking apart, and followed by a removal or storage. In Ancient Hebrew* ⟩⟨ *speaks of a shield of thorns protecting the seed against wickedness. The AH for wickedness, resha,* ⊙ᝣᏑ *reading from right to left pictures a head and two front teeth meaning to chew or, also to strike like a serpent and an eye; thus, a distorted perception.)*

1:10 The earth traces its foundation back to you, the heavens also are your invention; they are all hand-crafted by you. *(Psalm 102:25-27)*

1:11 They shall become obsolete, but you will remain; they shall wear like an old garment, *(The old order will be replaced with the new.)*

1:12 and you will fold them up as a mantle *[which reminds of the folded head-cloth in Jesus' grave after his resurrection - John 20:7]*; **they shall be [1]renewed, but you remain I am, and your years will never cease.** *(This is resurrection-language. The word,* חָלַף *[1]Chalap, to be renewed; to be made to sprout.*

> *See Hebrews 8:13 He announces the new dispensation to confirm that the old shadow system has been rendered redundant. See Colossians 3:9 That old life was a lie, foreign to our design. Those garments of disguise are now thoroughly stripped off us in our understanding of our union with Christ in his death and resurrection. We are no longer obliged to live under the identity and rule of the robes we wore before.)*

1:13 Neither was it any of the prophetic messengers he had in mind when he said, You are the extension of my right hand; my executive authority; take your position and witness how I make your enemies a place upon which you may rest your feet. *(See Hebrews 10:13; Luke 20:41-44; Psalm 109:1 LXX, also Isaiah 66:1)*

1:14 Are they not all Spirit-employed and commissioned on behalf of everyone who was about to become heirs of salvation. *(λειτουργικα 1 Peter 1:10-14.)*

Hebrews Chapter 1 Extended Notes:

Notes on Hebrews Chapter 1

Notes on Hebrews Chapter 1

The many and various ways in which God spoke of old to the fathers through the prophets is compared to the difference between an angelic messenger and the ultimate conclusion of the prophetic word in the Incarnate One, the Messiah. Who, in his sonship, revealed and redeemed mankind's sonship. Most of these examples and references mentioned in chapter one are from David's Psalms and clearly points to someone and a time beyond his own life and generation. If David himself or his generation were the subject of these prophecies, then Scripture would cease to be relevant and therefore merely reduced to a historical document. *[See 1 Peter 1:12 in these notes]*

When young Philip is commissioned to join the chariot of the chief treasurer of Ethiopia, he hears him read from Isaiah 53:7,8, Like a lamb led to slaughter, he did not open his mouth to defend himself... and immediately asks him, Sir, do you understand what you are reading? The Treasurer's question was very relevant, Was the prophet speaking about himself or did he have someone else in mind? And beginning with this verse, Philip told him the good news of Jesus. Acts 8:29-35.

Commentary to Hebrews 1: 5 *(Psalm 2:7,8, 'You are my Son, today I have* **begotten you.** *The word,* γεγεννηκα [1]**gegennēka,** *Perfect Active Indicative of* **gennaō** *refers to* **the incarnation** *[John 1:1-3 and 14] as well as to* **the resurrection.** *It is important to note that* **the incarnation is not the origin of Jesus.** *See my commentary note on John 1:1. See Acts 13:30-33 But God raised him from the dead; and for many days he appeared to those who came up with him from Galilee to Jerusalem, who are now his witnesses to the people. And we bring you the Good News that what God promised to the fathers, he has fulfilled to us their children by raising Jesus; as also it is written in the 2nd Psalm, Today I have begotten you. The resurrection of Jesus represents our new birth and our redeemed sonship. See 1Peter 1:3. Also my notes on the day of the Lord, Revelation 1.* **John 1:1 To go back to the very [1]beginning, is to find the [2]Word already [3]present there; [4]face to face with God. The one mirrors the other. The Word is [3]I am; God's [2]eloquence echoes and [4]concludes in him. The Word equals God.** *(In the beginning,* [1]**archē,** *to be first in order, time, place or rank. The Word,* [2]**logos,** *was with God; here and again in verse 2 John uses the Greek Preposition* [4]**pros,** *towards; face-to-face.*

Three times in this sentence John uses the Active Indicative Imperfect form of the verb [3]**eimi,** *namely* **aēn** *[ἦν] to continue to be, [in the beginning 'was' the Word etc...] which conveys no idea of origin for God or for the Logos, but simply continuous existence, I am. Quite a different verb* **egeneto,** *became, appears in John 1:14 for the beginning of the Incarnation of the Logos. The Word 'became' flesh. The incarnation is not the origin of Jesus. See the distinction sharply drawn in John 8:58, before Abraham was [born,* **genesthai** *from* **ginomai] I am. The word** **eimi,** *I am; the essence of being, suggesting timeless existence. See my commentary note on 1 Peter 1:16)*

John 1:2 The beginning mirrors the Word face to face with God. *(Nothing that is witnessed in the Word distracts from who God is. If you have seen me, you have seen the Father. [John 14:9] The Word that was from the beginning was not* *yet written or spoken; it was simply face to face with God. The beginning declares the destiny of the Word, image and likeness would be mirrored and redeemed in incarnate human form.)*

John 1:3 The Logos is the source; everything commences in him. He remains the exclusive Parent reference to their existence. There is nothing original, except the Word. The Logic of God defines the only possible place where mankind can trace their origin. *(All things were made by him; and without him was not any thing made that was made. KJV See Colossians 1:16.)*

Peter powerfully mirrors Hebrews chapter 1 in his own Epistle,

See 1 Peter chapter 1

He continues to quote Hebrews also in the next chapter - See **1 Peter 2:5-7***.*

.

2:1 I have said all this to help you realize the timeless relevance of the [1]message you have heard. [2]Constantly engage its mirror-meaning and thus you will never drift away from its influence and appeal. *([1]Hebrews 1:1-3. [2]The word προσεχειν prosechein, with pros, face to face, and echō; in the Present Infinitive, which suggests a continual engagement.)*

2:2 The words which God spoke through prophetic-messengers, were not to be taken lightly; considering the fact that the many and various ways in which God spoke to our fathers, *(1:1-3)* did not compromise the initial intention and [1]resolve of God; neither did the prophetic announcement distract from the [2]ultimate conclusion of the word, [5]realized in the Son of God. The prophetic word [2]stands above reproach in every way; the same [3]source is confirmed in our hearing today, and is to be [4]judged in the same integrity. *(Note the words, [1]bebaios, steadfast, from bainō, to stand, and [2]parabainō, and [3]parakoō are used here; para, closest possible proximity and bainō, footprint, to stand; and then also the word para combined with akoō, to hear, hearing from the original source. The word, [4]endikē, from en, in, and dikē, judged equal, two parties finding likeness in each other; a scale perfectly balanced. The word, [5]lambanō, to receive, to realize, to grasp, to associate with.)*

2:3 No one can afford to underestimate and be blasé about this final message; a salvation of such magnificent proportions. There is no alternative [1]escape. Salvation as it is articulated in Christ, is the message that God spoke from the beginning, and it was confirmed again and again by those who heard him. *(We are [1]rescued from the lies that we believed about ourselves under the law of performance.)*

2:4 The delightful resolve of God in every sign, miracle, and diffusion of Holy Spirit bears joint-testimony to the magnificence of this salvation.

2:5 God never intended to put celestial-messengers in charge of this [1]new world order that we are speaking of. *(The [1]age and dispensation of mankind's realized, redeemed sonship and identity.)*

2:6 [1]Somewhere in the Scriptures it is written, What is it about the human species that God cannot get them out of his mind? What does he [2]see in the son of man that so captivates his gaze? *([1]Psalm 8:4-6. The word [2]episkeptomai, from epi, continuous influence upon, and skopos, to view; to observe with keen interest.)*

2:7 It seems that man briefly descends to a [1]less elevated place than Elohim; yet he is crowned with God's own glory and dignity, and appointed in a position of authority over all the works of his hands. *(Possibly, a copyist felt that the reference to equality with our Maker [Genesis 1:26] was too bold, so the Greek text reads, he made us a little lower than the celestial messengers. Here is the reference, Psalm 8:4 What is man that you are mindful of him, and the son of man that you care so much for him? Psalm 8:5 Yet you made him little less than God, [Elohim] and crowns him with glory and honor. Psalm 8:6 You have given him dominion over the works of your hands; you have put all things under his feet.*
The word ἐλαττόω [1]elattoō [English, elation] suggests a little less than Elohim.)

2:8 God's intention was that human life should rule the planet. He subjected everything without exception to his control. Yet, looking at the human race, it does not seem that way at all.

2:9 But what is apparent, is Jesus. *[Now God spoke to us in a son. Hebrews 1:1-3]* Let us then consider him in such a way, that we may clearly perceive what God is saying to mankind in him. In the death he suffered, he briefly descended to a seemingly less elevated place than Elohim, *[Psalm 8:5]* in order to taste the death of the entire human race, and in doing so, to fulfill the grace of God and be crowned again *[as a man, representing all of mankind]* with glory and highly esteemed honor.

(Philippians 2:6 His being God's equal in form and likeness was official; his Sonship did not steal the limelight from his Father. Neither did his humanity distract from the deity of God.

Philippians 2:7 His mission however, was not to prove his deity, but to embrace our humanity. Emptied of his reputation as God, he fully embraced our physical human form; born in our resemblance he identified himself as the servant of the human race. His love enslaved him to us.

Philippians 2:8 And so we have the drama of the cross in context: the man Jesus Christ who is fully God, becomes fully man to the extent of willingly dying humanity's death at the hands of his own creation. He embraced the curse and shame of the lowest kind in dying a criminal's death. (Thus, through the doorway of death, he descended into our hellish darkness. Revelation 9:1 When the fifth celestial messenger blew his trumpet, I saw a star that had fallen to earth from the sky. The star was given the key to the shaft into the fathomless depths of the Abyss. [In his death, Jesus conquered the underworld and he has the keys; no-one else does.] Revelation 1:18 I am also the Living One; I died and now, see, here I am alive unto the ages of the ages and I have the keys wherewith I have disengaged the gates of Hadēs and death. Also, Ephesians 4:8-10.)

Philippians 2:9 From this place of utter humiliation, God exalted him to the highest rank. God graced Jesus with a Name that is far above every other name. (Ephesians 1:20 Do you want to measure the mind and muscle of God? Consider the force which he unleashed in Jesus Christ when he raised him from the dead and forever seated him enthroned as his executive authority in the realm of the heavens. The man, Jesus, is God's right hand of power. He was raised up from the deepest dungeons of human despair to the highest region of heavenly bliss. [See Ephesians 2:5,6 & 4:8,9] Ephesians 1:21 Infinitely above all the combined forces of rule, authority, dominion or governments; he is ranked superior to any name that could ever be given to anyone of this age or any age still to come in the eternal future. The name of Jesus endorses his mission as fully accomplished. He is the Savior of the world. Titus 2:11 The grace of God shines as bright as day making the salvation of mankind undeniably visible. See also Ephesians 3:15, Every family in heaven and on earth originates in him; his is mankind's family name and he remains the authentic identity of every nation.]

See Luke 10:18-24 in the Mirror)

2:10 He [1]towers in conspicuous prominence far above all things. He is both their author and their conclusion. All things exist in him and through him. He now, triumphantly leads everyone as sons to glory, through a perfect salvation. The extent of the suffering he bore is the measure of the perfection of the salvation over which he presides.

*(The word, [1]**prepo**, means to tower; see Hebrews 7:26 - 8:1 and **Ephesians 4:8-10**.*

*Also **Colossians 1:15** **In him the image and likeness of God is made visible in human form in order that everyone may recognize their true origin in him. He is the firstborn of every creature.** [What darkness veiled from us, he unveiled. In him we clearly see the mirror reflection of our original life. The Son of his love gives accurate evidence of his image in human form. The incarnation means that God can never again be invisible.]*

__Colossians 1:16 Everything that is, begins in him; whether in the heavenly realm or upon the earth, visible or invisible, he is the original blueprint of every order of justice and every level of authority, be it kingdoms or governments, principalities or jurisdictions; the original form of all things were founded by him and created for him.__ [Any order that does not mirror Christ is a distortion of man's own making.]

__Colossians 1:17 He is the initiator of all things, therefore everything finds its relevance and its true pattern only in him.__

__Colossians 1:18 The ekklesia-church is the bodily, incarnate expression of which Jesus is the head. He is the principal rank of authority who leads the triumphant procession of our new birth out of the region of the dead. His preeminent rank is beyond threat.__ (... leading the resurrection parade — The Message. See also Revelation 1:5 and Ephesians 4:8,9; Colossians 2:9 & 10.)

2:11 Because both he who carried out the rescue mission, as well as those whom he saved and restored to innocence, [1]originate from the same [2]source. Therefore he is not ashamed to introduce [3]each and everyone individually, as [4]his siblings. *(The word, εξ [1]**eks** [origin; source] [2]**henos** [one] [3]**pantes** [each and everyone]; [4]**adelphous**, with a as a connective particle and **delphus**, the womb; siblings, from the same womb. See Romans 8:29)*

2:12 He says, I will [1]reveal your name to my brothers as being their own; in this great [2]family reunion I will celebrate you in song.

*(This is a powerful reference to the great, dramatic **Psalm 22** which gives profound context to the entire conversation recorded in the book of Hebrews.*

*[**Psalm 22:22**] In Hebrew: I will [1]inscribe your name, in the core of my kindred; The word, ספר **safar**, means enumerate, detail; and the word, **tavek**, תוך means to cut to the core, sever, to bisect; it is a mathematical term which is the division of a given curve, figure, or interval into two equal parts, the one mirroring the other.*

***Psalm 22:27**, And all the ends of the earth shall remember and return to the Lord. All the families of every nation shall worship him face to face.*

This also dramatically reminds of the emotional moment when Joseph revealed himself to his brothers. [Genesis 45:1]

*The [2]**ekklesia** is the great family reunion. From **ek**, source or origin and **kaleō**, to surname - thus our authentic identity is redeemed, Simon, son of Jonah [surname], Who do you say that I, the Son of Man am? He replied, You are the Christ, the son of the living God. Jesus responded, Blessed are you. Flesh and blood has not revealed this to you, but my Father has. I say, you are Mr Rock [**petros**], a chip off the old block [**petra**]. Upon this rock [the revelation that the son of man is the son of God] I will build* *my ekklesia-church and the gates of Hadēs [ha, negative plus eidō, to see] will not prevail against you. In a walled city, the gates are the most strategic point - if the gates are disengaged, the city is taken. Thus, the blindfold mode of mankind's forgotten identity, will not prevail against you.)*

2:13 [1]I will rest my confident trust in him. I am surrounded by the children which God has given me. I am one of them.

(Precise [1]quote from Isaiah 8:17 in the Septuagint; And One [the Messiah] shall say, I will remain in seamless abiding [menō] in God and I will be yielding upon him. πεποιθὼς ἔσομαι ἐπ'αὐτῷ pepoithōs esomai Ephesians' autō - then, Isaiah 8:18. See also its context in Isaiah 7:14/ 8:8,10 -the only 3 places where Immanuel is mentioned.)

2:14 The fact that the children are flesh and blood-beings by design, explains the incarnation. In the genius of God, the Word was always destined to become flesh - he lived and died in a body as fully human as ours. Dying our death was his doorway into our deepest fears. He thus [1]disengaged the dominion of the death that trapped the human race in a [2]fallen mindset.

(Had he done all this in a superhuman body, the implications of his life, death and resurrection would be irrelevant. The word, καταργέω [1]katargeō means, to render entirely useless. Then, [2]diabolos, usually translated Devil, literally, dia + ballō, thus, as a result of the fall.)

2:15 As a fellow human, he re-defined death and delivered them from the lifelong dread of death. *(He brought final closure to the idea of judgment, which is what the system of works is all about. Hebrews 9:27,28. Evil is not immortal, love is. See 1 John 4:18.)*

2:16 This is why it is so relevant to understand that Jesus did not arrive on the planet in a celestial form *[or a Superman-suit];* **he is the seed of Abraham.** *(The seed of faith-righteousness and not flesh-righteousness. See **Galatians 3:16 It is on record that the promise** [of the blessing of righteousness by God's faith] **was made to Abraham and to his seed, singular,** [thus excluding his effort to produce Ishmael.] **Isaac, the child of promise and not of the flesh mirrors the Messiah.** Galatians 3:7 The conclusion is clear; faith and not flesh relates us to Abraham. [Grace rather than law is our true lineage. Ishmael represents so much more than the Muslim religion. Ishmael represents the clumsy effort of the flesh to compete with faith; the preaching of a mixed message of law and grace.] See also Galatians 4:21-31.)*

2:17 He therefore completely assimilated every detail of his human family so that, as Chief Priest standing face to face before God, his compassion and unwavering faith would prevail effectively over the [1]lies that they believed about themselves, having fully accomplished their [2]at-one-ment.

*(The Greek word, [1]hamartia, often translated as sin, is the word, **ha**, without, and **meros**, allotted portion; which is the stem of the word **morphē**, form; thus a distorted form; the lie that we believed about ourselves as a result of the futile ways we inherited from our fathers. See 1 Peter 1:18. The word [2]ἱλάσκομαι **hilaskomai**, means to conciliate, to bring about atonement/conciliation, from **hileos**, gracious, merciful.*

1 John 2:2 Jesus is our at-one-ment, he has reconciled us to himself and has taken our sins and distortions out of the equation. What he has accomplished is not to be seen as something that belongs to us exclusively; the same at-one-ment includes the entire cosmos.)

2:18 He experienced mankind's temptation with the same intensity, and under the same scrutiny, and powerfully represents them [1]with immediate effect. *(To run to their rescue. [βοή **boē** shout/cry for help; and θέω **theō** to run.] The word, βοηθησαι [1]**boethesai** is the Aorist Infinitive of βοηθέω, **boetheō** which means to reinforce, specifically a rope or chain for frapping a vessel in a storm. In his incarnate human body Jesus victoriously faced every onslaught that we would ever possibly encounter. See Hebrews 4:15,16. The Aorist Infinitive indicates the prior completion of an action in relationship to a point in time.)*

3:1 Friends, in the context of our co-inclusion in Christ, we are blameless; we ²participate in his heavenly ¹identity. ⁴Acquaint yourselves immediately and fully with Christ Jesus as the Ambassador and Chief Priest of our ³confession. Our lives co-echo the logic of God's eternal conversation in him. *(The word, ¹kaleō, means to identify by name, to surname; the word, ²metochos, comes from meta, meaning together with, and echō; to hold; to embrace; we echo his conversation. The word, ³homologeō, comes from homo, the same, and legō, to speak. The word, ⁴katanoeio, from kata, in this case a Preposition denoting direction towards, and noieō, to perceive, to contemplate; translates as fully acquainted. The Aorist Imperative is used here, katanoesate, which implies the urgency to get something done once and for all.)*

3:2 Jesus is proof of God's workmanship; he exhibits God's persuasion concerning us. Jesus is what God believes about us. In Moses we have the prophetic model, demonstrated in his complete belief in God's purpose displayed in the meticulous attention to detail regarding the construction of the tabernacle. *(See Hebrews 8:5 The prophetic model mirrors God's meticulous attention to detail when it comes to every aspect of your life. You are his tabernacle; you are his address on planet earth.)*

3:3 Yet his fame surpasses the glory of Moses, because the one who designs and constructs the house gets the greater glory. *(Hebrews 1:4; John 1:15.)*

3:4 Every house is an expression of someone's design; God is the ultimate architect and creator of all things. *(He owns the blueprint.)*

3:5 Moses took responsible charge of the administration of the tabernacle as a servant of, and witness to the prophetic voice.

3:6 But Christ is in charge of his own household, not as a servant but as a son. Understand this: we are part of this family; this is our real state now; we are not playing a role, or doing the dress rehearsal. We are no longer talking prophetically in figures and analogies. We are bursting with confidence. What good reason we now have for rejoicing. Our expectation, inspired by its foundation in prophecy, has now come to full fruition.

3:7 In Psalm 95:7-11, the Holy Spirit said, Discern the voice of the shepherd. Grasp the urgency of what God is saying to you today. *(Sonship is the Father's language. Hebrews 1:1.)*

3:8 Therefore, do not be calloused in heart as the people of Israel were: every time they faced any contradiction or temptation in the wilderness, their response immediately revealed their irritation, rather than their persuasion in God's belief.

3:9 Your fathers continued to scrutinize me suspiciously, examining me as though my intentions with them could not be trusted, even though they were eye-witnesses of my miraculous works for forty years.

3:10 They were a generation of people who grieved me deeply; instead of learning my ways, they habitually went astray in their hearts, intoxicated by their unbelief.

3:11 *(Even to this day they are still trapped in the wilderness of unbelief.)* **Hear the echo of God's cry through the ages, Oh. If only they would enter into my rest.**

3:12 Make sure that none of you tolerates the poison of unbelief in your hearts, allowing callousness to distract and distance you from the living God. *(Unbelief, believing a lie about yourself and your salvation [Numbers 13:33, Joshua 2:11]; unbelief exchanges the living God for a dead god of your own imagination. A calloused heart is a mind dominated by the senses.)*

3:13 Instead, [1]remind one another daily of your true identity; make today count. Do not allow callousness of heart to cheat any of you for even a single day out of your allotted portion. *(To encourage one another daily, from the word, [1]parakaleō, from para, a Preposition indicating close proximity, a thing proceeding from a sphere of influence, with a suggestion of union of place of residence, to have sprung from its author and giver, originating from, denoting the point from which an action originates, intimate connection, and kaleō, to identify by name, to surname. Jesus introduces the Holy Spirit in the same capacity, paraklētos [John 14:16] Greek, hamartia, sin,without form, or allotted portion. Sin would be anything that distracts from the awareness of our authentic likeness.)*

3:14 Who we are in our [1]union with Christ must be taken to its ultimate conclusion. Do not cancel out your confident start, by making a poor finish. *(Starting in faith, then going back to the law of works. Again the word, [1]metochos, is used, from meta, meaning together with, and echō; to hold; to embrace; we co-echo Christ in our union with him.)*

3:15 Every day is an extension of God's today; hear his voice, do not harden your heart. The stubborn rebellion of Israel brought them nowhere.

3:16 The same people who experienced God's mighty act of deliverance out of Egypt under the leadership of Moses were the very ones who rebelled.

3:17 They grieved him for forty years in the wilderness and died there.

3:18 God's invitation does not exclude anyone from possessing the promise of his [1]rest; their unbelief does. Persuasion cannot be compromised by unbelief. *(Our believing a lie about ourselves cannot compromise what God knows to be true about us. Futile striving to become cannot match the bliss of discovering and celebrating who you already are by his design and redemption. [1]His rest declares his perfect likeness revealed and redeemed in human form. See Genesis 1:26, 31, 2:1, 2.)*

3:19 The point is this: even though they survived by supernatural means in the wilderness for forty years, they failed to grasp what God had in mind for them. Their own unbelief disqualified them. *(They did not die because of an inferior salvation from Egypt; Pharaoh was taken out of the equation. They died because of unbelief, they believed a lie about themselves. [Numbers 13:33, Joshua 2:11] Don't blame Pharaoh or the Devil for your own unbelief. You can experience God's supernatural provision and protection and yet remain outside his rest. The ultimate proof of faith is not experience of the supernatural, but entering into his rest. His rest celebrates his perfect work; it finds its definition and reference in Genesis 1:31, 1 Kings 6:7 and Colossians 2:9, 10. He longs for you to discover your own completeness and perfection as seen from his point of view. His rest is sustained in you by what he sees, knows, and says about you in reference to the finished work of Christ. Jesus is what God believes about you.)*

4:1 What a foolish thing it would be if we should now fail in a similar fashion to enter into his rest, where we get to celebrate the full consequences of our redemption. *(Why waste another lap in the same wilderness of unbelief.)*

4:2 What God has now spoken to us in Jesus confirms that we were equally included in the prophetic message which was proclaimed to our ancestors; their unbelief disqualified them from possessing the promise; they could not make the vital connection with the promise while they remained enslaved to their dwarfed opinions of themselves. Because the word did not mingle with faith, there was no catalyst to ignite its effect in their hearts, and so the promise did not profit them at all. *(Even though they witnessed the supernatural on a 24/7 basis for 40 years, the supernatural is not proof of faith. They were absorbed with the typical fruit of the I-am-not-tree -mentality; they remained more persuaded about a perception of an inferior identity, than what they were about the largeness of their salvation from slavery, into the freedom of the authentic life of their design. Numbers 13:33; Joshua 2:11)*

4:3 Faith *(not willpower)* **realizes our immediate access into God's rest. Hear the echo of God's [1]cry through the ages, Oh! If only they would enter into my rest. His rest celebrates perfection. His work is complete; the [2]fall of mankind did not flaw its perfection.**

([1] Sadly most translations read, I have sworn in my wrath that they will never enter into my rest. The word, wrath is derived from **orgē***, from ὀρέγομαι* [1]***oregomai****, to stretch oneself out in order to touch or to grasp something, to reach after or desire something.*

*The text does not say, they will never enter my rest. Both the Greek Septuagint and the Hebrew text quoted here, read the same. [**Psalm 94:11** in the Septuagint, which is **Psalm 95:11** in the Hebrew], Oh that they would enter into my rest. Greek **ei** and Hebrew, אִם **im**.*

> *See* **Hebrews 4:6** *It is clear then, that there is still an opportunity to enter into that rest which Israel failed to access because of their unbelief, even though they were the first to hear the Good News of God's intention to restore mankind to the same Sabbath that Adam and Israel had lost. (Both Adam and Israel believed a lie about themselves. [Numbers 13:33, Joshua 2:11])*

> **Hebrews 4:7** *So, now again many years later, he points specifically to an extended opportunity when he announces in David's prophecy, Today when hearing my voice, do not do so with a calloused heart.*

> **Hebrews 4:8** *If Joshua, who led the new generation of Israel out of the wilderness of their parent's unbelief, had succeeded in leading them into the rest that God intended, David would not so many years later have referred to yet another day.*

First Adam failed to enter into God's finished work, and then Israel failed to enter into the consequence of their complete redemption out of slavery; and as a result of their unbelief, they perished in the wilderness. Now let us not fail in the same manner to see the completed work of the Cross. God desires for us to see the same perfection; what he saw when he first created mankind in his image and then again, what he saw in the perfect obedience [lit. hearing] of his Son.

God is not in their rest because they are exhausted, but because they are satisfied with what they see and know concerning us. We are now invited with urgent persuasion to enter into what they see. Elohim's rest was never at risk. Their works were finished from the foundation of the world.

*[2] The word, **apo**, translates as away from, and [2]**kataballō**, cast down, the fall of mankind, sometimes translated, foundation [see notes on Ephesians 1:4]*

This association goes back to before the fall of the world; their love knew that they would present us again face to face before them in blameless innocence. The implications of the fall are completely canceled out. The entire Fall was a falling away in our minds from our true identity as image and likeness bearers of Elohim. Just like Eve, were we all deceived to believe a lie about ourselves, which is the fruit of the I-am-not-tree . We all, like sheep, have gone astray. Isaiah 53:6.)

4:4 Scripture records the seventh day to be the prophetic celebration of God's perfect work. What God saw satisfied his scrutiny.

(Remember what happened on the 7th day? I celebrate you. I still do. Behold, it is very good, and God rested from all his work. [Genesis 1:31, 2:2] God saw more than his perfect image in Adam, he also saw the Lamb and his perfect work of redemption. The Lamb having been slain from the foundation of the world. [Revelation 13:8] That which has been is now; that which is to be, has already been. [Ecclesiastes 3:15] Also 2 Timothy 1:9.)

4:5 In Psalm 95 the same seventh day metaphor is reiterated: Oh, that they would enter into my rest.

4:6 It is clear then, that there is still an opportunity to enter into that rest which Israel failed to access because of their unbelief, even though they were the first to hear the Good News of God's intention to restore mankind to the same Sabbath that Adam and Israel had lost. *(Both Adam and Israel believed a lie about themselves. Numbers 13:33, Joshua 2:11.)*

4:7 So, now again many years later, he points specifically to an extended opportunity when he announces in David's prophecy, Today when hearing my voice, do not do so with a calloused heart. Be faith sensitive.

4:8 If Joshua, who led the new generation of Israel out of the wilderness *[where their parents perished through unbelief],* **had succeeded in leading them into the rest that God intended, David would not so many years later have referred to yet another day.** *(This moment still remains as an open invitation to mankind to enter into their rest: the living blueprint of their design. This confirms that the history of Israel was a mere shadow and prophetic type of that Promise that was yet to be fulfilled.)*

4:9 The conclusion is clear: the original rest is still in place for God's people. *(The people of this planet are the property of God. Psalm 24:1.)*

4:10 God's rest celebrates his finished work; whoever enters into God's rest immediately abandons his own efforts to improve what God has already perfected. *(The language of the law is do; the language of grace is done.)*

4:11 Let us therefore be [1]prompt to understand and fully appropriate that rest and not fall again into the same trap that snared Israel in [2]unbelief. *(The word, [1]**spoudatzo**, from **spoude**, I translated prompt, not labor; this word also reminds of the English word, speed; immediately. The word, [2]**apeitheia** [apathy] from **a** as a negative particle, not; and **peithō**, convince; is often, wrongly translated, disobedience.)*

4:12 The message God spoke to us in Christ, is the most life giving and dynamic influence in us, cutting like a surgeon's scalpel, sharper than a soldier's sword, piercing to the deepest core of human conscience, to the dividing of soul and spirit; ending the dominance of the sense realm and its neutralizing effect upon the human spirit. In this way a person's spirit is freed to become the ruling influence again in the thoughts and intentions of their heart. The scrutiny of this living Sword-Logos detects every possible disease, discerning the body's deepest secrets where joint and bone-marrow meet.

(The moment we cease from our own efforts to justify ourselves, by yielding to the integrity of the message that announces the success of the Cross, God's word is triggered into action. What God spoke to us in sonship (the incarnation), radiates his image and likeness in our redeemed innocence. [Hebrews 1:1-3] This word powerfully penetrates and impacts our whole being; body, soul and spirit.

The Sword would always point back to mankind's original identity. The Hebrew word in Genesis 3:24, הפך hâpak is a primitive root; meaning to turn about; by implication to change, to return, to be converted, turn back. Also in the Septuagint the same thought is communicated in the Greek word, strephō, which is the strengthened from the base of tropay; to turn around or reverse: - convert, turn again, back again, to turn self about. In Luke 15 the prodigal son returns to himself - Plato is quoted by Ackerman [Christian Element in Plato] as thinking of redemption as coming to oneself. See Notes on the splendor of the Gates Revelation 21.)

4:13 The entire person is thoroughly exposed to his scrutinizing agape-gaze. *(The thought of you intrigues your Maker with delight. There is nothing about you that he doesn't know. He knows your deepest thoughts and understands the secret longings of your heart. Psalm 139:2)*

4:14 In the message of the incarnation, we have Jesus the Son of God representing mankind in the highest place of spiritual authority. That which God has spoken to us in him is his final word. It is echoed now in our conversation.

4:15 As High Priest he fully identifies with us in the context of our frail human lives. Having subjected it to close scrutiny, he proved that the human frame was master over sin. His sympathy with us is not to be seen as excusing weaknesses which are the result of a faulty design, but rather as a trophy to mankind. *(He is not an example for us but of us.)*

4:16 For this reason we can approach the authoritative throne of grace with bold utterance. We are welcome there in his embrace, and are [1]reinforced with immediate effect in times of trouble.

(The word, [1]boētheia, means to be reinforced, specifically a rope or chain for frapping a vessel in a storm. In his incarnate human body Jesus represents us on the deepest possible level of every detail of our lives, spirit, soul and body. He victoriously faced every onslaught and scrutiny that we would ever possibly encounter.)

5:1 Traditionally a person would be appointed from among their fellows to fulfill the office of High Priest in presenting gifts and sacrifices before God on behalf of the people and for their own sins. *(The High Priesthood of Christ is in sharp contrast to the system of priesthood the Jews were familiar with.)*

5:2 Every Jew felt reassured by the fact that High Priests themselves were hemmed in by the same sins that snared the people they represented. By virtue of their own limitations and inadequacies they were able to sympathize with the ignorance and waywardness of the people under them.

5:3 It was accepted practice that they would offer sacrifices for both their own and the people's sins.

5:4 This honorable office was not by self-appointment but, as in Aaron's case, the priest was summoned to the work by God.

5:5 Neither did Christ assume the high priestly office by his own presumption, but in fulfillment of the prophetic word *(in Psalm 2)* concerning the Messiah, in which God, speaking through David, said, You are my Son, today I have begotten you.

5:6 Just as he has spoken in other Scriptures concerning this new priestly order: Thou art a Priest forever, after the order of Melchizedek. *(By translation, the King of Righteousness, [Genesis 14:18] In these Scriptures a new and eternal order of priesthood is introduced. [Psalm 110:4] Jesus knew that his priesthood was prophesied in Scripture, a priesthood neither passed on by natural birth, nor ending with natural death.)*

5:7 When he faced the horror of his imminent death, he presented his plea to God in an outburst of agonizing emotion and with tears. He prayed with urgent intent to be delivered from death, knowing God's power was saving him and that he enjoyed God's full attention - he had a [1]firm grip on the prophetic word. *(Not because he feared, as some translations have put it, but because he fully grasped that he was the fulfillment of Scripture; he knew that he would be raised on the third day; [Hosea 6:2] eu + lambanō- he had a firm grip; he grasped/embraced the goodness of God.)*

5:8 Acquainted with sonship he was in the habit of [1]hearing from above; what he heard [2]distanced him from the effect of what he had suffered. *(The word often translated as obedience is the word, [1]upoakuo, under the influence of hearing, or hearing from above. By the things he suffered, [2]apo, away from, distanced. Then I said, I read in your book what you wrote about me; so here I am, I have come to fulfill your will. [Hebrews 10:7])*

5:9 By his perfect hearing he forever freed mankind to hear what he had heard. *(He now makes it possible for us to hear in such a way that we may participate again in the full release of our original identity; the logos finding voice in the incarnation in us.)*

5:10 The authority of this high priestly order of Melchizedek [1]flows directly from God. *(Called of God is from the word, [1]prosagereo, from pros, a Preposition of direction, towards, face to face + agō, to lead as a shepherd leads his sheep, and* **+ reo** *[Strong's number: 4482] to flow, or to run like water. His High Priestly office originates in God.)*

5:11 On this subject there remains so much to be said; but oh, how difficult it is to explain something to someone who hears with an indifferent attitude.

5:12 By now you *[Jews]* **should have been professors, able to teach the rest of the world, but you are still struggling with the ABC's of God's Messianic-language.** *[Hebrews 1:1-3]* **The difference between the prophetic shadow and the real is like that between milk and meat in your diet. You cannot live on baby food for the rest of your lives.**

5:13 The revelation of righteousness is the meat of God's word. Babes live on milk *[the prophetic shadow of the real, which was to come]*; **so does everyone who is not** [1]**pierced in the ear of his heart by the revelation of Christ.** *(The word,*[1]***apeiros,*** *comes from* **a,** *negative, and* **peira,** *pierced, not pierced, tested by piercing. God's act of righteousness in Christ restored mankind to blameless innocence [Romans 1:17])*

5:14 This is the nourishment of the mature. They are those who have their faculties of perception trained as by gymnastic precision to distinguish the relevant from the irrelevant. *(The mature are those who know the difference between the shadow and the substance; between the futility of the law of works and willpower to work righteousness, and righteousness revealed by the faith of God in the finished work of Christ.)*

6:1 Consequently, as difficult as it may seem, you ought to divorce yourselves from your sentimental attachment to the foreshadowing doctrine of the Messiah, which was designed to carry us like a vessel over the ocean of prophetic dispensation into the completeness of the fulfilled promise. A mind shift from attempts to impress God by your behavior, to realizing the faithfulness of God, is fundamental. There is no life left in the old system. It is dead and gone; you have to move on. *(Romans 3:27.)*

6:2 All the Jewish teachings about ceremonial washings *[baptisms]*, the laying on of hands *[in order to identify with the slain animal as sacrifice]*, and all teachings pertaining to a sin consciousness, including the final resurrection of the dead in order to face judgment, are no longer relevant. *(All of these types and shadows were concluded and fulfilled in Christ, their living substance. His resurrection bears testimony to the judgment that he faced on mankind's behalf and the freedom from an obstructive consciousness of sin that he now proclaims. [Romans 4:25; Acts 17:31; John 12:31-33] Jesus said, and when I am lifted up on the cross, I will draw all judgment unto me. [airō to lift up] Hebrews 9:28.)*

6:3 So it is with God's prompting that we advance. *(From the prophetic types and shadows of Scripture into the substance of what God has now spoken to us in sonship. Hebrews 1:1-3.)*

6:4 Now it may be that someone may clearly see the light *[of the prophetic word]* and participate in the Holy Spirit by already having sampled the heavenly gift,

(The Prophets who prophesied of the grace that was to be yours searched and inquired about this salvation; they inquired what person or time was indicated by the Spirit of Christ within them when predicting the sufferings of Christ and the subsequent glory. 1Peter 1:10, 11.)

6:5 and they might even begin to feast on the beauty of the Word; already having experienced the power of the age of the promise that all were waiting for.

6:6 If such a person were to insist on relapsing into the old mindset of legalism, sin consciousness, and condemnation, it becomes impossible for him to be restored again and again to [1]repentance. The principle of repeated [1]repentance, as practiced under the law, does not make sense in the context of the new dispensation, because it would absurdly imply that Christ was being re-crucified and subjected to public shame over and over again. This new order is not to be confused with the old. Grace is not a cheap excuse for sin. C'mon, [1]awaken to faith-consciousness once and for all. You are free from the old rules and bondage of the duty-driven law of willpower. It is impossible for the old system to match the new.

(See Romans 3:27. Under the shadow system of the law, sacrifices were repeatedly slain because no permanent cleansing was possible. [Hebrews 10:1-4]

*[1] The word often translated, repentance, is the Greek word, **metanoia**, from **meta**, together with and νοιέω **noieō**, to perceive with the mind. It describes the*

awakening of the mind to that which is true; a re-alignment of one's reasoning; it is a gathering of one's thoughts, a co-knowing. Faith is not a decision; it is a discovery. It has nothing in common with the Latin word **paenitentia** *- where the idea of penance and repentance stems from.)*

6:7 For when cultivated soil is soaked by frequent showers and produces the useful, life-giving crop expected by the farmer, the harvest brings much celebration.

6:8 What a complete disappointment though, if the same soil produces nothing but thorns and thistles; it is a worthless yield, and fit for burning; like a dream that has gone up in smoke.

6:9 Having said all this, my dear friends, I am fully convinced of God's love for you; what God accomplished in salvation on your behalf is beyond comparison to anything you were familiar with before. Salvation realities echo what the law could only foreshadow.

6:10 God is not unfair, neither is he unaware of the affectionate way in which you have honored his Name, and the diligence you have shown in your unrelenting religious service in keeping all the sacred rituals and ceremonies, even to this the present day.

6:11 I urge you to employ that same sincere devotion to now realize the fulfillment of everything that the old system anticipated.

6:12 We do not want you to behave like ¹illegitimate children, unsure of your share in the inheritance. Mimic the faith of those who through their patience came to possess the promise of their allotted portion.

(The word, ¹nothros comes from **nothos**, *one born outside of wedlock, of a concubine or female slave. The child of the law and not of the promise. Galatians 3:29; Galatians 4:22-31.)*

6:13 Since God had no one greater by whom to swear, he swore by himself. He could give Abraham no greater guarantee but the integrity of his own Being; this makes the promise as sure as God is.

6:14 Saying, I will continue to speak well of you. I will confirm my intention always only to bless you, and to multiply you beyond measure. *(Genesis 2:17, In blessing I will bless you, and in multiplying I will multiply you.)*

6:15 And so Abraham continued in patience and secured the promise.

6:16 It is common practice in human affairs to evoke a higher authority under oath in order to add weight to any agreement between parties, thereby ¹silencing any possibility of quibbling. *(The word ¹peras, means the end of all dispute; the point beyond which one cannot go.)*

6:17 In the same context we are confronted with God's eagerness to go to the last extreme in his dealing with us as heirs of his promise, and to cancel out all possible grounds for doubt or dispute. In order to persuade us of the unalterable character and finality of his resolve, he [1]confined himself to an oath. The promise which already belongs to us by heritage is now also [1]confirmed under oath.

([1] The word [1]mesiteuō is used, interposed or mediated. Compare mesitēs, mediator, from mesos, midst. In the incarnation, God has positioned himself in the midst, of his creation. See Galatians 3:20 With Abraham there was no middleman; it was just God. [The Mosaic law spoke the language of the fallen mind and required mediators - the Levitical priesthood - because it was an arrangement whereby mankind had a part and God had a part. Mankind's part was to obey the commandments and God's part was to bless. God's covenant with Abraham was a grace covenant pointing to the man Jesus Christ, in whom God himself would fulfil mankind's part and therefore needed no mediator apart from himself.

In the incarnation Jesus fulfills both the proposal and the I do. M. Perez]

The Word is the promise; the Incarnate, crucified and risen Christ is the proof. He desires to show more convincingly to the heirs of the promise the unchangeable character of his purpose. RSV .

Mankind was not redeemed from the Devil; a thief never becomes an owner; neither did Jesus do what he did to change his Father's mind about us. It was our minds that needed persuasion. God was not to be reconciled to his creation; God was in Christ when he reconciled the world to himself. 2 Corinthians 5:18-20.)

6:18 So that we are now dealing with two irreversible facts which make it impossible for anyone to prove God wrong; thus our persuasion as to our redeemed identity is powerfully reinforced. We have already escaped into that destiny; our expectation has come within our immediate grasp.

*(The promise of redemption sustained throughout Scripture and the fulfillment of that promise in Jesus. See John 8:13-18 **John 8:17** That should settle it for you since it is written in your law that the testimony of two, is true. [This combined witness of two is not true just because they agree, unless true in fact separately. But if they disagree, the testimony falls to the ground. Deuteronomy 17:6; and Deuteronomy 19:15. - Robertson. Also Revelation 10:6 See notes on the Oath at the end of Revelation 10 also the Notes on the Testimony of Jesus at the end of Revelation 20.])*

6:19 Our hearts and minds are certain; anchored securely within the innermost courts of God's immediate Presence; beyond the *(prophetic)* **veil.**

6:20 By going there on our behalf, Jesus pioneered a place for us and removed every type of obstruction that could possibly distance us from the promise. In him we are represented for all time; he became our High Priest after the order of Melchizedek. We now enjoy the same privileged access he has.

(He said, I go to prepare a place for you so that you may be where I am. On that day you will no longer doubt that I and the Father are one; you will know that I am in the Father and you in me and I in you. John 10:30, 14:3, 20.)

7:1 This is the same Melchizedek, King of Salem, the Priest of God, who met Abraham after he had defeated the kings, and blessed him. *(Melchizedek, King* מלך *Melek and* צדק *Zedek of righteousness. For a better understanding of the word Zedek, see 2 Corinthians 6:14. Faith-righteousness has nothing in common with the philosophies of karma and performance-based approval; they could never [1]balance the scales or be evenly yoked together in any context. [The word [1]heterozugeō, an unequal or different yoke; from the Hebrew word, zugot, זגות indicates pairs of two identical objects; a yoke or a teaching; the yoke of a rabbi or philosopher represented their doctrine; reminds of the Hebrew word for righteousness, tzedek, צדק which also includes the idea of the wooden beam in a scale of balances. He who judges his neighbor according to the balance of righteousness, or innocence, judges him according to righteousness. [T. Bab. Sabbat, fol. 127. 2.] The Greek stem for righteousness is dikē - it is interesting to note that the Greek goddess of Justice is Dikē [pronounced, dikay] and she is always pictured holding a scale of balances in her hand.])*

7:2 It was to him that Abraham gave a tenth part of all the spoils, without keeping even a shoestring for himself! To begin to appreciate the significance of Melchizedek, we must first understand the profound meaning of his name: King of Righteousness and King of Peace. He is the one who administers God's promise and who prophetically represents mankind's restored and redeemed oneness, innocence and wholeness.

*(Genesis 15:1 in the Septuagint LXX reads, **Immediately after Abram meets Melchizedek, Jahweh speaks to him and addresses his fears** [no land; no child] **Fear not! Beyond all comparison** [υπερασπιζω from ὑπεράνω **huperanō**; uper + ano - over and above], **I am your priceless reward; exceedingly surpassing any possible reward you could wish for, as achieved in by your own efforts!***

Romans 4:3 Scripture is clear, Abraham reflected God's belief in him; this is the basis of the [1]rediscovery of [2]righteousness. ([1]One must remember that in Adam & Eve's communion with Elohim, something was lost which would be redeemed - there would be a return to the consciousness of this union. [2]This most significant, relational term, righteousness, points to a shared likeness, which includes one's authentic identity and innocence.)

7:3 There exists no record that can link Melchizedek to a natural father or mother; no birth certificate neither any account of his death, nor is there any record of his age. He resembles exactly the Son of God: his priesthood abides without beginning or end. *(This was at a time where detailed records were kept of every genealogy.)*

7:4 Now carefully consider this; the fact that Abraham the great Patriarch gave him a tenth portion of the spoil just goes to show what a distinguished man Melchizedek must have been in Abraham's estimation, and what an impression he had made on him. *(In the Hebrew mind, Abraham was the most important individual standing as a reference to their identity and tradition.)*

7:5 Levi's sons, who were priests by natural descent, were obliged by law to receive tithes from their brethren, even though they were equals and shared a common Father in Abraham.

7:6 However, Melchizedek here receives tithes from everyone associated with Abraham, despite his having no natural link to their lineage. In the blessing that he pronounced over Abraham he recognized Abraham as the holder of God's promises. *(He confirmed the Good News of the promise of righteousness represented by Abraham's faith.)*

7:7 In principle, the junior always receives the blessing from the senior person.

7:8 In the case of the Levites, the duration of their priesthood is concurrent with their lifespan; but Scripture declares that Melchizedek's life has no end.

7:9 My reasoning is that even Levi, who would later receive the tithe, had already paid the tithe to Melchizedek in Abraham.

7:10 When Melchizedek and Abraham met, Levi was already present in the loins of his father. *(By the time Levi was born, Melchizedek was still alive; since he has no beginning of time nor end of life, in him time and eternity meet.)*

7:11 The point that I wish to make is this: if the Levitical priesthood, linked to the law of Moses, was a flawless system *[by succeeding in presenting anyone in blameless innocence before God]*, there would surely be no further mention made of another order of priesthood presided over by Melchizedek and not by Aaron. *(Psalm 110:4.)*

7:12 If there is a new order of priesthood, there must obviously be a new law. *(Melchizedek reveals a new basis for righteousness, related not to a person's effort to keep the law by their own willpower, but based upon the perfect work of Christ. This new law is called the law of faith [Romans 3:27], the law of perfect liberty [James 1:25], and the law of the spirit of life in Christ Jesus [Romans 8:2].)*

7:13 The person who is prophetically implicated as being the leader of this new priesthood belongs to a completely different tribe. This implies a complete break with tradition because no one from any tribe other than the Levites ever touched the altar.

7:14 History is clear that the Lord's lineage is from Judah, concerning whom Moses made no mention of a priestly office.

7:15 Of far greater significance and even more apparent is the fact that Jesus is mirrored in Melchizedek in whom the new priestly office arises.

7:16 This new office is not based on the law of precepts constrained by the frailty of the flesh, but by the authority of an indestructible life. *(As demonstrated in his resurrection.)*

7:17 Thus Scripture confirms his perpetual priesthood exactly according to the pattern of Melchizedek.

7:18 This new order brought about an immediate end to the previous inferior and useless system of laws and commandments.

7:19 In its ability to reunite mankind with God, the law did not succeed even once; that is why it was superseded by the introduction of a far superior hope, a new order in which we are perfectly represented before God.

7:20 The previous priesthood was reduced to a mere tradition and passed on through natural descent from father to son. God had no say in the matter.

7:21 To give irrefutable integrity to the new Messianic priesthood, it was written, The Lord has sworn and will not change his mind, 'You are a priest forever after the order of Melchizedek.' *(Psalm 110:4.)*

7:22 Melchizedek mirrors Christ in the highest office of priesthood as [1]endorsing the human race. Jesus is now the living proof of God's covenant pledge to benefit mankind in a far better way than under any previous arrangement. *(The word ἔγγυος [1]egguos, surety, official endorsement.)*

7:23 The fact that there were so many priests shows how frequently they died and had to be replaced.

7:24 But there will be no successor to the Priesthood of Jesus because he remains forever.

7:25 Through him mankind's approach to God is forever secured; he continues to [1]communicate the full accomplishment of their salvation. *(The word, ἐντυγχάνω [1]entugchanō from en, in and tugchanō, to hit the mark: of one discharging a javelin or arrow. Thus to entirely represent the individual in his person as the incarnate son of man/son of God. See Hebrews 12:24,25.*

Also Hebrews 8:6 Jesus is now the fulfillment of all those promises towards which the old practices were merely pointing; as when an arrow strikes the bullseye. The dispensation he now administers is far superior to the old. He is the arbitrator of a more effective covenant; sanctioned by its being an announcement of far greater benefit to mankind.

See also, Hebrews 9:15 As fully representing mankind, Jesus' death brought an end to the Old, and introduced the New Testament. He thus redeemed us from the transgressions recorded under the first Covenant and identified us as heirs; qualifying us to participate in the full inheritance of all that he obtained on our behalf. [The concept of a mediator, **mesitēs***, in this analogy, is not a go-between, as if Jesus had to change the Father's mind about us; it was our minds that needed to be persuaded. Jesus did not save us from God; he is fully God and fully man, and in him mankind is most completely represented. See Galatians 3:20; also Hebrews 6:16-20. And 1 John 2:1,2.])*

7:26 As our High Priest he towers far above every other priestly system in conspicuous prominence and in holy character. His guileless, flawless life on earth was never compromised by sin, and he himself was exalted above the heavens where he occupies the highest rank of authority in the eternal realm.

7:27 Unlike the previous high priests whose system of daily sacrifices was a constant reminder of their own failures, he had no need to sacrifice on his own behalf. The sacrifice he offered was himself for all; a sacrifice never to be repeated.

7:28 Under the law, men were appointed as high priests regardless of their weaknesses. The word of the oath, which succeeded the law, appointed the Son in perpetual perfection.

8:1 The conclusion of all that has been said points us to an exceptional Person, who towers far above the rest in the highest office of heavenly greatness. He is the executive authority of the majesty of God. *(The right hand of God.)*

8:2 The office he now occupies is the one which the Moses-model resembled prophetically. He ministers in the holiest place in God's true tabernacle of worship. Nothing of the old man-made structure can match its perfection.

8:3 The task of bringing gifts and sacrifices was the duty of every High Priest; with Jesus there would be no exception. *(He would bring the perfect sacrifice.)*

8:4 So here on earth, since he had no further offering to sacrifice *(in terms of the Jewish priesthood)*, he would not qualify to be a priest among the Jews, who still have their own priesthood functioning to offer the various gifts presented in accordance with the prescriptions of their law. *(Animal sacrifice was still practiced at the time of this writing, this continued until 70 AD when the temple was destroyed by the Romans.)*

8:5 They are maintaining a shadow service to God; one which was originally intended as a prophetic picture of the real, just as Moses followed instructions to erect a tabernacle consistent with the accurate pattern that God had shown him on the mountain. *(The prophetic model mirrors God's meticulous attention to detail when it comes to every aspect of your life. You are his tabernacle; you are his address on planet earth.)*

8:6 Jesus is now the fulfillment of all those promises towards which the old practices were merely pointing; as when an arrow strikes the bullseye. The dispensation he now administers is far superior to the old. He is the arbitrator of a more effective covenant; sanctioned by its being an announcement of far greater benefit to mankind. *(See Hebrews 7:25)*

8:7 If there had been no flaw in the first dispensation, why bother to replace it by a second?

8:8 He had already faulted the first system when he said through Jeremiah, Behold the days will come when I will make an entirely new covenant with the house of Israel and the house of Judah.

8:9 We will be making a new agreement, completely unlike the previous one based on external ritual. I had literally to take your hand and lead you out of slavery from Egypt; yet you refused to spontaneously follow or trust in me; I could never abide your indifference. *(God prophesies a covenant that will not be subject to the same defect of the previous one; or one that was spoon-fed to Israel and whose obligations they yet failed to meet. God had to take them by the hand to lead them out of Egypt. This time, he promised, I will put my laws into their minds and write them it upon their hearts ...)*

8:10 Now, instead of documenting my laws on stone, I will chisel them into your mind and engrave them in your inner consciousness; it will no longer be a one-sided affair. I will be your God and you will be my people, not by compulsion but by mutual desire.

8:11 Knowing me will no longer be a Sunday-school lesson, or something taught by persuasive words of doctrine, neither will they know me on account of family tradition or door to door evangelism [*each one telling his neighbor*]. Everyone, from the most unlikely to the most prominent people in society, will know me inwardly.

8:12 This knowledge of me will never again be based on sin-consciousness. My act of mercy, extended in Christ as the new Covenant, has removed every possible definition of sin from memory. (*God's memory of our sins was not what needed to be addressed in the redemption of our innocence. God did not have a problem with sin-consciousness, we had. He wasn't hiding from Adam and Eve in the garden; they were hiding from him. What needed to be addressed were our perceptions of a judgmental God, which were the inevitable fruit of the I-am-not tree system and mentality.*

Revenge, judgment, guilt, condemnation, inferiority, shame, regret, suspicion etc. could not be treated lightly; they are the enemies of romance. If rules could do it, then the law would be our opportunity to save ourselves, simply by making the correct decisions. If willpower could save us then Moses would be our savior. But, alas. The good that I want to do I cannot. See Romans 7.

The scapegoat system would be introduced to somehow address and attempt to manage the consequences of sin. The typical eye for an eye, tooth for a tooth scenario would be substituted with the idea of a scapegoat. And so, every system of sacrifice carried some significance, but only as far as it pointed to its weaknesses in dealing with the root of the problem, and the need for a better solution. We needed more than forgiveness of our sins; we needed a savior who could rescue us from our sinfulness. This was not merely a means whereby we could get rid of the cobwebs; the spider needed to be killed. The pay now, sin later-system had a very real sell-by date.

See Hebrews 10:2 & 3 Had it been possible to present the perfect offering that had the power to successfully remove any trace of a sin-consciousness, then the sacrificial system would surely have ceased to be relevant. But in the very repetition of these ritual sacrifices the awareness of guilt is reinforced rather than removed.

God does not demand sacrifice; he provides the sacrifice. The ultimate sacrifice for sins would never be something we did, or brought to God, to appeal to him; but the shocking scandal of the cross, is the fact that mankind is confronted with the extravagant, embarrassing proportions of the love of their Maker; he would go to the most ridiculous extreme to finally convince us of his heart towards us. In order to persuade us of our worth to him, he speaks the most severe scapegoat language: Behold the Lamb of God, who takes away the sins of the world. This completely disarms religion. Suddenly there is nothing that we can do to persuade God about our sincere intentions; this is God persuading us of his eternal love dream.

God did not clothe Adam with the skin of an animal because of a divine need to be appeased, but because of their unconditional love for Adam; they spoke the language of Adam's own judgment: Adam, not God, was embarrassed about his nakedness. The clothing was not to make God look at Adam differently, but to make Adam feel better about himself. And ultimately it was to prepare Adam for the unveiling of the mystery of mankind's redemption in the incarnation. Here Deity would clothe themselves in human skin in a Son, and the Lion of Judah would become the Lamb of God in order to free our minds to re-discover his image and likeness in our skin. Mankind is tailor-made for God.

See also **1 Peter 1:19 but you were redeemed with the priceless blood of Christ; he is the ultimate sacrifice; spotless and without blemish. He completes the prophetic picture.** *(In him God speaks the most radical scapegoat language of the law of judgment, and brings final closure to a dead and redundant system. In Psalm 40:6,7, it is clearly stated that God does not require sacrifices or offerings. Jesus is the Lamb of God. He collides victoriously with the futile sacrificial system whereby offerings are constantly made to the pseudo, moody, monster gods of our imagination. This is the scandal of the cross. God does not demand a sacrifice that would change the way he thinks about mankind; he provides the sacrifice of himself in Christ in order to forever eradicate sin-consciousness from our minds and radically change the way we think about our Maker, one another and ourselves. [Sin-consciousness is a works-based consciousness which is the currency of religion.]*

Also John 5:28 Do not be alarmed by this, but the hour is coming when those in the [1]*graves will hear his voice. (No-one who ever lived will escape the extent of his righteous judgment. Those who have* [1]*forgotten who they are will hear his incarnate voice. The word for grave,* [1]**mnēmeion**, *memory, suggests a remembrance - to bring something from memory into the here and now! Like David prophesies in Psalm 22 when he sees the cross-crisis* [**krisis** - *judgment, means the 'decisive moment' or, turning point.*] *He prophesies in Psalm 22, a thousand years before it happens! His conclusion in verse 27 sums up the triumph of God's resolve! All the ends of the earth shall* [1]*remember and turn to the LORD; and all the families of the nations shall worship before him. See 1 Corinthians 15:21,22 The same mankind who died in a man was raised again in a man. In Adam all died; in Christ all are made alive.)*

8:13 He announces the new dispensation to confirm that the old shadow system has been rendered redundant.

9:1 The first system followed a specific pattern of worship which was conducted in a specific and sacred place of worship. *(The details of which spoke in shadows of the new.)*

9:2 The first tented area was called the Holy Place; the only light here came from the ¹lampstand illuminating the table upon which the ²showbread was presented. *[Leviticus 24:5-9]*

([1] The lampstand was a beautifully crafted golden chandelier portraying budding and blossoming almond branches. Remember that this is also what Jeremiah saw in **Jeremiah 1:12***, when God said, I am awake over my word to perform it. The same Hebrew word is used here,* שקד *shaqad; the almond was called the awake tree, because it blossomed first, while the other trees were still in their winter sleep.*

[2] The Hebrew word לחם הפנים *lechem haPānīm, face bread, or bread of the presence. What happened to us in Christ is according to God's eternal purpose [Bread of the Presence, or showbread, in Greek,* πρόθεσις *¹prothesis, pre-designed/prophetic purpose] which he has shown in every prophetic pointer and shadow; in the Hebrew tradition the showbread pointed to the true bread from heaven, the authentic word that proceeded from the mouth of God - Jesus, the incarnate word - sustaining the life of our design. The showbread pointed towards the daily sustenance of life in the flesh as the ultimate tabernacle of God, realized in the account of Jesus with the two men from Emmaus; their hearts were burning with resonance and faith while he opened the Scriptures to them, and then around the table their eyes were opened to recognize him as the fulfillment of Scripture, their true meal incarnated [Luke 24:27-31]. Mankind shall not live by bread alone, but by the authentic thought of God, the Word proceeding from his mouth, the original intent, his image and likeness incarnated, revealed, and redeemed in human life. See my note to* **1 Corinthians 11:34***.)*

9:3 The second veil led to the inner tent known as the Most Holy Place.

9:4 The golden ¹cencer *[fire-pan]* of incense was taken there ²once a year on the day of atonement. The heart of the entire sanctuary was represented in the ³ark of the covenant, also called the ark of testimony. It was a wooden chest, covered in pure gold, both inside and out. In it were kept the ⁴golden jar with a sample of the miracle manna from the wilderness, as well as the ⁵budding staff of Aaron, as also the ⁶two engraved tablets of stone with the ten commandments of the covenant.

[1] **Leviticus 16:12,13** *And once a year, Aaron shall take burning coals from the [bronze] altar in the golden fire-pan, and bring it to the golden altar of incense in the Holy Place. He would also take two hands full of fragrant perfumes, beaten small, and put it on the altar of incense, then carry it before Jahweh in the Most Holy place beyond the veil, and the cloud of the incense shall cover the mercy-seat on the Ark of testimony.*

*This was a preparation peculiar to the day of expiation. On other days it was the custom of the priest to take fire from the brazen altar in a silver censer, but once a year, on the great Day of Atonement the high priest took the fire from the bronze altar in a golden censer; he would take **incense** from one of the priests, who brought it to him, and went with it to the golden altar of incense in the Holy Place, and then within the veil, in the Most Holy Place, before the Ark of the Covenant, he would worship before God. Sir Isaac Newton.*

See Revelation 8:3 Then another celestial messenger arrived with a golden censer for frankincense and took charge of the altar in priestly fashion. Much perfume was given to him and this would be burned as a sweet smelling fragrance upon the golden altar of incense [in the Holy Place], before the throne [now, unveiled within the Most Holy place] to represent the prayers of every single saint. (The word libanōtos refers to the gum exuding from a frankincense tree; also the censer for burning the frankincense with the coals from the brazen altar of sacrifice. The verb estathē is the ingressive first Aorist Passive of histēmi [intransitive], took his place - was positioned; epi tou thusiastēriou - took up his priestly position over the altar.

See Exodus 30:1-10 on the altar of incense in The Holy Place. Exodus 30:6 And you shall put it before the veil that is by the ark of the testimony, before the mercy seat that is over the testimony, where I will meet with you.

[2] The once a year Day of Atonement - יוֹם כִּפֻּר *Yom Kippur, also known as the Sabbath of Sabbaths. Even in modern times the Jews are still celebrating this, as their most holy day. Oh for them to discover their true Sabbath in Jesus the Messiah!*

[3] The word, ¹kibotos, the wooden box, is the same word used for Noah's ark; the container of mankind's redemption. Genesis 6:14; see 1 Peter 3:18-20 in the Mirror.

[4] The ²manna prophetically pictured the true bread from heaven, not the bread that mankind's labor produces. John 4:35, 38.

[5] Moses' staff - but here referred to as Aaron's - when they first met with Pharaoh Aaron's staff turned into a snake - the symbol of Pharaoh's rule, and swallowed the snake staffs of the Egyptian magicians.

[6] Pointing prophetically to the rebooted life of our design where the law of agapē is inscribed in our inner consciousness.

Both the brazen altar as well as the altar of incense were made of acacia wood; [shittim wood] the brazen altar was overlaid with brass and the incense altar with pure gold. The Acacia tree derives its name from its scourging thorns - שטה shittah, from שטט shôțêt, to pierce; to flog; a goad: - scourge. The symbolic use of the acacia wood in the building of these altars presents us with powerful imagery of the crucifixion. Exodus 27:1-5; Exodus 30:1. *See my notes on the altars at the end of Revelation 16.)*

9:5 Hovering above and over the ark of the Covenant were the two Cherubim, images of glory, intent upon the mercy seat that covered the box on which the blood was sprinkled once a year by the High Priest to cover the sins of the people. Every detail is significant but cannot be discussed at length in this writing. *(The Hebrew word,* כפר *kopher, means to cover [specifically with bitumen], figuratively to cover by legal and equal exchange in order to restore a previously disturbed balance. The legal requirement according to human tradition and mythology, was an eye for an eye, etc. Jesus urges his followers to turn the other cheek: You have heard that it was said, An eye for an eye and a tooth for a tooth. But I say to you...*

The Ark represented a place of mercy where atonement would be made. Innocence had to be achieved at a cost equal to the replacement value of the peace sought between the different parties. See also Genesis 6:14, where the same word denotes the covering of Noah's ark with pitch. The Cross, where Jesus, the Lamb of God, died humanity's death, is the crux of the equation of atonement.

*See **1 Peter 1:18,19** how God speaks the most radical scapegoat language of the law of judgment, and brings final closure to a dead and redundant system. In **Psalm 40:6,7**, it is clearly stated that God does not require sacrifices or offerings. Jesus is the Lamb of God. He collides victoriously with the futile sacrificial system.)*

9:6 In the context of this arrangement the priests performed their daily duties, both morning and evening. *(The daily duties included their dress and preparations, washings, sacrificial offerings, lighting and trimming; then, on every Sabbath, replacing the old showbread with 12 fresh loaves, and sprinkling the blood of the sin offerings on the golden altar of incense before the veil of the sanctuary.)*

9:7 The routine was interrupted only once a year, when the High Priest alone would enter the second tent, the most sacred place of worship, with the blood sacrifice for his own and the people's accumulated errors.

9:8 Already in this arrangement the Holy Spirit indicated that there was a yet more sacred way, beyond the first tent, that was still to be opened. While the first pattern was still being upheld, its fulfillment in truth could not yet commence.

9:9 The tabernacle pattern of that time was an analogy of the hitherto imperfect system in which the gifts and sacrifices presented failed completely to cleanse the conscience of the worshipper.

9:10 All these external rituals pertaining to food and drink and the various ceremonial baptisms and rules for bodily conduct were imposed upon them until the anticipated time of restoration; the foretold moment when [1]all that was crooked would be made straight and restored to its natural and original condition. *(This word, [1]diothosis, is only used in this one place in the New Testament; what was crooked will be made thoroughly straight, restoring to its natural and normal condition something which in some way protrudes or has gotten out of line, as broken or misshapen limbs.)*

9:11 But now Christ has made his public appearance as High Priest of a perfect tabernacle. The good things that were predicted [1]have arrived. This new tabernacle is not a compromised replica of its shadow type, man-made one. This is the real deal. *(The verb, γενομενων [1]genomenōn, is the Aorist Participle, having come about. Sadly, some later copyist deliberately left out the word, γενομενων; they just copied 10:1 τῶν μελλόντων ἀγαθῶν, the blessings that are soon to come.*

Clearly, the restoration of God's original dwelling place in human life is again revealed. See The Restoration of all things at the end of this chapter; also at the end of Acts 3.)

9:12 As High Priest, his permission to enter the Holy Place was not secured by the blood of beasts. By his own blood he obtained access on behalf of the human race. Only one act was needed for him to enter the most sacred place of grace and there to institute a ransom of perpetual consequence. *(The perfection of the redemption he secured needs no further sacrifice. There are* *no outstanding debts; there is nothing we need to do to add weight to what he has accomplished once and for all. The only possible priesthood activity we can now engage in is to continually bring a sacrifice of the fruit of our lips, giving thanks to his Name; no blood, just fruit, even our acts of self-sacrifice, giving of time and money, etc. are all just the fruit of our constant gratitude.)*

9:13 The blood of beasts and the ashes of the burnt sacrifice of a heifer could only achieve a very temporal and surface cleansing by being sprinkled on the guilty. *(The word for heifer, is **damalis**, from **damatzo**, to tame; this was the most dear and expensive sacrifice. She was a strong, pristine, spotless female calf, she was raised as a family pet; A Little Princess. This was the best that the law-system could present; yet, no inner purging of conscience was possible; only the sense of temporal relief; whilst knowing that the entire process would have to be repeated again and again. In this arrangement, God addressed the dilemma of our sin consciousness; the deep-seated stain that it had left needed to be thoroughly exposed, and then brought to closure. The shadow system with its imperfections, as a possible means of obtaining a lasting and meaningful sense of innocence, had to be exhausted; ultimately proving that no sacrifice that anyone can bring at any expense of their own, could possibly match the sacrifice of God giving himself as scapegoat to the human race in order to persuade us that his love for us would go to the scandalous extreme, where we are finally confronted with the fact that it is not in a sacrifice that we bring where God's mind is favorably influenced towards us; but in the shocking sacrifice of himself, where he forever, in the most radical language, impact our ideas and thoughts about the Father, Son and Spirit's estimate of us. There is nothing dearer in the universe to them, but our redeemed innocence and our individual value realized. See Colossians 2:14,15 in the Mirror Bible.)*

9:14 How much more effective was the blood of Christ, when he presented his own flawless life through the eternal Spirit before God, in order to purge your conscience from its frustration under the [1]cul-de-sac rituals of the law. There is no comparison between a guilt and duty-driven, dead religious system, and the vibrancy of living your life free from a sin-consciousness. This is what the new testament priesthood is all about. *(Dead works, [1]nekros ergon. A dead, religious-routine system, can never compete with the resurrected Christ now realized in you.)*

9:15 As [1]fully representing mankind, Jesus' death brought an end to the old, and introduced the New Testament. He thus redeemed us from the transgressions recorded under the first Covenant and identified us as heirs; qualifying us to participate in the full inheritance of all that he obtained on our behalf. *(The concept of a [1]mediator, **mesitēs**, in this analogy, is not a go-between, as if Jesus had to change the Father's mind about us; it was our minds that needed to be persuaded. Jesus did not save us from God; he is fully God and fully man, and in him mankind is most completely represented. See Galatians 3:20; also Hebrews 6:16-20.)*

9:16 For a will to take effect the person who made it must be dead.

9:17 Before the testator dies the will is merely a future promise with no immediate benefit to anyone.

9:18 Even the first Covenant required a death for its actualization; the blood of the animal sacrifice represented that death.

9:19   After Moses uttered the detailed requirements of the law in the hearing of all the people, he would take the blood of calves and of goats, mix it with water and, dipping a bunch of hyssop bound with scarlet wool into the blood-basins, sprinkle the blood on the book and upon the people.

9:20 While performing this cleansing ritual, Moses would solemnly declare, This is the blood of the covenant which God has made binding upon you.

9:21 The same blood was then also sprinkled on the tabernacle, and on all the furniture and ministry utensils.

9:22 Thus, according to the law, all purging was by means of blood; [1]forgiveness was specifically associated with the shedding of blood. *(The idea of closure to the particular case was communicated in the death of an innocent victim. The blood symbolizes this currency. The word translated forgiveness, or remission is the word* [1]*aphiemi, from* **apo**, *away from, and* **hieimi** *an intensive form of* **eimi**, *I am; thus forgiveness is in essence a restoring of one's true 'I-am-ness.' The injury, insult, shame, hostility or guilt would no longer define the individual. See* **1 Peter 1:18** *It is clear to see that you were ransomed from the futile, fallen mindset that you inherited from your fathers, not by the currency of your own labor, represented by the fluctuating values of gold and silver, and the economy of your religious efforts;* **1 Peter 1:19** *but you were redeemed with the priceless blood of Christ; he is the ultimate sacrifice; spotless and without blemish. He completes the prophetic picture. (In him God speaks the most radical scapegoat language of the law of judgment and brings final closure to a dead and redundant system. In Psalm 40:6,7, it is clearly stated that God does not require sacrifices or offerings. Jesus is the Lamb of God. He collides victoriously with the futile sacrificial system whereby offerings are constantly made to the pseudo, moody, monster gods of our imagination. This is the scandal of the cross. God does not demand a sacrifice that would change the way he thinks about mankind; he provides the sacrifice of himself in Christ in order to forever eradicate sin-consciousness from our minds and radically change the way we think about our Maker, one another and ourselves. [Sin-consciousness is in essence a works-based consciousness.])*

9:23 If the methods of the law were only a shadow prefiguring the heavenly reality, the fulfillment of these examples surely requires a stronger and more efficacious sacrifice.

9:24   In Christ we have so much more than a type, reflected in the tabernacle of holy places which was set up by human hands. He entered into the heavenly sphere itself, where he personally mirror-exhibits us face to face with God. *(νῦν now, ἐμφανισθῆναι to exhibit τῷ προσώπῳ τοῦ Θεοῦ in the face; immediate presence; the words, ὑπέρ [with the Genitive case] across ἡμῶν, us; thus, he mirror-exhibits us.)*

9:25 Neither was it necessary for him to ever repeat his sacrifice. The High Priests under the old shadow system stood proxy with substitute, animal sacrifices that had to be offered every year.

9:26 But Jesus did not have to suffer again and again since the [1]fall of the world; the single sacrifice of himself, in the fulfillment of history, now [2]reveals how he has brought sin to naught. He was made manifest once and for all, at the [3]conclusion of the age, in order to do away with sin. *(The word, [1]kataballō, meaning to fall away, to put in a lower place, instead of themelios, meaning foundation [see Ephesians 2:20]; thus, translated the fall of the world, instead of the foundation of the world. The entire Fall was a falling away in our minds from our true identity as image and likeness bearers of Elohim. Just like Eve, we were all deceived to believe a lie about ourselves, which is the fruit of the I-am-not-tree. We all, like sheep, have gone astray. [Isaiah 53:6]) [2]God's Lamb took away the sins of the world. The word, [2]phaneroō, means to render apparent, to openly declare, to manifest. Here in the Perfect Passive Indicative tense, πεφανερωται which means that the progress of an action has been completed and the results of the action are continuing on, in full effect. The words συντέλεια τῶν αἰώνων [3]sunteleia tōn aiōnōn, at the conclusion of the age - only used here and 5 times in Matthew. Jesus is the end of the age; he is the end of the law; what he has done, now defines human life and not their performance measured under the law of works.)*

9:27 So, every person's [1]once-off appointment with death is mirrored in the full consequence of [2]this very judgment, which Jesus now disengaged. *([1]hapax as in once-off; μετὰ with δὲ [1]τουτο this κρίσις judgment. See John 12:31 Now is the judgment of this world; this is the moment where the ruler of the world-system is [1]conclusively cast out. [John uses a double-barrel word here, ekballō eksō - completely thrown out. Thus, taken out of the equation. Luke 10:18.] The serpent's head is about to be crushed. Genesis 3:15; Colossians 2:14,15. Also, John 16:11 Then the world will be convinced that the judgment that was their due was accomplished when the ruler of this world system was judged.)*

9:28 Thus, in this context *[of everyone's appointment with death]*, **Jesus is the ultimate sacrifice. What the first, shadow-dispensation merely prophetically pointed to, he fulfilled [1]once and for all, when he was [2]presented as an offering, to [3]take upon himself the sins of the [4]entire human race. Now, with sin no longer on the agenda, he appears a [6]second time, [5]out of this death, to be clearly seen in everyone's [7]whole-hearted embrace of him as Savior.**

[1] The word, απαξ [1]hapax here, mirrors the same 'once-off appointment with death' in the previous verse, now concluded in Christ.

[2] The Aorist Passive Participle προσενεχθεις of [2]prospherō, having been presented as an offering;

[3] ἀναφέρω [3]anapherō, [Aorist Infinitive describes the action expressed by the verb as a completed unit with a beginning and end] to take upon oneself as a load to be carried, once and for all!.

[4] The preposition εἰς eis, points to a final conclusion; then, τὸ πολλῶν [4]to pollōn, the many, the mass of humanity.

[5] Now, out of this death, he appears a second time; the Preposition [5]ek always denotes source, out of.

[6] The resurrection is thus his [6]second appearance in this conversation. The word, δεύτερος [6]deuteros, the other of two. His first appearance was in his birth, as the incarnate Word made flesh, and now, the second time, in his resurrection unveiled in his presence in Holy Spirit in our flesh! See Acts 3 in the Mirror Study Bible.

[7] In their whole-hearted embrace of him; the Dative case also points to location in, thus, τοις αὐτὸν ἀπεκδεχομένοις. ⁷apekdechomai, from apo, away from, [that which defined one before] and ek, out of, source; and dechomai, to take into one's hands to accept whole-heartedly, to fully embrace. In his resurrection he re-appeared as the victorious Savior of the world. Sin is no longer on the agenda; the Lamb of God has taken away the sins of the world. Jesus Christ fulfilled mankind's destiny with death and judgment! [1 Corinthians 15:3-5; Romans 4:25; Acts 17:30, 31; Romans 6:10.]

Many Scriptures have been translated and interpreted with only a futuristic value and have consequently neutralized many, like the Jews, to diligently wait for the Messiah still to come. The Messiah has come once and for all as Messiah. Jesus appeared again after his resurrection, and now his resurrection life in us as his body is the extension of his second appearance; God making his appeal to an already reconciled world to be reconciled. [Acts 3:26, 2 Corinthians 5:19, 20] The church continued to postpone the reality of what God introduced in Christ. We are already fully represented in his blamelessness. The traditional, second coming doctrine is not the context of these chapters at all. [See 1 Peter 1:10-13] The Aramaic word, maranatha, מרן אתא maran ata, means, Our Lord has come.

See my notes on The Day of the Lord at the end of Revelation 1 - also, End Times in Revelation 17

See Like a Thief in the Night at the end of Revelation 3

The Wedding [see notes on The City-Bride Revelation 3]

Also, my extended notes on The New Heaven and Earth end of Revelation 21

Hebrews Chapter 9 Extended Notes:

Notes on The First and Second Death

So, what about the Second Coming?

The Restoration of All Things

The same Cloud which took him from view now reveals him

The word Parousia does not mean 2nd coming

The Two Dispensations referenced in the book of Hebrews

Notes on The First and Second Death

Hebrews 9:27   So, every person's [1]once-off appointment with death is mirrored in the full consequence of [2]this very judgment, which Jesus now disengaged. *([1]hapax as in once-off; μετὰ **meta** with δὲ [1]τουτο **this** κρίσις judgment. See John 12:31 Now is the judgment of this world; this is the moment where the ruler of the world-system is [1]conclusively cast out. [John uses a double-barrel word here, ekballō eksō - completely thrown out. Thus, taken out of the equation. Luke 10:18.]The serpent's head is about to be crushed. Genesis 3:15; Colossians 2:14,15. Also, John 16:11 Then the world will be convinced that the judgment that was their due was accomplished when the ruler of this world system was judged.)*

Revelation 2:11 Now, listen up with your inner ears. Hear with understanding what the Spirit is saying to the ekklesia: the individual who [1]continues to see their triumph mirrored in mine *[their co-seatedness with me in the throne room]*, **is [2]most certainly not threatened by any [3]contradiction to their true likeness; there is nothing to fear [4]in the second death.** *(The word [1]**nikōn**, is the Present Active Participle Nominative, form of the verb **nikaō**, to emphasize a continual or habitual victory. Then the double negative, οὐ μὴ ἀδικηθῆ [2]**ou mē**, plus the verb, [3]**adikeō**, meaning unrighteous; out of sync with likeness - with **a**, negative and **dikeō**, two parties sharing likeness - **adikēthē** is the Aorist Subjunctive form, meaning a definite outcome that will happen as a result of another stated action. The preposition, ἐκ [4]**ek**, mostly pointing to source, but here used for the agent or instrument] τοῦ θανάτου τοῦ δευτέρου the second death.*

*So, in context of the previous verse [Revelation 2:10], You have no need to fear anything you might suffer at any time, the Second Death is not to distract from the once and for all death that Jesus died, but to endorse it. In the lake of fire, Death and Hadēs are eradicated from memory. The first death is the once and for all death that Jesus died, representing the global death of humankind. Jesus' death took mankind's death in Adam, out of the equation. The idea of the Second Death has to do with the fact that the revelation of the full extent of everyone's inclusion in the death of Jesus, has not yet dawned on some - so it will take a crisis, even their own death, to immediately engage them with the symbolic cleansing [from their doubts, ignorance and unbelief] represented by the lake of burning sulphur, purifying like in a furnace, separating the gold from the dross-mindsets. This is the ultimate awakening to the success of the cross - the realizing that even Death and Hadēs itself died in Jesus' death. It is indeed the death of Death. Revelation 20:14. See my notes on **The Lake of Fire and the Second Death** at the end of Revelation 19.*

But here, specifically in Smyrna's case, the intensity of their persecution is neutralized by their realizing that gold is never threatened by fire.

Remember the One talking is he who said, I am the Living One; I died and now, see, here I am alive unto the ages of the ages and I have the keys wherewith I have disengaged the gates of Hadēs and death. Revelation 1:18. Also Hebrews 9:25-28.

He thus broke the spell of the supposed claim of judgment and death over the Adamic race. The significance of the implications of Jesus' death cannot be exaggerated. It reaches into the entire past, present and future of human history.

As representative of the human race, Jesus Christ fulfilled mankind's destiny with death and judgment. [1 Corinthians 15:3-5, Romans 4:25, Acts 17:30, 31.] Note: Jesus did not come to condemn the world. The Father judges no one for he has handed over all judgment to the Son, who judged the world in righteousness.)

John 12:31 Now is the judgment of this world; this is the moment where the ruler of the world-system is conclusively cast out.

John 12:32 When I am lifted up from the earth, I will draw all of mankind and every definition of judgment unto me. (*He would be lifted up on a cross, descend into the depths of our hell, then, according to the prophetic word in Hosea 6:2, after two days, the entire human race he represents, will be co-quickened and on the third day, be co-raised, out of the lowest parts of the earth and elevated to the highest heavens. Ephesians 4:8,9; see also Ephesians 2:5,6 and Colossians 3:1-3. 'All' includes all of mankind and every definition of judgment. The subject of the sentence, as from the previous verse, is the judgment of the world - thus the primary thought here is that in his death, Jesus would draw all judgment upon himself. John 3:14; John 8:28; Acts 2:33. 1 John 3:5 We have witnessed with our own eyes how, in the unveiling of the prophetic word, when he was lifted up upon the cross as the Lamb of God, he lifted up our sin and broke its dominion and rule over us. John 1:29 Behold, the Lamb of God, who takes away [**airō**] the sin of the world. The word **airō** means to lift up.*)

John 12:33 This he said to point to the way in which he would die.

2 Corinthians 5:14 The love of Christ constrains us and resonates within us; leaving us with only one conclusion: when Jesus died, every individual simultaneously died. In God's logic, one has died for all, thus all have died.

Revelation 20:14 Then Death and Hadēs were cast into the lake of fire. This is the second death.

Hebrews 2:15 As a fellow human, he re-defined death and delivered them from the lifelong dread of death. (*He brought final closure to the idea of judgment, which is what the system of works is all about. Evil is not immortal, love is.*)

1 John 4:18 Fear cannot co-exist in this love realm. The perfect love union that we are talking about expels fear. Fear holds on to an expectation of crisis and judgment [*which brings separation*] **and interprets it as due punishment** [*a form of karma.*] **It echoes torment and only registers in someone who does not yet realize the completeness of their love union.** [*With the Father, Son and Spirit and with one another.*] (*See Hebrews 2:15.*)

So, what about the Second Coming?

Luke 18:8 I assure you, he will speedily vindicate you; the day of the Son of Man is about to dawn. Will the Messiah find a people standing on tip-toe in full expectation of his coming. *(Jesus is not talking about some future coming of the son of man. - Not in this, or in the previous chapter of Luke.)*

Meanwhile... **Luke 18:35 As they approached Jericho, a blind man was sitting beside the road; in eager expectation to receive something.** *(Here is a blind beggar from Jericho, standing on tip-toe in his eager expectation for Jesus, the son of David, to show up and heal him. He made the vital connection.)*

Remember what Jesus said about his Father in **John 14:11, The fact that the Father seems distant or invisible to you does not mean that he is absent. In me he is very present with you. You cannot claim to know me while you ignore him - we are inseparable.**

John 16:7 Now listen up. Hear me, my departure is not to disadvantage you; everything that is about to happen, brings conclusion and bears together what the Prophets pointed to. This will be to your absolute benefit. If I do not go away, your [1]Companion cannot come to you, but if I go I will send to you One to be [2]face to face with you, defining your very being. *([1]Parakletos, from **para** and **kaleō**; redefining our original being in the closest possible association and kindred companionship; closer to you than your breath. Again the word [2]**pros** is used.)*

John 16:16 For a brief while I will be absent from your view; then in another brief while you will see and know me.

John 14:10 Are you not convinced that I am in the Father and that the Father is in me? We are in seamless union. The words that I speak to you are not my independent opinion or ideas; the Father in me addresses you; this conversation then translates into the Father's action unveiled in my doing.

John 14:11 The fact that the Father seems distant or invisible to you does not mean that he is absent. In me he is very present with you. You cannot claim to know me while you ignore him - we are inseparable. I dare you [plural] to believe that I am in the Father and the Father in me - if it seems far fetched, then believe me because of what I have done and what I am about to do. It is the Father in me who defines me. My works exhibit his resolve. *(Jesus does not have to persuade the Father about us, he came to persuade us about the Father. There is nothing in the incarnate Word that is in conflict with who God is. John 1:1-3 If you underestimate me, you underestimate my Father - and you underestimate you.)*

John 14:12 I want you to be fully convinced about this, anyone whose belief concludes in who I am, will also do the works that I do. And because of my [1]relocation to continue to be [2]face to face with my Father, the works that the believer will do, will be of greater proportion and of global influence; the Father is as present in you as he is in me. *(The word, [1]**poreuomai**, to transfer, relocate, to travel. Again the word, [2]**pros**, face to face. Jesus is multiplied in us.)*

John 14:13 And whatever you desire in my name, that will I do that the Father may be glorified in the Son. Your sonship is endorsed in my sonship. *(The first occurrence of the phrase, In my name, en tōi onomati mou. See also John 14:26; 15:16; 16:23, 16:24, 16:26. If this name, Jesus Christ is in the believer's consciousness, the element in which the prayerful activity moves; so that thus, that Name, embracing the whole revelation of redemption, is that which specifically measures and defines the disposition, feeling, object, and contents of prayer. The express use of the name of Jesus therein is no specific token; the question is of the spirit and mind of him who prays Meyer. [Vincent])*

John 14:14 If you ask me anything, in knowing what my name entitles you to, that will I perform. *(The use of 'me' here is supported by Aleph B 33 and the Vulgate Syriac Peshitta manuscripts. Aleph is the famous Sinaiticus, the great discovery of Constantine von Tischendorf, the only surviving complete copy of the New Testament written prior to the ninth century; [4th century].)*

John 14:15 In your loving me you will greatly value and treasure ¹the prophetic conclusion of my ministry. *(The word ¹entolē, which is often translated commandment or precept, or assignment, has two components, en, in and telos, from tellō, to set out for a definite point or goal; properly the point aimed at as a limit, that is, by implication, the conclusion of an act or state, the result; the ultimate or prophetic purpose. Strong's 5056. See 1 John 2:3.)*

John 14:16 In my prayerful engagement with the Father, he will give you ¹another ²close companion to be with you - in such an intimate way that ³my immediate presence will continue to be ⁴inseparably one with you in ⁵timeless ages to come. *(The word **allos** is used here. The words ¹**allos** and **heteros** are both usually translated as another in English. Yet **allos** means another of the same kind and **heteros** means another of a different type. The word, ²**parakaleō**, alongside, closest possible proximity of nearness; and **kaleō**, to identify by name, to surname. Also, kinsman; intimate companion. See Romans 12:8. ...just be there alongside someone to remind them of their true identity. 1 Thessalonians 5:11 Continue, as you so eloquently do, to edify one another by cultivating the environment of your close association in your joint-genesis. [The word **parakaleō** is here translated as our joint-genesis] The words, **ina he meth** [meta] **umōn eis ton aiona he** - ινα η μεθ υμων εις τον αιωνα - the verb ³**he** from **eimi**, I am, is in the Present Active Subjunctive form, to continue to be; ⁴**meta**, with, inseparably one with you in ⁵**aiona**, the timeless ages.)*

John 14:17 Your eternal companion is the Spirit of truth, whom those trapped in the sense-ruled world, just cannot ¹get to grips with. Their visual horizon is veiled, and they are unable to understand what they cannot see. But, *[in your acquaintance with me],* **you are familiar with this ²seamless, intimate union, and the Spirit's continued presence within you.** *(The word, ¹**lambanō**, to grasp; to get to grips with. The following 3 verbs are all in the Present Active Indicative tense, which is the timeless present tense, and indicates continued action, something that happens continuously or repeatedly, or something that is in the process of happening: to know, **ginōskō**; to abide **menō**; and to be **eimi**. Thus, ²**ginōskete**, a knowing that is extended beyond the moment. The absence of Jesus will not interrupt this knowing. [See verse 20.] Then, ὅτι παρ᾽ ὑμῖν μένει **hoti** because, **para**, closest possible nearness and intimate acquaintance, and*

[2]*menō - to abide in seamless oneness; and is present in you.* καὶ ἐν ὑμῖν ἐστίν *kai en humin estin- the Spirit already resides in you. In the Incarnate Word, spirit dimension is not a foreign place, neither is the Spirit a foreign person to you.)*

John 14:18 At no time will you be orphaned or abandoned by me; I come to abide [1]**face to face with you.** *(I come to be no less face to face with you, than what I've always been face to face with the Father, from the beginning and for all eternity. The Holy Spirit does not replace, but reinforces the presence of Jesus and the closeness of the Father. Again, John uses the word* [1]*pros, face to face. See John 1:1)*

John 14:19 In yet a little while the world will no longer see me, but I will be tangibly visible to you in the very life we share together.

John 14:20 In that day you will know that we are in seamless union with one another. I am in my Father, you are in me and I am in you. *(The incarnation does not divide the Trinity; the incarnation celebrates the redeemed inclusion of humanity. Picture 4 circles with the one fitting into the other - The outer circle is the Father, then Jesus in the Father, then us in Jesus and the Holy Spirit in us. This spells inseparable, intimate oneness. Note that it is not our knowing that positions Jesus in the Father or us in them or the Spirit of Christ in us. Our knowing simply awakens us to the reality of our redeemed oneness. Gold does not become gold when it is discovered but it certainly becomes currency.)*

The mystery that was hidden for ages and generations is now the unveiling of Christ in us. This is second coming-language, and ultimately the earth will be flooded with the revelation of his glory. As the waters cover the sea. And all flesh shall see it together. According to Peter in Acts 3:25,26 Pentecost celebrates the second coming of the risen Christ, in the nations.

John 12:24 Most certainly shall the single grain of wheat fall into the earth and die - if it doesn't die it remains alone - but in its death it produces much fruit.

John 4:35 Would you say that it will take another four months for the seed to ripen in the ear? This is not the food that I am talking about. The fruit of your own toil will never satisfy permanently. I want to show you the real harvest. From now on, look at people differently; see them through your Father's eyes, and you will know that they are ripe and ready to discover how perfectly mirrored they are in me. *(Jesus canceled every definition of delay. We've been waiting for the wrong harvest for centuries - the one we've labored for all our lives. A harvest is ripe when the seed in the ear matches the seed that was sown.)*

The Restoration of All Things

Hebrews 9:9 The tabernacle pattern of that time was an analogy of the hitherto imperfect system in which the gifts and sacrifices presented failed completely to cleanse the conscience of the worshipper.

Hebrews 9:10 All these external rituals pertaining to food and drink and the various ceremonial baptisms and rules for bodily conduct were imposed upon them until the anticipated time of restoration; the foretold moment when [1]all that was crooked would be made straight and restored to its natural and original condition. *(This word, [1]diothosis, is only used in this one place in the New Testament; what was crooked will be made thoroughly straight, restoring to its natural and normal condition something which in some way protrudes or has gotten out of line, as broken or misshapen limbs.)*

Hebrews 9:11 But now Christ has made his public appearance as High Priest of a perfect tabernacle. The good things that were predicted [1]have arrived. This new tabernacle is not a compromised replica of its shadow type, man-made one. This is the real deal. *(The verb, γενομενων [1]genomenōn, is the Aorist Participle, having come about. Sadly, some later copyist deliberately left out the word, genomenōn; they just copied 10:1, τῶν μελλόντων ἀγαθῶν, the blessings that were soon to come.*

Clearly, the restoration of God's original dwelling place in human life is again revealed.)

See Peter's powerful testimony in Acts 3:11-26. This is just after he and his partner John, healed a cripple beggar at the temple. [Only a few days after Pentecost.] Now remember, they did not say to him, sorry Sir, you've missed Jesus by 50 days. Nor did they point this man to an invisible Jesus who disappeared into the sky; they boldly said to him, Sir, look at us. What we have, belongs to you.

When everyone gathered in awe of this fantastic miracle, performed by two illiterate fishermen, Peter boldly addressed them:

Acts 3:19 Let this be your [1]wake-up call once and for all. Face the fact that your sins and scars were [2]completely blotted out, and [3]return to the one you have wandered from. Now you may encounter times of [4]total rejuvenation in the [5]face to face, immediate embrace of the Lord.

([1] The word, [1]metanoēsate, μετανοησατε - be awakened in your mind - this is the Aorist Active Imperative tense, which means, get it over and done with] -

[2] Then Peter uses the Aorist Passive Infinitive tense εξαλειφθηναι, which **clearly does not refer to a future event.** *The Aorist Infinitive presents the action expressed by the verb as a completed unit with a beginning and end. From the verb, [2]exaleiphō, with three components, ek, out of, and aleiphō, with a, as a particle of union, and liparos, to grease, to leave a stain; scars of hurtful experiences were like grease stains stored in memory.*

[3] and return to where you've wandered from, [3]epistrepsate also the Aorist Active Imperative tense as in [1].

[4] The word αναψυξεως, [4]anapsuxis from ana upwards, and ψύχω psuchō to breathe again; a unique word only used this once by dr Luke, meaning to catch your breath; heavenly breath from above; spiritual rejuvenation/refreshing.

*[5] The man Jesus, the Messiah has given a face to the invisible Father! The word, πρόσωπον ⁵**prosopon** countenance; face. Jesus is the face of the Father. If you have seen me you have seen the Father. This was his purpose, to resonate and redeem the Abba echo in every human heart.)*

Acts 3:20 Jesus is the ¹authentic Christ, the one whom the prophets spoke about all along; he is the desire of the nations, the very ²One you longed for; the one and only Messiah, who was to be sent to you.

*([1] The best texts read προκεχειρισμένον, ¹**prokecheirismenon**, meaning, the prophetic and authentic, handpicked for you. The handpicked one, gives a powerful, personal touch to the fact that in his incarnation, Jesus is the tailor-made, anticipated Messiah. Used by Luke only, Acts 22:14; Acts 26:16. The verb originally means to take in hand. Thus, he was handpicked/tailor-made for you. [It is the Perfect Passive Participle, describing a state that exists, as a result of something that happened previously]*

*[2] Then the word, αποστειλη ²**aposteilē**, which is the Aorist Active Subjunctive, expressing a wish, regarding a single event. The Aorist Active Subjunctive is a pure form denoting a definite outcome that will happen as a result of another stated action [the prophetic word]. See **John 12:23**, Jesus, immediately understanding the prophetic significance of the moment, knew that he, the Messiah, was who all the nations were longing for, and answered, The hour is here for the Son of man to be glorified. [Jesus studied Scripture as in a mirror - he knew that in the book, it is written about me.] **Haggai 2:7** and the desire of the nations shall come...)*

Acts 3:21 Jesus is the theme of God's conversation, from the earliest ages; through the lips of the prophets who carried the Messiah in the womb of their words. He was to be held all along in the unseen heavenly realm for a time such as this. He is the ¹restoration of all things.

*([1] **The idea of restoration** was part and parcel of the Messianic expectation. Here, in context with the healing of a cripple man, Luke records Peter, using the noun, ἀποκαταστάσεως ¹**apokatastaseos**. The verb, αποκαταστησει to restore to its natural and original condition; as a technical medical term, it denotes complete restoration of health; the restoring to its place of a dislocated joint.*

> *See also its synonym, diothosis, used in **Hebrews 9:10** All these external rituals pertaining to food and drink and the various ceremonial baptisms and rules for bodily conduct were imposed upon them until **the anticipated time of restoration**; the foretold moment when ¹all that was crooked would be made straight and **restored to its natural and original condition**. (This word, ¹diothosis, is only used in this one place in the New Testament; what was crooked will be made thoroughly straight, restored to its natural and normal condition something which in some way protrudes or has gotten out of line, as broken or misshapen limbs.*

> *Faith sees him first, then all flesh shall see it together! Isaiah 40:3-5.*

*Peter clearly remembers his, James and John's encounter on the mount of transfiguration with Jesus, when Moses and Elijah also appeared. Then, a voice **from within the cloud** spoke, this is my Son, the Incarnate Logos [**eklegō**] - hear him. **Luke 9:35.***

*See **Matthew 17:9** And as they were coming down the mountain, Jesus commanded them, Tell no one the vision, **until the Son of man is raised from the dead.***

*Matthew 17:10** And they asked him, **Then why do the scribes say that first Elijah must come?***

*Matthew 17:11** He replied, Elijah does come, and he is **to restore all things;***

*Matthew 17:12** **but I tell you that Elijah has already come,** and they did not know him, but did to him whatever they pleased. So also the Son of man will suffer at their hands.*

*Matthew 17:13** Then the disciples understood that he was speaking to them of **John the Baptist**. See Luke 3:3-6 in the Mirror])*

Acts 3:22 Has not Moses told us: the Lord your God will raise up a prophet out of your midst who is like me. Give your undivided attention to every detail of his conversation and dealings with you. *(The Jews understood Moses to be a type of Christ. **John 1:21** Could you possibly be the re-incarnate Elijah? To which he answered, No, I am certainly not. Then you must be The Prophet who Moses said would come? No. He said, I am not. [Deuteronomy 18:15; John 6:14; Acts 3:22])*

Acts 3:23 What a foolish thing it is to reject Jesus. There is no second Messiah on the prophetic menu. So, if you've already missed out on linking Jesus with Moses' word, then your entire Messianic expectation has come to nothing. *(Lit. - ignoring who Jesus is, by not hearing Moses **in verse** 22 [who very much defines the Jewish people], completely nullifies your Messianic expectation.)*

Acts 3:24 All the prophets, from Samuel onwards, spoke and announced this present time. *(1 Samuel 3:1 Now the boy Samuel was ministering to the LORD under Eli. And the word of the LORD was rare in those days; there was no frequent vision.*

*Samuel's father was from **râmâthayim tsôphîym** רָמָתַיִם צוֹפִים - From the dual of H7413 and the plural of the active Participle of H6822; double height of watchers. A powerful prophetic picture of seeing into the future.)*

Acts 3:25 And you are the sons of the prophets, and the covenant that God initiated with your fathers who were mirrored [pros] in Abraham's face when he declared, in your seed will I [1]bless all the families of the earth.

*([1] ἐνευλογέω [1]**eneulogeō** only used here and in Galatians 3:8. Literary, to be immersed in the well done announcement - the blessing.*

Galatians 3:8 Scripture records prophetically that the mass of non-Jewish nations would be justified by faith and not by their own ability to be righteous. This announcement by God over Abraham is the gospel in advance. God saw every nation included in the same principle of the faith that Abraham pioneered. In you all the nations of the earth are equally represented in the blessing of the faith. *([Genesis 22:17] I will indeed bless you, and I will multiply your seed as the stars of heaven and as the sand which is on the seashore. And your seed shall possess the gate of their enemies, Genesis 22:18 and by your seed shall all the nations of the earth bless themselves. Righteousness by faith is the revelation of the gospel; [Romans 1:17 and Habakkuk 2:4] the just shall live by his (God's) faith Righteousness by God's belief defines your life.)*

Also, **Matthew 26:28** *for this is my blood which is to be poured out for the multitudes, for the remission of sins--the blood which ratifies the Covenant. See* **1 Peter 1:18,19.***)*

In the next verse Peter clearly announces the fact that after his resurrection, Jesus has now appeared again, mirrored in this miracle, performed by ordinary people who have realized the essence of the incarnate Christ in his first coming. The single grain of wheat that fell into the earth and died, did not abide alone. It bore much fruit. *[Remember,* **Matthew 17:9** *And as they were coming down the mountain, Jesus commanded them, Tell no one the vision,* **until the Son of man is raised from the dead.***]*

Acts 3:26 Having raised his ¹child, Jesus from the dead, he ²commissioned him <u>first of all to you</u>; in order to bless you in turning you away from the ³ponēros *[evil]* **system of wearisome labors and annoyances.**

([1] Note, NOT his servant as in some translations - The word, παῖς *¹***pais***, boy [G3816] - is in the LXX in most places where the Hebrew text prefers* עֶבֶד,***ebed***, slave. See* **Isaiah 52:13** *in the Septuagint, Behold. My boy shall be full of* **understanding***; he shall be exalted and decorated with exceedingly great esteem.* Ἰδοὺ **Idou** *- Behold. [*συνήσει **suniesei** *from* **suniemi***, to understand; as in two rivers flowing together. Also carrying in it the idea of the Incarnation - the word made flesh - In the Scriptures it is written about me. [*ὁ παῖς μου **ho pais mou** *- my boy -* **kai hupsothesetai***] he shall be exalted [***kai doxasthesetai sphorda,***] and decorated with exceeding great esteem. The Masoretic Text dates a thousand years later than the Greek Septuagint - LXX.*

[2] He has ²sent ἀπεστειλεν *- [commissioned] him to you [Jews] first.*

*[3] The word, ³***ponēros***, means full of labors, hardships and annoyances; the fruit of the tree of the knowledge of good and labor ponēros. This concludes in a judgment based on performance. Which is the opposite to an opinion of approval based on value.*

Hebrews 9:16 For a will to take effect, the person who made it must be dead.

Hebrews 9:17 Before the testator dies, the will is merely a future promise with no immediate benefit to anyone.

Hebrews 9:27 So, every person's ¹once-off appointment with death is mirrored in the full consequence of ²this very judgment, which Jesus now disengaged.

*(¹***hapax** *as in once-off;* μετὰ *with* δὲ *²*τουτο **this** κρίσις *judgment. See John 12:31 Now is the judgment of this world; this is the moment where the ruler of the world-system is ¹conclusively cast out. [John uses a double-barrel word here, ekballō eksō - completely thrown out. Thus, taken out of the equation. Luke 10:18.]The serpent's head is about to be crushed. Genesis 3:15; Colossians 2:14,15. Also, John 16:11 Then the world will be convinced that the judgment that was their due was accomplished when the ruler of this world system was judged.)*

Hebrews 9:28 Thus, in this context *[of everyone's appointment with death]***, Jesus is the ultimate sacrifice. What the first, shadow-dispensation merely prophetically pointed to, he fulfilled ¹once and for all, when he was ²presented as an offering, to ³take upon himself the sins of the ⁴entire human race. Now, with sin no longer on the agenda, he appears a ⁶second time, ⁵out of this death, to be clearly seen in everyone's ⁷whole-hearted embrace of him as Savior.**

([1] The word, απαξ, [1]**hapax** here, mirrors the same 'once-off appointment with death' in the previous verse, now concluded in Christ.

[2] The Aorist Passive Participle προσενεχθεις of [2]**prosphero**, having been presented as an offering;

[3] ἀναφέρω [3]**anaphero**, [Aorist Infinitive describes the action expressed by the verb as a completed unit with a beginning and end] to take upon oneself as a load to be carried.

[4] The preposition εἰς **eis**, points to a final conclusion; then, τὸ πολλῶν [4]**to pollōn**, the many, the mass of humanity.

[5] _Now, out of this death, he appears a second time;_ the Preposition [5]**ek** always denotes source, **out of.**

[6] The resurrection is thus his [6]**second appearance** in this conversation. The word, δεύτερος [6]**deuteros**, the other of two. His first appearance was in his birth, as the incarnate Word made flesh, and now, the second time, in his resurrection unveiled in his presence in Holy Spirit in our flesh!

[7] In their whole-hearted embrace of him; the Dative case also points to location in, thus, τοις αὐτὸν ἀπεκδεχομένοις. [7]**apekdechomai**, from **apo**, away from, [that which defined one before] and **ek**, out of, source; and **dechomai**, to take into one's hands to accept whole-heartedly, to fully embrace. In his resurrection he re-appeared as the victorious Savior of the world. Sin is no longer on the agenda; the Lamb of God has taken away the sins of the world. Jesus Christ fulfilled mankind's destiny with death and judgment! [1 Corinthians 15:3-5, Romans 4:25, Acts 17:30, 31. Romans 6:10.]

Many Scriptures have been translated and interpreted with only a futuristic value and have consequently neutralized many, like the Jews, to diligently wait for the Messiah still to come. The Messiah has come once and for all as Messiah. Jesus appeared again after his resurrection, and now his resurrection life in us as his body, is the extension of his second appearance; God making his appeal to an already reconciled world to be reconciled. [Acts 3:26, 2 Corinthians 5:19, 20] Through centuries, the church continues to postpone the reality of that which God has already fully accomplished in the incarnate Christ.

We are now already fully represented in his blamelessness. The traditional, second coming doctrine is not the context of these chapters at all. [See 1 Peter 1:10-13] The Aramaic word, **maranatha**, מרן אתא **maran ata**, means, Our Lord has come.

See **Galatians 1:4** Grace and peace have their reference in the fact that Jesus gave himself as the scapegoat for our sins and plucked us out from the evil of this present religious age that encroached on us. This was exactly what the Father had planned in his love for mankind.

Galatians 1:5 His glorious reputation is ageless; it extends beyond all times and seasons. We salute him with our amen. (Nothing that religion communicates in any age or context can match him.)

Galatians 1:6 I am amazed that you can so easily be fooled into swapping the Gospel for a gimmick. The Gospel reveals the integrity of your original identity rescued in Christ; the gimmick is a conglomeration of grace and legalism. This mixture boils down to a do-it-yourself plan of salvation. (Which is a recipe for disaster.)

Galatians 1:7 There is no other gospel in spite of the many so-called Christian products branded gospel. If any hint of the law remains, it is not good news but merely religious people's ideas, detracting from the gospel of Christ. (Some seek to unsettle your minds by perverting the Gospel to accommodate their own opinion.))

The same Cloud which took him from view now reveals him

Acts 1:9 And saying these things, while they were gazing at him, he was taken up, and a ¹cloud veiled him from their sight. *(The Jews were familiar with the cloud. See Exodus 13:21 in LXX the cloud of his presence, which led the Israelites in the wilderness - νεφέλη **nephelē**, from nephos. In Hebrew, ענה annah, and Ancient Hebrew, ⼲⼳⼳◉ reading from right to left, an eye, ◉ seeing the multiplied seed,⼳⼳ then, a picture of a man with his arms raised in wonder, looking at a great sight, ⼱.)*

In his message recorded in Acts chapter 3, Peter clearly remembers his, James and John's encounter on the mount of transfiguration with Jesus, when Moses and Elijah also appeared.

2 Peter 1:16 We are not con-artists, fabricating fictions and fables to add weight to our account of his majestic ¹appearance; with our own eyes we have witnessed the powerful display of the illuminate ²presence [²parousian] of Jesus the Master of the Christ-life. *(His ¹appearance here, is obviously referring to this specific moment of seeing Jesus like they have never seen him before. His face shone like the sun, even his raiment was radiant white. Matthew 17.)*

2 Peter 1:17 He was spectacularly endorsed by God the Father in the highest honor and glory. Then, a voice from within the cloud spoke, this is the Son of my delight; he completely pleases me. *(Matthew 17:5 a radiant cloud enveloped them.)*

2 Peter 1:18 For John, James, and I, the prophetic word is fulfilled beyond doubt; we heard this voice loud and clear from the heavenly realm while we were with Jesus in that sacred moment on the mountain.

2 Peter 1:19 For us the appearance of the Messiah is no longer a future promise but a fulfilled reality. Now it is your turn to have more than a second-hand, hearsay testimony. Take my word as one would take a lamp at night; the day is about to dawn within you, in your own understanding. When the Morning Star appears, you no longer need the lamp; this will happen shortly on the horizon of your own hearts.

Luke 9:34 While Peter was still chatting away, they were suddenly struck with awe, being overshadowed by a cloud and enveloped in it.

Luke 9:35 Then, <u>a voice from within the cloud spoke</u>, this is my Son, the Incarnate Logos *[eklegō]* **- hear him.** *(The voice of his Father confirms that **his beloved son** is the conclusion of the conversation represented in both Moses, [the law] and Elijah, [the prophets] Mark, Matthew and Peter quotes, the Son of my delight instead of chosen eklegō; Mark 9:7; Matthew 17:5. 2 Peter 1:16-19.)*

*Peter, however, knows exactly what he's saying in 1 Peter 2:9, You are proof of the authentic [**eklegō**] generation; you give testimony to the original idea of the royalty of true priesthood [the order of Melchizedek;] you are a perfect prototype of the mass of the human race. You are the generation of people who exhibit the conclusion [**eis**] of the prophetic, poetic thought of God that has come full circle. [See 1 Peter 1:3] You publish the excellence of his elevation and display that* *your authentic identity has been rescued out of obscurity and brought into his spectacular light. [The word **eklegō** has traditionally been translated to mean election - I would prefer to emphasize the fact that **ek** is a preposition always pointing to origin or source and the verb **legō**, is associated with its noun **logos** as in the context of John 1:1,14. The original conversation.] See Hebrews 1:1-3 - Jesus is the conversation of God - he is the Logos - Also, John 1:1,2,5,9,14, To go back to the very beginning, is to find the Word already present there; face to face with God. The Word is I am; God's eloquence echoes and concludes in him. The Word equals God. The beginning mirrors the Word face to face with God. [Nothing that is witnessed in the Word distracts from who God is. If you have seen me, you have seen the Father.] The darkness was pierced and could not comprehend or diminish this light. A new day for mankind has come. The authentic light of life that illuminates everyone was about to dawn in the world.)*

Luke 9:36 In the silence following the voice, Moses and Elijah were gone; it was just Jesus. The disciples were speechless and for the time being, kept their encounter secret. *(See Matthew 17:9 As they were descending the mountain, Jesus emphatically instructed them not to tell anyone about their encounter until they see the Son of Man risen from the dead.)*

1 Corinthians 10:1 Now remember how the people of Israel were all delivered from slavery; the cloud of God's presence, protection, and provision included everyone equally. They were all miraculously led through the Red Sea on dry land and witnessed how their oppressors were completely defeated. *(These Egyptians whom you see today you will never see again. [Exodus 14:13]. Their own unbelief, and not Pharaoh was the reason for their forty-year detour in the desert.)*

1 Corinthians 10:2 The cloud and sea was a type of baptism that they underwent to identify with Moses leading them out of slavery. *(This was all a prophetic picture of Christ leading us out of bondage and slavery in his death and resurrection.)*

Revelation 1:7 Behold he comes with a [1]large dense multitude; an innumerable throng of people, united as one, like the particles of water in a cloud. Every eye will see him, not merely as observers, but they will perceive him for who he really is - even those who participated in his murder, when they pierced his hands and his side. Every single tribe of the earth will see him and weep greatly at the thought of their foolish rejection of him. This will surely be. *(The word **nephos** is a cloud, a large dense multitude, a throng. See Philippians 2:8-12.)*

Revelation 1:8 The God who is Lord over all things says: I am the Alpha and the Omega - my I-am-ness defines time - I am present, past and future. *(The union of **Alpha** and **Omega**, in Greek, makes the verb αω aō, I breathe. And in Hebrew the union of the first and last letter in their alphabet, **Aleph** [bull's head] and **Tav** [the cross] makes ✝ﬡ in Ancient Hebrew or את in modern Hebrew - et, which the Rabbis interpret as the first matter out of which all things were formed, [see Genesis 1:1]. The particle et, is untranslatable in English but, says Rabbi Aben Ezra, it signifies the substance of the thing. Jesus is the [1]**Alpha***

*and **Omega** in whom we live, and move, and have our being. He is indeed closer to us than the air we breathe. Don't waste a day waiting for another day.)*

1 Thessalonians 4:17 In the wake of their arising, we will all be gathered into a large dense multitude of an innumerable throng of people, united as one, like the particles of water in a cloud, and we will encounter the Lord in the very air we breathe and so shall we continually celebrate our I-am-ness in our union with him. *(All flesh shall see his glory together - ultimately every single one will realize that Deity and humanity are married - the Bride and her Groom are united.)*

Hebrews 12:1 So now the stage is set for us: all these faith-heroes cheer us on; they are the [1]cloud of witnesses; as it were, like a great multitude of spectators in the amphitheater. This is our moment. As with an athlete who is determined to win, it would be silly to carry any baggage of the old law-system that would weigh one down. Make sure you do not get your feet clogged up with sin-consciousness. Become absolutely streamlined in faith. Run the race of your spiritual life with total persuasion. *(νέφος [1]nephos, a cloud, a large dense multitude, a throng.)*

Luke 9:27 The Kingdom of God is not a future event beyond your reach. You don't have to wait till you're dead to see it; some of you standing here are about to [1]dramatically witnesses what I am talking about. *[The word, ὁράω [1]horaō, to stare; to gaze with wonder; to encounter; to see for yourselves.)*

Saul encounters an unexpected, sudden and spectacular conversion when Jesus appears to him, engulfing him in light. Introducing himself to him saying, I am Jesus of Nazareth whom you are persecuting. *Acts 22:6,8.* He later testifies in, **2 Corinthians 4:6 The light source is founded in the same God who said, Light, be. And light shone out of darkness. He lit the lamp in our understanding so that we may clearly recognize the features of his likeness in the face of Jesus Christ reflected within us.**

Titus 3:3 Do not be harsh on others. Remember that we too were typically foolish; we were stubborn and indifferent to spiritual things, our addiction to the sensual and sexual kept us running around in circles, we were engaged in malice and spiteful jealousies, we were bored and lonely, often utterly disliking ourselves and hating one another. *(The only difference in who we are now and who we were then is in what we now know to be true about ourselves.)*

Titus 3:4 But then, oh happy day. It was the generosity of God and his fondness for mankind that dawned on us like a shaft of light. Our days of darkness were over. Light shone everywhere and we became aware: God rescued the human race. *(See Titus 2:11.)*

The word Parousia does not mean 2nd coming

1 Thessalonians 2:19 We expect nothing less in the context of the gospel than you enjoying a face to face encounter in the [1]immediate presence of our Lord Jesus Christ. This is our delight and wreath of honor. *(The word [1]parousia speaks of the immediate presence of the Lord. From para, a Preposition indicating closest possible proximity; intimate connection, and eimi, I am. There is not even a hint of judgment or punishment in this word. While there are great and accurate definitions in Strongs, please do not believe everything you read there. G3952 parousia from the Present Participle of G3918 pareimi; a being near, that is, advent; often, return; specifically of Christ to punish Jerusalem, or finally the wicked.!?*

The Greek word parousia, occurs 24 times in the NT, and 22 times it wrongly implies a 2nd coming or coming judgment. Only twice it is translated as presence. 2 Corinthians 10:10, Philippians 2:12. Of all the English translations that I have checked, only the Young's Literal has it correct. What a shame that this word has been so dramatically twisted over the years.

In the Greek Septuagint Psalm 138:8 [in the Hebrew it is Psalm 139] reads, If I make my bed in Hadēs, your presence already fills it. LXX - πάρειμι pareimi your immediate presence - I am.)

1 Thessalonians 3:13 The [1]dominion of the Christ-life establishes you in blameless innocence, face to face before our God and Father, in the constant awareness of his [2]presence in our mutual togetherness with all the saints. *(The subject of the sentence is the Lord Jesus Christ from the previous verse. His lordship endorses the reign of the Christ-life in us. Again the word parousia is translated in all other translations [Except YLT] as second coming.)*

2 Peter 1:16, We are not con-artists, fabricating fictions and fables to add weight to our account of his majestic [1]appearance; with our own eyes we have witnessed the powerful display of the illuminate presence [[2]parousian] of Jesus the Master of the Christ-life. *(Peter was certainly not referring to a possible future event. His [1]appearance here, is obviously referring to this specific moment of seeing Jesus like they have never seen him before. His face shone like the sun, even his raiment was radiant white. Matthew 17.)*

1 Thessalonians 4:13 I do not want you to be ignorant concerning those who seem to be fast asleep in their indifference and unbelief. There is no need for you to grieve as if they are beyond hope. *(See 1 Corinthians 15:51 [1]Ponder this mystery, I want to show you something that you have never seen before: [2]everyone will awaken out of sleep; we will [3]all experience exactly the same change. Look. A Mystery - [1]idou musterion; [2]pantes ou koimethesometha, means no one will sleep; [3]pantes de allangesometha; everyone will be changed.)*

1 Thessalonians 4:14 We believe that Jesus died and rose again, and that he fully represents and includes even those who have not awoken unto him yet. God will [1]lead them to realize that they are indeed in Jesus. *(The word [1]agō means to lead as a shepherd leads his sheep. See 1 Corinthians 1:30, Ephesians 1:4.)*

1 Thessalonians 4:15 We give voice to the word of the Lord; we are God's wake-up call to them that are asleep. We are exhibiting the [1]immediate tangible

presence of the Lord and shall not ²exclude them. *(The word ¹parousia means immediate presence. See my comment in 1 Thessalonians 2:19. See the use of the word ²phthanō, to prevent, to hinder or exclude, also in 2 Corinthians 10:14, Our ministry to you is proof that there are no geographic limitations which could possibly exclude you from the gospel of Jesus Christ. See also 1 Thessalonians 3:12, We can already see how the Lord causes the love we have for you to dynamically impact each of you and burst its banks to flood the entire world. The people who dwelt in darkness have seen a great light. The true light that enlightens everyone has come. And the glory of the Lord shall be revealed and all flesh shall see it together.)*

1 Thessalonians 4:16 *(There remains no disconnect between those who are dead and those who are alive; everyone will encounter the great awakening, where the invisible meets the visible.)* **In their awakening, the dead will all, first-hand witness the Lord stepping out of the invisible heavenly realm into their immediate visible horizon with an inciting shout, announcing his triumphant reign in the trumpet-like billowing voice of God.**

1 Thessalonians 4:17 In the wake of their arising we will all be gathered into a large dense multitude of an innumerable throng of people, united as one, like the particles of water in a cloud, and we will encounter the Lord in the very air we breathe and so shall we continually celebrate our I-am-ness in our union with him. *(All flesh shall see his glory together - ultimately every single one will realize that Deity and humanity are married - the Bride and her Groom are united.*

1 Thessalonians 4:18 The fact that we are all deeply connected in the same source of our 'beingness' causes us to be constantly engaged in this conversation with one another.

The Two Dispensations referenced in the book of Hebrews

Clearly, **the first and the second** *manifestations of Jesus referenced again and again in the book of Hebrews, mirror the* **two distinct dispensations** *of the old and the new; the prophetic shadow in the Scriptures, and the substance unveiled in the incarnate Christ.*

Hebrews 9:11 But now Christ has made his public appearance as High Priest of a perfect tabernacle. The good things that were predicted have arrived. This new tabernacle is not a compromised replica of its shadow type, man-made one. This is the real deal.

Hebrews 6:17 In the same context we are confronted with God's eagerness to go to the last extreme in his dealing with us as heirs of his promise, and to cancel out all possible grounds for doubt or dispute. In order to persuade us of the unalterable character and finality of his resolve, he ¹confined himself to an oath. The promise which already belongs to us by heritage is now also ¹confirmed under oath. *(The word ¹mesiteuō is used, interposed or mediated. Compare* **mesitēs***, mediator, from* **mesos***, midst. In the incarnation, God has positioned himself in the midst, of his creation. See Galatians 3:20*

The Word is the promise; the Incarnate, crucified and risen Christ is the proof. He desires to show more convincingly to the heirs of the promise the unchangeable character of his purpose. RSV .

Mankind was not redeemed from the Devil; a thief never becomes an owner; neither did Jesus do what he did to change his Father's mind about us. It was our minds that needed persuasion. God was not to be reconciled to his creation; God was in Christ when he reconciled the world to himself. 2 Corinthians 5:18-20.)

Hebrews 6:18 So that we are now dealing with two irreversible facts which make it impossible for anyone to prove God wrong; thus our persuasion as to our redeemed identity is powerfully reinforced. We have already escaped into that destiny; our expectation has come within our immediate grasp. *(The promise of redemption sustained throughout Scripture and the fulfillment of that promise in Jesus. See John 8:13-18* **John 8:17** *That should settle it for you since it is written in your law that the testimony of two, is true. [This combined witness of two is not true just because they agree, unless true in fact separately. But if they disagree, the testimony falls to the ground. Deuteronomy 17:6; and Deuteronomy 19:15. - Robertson. Also Revelation 10:6 See notes on the Oath at the end of Revelation 10 also the Notes on the Testimony of Jesus at the end of Revelation 20.])*

Hebrews 6:19 Our hearts and minds are certain; anchored securely within the innermost courts of God's immediate Presence; beyond the *(prophetic)* **veil.**

Hebrews 6:20 By going there on our behalf, Jesus pioneered a place for us and removed every type of obstruction that could possibly distance us from the promise. In him we are represented for all time; he became our High Priest after the order of Melchizedek. We now enjoy the same privileged access he has. *(He said, I go to prepare a place for you so that you may be where I am. On that day you will no longer doubt that I and the Father are one; you will know that I am in the Father and you in me and I in you. John 10:30, 14:3, 20.)*

Hebrews 8:7 If there had been no flaw in the first dispensation, why bother to replace it by a second? Jesus was made apparent as the conclusion of the dispensation of condemnation; he fulfilled every single prophetic pointer to the mission of the Messiah-Christ.

Hebrews 9:1 The first system followed a specific pattern of worship which was conducted in a specific and sacred place of worship. *(The detail of which spoke in shadows of the new.)*

Hebrews 9:2 The first tented area was called the Holy Place; the only light here came from the lampstand illuminating the table upon which the [1]showbread was presented. *(The lampstand was a beautifully crafted golden chandelier portraying budding and blossoming almond branches. Remember that this is also what Jeremiah saw in Jeremiah 1:12, when God said, I am awake over my word to perform it. The same Hebrew word is used here, שקד shaqad; the almond was called the awake tree, because it blossomed first, while the other trees were still in their winter sleep. The Hebrew word לחם הפנים lechem haPānīm, face bread, or bread of the presence. What happened to us in Christ is according to God's eternal purpose [Bread of the Presence, or showbread, in Greek, πρόθεσις [1]prothesis, pre-designed/prophetic purpose] which he has shown in every prophetic pointer and shadow; in the Hebrew tradition the showbread pointed to the true bread from heaven, the authentic word that proceeded from the mouth of God - Jesus, the incarnate word - sustaining the life of our design. The showbread pointed towards the daily sustenance of life in the flesh as the ultimate tabernacle of God, realized in the account of Jesus with the two men from Emmaus; their hearts were burning with resonance and faith while he opened the Scriptures to them, and then around the table their eyes were opened to recognize him as the fulfillment of Scripture, their true meal incarnated [Luke 24:27-31]. Mankind shall not live by bread alone, but by the authentic thought of God, the Word proceeding from his mouth, the original intent, his image and likeness incarnated, revealed, and redeemed in human life. See note to 1 Corinthians 11:34.)*

Hebrews 9:3 The second veil led to the inner tent known as the Most Holy Place.

Hebrews 9:4 Therein were the golden altar of incense, and the ark of the covenant. The [1]box was completely covered in gold, both inside and out. In it were kept the golden jar with a sample of the miracle [2]manna from the wilderness, as well as the budding staff of Aaron, *[Moses' staff - but here referred to as Aaron's - when they first met with Pharaoh Aaron's staff turned into a snake - the symbol of Pharaoh's rule, and swallowed the snake staffs of the Egyptian magicians]* **as also the two engraved tablets of stone with the ten commandments of the Covenant.** *(Pointing prophetically to the rebooted life of our design where the law of agapē is inscribed in our inner consciousness. A golden fire-pan was for the purpose of carrying fire, in order to burn incense on the day of Atonement [at-one-ment] once a year in the ultimate place of worship. The word, [1]kibotos, the wooden box, is the same word used for Noah's ark; the container of mankind's redemption. Genesis 6:14 The [2]manna prophetically pictured the true bread from heaven, not the bread that mankind's labor produces. John 4:35, 38.* **Noah** נֹחַ *rest. Noah* נֹחַ *rest. Noach* נֹחַ *found favor* חֵן *in the eyes of the Lord. See Genesis 6:8, the same letters in reverse, as in a mirror reflection,* חֵן *chen, means, grace/favor.)*

414

Hebrews 9:5 Hovering above and over the ark of the Covenant were the two Cherubim, images of glory, intent upon the mercy seat that covered the box on which the blood was sprinkled once a year by the High Priest to cover the sins of the people. Every detail is significant but cannot be discussed at length in this writing. *(The Hebrew word, כפר kopher, means to cover [specifically with bitumen], figuratively to cover by legal and equal exchange in order to restore a previously disturbed balance. The legal requirement according to human tradition and mythology, was an eye for an eye, etc. Jesus urges his followers to turn the other cheek: You have heard that it was said, An eye for an eye and a tooth for a tooth. But I say to you...*

The ark represented a place of mercy where atonement would be made. Innocence had to be achieved at a cost equal to the replacement value of the peace sought between the different parties. See also Genesis 6:14, where the same word denotes the covering of Noah's ark with pitch. The Cross cannot be taken out of the equation of atonement.

God did not clothe Adam with the skin of an animal because of a divine need to be appeased, but because of their unconditional love for Adam; they spoke the language of Adam's own judgment: Adam, not God, was embarrassed about his nakedness. The clothing was not to make God look at Adam differently, but to make Adam feel better about himself. And ultimately it was to prophetically prepare Adam for the unveiling of the mystery of mankind's redemption in the incarnation. Here Deity would clothe themselves in human skin, in a Son; and the Lion of Judah, would become the Lamb of God, in order to free our minds to re-discover his image and likeness in our skin. See 1 Peter 1:2.

See 1 Peter 1:18,19 how God speaks the most radical scapegoat language of the law of judgment, and brings final closure to a dead and redundant system. In Psalm 40:6,7, it is clearly stated that God does not require sacrifices or offerings. Jesus is the Lamb of God. He collides victoriously with the futile sacrificial system.)

Hebrews 9:6 In the context of this arrangement the priests performed their daily duties, both morning and evening. *(The daily duties included their dress and preparations, baptisms, sacrificial offerings, lighting and trimming, removing the old showbread and replacing it with fresh bread, and sprinkling the blood of the sin offerings before the veil of the sanctuary.)*

Hebrews 9:7 The routine was interrupted only once a year, when the High Priest alone would enter the second tent, the most sacred place of worship, with the blood sacrifice for his own and the people's accumulated errors.

Hebrews 9:8 Already in this arrangement the Holy Spirit indicated that there was a yet more sacred way, beyond the first tent, that was still to be opened. While the first pattern was still being upheld, its fulfillment in truth could not yet commence.

Hebrews 9:9 The tabernacle pattern of that time was an analogy of the hitherto imperfect system in which the gifts and sacrifices presented failed completely to cleanse the conscience of the worshipper.

Hebrews 9:10 All these external rituals pertaining to food and drink and the various ceremonial baptisms and rules for bodily conduct were

imposed upon them until the anticipated time of restoration; the foretold moment when [1]all that was crooked would be made straight and restored to its natural and original condition. *(This word, [1]diothosis, is only used in this one place in the New Testament; what was crooked will be made thoroughly straight, restoring to its natural and normal condition something which in some way protrudes or has gotten out of line, as broken or misshapen limbs.)*

Hebrews 9:11 **But now Christ has made his public appearance as High Priest of a perfect tabernacle. The good things that were predicted [1]have arrived. This new tabernacle is not a compromised replica of its shadow type, man-made one. This is the real deal.** *(The verb, γενομενων [1]genomenōn, is the Aorist Participle, having come about. Some later copyist deliberately left out the word, γενομενων; they just copied 10:1 τῶν μελλόντων ἀγαθῶν, the blessings that are soon to come. The restoration of God's original dwelling place in human life is again revealed.)*

Hebrews 7:25 **Through him mankind's approach to God is forever secured; he continues to [1]communicate the full accomplishment of their salvation.** *(The word, ἐντυγχάνω [1]entugchanō from en, in and tugchanō, to to hit the mark: of one discharging a javelin or arrow. Thus to entirely represent the individual in his person as the incarnate son of man/son of God. See Hebrews 12:24,25.*

Hebrews 8:6 **Jesus is now the fulfillment of all those promises towards which the old practices were merely pointing; as when an arrow strikes the bullseye. The dispensation he now administers is far superior to the old. He is the arbitrator of a more effective covenant; sanctioned by its being an announcement of far greater benefit to mankind.**

Hebrews 9:15 **As [1]fully representing mankind, Jesus' death brought an end to the old, and introduced the New Testament. He thus redeemed us from the transgressions recorded under the first Covenant and identified us as heirs; qualifying us to participate in the full inheritance of all that he obtained on our behalf.** *(The concept of a [1]mediator, mesitēs, in this analogy, is not a go-between, as if Jesus had to change the Father's mind about us; it was our minds that needed to be persuaded. Jesus did not save us from God; he is fully God and fully man, and in him mankind is most completely represented. See Galatians 3:20; also Hebrews 6:16-20.)*

Hebrews 9:28 **Thus, in this context** [*of everyone's appointment with death*], **Jesus is the ultimate sacrifice. What the first, shadow-dispensation merely prophetically pointed to, he fulfilled [1]once and for all, when he was [2]presented as an offering, to [3]take upon himself the sins of the [4]entire human race. Now, with sin no longer on the agenda, he appears a [6]second time, [5]out of this death, to be clearly seen in everyone's [7]whole-hearted embrace of him as Savior.**

See my extended chapters on these subjects following Hebrews chapter 9 in the 2020 revision of my book, DIVINE EMBRACE [in print or Kindle]

10:1 For the law presented to us a faint shadow, outlining the promise of the blessings anticipated in the coming of Christ, even detailing its future significance. The mere sketch however, could never be confused with the actual object that it represented. The annual sacrificial rites as shadow of the eventual object would always leave the worshipper feeling inadequate and be a reminder year after year of the sinfulness of mankind. *(Barnes Notes on Hebrews 10:1, For the law having a shadow: That is, the whole of the Mosaic economy was a shadow; for so the word Law is often used. The word shadow here refers to a rough outline of anything, a mere sketch, such as a carpenter draws with a piece of chalk, or such as an artist delineates when he is about to make a picture.*

He sketches an outline of the object which he desires to draw, which has some resemblance to it, but is not the very image; for it is not yet complete. The words rendered the very image refer to a painting or statue that is finished, where every part is an exact representation of the original. The good things to come here refer to the future blessings which would be conferred on mankind by the Gospel. The idea is, that under the ancient sacrifices there was an imperfect representation; a dim outline of the blessings which the Gospel would impart to people. They were a typical representation; they were not such that it could be pretended that they would answer the purpose of the things themselves which they were to represent, and would make those who offered them perfect.

Such a rude outline; such a mere sketch, or imperfect delineation, could no more answer the purpose of saving the soul than the rough sketch which an architect makes would answer the purpose of a house, or than the first outline which a painter draws would answer the purpose of a perfect and finished portrait. All that could be done by either would be to convey some distant and obscure idea of what the house or the picture might be, and this was all that was done by the Law of Moses.

The Gospel is no longer a future prediction; it is a now and relevant revelation. We are talking good news, and not just good predictions. News already happened. Every definition of distance or delay is canceled in Christ.)

10:2 Had it been possible to present the perfect offering that had the power to successfully remove any trace of a sin-consciousness, then the sacrificial system would surely have ceased to be relevant.

10:3 But in the very repetition of these ritual sacrifices the awareness of guilt is reinforced rather than removed.

10:4 The conclusion is clear: animal sacrifices failed to remove anyone's sinfulness or their sin-consciousness.

10:5 So when Jesus, the Messiah, arrives as the fulfillment of all the types and shadows, he quotes Psalm 40:6-8, and says, In sacrifices and offerings God takes no pleasure; but you have ordained my incarnation. *(Adam Clark writes the following commentary: A body hast thou prepared me - The quotation of this and the two following verses by the apostle, is taken from the Septuagint, with scarcely any variety of reading: they are widely different in verbal expression in the Hebrew. In the Hebrew text David's words are, **oznayim caritha li,** אזנים כרית לי which we translate, My ears hast thou opened; but the writer of this*

*Epistle quotes, **soma** [body] **de katertiso moi**; [which I translated in the mirror as, **You have ordained my incarnation**.] How is it possible that the Septuagint and the Apostle should take a meaning so completely different from the sense of the Hebrew? Dr. Kennicott has a very ingenious conjecture here: he supposes that the Septuagint and Apostle express the meaning of the words as they stood in the copy from which the Greek translation [LXX - Septuagint] was made; and that the present Hebrew text is corrupted in the word **aznayim**, ears, which has been written through carelessness for **az gevah**, then, a body... The first syllable אז, **az**, Then, is the same in both; and the latter, נים **nyim**, which, joined to **az** makes **oznayim**, might have been easily mistaken for **geviah**, גויה body; the letter נ **nun** being very like the letter ג **gimel**; and י **yod** like ו **vau**; and ה **he** like final ם **mem**; especially if the line on which the letters were written in the manuscript happened to be blacker than ordinary, which has often been a cause of mistake, it might then have been easily taken for the under-stroke of the **mem**, ם and thus give rise to a corrupt reading; add to this, the root of כרית **carah** כרה signifies as well to prepare, as to open, dig, etc. On this supposition the ancient copy translated by the Septuagint, and followed by the apostle, must have read the Hebrew text thus: **az geviah charitha li**; and therefore wrote the Greek text thus, **soma de katertitsoo moi - Σωμα δε κατηρτισω μοι**. Then a body thou hast prepared me: thus the older Hebrew text, the version of the Septuagint, and the Apostle, will agree in what is known to be an indisputable fact in the Christian faith; namely, that Jesus Christ is the incarnate prophetic word; he is the Lamb of God who took away the sin of the world.*

It is remarkable, that all the offerings and sacrifices which were considered to be of an atoning or cleansing nature, offered under the law, are here enumerated, to show that none of them, nor all of them, could take away sin; and that the grand sacrifice of Christ was that alone which could do it. Adam Clarke)

10:6 **None of the prescribed offerings and sacrifices, including burnt offerings and sin offerings were your request.**

10:7 **Then I said, I read in your book what you wrote about me; so here I am, I have come to fulfill my destiny.** *(Psalm 40:7, Luke 4:17, Luke 24:27, 44.)*

10:8 **Having said what he did in the above quote, that the prescribed offerings and sacrifices were neither his desire nor delight, he condemned the entire sacrificial system upheld by the law.**(*These only served to sustain a sin-consciousness and was of no redemptive benefit to anyone.)*

10:9 **Also by saying, I am commissioned to fulfil your will, he announces the final closure of the first in order to introduce the second.** *(Grace replaces the law; innocence supersedes sin-consciousness.)*

10:10 **So, by this fulfilled will, in the mind of God and by his resolution he declares mankind immediately sanctified through one sacrifice; the presentation of the body of Jesus Christ.**

10:11 **Every priest continually repeats the same daily rituals and sacrifices, knowing that they have always proved incapable of removing sins.**

10:12 **But now we have an exception. In complete contrast to the previous priesthood, this priest offered a single sacrifice of perpetual efficacy for sins. To celebrate the perfection of what was attained through his single sacrifice, he sat down as the executive authority of God.**

(God's right hand [Hebrews 1:3]. He occupies the highest seat of dominion to endorse mankind's innocence. Having accomplished purification of sins, he sat down.)

10:13 His seat of authority is established upon ¹the fully realized, prophetic expectation that every opposing threat to human life ²was made the resting place of his feet. *(See Hebrews 1:13 You are the extension of my right hand, my executive authority; take your position and witness how I make your enemies a place upon which you may rest your feet. [Matthew 22:42-45.] The neck supporting and turning the head suggests that the mindset of every hostile influence is thus conquered. This act was done symbolically, as a token, not only of the present complete victory, but of continued and sustained triumph over all adversaries. The word, εκδεχομενος ¹ekdechomenos, [to accept from the source] is the Present Participle Passive. Participles are verbal adjectives. [Nearly a third of Greek verbal forms are Participles.] For the Present Participle this implies that the action of the Participle is going on at the same time as the action of the main verb in the sentence, which is the verb in the previous verse where the sentence begins, ἐκάθισεν ekathisen, the Aorist Indicative Active, he sat down having offered a single sacrifice of perpetual efficacy for sins... Then the word, τεθωσιν ²tethōsin, to be subdued; the Aorist Subjunctive Passive - a definite outcome that will happen as a result of another stated action. See 1 Corinthians 15:25 His dominion is destined to subdue all hostility and contradiction under his feet. (The Lord said to my Lord, Sit at my right hand until I make your enemies your footstool. [Psalm 110:1] Jesus is Lord of Lords; in his victory mankind is restored to lordship; I say you are gods, all of you are sons of the Most High [Psalm 82:6 RSV]. See Revelation 3:11.)*

10:14 By that one perfect sacrifice he has ¹perfectly ²sanctified sinful mankind forever. *(The word, ²hagiazomenous, means sanctify, the present Participle describes an action thought of as simultaneous with the action of the main verb, perfectly; ¹teteleioken, in the Perfect tense denotes an action which is completed in the past, but the effects of which are regarded as continuing into the present. [See Hebrews 2:11] For he who sanctifies and those who are sanctified have all one origin.)*

10:15 This is exactly what the Holy Spirit now endorses in us having already foretold it in Scripture. *(Jeremiah 31:33, 34.)*

10:16 This is my covenant that I will make with you during those days, says the Lord; I will greatly advantage you by ¹giving my laws in your hearts and engrave them in your inmost thoughts. *(The word, ¹didomi, means to give someone something to their advantage.)*

10:17 This is final: I have no record of your sins and misdeeds. I cannot recall them. *(Nothing in God's reference of mankind, reminds him of sin. See Hebrews 8:12.)*

10:18 Sins were dealt with in such a thorough manner that the idea of future offerings would never again be considered. Nothing that we can personally sacrifice could add any virtue to our innocence.

10:19 So, fellow family, what the blood of Jesus communicates, seals our immediate access into this ultimate place of sacred encounter, with unashamed confidence.

10:20 This is the official inauguration of a brand new way of life. The torn flesh of Jesus opened the veil for us. Our own flesh can no longer be a valid excuse to interrupt the expression of the life of our design from within our innermost shrine.

10:21 We have a High Priest in the house.

10:22 We are free to approach God with absolute confidence, fully persuaded in our hearts that nothing can any longer separate us. We are invited to draw near now. We are thoroughly cleansed, inside and out, with no trace of sin's stains on our conscience or conduct. The sprinkled blood purges our inner thought-patterns; our bodies also are bathed in clean water. *(1 Corinthians 6:19 Do you not realize that your body is the sacred shrine of the Spirit of God, echoing within you. You do not own your life. 1 Corinthians 6:20 You are bought and paid for. All of you are his. Live your life conscious of how irreplaceable priceless you are. You host God in your skin.)*

10:23 Our conversation echoes his persuasion; his faithfulness backs his promises. *(His integrity inspires our confession. Let us hold fast the confession of our hope without wavering, for he who promised is faithful.)*

10:24 Let us also think of creative ways by which we can influence one another to find inspired expression in doing things that benefit others. Good actions give voice and volume to the love of God. *(Let us consider how to stir up one another to love and good works. RSV.)*

10:25 In the light of our free access to the Father, let us extend that embrace to one another. Our gatherings are no longer a repetition of tradition but an essential fellowship where we remind one another of our true identity. Let us do so with greater urgency now the day has dawned in our understanding. *(The prophetic shadow has been replaced by the light of day.)*

10:26 To know the truth, as we now do, and still persist in deliberate sinning is to openly discard God's provision in Christ. But unlike the old sacrificial system, no further sacrifice can be offered in the new.

10:27 To despise and reject his gift inevitably brings the self-inflicted judgment of the law of works; this destructive judgment devours lives like stubble in a fire. *(To know that Jesus bore your judgment and still prefer to carry it yourself by remaining under the law is absurd.)*

10:28 There was no mercy under Moses's law; two or three witnesses could sentence a suspect to death. *([See also Hebrews 6:6-17; James 2:13] Judgment shows no mercy to those who do not walk in mercy, but [the law of liberty/mercy] fears no judgment. [Galatians 5:22, 23] There is no law against love. See also 1 John 4:18.)*

10:29 With how much closer scrutiny do you suppose someone will be viewed who has trampled the Son of God underfoot and scorned the blood of the Covenant by publicly insulting the Spirit of grace. *(Preferring the law above the revelation of grace brings you back under judgment of the law without the possibility of further sacrifice. There is no alternative mercy outside of God's grace gift in Christ.)*

10:30 As Jews we are familiar with Scripture, which says that God is the revealer of righteousness, jealous to restore the order of peace. He is the umpire of his people. *(Deuteronomy 32: 36.)*

10:31 What a foolish thing it would be to deliberately shun the hands that bled for your salvation.

10:32 Remember how strongly you stood against painful contradictions in those early days when you first saw the light.

10:33 As if on a theatre stage, you were publicly ridiculed and afflicted for your faith, both personally and in your association with others that were similarly abused.

10:34 I remind you of the sincere sympathy you felt for me then, during my imprisonment; how you also cheerfully accepted the plundering of your personal property. You were convinced that the treasure you have within you is of far greater and more permanent value, secured as it is in the heavenly dimension.

10:35 I urge you not to relinquish your confident conversation. [1]Persuasion in God's achievement in Christ, redefines the idea of [2]reward and confirms what grace reveals. *(See Hebrews 11:6. Jesus Christ defines God's [1]faith; he is Immanuel. He is the substance and evidence of all that God believes. The word translated reward is the word [2]**misthapodotes**. This word is only used in the book of Hebrews, (6 times) and is an interesting combination of two words, **misthoo**, a wage and **apodidomi** to give away; righteousness is revealed by faith as a gift and not as a reward for keeping the law; faith pleases God, not good or bad behavior. Just love living in the awareness and full persuasion of the closeness of God...He is not far from each one of us, says Paul to a bunch of idol worshipping Greek philosophers. Acts 17:27, 28. Even in our ignorance or indifference to him - even in our hostility, he successfully reconciled the human race to himself in Christ. The incarnation celebrates that Immanuel means that God has no desire to be without us.)*

10:36 Employ patience as you continue to echo the poetry of God's desire for you to possess the promise. *(The word, [1]**poeima**, means to make poetry of the promise; your doing is to echo the promise and the desire of God. The promise is a gift of faith and not a reward for behavior.)*

10:37 Time becomes insignificant once the promise is realized. Remember how the promise of his imminent appearance was recorded in Scripture. *(The arrival of Jesus is the fulfillment of the promise and the realizing of righteousness by faith, as Habakkuk prophesied. Habakkuk 2:2-4. He is the fullness of time. Galatians 4:4.)*

10:38 Righteousness by God's faith defines life; reverting to the law of works grieves God's work of grace. *(Instead of reading the curse when disaster strikes, Habakkuk realizes that the Promise out-dates performance as the basis to mankind's acquittal. Deuteronomy 28 would no longer be the motivation or the measure of right or wrong behavior. Though the fig tree does not blossom, nor fruit be on the vines, the produce of the olive fails and the fields yield no food, the flock be cut off from the fold and there be no herd in the stalls, yet I will rejoice in the Lord, I will joy in the God of my salvation. God, the Lord, is my strength; he makes my feet like hinds' feet, he makes me tread upon my high places. Habakkuk 2:4, 3:17-19 RSV.)*

10:39 But we are not of the quitting kind; we possess a persuasion of soul that believes against all the odds.

11:1 Persuasion confirms confident expectation and proves the unseen world to be more real than the seen. Faith celebrates as certain what hope visualizes as future. *(The shadow no longer substitutes the substance. Jesus is the substance of things hoped for the evidence of everything the Prophets foretold. The unveiling of Christ in human life completes mankind's every expectation. Colossians 1:27.)*

11:2 People of previous generations received the testimony of their hope in faith. It was faith that made their hope tangible. *(Only the Messiah can give substance to the Messianic hope. No substitute will suffice.)*

11:3 Faith alone explains what is not apparent to the natural eye; how the ages were perfectly framed by the Word of God. Now we understand that everything visible has its origin in the invisible.

11:4 It was faith that made the difference between the sacrifices of Abel and Cain, and confirmed Abel's righteousness. God bore witness to righteousness as a gift rather than a reward. Even though he was murdered, his faith continued to be a most relevant prophetic voice. *(See Hebrews 12:24.)*

11:5 Enoch enjoyed God's favor by faith, in spite of Adam's fall; he proved that faith defeats death. *(His absent body prophesied the resurrection of Christ; faith does not die.)*

11:6 There is no substitute [1]reward for faith. Faith's return exceeds any other sense of achievement. Faith knows that God is; those who desire to respond to his invitation to draw near, realize by faith that he is life's most perfect gift. *(If he is the desired one then no substitute will suffice. Jesus Christ defines God's faith; he is Immanuel. He is the substance and evidence of all that God believes. Jesus is what God believes. The word translated reward is the word [1]misthapodotes. This word is only used in the book of Hebrews, (6 times) and is an interesting combination of two words, misthoo, a wage and apodidomi to give away; righteousness is revealed by faith as a gift and not as a reward for keeping the law; faith pleases God, not good or bad behavior. See Hebrews 10:35.)*

11:7 Noah received Divine instruction to save his household from judgment; faith prompted him to construct the Ark immediately, long before the rains were evident. His faith demonstrated the difference between judgment and justification.

11:8 By faith Abraham acknowledged the [1]call of God which gave him his identity and destiny, as evidence of his inheritance as he journeyed into the unknown. *(The word, [1]kaleō, means to call, to identify by name, to surname. This is the essence of ekklesia - see my note in verse 10)*

11:9 Nothing but his faith seemed permanent while Abraham camped in tents like a stranger in the land of promise. His sons Isaac and Jacob joined him as sojourners; equally persuaded that they were heirs of the same promise.

11:10 His faith saw a city with permanent foundations, designed and constructed by God. *(In Matthew 16:13-19 Jesus asks the most important question* *in the Bible, Who do people say, that I, the Son of Man am? Then he asked his followers, Who do you say that I am? The Rock foundation of the ekklesia that Jesus is both the Architect and Master-builder of, is the unveiling of the Father. The son of man [Revelation 1:13] is the son of God. Blessed are you, Simon, son of Jonah. [Bar Jonah, his surname identity] Flesh and blood did not reveal this to you, but My Father. I say, you are Rock, a chip [**petros**] of the old Block [**petra**]. And upon this revelation, that the son of man is the son of God, I will build my ekklesia and the gates of Hadēs will not prevail against it. The word, translated church is* **ekklesia** *from* **ek***, origin and* **kaleō***, to surname; original identity.* **Hadēs***, from* **ha***, negative particle, and* **eidō** *to see. In a walled city, the gates are the most strategic point - if the gates are disengaged, the city is taken. Thus, the blindfold mode of mankind's forgotten identity, will not prevail against you.*

Also, Hebrews 3:2 Jesus is proof of God's workmanship; he exhibits God's persuasion concerning us. Jesus is what God believes about us. In Moses we have the prophetic model, demonstrated in his complete belief in God's purpose displayed in the meticulous attention to detail regarding the construction of the tabernacle. (See Hebrews 8:5 The prophetic model mirrors God's meticulous attention to detail when it comes to every aspect of your life. You are his tabernacle; you are his address on planet earth.)

Hebrews 3:3 Yet his fame surpasses the glory of Moses, because the one who designs and constructs the house gets the greater glory. (Hebrews 1:4; John 1:15.)

Hebrews 3:4 Every house is an expression of someone's design; God is the ultimate architect and creator of all things.)

11:11 Sarah's testimony of faith is just as amazing: she conceived and bore a child when it was humanly impossible. She believed that God would be faithful to his promise, and ¹gave that belief authority over her life. *(The word, ¹***hegeomai***, strengthened form of* **agō***, to officially appoint in a position of authority.)*

11:12 Faith brought into reality an offspring beyond calculation; from one as good as dead children would be born more numerous than the stars and as impossible to count as the grains of sand on every distant sea shore. *(The uttermost parts of the earth, bordered by the sea shore, will know the blessing of righteousness by faith which is the blessing of Abraham, meant for the entire world. 1 Peter 1:3.)*

11:13 These heroes of faith all died believing. Although they did not witness the promise in their lifetime, they saw its fulfillment in the future and embraced the promise by their persuasion. Convinced of its reality; they declared by their way of living that they were mere sojourners and pilgrims in a shadow land whose geography could neither confine nor define their true inheritance.

11:14 They clearly declared by faith a hinterland beyond their immediate horizon. *(A place of promise where God and mankind would be one again.)*

11:15 They did not regret the country they had left behind. Their faith took them beyond the point of no return. *(Do not allow the contradictions*

in your past or present to become your reference once again. James says that the
person who goes back into an old mindset immediately forgets what manner of
person they are. James 1:24, 25. The old things have passed away [in his death].
Behold, everything has become new. In his resurrection we were born anew. 2
Corinthians 5:14-17, 1 Peter 1:3.)

11:16 Their faith saw a greater reality in the spiritual realm than that
which they experienced in their present situation; they reached for their
true native city designed by God where he himself is proud to be their
permanent address. *(The fulfillment of the promise is Christ. He is both our*
native land and our eternal city.)

11:17 Faith became a more tangible evidence of the promise than even
Isaac could ever be to Abraham. Isaac neither fulfilled nor replaced
the promise. Inspired by what faith saw, Abraham was ready to do the
ridiculous; to sacrifice his only son, convinced that not even Isaac's death
could nullify the promise that God had made to him. *(If Isaac was not the*
substance of Abraham's faith then who was? Abraham saw beyond Isaac. Jesus
said, Abraham saw my day. [John 8:56-58] Before Abraham was, I am.)

11:18 Yet Abraham knew that God had said that his lineage of faith
would be traced through Isaac.

11:19 He made a prophetic [1]calculation by faith to which there could only
be one logical conclusion based on the word he had received: that God
would raise the promise from the dead. *(In the context of Abraham's vision,*
this was an analogy pointing to the parable of the death and resurrection of Christ.
A calculation, logical conclusion, from the word, [1]logitzomai, from logos; God's
faith is God's logic.)

11:20 By the same faith Isaac extended the future of the promise in the
blessing he pronounced over his sons, Esau and Jacob.

11:21 In his dying moments, Jacob, in worship to the God of Abraham,
as the father of the nations, included in the promise [1]the sons of Joseph
who were born in Egypt. *([1]In exalting the two grandsons into the rank and*
right of Joseph's brothers, he bestowed on them, rather than on Reuben, the double
portion of the first-born. Again, faith exceeds the natural. Even though they had
an Egyptian mother, they would have an equal interest in all the spiritual and
temporal blessings of the covenant of promise.)

11:22 At the end of his life, Joseph prophetically reminded his sons of
the exodus. He had such a firm belief that they would possess the land
of promise that he exacted an oath from them: they were not to leave his
bones in Egypt.

11:23 By faith the parents of Moses did not fear the king's decree, but
hid him from Pharaoh for three months, because they saw a future in the
child.

11:24 It was faith that made Moses realize that he was not the son of
Pharaoh's daughter.

11:25 By faith he preferred to be associated with the affliction of God's people rather than with the fleeting privileges of Pharaoh's house, which did not constitute the true [1]portion of his inheritance. *(The word, [1]hamartia, from ha, meaning negative, and meros, meaning form or portion, without your portion, to fall short of your portion; often translated as sin.)*

11:26 He was not embarrassed to be associated with the Messianic promise at the expense of the treasures of Egypt. He deliberately looked away from those towards the greater riches of his reward in Christ. *(No reward of the flesh can compare with the wealth of faith.)*

11:27 The rage of the King did not scare him when he abandoned Egypt; faith, giving substance to the invisible, made him brave.

11:28 His faith saw the Paschal Lamb and the sprinkled blood on the door posts as the salvation of the people.

11:29 By faith they crossed the Red Sea on dry ground, but the Egyptians drowned when they followed them.

11:30 By faith the walls of the city of Jericho collapsed when Israel marched around the city for seven days. *(They did not conquer through the strength of their army.)*

11:31 Rahab the prostitute's faith saved her even though her house was built in the wall. While all the other houses collapsed around her, her own remained. She welcomed the spies and acknowledged the God who saved them out of Egypt. *[Joshua 2:11]* Her family also was given an equal opportunity to be saved through her faith. *(Imagine their surprise, bearing in mind her life and shameful reputation.)*

11:32 And so the list of faith-heroes continues. There is not enough time to tell the stories of Gideon and Barak and Sampson and Jephtah, of David, Samuel and the Prophets.

11:33 These are they who conquered kingdoms by faith. They accomplished righteousness by that same faith and thus secured the promise. By faith they shut the mouths of lions. *(Gideon, like Rahab, was in no position to claim any credit for his achievement; faith nullifies boasting. See Romans 3:27, Judg 6:11-16. By faith and not by performance, Deborah told Barak the son of Abinoam that, although he would deliver Israel, he would not get the honor, since a woman would do it for him. See Judg 4:21. In the principle of righteousness by faith, the flesh will take no glory. Barak, means to worship in adoration, and Abinoam means, my father's delight or grace. Samson's mighty achievements were immediately accredited to the Spirit of the Lord who moved upon him. Again there was no occasion to glory in the flesh.)*

11:34 Their faith extinguished powerful fires. They escaped from fierce battles. They were empowered in spite of their frailty. They became heroes in battle and caused hostile armies to flee before them. *(Jephtah whose own brothers disinherited him because his mother was a prostitute became the captain of the army of Israel.)*

11:35 By faith women received their children back from the dead. Others were severely tortured for their faith and refused to accept release when it was offered them on condition that they would renounce their opinions. To have accepted deliverance then could have saved their lives, but their faith saw a more honorable and glorious resurrection. *(1 Kings 17:18-24, 2 Kings 4:32-34.)*

11:36 Still others were mocked and ridiculed for their faith: they were beaten up, shackled and imprisoned.

11:37 While some were stoned to death, others *[like Isaiah the Prophet]* were sawn asunder with a wood saw. There were yet others who were tempted by the promise of possible release from torture, and then were brutally slaughtered with the sword. Many became wandering refugees with nothing but sheep and goatskins for clothing. They lost everything and were harassed and tormented.

11:38 The world did not realize their worth. These faith-heroes were often driven from their homes and forced to live in the deserts and mountains; sleeping like animals in caves and holes in the ground.

11:39 Their lives were trophies to their faith, as the substance of what was visualized by their hope, and the evidence of things their natural eyes never saw.

11:40 God saw the perfect picture in us; we now complete the history of their lives. *(Everything that the shadows prefigured has now found its substance through Christ in us.)*

12:1 So now the stage is set for us: all these faith-heroes cheer us on; they are the [1]cloud of witnesses; as it were, like a great multitude of spectators in the amphitheater. This is our moment. As with an athlete who is determined to win, it would be silly to carry any baggage of the old law-system that would weigh one down. Make sure you do not get your feet clogged up with sin-consciousness. Become absolutely streamlined in faith. Run the race of your spiritual life with total persuasion. (νέφος *[1]nephos, a cloud, a large dense multitude, a throng. See my note on The Cloud at the end of Hebrews chapter 9.)*

12:2 Look away from the shadow dispensation of the law and the Prophets and fix your eyes upon Jesus. He is the source, sustenance and conclusion of faith. He saw the joy *[of mankind's salvation]* when he braved the cross and despised the shame of it. As the executive authority of God *[the right hand of the throne of God]* he now occupies the highest seat of dominion to endorse mankind's innocence. *(Having accomplished purification of sins, he sat down. Hebrews 1:3, Isaiah 53:11.)*

12:3 [1]Ponder how he overcame all the odds stacked against him; this will boost your soul-energy when you feel exhausted. *([1]analogitsomai, upward calculation.)*

12:4 Would you be willing to die for your faith? *(Are you as persuaded of your faith in the substance of Christ as your predecessors were in their believing a mere shadow?)*

12:5 The word in Scripture that confirms your genesis in God addresses you as sons, My son do not undervalue the [1]loving instruction of the Lord; neither become despondent when you are corrected. *(See note in verse 7 on [1]loving instruction. The word, [1]parakletos, in the King James Version is translated as exhortation, but here it is translated rather as loving instruction, comfort as in John in relation to the Holy Spirit, the Comforter. The word consists of two components, para, a Preposition indicating close proximity, a thing proceeding from a sphere of influence, with a suggestion of union of place of residence, to have sprung from its author and giver, originating from, denoting the point from which an action originates, intimate connection, and kaleō, to identify by name, to surname.)*

12:6 For every instruction is inspired by his love, even as a father would teach his sons with affection, though it might seem harsh at the time.

12:7 Embrace correction. His [1]instruction confirms your true sonship; just as a father would take natural responsibility for the education of his children. *(The word, [1]paideo, comes from pais, for a boy or a girl and deō, to bind, to tie [relational]; thus to correct with education, instruction and the schooling of a child. The word, education in English comes from the Latin word, educare, which means to draw out. Discipline means to teach, not punish.)*

12:8 See yourselves as sons, not as illegitimate children, *[children of faith, not of the slave woman]* welcoming your spiritual education together with the rest of the family of faith.

12:9 As we have shown respect to our natural fathers in the process of our education, how much more should we value the instruction of the Father of our spiritual origin who upholds the life of our design.

12:10 In their opinion they gave us the best possible education during the brief time that we were under their roof; God has our ultimate wellbeing in mind.

12:11 The process of education is not immediately appreciated; at the time it seems to be more pain than pleasure, but it certainly yields the harvest of righteousness for the faith athlete.

12:12 Shake off your weariness, loosen your limbs, catch your breath. *(Get back into faith-mode, quit the flesh-mode.)*

12:13 Get rid of all obstacles that could possibly cause you to stumble and sprain an ankle. Don't let a recurrent injury force you out of the race. [1]Recover and carry on running. Don't allow old legalistic mind-sets to trip you up again. *(Isaiah 40:28-31, the [1]kawa principle, [1]intertwining with God's thoughts concerning you immediately causes you to escape the weariness of the old DIY times and mount up with wings like an eagle, to run and not be weary, to walk and not faint. Hebrew קוה kawa, to intertwine.)*

12:14 Pursue peace with all people; true friendship can only be enjoyed in an environment of total forgiveness and innocence. This makes God visible in your life.

12:15 You must understand that this is a grace-race and not a law-race. While we're in compete- and compare-mode we create the opportunity for resentment to flourish and to poison many in the process. *(We are all equally included in the same victory in Christ.)*

12:16 A performance-driven mindset triggers the law system into action and [1]distorts the picture: suddenly the fleeting moment of pleasure seems more attractive than your true portion This is exactly what happened to Esau, when he traded his birthright for a morsel of meat. *(Sin is a distorted picture; the word, [1]hamartia, often translated as sin is made up of two words, ha, meaning without, and meros, meaning form, or allotted portion.)*

12:17 Esau's regret could not change Isaac's mind. God's mind is made up about our salvation. *(We are saved by faith in his finished work and not by our own works; his system of faith cannot be challenged or replaced by another law system. It's not about our sincerity; it's about seeing what God's faith sees.)*

12:18 We are not talking of a visible and tangible mountain here, one spectacularly ablaze in a setting of dark blackness and tempestuous winds. *(Witness the vivid contrast between the giving of the law and the unfolding of grace; the exclusiveness of the one and the all inclusive embrace of the other. The dramatic encounter of Moses on the mountain is by far exceeded by the mountaintop experience to which we are now welcomed and elevated through Christ. Mankind is now fully represented and co-seated together with Christ in heavenly places. Ephesians 2:5, 6, Hosea 6:2.)*

12:19 Shrill trumpet sounds and a thunderous voice uttering human language. This filled the people with such terror that they begged for silence. *(The word, ἤχος ēchos means a sound, noise, like the roar of the sea waves. Only used here and in Acts 2:2 and Luke 4:37.)*

12:20 Beast and humans alike felt threatened and excluded from that terrible mountain.

12:21 Even Moses, the representative of the people, was extremely terrified. He was shivering and shaking. Who could approach God and live? How impossible it seemed to find favor with such a 'terrifying' God.

12:22 By contrast, we have been welcomed to an invisible mount Zion; the city of peace *(Jerusalem)***, the residence of the living God, the festive assembly of an innumerable celestial host.**

12:23 We are participating in a mass joint-celebration of heavenly and earthly beings; the ¹Ekklesia-church of the firstborn mirror-inscribed in the heavenlies. *(Our original identity, ¹Ekklesia, from ek, a Preposition that always denotes origin, and kaleō, meaning to identify by name, to surname], is endorsed by Jesus, patterned in him, the first born from the dead.)*

12:24 Jesus is the spokesman and arbitrator of the New Testament order. His blood signature sanctions mankind's innocence. This is a complete new language that communicates better things, in that it is the very substance of what was spoken in the shadow-type message of the blood sacrifice that Abel brought. *(Abel's faith was a prophetic introduction to the sacrificial shadow system of the Old Covenant. Jesus is the substance of things hoped for. Hebrews 11:4 It was faith that made the difference between the sacrifices of Abel and Cain, and confirmed Abel's righteousness. God bore witness to righteousness as a gift rather than a reward. Even though he was murdered, his faith still has a most relevant prophetic voice.*

*See my **Extended Notes on the Blood** at the end of the book.)*

12:25 If Jesus is the crescendo of God's final message to mankind, you cannot afford to politely excuse yourself from this conversation. Consider the prominent place that Moses plays in the history of Israel: if you think that Moses or any of the Prophets who spoke with authority on earth deserve honor, how much more should this word that God declared from heaven concerning our sonship, and our redeemed innocence revealed in the Messiah himself, deserve our undivided attention.

12:26 When he introduced the prophetic shadow of what was to come *[the Law system]***, his voice visibly shook the earth.** *[Exodus 19:18.]* **But now the Messiah has come** *[he is the one the law and the prophets pointed to; the desire of the nations; he is what heaven and earth were waiting for. Haggai 2:6,7]* **The voice of God** *[articulated in Christ's birth, life, ministry, death, and resurrection]***, has rocked not only the systems on the earth, but also every unseen principality in the heavens, to their very foundations.**

12:27 In the words of the Prophet, Yet once more will I shake every unstable system of man's effort to rule himself. God clearly indicates his

plan to remove the old and replace it with the new. The second shaking supersedes any significance in the first shaking. Then it was a physical quaking of the earth; now the very foundations of every man-made system was shaken to the core while the heavens were impacted by the announcement of his permanent rule on earth as it is mirrored in heaven.

12:28 We are fully associated in this immovable Kingdom; an authority that cannot be challenged or contradicted. Our participation echoes grace *[and not law and fear-inspired obedience]* as we [1]accommodate ourselves to God's delight, yielding in awe to his firm embrace. *(The word, [1]euarestos, means well pleasing, to accommodate yourself to God's delight.)*

12:29 His zeal for us burns like fire. *(Deuteronomy 4:24.)*

Hebrews Chapter 12 Extended Notes:
Extended Notes on the Blood - Hebrews 12:24

Extended Notes on the Blood - Hebrews 12:24

What makes his blood most powerfully significant is in what it communicates. His blood speaks of better things...

The blood of Jesus was not different to the blood of any other person. If there was some mysterious power in the blood of Jesus, then all we needed was a blood transfusion.

If so-called born again people have received some mystical blood transfusion, then why are they still capable and do they actually still commit sins?

Hebrews 12:24 Jesus is the spokesman and arbitrator of the New Testament order. His blood signature sanctions mankind's innocence. This is a complete new language that communicates better things, in that it is the very substance of what was spoken in the shadow-type message of the blood sacrifice that Abel brought. *(Abel's faith was a prophetic introduction to the sacrificial shadow system of the Old Covenant. Jesus is the substance of things hoped for. Hebrews 11:4 It was faith that made the difference between the sacrifices of Abel and Cain, and confirmed Abel's righteousness. God bore witness to righteousness as a gift rather than a reward. Even though he was murdered, his faith still has a most relevant prophetic voice.*

Unlike the idea that the ultimate, most expensive sacrifice would perhaps persuade Deity to look differently and favorably upon sinful mankind, this is not Deity getting even with mankind in the typical language of an eye for an eye, and a tooth for a tooth judgment; this is Deity reconciling mankind to themselves. Jesus did not do what he did to reconcile God with us; this is Father Son and Spirit clothed in human skin, lovingly and willingly going to the gruesome extreme of a ridiculously unfair trial by a human court, and the scandalous execution of innocent life, in order to persuade us most convincingly of their priceless esteem of us and their relentless love for us, and to forever rescue our minds from every definition of unworthiness and condemnation, and every sense of separation.

In the broken, bleeding body of Jesus, the incarnate Engineer of the universe, willingly dies mankind's death at the hands of his own creation in order to redeem our minds from the plague of a sin-consciousness that left us distanced and indifferent for ages and generations, stuck in the wilderness of our self-help religious and survival programs.)

Hebrews 2:14 Being one with the children of God presupposes the fact that he lived and died in a body exactly like theirs; being as fully human as we are, he is qualified to remove the dominion of death that was introduced [1]as a result of Adam's fall. *(Had he done all this in a superhuman body, the implications of his life, death and resurrection would be irrelevant.)*

Hebrews 2:16 This is why it is so relevant to understand that Jesus did not arrive on the planet in a celestial form *(or a Superman-suit);* **he embraced the seed of Abraham.**

Hebrews 2:18 He experienced mankind's temptation with the same intensity, and under the same scrutiny, and was therefore qualified to represent them with immediate effect. *(To run to their rescue. See Hebrews 4:15,16.)*

Hebrews 9:15 As [1]fully representing mankind, Jesus' death brought an end to the old, and introduced the New Testament. He thus redeemed us from the transgressions recorded under the first Covenant and identified us as heirs; qualifying us to participate in the full inheritance of all that he obtained on our behalf. *(The concept of a [1]mediator,* **mesitēs***, in this analogy, is not a go-between, as if Jesus had to change the Father's mind about us; it was our minds that needed to be persuaded. Jesus did not save us from God; he is fully God and fully man, and in him mankind is most completely represented. See Galatians 3:20; also Hebrews 6:16-20)*

Hebrews 9:22 Thus, according to the law, all purging was by means of blood; [1]forgiveness was specifically associated with the shedding of blood. *(The idea of closure to the particular case was communicated in the death of an innocent victim. The blood symbolizes this currency.)*

The shedding of blood was the language of judgment; in Jesus God speaks our scapegoat language, not to manage our sin consciousness, but to remove it! *[See Hebrews 10:2-5]*

Hebrews 10:2 Had it been possible to present the perfect offering that had the power to successfully remove any trace of a sin-consciousness, then the sacrificial system would surely have ceased to be relevant.

Hebrews 10:3 But in the very repetition of these ritual sacrifices the awareness of guilt is reinforced rather than removed.

Hebrews 10:4 The conclusion is clear: animal sacrifices failed to remove anyone's sinfulness or their sin-consciousness.

Hebrews 10:5 So when Jesus, the Messiah, arrives as the fulfillment of all the types and shadows, he quotes Psalm 40:6-8, and says, In sacrifices and offerings God takes no pleasure; but you have ordained my incarnation.

1 Peter 1:18 It is clear to see that you were ransomed from the futile, fallen mindset that you inherited from your fathers, not by the currency of your own labor, represented by the fluctuating values of gold and silver, and the economy of your religious efforts;

1 Peter 1:19 but you were redeemed with the priceless blood of Christ; he is the ultimate sacrifice; spotless and without blemish. He completes the prophetic picture. *(In him God speaks the most radical scapegoat language of the law of judgment, and brings final closure to a dead and redundant system. In Psalm 40:6,7, it is clearly stated that God does not require sacrifices or offerings. Jesus is the Lamb of God. He collides victoriously with the futile sacrificial system whereby offerings are constantly made to the pseudo, moody, monster gods of our imagination. This is the scandal of the cross. God does not demand a sacrifice that would change the way he thinks about mankind; he provides the sacrifice of himself in Christ in order to forever eradicate sin-consciousness from our minds and radically change the way we think about our Maker, one another and ourselves. [Sin-consciousness is in essence a works-based consciousness.] God did not clothe Adam with the skin of an animal because of a divine need to be appeased, but because of their unconditional love for Adam; they spoke the language of Adam's own judgment: Adam, not God,* *was embarrassed about his nakedness. The clothing was not to make God look at Adam differently, but to make Adam feel better about himself. And ultimately it was to prophetically prepare Adam for the unveiling of the mystery of mankind's redemption in the incarnation. Here Deity would clothe themselves in human skin, in a son; and the Lion of Judah, would become the Lamb of God, in order to free our minds to re-discover his image and likeness in our skin. See 1 Peter 1:2.)*

1 Peter 1:20 He was always destined in God's prophetic thought; God knew even before the [1]fall of the world order that his son would be the Lamb, to be made manifest in these last days, because of you. *(You are the reason Jesus died and was raised. The word, [1]kataballō, meaning to fall away, to put in a lower place, instead of* **themelios**, *meaning foundation [see Ephesians 2:20]; thus, translated the fall of the world, instead of the foundation of the world.)*

1 Peter 1:21 He is the conclusive cause of your belief in God. Seeing then how perfectly you fit into the scheme of things, it is no wonder that your faith in God's act of raising Jesus from the dead becomes the glorious reference to your own new birth. The glory that God gave Jesus by raising him from the dead, is the conclusion of everything that your faith longed for. *(This is the redeemed glory that the Prophets pointed to. Hosea 6:2 After two days he will revive us; on the third day he will raise us up. Isaiah 40:5 And the glory of the Lord shall be revealed, and all flesh shall see it together.)*

2 Corinthians 5:18 The idea of mankind's co-inclusion in the death and resurrection of Jesus Christ is entirely God's doing. To now realize that God has indeed brought final closure to the old and for us to see everything and everyone in this new light is to simply see what God has always known to be true about us in Christ; we are not debating human experience, opinion, or their contribution; this is exactly what God believes. In Jesus Christ, God [1]exchanged equivalent value to redeem us to himself. He went to the highest extreme in this act of reconciliation to persuade us of our original worth. This, God has given us as the mandate of our ministry. *(The word, [1]katallassō, translates as reconciliation; it is a mutual exchange of equal value. This transaction was not to buy us back from the devil; a thief never becomes an owner; it was God redeeming our minds from the lies that we believed about ourselves - reconciliation is the bold unveiling of the value of the hidden treasure in everyone. See 2 Corinthians 4:7 and Matthew 13:44 The kingdom of heaven is like treasure hidden in an agricultural field, which a man found and covered up; then in his joy he goes and sells all that he has and buys the entire field. There is so much more to you than what meets the eye.)*

Hebrews 6:16 It is common practice in human affairs to evoke a higher authority under oath in order to add weight to any agreement between parties, thereby [1]silencing any possibility of quibbling. *(The word [1]peras, means the end of all dispute; the point beyond which one cannot go.)*

Hebrews 6:17 In the same context we are confronted with God's eagerness to go to the last extreme in his dealing with us as heirs of his promise, and to cancel out all possible grounds for doubt or dispute. In order to persuade us of the unalterable character and finality of his resolve, he

[1]**confined himself to an oath. The promise which already belongs to us by heritage is now also confirmed under oath.** *(The word [1]*mesiteuō* is used, interposed or mediated. Compare* **mesitēs,** *mediator, from* **mesos,** *midst. In the incarnation, God has positioned himself in the midst, of his creation. See Galatians 3:20 With Abraham there was no middleman; it was just God. [The Mosaic law required mediators [the Levitical priesthood] because it was an arrangement whereby mankind had a part and God had a part. Mankind's part was to obey the commandments and God's part was to bless. God's covenant with Abraham was a grace covenant pointing to the man Jesus Christ, in whom God himself would fulfil mankind's part and therefore needed no mediator apart from himself.*

The Word is the promise; the Incarnate, crucified and risen Christ is the proof. He desires to show more convincingly to the heirs of the promise the unchangeable character of his purpose. RSV

Mankind was not redeemed from the devil; a thief never becomes an owner; neither did Jesus do what he did to change his father's mind about us. It was our minds that needed persuasion. God was not to be reconciled to his creation; God was in Christ when he reconciled the world to himself. 2 Corinthians 5:18-20.)

I deal with the following issues in my book, Divine Embrace *(In print or on Kindle)* There is nothing wrong with the human race - What about the sinful nature? - A new perspective on the New Birth - The great awakening. - The Metanoia-moment! - The logic of God's economy of inclusion - How does this gospel translate into a transformed life? - Thoughts on hell.

See my rendering of the Genealogy of Jesus as Luke records it

Now, Luke cleverly brings in the genealogy of the Incarnate word, immediately after Jesus' baptism. Leading us through the natural lineage of Jesus via the woman's seed. [The seed of the woman shall crush the serpent's head! Genesis 3:15.]

He brings in Joseph's Father-in-law, *[Eli was the father of Mary.]* Matthew writes the genealogy of Joseph, descended from David via Solomon, while Luke connects Jesus through Mary's lineage with David via Nathan! David named his son after the prophet Nathan who prophesied the Messianic kingdom over David's seed. *[See **Luke 3:21-38**]*

In order to highlight the significant meaning of the names that feature in the genealogy of Jesus, I have also employed the Ancient Hebrew alphabet, related to the Proto-Sinaitic alphabet. The earliest Proto-Sinaitic inscriptions are mostly dated to between the mid-19th (early date) and the mid-16th (late date) century BC. The discovery of the Wadi El-Hol inscriptions near the Nile River shows that the script originated in Egypt. These inscriptions strongly suggest a date of development of Proto-Sinaitic writing from the mid-19th to 18th centuries BC.

https://en.wikipedia.org/wiki/Proto-Sinaitic_script

Some hints on practical kingdom living, including family, friends, fellowship, marriage, money and ministry:

13:1 Treasure family bonds and friendship. Family fondness remains the essence of this kingdom. *(Relationship is long-term in every sense of the word.)*

13:2 Do not neglect to treat strangers with hospitality and affection; they are probably a messenger of God in disguise. *(The ancient Greeks saw any stranger is a god in disguise. When Mother Teresa was asked what motivates her to go out into the streets of Calcutta in the odd hours of the night, her reply revealed her mission, I go to minister to my Lord in his most disturbing disguises.)*

13:3 Identify with those who are in prison or suffering abuse for their faith as if you were the one afflicted.

13:4 Treasure marriage - take sides with God on all matters of intimacy - do not trade what is precious for something profane and casual.

13:5 Don't give money a prominent place in your thoughts; realize that what you already have is priceless. He has said that he will never quit on you or abandon you. *[Joshua 1:5.]* **This is reason enough for total and continual contentment.**

13:6 What he said concerning us gives our confession the edge; we boldly echo Scripture, The Lord is for me, I cannot be afraid of anything that anyone could possibly do to harm me. *(Psalm 118:6.)*

13:7 Be mindful of those who guide you in the revelation of God's word; follow their faith, consider the conclusion of their lives. *(Do not follow a counterfeit. This would be someone who fakes faith while actually living the law.)*

13:8 Take your lead from Jesus. He is your reference to the most complete life. In him yesterday is confirmed today and today mirrors tomorrow. What God spoke to us in Christ is as relevant now as it was in the prophetic past and will always be in the eternal future. *(Jesus is the same yesterday, today, and forever; there is a history to our salvation that carries more authority and relevance than anything that ever happened in our past, or anything present in time or still to happen in the future. Imagine the enormity of eternity in his sameness before time was; and we were there in him all along. See Romans 8:34 What further ground can there possibly be to condemn mankind? In his death he faced our judgment; in his resurrection he declares our innocence; the implications cannot be undone. He now occupies the highest seat of authority as the executive of our redemption in the throne room of God. See Romans 8: 1, also Romans 4:25. The heavens declare his glory, night to night exhibits the giant solar testimony that is mathematically precise, revealing that God knew before time was the exact moment he would enter our history as a man, and the exact moment the Messiah would expire on the cross and be raised again from the dead.)*

13:9 Do not be swayed by distracting speculations. Any influence foreign to what grace communicates, even if it seems very entertaining and carries the Christian label, is to be shunned. Feast on grace; do not dilute your diet with legalism. There is no nourishment left in the law.

What's the use of being busy but not blessed? (*Legalism includes any form of self-sacrifice or self-effort with the illusion of gaining further favor from God or improving your spiritual standing before God.*)

13:10 For us there is only one altar and one sacrifice; we can never again confuse him with the rituals of the old redundant system. It seems that some would like to eat the meat of their own sacrifices and at the same time indulge in the benefits of grace. This is not possible. (*It is like trying to go in opposite directions at the same time.*)

13:11 When it comes to the sin offering, the carcasses of the slain animals were burnt outside the camp.

13:12 According to the prophetic pattern, Jesus, as the final sin sacrifice, was slain outside the city walls.

13:13 There are two opposing systems; you cannot associate with Christ for your convenience while still hanging on to your Jewish sentiment. If you're going to take your stand for Jesus, go all the way. Break your ties with the old shadow-system. Go outside the city-system. Be prepared to share his shame when your fellow Jews mock your commitment to Jesus.

13:14 We are not finding our identity or security in the walled city of popular legalistic religious opinion. Our interest is captured by a different kind of city, much closer to us than the visible one.

13:15 Praise replaces sacrifice; the harvest we bring is the tribute of our lips acknowledging his Name. (*His Name represents the authority of our identity and redeemed innocence.*)

13:16 God delights in good deeds. These deeds are like beautiful poetry giving a voice to your fellowship. (*They are inspired by your innocence; rather than offered as guilt-driven sacrifices.*)

13:17 Trust your guides [*in this grace revelation*] **and yield to their instruction.** (*Even though it seems different to the law system that you were formerly acquainted with.*) **They are genuinely alert to your well-being.** (*Just as with shepherds guarding their sheep, you are their total concern.*) **They have taken official accountability for you.** (*They represent to you all that grace reveals rather than what the law requires.*) **It is to your advantage to embrace their care with joy; this makes their work a pleasure and not a burden.**

13:18 Worship prayerfully with us; we believe that our joint seeing inspires a beautiful life.

13:19 Pray also that I might be able to re-join you speedily; I can hardly wait.

13:20 This is my prayer for you: that the God who made peace with the human race through the blood of the eternal Testament, who raised Jesus from the dead as the supreme shepherd of the sheep,

13:21 will thoroughly equip you in the most distinguished way possible, to give expression to his design in you according to his delight realized in Jesus Christ, who is the blueprint of the ages. Jesus is the accurate expression of God's glory. Our lives confirm and echo the Amen.

13:22 My friends, I have written to you briefly, [1]reminding you of your original identity in order to [2]increase the volume of its resonance in your hearts. *(The word, [2]anechomai, means to hold oneself up against, from ana, often means by repetition in order to increase intensity, and echō, to hold, embrace or echo, resonance. The word, [1]parakaleō, from para, originating from a sphere of influence, and kaleō, to call by name, to surname. See notes on ekklesia, Hebrews 12:23.)*

13:23 Brother Timothy has already been released from prison; as soon as he arrives we will visit you together.

13:24 Greet all your leaders and the saints; the Italian believers salute you.

13:25 Grace is our embrace. YES.

JAMES - THE BROTHER OF JESUS

Lost and found identity

James, the younger brother of Jesus, brilliantly engages the subject of humanity's forgotten identity revealed and redeemed in the Incarnate Word.

From the first and the last verse of chapter one, James sets his teaching up against the sense of a lost identity: the twelve scattered tribes, and the widows and the orphans.

To lose one's land of heritage or immediate family, would be the greatest and most challenging test or temptation anyone can face: to forget what manner of person you are. *(James 1:24, Deuteronomy 32:18.)*

There was a time when neither he nor any of his family believed in Jesus. *[John 7:5]* It was only after the resurrection when Jesus appeared to him that the truth dawned on him; now he understood that his brother Jesus was indeed the one who all the rumors and prophetic pointers throughout time said he was. Jesus is God unveiled in flesh, the incarnate Word who redeemed the lost identity of mankind in his death and resurrection. James' eyes were opened to the fact that neither Jesus nor he began in Mary's womb. *[1 Corinthians 15:7; James 1:17,18.]*

Man began in God. We are not merely the desire of a parent, we are the desire of God. Mankind shares a common origin, the *boulomai*, the affectionate desire and deliberate resolve of God, the Father of lights, with whom there is no distortion or hidden agenda. The unveiling of our redemption also reveals our true genesis; we are God's personal invention. We are ***anouthen***, from above. We are perfect and complete and lacking in nothing. God's Sabbath is the celebration of our perfection, both by design and redemption. Every good and perfect gift comes from above, *(anouthen)* from the Father of lights with whom there is no variableness and no shadow due to change, he brought us forth by the Word of truth.

Born from above

John sees the same genesis. He only begins to write when he is already more than 90 years old. Unlike Luke and Matthew, he skips the genealogies of Joseph, he declares, In the beginning was the Word, what God was, the Word was, and the Word became flesh. He sees that the destiny of the Word was not the book, but human life. God finding accurate expression of himself, his image and likeness revealed in human form. Genesis 1:26 lives again; mankind is standing tall in the stature of the invisible God. If you have seen me, you have seen the Father. Unless a someone is born from above *(anouthen)*, they cannot see the Kingdom of God. The kingdom of God *(the reign of God's image and likeness in human life)* is made visible again on earth as it is in heaven; tangible in human form. *(John 3:3)*

In John 3 Nicodemus discovers that his irresistible attraction to Jesus was because of the fact that our natural birth is not our beginning. We come from above. God knew us before he formed us in our mother's womb. [Jeremiah 1:5] If people did not come from above, the heavenly realm would offer no attraction to them. In our make-up we are the God-kind with an appetite for more than what bread and the senses could satisfy us with. We are designed to hunger for and feast from the Logos that comes from above. From a dimension where the original thought remains preserved and intact without contamination; the Logos that comes from his mouth is the unveiled mirror radiance of our authentic origin, quickening and sustaining the life of our design. No one ascended into heaven, who did not also descend from heaven, even the son of man. (John 3:13)

Paul celebrates the same theme in **Galatians 1:15** *God's eternal [1]love dream separated me from my mother's womb; his grace became my [2]identity. ([1]**eudokeō**: his beautiful intention; the well done opinion. My mother's womb, my natural lineage and identity as a son of Benjamin. [2]**kaleō**, to surname, to summon by name.)* **Galatians 1:16** This is the heart of the gospel that I proclaim; it began with an unveiling of sonship [1]in me, freeing me to announce the same sonship [2]in the masses of non-Jewish people. I felt no immediate urgency to compare notes with those who were familiar with Christ from a mere historical point of view. *(The Greek text is quite clear, It pleased the Father to reveal his son in me in order that I may proclaim him in the nations. [1]**en emoi**, in me, and [2]**en ethnos**, in the Gentile nations, or the masses of non Jewish people. Not 'among' the Gentiles as most translations have it. Later when Barnabas is sent to investigate the conversion of the Greeks in Acts 11, instead of reporting his findings to the HQ in Jerusalem, he immediately finds Paul, knowing that Paul's gospel is the revelation of the mystery of Christ in the nations. Colossians.1:27. No wonder then that those believers were the first to be called Christians, or Christ-like.)*

Paul reminds the Greek philosophers in Acts 17 that we live and move and have our being in God; mankind is indeed the offspring of God. He is quoting from their own writings. [Epimenedes 600 BC and Aratus, 300 BC.] The incorruptible seed of sonship is as much in every person as the seed is already in all soil, even in the desert, waiting for the rain to awaken and ignite its dormant life. Mankind only has one Father. Matthew 13:44 the treasure was already in the field before it was discovered. 2 Corinthians 4:4 & 7. God wrote the script of every individual's innermost being when he knitted us together in our mother's womb; the code is Christ in you. Colossians 1:27.

Jesus has come to reveal that the son of man is the son of God. If you have seen me you have seen the Father. Matthew 23:9 Call no man your father on earth, for you have one Father, who is in heaven. He says to Peter, Flesh-and-blood cannot reveal to you who the son of man is, but my Father who is in heaven; blessed are you, Simon son of Jonah, I give you a new name that reveals your original identity: you are Mr Rock, a chip off the old Block. *[**Petros**, hewn out of the rock, **petra**. Isaiah 51:1, Deuteronomy 32:3, 4, 18.]* This revelation is the rock foundation that I will build my identity upon, *[my image and likeness]* - upon this rock will I build my church, *[literally, my **ekklesia**, from **ek**, denoting source or origin and **klesia** from **kaleō**, to surname or identify by name]* and the gates of Hadēs that trapped mankind into the walled city of the senses, will not prevail against the voice that surnames and summons them again. *[The word Hadēs, is from **ha** + **eidō**, not to see.]* Matthew 16:13, 17.

Therefore, Paul did not consult with flesh and blood. He deliberately avoided the opportunity to get to know Jesus from a human point of view by visiting the eleven disciples who were still alive and living in Jerusalem. They could have informed him first-hand about the life, ministry, parables, and miracles of Jesus. *[2 Corinthians 5:16.]* But Paul does not make mention in any of his writings even of a single parable Jesus told or miracle he performed, because his mandate and revelation was not to merely relate Christ in history, but to reveal Christ in mankind.

Only three years later he returned briefly to Jerusalem specifically to visit Peter and James, the Lord's brother. *[Galatians 1:18, 19.]* One is not surprised to discover that the first believers ever to be called Christians were the Greeks in Antioch who sat under Paul's ministry. *[Acts 11.]*

After his encounter with the risen Jesus, James writes in chapter 1:17 that the Father of lights brought us forth by the word of truth. When anyone hears this word, he sees the face of his birth *[genesis]* as in a mirror - for he sees himself.

What James, Peter and Paul had in common was an understanding that their flesh and blood birth did not define them. Jesus came to reveal and redeem our authentic spirit identity.

Humanity share three births in common:

1/ Man began in God. Malachi 2:10. Have we not all one father? Has not one God created us? See John 3:13 No one ascends into heaven but he who also descended from heaven, even the son of man. See also Matthew 22:41-46 and Matthew 23:9.

2/ The only passport to planet earth is the womb of a mother. Before I formed you in the womb I knew you. Jeremiah 1:5. It is not our brief history on earth that introduces us to God.

3/ In God's faith every human life is equally represented and included in Jesus Christ. One has died for all; therefore all have died. 2 Corinthians 5:14. While we were still dead in our sins, God made us alive together with Christ and co-raised us together with Christ. Ephesians 2:5. We have been born anew through the resurrection of Jesus Christ from the dead. 1Peter 1:3. Now if all were included in his death they were equally included in his resurrection. 2 Corinthians 5:15; Hosea 6:2.

Paul describes the metanoia-moment in Titus 3:4 But then, oh happy day. It was the generosity of God and his fondness for mankind that dawned on us like a shaft of light. Our days of darkness were over. Light shone everywhere and we became aware: God rescued the human race. See Titus 2:11.

Titus 3:5 Salvation is not a reward for good behavior. It has absolutely nothing to do with anything that we have done. God's mercy saved us. The Holy Spirit endorses in us what happened to us when Jesus Christ died and was raised. When we heard the glad announcement of salvation it was like taking a deep warm bath. We were thoroughly cleansed and resurrected in a new birth. It was a complete renovation that restored us to sparkling newness of life.

In 2 Corinthians 5:16 Paul declares: From now on therefore, we no longer know anyone according to the flesh.

James says, We can say beautiful things about God the Father but with the same mouth curse a person made in his mirror likeness. *(True worship is to touch someone's life with the same devotion and care you would touch Jesus himself; even if the other person seems a most unlikely candidate. James 3:9.)*

1:1 My name is James, I am bonded to God and the Lord Jesus Christ. It is in this capacity that I am writing to you, wherever you are. You might even be part of the twelve tribes which are scattered like seed all over the world. I greet you with joyful encouragement.

1:2 Temptations and contradictions come in different shapes, sizes, and intervals; their intention is always to suck you into their energy field. However, my friends, your joy in who you know you are [1]leads you out triumphantly every time.

([1] The word, [1]hegeomai, comes from a strengthened form of agō, to lead, thus, to officially appoint in a position of authority; to lead with distinguished authority. Joy is the official voice of faith. Count it all joy, make a calculation to which joy can be the only logical conclusion. The objective of every contradiction is to lure you into a place where you forget what manner of person you really are.)

1:3 Here is the secret: joy is not something you have to fake, it is the fruit of what your faith knows to be true about you. You know that the proof of faith results in a persuasion that remains constant in contradiction.

1:4 *(Just like a mother hen patiently broods over her eggs,)* steadfastness provides you with a consistent environment, and so patience prevails and proves your perfection; how entirely whole you are and without any shortfall.

1:5 The only thing you could possibly lack is wisdom. *[One might sometimes feel challenged beyond the point of sanity.]* However, make your request in such a way that you draw directly from the [2]source. *[Not filtered through other opinions]* God is the origin and author of wisdom; he [1]intertwines your thoughts with good judgment. His gifts are available to all, without regret.

([1] The word, [1]haplos, from ha, particle of union; hama, together with + plekō, meaning to plait, braid, weave together. See Luke 11:34 The eye is the lamp of the body; if the eye is single [entwined with light], the whole body is full of light. Entwining our eyes with Papa's eyes is what enlightens our entire being. Which is exactly what the word קוה Kawa in Hebrew means in Isaiah 40:31, they that entwine with the Lord's thoughts mount up with wings like eagles. We are wired by design to entwine. Also, Matthew 6:22. See 2 Corinthians 1:12. Wisdom that comes from above remains unaffected by the contradictions of the senses.

[2] The word, [2]didomi, to give; to be the author or source of a thing — Wesley J. Perschbacher.)

1:6 Your requests give voice to faith. Faith is the stabilizing factor; otherwise you become driven by emotions *(inconsistent judgments)* that get out of control like rough seas tossed by tempest winds.

1:7 A haphazard request makes it impossible to interpret God's wisdom accurately. *(Faith is the grace that reveals one's capacity to receive from God. The Greek word, para, with the Genitive, indicates source or origin, coming from — [Wesley J. Perschbacher] and the word, lambanō, to receive, to comprehend.)*

1:8 Someone of two opinions *[concerning their authentic identity]* remains jittery in all their judgments and seems always lost for direction.

1:9 *(Adverse circumstances can make or break you, depending on how you respond under pressure and allow these conditions to influence your judgment.)* **Let the down and out brother boast in his elevation in the Lord.** *(God's wisdom makes you see things differently. Begin by seeing yourself co-seated together with Christ in heavenly places. Colossians 3:1-3.)*

1:10 The rich should boast with confidence when things seem to threaten their position of financial strength. Flowers fade; so does fame when wealth is lost. *(Neither poverty nor wealth is a true measure of your life; faith is.)*

1:11 A severe sun combined with scorching eastern winds can completely destroy a harvest before it ripens; something that looked so beautiful and promising the one day, can be gone the next day; even so a wealthy person can suddenly perish in his pursuits. *(We are defined by a reference that is more stable than changing conditions.)*

1:12 Blessed is the one who does not lose their footing when temptation strikes; they are [1]crowned the victor; their lives prove the [2]currency and character of their [3]design. The [4]verdict: No contradiction can distract from the love of the Lord.

([1] Love inspires faith. [Galatians 5:6] The word, **stephanos***, means a mark of royal rank, or a wreath or garland, which was given as a prize to victors in public games. Yet life as God sees it is a gift, not a reward. [James 1:17-25] Thus even our reward is a gift because our enduring and steadfastness is not something we engage in with our diligence and willpower, but the energy ignited within us by the revelation of the Word of truth [verse 18].*

[2] The word, **dokimos***, means accepted, particularly of coins and money; thus, currency.*

[3] The Greek word for [3]birth, **ginomai***.*

[4] The verdict, **epaggellō***, official announcement.)*

1:13 When you feel enticed, never say, This test is from God! God is not in the teasing business; evil offers no attraction to God for God to be the author of it; neither is God experimenting with your design, since, in God's belief, the fabric of your authentic being is never in question!

(God cannot be both the source of light and darkness. There is no trace of darkness or a hidden agenda in God. [James 1:17]

The word, ἀπείραστος **apeirastos** *is only used here in the New Testament. Hort notes* **apeiratos kakōn** *as a proverb [Diodorus, Plutarch, Josephus] free from evils. Lit., God is incapable of tempting or being tempted. Some of the best expositors render it as, God is unversed in evil things.)*

1:14 Instead, every opportunity to be distracted into temptation is activated by a person's own private desires and thoughts, luring them away from their safe place *[of deeply engaging with who they are; verses 3, 4, & 17,18],* **in order to snare them** *[into forgetfulness - verses 23,24].*

([1] The word, **exelkō***, means to lure as in hunting; drawn away from their safe place, into a place beset with snares - [ἐξελκόμενος* **exelkomenos***]. Only here in New Testament.*

*[2] Then the word [2]deleatzō, from the word, **dolos**, to deceive by bait, as in fishing. Note the Present Participle, as indicating the progress of the temptation: is being drawn away. Vincent)*

1:15 In the nurturing of such an ill and all consuming passion, it [1]conceives [2]sin, which inevitably enforces its own likeness, patterned in [3]the same darkness which conceived it. It is a cul de sac to begin with!

*([1] The word, ἀποκύει, **opokuei**, to bring forth, is used by James only, here and at James 1:18. [Reminding of the father of lies vs, the Father of truth.]*

*[2] The word translated sin [**hamartia**] is a distorted identity. From the words, **ha**, without and **meros**, form. To walk in the light as he is in the light means to see your life and everything that concerns you, exclusively from your Father's point of view. Psalm 36:9. 1 Peter 1:18,19*

*[3] The word, θάνατος **thanatos** translated death, is the equivalent to the region of thickest darkness, a region enveloped in the darkness of ignorance. See 1 Thessalonians 5:3-6.)*

1:16 My dear friends, do not go [1]wandering off into deception.

*([1]The word πλανάω [1]**planaō**, to lead astray into deception; wander off. By giving credit to temptation, thinking that it could possibly be God's way of speaking to you.*

So what about the Lord's prayer? Lead us not into temptation, but deliver us from evil. This sounds like God had temptation on today's agenda for you, but if you pray this prayer then maybe he'll change his mind.

*To lead' in this sentence is the Greek word **eisphero**, to carry inward, to reach within; and temptation is the word **peiratzo**, to test through piercing, to examine closely, from **peira**, to pierce; a test to determine the hidden value of something; also from the word **peras**, which speaks of extremity or the furthest boundary. But as James clearly points out in verse 13, God is not in the teasing business. He is not the source of good and evil. The deliverance from evil, **poneros**, is the intent of this sentence; that a hidden alignment to the law of works will not be found within me; giving evil a foothold as it were. The word **poneros**, translated, evil, means full of hardships, annoyances and labors. Sounds like the wrong tree to me. Rather pray, Father, you know me inside-out. Free me thoroughly from any hidden alliance with the old system of performance based living. Remove any trace of the fruit of the I am not-tree system.*

*See also **2 Corinthians 13:5**, I implore you to examine faith for yourselves in order to test what it is that you really believe. Faith is so much more than the mere veneer of a superstitious belief in a historical Christ; faith is about realizing Jesus Christ in you, in the midst of contradiction. Just as ore is placed into a crucible, where the dross is separated from the gold in a furnace, come to the conclusion for yourselves of his indwelling. Should it appear to you that he is absent in your life, look again, you have obviously done the test wrong.)*

The Face of Your Birth

1:17 Without exception God's [1]gifts are only good; its perfection cannot be flawed. They come from [2]above *(where we originate from)***; proceeding like light rays from its source, the Father of lights, with whom there is no distortion, or even a shadow of shifting to obstruct, or intercept the light; nor any hint of a hidden agenda.**

[1] The principle of a ¹gift, puts reward-language out of business.

[2] The word, ²anouthen, means, from above. John 3:3, 13.

1:18 We were brought forth by the Word of truth. Our true origin is preserved in God's resolve. It was according to the Father's ¹delight that he ²birthed us; giving ³authentic, incarnate expression to the Word. *[The face to face-ness of the Logos that was before time was. John 1:1]* **Just like the first-fruits mirror the harvest, so we mirror the ⁴conclusion of his ⁵workmanship in the core of our ⁶being.**

[1] The word, ¹boulomai, means the affectionate desire and deliberate resolve of God.

[2] Only James uses the word, ²apokueō from apo + kuma; from apo, away from and kuō, to swell with young; bend or curve. Same word in v 15, where sin's passion parented death, vs. God's passion parenting authentic life in us. Thus, the effect of a mindset embracing temptation rather than truth. [The Father's resolve stands in total contrast to the perverted passions of sin, claiming its illegitimate parenthood of mankind. James 1:2; James 1:12-16.]

[3] Truth, ³alethea, from a, negative + lanthanō, meaning hidden; that which is unveiled; the Word [logos] of truth is the ³unveiled logic of God.

[4] The Preposition ⁴eis, points to conclusion.

[5] The word, κτίσμα ⁵ktisma meaning creation with reference to the proprietorship of the manufacturer - God owns the idea of our invention - he holds the copyright.

[6] The words, εἰς τὸ εἶναι ἡμᾶς ἀπαρχήν - ⁶einai hemas - our beingness from eimi, I am.

> *See Romans. 8:29, He pre-designed and engineered us from the start to be jointly fashioned in the same mold and image of his Son according to the exact blueprint of his thought. We see the original and intended pattern of our lives preserved in his Son. He is the firstborn from the same womb that reveals our genesis. He confirms that we are the invention of God. Also, John 1:1-18; 1 Peter. 2:9,10.*

1:19 Consequently my beloved friends, *[when you are faced with temptation,]* **give your immediate attention to the Word that reveals your true origin; do not ponder the contradiction. Rather remain silent, than to quickly give your vote and voice to the ¹emotions that arise in the heat of the moment.** *(Quick to hear, slow to speak, slow to ¹anger. The word ὀργή ¹orgē from oregomia, means the excitement of the mind; to stretch oneself out in order to grasp something, to reach after or desire.)*

1:20 These outbursts of emotion would typically distort the picture, and bring no credit to compliment God's ¹righteousness. *(¹What God achieved in redeeming our identity and innocence.)*

1:21 Therefore, by embracing the ¹infused word, you discover how thoroughly freed you already are from any kind of perverted passion that spirals out of control, polluting your lives like a filthy garment; your ²gentle abandonment to this logic, powerfully ²realizes the full

³extent of your salvation from the dictates of the soul ruled realm. *(Again, a word only James uses, ἔμφυτος ¹emphutos impregnated. The words, ²en prauteti - in gentleness are used in contrast to orgē. Rescuing you from negative thought patterns and depressing emotional traits. The verb σωσαι ³sōsai is the Aorist Infinitive tense, which presents the action expressed by the verb as a completed unit with a beginning and end.)*

1:22 Give the mirror-word your ¹undivided attention; do not underestimate yourself. ³Make the calculation. There can only be one logical conclusion: your authentic origin is mirrored in the word. You are God's poem; ²let his voice make poetry of your life. *(The word, ¹akroatēs, means intent listening. James is not promoting the doing of the law of works; he is defining the law of perfect liberty. Doing the word begins with your undivided attention to the face of your birth. ²A doer of the Word, poiētēs, means poet. Make the calculation, ³paralogizomai, from para, a Preposition indicating close proximity, union, and logizomai, to reckon the logic in any calculation.)*

1:23 Anyone who hears the word, sees the face of their birth, as in a mirror. The difference between a mere spectator and a participator is that both of them hear the same voice and perceive in its message the face of their own genesis reflected there;

1:24 they realize that they are looking at themselves, but for the one it seems just too good to be true; this person departs *[back to the old way of seeing themselves],* **and immediately forgets what manner of person they are; never giving another thought to the one they saw there in the mirror.**

1:25 The other is ¹mesmerized by what they see; ²captivated by the effect of a law that frees them from the obligation to the old written code that restricted them to their own efforts and willpower. No distraction or contradiction can dim the impact of what is seen in the mirror concerning the law of perfect ³liberty *[the law of faith]* **that now frees one to get on with the act of living the life** *[of their original design.]* **They find a new ³spontaneous lifestyle; the poetry of practical living.**

The law of perfect liberty is the image and likeness of God revealed in Christ, now redeemed in human form, as in a mirror. Look deep enough into the face of your birth, reflected in Christ, that you may see there in its perfection, a portrait that so resembles the original, that he becomes distinctly visible in the spirit of your mind and in the face of every person you behold.

[1] I translated the word, ¹parakuptō, with mesmerized from para, a Preposition indicating close proximity, originating from, denoting the point from which an action originates; intimate connection, and kuptō, to bend, stoop down to view at close scrutiny;

[2] Then, ²paramenō, to remain captivated under the influence of; again the Preposition para, with menō, to continue to be present.

[3] The word often translated as freedom, ³eleutheria, means without obligation; spontaneous.)

1:26 Meaningless conversation is often disguised in religious eloquence. Just because it sounds sincere, doesn't make it true. If your tongue is not bridled by what your heart knows to be true about you, then you cheat yourself.

1:27 The purest and most uncompromising form of religious expression is found at its [1]source. God is the Father of mankind. He inspires one to take a genuine interest in helping the fatherless and the widows in their plight and to make sure that one's own life does not become blemished in the process. *(The word [1]para, is a Preposition indicating close and immediate proximity, intimate connection.)*

2:1 Jesus heads up the kind of faith that does not judge on face value, neither is it influenced by popular opinion or [1]outward appearance. *([1]Face value, prosopolepsia.)*

2:2 Here is a typical example: an influential impressive looking man, dressed in glitter and fine jewelry may visit your assembly; then a shabby looking poor man may walk into the same gathering;

2:3 the smart guy gets the best seat while the shabby looking chap gets told to stand in the back or sit on the ground like a slave at your feet.

2:4 To discriminate in your heart against anyone conceives a judgment in you that can cause great ill; can you imagine how it hurts to be rejected like that?

2:5 May I have your full attention on this issue my dear friends, faith in who you really are according to [1]your original identity is the real measure of your wealth; you might be poor according to the standards of this world but according to God you possess your allotted portion which is the kingdom of his promise to those who love him. *(The word, [1]eklegomai, comes from ek, a Preposition denoting origin, and legō, meaning to speak; thus, the original blueprint-word, logos.)*

2:6 But you insult the poor, in your effort to impress the rich; meanwhile you fail to realize that the rich have abused their influence against you. They have conned you into their prejudices and discriminatory judgments. They bought your vote with cheap currency. *(Any value outside of the price God paid in Christ is an inferior value to human life.)*

2:7 Their apparent position of influence is just a disguise they employ to blaspheme the name that defines your true identity.

2:8 Scripture confirms that the law of the kingdom is fulfilled in you realizing the same value in your neighbor as you would see in yourself; this is what doing the word is all about, and it makes beautiful poetry. *(Lev 19:18; Luke 10:27, Matthew 22:37-40. By not forgetting what manner of person you are, you will not forget what manner of person your neighbor is according to the mirror principle.)*

2:9 To judge anyone on outward appearance is a [1]sin. This violates the law of liberty and revives condemnation and guilt. *(The word, [1]hamartia, from ha, meaning negative and meros, meaning form or allotted portion; sin represents any thing that robs you of your allotted portion which is the true measure of your life.)*

2:10 If you lower the standard of the law in just one aspect of it you have [1]failed entirely. *(To fail, stumble, err, [1]piptō, to descend from a higher place to a lower, from petomai, to fly; thus, to stop flying.)*

2:11 For he who said you shall not commit adultery also said you shall not kill. Here is an example, you might be faithful to your wife, yet you have killed someone; your not committing adultery does not cancel out the murder. *(And vice versa.)*

2:12 Let the law of liberty set the pace [be the judge] **in your conversation and conduct.** (The law of perfect liberty is the image and likeness of God revealed in Christ, now redeemed in mankind as in a mirror. Look deep enough into that law of faith that you may see there in its perfection a portrait that so resembles the original that he becomes distinctly visible in the spirit of your mind and in the face of everyone you behold. [Hebrews 10:25])

2:13 Judgment showed no mercy to those who do not walk in mercy, but mercy triumphs over judgment. (Those who walk in mercy walk in the law of liberty. [Galatians 5:22, 23.] There is no law against love. While judgment threatens condemnation, mercy interposes and prevails over judgment. See 1 John 3:20 So, even if our own hearts would ¹accuse us of not really being true to ourselves, God is greater than our hearts and he has the full picture. His knowledge of us is not compromised. [This word, ¹**kataginōskō** is only used three times in the NT, translated, to blame, or condemn. From **kata**, down and **ginōskō**, to know; thus to know from below; from a fallen mindset perspective.] 1 John 3:21 Beloved when we know what God knows to be true about us, then instead of condemning us, our hearts will endorse our innocence and ¹free our conversation before God. [The word ¹**parresia**, from **para**, a Preposition indicating close proximity, and **rheō**, to pour forth; to flow freely, suggesting an unreservedness in speech; bold utterance.]

Also 1 John 4:18,19 Fear cannot co-exist in this love realm. The perfect love union that we are talking about expels fear. Fear holds on to an expectation of crisis and judgment [which brings separation] and interprets it as due punishment [a form of karma.] It echoes torment and only registers in someone who does not realize the completeness of their love union [with the Father, Son and Spirit and with one another.] We love because he loved us first. [We did not invent this fellowship; we are invited into the fellowship of the Father and the Son.])

2:14 My friends, if your faith [in your true identity] **is not practical and visible in your conduct it is fake and cannot benefit you in any way.**

2:15 Let's bring it closer to home [I am not even talking about your duty to strangers], **someone in your own family might be struggling financially to the extent that they do not even have the basics as far as clothes and food are concerned.**

2:16 What's the good if you keep your contact with them very brief and distant and wave them goodbye with empty words, something like, May the Lord richly bless you brother. Be warm, be fed, ok, bye. Have a great day. A coat and a cup of soup is going to say so much more.

2:17 It is clear then, that without corresponding acts of kindness, faith on its own is fake.

2:18 Faith is not in competition with works; the one cannot operate without the other. Faith remains invisible without action; indeed the only way to communicate faith is in doing the things prompted and inspired by faith.

2:19 Congratulations. So you believe in one God; so do demons; however, their belief in God doesn't change them it just gives them the shivers.

2:20 Hey man, if you have nothing to show for your faith your faith is meaningless; it remains a dead doctrine.

2:21 Abraham's righteousness inspired his act of faith when he presented his son Isaac as a sacrifice upon the altar. *(Genesis 15:1, 6 confirms that Abraham was justified long before Isaac was born. God was his reward, not Isaac. No amount of good works can justify a person; good works follow faith, not the other way around. Here James asks the question, Was not Abraham our father justified by works, in that he offered up Isaac his son upon the altar? The answer is clearly, No. Abraham was justified when he believed God's Word concerning his offspring, many years before Isaac was born.)*

2:22 His works were in synergy with his faith, and completed it. The one compliments the other.

2:23 Abraham's friendship with God was the fruit of the righteousness he received by faith; this was announced in Genesis 15:6 and prompted a lifestyle that confirmed his faith. *(2 Chr 20:7 calls Abraham the friend of God.)*

2:24 It is obvious then that justification does not stop at faith but continues into action.

2:25 By protecting the messengers Rahab the prostitute showed her faith in their message and was justified. *(Hebrews 11:31.)*

2:26 Just as the body gives expression to the spirit, so actions give expression to faith.

3:1 My friends, let's not be quick to assume the title of teacher. Remember when we teach we subject ourselves to greater scrutiny.

3:2 It is a common habit to [1]descend from a higher place *[of faith]* to a lower *(of the senses)*, especially in conversation. However, if you want to be in perfect charge of your whole person, the best place to begin is to take charge of your tongue. *(To reflect the word that confirms your true genesis [James 1:18, 19]. The word,* [1]*peripiptō, comes from,* **peri**, *meaning surrounded* + **piptō**, *from* **petomai**, *meaning to fly; thus, to descend from a higher place to a lower, to stop flying.)*

3:3 With bit and bridle we are able to direct the strong body of a horse; it's the little bit in the mouth that makes the difference.

3:4 Consider the effect of a small rudder on a large ship, when the seasoned captain skillfully steers that vessel on a straight course contrary to fierce winds and weather.

3:5 As small a member the tongue might be it can make great claims. A little fire can go out of control and consume a large forest.

3:6 A tongue can strike like lightning and turn the harmony of your world into chaos; one little member can stain the whole body. It can disrupt the pattern of your design, taking its spark from the smoldering garbage heaps of [1]Gehenna. *(*[1]*The garbage heap outside Jerusalem, commonly related to hell.* **Gehenna**, *is the Latin word;* **Geenas** *is the Greek word used for the Hebrew* **Valley of Hinnom**, גיא בן הינום *which is modern day* **Wadi er-Rababi**. *A fiery place for the disposal of waste matter from the city of Jerusalem. The Valley of Hinnom lies outside of ancient Jerusalem. Thus to slander someone is to reduce that person to rubbish.)*

3:7 From tigers to eagles, cobras to dolphins, humans have succeeded in curbing the wild nature of beasts and birds, reptiles and sea creatures.

3:8 Yet no-one can tame a tongue; no-one can restrain the evil in its fatal venom. *(The law of works operated by willpower cannot match the effect of the law of perfect liberty. Mirror likeness ignites true freedom to utter that which is precious.)*

3:9 We can say beautiful things about God the Father but with the same mouth curse a fellow human made in his mirror likeness. *(The point is not what the person did to deserve the insult. The point is that people are image and likeness bearers of God by design. True worship is to touch someone's life with the same devotion and care you would touch Jesus himself; even if the other person seems a most unlikely candidate.)*

3:10 My friends, a blessing and a curse cannot originate from the same source. *(Discovering our true source brings true freedom. James 1:17,18.)*

3:11 Not even a natural fountain produces both bitter and sweet water.

3:12 As impossible as it is for a fig tree to bear olives, and a vine to produce figs, so a fountain cannot yield salt and fresh water from the same source.

3:13 Humility advertises wisdom; it shows in the quality of your conversation and actions. This distinguishes you with the reputation of someone who is acquainted with wisdom and skilled in understanding.

3:14 If there is any hidden agenda, secretly driven by bitter jealousy and contention, you have nothing to be proud of. Your big talk sounds superficial and offers no disguise. *(The fountain of your heart always shows.)*

3:15 This wisdom does not originate from above, but is clearly reduced to a kind that is earthly, ruled by the senses and dictated to by demons. *(Or daimōn; from daiō (to distribute fortunes). The Greeks gave the word daimōn the same meaning as god. What they meant by the word; however, is still a conjecture. They may have related a demon with daemmonas, knowing or being experienced in a thing, or they may have derived the word from daíomai, meaning to assign or award one's lot in life (diaítētai kai dioikemtai tōn ánthrōpōn), the arbitrators or umpires and governors of men.*

They conceived of them as those who ruled and directed human affairs, not as a personality, but primarily as a destructive power. Thus they called the happy or lucky person eudaímōn, one who is favored by this divine power. The adjective, daimónios, was used for one who demonstrated power irrespective of whether it was saving or destructive. The Tragic Poets use daimōn to denote fortune or fate, frequently bad fortune, but also good fortune if the context represented it as such. Thus, daimōn is associated with the idea of a gloomy and sad destiny independent of a person, coming upon and prevailing over them. Consequently, daimōn and túchē, luck, are often combined, and the doctrine of demons developed into signifying either a beneficent or evil power in the lives of people. — Zodhiates Complete Word Study Lexicon.)

3:16 An environment of envy and rivalry is conducive to confusion and disorder and all kinds of worthless pursuits.

3:17 The wisdom that originates from above sets the pace in innocence; it loves peace; it is always appropriate *(polite)*; persuaded about that which is good; filled with compassion; these fruits are pure goodness and [1]without discrimination. *(From [1]anhupokritos, without hypocrisy. See James 1:17.)*

3:18 Seed always predicts the harvest. Righteousness inspires the kind deeds of those who embrace peace; these are like seeds sown into fertile soil.

4:1 What is it that triggers disputes and fighting? Is it not selfish desires and greedy agendas that ¹both parties host within themselves? Hence wars are born. It is a global identity crisis. *(The word, ¹enteuthen, means, repeated on both sides; also translated, hence, from this point. This is in such contrast to the wisdom from above, see 1:17 & 3:17. Any sense of lack causes you to forget what manner of person you are, and how perfect and complete and without lack you are by design, as mirrored in Christ. This is again the typical arena of the law of works and striving against the law of perfect liberty.)*

4:2 You allow your heart to become so consumed with longing for something until you are ready to kill for it. Then you are still not satisfied. What you want keeps evading you; you quarrel and strive, and you just can't get it. If you are desperately unfulfilled why don't you simply ask God to give you what you need? *(This is in such contrast to the wisdom from above, see 3:17. Also James 1:5, The only thing you could possibly lack is wisdom [One might sometimes feel challenged beyond the point of sanity]; however, make your request in such a way that you draw directly from the source [not filtered through other opinions]. God is the origin and author of wisdom; he intertwines your thoughts with good judgment. His gifts are available to all, without regret.)*

4:3 You have asked, but God seems reluctant to give it to you, you may say. But when your motivation is to get something just so that you can squander it on yourself, you are doing it all wrong. *(This is like expecting God to support your own futile efforts to justify yourself. See James 1:2-4, 17, 18, 23-25.)*

4:4 Adultery, whether it is the husband or the wife who does the flirting, is destructive. Can't you see that even though the world system might approve of such behavior, it is contrary to God's design for you? Whose friend do you want to be? Are you prepared to distance yourself from God *[and the life of your design]* just to win the plastic applause of the world?

4:5 Scripture is not quoting empty words when it states that God yearns with jealous expectation over the spirit which he has made to inhabit us.

4:6 His gift of grace *[1:17]* is in direct opposition to the vanity of the proud mindset of self-effort, whereby people strive to prove themselves as superior to others. Gift and reward are opposites. Humility attracts grace.

4:7 Your most effective defense against any diabolical mindset, is to yield yourselves in total abandonment to God, and there encounter his dream-life for you. You will witness how effortlessly those thoughts flee from you. *(The word diabollos, from diaballō, dia, because of, and ballō, to cast down; to accuse, to make false and defamatory statements against someone. This points to the devilish fallen mindset-system which has engaged generations in the blind-fold mode of pride and accusation, by not seeing the image of God in human life.)*

4:8 Snuggle up to the warm embrace of God; experience his closeness. The sinner can come with all stains washed from his hands; the double-minded can come with a purified heart. *(In Christ every definition of distance or delay is canceled.)*

4:9 This is not a mere blase yielding. Realizing the misery that you have brought upon yourself and others is often accompanied by intense grief and weeping. This is no place for superficial laughter and make-belief joy; nor any occasion for boasting. *(Your futile efforts to justify yourself through striving and fighting only reinforce your nakedness. The perfect law of liberty, unveiling the mirror message declares your redeemed innocence through the finished work of Christ.)*

4:10 Put down your own efforts to fight for your rights; let him lift you up to the dignity of his [1]presence. *(The word translated, presence, [1]enopion means in the gaze of; face to face. See your own face reflected in his. There is no higher elevation to engage in.)*

4:11 Gossip is out; to bad-mouth and point your finger at your brother is to insult the law of liberty; you put yourself up as a law enforcer and thereby assume that you are above scrutiny.

4:12 God is the one who endorses the law of perfect liberty. That makes him the only judge with power to save. He rendered the law of performance completely irrelevant. He never handed you the power of attorney to judge anyone.

4:13 Hey, you've got your year planner out and can already taste the profits in all your business ventures; you're going big; travel, and trade from city to city.

4:14 Meanwhile, you have no handle on tomorrow. Your life is like a mist that is visible for a short while before it evaporates.

4:15 My best advice for you is to wrap up all your plans and conversations in the delightful resolve of God.

4:16 Don't be so cocksure about your dreams for the future. Plans that presumptuously exclude God's opinion end up to be [1]full of labors, annoyances, and hardships. *(The word, [1]poneros, is described in Thayer's Lexicon to mean, full of annoyances, hardships, and labors; often translated as evil.)*

4:17 To turn a blind eye to an obvious opportunity to do good is [1]out of character. *(The word, [1]hamartia, comes from ha, meaning without and meros, meaning portion or form, distorted behavior, often translated as sin.)*

5:1 Your wealth cannot disguise your weakness when calamity strikes. Then it is too late to scream and cry.

5:2 Whatever you have hoarded to show how strong you are financially shows signs of rot; your wardrobes of fine clothing are moth eaten.

5:3 Your tarnished treasures of gold and silver bear witness against you; instead of exhibiting your riches they show off your shame. Your wealth worries have given you ulcers that consume you like a fire from within. You would have thought that you stored up enough insurance to last you to the end of days.

5:4 In the process you have short paid your laborers who reaped your harvests; those wages have now become a loud voice together with the groans of the workers you have cheated and abused; they shout out against you in earshot of the Lord of the masses.

5:5 You have indulged in a delicate lifestyle on all your properties; you have stuffed yourselves; grabbing and looting like soldiers on the battlefield.

5:6 In your quest to get to the top you have stepped on others and ruined innocent lives; while no one opposed you.

5:7 My friends, if you are the ones abused, remain passionate about the [1]presence of the Lord. Consider how the farmer lays hold of the harvest by patiently letting the early and latter rain do its work in the soil to prepare its precious yield. *(The word, [1]parousia, means presence, from para, closest possible proximity, and eimi, I am. Sadly this beautiful word has always been traditionally translated to point to yet another future event—the coming of the Lord. Religion thrives on two lies, distance and delay. Immanuel canceled both in Christ. Jesus says in John 4, Do you not say, there are yet four months then comes the harvest. Yet you are looking at the wrong harvest. Lift up your eyes, look away from your own labor and see the harvest that is already ripe.)*

5:8 Let your hearts also be firm in patience while the [1]closeness of the embrace of his presence sustains you. *(The word, [1]engidzo, means to bring near, reflexively — Strong's Concordance; here translated as the closeness of his embrace.)*

5:9 When circumstances [1]squeeze you into tight spots, don't make your problem your topic of conversation with one another *(there is no relief in feeling sorry for yourselves)* while the Lord is left standing outside behind closed doors. Let him be the judge of your situation. *(The word, [1]stenadzo, means to groan, complain; from stenos, meaning narrow.)*

5:10 The Prophets who spoke in the Name of the Lord are our [1]mentors; consider what they had to put up with and what hardships they went through, and with what fortitude they prevailed. *(The word, [1]upodeigma, means an exhibit, pattern for imitation.)*

5:11 To look back at the faith heroes of yesterday is always an inspiration. Even Job's life was prophetic. Consider how God came through for him in the end; his endurance proved God's extreme compassion and tender mercies. *(The first part represents life under the law of fear, the latter the law of faith.)*

5:12 Making foolish oaths does not add weight to your intentions. It makes no difference whether you attempt to tap into heaven's magic or swear by some earthly institution, or any other binding authority. Keep it simple, yes cannot mean no at the same time. Swearing silly oaths makes you look phony anyway. *(Live your life, convinced of God's tender feelings towards you.)*

5:13 If anyone is going through a tough time, let him worship; when times are good, sing praises. *(Don't take your lead from your negative or your positive circumstances.)*

5:14 If you feel too [1]weak to [2]worship, find encouragement in the care of those who are mature in their faith. Let them anoint you with oil and worship with you in [3]prayer. Identify yourself in all that the Lord's name represents. *(The words, [1]astheneo, means weak, feeble; [2]proseuxomai, worship; and [3]euxomai, prayer.)*

5:15 The prayer *[environment]* of faith shall restore the feeble. The Lord revitalizes and quickens you; he has already forgiven you of anything stupid you might have done to have caused the situation.

5:16 *(Do not tolerate vibes)* if you have wronged someone talk to him about it; pray for each other to maintain a healthy fellowship. Righteousness is the fuel of effective prayer. *(How right things are, not how wrong things are now motivate your every prayer and conversation. Not the size or the detail of the problem.)*

5:17 Elijah wasn't superman, yet his prayers had supernatural results with global impact. Remember how he prayed. He prayed with such resolve that he stopped the rain for three and a half years.

5:18 He prayed again and everything was back to normal; rain and harvest in season.

5:19 If a brother strays off from the truth, go and fetch him.

5:20 To turn a sinner back from error not only rescues the individual but stops the ripple effect of the rot in a community.

1:1 I am Peter, an ambassador of Jesus Christ to the many [1]foreigners who are scattered throughout Pontus, Galatia, Cappadocia, Asia and Bithynia. *(The word, [1]parepidēmos, from para, proceeding from a sphere of influence, originating from; and epidēmeō, from epi, continuous influence upon, and demos, to bind together; thus, a people who are bound together socially, whilst living in a foreign country. The picture of mankind's scatteredness away from home-in the Father's bosom, is captured here.)*

1:2 Your [1]original identity is defined by what God, the Father of mankind has [2]always cherished about you; knowing that your pre-Adamic innocence in spirit, would be preserved in the prophetic word, and redeemed through the obedience of Jesus Christ, and the effect of the sprinkling of his blood. Realizing his grace and peace exceeds any definition of contradiction or reward. *(The word [1]eklektos, derives from eklegomai, which has two components, ek, a Preposition that indicates source or origin, and legō, to speak; translates, original logic; see John 1:1-3 and 12. The word [2]prognosis means to know in advance. Peter emphasizes the priceless value of our redeemed innocence through the obedience of Christ and the shedding of his blood. See 1 Peter 1:18,19; 2 Peter 1:9.)*

1:3 Let us [1]celebrate the God and Father of our Lord Jesus Christ with articulate acclaim. According to his matchless mercy and tender compassions, he [2]birthed us again when Jesus was raised from the dead. In him, we were rebooted to live the authentic life of our design; while [3]participating in a living hope, witnessing the Father's [4]expectation of the ages unfold in us. *(The word, [1]eulogetos, means to brag, to bless, to speak well of. Jesus reminds Nicodemus that we are born anouthen, from above. [John 3:3, and John 3:13] No one can fully engage in heaven's perspective, unless one's heavenly origin is realized. The Son of man declares mankind's co-genesis from above and now through our joint resurrection, we are reconnected again to our original identity as sons. The word [2]anagennaō, from ana, upward, [reconnecting with anouthen - John 3:3 - from above, where we came from in the first place]; and gennaō, to regenerate, to give birth. As much as his death brought dramatic closure to our futile and failed attempts to justify and define ourselves, our co-resurrection rebooted the original blueprint of our Maker's image and likeness in us. - The mystery of the ages is unveiled. Christ in us. The verb, ζωσαν tzōsan from ζάω tzaō is a Present Active Participle, being alive to participate and witness [3]a living hope - ελπιδα elpida, the expectation of the ages concluding in life. Your life is the Father's dream come true. See Colossians 1:27)*

1:4 We are reintroduced to an [1]imperishable inheritance, which has been [2]flawlessly [3]preserved for us in the heavenly realm, where neither Adam's fall, nor mankind's failure to justify themselves, could possibly [2]contaminate, discredit or diminish the original portion of our true sonship realized in Christ Jesus. *(Here Peter employs three adjectives to reinforce the idea of the absolute imperishable integrity of our inheritance. The word, [1]aphthartos from a + ptheirō, incorruptible, indestructible, that which time cannot decay or decrease; the word, [2]amiantos, a + miainō, discredit, dishonor, flaw; also, [3]amarantos, from a + marainō, extinguish, neither time nor decay* *could touch or contaminate it in any way. The verb,* **teteremenen,** *is in the perfect Passive tense, which translates having been kept. See also Hebrews 6:16,17.)*

1:5 Your legitimate inheritance was guarded all along by God's belief in you, to be fully unveiled in the [1]conclusion of time as the perfect solution to mankind's predicament. *([1]Jesus is the incarnate Word, Hebrews 1:1-3; Galatians 4:4.)*

1:6 So, regardless of any degree of contradiction, whether prolonged, or swift, your reason for exuberant joy remains uninterrupted; even at times where you might have occasion to feel utterly miserable.

1:7 This will help you in those difficult times: think of your belief as something much more precious than any possible evaluation of gold; remember that fire does not destroy the metal, it reveals it. Now even gold is an inferior comparison to faith. Gold as a currency has only temporal and unpredictable value; it fluctuates as the market changes. Now, in the same way that fire reveals gold, your faith in the midst of contradiction, makes Jesus Christ visible and gives much reason to testimony [1]stories worth telling. This is what has permanent [2]value, and exhibits the glory of Christ in you. *(The word often translated as praise,* **[1]epainos,** *has two components,* **epi,** *continuous influence upon, and* **ainos,** *which often reflects a story worth telling; the word* **[2]timay,** *honor, suggests a valuing by which the price is fixed. See 2 Corinthians 13:5.)*

1:8 So even though you have never seen Jesus in the flesh you love him; even at times where he seems remote and invisible, your awareness of your union in him continues to ignite belief. You are leaping with indescribable and exuberant joy as you hold him in high esteem.

1:9 In this place of joy, you are [1]beyond the reach of any harm. Joy gives your faith a voice announcing the perfection of your soul's salvation. *(Joy celebrates the fulfillment of Scripture. Belief gives evidence of everything the Prophets pointed to. The word,* **kolumbaō,** *to carry off from harm. See 2 Corinthians 5:10.)*

1:10 This salvation which you now know as your own, is the theme of the prophetic thought; this is what intrigued the Prophets' minds for generations and became the object of their most diligent inquiry and scrutiny. They knew all along that mankind's salvation was a grace revelation, sustained in their prophetic utterance. *(Salvation would never be by personal achievement or a reward to willpower-driven initiative. The law of works would never replace grace.)*

1:11 In all of their conversation there was a [1]constant quest to determine who the Messiah would be, and exactly when this would happen. They knew with certainty that it was the spirit of Christ within them, pointing prophetically and giving testimony to the sufferings of the Christ and the subsequent glory. *(The [1]big question was, Who and When? In Acts 17:31 Paul addresses the Greek Philosophers and reminds them of their own ancient writings* *and he quotes two of their well-known philosophers: in 600BC Epimenedes wrote a song saying, We live and move and have our being in God; and Aratus wrote in 300BC that we are indeed God's offspring. Paul then announces to them that the God whom they worship in ignorance is not far from each one of us. He is not more Immanuel to the Jew than what he is to the Gentile. Now follows the punch line of the gospel: in the context of his Jewish background and personal encounter with Jesus Christ, Paul declares to them the Good News of mankind's redeemed innocence. God has overlooked the times of ignorance, and is now urging all of mankind, whoever and wherever they are, to a radical mind-shift, since he has prophetically **fixed a day** on which he would judge the world in righteousness **by a man whom he has appointed**, and of this [righteous judgment] he has given proof to all by raising him from the dead. Acts 17:30,31. See also Romans 4:25 where, in Paul's understanding, the resurrection of Jesus from the dead includes mankind's co-resurrection and seals their acquittal and redeemed innocence. This is the predicted subsequent glory that was to follow the cross. Hosea 6:2, After two days he will revive us; on the third day, he will raise us up. Whatever glory was lost in Adam, would be redeemed again in Jesus Christ.)*

1:12 It was revealed to them that this glorious grace message that they were communicating pointed to a specific day and person beyond their own horizon and generation; they saw you in their prophetic view. This [1]heavenly announcement had you in mind all along. They proclaimed glad tidings to you in advance, in the Holy Spirit, commissioned from heaven; the prophetic messengers themselves longed to gaze deeply into its complete fulfillment. *(Peter uses the word, [1]anaggellō, where the Preposition, **ana**, points upward to the source of the announcement.)*

1:13 How amazing is that. Jesus is what the Scriptures are all about; and you are what Jesus is all about. Now wrap your minds around that. This unveiling is [1]what tied up all the loose ends that would trip you and frustrate your seamless transition from the old to the new. The revelation of Jesus is no longer a future expectation. Do not allow the old mindset of a future tense glory to intoxicate you and distract you from the relevance of this moment. Stop pointing to a future Messiah. Jesus is who the Prophets pointed to. You are the fruit of his sufferings; you are the glorious resurrection generation. Fully engage your [2]minds with the consequence of this grace in the revelation of Jesus Christ. He [3]completes your every [4]expectation. *(The word [1]anazōsamenoi, to gird up, is an Aorist Participle, which translates, having girded up the loins of your mind, be sober. The word [2]dianoia, suggests deep contemplation, thinking something thoroughly through, in order to reach a sober conclusion. Then Peter writes, [3]teleios [4]elpisate, this is the completeness of every expectation. See Colossians 1:27.*

In one act of righteousness, God removed every possible definition of distance and delay. Every excuse that we could have to feel separated from God was canceled. This is what the Prophets saw: Every valley shall be lifted up, and every mountain and hill be made low; the crooked places shall be made straight, even the rough places shall be made smooth. And the glory of the LORD shall be revealed, and all flesh shall see it together, for the mouth of the LORD has spoken. Isaiah 40:4,5.)

1:14 Your ¹accurate hearing is what distinguishes you as the resurrection generation; the days of being driven by every ²desperate, distorted passion of your former ignorance are over. The ³fashions and patterns of a redundant system are no longer relevant. *(The word, ¹upoakoō is often translated, obedience, from **upo**, meaning under, as in under the influence of, and akoō, to hear. In the context of this chapter, Peter urges us to hear accurately what was communicated in the prophetic word concerning the life of our design, now rebooted into newness by our joint resurrection with Jesus Christ. The word, ²**epithumia**, translates, desire, craving, longing, desire for what is forbidden, lust. The word, ³**suschēmatizō**, from **sun**, union, and **schema**, pattern; a typical template.)*

1:15 The one whose ¹idea you are to begin with, designed you to radiate their image and likeness; as the true pattern of your beingness. So, ²be who you are in realizing the exact detail of your genesis. You are ³whole and in perfect harmony; seamlessly one with God. *(The word ¹kaleō, to define by name; to surname. The word ²**genēthēte**, referring to genesis, or birth, is in the Aorist, Passive, imperative case; the distinction between the Aorist Imperative and the Present Imperative is one of aspect, not tense. Thus, to get something over and done with. The word, ³**hagios**, holy, separate from common condition and use. See Hebrews 10:14-16 Mirror Bible)*

1:16 On the very account that what is ¹written in prophetic Scripture, *[and echoes in your innermost being],* **already mirrors the life of your design, you are free to ²be who you are. As it is written, I am, therefore you are. I am wholly separated unto you, and invite you to explore the same completeness of your being in me.** *(The word, ¹graphō, to engrave, often refers to the prophetic writings, Old Testament Scripture. The appeal of truth is confirmed in the resonance within us due to the echō of that which is already written in our innermost being by design. Did not our hearts ignite within us while he opened to us the Scriptures. Luke 24:27,32,44,45. The Textus Receptus uses the word **genēsthe**, instead of ²esesthe, from eimi, as in the Westtcott & Hort text. This makes a massive difference. So, instead of **ginomai**, to become, it is the word, **esesthe** be, from **eimi**, I am. See note in John 1:1 Three times in this sentence John uses the Active Indicative Imperfect form of the verb **eimi**, namely **aēn** [ἦν] to continue to be, [in the beginning 'was' the Word etc...] which conveys no idea of origin for God or for the Logos, but simply continuous existence, I am. Quite a different verb **egeneto**, became, appears in John 1:14 for the beginning of the Incarnation of the Logos. The Word 'became' flesh. The incarnation is not the origin of Jesus. See the distinction sharply drawn in John 8:58, before Abraham was [born, **genesthai** from **ginomai**] I am. The word **eimi**, I am; the essence of being, suggesting timeless existence. You did not begin in your mother's womb. You began in God's I-am-ness. You are the most magnificent idea that the Engineer of the Universe has ever had. I knew you before I formed you in your mother's womb. Jeremiah 1:5. In him we live and move and have our being. Acts 17:28.)*

1:17 Now since you are defined in your Father, who does not judge anyone on face value, but always only according his work; *(his finished work in Christ)* **wherever you find yourself located geographically or emotionally, ¹return**

to your 'at home-ness' in him, with a deep sense of God-consciousness; you are not defined by your circumstances. *(The word ¹anastrephō, suggests a radical returning; literally a turning upside down. Actually **ana**, means upward- so, it's actually a turning downside up. See 2 Corinthians 3:16.)*

1:18 It is clear to see that you were ransomed from the futile, fallen mindset that you inherited from your fathers. This was not concluded by the currency of your own labor, represented by the fluctuating values of gold and silver, and the economy of your religious efforts;

1:19 but you were redeemed with the priceless blood of Christ. He is the ultimate sacrifice; spotless and without blemish. Jesus completes the prophetic picture. *(In him God speaks the most radical scapegoat language of the law of judgment and brings final closure to a dead and redundant system. In Psalm 40:6,7, it is clearly stated that God does not require sacrifices or offerings. Jesus is the Lamb of God. He collides victoriously with the futile sacrificial system whereby offerings are constantly made to the pseudo, moody, monster gods of our imagination. This is the scandal of the cross. God does not demand a sacrifice that would change the way he thinks about mankind; he provides the sacrifice of himself in Christ in order to forever eradicate sin-consciousness from our minds and radically change the way we think about our Maker, one another and ourselves. [Sin-consciousness is in essence a works-based consciousness.] God did not clothe Adam with the skin of an animal because of a divine need to be appeased, but because of their unconditional love for Adam; they spoke the language of Adam's own judgment: Adam, not God, was embarrassed about his nakedness. The clothing was not to make God look at Adam differently, but to make Adam feel better about himself. And ultimately it was to prophetically prepare Adam for the unveiling of the mystery of mankind's redemption in the incarnation. Here Deity would clothe themselves in human skin, in a Son; and the Lion of Judah would become the Lamb of God in order to free our minds to re-discover his image and likeness in our skin. See 1 Peter 1:2.)*

1:20 He was always destined in God's prophetic thought; God knew even before the ¹fall of the world order that his Son would be the Lamb, to be made manifest in these ²last days, because of you. *(You are the reason Jesus died and was raised. The word, ¹**kataballō**, meaning to fall away, to put in a lower place, instead of **themelios**, meaning foundation [see Ephesians 2:20]; thus, translated the fall of the world, instead of the foundation of the world. The entire Fall was a falling away in our minds from our true identity as image and likeness bearers of Elohim. Just like Eve, were we all deceived to believe a lie about ourselves, which is the fruit of the I-am-not-tree. We all, like sheep, have gone astray. Isaiah 53:6.*

*The word ²**eschatos** means extreme; last in time or in space; the uttermost part, the final conclusion. What God said about 'you-manity' in Jesus defines eschatology.)*

1:21 He is the conclusive cause of your belief in God. Seeing then how perfectly you fit into the scheme of things, it is no wonder that your faith in God's act of raising Jesus from the dead becomes the glorious reference to your own new birth. *[1:3]* The glory that God gave Jesus by raising him

from the dead, is the conclusion of everything that your faith longed for. *(This is the redeemed glory that the Prophets pointed to. Hosea 6:2, After two days he will revive us; on the third day he will raise us up. Isaiah 40:5, And the glory of the Lord shall be revealed, and all flesh shall see it together.)*

1:22 As a result of your [1]accurate hearing of the unveiled truth, and through the agency of the Spirit, you have engaged your souls fully with the purifying effect of your inclusion in his glorious work of redemption. *(See [1]commentary note in 1 Peter 1:14. The same Spirit of Christ who spoke from within the Prophets of old, now endorses truth within your spirit.)*

1:23 This co-resurrection-new-birth does not compare to the fading qualities of that which is produced by the perishable seed of the carnal works- and performance-based mindsets. The indestructible living seed of the word of God conceives resurrection life within you; this life is [1]equal to its source. *(The word, [1]menō means, abiding in seamless union, or, to remain the same. You are giving stature to the rise of a new person; a new resurrection generation of a people who are coming out of obscurity into his marvelous light.)*

1:24 All flesh is grass, and all its glory is like the flower of the field. The grass withers, the flower fades,

1:25 but the word of our God is [1]risen forever. This word is the [2]exact same message of the glad tidings announced by the Prophets and now proclaimed unto you. *(Peter again quotes from Isaiah 40, this time verses 6 and 8. The Hebrew word [1]Qum, קוּם means to rise up; like in Hosea 6:2, After two days he will revive us, on the third day, he will raise us up. Isaiah 40:6,8; also see note on 1 Peter 1:13. The word [2]menō is used in the Septuagint and also here in the Greek text, Peter uses the word, menō, to remain the same; to continue to be present. He continues to quote Isaiah also in the next chapter - 1 Peter 2:5.)*

2:1 Now, since you are rebooted and redefined in this eternal conversation, any distracting talk is inappropriate. Do away with everything associated with the old performance based mindsets. Anything perverse, all manner of guile and hypocrisies and spiteful jealousies as well as any kind of backbiting is to be shunned. There is zero nourishment in such conversation.

2:2 Imagine how a newborn babe would crave nothing else but pure mother's milk; in just the same way, become addicted to the unmixed milk of the word. This is your true nourishment. *(Approach the Scriptures with an attitude of a newborn babe, drawing milk from the mother.)*

2:3 Once you've tasted pure grace, you are spoilt for life. Grace rules. The Lordship of Jesus is established upon the dynamic of his goodness. *(χρηστὸς ὁ Κύριος Chrestos ho kurios. Grace is the throne of his Lordship.)*

2:4 The irresistible attraction seen in him, the living stone, is not at all compromised by the fact that man-made religious structures rejected him; he is esteemed most precious and remains the original and pivotal idea of God.

2:5 Now, present yourselves [1]likewise as living stones *[co-quickened in his resurrection; 1 Peter 1:3]* to be co-constructed, and seamlessly joined into a [2]spiritual house; you are a priestly people, wholly consecrated to engage the [2]new spiritual order; instead of a mere symbolic, prophetic picture, [3]you have now presented yourselves, entwined in Christ, reflecting God's [4]delight and face to face embrace in this union.

(Everything that was prophetically mirrored in the shadow tabernacle of Israel, has finally found its relevance in Jesus Christ. He fully unveils the real deal, in our union with him; we are the living skin-tabernacle temple, the new priestly-order.

[1] Jesus is the Living Stone and [1]we are like him. Even as newborn babies we share his perfection; no chiseling required, only nurturing. See 1 Kings 6:7.

[2] The word πνευματικός pneumatikos, spritual realities, is used twice in order to emphasize the fact that the old symbolic system is now replaced in the new, incarnate order of human life, mirrored in Christ.

[3] The word ανενεγκαι anenengkai is the Aorist Infinitive of ἀναφέρω [2]anapherō, to lift up oneself; to present oneself [as a living sacrifice]. See Romans 12:1. The Aorist Infinitive takes the thought beyond the prophetic; it is the inevitable consequence of that which is now accomplished.

[4] The word, εὐπρόσδεκτους from [3]euprosdechomai, having 3 components, eu, favorable; well pleased; pros, preposition meaning face to face, and dechomai, to embrace intimately.)

2:6 This is [1]central to the prophetic theme of Scripture: as voiced in Isaiah 28:16: Behold, I am laying in Zion a stone, a [2]cornerstone, the [3]exact and precise reference to the authentic thought of God; the one who exhibits the perfect idea of human life indwelt by God. This makes him most precious and desirable; he will not disappoint anyone's belief that he is indeed the Messiah, the Savior of the world. He exhibits human life as the true temple of God.

([1] The word ¹periechō, from peri, which, in compounds, retains substantially the same meaning of circuit (around), excess (beyond), or completeness (through), with echō, to hold, to resonate.

[2] The ²cornerstone is the foundation stone, which is the setting stone. It is the first stone set in the construction of a masonry foundation. All other stones will be set in reference to this stone, thus determining the position of the entire structure.

It is the primary foundation-stone at the angle of the structure by which the architect fixes a standard for the bearings of the walls and cross-walls throughout. [W. W. Lloyd]

See 1 Kings 6:7 Not a sound of a hammer or chisel while the temple was built. Every stone was perfectly cut in the quarry [the cross], to exactly mirror the pattern of the chief cornerstone. Also Isaiah 51:1. And, Romans 9:30-33, Isaiah 8:14, Isaiah 28:16.

[3] The word, ³eklegō, from ek, origin, and legō, idea, thought.

See Ephesians 2:20 Your lives now give tangible definition to the spiritual structure, having been built into it by God upon the foundation of the Prophets and Apostles. Jesus Christ himself is the ¹chief cornerstone.

Also Romans 9:33 The conclusion of the prophetic reference pointed towards the rock as the spirit identity of a person. God placed his testimony of their identity in front of their eyes, in Zion, the center of their religious focus, yet, blinded by their own efforts to justify themselves, they tripped over him.

But those who recognized him by faith, as the Rock from which they were hewn are freed from the shame of their sense of failure and inferiority. [See Deuteronomy 32:18, you have forgotten the Rock that birthed you; and in Isaiah 51:1, Look to the Rock from which you were hewn.] It is only in him that mankind will discover what they are looking for.

Who is the son of man? His physical identity is defined by his spiritual origin, the image and likeness of God, I say you are Petros, Mr Rock - a chip of the old Block! [See Matthew 16:13-19]. Mankind's origin and true identity is preserved and revealed again in the Rock of Ages. The term rock in those days, represented what we call the hard drive in computer technology today; the place where data is most securely preserved. Also interesting to note that rock fossils carry the oldest data and evidence of life.

See also Romans 10:11 Scripture declares that whosoever believes in Christ [to be the fulfillment of the promise of God to redeem mankind] will not be ³ashamed. [See Isaiah 28:16] These two Hebrew words, chush, חוּשׁ to make haste, and [Isaiah 49:23] ³bush, בּוּשׁ to be ashamed, look and sound very similar and were obviously confused in some translations—the Greek from Hebrew translation. The Septuagint was the Scriptures Paul was familiar with and there the word was translated from the word ³bush בּוּשׁ.)

2:7 His irreplaceable and priceless value is realized in your conviction; the very stone rejected by the unbelief of the religious leaders of the day, has become the cornerstone. It is in fact the most important stone in which the entire structure is defined. *(The cornerstone is the foundation stone, which is* *the setting stone. It is the first stone set in the construction of a masonry foundation. All other stones will be set in reference to this stone, thus determining the position of the entire structure. See Luke 20:17, Psalm 118:22, Matthew 21:42.)*

2:8 Unbelief is such a predictable set-up where that which is highly esteemed by faith, seems scandalous and offensive to the self-righteous mind. Since there is no ground left for boasting, grace offends the typical law of works-mentality. They are the ones who refuse to see the reference to their original identity revealed and redeemed in Christ.

2:9 You are proof of the [1]authentic *[eklegō]* generation; you give testimony to the original idea of the royalty of true priesthood *[the order of Melchizedek;]* you are a perfect prototype of the mass of the human race. You are the generation of people who exhibit the conclusion *[eis]* of the prophetic, poetic thought of God that has come full circle. *(See 1:3)* You publish the excellence of his elevation and display that your authentic identity has been rescued out of obscurity and brought into his spectacular light. *(The word [1]eklegō has traditionally been translated to mean election - I would prefer to emphasize the fact that ek is a Preposition always pointing to origin or source and the verb legō, is associated with its noun logos as in the context of John 1:1 The original conversation. See Hebrews 1:1-3)*

2:10 You were once a people without identity, but have now discovered the integrity of your original identity in God; where there was no mercy *[under the cruel judgment of the law of works, sponsored by the I am not-tree-system]*, you have now received much mercy.

2:11 It does not matter how appealing the system of the flesh-glory seems, it can never define or fulfill you; do not allow yourself to be lured into its strategies and sway. You are dearly loved. I urge you from within this place of our joint oneness to remain like pilgrims and strangers to the subtleties of a world-system that is foreign to your design. Avoid any influence that does not [2]resonate with your innocence. *(The word, [1]parakaleō has two components; para, suggesting close proximity and kaleō, to surname or to identify by name; suggesting close and intimate companionship; the word [2]apechomai, apo, away from and echō, to abstain from that which does not resonate.)*

2:12 The beautiful way in which you conduct yourselves in the company of people who are not familiar with your beliefs, will attract their attention to the resonance of their hearts as they witness for themselves God's intentions as evidenced in your good works. This will be as clear as daylight to them and will completely disarm the rumors that they have heard about you.

2:13 Reflect the Lordship of Jesus in your life in the way that you submit to every man-made ordinance, by acknowledging the supremacy of a king.

2:14 Recognize their leadership and structures as their objective to manage the evil doers in a righteous way as well as to commend those who do well.

2:15 God desires that your good conduct will silence those foolish people who see you as a threat to society.

2:16 Yes you are free *[from man-made rules and institutions to govern your behavior]* but do not use your freedom in a way that others may read it as a disguise for an evil agenda. You are God-governed. *(Where love rules.)*

2:17 Esteem all people with equal respect. Love family with much affection. Revere God. Respect the King.

2:18 Servants be subject to your masters in every possible way; not only to those who are nice to you but even to the crooked ones.

2:19 Seeing together with God enables you to suffer wrongfully, gracefully.

2:20 For someone to get beaten up for his sins and then to bear it patiently is one thing; but suffering such abuse while you are doing well is pure grace before God.

2:21 These are defining moments for us, since Christ suffered our judgment in his innocence, thus leaving us a perfect example. In this way, our attitude in bearing insults we do not deserve, reveals the grace of God to the ones mistreating us.

2:22 He never said or did anything wrong.

2:23 Even when they heaped abuse upon him, he never retaliated; he suffered much, but never threatened; instead he fully yielded himself to the righteous judgment of God; which is God declaring the unjust righteous because of what Christ has done.

2:24 In his person he bore our sins in his own body upon the tree and thus [1]brought closure to every distorted pattern of sin's influence upon us; we were made alive unto righteousness; we were healed by the blows he took in his body. *(The word [1]apogenōmenos from apo, away from and ginomai, to cause to be, to generate; in giving up his body to death, he removed us from the deadly influence of every distortion that sin could possibly generate in us. See 1 Peter 1:11.)*

2:25 You were completely vulnerable, just like sheep roaming astray without direction or protection, but now, you have [1]returned and are restored to the shepherd and Guardian of your souls. *(The word, [1]epistrephō means to return to where we've wandered from. See 1 Peter 1:17 also 2 Corinthians 3:16.)*

3:1-17 *(Still to be translated.)*

3:18 *[From Adam till Noah to Now.]* **Christ** [1]**died** [2]**once and for all, in order to** [4]**conclusively** [3]**separate you from a** [5]**distorted identity. Thus, restored righteousness** *[shared likeness]* **triumphed** [6]**beyond the reach of any identity that is not in sync with innocence and oneness,** *[righteousness bringing closure to* [7]*unrighteousness]*— **in order that he might** [8]**lead you-manity to be face to face with God; his body was** [9]**murdered, but he was made alive in spirit.** *(The best manuscripts have,* [1]*apethanen [Aorist form of* ἀποθνῄσκω, *to die], later manuscripts were changed to* **epathen** *[suffered]. Then the word,* [2]**hapax** *once for all; not once upon a time [**pote**]. Oldest manuscripts have* **humas** *[su]* **you**-manity not **hemas** *us believers. The words,* περὶ ἁμαρτιῶν [3]**peri hamartiōn** *[here, the Genitive suggests, separation from] The Preposition* [4]**peri**, *encircling; circuit [around], excess [beyond], completeness; all inclusive. The word often translated, sin,* [5]**hamartia**, *from* **ha**, *without and* **meros**, *which is the stem of the word* **morphē**, *form; thus a distorted form; the lie that we believed about ourselves. As in 2 Corinthians 3:18 the word* **metamorphē**, *with form, which is the opposite of* **hamartia** - *without form. Sin is to live out of context with the blueprint of one's design; to behave out of tune with God's original harmony. Then, the preposition* ὑπέρ [6]**huper**, *means above; beyond. The word often translated, unrighteous,* [7]**adikē**, *from* **a**, *negative and* **dikē**, *two parties in sync with one another; shared likeness - thus,* **adikē** *means to be out of sync. The word,* [8]**prosagagē**, προσαγαγη *with* **pros**, *face to face and* **agō**, *to lead as a shepherd leads his sheep.* θανατωθεις, [9]**thanatōtheis**, *the Perfect Passive Participle is a hebraistic equivalent for the superlative; he was murdered.)*

3:19 Thus, through the doorway of death, his spirit entered the very domain where those who died before were imprisoned. There, he announced his message. *[See my rendering of Ephesians 4:8,9 with commentary.]*

3:20 His audience included all who died in unbelief, in the days of Noah when he built the [1]**Ark. Jesus is the extension of the patience of God, who waited for mankind at a time when only 8 survived the flood. There is a new baptism. Immersed in his death and co-quickened in his resurrection, mankind once dead and drowned are now made alive and crowned.** *(See Hebrews 9:4 Pointing prophetically to the rebooted life of our design where the law of agapē is inscribed in our inner consciousness. A golden fire-pan was for the purpose of carrying fire, in order to burn incense on the day of Atonement [at-one-ment] once a year in the ultimate place of worship. The word,* [1]**kibotos**, *the wooden box, is the same word used for Noah's ark; the container of mankind's redemption. Genesis 6:14 The manna prophetically pictured the true bread from heaven, not the bread that mankind's labor produces. John 4:35, 38. Noah* נֹחַ *rest. Noach* נֹחַ *found favor* חֵן *in the eyes of the Lord. See Genesis 6:8, the same letters in reverse, as in a mirror reflection,* חֵן **chen**, *means, grace/favor.)*

Jesus emptied whatever definition we have of hell, and came back with the trophies *[humanity]* and the keys *[Isaiah 22:22]*. Oh, what an insult it is to the entire gospel, to continue to preach a defeated devil and an empty hell, back into business. *See Revelation 1:18 I am also the Living One; I died and now, see, here I am alive unto the ages of the ages and I have the keys wherewith I have disengaged the gates of* **Hades** *and death.)*

5:1-6 *(1 Peter Chapter 4 as well as chapter 5:1-6 is still to be translated)*

Cast your cares!

5:7 Take immediate action when it comes to distractions and cares! [1]Fling them upon the Lord! He's got your best interest at heart! And he's got your back!

[1] The word [1]epirhiptō, means to fling or cast, through the idea of sudden motion.

[2] The word [2]merimna refers to distractions or cares,

[3] while the word [3]mellō, means to be of interest or concern to.

LITV casting all your anxiety onto him, because it matters to him concerning you.

This is a direct quote from the Greek Septuagint, LXX- Psalm 54:22 Cast your care upon the Lord, and he will sustain you; he will never let the righteous be moved.

Also in the Hebrew Masoretic text Psalm 55:22.

Now, any Jew would immediately recognize this verse as being a direct quote from the Psalms and also remember that in the Psalms it speaks about one's immovable standing in righteousness!

So Peter immediately continues in the next verse...

5:8 Do not be [1]intoxicated by cares! Keep your mind clear; be wide awake! The [2]fallen mindset-system would seek to snare and paralyze you with fear, like a roaring lion. This system is in complete [3]opposition to your righteousness! It would want to employ a sense of unworthiness and sin-consciousness to question your righteousness. Do not go there! Do not allow distractions to devour you!

[1] The word [1]nepsate, from nēphō to to be sober; not intoxicated. Peter compares these distractions and cares to the effect of the roar of a lion – if you don't deal with the distractions they can devour you!

[2] The [2]diabolos [devil] literally, because of the casting down - thus, the fallen mindset system will want to take advantage by questioning your righteousness!

[3] The adversary, [3]ho antidikos from anti, against and dikē, that which balances the scales - suggesting to be judged equal; it implies the idea of two parties finding likeness in each other - which is the root word for dikaiosunē, righteousness.

[Your righteousness has nothing to do with anything you did right or wrong! See 2 Peter 1:1]

To be continued.

1:1 I am Simon the Rock, bondman and ambassador of Jesus Christ. We are in this together; it is not something we had to compete for, since we are equal [1]shareholders in a faith of exactly the [2]same, priceless value. This rests entirely upon the merit of the righteousness of God and our Savior Jesus Christ.

([1] He rescued us from the lies that we believed about ourselves. The word, [1]lanchanō, means to be measured out beforehand; to be allocated something by allotment. This emphasizes the fact that nothing we did or determined to achieve had any influence upon God to qualify us. Faith is not something we do to persuade God; faith is what happens to us when we realize how persuaded God is about us. Salvation belongs to everyone based on exactly the same merit. God's righteousness persuades us. What God did right in Christ cancels out everything that Adam, or we did wrong. See Romans 1:17 Herein lies the secret of the power of the Gospel; there is no good news in it until the righteousness of God is revealed. The dynamic of the gospel is the revelation of God's faith as the only valid basis for our belief. The Prophets wrote in advance about the fact that God believes that righteousness defines the life that he always had in mind for us. Righteousness by his (God's) faith defines life.

[2] The word, ἰσότιμος [2]isotimos, from isos, means that which is similar; equal, and τιμή timey value, esteem, thus, reckoned as equally precious.)

1:2 God's [1]desire is that we may now increasingly be overwhelmed with grace as his divine influence within us and become fully acquainted with the awareness of our [2]oneness. The way he has always [3]known us is realized in Jesus our Master.

([1] The verb [1]plethunthein, meaning to increase, to multiply, is in the Optative mood which expresses a wish.

[2] The word [2]eirēnē, means peace, from eirō, to join, to be set at one again, in carpentry it is the strongest joint, referred to as the dovetail joint.

[3] The [3]knowledge of God is not our knowledge of him; it is God's knowledge of us. He knew us before he formed us in our mother's womb. Jeremiah 1:5. In this context no one can ever feel ignored or neglected again.)

1:3 By his divine [1]engineering <u>he gifted us with all that it takes to live life to the full</u>, where our ordinary day to day lives mirror our [2]devotion and romance with our Maker. His [3]intimate knowledge of us [4]introduces us to ourselves again and [5]elevates us to a position where his [6]original intention is clearly perceived.

([1] I have translated the word, [1]dunamis, power or ability, as engineering, in this context.

[2] The word [2]eusebeia means devotion or worship.

[3] The word [3]epignoseos suggests an intimate knowledge; here it is in the Genitive case, which means God is the owner of this knowledge. Jeremiah 1:5, 1 Corinthians 13:12.

[4] The word [4]kaleō, means to surname, I translated it, he introduced us to ourselves again, which reminds of Jesus declaring to Simon, son of Jonah his original identity and thus laying the rock-foundation in our understanding that the son of man is

indeed the son of God, now celebrated in the ekklesia, which literally means our original identity. Matthew 16:17,18.

*[5] The word [5]arētē from **aireō** means to elevate, to lift one's perspective; often translated, virtue.*

*[6] The word [6]**doxa**, often translated, glory, from **dokeō**, original intention, opinion.)*

1:4 This is exactly what God always had in mind for us; everyone of his abundant and priceless promises pointed to our restored participation in our [1]godly origin. This is his gift to us. In this fellowship we have escaped the distorted influence of the corrupt cosmic virus of greed. *([1]His image and likeness is redeemed in us. The default settings are restored. We are re-booted to fully participate in the life of our design. Sadly, my mother tongue language, in the old Afrikaans translation says, Once you have escaped the corruption of the lusts of the flesh, you'll be rewarded with the divine nature. Now that is putting the cart before the horses.*

*Unfortunately our Authorized Bibles all repeat the same mistake in the next verse, 2 Peter 1:5, by saying, **Add to your faith** virtue, etc... This is after Peter clearly states in verse 1 that, to begin with, we already are equal shareholders in a faith of exactly the same, priceless value. Then in verse 3, ...by God's divine engineering, we are gifted with all that it takes to live life to the full.*

One cannot add to something that is already complete. However, one can engage in the adventure of a limitless discovery. I often use an 8-piece Babushka doll to illustrate that there is so much more than just the outer image. This is a traditional Russian doll, beautifully carved out of wood and painted with a colorful image. The outer image is repeated again and again in smaller, identical inner pieces - each one fitting perfectly into the other. Until it almost seems impossible that yet another piece could follow the little figures that emerge. Our 5-year-old granddaughter, Nicola, calls this the Reflection Doll.

Faith unfolds into these amazing attributes that each person is equally gifted with:

*1/ **Faith**; 2/ **Elevation**; 3/ **Spiritual insight**; 4/ **Inner strength**; 5/ **Patient perseverance** - like a broody hen; 6/ **Meaningful devotion and worship**; 7/ **Genuine fondness for others** and finally, the heart of faith is 8/ the **Agapē** of God.*

Now, acquaint yourselves with these.

*The keyword here, in Peter's illustration is the word, **epichoregeō** which was traditionally translated to 'add to'. The etymological values in the components of this word clearly describe a conductor of music.)*

1:5 Now *[in the light of what we are gifted with in Christ]*, **the stage is set to display life's excellence. Explore the adventures of faith. Imagine the extreme dedication and focus of a [1]conductor of music; how he would [2]diligently [3]acquaint himself with every individual voice in the choir, as well as the contribution of every specific instrument, to follow the precise sound represented in every single note in order to give maximum credit to the original composition. This is exactly what it means to exhibit the divine character. You are the choir conductor of your own life. Familiarize yourselves with every ingredient that faith unfolds. See there**

how [4]elevated you are, and from within this position [*of your co-seatedness in Christ*], [5]enlightened perspective will dawn within you.

([1] *The word,* [1]***epichoregeō****, comes from* ***epi****, a Preposition of position, over, in charge, indicating continuous influence upon,* + ***chorus****, choir, orchestra, or dance* + ***agō****, meaning to lead as a shepherd leads his sheep; thus, the conductor of music.*

[2] [2]*Giving all diligence, extreme devotion. The word,* [2]***spoude****, means to interest oneself immediately and most earnestly.*

[3] *The word,* [3]***pareisphero****, means to introduce simultaneously. I translated it, to acquaint yourself with every detail of the whole. From* ***para****, a Preposition indicating close proximity, a thing proceeding from a sphere of influence, with a suggestion of union of place of residence, to have sprung from its author and giver, originating from, denoting the point from which an action originates, intimate connection,* + ***eispherō****, to reach inward. Before a performance, the first violinist will give the exact key of the piece to be played; now every instrument can be finely tuned to that note, in the same way the faith of God gives that exact pitch.*

[4] *The word,* [4]***arete****, often translated, virtue, comes from the word* ***airō****, to raise up, to elevate. Faith unfolds the secret of our joint-elevation with Jesus. See yourself seated together with Christ. Colossians 3:1-3. Now from this position of elevation we begin to see new horizons; in fact we begin to see everything differently. There is a level of understanding,* [5]***gnosis****, a knowing, that can only be accessed by faith. In Hebrews 11:3, by faith we understand that the ages were framed by the Word of God.*)

1:6 Here you will realize your [1]inner strength and how fully competent you are to prevail in [2]patient perseverance in the midst of any contradiction. It is from within this place of enlightened perspective that meaningful devotion and worship ignite.

([1] *Spiritual strength exceeds mind-, muscle- or willpower by far. Isaiah 40:31.*

See **Ephesians 1:19** *I pray that you will be* [1]*overwhelmed with the unequalled greatness and magnitude of his power,* [2]*which he has wrought in us, in Christ; according to the working of his great might! This is the* [3]*conclusion and dynamic of* [4]*faith.*

Ephesians 1:20 *Do you want to measure the mind and muscle of God? Consider the force which he unleashed in Jesus Christ when he raised him from the dead and forever seated him enthroned as his executive authority in the realm of the heavens. Jesus is God's right hand of power. He was raised up from the deepest dungeons of human despair to the highest region of heavenly bliss. (See Ephesians 2:5,6 & 4:8,9.)*

Ephesians 1:21 *Infinitely above all the combined forces of rule, authority, dominion or governments; he is ranked superior to any name that could ever be given to anyone of this age or any age still to come in the eternal future.*

[2] *See* **James 1:4** *(Just like a mother hen patiently broods over her eggs,) steadfastness provides you with a consistent environment, and so patience prevails and proves your perfection; how entirely whole you are and without any shortfall.*)

1:7 In worship you will find a genuine fondness for others. At the heart of everything that faith unfolds is [1]the agapē-love of God. *(Worship and* *devotion includes esteeming people and honoring friendship [James 3:9]; the same voice that magnifies God cannot insult a person made in God's image. True worship is to touch someone's life with the same devotion and care you would touch Jesus himself; even if the other person seems a most unlikely candidate. The word, ¹agapaō, is from agō, meaning to lead as a shepherd leads his sheep, and paō, to rest; as in Psalm 23, he leads me besides still waters, he restores my soul; or, by the waters of reflection, my soul remembers who I am. The Message reads, each dimension fitting into and developing the other.)*

1:8 While you diligently ¹rehearse the exact qualities of every divine attribute within you; the volume will rise with ever increasing gusto, guarding you from being ineffective and barren in your knowledge of the Christ-life, displayed with such authority and eloquence in Jesus. *(These things being in you. The word, ¹uparcho, translates rehearse, from upo + archomai, to commence or rehearse from the beginning. The word archē, suggests commencement or beginning.)*

1:9 If anyone feels that these things are absent in his life, they are not; spiritual blindness and short-sightedness only veil them from you. This happens when one loses sight of one's innocence. *(The moment one forgets the tremendous consequence of the fact that we were cleansed from our past sins, one seems to become pre-occupied again with the immediate sense-ruled horizon, which is what short-sightedness is all about; this makes one blind to his blessings. Spiritual realities suddenly seem vague and distant. Become acquainted with your innocence.)*

1:10 Therefore I would encourage you, my fellow family, to make every immediate effort to become cemented in the knowledge of our ¹original identity ²revealed and confirmed in the logic of God. Fully engage these realities in your lifestyle, and so you will never ³fail. *(Your original identity, ¹kaleō, often translated as calling, to surname, to identify by name; ²eklogen, often translated as election; yet the two parts of this word, ek, a Preposition denoting origin or source, and legō, from logos, suggests the original word (the logic of God) as our source [John 1:1,14]. The word, ³ptaio, means to fail, falter, or get out of tune again in the context of verse 5, literally to fall, lose height, to stop flying.)*

1:11 Thus the great ¹Conductor of music will draw your life into the full volume of the harmony of the ages; the ²royal song of our Savior Jesus Christ. *(In Colossians 2:19, You are directly connected to Christ who, like a choir conductor, draws out the music in everyone like a tapestry of art that intertwines in harmony to reveal the full stature of divine inspiration, which is Christ in you. Again the word ²epichoregeō is used, the choir conductor; this time, God is doing the conducting and is leading us into his harmony; ²eis + odos, meaning access into the road. Yet, in this context I prefer the thought that we are led into a song, an ode; a ceremonious lyric poem. The form is usually marked by exalted feeling and style. The term ode derives from a Greek word alluding to a choir song, usually accompanied by a dance; also a poem to be sung composed for royal occasions.)*

1:12 Having said all this I am sure that you can appreciate why I feel so urgent in my commitment to you to repeatedly bring these things to your

attention; as indeed you have already taken your stand for the truth as it is now revealed.

1:13 So while I am still in this body-suit, I take my lead from the revelation of righteousness and make it my business to thoroughly stir you until these truths become permanently molded in your memory.

1:14 All the more since I know that my time in this tabernacle is almost done; our Lord Jesus Christ has prepared me for this.

1:15 In the meantime, I will do whatever it takes to make it possible for you to always be able to easily recall these realities even in my absence.

1:16 We are not con-artists, fabricating fictions and fables to add weight to our account of his majestic appearance; with our own eyes we have witnessed the powerful display of the illuminate presence of Jesus the Master of the Christ-life. *(His face shone like the sun, even his raiment was dazzling white. Matthew 17.)*

1:17 He was spectacularly endorsed by God the Father in the highest honor and glory. Then, a voice from within the cloud spoke, this is the Son of my delight; he completely pleases me. *(Matthew 17:5 a radiant cloud enveloped them.)*

1:18 For John, James, and I, the prophetic word is fulfilled beyond doubt; we heard this voice loud and clear from the heavenly realm while we were with Jesus in that sacred moment on the mountain.

1:19 For us the appearance of the Messiah is no longer a future promise but a fulfilled reality. Now it is your turn to have more than a second-hand, hearsay testimony. Take my word as one would take a lamp at night; the day is about to dawn within you, in your own understanding. When the Morning Star appears, you no longer need the lamp; this will happen shortly on the horizon of your own hearts.

(Peter reflects on the Jewish custom to light lamps in their houses in preparation for the day of the Sabbath. See Luke 23:54 It was the day of Preparation and the Sabbath [1]was already glimmering with light.

[1] The word, ἐπιφώσκω epiphōskō - the Jews would light lamps in their houses just before sunset on the evening of the Sabbath.

See my extended notes on the day of Preparation at the end of Luke 23)

1:20 It is most important to understand that the prophetic word recorded in Scripture does not need our interpretation or opinion to make it valid.

1:21 The holy men who first spoke these words of old did not invent these thoughts, they simply voiced God's oracles as they were individually inspired by the Holy Spirit.

2 Peter to be continued in a future edition of the Mirror Study Bible.

Lydia and Francois met on the 25th of August 1974, while he was working with Youth For Christ. She was sixteen and he, nineteen. The following year he studied Greek and Hebrew at the University of Pretoria for three years while Lydia completed her nursing training. In 1978 Francois also spent a year with YWAM. They married in January 1979 and are blessed with four amazing children, Renaldo, Tehilla, Christo and Stefan; also, four darling grandchildren: Nicola, Christiaan, *[Tehilla & Pieter's]*; Lydie-Anne, *[Stefan and Yaël's]*. With Christo and Keryn's Sadie turning 2 in July 2023. And Stefan and Yaël expecting in January '24!

They pioneered and worked in full-time mission for fourteen years, during which time they also pastored a church and led a training facility for more than 700 students over a five-year period. During this time he translated several of the Pauline Epistles [The Ruach Translation], which were never published; although printed along with other booklets he wrote and distributed amongst their students.

They then left the ministry and for ten years did business mainly in the tourism industry. They built and managed a Safari Lodge in the Sabi Sand Game Reserve and eventually relocated to Hermanus where they started Southern Right Charters boat-based whale watching.

In December 2000 Francois began to write the book, "God believes in You" which led to him being invited to speak at various Christian camps and churches. Since February 2004, they have traveled regularly abroad and into Africa as well as South Africa.

Francois has written several books in both English and Afrikaans, including God Believes in You, Divine Embrace, The Logic of His Love; these are also available on Kindle. Also, The Mystery Revealed and Done, which are no longer in print - although still available in Afrikaans.

In order to focus their time on writing and translation, they relocated from Hermanus in 2015, to a remote farm in the Swartberg Mountains. They have since, also stopped most of their travelling.

Lydia has written 5 amazing children's stories of which Stella's Secret, The Little Bear And The Mirror, Kaa of the Great Kalahari as well as The Eagle Story, are already published in print and on Kindle. Her most recent story "King Solitaire's Banquet" was released in December '20.

Francois passionately continues his translation of the Mirror Bible, which will eventually include the entire NT as well as select portions of the Old. The 1st 250 page, A5 edition, was published in 2012. The 10th edition Mirror Study Bible is a 7 x 10 inch book, of 1194 pages, released in May 2021.

Lydia's books are already available in English Afrikaans, German and Spanish.

The Mirror Bible is currently available in Spanish, Shona, Xhosa and large portions in German.

More than 50000 people subscribe to their daily posts on Social Media; Lydia has her own fb page and Francois his own profile page and a Mirror Translation Group as well as an Afrikaans, Spanish, Hungarian, French, Dutch and Russian group on Facebook.

Their email address is info@mirrorword.net
You can get more detail about them on www.mirrorword.net
The Mirror Bible is also on Kindle as well as an App, app.mirrorword.net

There are many of Francois' teachings on YouTube but they recently started their own

Mirror Word YOUTUBE channel, *https://m.youtube.com/channel/UC63YHkpabON9nHgQq-WeIPkA/videos*

Mirror Word PODCAST https://open.spotify.com/show/3qsgRsf2SNDx1bubxngw0W?fbclid=I-wAR0zLo_wkVymqouQA3CvYxZ3lINrK-zUyXf4PuCql7bG-OGns4BTcgAgRLQ

REFERENCES & RESOURCES

Referred to by the author's name or by some abridgment of the title.

Adam Clarke (1762–1832 A British Methodist theologian)

Ackerman [*Christian Element in Plato*]

Bruce Metzger *(Textual Commentary on the Greek NT)*

Barnes Notes (Notes on the Bible, by Albert Barnes, [1834], at sacred-texts.com)

BBE (1949, Bible in Basic English)

Doddrich (Philip Doddridge 1702-1751 www.ccel.org/d/doddridge)

Dr. Robinson (Greek Lexicon by Edward Robinson1851)

E-Sword by Rick Meyers (www.e-sword.net)

Greek English Lexicon by C.Grimm Wilke - translated from Latin by J.H. Thayer DD - Edinburgh - T&T CLARK - Fourth Edition 1901)

JB Phillips Translation (Geoffrey Bles London 1960)

Jeff Benner http://www.ancient-hebrew.org/

KJV (King James Version - In 1604, King James I of England authorized that a new translation of the Bible into English. It was finished in 1611)

Knox Translation (Translated from the Vulgate Latin by Ronald Knox Published in London by Burns Oates and Washbourne Ltd. 1945)

Liddell, Scott & Jones, Greek-English Lexicon

Marvin R. Vincent (1834-1922) Word Studies.

NEB (New English Bible New Testament - Oxford & Cambridge University Press 1961)

Robert Charles *R. H. (Robert Henry), 1855-1931*

RSV (The Revised Standard Version is an authorized revision of the American Standard Version, published in 1901, which was a revision of the King James Version, published in 1611.)

Strongs (James Strong - Dictionary of the Bible)

The Message (Eugene H. Peterson Nav Press Publishing Group)

Walter Bauer (Greek English Lexicon - a translation of Walter Bauer's Griechisch-Deutches Worterbuch by Arndt and Gingrich 1958)

Wesley J. Perschbacher (The New Analytical Greek Lexicon Copyright 1990 by Hendrickson Publishers, Inc)

Westcott and Hort *The New Testament in the Original Greek 1881*

Weymouth New Testament *(M.A., D.Lit. 1822-1902)*

Zodhiates Complete Word Study Lexicon Mantis Bible Study for Apple

Printed in the USA
CPSIA information can be obtained
at www.ICGtesting.com
CBHW080443041224
18361CB00040B/486